MALT
WHISKY
YEARBOOK
2018

www.maltwhiskyyearbook.com

First published in Great Britain in 2017 by
MagDig Media Limited

© MagDig Media Limited 2017

ISBN 978-0-9576553-4-8

MagDig Media Limited
1 Brassey Road
Old Potts Way, Shrewsbury
Shropshire SY3 7FA
ENGLAND

E-mail: info@maltwhiskyyearbook.com
www.maltwhiskyyearbook.com

Previous editions

Contents

Introduction and acknowledgements, 6

Secrets of the Stillmakers, 8
by Gavin D Smith

Guardians of the Whisky Galaxy, 16
by Neil Ridley

The Rise of English Whisky, 24
by Dominic Roskrow

Brand New Whisky, 30
by Jonny McCormick

Scotch Whisky and the Law, 38
by Charles Maclean

Sweet and Dry, 46
by Ian Wisniewski

Malt Whisky Distilleries of Scotland, 52-169

Websites to Watch, 81

New Distilleries, 170

Distilleries per owner, 183

Closed Distilleries, 184

Single Malts from Japan, 194
by Stefan Van Eycken

Distilleries Around The Globe, 204

The Year That Was, 258

Independent Bottlers, 274

Whisky Shops, 282

Tables & Statistics, 288

Maps, 294

Index, 296

Introduction

Even though single malts are still only 10% of all the Scotch whisky sold in terms of volumes, it is a category that has become increasingly more important. The fact that it makes up 26% of the total values is evidence enough. At the same time, single malts are not just about Scotland anymore or even Japan or Ireland for that matter. Single malt whisky is now produced in more than 30 countries. Most of these are still young and sometimes made in an unorthodox way but it will be interesting to see in a few years time how the whiskies from new territories ar beeing accepted by the consumers and if they have any impact on the industry as a whole.

Whisky as a category continues to grow despite fierce competition from other spirits. Meanwhile, the traditional producers are walking a tight rope, balancing between reinventing themselves to make them interesting to a new generation while at the same time nurturing the traditions and the heritage that made whisky the world´s most popular spirit.

As usual, my excellent team of whisky writers have excelled themselves this year and have contributed with some fascinating articles;

Before you can start the distillation you obviously need a still. Gavin D Smith lets us in on all the secrets of the stillmakers.

Is the whisky category becoming a lawless country in danger of consuming itself? Neil Ridley went looking for the guardians of the whisky galaxy.

Surely they can´t make whisky south of the border, can they? Dominic Roskrow tells the story of how English whisky is slowly winning the battle for credibility.

As if producing whisky wasn´t complicated enough - wait until you have to sell it.
Jonny McCormick explains the difficulties of branding .

Some say it is the cornerstone of the Scotch whisky success - others say it´s an impediment to innovation. Charles MacLean examines the laws regulating Scotch whisky.

We all find them in our whisky - the sweet and dry notes - but how do they affect our interpretation of the taste and how did they get there in the first place? Ian Wisniewski will give you the answers.

Everyone wants Japanese whisky but where to get it these days? Stefan Van Eycken has found a stream of hope with the new producers.

In Malt Whisky Yearbook 2018 you will also find the unique, detailed and much appreciated section on Scottish malt whisky distilleries. It has been thoroughly revised and updated, not just in text, but also including numerous, new pictures, new distilleries and tasting notes for all the core brands. The chapter on Japanese whisky is completely revised and the presentation of distilleries from the rest of the world has been expanded. You will also find a list of more than 150 of the best whisky shops in the world with their full details and suggestions where to find more information on the internet. The Whisky Year That Was provides a summary of all the signficant events during the year. Finally, the very latest statistics gives you all the answers to your questions on production and consumption.

Thank you for buying Malt Whisky Yearbook 2018. I hope that you will have many enjoyable moments reading it and I can assure you that I will be back with a new edition next year.

Malt Whisky Yearbook 2019 will be published in October 2018.
To make sure you will be able to order it directly, please register at
www.maltwhiskyyearbook.com.

If you need any of the previous twelve volumes of Malt Whisky Yearbook,
some of them are available for purchase (in limited numbers) from the website
www.maltwhiskyyearbook.com

Acknowledgements

First of all I wish to thank the writers who have shared their great specialist knowledge on the subject in a brilliant and entertaining way – Stefan Van Eycken, Charles MacLean, Jonny McCormick, Neil Ridley, Dominic Roskrow, Gavin D. Smith and Ian Wisniewski.

A special thanks goes to Gavin who put in a lot of effort nosing, tasting and writing notes for more than 100 different whiskies. Thanks also to Suzanne Redmond for the tasting notes for independent bottlings and to Stefan for the Japanese notes. I am also deeply grateful to Philippe Jugé for his input on French distilleries.

The following persons have also made important photographic or editorial contributions and I am grateful to all of them:

Kevin Abrook, Iain Allan, Stephanie Allison, Alasdair Anderson, Russel Anderson, Nuno Antunes, Duncan Baldwin, Hannah Bambra, Adam Barber, Jan Beckers, Graeme Bell, Jodi Best, Keith Brian, Ross Bremner, Andrew Brown, Graham Brown, James Brown, Jennifer Brown, Alex Bruce, Gordon Bruce, Simon Buley, Stephen Burnett, Pär Caldenby, Neil Cameron, Peter Campbell, Jim Casey, Ian Chang, Oliver Chilton, Ashok Chokalingam, Tor Petter Christensen, Stewart Christine, Claire Clark, Gordon Clark, Joe Clark, Suzanne Clark, Shelagh Considine, Nicole Cook, Graham Coull, Jason Craig, Georgie Crawford, Andrew Crook, Iain Croucher, Gloria Cummins, Alasdair Day, Paul Dempsey, Scott Dickson, Ludo Ducrocq, Lukasz Dynowiak, Graham Eunson, Diane Farrell, Andy Fiske, Robert Fleming, Camden Ford, John Fordyce, Richard Forsyth, Dave Francis, Callum Fraser, Hamish Fraser, Sarah Fraser, Ewan George, Gillian Gibson, Adele Goodfellow, Kenny Grant, Pierrick Guillaume, Wendy Harries Jones, Stuart Harrington, Annelise Hastings, Mickey Heads, Lucas Hohl, Paul Hooper, Liam Hughes, Robbie Hughes, Kevin Innes, Emma Jackson, Akshat Jain, Sandy Jameson, Jemma Jamieson, Matthew Jamieson, Michael John, Steven Kersley, Michael Kinstlick, Tyler LaCorata, Laura Laden, Nico Liu, Mark Lochhead, Jay Lockwood, Rich Lockwood, Allan Logan, Graham Logan, Polly Logan, Alistair Longwell, Bill Lumsden, Horst Lüning, Iain MacAllister, Katy Macanna, Christine McCafferty, Des McCagherty, Brendan McCarron, Alan McConnochie, Alistair McDonald, Andy Macdonald, John MacDonald, Lynne McEwan, Christy McFarlane, Sandy Macintyre, Doug McIvor, Brenton Mackechnie, Alistair Mackenzie, Bruce Mackenzie, Drew McKenzie Smith, Jaclyn McKie, Ian MacMillan, Emily McQuade, Ian McWilliam, Dennis Malcolm, Johanna Malmgren, Martin Markvardsen, Christine Marshall, Jennifer Masson, Neil Mathieson, Santiago Mignone, Amy Millen, Andrew Millsopp, Katy Moore, Carol More, Gareth Morgan, Gordon Motion, Jake Mountain, Robert Muir, Bridgeen Mullen, Alex Munch, Jari Mämmi, Andrew Nairn, Andrew Nelstrop, Ingemar Nordblom, Laura Nussbaumer, Nathan Nye, Cordelia O´Connell, Ewan Ogilvie, Sean Olivier, Wouter Peeters, Sean Phillips, Struan Grant Ralph, Chad Ralston, Brandy Rand, Tony Reeman-Clark, David Robertson, Jackie Robertson, James Robertson, Stuart Robertson, Colin Ross, Suzanne Russell, Zoe Rutherford, Emily Senn, Nestor Serenelli, Steven Shand, Sam Simmons, Daniel Smith, Colin Spoelman, Alison Spowart, Greig Stables, Marie Stanton, Vicky Stevens, Karen Stewart, Reto Stoeckli, Heinfried Tacke, Duncan Tait, Elizabeth Teape, Eddie Thom, Annabel Thomas, Phil Thompson, Simon Thompson, Ruth Thomson, Louise Towers, Jennifer Turkington, David Turner, Sandrine Tyrbas de Chamberet, Perry Unger, Kyle VanStrien, Stewart Walker, Grace Waller, Arch Watkins, Ranald Watson, Mark Watt, Iain Weir, Nick White, Ronald Whiteford, Anthony Wills, Alan Winchester, Jaime Windon, Stephen Woodcock, Kenneth Wortz, Allison B Young, Derek Younie.

Finally, to my wife Pernilla and our daughter Alice, thank you for your patience and your love and to Vilda, our labrador and my faithful companion in the office during long working hours.

Ingvar Ronde
Editor
Malt Whisky Yearbook

Secrets of the Stillmakers

by Gavin D Smith

The gleaming copper pot still is, together with the pagoda roof,
the most recognisable feature of a malt whisky distillery. Made from plain
sheets of copper, they are the result of hard work and years of experience.
They are the pride of the stillmakers.

It is thought that the distillation of alcohol was first developed in the 11th century AD, and that water cooling did not take place until five centuries later. With the discovery that cold water could condense the distilled vapours efficiently, the still shape began to evolve into something we might recognise today: at its simplest, a pear-shaped vessel with neck, head and lyne arm, leading into a tub containing cold water.

According to third-generation coppersmith Richard Forsyth, "Early stills were small enough that they could be lifted up and carried away if the excise officers came along and they were distilling without a licence. They were basically tin cans with conical copper shoulders and a copper tube for a worm. The shapes we see today have evolved from that".

"Copper was first used for pots stills and worms because it was soft, pliable and could be rolled. The first distillers almost certainly didn't know that it was a good conductor of heat or removed unwanted sulphides from the spirit. It makes for a clear spirit, which you can't get if you use stainless steel."

To describe Forsyth as a 'coppersmith' is somewhat to undersell the man and his achievements. As Chairman of Forsyths Ltd he presides over a workforce of around 380. The company has created distilleries in dozens of countries, across several continents and is the world's biggest and brightest name in still design and construction.

The Forsyth empire is based in the small Speyside town of Rothes, which is also home to Glen Grant, Speyburn, Glen Spey and Glenrothes distilleries. The first recorded Rothes coppersmith operation was established during the 1850s, with legal whisky-making in Scotland having grown significantly since the 1823 Excise Act, making such a business viable.

"The first one was owned by a man named Bailey," says Richard Forsyth, "but it was bought out by a bigger player from the Central Belt called Robert Willison. He bought it during the 1880 and my grandfather Alexander started serving his time there in the early 1890s. He worked for Willison in Rothes, and also in his works at Alloa, in central Scotland, He also had a place in Sunderland, on the River Wear in north-east England where they made copper piping for ships."

"After spending time in Alloa and Sunderland, my grandfather came back to Rothes as working manager. When Willison retired he sold off the three parts of the business to his three working managers, and my grandfather took over in Rothes in 1933 and formed A Forsyth & Son Ltd. The Alloa works became Abercrombie's, which is now owned by Diageo."

The Second World War saw virtually all of Scotland's distilleries shut down, and Forsyth's endured lean times, but after the war, Richard's father, Ernest – known locally as 'Toot,' – joined the firm, which was boosted by the boom in Scotch whisky during the 1950s, '60s and '70s. "He had learnt how to weld in the REME [the army's Corps of Royal Electrical and Mechanical Engineers], and welding replaced riveting in still construction," recalls Richard Forsyth.

Richard began to work from time to time in his father's workshop at the age of around 13, and soon decided that he wanted to follow the family trade. By the mid-1970s, he was running the company, but as has so often been the case in the Scotch whisky business, boom times were to be followed by a contraction during the early to mid-1980s due to over-supply, and diversification became essential if the firm was to survive and prosper.

"We got involved in paper mills and built up a major engineering and draughtsmanship operation,"

explains Forsyth. "We were ideally placed to go into the oil and gas business in the 1990s, and by around 2005/6 oil and gas and the whisky side of things were doing very well, and we grew substantially. We bought a site in Buckie Harbour on the Moray Firth coast and developed that for oil and gas projects."

Meanwhile, back in Rothes, Forsyth's acquired the silent Caperdonich distillery from Chivas Brothers in 2010, and proceeded to demolish it, in order to expand the firm's adjacent site. The company has been based in its current Rothes premises since 1974, and it is from this headquarters and fabrication facility that Richard and his son, Richard E Forsyth, company managing director, run operations.

A downturn in North Sea oil and gas enterprises during the past few years has conveniently coincided with an upturn in global demand for Scotch whisky and for the kitting out of new distilling ventures.

Richard Forsyth notes that "A few years ago, split was probably 70:30 oil and gas to distilling, but now it's closer to 70:30 distilling to oil and gas, and we have shed the paper business. Our whisky activities have increased three or fourfold over the last seven or eight years, not only in Scotland, but all over the world."

Kavalan distillery in Taiwan has been a major project for the Forsyth team, with Richard noting that "Initially we put in six stills to make 1 million lpa, but we have now installed a total of 20 stills and four mashtuns, giving a capacity of 8 million lpa."

In 2017, the company was commissioned to produce four distilleries for Japan, and Forsyth says that "We've previously built one in China and this year got a sizeable order for a second one there. We're also working on a distillery in Thailand. Other projects have been in Brazil, Russia, New Zealand, Sweden and Finland. We've made pot and column stills for rum in the Caribbean, and six tequila stills for Mexico, and have priced 81 for future expansion next year."

Several new distilleries per year are commissioned from the USA, and the growth in Irish distilling during the past few years has also led to lucrative contracts to build both pot and column stills, with Forsyth noting that "We built three pot stills for Midleton distillery in County Cork, and each had a capacity of 80,000 litres content. They're the three biggest stills we've ever made."

Closer to home, many of Scotland's start-up distilleries have been created by Forsyth, including Wolfburn, Annandale, Kingsbarns, Lindores and Ballindalloch on Speyside. Indeed, Speyside is currently the venue for three of Forsyth's largest projects, as Glenlivet, Glenfiddich and Macallan

A few of the new stills that were delivered to Kavalan in Taiwan in 2016

Copper plates are cut to size using a water jet

all strive to outdo each other in terms of potential capacity.

Glenlivet is currently developing a brand-new distillery alongside its existing facilities, and there is talk of ultimately trebling capacity from the present 10.5mla to in excess of 30mla. Meanwhile, Glenfiddich's second distillery will give a total capacity of 20mla.

Most impressive of all, however is the ongoing creation of an entirely new Macallan distillery alongside the existing plant, with Forsyth's acting as main contractors for the processing side of the project. "This is a £30 million contract in total," notes Richard Forsyth, "the biggest ever construction job in the Scotch whisky industry, and we have fabricated 36 stills for it."

From sheet to pot

It is easy to mention glibly '81 tequila stills' and '36 Macallan pot stills,' but just how does a company like Forsyth go about the business of turning sheet copper into curvaceous, visually pleasing, but also highly efficient distilling vessels?

Coppersmiths serve a four-year apprenticeship in order to be able to do the skilful and demanding work, and around 50 people are employed on the whisky side of the business. At any one time up to 20 per cent of them will be apprentices.

"Flat plate is bought from one of two copper mills in the former East Germany," explains Forsyth, "and in effect, stills are made from cones. Cutting of the sheet copper used to be done with hand shears, but now we use a water jet to cut. It's precise and very clean. The design is all done on computer and sent to the cutting machine. We used to have to mark it all out on the sheets of copper on the floor!"

"We draw out segments, cut and shape them, weld them together, then hammer the copper to put the strength back into it, to harden it. We have six mechanical 'planishing' hammers, which takes some of the labour out of it, but working on the big still body shoulder plates remains a physical business, and it's really a young man's game."

"A swan neck is completely hand-shaped and hand planished, because it's an awkward shape and can't fit onto mechanical hammers. In terms of still shape and size, everything has to look right, it has to be

Welding replaced riveting after the Second World War

aesthetically pleasing. It's like looking at an attractive woman – the curves must be in the right place!"

Aesthetics aside, what influences do still sizes and shapes have on spirit character? Dr Harry Riffkin of analytical and consulting chemists Tatlock & Thomson Ltd declares that "Whisky is made in the wash still, not the spirit still. Wash still design is key to quality. Spirit character depends on the shape of the wash still and how the condenser operates. The faster you run your stills the hotter the condenser will run. Reflux will be reduced, which will affect spirit quality. In the spirit still you're looking for high reflux, and factors here include the height of the head, the direction of the lyne arm, and even the fitting of purifiers."

Richard Forsyth notes that "The area that affects spirit character is the head and neck, as that's where you get reflux. For example, Glenmorangie's stills are very tall and produce a light-bodied spirit, while Macallan's are small and dumpy and make a heavy spirit. However, yeast, malt, and fermentation times are also very important. The size of the stills is not a major factor, and the shape is only part of the equation. Fermentation times can vary from 50 hours to 120 hours plus, so that's obviously a factor in ultimate spirit character, as are the points where you 'cut' the spirit"

Forsyth highlights two major changes to the business of distillation, namely the introduction of 'shell and tube' condensers and the switch from direct to indirect firing of stills. "Cooling worms in worm tubs were used by everyone until after the war," he notes. "Shell and tube condensers give very intense copper contact. They are more efficient than worms and take up much less space."

In terms of heating stills, he points out that "When coal-firing was taking place the fires got up to over 1,000 degrees centigrade, so you needed thicker still bottoms and flue plates to withstand the heat, as they effectively sat in the fire. The bottom would be around 16mm thick and the sheets of copper the flues were made from would be 12mm. With steam heating of stills, those thicknesses drop to 6mm."

"The wash still contains seven per cent of solids, so with direct firing it had to be stirred, like porridge in a pan. The stills were fitted with rummagers [rotating chains], which had high capital and maintenance costs."

Parts of the new Glenfiddich stills

The 64,000-dollar question is, of course, did the switch from direct to indirect firing affect spirit character. Opinion is divided, but Richard Forsyth says that "Before they converted from direct firing, distilleries like Glen Grant and Glenlivet took one set of stills and trialled them with steam. Overall, I think, there was a feeling that there was a slight character difference, but not enough to be a game changer."

"Steam is very efficient, fuelled by oil or gas, with gas being the cleanest and cheapest. It made economic sense to switch to steam, and all the distillers were competing keenly on economics. Today, on Speyside, only Glenfarclas and Glenfiddich have stills that are direct-fired – using gas."

He explains that "The earliest steam heating was through copper coils, then stainless steel coils were brought in, and pans – which were effectively percolators. We now use a radiator-type of system."

"Also, we now have external heating now via plate heat exchangers, which are easy to clean. All 12 of the new wash stills we've fitted at the new Macallan distillery are heated externally, but the spirit stills are heated internally. That is because you only need to clean the spirit stills twice a year, but with wash stills it's once a week because of that seven per cent solids content."

New technique saves energy

One relatively recent innovation has been the equipping of stills for thermo-vapour recompression, with all of Chivas Brothers' 14 malt distilleries operating what is usually referred to as 'TVR.'

Richard Forsyth explains the process by noting that "Essentially, the condenser design is altered to produce hotter water than normal – up to 80-plus degrees centigrade, instead of 45-60 degrees centigrade. The hot water is drawn off and passes through a thermo-compressor, creating steam which is fed back into the still."

"Up to 30% fuel savings can be achieved with TVR. However, because the water is so much hotter, the life of the condenser tends to be reduced, and they will last for something like six or seven years, instead of eight to ten years. We've been making TVR stills for around ten years now – and as well as Chivas distilleries, Speyburn and Glenfiddich also have them."

Increased computerisation of distilling processes has been ongoing for several decades now, and Forsyth point out that "There are even instruments in some stills to stop spirit rising too far up inside them, to control reflux, if you like. The 'sight glasses' on the still are there, but they're not actually used to see how the spirit is performing. The instrumentation in the still will automatically knock the spirit back down."

"Similarly, the spirit safe is now sometimes just there for appearance. A density meter can measure strength and temperature – exactly what would previously have been done manually in the spirit still. Distillers are really looking for consistency, and there is greater consistency than ever before."

Forsyth's principal competitors for distillery equipment in the UK are Diageo-owned Abercrombie and McMillan Ltd, based at Prestonpans, near Edinburgh, and with a heritage dating back to 1867. Although most of Scotland's distilleries are fitted out with plant from one of these three operators, an increasing number of start-up distilling ventures are looking overseas to source their kit.

For example, Arbikie on the east coast between Dundee and Aberdeen and Glasgow distillery both use stills produced by the German fabricator Carl, an independent company based near Stuttgart, established in 1869.

According to distillery consultant and Glasgow's former master distiller Jack Mayo, "The only major difference is that the Carl stills have steam jackets rather than steam coils and so run much cooler," making for a 'cleaner' spirit during the wash distillation.

Harry Riffkin notes that "Some of the new stills, like those from Carl, tend to be cylindrical because there's no need for the traditional shape, which was designed to accommodate direct firing, and the style has just been copied and carried on."

Another German manufacturer, Arnold Holstein of Markdorf, has been responsible for producing the stills at Lone Wolf distillery in Aberdeenshire. This is the first instance of Holstein stills being used for Scotch whisky distillation, as the company is principally associated with brandy and eaux de vie vessels.

The pair of pot stills vary significantly in style,

with the first having a distinctive triple 'bubble' in the neck, allowing for high levels of reflux. Master distiller Steven Kersley says that "Sometimes that's good, but sometimes you want a more a more 'meaty' spirit – so we'd run the still harder in that case."

The second still is more conventional in appearance, but has two condensers, the second of which has a very large amount of copper for optimum levels of reflux, though it may be bypassed if Kersley's 'meaty' spirit style is required. Finally, Lone Wolf's still room boasts a rectification column, which is used to make grain spirit or US-style Bourbon or rye whisky.

Equally unconventional for the Scotch whisky industry are the Hoga stills in use at Strathearn and Eden Mill distilleries, manufactured in Galicia, Italy. They are small, alembic-style stills, significantly cheaper than the products of Forsyth, Abercrombie or McMillan, and fitted with larger heads than is usual on this style of still, in order to increase reflux.

Meanwhile, Inchdarnie distillery in Fife and Harris in the Outer Hebrides opted for stills made by the Italian family firm of Frilli, established in Tuscany back in 1912. These are relatively conventional copper pots, and when an expansion of Glen Moray distillery in Elgin took place in 2017, the three new stills, complete with thermo-vapour recompression capability, were also supplied by Frilli.

Not that anyone need be too concerned that the great Scottish tradition of copper pot still fabrication is under any real threat. Forsyth's recorded turnover of £52 million in the 12 months to the end of October 2016, and pre-tax profits stood at £5.7 million. As Richard Forsyth says, "Due to a combination of project at home and overseas, it was our best year ever."

Those pear-shaped, gleaming copper stills, with their Loch Ness monster necks seem certain to keep finding their way from the back streets of Rothes to spirit-makers all over the world.

Gavin D Smith is one of Scotland's leading whisky writers and Contributing Editor Scotland for Whisky Magazine. He regularly undertakes writing commissions for leading drinks companies and produces articles for a wide range of publications, including Whisky Magazine, Whisky Magazine & Fine Spirits – France, Whisky Etc, Whisky Advocate, Whiskeria, Whisky Quarterly and The Cask.
He is the author and co-author of some 30 books, and recent publications include The Dalmore Presents History in the Making – Richard Paterson 50 Year Anniversary and a new and fully updated edition of Michael Jackson's Whisky the Definitive World Guide, co-written with Dominic Roskrow.

Guardians
of the Whisky Galaxy

by Neil Ridley

With the huge growth in the number of craft distilleries across both Scotland and Ireland, do the major whisky stakeholders feel the need to protect the category as a whole, which could be in danger of consuming itself?

Every major big-budget-Hollywood-block-buster film needs a sense of drama to capture the attention of the viewer. As a man fast approaching middle age, my enthusiasm for the edge-of-your-seat dramatics in the Star Wars films has occasionally bordered on the fanatical (ok, with the exception of the rubbish 'trilogy' made as the new millennium arrived) and I have taken great delight in following the almost pantomime personas of the main characters. For every Darth Vader out there, (boooo, hiss…) there needs to be a Luke Skywalker or Obi-Wan Kenobi (hooray!) to balance the yin and yang of the fabric of the galaxy.

Now, it might seem a little tenuous here, but for me, we're sort of reaching a Star Wars'esque story-line in whisky. One where the small, independent - and often maverick - distiller or whisky maker challenges the established order, often causing extremely newsworthy friction along the way. We feel their pain as they face setbacks and run-ins with the regulatory authorities, their innovative wings clipped, by dark, insidious overlords, to make an example for anyone else who might dare to dream differently. Or something like that.

In all seriousness though, when you begin to tot up the swelling numbers in the ranks of the new craft distilling movement in both Scotland and Ireland, one actually starts to feel genuine change in the

The new micro distillery at Midleton

waters, which is clearly inspiring. At the same time though, there's potentially trouble brewing.

Cast your eye over the following stats. In 2013, there were just four distilleries making whiskey in Ireland. Today there are 16 in production and 13 more being planned across Ireland, bringing the total to 29 distilleries over the next ten years. In Scotland, the picture is very similar. Since 2013, 14 new distilleries have emerged blinking from the shadows, with another 20 currently going through the process of establishing themselves over the next few years.

Great stuff. Or is it?

Yes, on one hand, it reflects the true vibrancy of the spirit at this given moment. However, it's probably fair to say that not all of these new operations are going to be turning out outstanding whisk(e)y - or can even afford to stay in the game long enough to actually produce the spirit. Herein lies the problem. Whisky has survived for so long by painstakingly building its fearsome reputation for consistent quality. Throw in a few mavericks with loud mouths and voracious appetites for using social media and suddenly that stability is potentially under threat, the worst case scenario being that the consumer is left fearing and distrusting what's in their glass; where flavour profile and quality are sent spiralling out of control like a stricken Millennium Falcon, despite

the authorities' best attempts to control it. To quote my learned friend Joel Harrison for a second, 'yes, a rising tide floats all boats, but it also dredges up a load of sunken trash at the same time…'

Custodians of whisky

All this got me thinking about the concept of 'Custodianship'. What if some of the bigger players took it upon themselves to become not the big, bad Darth Vaders of the industry, but the facilitators; the mentors; and ultimately the guiding lights to the new generation of distillers: the Obi-Wans of Whisk(e)y.

My first port of call in this respect was to visit Irish Distillers, (I.D.L.) a company, which has openly discussed its support for this sort of concept, when it comes to its broader role in the Irish whiskey industry. The vast Midleton distillery in Cork is now home to a brand new high-tech on-site micro distillery with a capacity of 2,500 litres, (compared to the 75,000-litre capacity stills on display in the main distillery,) aiming to enable a greater level of innovation for its whiskey makers. It is also one of the first to offer a mentoring programme, alongside a Whisky Academy course to learn directly from the IDL distilling experts.

'Clearly Irish whiskey is on a significant rise and

Brendan Buckley - Strategy, Innovation & Prestige Whiskeys Director for Irish Distillers

we see our role in the industry certainly as a company who can help engender the most important thing in its production, which is quality,' explains Brendan Buckley, Strategy, Innovation & Prestige Whiskeys Director. 'In opening the Irish Whiskey Academy and mentoring scheme, [led by Dave Quinn, Head Of Whiskey Science, along with tutor, Ciarán O'Donovan,] we very much felt that we could give aspiring distillers a chance to learn the best technical ability. It's empowering them to produce quality whiskey of their own, which at the end of the day, leads to the betterment of the industry as a whole. There's absolutely nothing to be gained for the business if there's poor quality whiskey out there,' he continues, 'so this is a long term investment in the category for Irish Distillers.'

In some ways, despite being one of the largest producers of whiskey in the world, what's crucial here is the willingness of I.D.L. to understand the complexities and future pitfalls of the category, now there are so many more players in it. Clearly, the makers of Jameson and Redbreast et al aren't going to be feeling a major financial pinch from the newcomers anytime soon, but by reaching out to the wider Irish whiskey industry with this scheme, what they can learn is how to be more fleet-of-foot and open-handed with the burgeoning community of new distillers, giving them the genuine right to play the elder statesman.

Back in Scotland, i'm keen to catch up with arguably one of the most vocal - and controversial - companies in the drinks business, which has, over the past decade, been highly critical of some of the major players, particularly when it comes to their influence over the rules and regulations.

Last year, maverick brewers Brew Dog entered the spirits business, announcing the opening of its new distillery, Lone Wolf, in Ellon, Aberdeenshire, claiming it 'wants to stretch the boundaries of what a distillery can do – and what a distillery should do.'

The man tasked with piloting the ship through the spirity asteroid belt is Head Distiller Steven Kersley, who previously worked for Diageo, managing several of its distillery sites. As a distiller with experience in both an established organisation and now, with an unconventional and more esoteric-focused one, Does Steven think that the major stakeholders should be concerned about the potential 'threat' from the new breed of savvy, forward-thinking independents?

'The 'established' are not likely losing any sleep just yet, however they absolutely should be taking note of the fundamental progress happening within our industry,' he feels. 'One is the globalisation of whisky. The international whisky surge shows no

Lone Wolf Distillery's manager, Steven Kersley

sign of rest as more distillers from across the globe are putting their own interpretation of whisky into a bottle. The creation of the 'global distiller' means that we're moving toward a post-geographical era in whisky; where the link between a whisky style's quality and its country of origin will no longer be recognised. And rightly so,' he continues, 'irrespective of style, a pre-requisite for quality should never be influenced by the country in which it was distilled. With this, 'established' distillers will see consumers enjoying new global expressions and this will begin to erode long standing loyalties to Scotch.'

It's a bold statement - especially given that Lone Wolf is essentially a Scottish distillery, who will be producing a 'Scotch whisky' at some point in the next few years, under the regulations of the Scotch Whisky Association.

'In terms of a 'threat' to Scotch's flavour profile, there first needs to be an appetite for moving beyond traditional distilling methods – an appetite which I have,' continues Kersley. 'The traditional approach to distilling whisky has served Scotland well but it's time to accept that we can do even more in pursuit of flavour. As a distiller, my allegiance can never be to a single spirit style. I want to move beyond tradition by exploring many styles of whisky and putting our unique interpretation of these into the glass.'

I ask Steven for his thoughts on whether the bigger companies have a duty to protect how the Scotch whisky industry develops, given the rise in smaller voices, or whether ultimately too much interference could lead to its downfall. Naturally, he doesn't hold back…

'There's a thin line between 'protecting' and 'controlling' how the industry develops. Large stakeholders currently hold too much influence over how the future of this industry will develop. We only have to look at the S.W.A. council to understand who steers the ship and it is this dynamic that causes me concern,' he points out. 'Without visibility of alternative concepts designed to challenge mindsets in a progressive way, in all likelihood, they will stymie; never advancing the methods, knowledge and ultimately, the whisky of the companies that they represent.'

Moment of truth - first bottling

'I think the regulations have helped to ensure that people who are actually committing to make whisky aren't simply in it for a quick buck, thinks Michael Vachon, founder of Maverick Drinks, who distribute a wide range of craft distillery releases, including American whiskeys and now, the new Wolf Burn distillery in Thurso, Scotland. 'If you've got to wait three years, I think you're going to want it to be good when it comes out of the barrel. It does mean you've got to have a lot of capital on hand and I'm just waiting for the flood of distilleries who've been making gin to pay the bills, while they make their whisky. That's when we'll really separate the kids from the adults – and the whiskies that can stack up will really shake things up.'

On the flip side, I ask Nick Morgan, Head Of Whisky Outreach for Diageo for his thoughts regarding the rise in craft distilleries and whether there is cause for concern from within the major stakeholders in

Impression of the expanded Stauning Distillery

how these new whiskies will be perceived, given the hard fought reputation of Scotch worldwide.

'The market for Scotch whisky, whether from very small or very large distilleries, is on a long-term upward trend: there is room for everyone, IF they can produce something that people want to buy - time and again. Indeed, we believe that current trends will add even greater momentum to the Scotch category and inspire new generations of consumers to fall in love with Scotch. That is good for everyone in the industry, whether large or small.'

So has Diageo ever viewed itself as a potential 'custodian' to the ranks of smaller emerging distillers?

'Well, we have privately offered support and advice to a number of start-ups in Scotland, as well as to new distillers throughout the world who are associated with Distill Ventures,' [a Diageo-backed development company, which provides investment and support to spirits entrepreneurs, so far committing over £25m to distilling projects since 2013,] continues Morgan. 'In Scotch, producers have a long history of collaboration and knowledge sharing. In addition, our micro distillery at Leven [containing a pair of 1,000 litre stills] operates as an experimental facility to support our extensive innovation agenda in Scotch.'

It seems rather timely to turn my attention away from Scotland for a second to speak to someone who, in many respects, has the benefit of being part of the growing independent community, but with the added benefit of financial support, advocacy and counsel from Distill Ventures. Alex Munch is

Alex Munch, managing director and co-founder of Stauning

the Managing Director and co-founder of Stauning distillery in Denmark, which first began distilling in an old abattoir in the western part of Jutland back in 2005. A decade later, the distillery received a £10 million investment from Distill Ventures with plans to upscale production from the current 15,000 litres to around 900,000, so you could say a significant increase in size - and indeed, expectation.

'The bigger stakeholders need to embrace and follow the way the whisky industry develops,' thinks Munch. 'Protection will only make them unpopular. It will not trigger the industry's downfall but it will decrease the interest in larger distilleries and ultimately decrease revenue. You already see more and more of the 'big' players in the industry invest in - and work with - new small craft distilleries.'

As an independent - and a recipient of support

Eden Mill Brewery/Distillery (top)
and the column at Lone Wolf, 19 metres tall with 60 plates

from Distill Ventures, is Munch keen to keep the focal point of his whisky as different as possible (within the regulations) or would he welcome input from larger players if he felt it improved his production capability?

'We very much welcome input from the larger players. We do not aim to make 'different' whisky. We try to make 'great' whisky' he explains. 'The larger players have a lot of experience in the production of whisky. Often they are restricted in making new styles by the size of their production. But they possess the knowledge, people and money to be able to do fantastic new stuff. We can learn a lot from them.'

Similarly, what can the bigger players learn from the likes of Stauning?

'The larger players need to be more versatile,' thinks Munch. 'They need to understand that the spirits world wants to see more craftsmanship. Drinkers also want to experiment with their own tastes. They want to be challenged. But they also want to have a 'safe haven'. A place to go back to. A favourite. A Brand. It is like cars. You like to drive different ones, but you have favourite. I like Porsche, but I love to try other cars! So the big players need to put out more small scale 'experiments'. Johnnie Walker is doing some of that with its limited releases.'

Back in Scotland I head over to Eden Mill, arguably one of Scotland's more progressive new distilleries, helping to mark the resurgence of the Lowland region. Here, co-founder Paul Miller and his team of distillers have gone against the grain (excuse the pun) in terms of how they perceive a distillery set up. You'll find small alembic-style pot stills from Portugal rather than a traditional Forsyth template, and an extensive knowledge of brewing has widened the net in terms of unusual mash bills - of course, all needing to stay well within the regulations of the S.W.A.

Like Stauning's Alex Munch, I also ask Miller whether if he would be keen to keep the ethos and DNA of Eden Mill's whisky as unique as possible, or given the opportunity, would he welcome the input of the larger players, if he felt it would improve his production capabilities.

'That's a difficult question. I think the advantage of 'small' probably comes with less risk and more scope to be creative and interesting. That said, around the whisk(e)y globe there are great examples of fantastic collaborations created by smaller distillers and whisky makers aligning themselves with big players. Whether it is great blended Scotch [think Compass Box, who, since 2015, have a long-term whisky supplier and a minority stake investor in the shape of Bacardi's John Dewar & Sons,] or at the extreme, bigger brands such as the fantastic High West range, [now part of an acquisition deal with Constellation Brands Inc,] there is definitely scope for clever marriage of the two.'

So where can changes - perhaps concessions - be made by the bigger companies and the regulators, allowing small players to continue to thrive and survive?

'The rules and regs can be very limiting and definitely restrict commercial advantage versus other whisk(e)y regions and countries,' feels Miller. 'An example is the flexibility for new Irish distilleries to drive early revenue from blended malts and create brand engagement before their own spirit is mature. This is not allowed in Scotland. This forces the need for more creativity in both the marketing and the production of the products with Scotch. At Eden Mill we have created a range of exciting blended whiskies but cannot market them under our own name as the [regulatory] view is that the consumer is not clever enough to understand the difference between a malt and a blend. That is clearly ridiculous,' he continues. 'This, along with the obvious crazy notion that drinkers don't want to know, or be better informed as to the transparency of the major components of their blended whisky, are clearly absolute

nonsenses which should be addressed.'

Ah. The T Word. Good old transparency. Back over at Lone Wolf, I get the sense that Steven Kersley has a few more choice things to say, especially on this industry buzz word, currently butting heads with the powers-that-be. A fight brilliantly highlighted by John Glaser, Compass Box's very own Han Solo a little over a year ago, it feels like we certainly haven't heard the last of it yet… certainly not from Mr Kersley at any rate.

'The industry needs and should become fully transparent in what it's doing,' he argues. 'Forget Age Statements vs NAS… just tell me what the fuck is in the bottle! I want to know where your casks are from? Are you using virgin oak, ex-bourbon or re-fill? If so, what char level is on your virgin oak wood? What was in your bourbon cask before - and for how long?'

The more I hear and read about the likes of Lone Wolf, Stauning, Eden Mill and a host of other smaller players who are just establishing themselves, the more I feel that there clearly needs to be a broader symbiotic relationship in place between the mavericks, the major players and, as the overarching governing bodies, the Scotch and Irish Whisk(e)y Associations. Yes, it's easy to paint them as the Dark Side, set up so support the interests of the few rather than the many, but when you think of whisk(e)y as a galaxy of distilleries and flavours, there needs to be some higher level of regulation to stop the whole thing imploding. That said, for European whiskies to continue to develop and delight new consumers, who now have a greater choice of flavours and styles coming from the growing number of innovative American craft whiskies too, the bigger players, including the respective authorities need to listen more closely to those pushing the envelope, rather than rattling their (light) sabres at them.

Come on guys. Let's make the next decade in whisky A New Hope. Not The Empire Strikes Back.

Neil writes about whisky and other fine spirits for a number of publications globally, including The Daily and Sunday Telegraph, and is also the deputy editor for Whisky Quarterly. He is the former chairman of the World Whiskies Awards and regularly presents a drinks feature on the popular TV show, Channel 4 Sunday Brunch. His first book, (written with Gavin D. Smith) 'Let Me Tell You About Whisky' was published in 2013 and since then, he has co-authored 'Distilled', which is now printed in nine languages, winning the Fortnum & Mason Drink Book Of The Year in 2015. His latest book, 'Straight Up...' celebrates the finest drinking experiences on every continent.

Daniel Szor - founder and owner of Cotswolds Distillery

The Rise
of English Whisky

by Dominic Roskrow

By the end of 2018 there will be nine distilleries
in England with whiskies ready to bottle, and by the end of 2020
there will be 14. Dominic Roskrow looks at how the English are slowly
and surely winning the battle for credibility.

"When we launched our distillery we were considered whisky makers who were doing some gin while we waited for the whisky spirit to mature. That is often what whisky distillers do. But in the three years since, we have gone from being whisky makers doing gin on the side, to an award winning gin distillery that has a new single malt whisky. The whole perception has changed. It's quite strange."

Daniel Szor is the owner of Cotswolds Distillery at Stourton, Warwickshire in England and he is committed to making great malt whisky. The distillery's first release came in late 2017. But the three years it took to mature happens to coincide almost exactly with the revolution in gin production. Over those three years gin is being made pretty much everywhere, but it's being made pretty much everywhere more in England than anywhere else. And it turns out that the Cotswold Distillery is pretty good at making it,

The English Whisky Company's Master Distiller David Fitt (left) and founder and managing director Andrew Nelstrop

picking up award after award for its richly flavoured, premium quality spirit.

English whisky is still learning to walk, and might be considered vulnerable. So has the gin boom in England been a cause for celebration for the country's whisky producers, or has it over-shadowed their hard work and even damaged their potential to be taken seriously as malt makers? Andrew Nelstrop, founder and managing director of the English Whisky Company, says it hasn't made much of a difference.

"There is no question the gin boom has taken the media eye off whisky," he says. "It has also taken a share of the shelf space in both shops and bars – so yes there must have been a detrimental effect. However we haven't felt it much with The English brand, so one can only assume it is more likely to be hurting the big generic brands."

Paul Currie, founder and managing director of the Lakes Distillery, argues that the gin boom has been positive for English whisky producers.

"From the outset we always planned to produce whisky, gin and vodka, and all three are important to us," he says. "The rapid growth in gin has only helped the credibility of English spirit production in general, as there are some outstanding products, not least from those distilleries also producing whisky."

One of the newest English distilleries, Spirit of Yorkshire, has not succumbed to the gin trend, and is proudly producing malt spirit. In fact the distillery's whisky director Joe Clark dismisses gin out of hand.

"We make every drop of our spirit from first principles and from barley we grow on our farm. This is at the core of our distillery and everything we do," he says. "To take any of this spirit forward to make a pot distilled gin at this stage just wouldn't make sense from a long term point of view."

All the evidence is that the new whisky producers will not be rocked off course by anything as trivial as a rival spirit. After all, its Northern neighbour is Scotland and its Western one is Ireland, both heavyweight whisky makers. No pressure then.

Struggling with the councils

England, led by Nelstrop and his team, has had to fight a constant credibility battle on the one hand, and has faced hurdles unlike most other countries.

Right from the start, there were problems. Armed with an antiquated, cumbersome, and ambiguous law about the minimum size of a distillery's stills, Britain's customs and revenue officers proved to be remarkably intransigent when it came to issuing distilling licences. Ignoring the craft industry in the United States, where job creation, tax generation, and a tourism boom were by-products of it, English planners brought an ill informed and inaccurate view

Spirit of Yorkshire - one of the latest distilleries to open up in England

of whisky making to the decision making table.

Andrew Nelstrop takes up the story. "When we sought planning permission for the distillery we wanted it to be on a greenfield site, but the council officers wanted to advise the councillors to only approve a site on an industrial estate in a nearby town. They had no understanding of what malt whisky distilleries were, and how they operated elsewhere in the world, especially in Scotland."

Nelstrop approached Whisky Magazine, which is based in nearby Norwich, and asked its Editor to write to councillors explaining the tourism benefits, and how distilleries in Scotland had nestled among the bens, glens and lochs for generations, with little or no detrimental environmental effect.

It worked. Not only did St George's get a unanimous vote in favour of the site it is now based on, but also the council officers were reprimanded for their failure to research the issue properly.

That wasn't the absolute end of it, though. Four years later your writer received a call from Paul Currie, stating that he was fighting the very same objections in the pretty tourist region of the Lake District. He won, too, and irony of ironies, now presides over one of the region's most visited tourist sites.

"Tourism is an important part of our business, and we have enjoyed great success in establishing The Lakes Distillery as a major tourist destination," says Currie. "Already in only our third year we are a Top 10 visited distillery in the United Kingdom (including Scotland)."

"Tourism is very important," says Nelstrop. "We now receive more than 50,000 visitors a year. A good proportion of these have come to the region specifically to visit us, so we are acting as a draw to the local tourism industry."

Both St George's with the Norfolk Broads and extensive coastline, and Lakes with the Lake District, are aided by the fact that they can tap in to a ready supply of natural tourist traffic. That's true of the Cotswolds Distillery, too, though Zsor and his partners steered around the potential for objections by involving the community from the very start, calling a parish meeting, unveiling his plans and asking for questions and suggestions from the local community.

"They were fully supportive when they saw what we planned. And we have made sure we have stayed at the heart of the community since. People from the village come and label our bottles for us and this has become quite a social event."

It's still very early days for English whisky but it's already clear that it's highly unlikely that its distillers will follow Scotland and Ireland down the road of forming an Association to define and dictate what can and cannot bear the national name on the bottle. That's in the main because there is a definite independence about the current batch of distillers and while some of them are making single malt in pretty much the same way as Scotland does, they're reluctant to give up the right to do something different should they so wish. Indeed some English producers have done something different from the off.

Adnams' Copper House Distillery, The London Distillery Company and The Oxford Artisan Distillery (TOAD) are experimenting with different grains including rye. Unusual wood types have been employed, and spirit matured in virgin oak has been used. Even St George's has moved from its peated and non peated formula and has successfully launched The Norfolk, a zesty and sweet grain whisky.

Paul Currie says that while Lakes will experiment with styles, the distillery's principle aim is to make good quality malt whisky.

"It really depends on the distillery, as I am sure we each have our different plans," he says. "At The Lakes Distillery we are very much taking the best of Scotch whisky making and bringing that to the Lakes. Just as in Scotland, where there is a large range of styles, there is likely to be a range of styles amongst the English distilleries."

What characterises the first wave of English distillers is their serious approach to whisky making. There is no corner cutting, no dubious practices, and a great deal of emphasis on the very best equipment and the finest resources. This has partially been born of necessity. St George's, Adnams and Cotswolds all bottled whisky at its minimum age of three years and so they had to do everything to ensure the quality was good. Different climate conditions to Scotland helps. So does the move by Scottish distillers to market younger non aged statement whiskies.

"Every time a new Scottish single malt whisky comes out without an age statement, my life gets a little bit easier," says Nelstrop.

Is there an English whisky style?

So far, there has been no need or great call for an Association. The upside of an Association is that it can enforce a minimum quality standard but the down side is that it can harness creativity. The current distillers seem universally happy to focus on their own whisky and not to look or a specific style of English whisky.

"I think it will be a long time before we see an accepted style (of English whisky)," says The English Whisky Company's Andrew Nelstrop. "Maybe never, given a lot of the newcomers are using part pot/part column stills to make whisky – which definitely make a different style of whisky to the more

traditional set up."

Joe Clark at the Spirit of Yorkshire Distillery tends to agree, but adds a note of caution.

"If regional styles develop across English whisky distilleries or an overall style emerges that would be a great thing, but it would almost certainly be a coincidence," he says.

"A distillery character is generally being shaped by choices rather than geography these days anyway. We have been able to do some really interesting things in terms of production by not being tied down by SWA regulations. However, it's very much a double edged sword. The lack of rules in English whisky production could allow for some less than excellent whisky to emerge, and this in turn could potentially damage all English whisky. Overall I would say it's a positive having less rules to abide, so long as quality is always at the forefront."

The quality issue is essential if English whisky is going to be fully accepted in the medium to long term. All the distillers accept that the battle to establish credibility in international markets is far from won.

"Consumers are now much more interested in trying whiskies from different countries, and there is a huge choice now," says Lakes Distillery's Paul Currie. "As a result English whisky is no longer that different a concept, although it is still relatively new and the number of whiskies available at present is small. But over the coming years there will be quite a few more launching (including The Lakes Malt), and then the reputation will spread."

Joe Clark still thinks there is no real perception of what English whisky is.

"The English whisky industry is still very young, but as more distilleries appear and start coming of age in the coming years I'm sure a positive perception will emerge."

So the burning questions are if English whisky going in a different direction to its Scottish neighbour, and can it better the famous spirit from North of the border?

"Dare I say it but I think you're asking the wrong question," says Nelstrop. "The real question is 'are there differences between what Independent whisky producers are trying to achieve and what the Big Five are doing'?"

As independent start ups, all of us are free to create a whisky style of our own, along with a brand image to make us attractive to our target audience. Those of us based outside of Scotland have a simpler set of rules we have to adhere to, which should have the advantage of letting us be more creative – which we need to be."

Mor than 70,000 visitors come to The Lakes Distillery every year

The Spirit of Yorkshire's Joe Clark also picks up on the big distillery versus craft angle.

"The English whisky scene is yet to really find its feet," he says. "We also have an absence of the big distilling companies, so on the whole you could say we are looking to achieve very different things at the moment. Mainly that we need to establish ourselves as a credible and serious whisky making country. St George's efforts have gone a long way already, to which we doff our caps. Here at SOY we are motivated largely by flavour and are hugely excited about what we're doing. I think the excitement levels in some of Scotland's older distilleries might have diminished as a result of decades of automation."

Nevertheless, the pressure is on for the English producers to get it right – and get it right first time. Daniel Zsor, for instance, admits to nervousness as his whisky enters the whisky arena.

"Of course we all hope consumers like the whisky as much as we do," he says. "But it's exciting too. All the work we have done and time we have spent comes down to this. And yet we have no idea what people's buying habits will be, and how much we will sell."

So is English whisky set for an exciting future? The answer is unanimous.

"Almost certainly yes," says Clark. "There's an English whisky boom in the pipeline and it's going to make for some interesting tasting and debate in the coming decades."

Andre Nelstrop goes one further. "If anyone making English whisky spirit says no to this – they probably need a new career," he says. "It will have its highs and lows financially but I am pretty sure it will always be exciting – after all there are three billion customers we have to go out and meet!"

A firm future for English whisky? I'll raise a glass of gin and tonic to that.

Dominic is a freelance writer and consultant, specialising in whisky from non traditional regions. He has written 11 spirits books, and has another five due for publication in 2018. He has worked as a writer on a range of newspapers and magazines, and the titles he has edited include Whisky Magazine, The Spirits Business, Whiskeria, Pub Food, The Pub Business, and Club Mirror. He was Fortnum & Mason's Drink Writer of the Year in 2015, and his book Whisky: Japan was granted 'Best in the World' status at the 1917 Gourmand Awards in China. Dominic lives in Norfolk and he is one of the few people to be both a Kentucky colonel and a Keeper of the Quaich.

Lone Wolf Distillery

Brand New Whisky

by Jonny McCormick

Building a new distillery is a complicated
and time consuming commitment, not to mention running it once it has
been commissioned. But three or more years ahead, lies another
daunting task. Branding and selling your mature product.

Imagine you own a newly built distillery. From inception to opening, your whole project has been scrutinized and debated on social media, speculated upon at festivals and whisky club nights, eyed-up by a sceptical local press, and watched closely by your long-suffering family, friends, and curious neighbours. There's a lot riding on this. Finally, you believe you are ready to put the liquid into a bottle and send it out into the world, but it's a nerve-wracking moment, like a parent letting their child's hand slip free on the first day of school. How will the world react to your new product, your new brand, your brand new whisky?

This is the time of distilleries with brief histories. By the Twenties, dozens of new, young single malt Scotch whiskies will be vying for your attention. Where will you be when you drink your first dram of Port of Leith, Toulvaddie, or GlenWyvis? Will whisky drinkers be able to buy any of these whiskies for under £50, or £100 by then? What lessons and pitfalls can whisky consumers and distillers with big time dreams learn from reviewing the strategies adopted by new distillers over the last 30 years?

From flogging branded new make spirit to wooing enthusiasts into cask sales, through exclusive founder's clubs to the critically important inaugural release, these fledgling distillers have a lot of decisions ahead of them. Let's begin by meeting

Tony Reeman-Clark – founder and owner of Strathearn Distillery

someone who developed his own unique solution to the quandary of the first release.

Strathearn distillery in Methven may be one of Scotland's smallest, but it has plenty of space for ambition. As the first distillate approached three years in cask, distillery owner and founder Tony Reeman-Clark contemplated what to do.

"I didn't have any idea what price to put on the bottles," he admits. "The first bottling sets the benchmark. If it's too low, they fly off the shelves and I kick myself. If it's too high, they wouldn't sell and that would be it." Mulling this predicament over, Reeman-Clark had a brainwave. He knew it was risky, but it might just work. "I suddenly thought, let's give everyone the opportunity to get involved. Why don't we put one hundred 50cl bottles up for auction?"

Reeman-Clark approached Iain McClune at Whisky Auctioneer, Perth, and they conceived an exciting new venture for both parties. Firstly, they created a dedicated Strathearn microsite within Whisky Auc-

tioneer. Secondly, they stretched the online format way beyond the normal duration. Reeman-Clark stipulated that the sale would last from August 23rd, the date that Strathearn received its licenses in 2014, until December 1st, the distillery's third anniversary. He could scarcely believe his eyes when all 100 bottles met the reserve within the first 10 hours.

Using an auction, Reeman-Clark circumvented people buying his first release and flipping it for profit, yet it enabled the distillery to nimbly sidestep any criticism of setting a prohibitively high price for young whisky. That's not the kind of publicity you want to attract. When Abhainn Dearg released 2,011 bottles of 3 year old whisky for £150, some balked at the asking price for a 50cl bottle. Six years later, the inaugural release is still listed for sale on the distillery's website, a salutary lesson for new distillers and collectors. Isle of Arran has earned a highly regarded reputation for innovative packaging, but their first production 3 year old was an unlabelled decanter with a clear plastic seal over the cork. If the neck tag was lost, it was difficult to prove provenance and authenticity.

Two distilleries stand out for delivering effective campaigns that helped to cultivate a loyal following. Family-run Glengyle distillery in Campbeltown released generous quantities of their annual 'Work in Progress' bottlings from 2009 onwards, all based on their 2004 production. The packaging was eye-catching, bottles were never numbered, and prices were eminently affordable. At each subsequent release, the whisky was a little more mature, and they began to showcase the influence of bourbon and sherry wood maturation until the whisky turned 12 years old.

Kilchoman, Islay's eighth distillery, delivered an inaugural release of 3 year old whisky that sold out quickly. Eager fans snapped up the regular supply of seasonal releases and cask strength single cask bottlings that followed. Quite rightly, Kilchoman are regarded as the master architects of the perfect distillery launch. Welcome similarities are apparent in the pace of young whiskies emerging from Wolfburn distillery in Thurso: while 875 bottles of their inaugural release cost £200 each (but now sell for two to three times the price), simultaneously, they released a regular bottling for £45 to enable drinkers to taste the single malt.

Given that history, did the auction help Tony Reeman-Clark set his prices for future releases?

"I thought this would give me an indication," he says optimistically. "I knew the first 100 bottles would probably go at a premium. I thought, 'If they go for £120 on average, then the retail price would be £60–80. It'll give me a guideline.' How wrong I was!" The 100 bottles sold for a total of £40,000, achieving a median hammer price of £333. Giuseppe Begnoni, the well-known Italian whisky collector, purchased bottle No. 1 for £4,150, which may be the most expensive first bottle ever released by a distillery.

"There was a huge amount of interest from all around the world. It means people know Strathearn; they believe in what we do, they believe in the quality of the spirit, and it's good for small-scale distillers everywhere."

After pioneering the Strathearn sale, Whisky Auctioneer secured another inaugural release exclusive from Israel's Milk & Honey distillery in August 2017. What next for Strathearn?

"I think if I were to go to auction with the second lot, it possibly appears that I'm being greedy and I'm not," explains Reeman-Clark. "A lot of people asked why I didn't keep bottle No.1? Well, I've got the distillery!" he says with a broad grin.

Money up front

Launching a distillery is an expensive business. It's more than just covering the building, distillery equipment, production staff, malt, and casks. Don't forget to budget for the costs of marketing, developing branded packaging and bottles, and employing a sales team. Properly financed projects have all this covered, cognisant that the return on their investment will not be realised for many years. You are more likely to hear about companies with a funding gap separating their ambitions from their bank balance.

Companies with tighter resources try to bolster their cash flow by connecting with high-end consumers and investors. Raising additional funds can take the form of crowdfunding, private investments, cask sales, and founder's clubs. What's in it for us, the consumer? An opportunity to be part of something new from the beginning, guaranteed access to early bottlings and distillery privileges, and the pleasure of following the maturation of your own cask.

The downside can be summarised in two words: Ladybank distillery. Just over a decade ago, the public were invited to invest thousands of pounds to join an exclusive founder's club for this yet to be built farm distillery in Fife. Founding members could enjoy access to exclusive club facilities and look forward to receiving a case of whisky every year once it was mature. Hundreds of people handed over their cash. But then the project floundered. The company approached existing club members for even more money, but in the end, the project collapsed and the distillery was never completed. Nobody received any whisky. Nobody got a penny back.

Learn to discriminate between working distilleries already producing spirit from schemes that have yet to break ground; despite the best intentions, the latter may not have the money, requisite approvals, or required permissions to build. Regrettably, the Gartbreck distillery project was scuttled in this manner, quite literally holed below the water line (though they never sought outward investment from whisky drinkers). If you are considering obliging new distillers with alternative forms of finance, you need to decide the level of risk you are prepared to take and what you expect in return.

Holyrood Park distillery hope to raise £5.5 million through an Enterprise Investment Scheme, the same tax-efficient investment vehicle that Holyrood Park co-founder David Robertson used to launch an ambitious £4 million fundraising drive for his Whisky Trading Company in 2013. The GlenWyvis distillery

Richard Beattie, Distilling Director for Mossburn Distillers and Anthony Wills, founder and owner of Kilchoman Distillery

community share scheme exceeded expectations and a second wave of £250 shares was launched to meet demand. Crowdfunders who invested £2,000 with the Thompson Brothers at Dornoch distillery are happily seeing their freshly filled-octaves heavy with spirit.

Founder's Clubs currently seeking members from distilleries either side of their first distillation runs include Isle of Harris, Isle of Raasay, Kingsbarns, Lindores Abbey, and Toulvaddie. Given the abundance of choice, there may be more schemes than participants. Cask schemes require greater investment; a decade ago, Macallan filled private casks for £10,000 each, nowadays, that's the price that new distillers like Arbikie charge for their 1794 Founders cask. If you want one of the early casks from Annandale distillery, they cost £100,000 each, except for cask No.1, which they've valued at £1 million (don't worry, their 2017 casks start at a more sensible £2,100).

Cask offers vary enormously; read the small print on the current schemes from Ardnamurchan, Arran, Glasgow, Isle of Harris, Isle of Raasay, Strathearn, and Toulvaddie. Down the line, private casks can potentially compete against the distillery brand so typically numbers are limited each year. Certainly, aged casks from well-known distilleries have performed well at auction on occasion, but new distilleries have yet to earn their credentials. Do it for pleasure,

club together for the experience, but despite the less than subtle hints in the brochure, don't buy one as an investment. Remember, your cask will not be particularly rare once mature. The distillery's official branded whisky will be bottled concurrently, and every cask owner like you will be trying to sell the same type of whisky from the same place.

The Spirit of Skye

What you have to watch are the quiet ones. New distilleries that opened without asking for your money up front, and just got on with the business of distilling. Think of distilleries such as Ballindalloch, The Clydeside distillery and The Borders distillery from Three Stills.

Meet Richard Beattie, the enthusiastic Distilling Director for Mossburn distillers. His job utilises his wealth of industry experience: the former Speyside distillery manager has also worked for a commercial malting company and a brewing and distilling engineering firm. You could say he's had an exciting year. Production commenced at Torabhaig distillery on the Isle of Skye and he expects to have produced 250,000 litres of alcohol (lpa) by the end of 2017, with a target of 450,000 lpa for 2018. They have a classic Forsyth still, semi-lauter mashtun, and wooden washbacks designed to produce specific attributes in the distillate.

The inaugural bottling from Wolfburn in Thurso was launched in early 2016

"It's a traditional island spirit," describes Beattie. "You would expect an island whisky to have a peat level. Ours comes in at a high level to begin with, though it's not excessive. All these fruity esters in the background give it a really interesting character."

Boasting panoramic views across the water to the west coast mainland, Torabhaig should benefit from the hundreds of thousands of visitors who make the excursion to Skye each year. But when your spirit is too young to bottle, what do you serve at the end of the distillery tour?

"We want people to feel they have really benefitted from the experience," Beattie begins. His intention is to pour Torabhaig new make, and surprisingly, some specially selected whiskies from other companies, though with good reason, "We're showing those whiskies because they have the attributes we're looking for in Torabhaig." There won't be casks sales nor should you expect Torabhaig single malt whisky to be bottled at 3 years and a day,

"We're very fortunate that the business is structured so we're looking at the slightly longer term. It'll be a limited release, but there won't be big volumes. The discussions will be more about how it has matured and if we feel comfortable to bottle what we've got. What is key is to get the best spirit we can."

Beattie's next task is to work on Mossburn distillery near Jedburgh in the Scottish Borders. This will become the main hub for the company and its future endeavours. Mossburn will comprise of a large malt distillery with a similar sized grain distillery, warehousing, offices, and a bottling hall. He's a busy man, but there's more. Mossburn distillers, he reveals, are building a new distillery in Japan.

"It's at the south end of Osaka bay, along the road from the White Oak distillery." The company owns a share of White Oak, and this new unnamed site will be built beside the Akashi-Kaikyo suspension bridge at the Akashi brewery. They will use a Forsyth's pot still in a 'one still does all' model (meaning it requires washing out between runs). A southerly location at sea level brings its own challenges. While there will be some token maturation on site, they are seeking a specific location to bring out the best from the wood.

"The Japanese are incredibly innovative, but I want to bring back some of the traditions of the Scotch whisky industry that helped start the Japanese industry," he explains. "Without realising it, it's become kind of industrialised. That's not a nice word to use, but I want to go back to the origins, look at maturation steps, and take it back to where we used to be: back to the roots of distilling. It's easier for a small company like us. Think about the things Barnard was looking at. We can take inspiration from that and produce a really high quality product. Both peated and unpeated spirit will be produced, though

Head of Distillation at Lone Wolf Distillery – Steven Kersley

initially, we're experimenting by adding a little peated grist to the mash to see what happens."

Two aspects in the purview of brand new whisky have been deliberately overlooked as beyond the scope of this discussion. Firstly, new distilleries built by existing multinational companies to augment their blending requirements, such as Kininvie, Ailsa Bay, Roseisle, and Dalmunach.

Secondly, reopened mothballed distilleries such as Ardbeg, Bladnoch, Benromach, Bruichladdich, Glendronach and others, where the new owners worked through the gems in the newly acquired inventory while they built up stocks of new spirit. Belatedly, Kininvie and Ailsa Bay became new single malt brands in their own right, and Octomore and Port Charlotte from Bruichladdich proved exceedingly popular. Both situations can result in brand new whisky but the companies often have additional advantages over new start-ups.

At the other end of the scale, new make spirit sales were pioneered by Kilchoman, adopted by a revived Glenglassaugh, with elegant interpretations from Kingsbarns, Eden Mill, and Annandale, heck, even Highland Park got in on the act at one point. Most new distillers regard spirit sales as an optional step before they can legally sell their whisky, but you can be pretty certain they will disappear from the shelves after the inaugural release. Steven Kersley thinks differently. The Head of Distillation at Lone Wolf distillery has spent months perfecting batches of spirit in their incredible stillroom in Ellon, and he's passionate he can make young spirit like you've never tasted before.

"When you distil purposely with a viewpoint of making this spirit really tasty and approachable at 2-2.5 years, you look at grain selection, fermentation, and adapt your stillhouse to affect flavour. If we give that spirit the right cask and the right warehouse environment to mature in, there's no reason we can't get awesome flavour in a shorter space of time."

The Brewdog-backed distillery has already released Lone Wolf gin and vodka. "I've designed this distil-

important to explore those different styles of liquid as well."

Distillers pour all their knowledge and expertise into brand new whisky, so it's only natural to want people to taste it.

"I mean, that's the whole point," says Kersley, slightly exasperated. "That's why we do this! It's not a luxury we have once in a while, or something you just reach for when you're celebrating. This is a liquid that should be celebrated every day because it's fantastic. Every whisky you drink is unique, and not having the opportunity to explore all these different nuances is a complete waste for me." Kersley voices further concerns about the pull toward premiumisation, "It's limiting the audience, and I don't want to limit anyone from drinking my spirits. Hyper-premiumisation within the industry is not sustainable. We are super premium at the moment: where do you go from there? Are we going to start paying £150 for a 10 year old? Where does this trend stop?" For those raising prices of brand new whisky to generate cash flow, he delivers a sobering warning, "I think it's a short-sighted, quick buck that perhaps will set the wrong tone for their brand. It sends out entirely the wrong message."

It's too early to tell if Lone Wolf will have the same impact on spirits that Brewdog had on beer culture. In Kersley, they have appointed a talented, instinctive, thoughtful distiller who is willing to push the boundaries for the benefit of the inquisitive imbiber.

"Consumers care about provenance and authenticity. Who's making it is a big thing: the visibility of the men and women that work in the distillery crafting that spirit. That's a key thing. Quality has to underpin everything. Innovation, experimentation, and having that creative freedom is important, but ultimately, you'll be judged on what's in the bottle."

This is the age of distilleries too young for age statements. In five years' time, there may a lot of people persuading you to buy and drink their bottle of young spirits. We've only considered Scotland, but similar trends are spreading across Ireland, the U.S., and Japan. Our cup will run over with brand new whisky.

lery to make sure we're not just looking at single malt or grain whisky: we have the ability to do different styles of spirit as well," says Kersley. "We're fortunate that we have a world-class brewing facility next door. The older brewhouse will be producing our wash, so we can play tunes with variance in mashing and fermentation. The stillhouse is really agile, flexible, and diverse in its capabilities. We can put our own interpretations on different whisky styles from around the world, but ultimately, we will create our own signature house style by combining all of those variations."

It's clear that Kersley has no interest in running with the pack; their approach sets them apart from other distillers. "A big part of what Lone Wolf stands for is forging its own path, and doing things on our terms. My philosophy is that I should be able to distil any style of whisky that I wish. To me, that is part of the art of being a distiller. Working with grain is awesome, but what about sugarcane compounded with different flavours to make an absinthe? Those things are still within a distiller's remit, and it's

Whisky writer, author, and photographer Jonny McCormick has written hundreds of whisky articles for publications including Whisky Advocate, Whisky Magazine, Wine Spectator and the Malt Whisky Yearbook. McCormick created the Whisky Magazine Index and the Whisky Advocate Auction Index to track trading and value in the secondary market. He is a Keeper of the Quaich and he has led presentations about whisky in Europe, Asia, and North America.

Scotch Whisky and the Law

by Charles MacLean

The rules and regulations governing the manufacture
and sale of Scotch whisky have shaped the industry over many years.
Their adoption, evasion or avoidance has played a key role in the
evolution of Scotch as we know it today.

The amount of whisky that can be made is in direct proportion to the quantity of grain available to the distiller. As a result, until the mid-eighteenth century, distilling in Scotland was small-scale and communal. It was also closely linked to farming: the residues of brewing and distilling (spent grains and draff) were essential winter feed for cattle, and much of Scotland's rural economy was pastoral. 'Private' distilling from grain grown by a community was perfectly legal, so long as the spirits were not offered for sale (in which case they attracted excise duty). Of course, much of it was: smuggling – the illegal transportation and sale of whisky – was widespread, indeed it was estimated that during the 1760s private distillers were selling ten times the quantity of whisky made by licensed distillers.

By the 1770s, improvements in agriculture, especially in the Lowlands, led to grain surpluses, which in turn made it possible for entrepreneurs – especially the Stein family and their cousins, the Haigs – to build huge commercial distilleries in Alloa, Edinburgh and Fife, described by Professor Michael Moss as: "the largest manufacturing undertakings of any kind to emerge during the first decade of the industrial revolution in Scotland".

From the government's perspective, if distilling was concentrated in the large Lowland operations it would be easier to collect tax. Accordingly, in 1774, the use of wash stills of less than 400 gallons and spirit stills less than 100 gallons was banned. While this favoured the larger concerns, it effectively prohibited legal distilling in the Highlands, where small stills were used. In 1781 private distilling was banned altogether, but this simply stimulated smuggling: the following year 1,940 illicit stills were seized by the Excise, most them in the Highlands.

Illicit distilling as Sir Edwin Landseer saw it in his famous painting "The Highland Whisky Still"

The government now sought to encourage legal distilling in the Highlands by introducing different fiscal and other provisions above and below a notional boundary – the 'Highland Line'. In both areas duty was based on still capacity, but at a lower rate above the Line, where smaller stills (of between 30 and 40 gallons capacity were allowed, although the movement of spirits beyond the Highland region was prohibited. Below the line the minimum still capacity remained at 400 and 100 gallons. Based on a declaration by London distillers to a House of Commons Committee, duty was "settled on the supposition that stills could be discharged about seven times a week" if quality spirits were to be produced.

Notwithstanding this caveat, Lowland distillers sought ways to speed up the rate of distillation by using stronger, thicker washes and shallow saucer-shaped stills, which could be charged and run off very rapidly – 25 times in 24 hours, rather than the

expected two or three times. While this lessened the impact of the increased duty, it did not allow for much contact between the alcohol vapour and the copper walls of the still, and as a result produced coarse, impure whisky, fit only for rectification or for drinking as toddy (with added sugar, lemons and spices).

Running such stills also required investment in new equipment, especially larger and more powerful steam engines to pre-heat the wash and keep the worts at a constant temperature. Lengths of copper chain mail, called rummagers, were fitted within the wash stills to revolve mechanically in order to prevent solids in the wash burning onto the base and contaminating the low wines.

As we have seen, licensed distilleries above the Highland Line were constrained as to still size and the availability of grain (mostly, but not exclusively, malted barley, grown locally), so they did not adopt the shallow stills and rapid distillation employed by the large Lowland distilleries. As a result, their whisky was much superior, and although the law required that it be consumed within the Highland region, much found its way south.

Of course, illicit distillers could distil as they chose – slowly, in small stills with weak washes – and their product was even more esteemed than the legally made Highland whisky. Smuggling increased dramatically, some of it large scale and well organized. A 1790 Report on Smuggling in the Highlands noted hosts of such smugglers operating below the Highland Line: "travelling in bands of fifty, eighty or a hundred and fifty horses remarkably stout and fleet [having] the audacity to go in this formidable manner in the open day upon the public high roads and through the streets of such towns and villages as they have occasion to pass".

Output doubled in 1786 and 881,969 gallons [2.3 million litres] were sent south for rectification into gin - one quarter of all sprits produced in England. The Steins, with support from distillers in Liverpool and Bristol, sought to challenge the London distillers' virtual monopoly by cutting their prices below production costs. The London distillers replied by also dropping their prices in order to "drive their Scotch competitors from the market", by bribing Excise officers to impose restrictions on shipment and by lobbying Parliament, alleging that the Scotch distillers were now charging their stills upwards of 40 times a week.

The resulting Lowland License Act of 1788 required Scottish distillers to give a year's notice to export to England, which effectively put them out of production for twelve months. Five of the largest Scottish distilleries, all owned by members of the Stein and Haig families, ceased trading, with debts (mainly to the Excise) of £700,000 [roughly £100 million in today's money].

With the English market closed, large quantities of cheap grain whisky became widely available in the Central Belt of Scotland and consumption increased rapidly, especially among those who could least afford it. In the Highlands, by contrast, it was more usual to take a 'dram' of plain malt spirit at around 60%Vol, either straight or 'qualified' with a little water. A dram was one-third of a pint.

In his reflections on Scottish Life & Character in the late 18th Century, Dean Ramsay sums up the general attitude towards drinking throughout Scotland and among all classes as: "These were the notions of a people in whose eyes the power of swallowing whisky conferred distinction. And with whom inability to take a fitting quantity was a mark of a mean and futile character. Sad to tell, the funeral rites of Highland chieftains were not supposed to have been properly celebrated except that there was an immoderate and often fatal consumption of whisky… at the last funeral in the Highlands conducted according to the traditions of olden times, several guests fell victims to this usage, and actually died of the excesses".

Dramatic raise of license fees

Soon after the declaration of war with France in 1793 the license fee for Lowland distillers was tripled (to £9 per gallon of still capacity), then doubled again in 1795, and tripled again in 1797 (to £54). In the Highlands it rose from £1.10s to £6.10s.

Such increases served only to encourage illicit distilling. As one Excise Officer wrote at the time: "The extent of illicit distillation depended in great measure on the amount of duty… The smuggler's gain was in direct proportion to the amount of the spirit duty: the higher the duty, the greater the gain and the stronger the temptation… Under the operation of the still license, the legal distiller, in his endeavours to increase production, sacrificed the quality of his spirits, until the illicit distiller commanded the market by supplying whisky superior in quality and flavour."

With the (temporary) defeat of Napoleon in 1814 the British economy, stimulated by Government spending since 1793, faltered. In October that year the rules under which the English distillers worked were extended to both Highland and Lowland distillers: duty was increased, stronger washes (designed for rectification, not flavour) were required, the use of wash stills less than 500 gallons in the Highlands and 2000 gallons in the Lowlands was banned. Highland distillers remained debarred from the English market and Lowland distillers still had to give a year's notice.

The effects of these measures were catastrophic for the smaller Scottish distilleries and many closed. Failed harvests in 1815 and 1816 compounded their plight, and in 1816 there were only twelve licensed distilleries in the Highlands. Distillers, maltsters and landowners urged the chairman of the Scottish Excise Board to reduce duty (as a means of combating smuggling), reduce the required size of stills (to encourage more distillers to take out licenses) and to allow for weaker washes (to improve the quality of the spirit).

The Small Stills Act 1816 and its Amending Act 1818 addressed these grievances, but smuggling continued to grow: thousands of de-mobilised servicemen had returned home to malnourishment and despair. Landowners feared anarchy: if the excise

Cameronbridge Distillery where the first continuous still was tested

laws could be flouted, all laws could be. There were inconclusive debates in the House of Commons in 1820, and in the House of Lords, Alexander, 4th Duke of Gordon and one of the largest landlords in the Highland, urged his fellow peers to extend the provisions of the 1816 and 1818 Acts, in order to allow small distillers to make good whisky and sell it at a reasonable profit.

An 'Inquiry into the Revenue' was set up under the chairmanship of Lord Wallace, Vice President of the Board of Trade. During its deliberations the Illicit Distillation (Scotland) Act 1822 dramatically raised the penalties associated with smuggling and the powers of excisemen and magistrates to prosecute such cases. But the Commission's report the following year, embodied in the significant 1823 Excise Act, laid the foundations of the modern whisky industry.

Let Professor Moss sum up its importance: "The Act broke the Stein's and Haig's monopoly of the English trade and the smugglers' monopoly of the quality whisky market. The small distilleries in both the Highlands and the Lowlands could now make whiskies that tasted good and sell them at a lower price… The new regulations allowed each distiller to choose his own method of working, the strength of his wash within a broad limit, the size and design of his stills and the quality and flavour of his whisky. The only restraint on the industry was now the market. If demand… grew, the industry expanded; if it fell, it would contract."

The number of licensed distilleries grew from 111 in 1823 to 263 in 1825, most of them small (under 500 gallons [1,300 litres] still capacity), many of them established by former smugglers, with the support and encouragement of their landlords, but often with the – sometimes violent – opposition of their former colleagues. The amount of spirit which could be distilled increased from 3 million gallons [c.8 million litres] in 1823 to a little over 10 million gallons [c.26 million litres] in 1828.

Although the benefits of maturation were known, the whisky was mainly drunk 'straight from the still' and was highly variable in flavour. There was no significant increase in demand from Scotland, and although exports to Ireland, England and overseas moved up, the demand was insufficient to sustain the increased level of production: many of the new ventures failed after only a couple of years. The new regulations did have the desired affect in regard to smuggling, however. George Pope of the Edinburgh Excise Office reported in 1825 that: "smuggling is nearly driven out of the Lowlands". Traditionalists had reservations: an un-named contributor to the Inverness Courier in 1830 stated that smuggling had not been eradicated in the Highlands and the spirit was "infinitely more wholesome, of finer flavour, and in every way more highly prized than licensed whisky, owing to the large size of the [licensed] stills".

In 1828 the first continuous still was installed for

John Haig founded Cameronbridge Distillery in 1824

William Gladstone was responsible for the Spirits Act of 1860

testing at John Haig's Cameronbridge Distillery in Fife. It had been invented by his cousin Robert Stein of Kilbagie Distillery. Another was installed by Andrew Stein at Kirkliston Distillery, but even as these stills went into production, Aeneas Coffey, former Director General of Excise in Dublin, patented an improved continuous still to produce whisky from mixed grains. The first to be installed in Scotland was at Grange Distillery, Alloa, by Andrew Philp, also a cousin of Robert Stein, in 1834.

Although the stills were expensive, their product was pure, bland, of high strength (94%-96%) and much more palatable than previous rapidly distilled spirits. It was also cheaper and ideal for rectification into gin. Continuous stills were soon adopted by many Lowland grain distillers.

Until the mid-1830s the massive increase in production was taken up by a thirsty populace. It was estimated that "in the 1830s, the population aged fifteen and over was drinking, on average, the equivalent of a little under a pint each of duty-charged whisky a week". Then came the 'Hungry Forties'. Harvests failed, destitution and starvation were commonplace, cholera and typhus stalked the land. Whisky consumption dropped by a million gallons between 1836 and 1843, and the number of licensed distilleries dropped from 230 to 169.

Following the accession of Queen Victoria in 1837 there was a gradual change in social attitudes and a growing concern among the middle and artisan classes that whisky was not 'respectable'.

Temperance movements began to proliferate and to influence Government thinking. The Forbes-Mackenzie Act of 1853 required that pubs close at 11.00 p.m. on weekdays and all day on Sundays, increased the power of the police to enter unlicensed drinking dens and introduced 'on' and 'off premise' licensing. The Act also permitted the vatting of malt whiskies before duty had to be paid.

The last was a significant measure. The random mixing of whiskies at different ages and from different distilleries had long been practiced by wine and spirit merchants, mainly in the interest of reducing cost. Now they were able to produce quality whiskies with consistent flavours at reasonable prices. They were also able to brand their creations: without consistency you cannot brand.

The birth of blended Scotch

The first to seize this opportunity was Andrew Usher & Company, Edinburgh agents for Smith's Glenlivet, who released Usher's Old Vatted Glenlivet in 1853. Other companies soon followed suit, and when Gladstone's Spirits Act 1860 allowed the mixing of malt and grain whiskies under bond, blended Scotch whisky as we know it today, became possible.

Blended Scotch has two great virtues: its flavour

David Lloyd George was no big fan of Scotch whisky

Dubious spirit was sometimes served in the pubs in London

may be designed to have broad popular appeal, and this can be repeated batch by batch, so consumers know what they are paying for. Single malt whiskies were known to be highly variable in flavour and were often too pungent for non-Scots, and single grain whiskies were bland and fiery. A mix of the two ironed out cask and age differences, modified the impact of malt whiskies and added flavour to the grain whiskies. As early as 1864, Charles Tovey was able to write in British & Foreign Spirits: "The prevalent notion among whisky drinkers, especially in Scotland, is that several varieties of whisky blended is superior to that of any one kind".

Henceforward, the fortunes of both malt and grain distillers would be tied to those of the blending houses. In effect, the blenders became their key – often, only – clients and production was geared to filling orders. Single malts continued to be esteemed, even in London – The Wine Trade Review for January 1871 lists a number of malts being shipped there in bulk, including Glenlivet, Glen Grant, Laphroig and Aberlour. They were sold by the cask and bottled by spirits merchants or private customers, but were increasingly eclipsed by blends.

Some malt distillers resented this, and when it was revealed during the trial of the Pattinson brothers in 1901 that some of the 'single' whiskies they sold were actually blends with only a tiny amount of malt, the North of Scotland Malt Distillers Association mounted a press campaign to limit the term 'whisky' to malt alone.

Then, in 1905, Islington Borough Council sued two spirits' merchants for passing off as 'Fine Old Scotch Whisky' a blend which contained 90% grain whisky. The magistrate hearing the case held that to be called 'Scotch whisky' the product must be distilled in a pot still. The blenders and patent grain distillers were dismayed, appealed the decision and petitioned the Government for an inquiry.

The result was the Royal Commission on 'Whiskey [sic] and other Potable Spirits' 1908/09 which, after examining 116 witnesses during 37 sittings, concluded that: "Whiskey is a spirit obtained by distillation from a mash of cereal grains saccharified by the diastase of malt [and] 'Scotch whiskey' is whiskey as above defined distilled in Scotland…We have received no evidence to show that the form of still has any necessary relation to the wholesomeness of the spirit produced".

During the inquiry, some malt distillers urged that blends should contain at least 50% malt to be termed 'Scotch', and that all whisky should be matured for two years before use, but the Commission dodged these issues, although the latter was enacted by the Immature Spirits Act 1915 and extended to three years in 1916.

In parallel with this Act, David Lloyd George, Minister of Munitions, established the Central Control Board (Liquor Traffic), with widespread powers to restrict liquor consumption as it saw fit. Lloyd George was a passionate tee-totaller and would have liked to prohibit the sale of all alcohol for the duration of the War. The most serious of the many measures introduced by the Board was the requirement, in April 1917, that the strength of spirits be no greater than 40%Vol (70 Proof), nor less than 37.2%Vol (65 Proof).

Prior to this the minimum strength at which spirits could be offered for sale had been fixed at 75 Proof (42%Vol), although in truth most were bottled at around 50%Vol since further dilution tended to cause the whisky to go cloudy. Chill-filtration was unknown. Neither the licensed trade nor the whisky industry was happy about this. A memorandum to the Control Board from the Wine & Spirit Brands Association pointed out: "Compulsory dilution to a degree that would rob high-class brands of their distinctive characteristics, and practically reduce all brands to a common level of mediocrity, would obviously be to the advantage of those whose aim is cheapness rather than quality". This fell on deaf ears. While 40%Vol remains the minimum strength at which whisky can be sold, the maximum strength was fixed at 94.8%Vol by the Scotch Whisky Act 1988. This important piece of legislation expanded the 1909 definition of Scotch whisky. It must be:

• Produced in a distillery in Scotland from water and malted barley (to which whole grains of other cereals may be added) all of which have been mashed at that distillery using only enzymes within the grain and fermented only with yeast.

• Distilled at an alcoholic strength less than 94.8%Vol, so the distillate has an aroma and taste derived from the raw materials its production.

• Matured in an excise warehouse in Scotland for no less than three years in oak casks of under 700 litres capacity. [while oak has always been the most desirable cask material, prior to 1988 other woods were permissible]

• Nothing other than water and spirit caramel may be added. [prior to this paxarette, an intensely sweet sherry derivative, was commonly used to colour whisky. Other additives such as brandy or prune juice seem also to have been legal. The EC Regulation recognizing Scotch whisky (1989) specifically states that it "shall not be sweetened or flavoured"].

• No other whisky than Scotch may be made in Scotland. [in the late 19th Century several distilleries made 'Irish whiskey'. Also, there was a confusing category of 'Whisky – Product of Scotland']

In 2009 the 1988 Act was up-dated and superceded by the Scotch Whisky Regulations, which embraced not only production, but also label design, packaging and advertising, in order to protect the product's 'Geographical Indication' (G.I.). In addition to the provisions listed above:

• Five categories of 'Scotch whisky' were defined: Single Malt, Single Grain, Blended Whisky, Blended Malt (formerly 'vatted') and Blended Grain. The category name must appear on the bottle label. [this was 'in the interests of consumer clarity', as well as for G.I. protection, though many of us find the various 'blended' categories more confusing than the old fashioned 'vatted'. Terms like 'pure malt' or 'straight malt' are banned].

• In addition to the category names, five regional names were defined: Highland, Lowland, Speyside, Campbeltown and Islay. Whisky bearing such names must be wholly made within the region. [these regions have been recognized by blenders since the nineteenth century].

• No whisky may be labeled with the name of a distillery if it is not the product of that distillery; no single malt to be packaged or promoted in a way which suggests it was made at a distillery other than where is actually was made.

• No whisky that is not truly Scotch may be passed off as such by a misleading brand name.

• While the bulk export of Scotch whisky is permitted (but not in wooden casks), single malt must be bottled in Scotland.

Scotch whisky is now the most tightly defined of any spirit. Some would say it is too tightly defined, inhibiting innovation and making it difficult to compete with non-Scotch whiskeys which are not so rigorously defined. Consider the popularity of bourbons flavoured with honey or maple syrup.

But the legal framework is designed to protect the reputation, quality, authenticity and uniqueness of the product, and to assist the Scotch Whisky Association in taking action against counterfeiters – the premium nature of Scotch makes it especially vulnerable to counterfeiting.

Charles MacLean has spent the past thirty-five years researching and writing about Scotch whisky and is one of the leading authorities. He spends his time sharing his knowledge around the world, in articles and publications, lectures and tastings, and on TV and radio. His first book (Scotch Whisky) was published in 1993 and since then he has published nine books on the subject. He was elected a Keeper of the Quaich in 1992 and became Master of the Quaich in 2009. In 1997, Malt Whisky won the Glenfiddich Award and in 2003 A Liquid History won 'Best Drinks Book' in the James Beard Awards. In 2012 he also starred in Ken Loach's film The Angel's Share.

Sweet and Dry

by Ian Wisniewski

The combination of sweet and dry notes
and how they interact with other flavours, is crucial to how we perceive the
whiskies we drink. Yet very little attention is given to the impact of these
two attributes and how they are created.

Earthy, peaty, smokiness, and plenty of it, is something I frequently crave. Though at other times all I desire is elegance and abundant fruit, particularly citrus. But whatever my preference, there are two characteristics which are an integral part of the experience: sweetness and dryness. However, they don't seem to receive much attention, as though merely playing a supporting role among the cast of characteristics, rather than being star performers in their own right.

Sweetness and dryness have also been less researched than various other whisky subjects (with dryness, in turn, less researched than sweetness). Consequently, this article is not intended as an explanation, but an exploration: looking at sweetness and dryness individually, how they work together as a double act, and how they influence the perception of other flavours; followed by an exploration of how sweetness and dryness are created, and how they evolve during the production process.

Whether sweetness and dryness are classified as flavours, rather than characteristics, depends on your

Brian Kinsman - Master Blender, William Grant & Sons

point of view (I consider them flavours). Either way, their influence is the same.

"Sweetness and dryness are always there in a malt whisky, though how much to the forefront varies. The role of sweetness and dryness is quite fundamental, it's the initial impression of taste, with all the layers of complexity beyond that. In some ways sweetness is a more definite flavour and more tangible than dryness, with dryness more of an experiential characteristic, so I think of them slightly differently," says Brian Kinsman, Master Blender, William Grant & Sons.

When assessing a malt, and experiencing sweetness and dryness, we inevitably focus on what's happening on our palates. But there is of course a higher authority at work. The brain.

"Sweetness is processed by the brain as something highly desirable, it's a reward and is also comforting. Dryness is fascinating as it entails a paradox, how can a liquid be dry? There's also an intuitive response to dryness programmed into our brains, which is to drink more liquid. That's why dryness is such a powerful factor," says Greg Tucker, a taste psychologist at The Marketing Clinic.

One role of sweetness and dryness is providing 'parameters' at either end of the flavour spectrum. But then sweetness and dryness also combine to create a related characteristic, richness, which adds a sense of indulgence and complexity.

"Sweetness and dryness work very effectively together, as each provides a context for the other, dryness accentuates sweetness and vice-versa. A good malt needs this combination, and is much more interesting when they're together," says Jim Beveridge, Master Blender, Diageo.

The relationship between sweetness and dryness also raises the question of where the balance lies between them.

"Sweetness is the central part of any whisky, you must have that as it also gives roundness and lusciousness. However, sweetness mustn't be allowed to dominate, my ideal ratio is 75% sweetness and 25% dryness. That may seem a lot of sweetness, but I'm thinking about the multitude of other flavours associated with sweetness, and of course it's not an exact science, it is indeed a highly complex one which varies from one whisky to another," says Richard Paterson, Master Blender, Whyte & Mackay.

Part of other flavours or what?

Another consideration is the extent to which sweetness and dryness exist in their own right, as independent characteristics, or are part of other flavours ?

Gordon Motion - Edrington´s Master Whisky Maker

"I think on many occasions they're part of another flavour, for example vanilla or honey notes incorporate sweetness, while spices give you dry notes," says Richard Paterson.

Gordon Motion, Edrington's Master Whisky Maker, continues this theme. "Vanilla is always delivered in a context of sweetness. However, whether you can say a particular compound is sweet or not is a different matter. There are compounds which give the impression of sweetness, but which may not deliver sweetness in themselves, and there's no way of analysing or establishing whether they do."

Meanwhile, sweetness and dryness also influence the perception of other flavours, even if the level of sweetness and dryness is so subtle that it's not actually discernible on the palate.

"Sweetness makes fruit flavours seem richer and riper, and so accentuates fruitiness, while dryness adds a counter-point, and this interaction also helps to create complexity," says Brian Kinsman.

Richard Paterson adds, "Sweetness enriches an assemblage of various other flavours, and this must be counter-pointed by dryness. However, if a whisky is too dry it stops the richness coming through, so dryness must be kept under control."

As sweetness and dryness have such a significant role, they are always a focal point when I write tasting notes, and I've noticed a certain pattern. Sweetness often appears in the opening stage of the palate (either in its own right, or in association with other flavours). Dryness usually appears mid-way (also, either in its own right, or in association with other flavours), and this is a significant moment, as both are present simultaneously. Sweetness is typically the 'top' note, with dryness generally subtler and the underlying note at the 'base' of the palate. In the finish, dryness typically appears first, and remains the key note, while other nuances emerge alongside, including sweetness.

So, how does this work ? Do sweetness and dryness (as well as other flavours) appear in a particular order determined by the malt whisky, or is it down to our perception ?

"Every taste bud in the mouth can detect all of the five main flavours, sour, sweet, salt, umami and bitter, but the brain would effectively suffer from overload if it tried to work out all the flavours at once. Consequently, the brain works in a certain sequence, so that it can give its full attention to each flavour," says Greg Tucker.

This sequence is both strategic and multi-functional.

"The first flavour identified by the brain is sour, which is a 'risk' mechanism essentially checking for freshness, and whether it's off, or safe to consume. Then comes the 'reward' element, sweetness, followed by salt and umami, and last of all is bitterness. Dryness is not categorised as one of the five basic tastes, I'd say it's a 'blended concept,' it can for example be a blend of sweet and salt which may be detected mid-way. So, while we're tasting, the brain is continually decoding sensory triggers, and attributing values to them," says Greg Tucker.

Our palates are of course individual, with varying preferences and sensitivities to flavours including sweetness and dryness.

"We're all looking for different notes and attributing particular qualities to them. You might think peaty malt is fantastic and the brain tunes into this. But how we judge flavours also changes according to the time of day, how we're feeling, who we're with, and so on. Additionally, the first sip of a malt can taste significantly different to the second sip, because the starting point for the palate is different. And as flavours can accrue, particularly sweetness, perception of the same malt can change in the course of an evening. This means the question of taste is very complex," says Greg Tucker.

How sweet and dry are created

With sweetness and dryness so integral to the character of a malt, how they are created, and how they evolve during production and ageing, is a fascinating subject.

Let's look at sweetness first. Barley provides the starches which mashing converts into sugars, and if peated this adds another dimension.

"Peat predominantly adds dryness, but some peat compounds can also add sweetness, and sweet compounds can also add dryness. It's the concentration that matters, as the same compounds that add sweetness can also, above a certain level, add dryness. But the level at which a compound changes from one to the other is very difficult to calculate. Distilling peated barley is certainly a way of introducing more complexity, depth and gradation of flavour," says Brian Kinsman.

Fermentation sees the sugars converted into alcohol, with a range of flavours also created which can contribute to sweetness, such as esters (fruity notes). But fermentation also creates sulphur compounds which have an altogether different influence. Characterised by vegetal, meaty, rubbery notes, sulphur compounds are only present in tiny quantities, but nevertheless sufficient to 'override' lighter notes such as sweetness.

The level of sulphur compounds reduces during distillation, as the copper surface of the still is able to 'absorb' a certain amount, and this reduction helps to reveal the (underlying) sweetness. A small amount of fruit notes are also created during distillation, adding to the level of sweetness. Meanwhile, dryness is also evident in new make spirit.

"Balvenie new make spirit contains sweetness, some of this is from the malted barley, though esters (fruit notes) for example also give sweetness. However, there are a whole range of contributors, and it's more a case of interaction between various flavour compounds, rather than sweetness coming across in its own right. I also pick up dryness, an almost crisp and astringent note," says Brian Kinsman.

Gordon Motion provides another perspective.

"Each of our distilleries produce new make spirit with varying levels of sweetness and/or dryness. Glenturret new make spirit has fresh orange, citrus notes with a background sweetness, while Macallan has a cereal character which is more dry than sweet. Highland Park has a level of sweetness balanced by light, dry phenolic compounds."

Meanwhile, Richard Paterson highlights dryness. "New make spirit is where it is at its driest point, and it's gasping for development. Wood management is key, up to 70% of the final flavour develops during the ageing process, and that's what will determine the concentration and balance of sweet and dry flavours."

The essential choice is American oak (ie. bourbon barrels) or European oak (ie. sherry casks, though sherry casks are also made from American oak). Both types of oak for example deliver vanilla notes, with bourbon barrels delivering a greater level than European oak sherry casks. It's essentially tannins that deliver dryness, with European oak having higher tannin levels than American oak.

"Tannins and oak add dryness, and longer ageing increases the dryness. But sweetness also increases during ageing, and retaining the right balance is the key," says Brian Kinsman.

Another aspect of the ageing process is a further reduction in levels of sulphur compounds, partly due to evaporation, and to 'adsorption' by the cask.

"As the level of sulphur compounds declines the sweetness becomes more visible, but at the same time sweetness is increasing through cask derived notes, such as vanilla. It's very difficult to quantify how much sweetness increases due to a reduction in the level of sulphur compounds, and so greater visibility, and how much sweetness increases due to cask derived sweetness," says Brian Kinsman.

The 'fill' is another significant factor (referring to

Two Master Blenders - left, Richard Paterson, Whyte & Mackay and right, Jim Beveridge, Diageo

the number of times a cask has been filled with new make spirit). The usual limit is 3-4 fills, with each fill seeing a reduction in the cask's influence.

"Second and third fill casks contribute less dryness and less richness, so it's a different balance of flavours compared to a first fill. Typically, refill casks allow for greater distillery character to show through, which means that the flavour profile from a second and third fill cask is mainly from distillation, while the flavours from a first fill are mainly extracted from the cask. Various malts are a blend of American oak and European oak casks, as well as using different fills which give different opportunities. You want a blend of influences, then you can tailor the cask selection to produce the sweet-dry-rich balance that you're looking for," says Jim Beveridge.

And that takes us from what happens in a cask to what happens in a glass. What a malt whisky has to offer also depends on how it's served. Adding water, for example, reduces the alcoholic strength, which is one of the factors that determine the flavour profile a malt shows.

"If the strength of the whisky is high, for example around 55% abv, that can mask some lovely fla-

vours. The ideal strength to taste a whisky is around 40-45-47% abv. This range allows a malt to show it's refinement and sweetness, with a lovely melange of rich flavours and some dryness, and it's important to hold it momentarily on the palate to really appreciate those flavours. Taking the strength below 40% abv entails a risk of loosing some flavours," says Richard Paterson.

And after all the skill and experience that goes into producing a malt whisky, as well as all the years of ageing, the risk of loosing any flavour is a daunting prospect.

Ian Wisniewski is a freelance drinks writer focusing on spirits, and particularly Scotch whisky. He contributes to various publications including Whisky Magazine and Whisky Quarterly and is the author of ten books, including Classic Malt Whisky. He regularly visits distilleries in Scotland, in order to learn more about the production process which is of particular interest to him.

Picture of Ian Wisniewski courtesy of Finlandia vodka

Caol Ila Distillery

Malt distilleries

Including the subsections:
Scottish distilleries | New distilleries | Closed distilleries
Japanese distilleries | Distilleries around the globe

Explanations

Owner: Name of the owning company, sometimes with the parent company within brackets.

Region/district: There are five protected whisky regions or localities in Scotland today; Highlands, Lowlands, Speyside, Islay and Campbeltown. Where useful we mention a location within a region e.g. Orkney, Northern Highlands etc.

Founded: The year in which the distillery was founded is usually considered as when construction began. The year is rarely the same year in which the distillery was licensed.

Status: The status of the distillery's production. Active, mothballed (temporarily closed), closed (but most of the equipment still present), dismantled (the equipment is gone but part of or all of the buildings remain even if they are used for other purposes) and demolished.

Visitor centre: The letters (vc) after status indicate that the distillery has a visitor centre. Many distilleries accept visitors despite not having a visitor centre. It can be worthwhile making an enquiry.

Address: The distillery´s address.

Tel: This is generally to the visitor centre, but can also be to the main office.

Website: The distillery's (or in some cases the owner's) website.

Capacity: The current production capacity expressed in litres of pure alcohol (LPA).

History: The chronology focuses on the official history of the distillery and independent bottlings are only listed in exceptional cases.

Tasting notes: For all the Scottish distilleries that are not permanently closed we present tasting notes of what, in most cases, can be called the core expression (mainly their best selling 10 or 12 year old).

We have tried to provide notes for official bottlings but in those cases where we have not been able to obtain them, we have turned to independent bottlers.

The whiskies have been tasted by Gavin D Smith (GS), a well-known and experienced whisky profile and author of 20 books on the subject.

There are also tasting notes for Japanese malts and these have been written by Stefan Van Eycken.

All notes have been prepared especially for Malt Whisky Yearbook 2018.

Aberfeldy

[ah•bur•<u>fell</u>•dee]

Owner:
John Dewar & Sons
(Bacardi)

Region/district:
Southern Highlands

Founded: | **Status:** | **Capacity:**
1896 | Active (vc) | 3 400 000 litres

Address: Aberfeldy, Perthshire PH15 2EB

Website:
aberfeldy.com

Tel:
01887 822010 (vc)

The malt range for all five of Dewar's distilleries was relaunched in 2014 and the most recent sales figures show that the upgrade has given a well needed boost to Aberfeldy.

For many years the sales figures sat just under 500,000 bottles per year but since 2014 there has been an increase of more than 100% and in 2016, Aberfeldy single malt was just 1400 bottles short of reaching the impressive 1 million bottle milestone. Dewars blended Scotch, on the other hand, where Aberfeldy plays an important role, has gone in the opposite direction. Over the last decade sales figures show a loss of 12 million bottles. It is, however, still number one in the USA and this could be down to a letter sent to Dewars in 1891. The sender was the great industrialist Andrew Carnegie and he requested a cask of Old Highland Whisky to be sent to President Benjamin Harrison as a gift. This was of course used cleverly by Dewar's in their marketing.

The distillery has been a part of John Dewar & Sons since the start, even though the company itself has changed hands many times, but since 1998 it has been run by Bacardi. Aberfeldy single malt is not just an essential part of Dewar's blended whisky. The distillery itself also illustrates its colourful heritage dating back to the Dewar brothers and this heritage is emphasized by Dewar's World of Whiskies, an excellent visitor centre where you can also bottle and buy your own exclusive Aberfeldy malts.

The equipment at Aberfeldy consists of a 7.5 ton stainless steel mash tun, eight washbacks made of Siberian larch and three made of stainless steel with an average fermentation time of 70 hours and four stills. With an additional washback, installed in 2014, production has now escalated to 22 mashes per week and 3.4 million litres of alcohol. The owners have also invested £1.2m in a biomass boiler that will reduce greenhouse gas emissions by up to 90%.

Since 2014, the core range from Aberfeldy is **12, 16** and **21 year old** and they have also introduced the first Aberfeldy duty free exclusive expression – an **18 year old**.

History:

1896 John and Tommy Dewar embark on the construction of the distillery, a stone's throw from the old Pitilie distillery which was active from 1825 to 1867. Their objective is to produce a single malt for their blended whisky - White Label.

1898 Production starts in November.

1917 The distillery closes.

1919 The distillery re-opens.

1925 Distillers Company Limited (DCL) takes over.

1972 Reconstruction takes place, the floor maltings is closed and the two stills are increased to four.

1991 The first official bottling is a 15 year old in the Flora & Fauna series.

1998 Bacardi buys John Dewar & Sons from Diageo at a price of £1,150 million.

2000 A visitor centre opens and a 25 year old is released.

2005 A 21 year old is launched in October, replacing the 25 year old.

2009 Two 18 year old single casks are released.

2010 A 19 year old single cask, exclusive to France, is released.

2011 A 14 year old single cask is released.

2014 The whole range is revamped and an 18 year old for duty free is released.

2015 A 16 year old is released.

12 years old

Tasting notes Aberfeldy 12 years old:

GS – Sweet, with honeycombs, breakfast cereal and stewed fruits on the nose. Inviting and warming. Mouth-coating and full-bodied on the palate. Sweet, malty, balanced and elegant. The finish is long and complex, becoming progressively more spicy and drying.

Aberlour

[ah•bur•lower]

Owner:
Chivas Brothers Ltd
(Pernod Ricard)

Region/district:
Speyside

Founded: 1879
Status: Active (vc)
Capacity: 3 800 000 litres

Address: Aberlour, Banffshire AB38 9PJ

Website: aberlour.com
Tel: 01340 881249

Glenlivet may be the jewel in the crown in Pernod Ricard's Scotch whisky portfolio but it was actually Aberlour distillery which was the company's entry ticket into the Scotch whisky segment.

It was acquired in 1974 (27 years before Glenlivet) when the newly formed Pernod Ricard took over Campbell Distillers. Since then a structured work plan has positioned Aberlour single malt today as the fifth best-selling single malt in the world (or actually sixth if you count the combination of three distilleries forming The Singleton). In the past six years alone, sales have increased by 67% to reach 4.1 million bottles in 2016. France is by far the biggest market, and in 2008 Aberlour managed to surpass Glenfiddich as the most sold single malt in the country.

The distillery is equipped with a 12 ton semi-lauter mash tun, six stainless steel washbacks and two pairs of stills. Aberlour was one of the first distilleries to tailor its distillery tours for the discerning whisky aficionados, rather than for large groups of tourists. The basic tour lasts for two hours and includes a tasting of no less than six expressions. One can also add on an additional tasting (Casks of the Past) of bottlings that are no longer available for purchase.

The core range of Aberlour includes **12, 16** and **18 year olds** – all being matured in a combination of ex-bourbon and ex-sherry casks. Another core expression is **Aberlour a'bunadh,** matured in ex-Oloroso casks. It is always bottled at cask strength and up to 59 different batches have been released by July 2017. Four bottlings have been released for the French consumers (but are available in other selected markets as well). These include **10 year old, 12 year old un chill-filtered, 15 year old Select Cask Reserve** and **White Oak Millennium 2004.** Two exclusives are available for duty free – a **12 year old Sherry Cask** and a **15 year old Double Cask.** There is also a cask strength bottling from the new Distillery Reserve Collection which is available at all Chivas' visitor centres – a **17 year old bourbon cask matured.**

History:

1879 The local banker James Fleming founds the distillery.

1892 The distillery is sold to Robert Thorne & Sons Ltd who expands it.

1898 Another fire rages and almost totally destroys the distillery. The architect Charles Doig is called in to design the new facilities.

1921 Robert Thorne & Sons Ltd sells Aberlour to a brewery, W. H. Holt & Sons.

1945 S. Campbell & Sons Ltd buys the distillery.

1962 Aberlour terminates floor malting.

1973 Number of stills are increased from two to four.

1974 Pernod Ricard buys Campbell Distilleries.

2000 Aberlour a'bunadh is launched.

2001 Pernod Ricard buys Chivas Brothers and merges Chivas Brothers and Campbell Distilleries under the brand Chivas Brothers.

2002 A new, modernized visitor centre is inaugurated in August.

2008 The 18 year old is also introduced outside France.

2013 Aberlour 2001 White Oak is released.

2014 White Oak Millenium 2004 is released.

12 years old

Tasting notes Aberlour 12 year old:

GS – The nose offers brown sugar, honey and sherry, with a hint of grapefruit citrus. The palate is sweet, with buttery caramel, maple syrup and eating apples. Liquorice, peppery oak and mild smoke in the finish.

Allt-a-Bhainne

[alt a•vain]

Owner:
Chivas Brothers Ltd
(Pernod Ricard)

Region/district:
Speyside

Founded: 1975
Status: Active
Capacity: 4 200 000 litres

Address: Glenrinnes, Dufftown, Banffshire AB55 4DB

Website:
-

Tel:
01542 783200

There have been three distinctive golden eras for Scotch whisky; the first in the late 1800s which ended with the Pattison crash, then from the late 1950s to the late 1970s and finally the one we are in now which started at the end of the 1990s.

Allt-a-Bhainne was built towards the end of the second era by Seagrams, but by the time they started up the production, dark clouds had gathered on the horizon. The Arab-Israel war in 1973 caused an oil crisis which sent the world into economic turbulence and the Vietnam War, which had stimulated the American economy, also ended at this time. On top of that there was a change in consumption attitudes where the younger generation preferred vodka or white wine to whisky. It would take another 20 years before Scotch whisky was seriously on the move again.

The reason for Seagrams building Allt-a-Bhainne was that the blend 100 Pipers, which had been introduced in 1966, proved to be a bigger success than expected. They simply needed more malt spirit to keep up with demand. Since then, sales of 100 Pipers have declined but it is still one of the 15 biggest blends in the world with 18 million bottles sold annually.

In the summer of 2015, a new, modern lauter mash gear was fitted into the existing traditional tun which had previously been equipped with rakes and ploughs. The rest of the equipment consists of eight stainless steel washbacks and two pairs of stills. The distillery is currently a busy place working 7 days a week with 25 mashes resulting in four million litres of alcohol per year. Chivas Brothers has no distillery on Islay so, to cover their need of peated whisky for their blends, they need to resort to other solutions. During the last few years, 50% of the production at Allt-a-Bhainne has therefore been peated spirit with a phenol content in the malted barley of 10ppm.

There are no official bottlings of Allt-a-Bhainne single malt but it has been used for bottlings of the Deerstalker brand from time to time with a limited 18 year old, bottled at cask strength, having been released in summer 2015.

History:

1975 The distillery is founded by Chivas Brothers, a subsidiary of Seagrams, in order to secure malt whisky for its blended whiskies. The total cost amounts to £2.7 million.

1989 Production has doubled.

2001 Pernod Ricard takes over Chivas Brothers from Seagrams.

2002 Mothballed in October.

2005 Production restarts in May.

Deerstalker 18 years old

Tasting notes Deerstalker 18 year old:

GS – Honey, icing sugar, lanolin; becoming buttery. Soft fruits, and finally toffee bonbons. Silky mouth-feel, slightly oily, vanilla, white pepper and tangerines. Relatively long finish and persistently spicy.

Ardbeg

Given that Ardbeg is such a well-known and appreciated single malt, it is surprising that the core range used to consist of only three expressions – the 10 year old, Uigeadail and Corryvreckan.

However, this was rectified in September 2017 when the first new core malt in almost ten years was added to the range. Ardbeg An Oa is a vatting of whiskies matured in several types of casks, i.a. PX sherry, ex-bourbon barrels and virgin oak. They have all been married together in a new "gathering vat" made of French oak in what is called the Gathering Room - a former grain store. Pricewise, it will sit between the 10 year old and Uigeadail.

It is no secret that Ardbeg distillery has been struggling for some time to produce enough whisky for future needs. Distillery manager Mickey Heads is a master of tweaking small details in the production in order to get more from the stills while at the same time not jeopardising the quality and character of the spirit. In 2013, the distillery went from running 5 days per week to a 7-day production but that just isn´t enough. An expansion in the near future is highly likely but whether that will involve "just" adding more washbacks or a new pair of stills remains to be seen. It is an interesting fact that when Alfred Barnard came to the distillery in the late 19th century, the distillery was producing 1.1 million litres and today it has increased by just 300,000 litres.

Sales of Ardbeg single malt is increasing rapidly. In the last two years, volumes are up by 20% and 1.2 million bottles were sold in 2016. This means Ardbeg is the fourth biggest seller on Islay after Laphroaig, Lagavulin and Bowmore.

The distillery is equipped with a 5 ton stainless steel semi lauter mash tun, six washbacks made of Oregon pine with a fermentation time of 56-57 hours and one pair of stills. A purifier is connected to the spirit still to help create the special, fruity character of the spirit. In 2017 they will be making 16-17 mashes per week, thereby accounting for 1.4 million litres of pure alcohol – another production record for the distillery.

The core range, all non-chill filtered, consists of the **10 year old**, a mix of first and re-fill bourbon casks, **Uigeadail**, a marriage of bourbon and sherry casks and bottled at cask strength, **Corryvreckan**, also a cask strength and a combination of bourbon casks and new French oak and the new **An Oa** which is bottled at 46.6%. Recent, limited releases have included last year´s bottling for Feis Ile and the Ardbeg Day, **Dark Cove**, which had been partly matured in "dark sherry casks". It was followed by a **21 year old** in September. The Ardbeg Day expression for 2017 was **Kelpie**, made from whisky that had been matured in virgin Black Sea oak casks and then married together with ex-bourbon matured Ardbeg. Bottled at 46% for Ardbeg Day, it was preceded as usual by a Committee bottling at 51.7%. Another limited expression has been announced for release later in 2017. **Ardbeg Twenty Something** is a 23 year old made from spirit distilled in the mid-nineties when Allied Distillers used to own the distillery.

[ard•beg]

Owner:
The Glenmorangie Co
(Moët Hennessy)

Region/district:
Islay

Founded: **Status:** **Capacity:**
1815 Active (vc) 1 400 000 litres

Address: Port Ellen, Islay, Argyll PA42 7EA

Website: **Tel:**
ardbeg.com 01496 302244 (vc)

History:

1794 First record of a distillery at Ardbeg. It was founded by Alexander Stewart.

1798 The MacDougalls, later to become licensees of Ardbeg, are active on the site through Duncan MacDougall.

1815 The current distillery is founded by John MacDougall, son of Duncan MacDougall.

1853 Alexander MacDougall, John's son, dies and sisters Margaret and Flora MacDougall, assisted by Colin Hay, continue the running of the distillery. Colin Hay takes over the licence when the sisters die.

1888 Colin Elliot Hay and Alexander Wilson Gray Buchanan renew their license.

1900 Colin Hay's son takes over the license.

1959 Ardbeg Distillery Ltd is founded.

1973 Hiram Walker and Distillers Company Ltd jointly purchase the distillery for £300,000 through Ardbeg Distillery Trust.

1977 Hiram Walker assumes single control of the distillery. Ardbeg closes its maltings.

1979 Kildalton, a less peated malt, is produced over a number of years.

1981 The distillery closes in March.

1987 Allied Lyons takes over Hiram Walker and thereby Ardbeg.

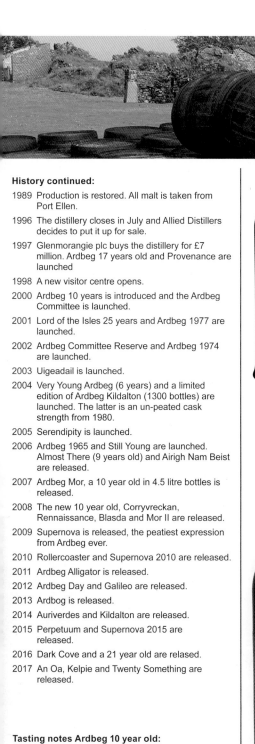

History continued:

1989 Production is restored. All malt is taken from Port Ellen.

1996 The distillery closes in July and Allied Distillers decides to put it up for sale.

1997 Glenmorangie plc buys the distillery for £7 million. Ardbeg 17 years old and Provenance are launched

1998 A new visitor centre opens.

2000 Ardbeg 10 years is introduced and the Ardbeg Committee is launched.

2001 Lord of the Isles 25 years and Ardbeg 1977 are launched.

2002 Ardbeg Committee Reserve and Ardbeg 1974 are launched.

2003 Uigeadail is launched.

2004 Very Young Ardbeg (6 years) and a limited edition of Ardbeg Kildalton (1300 bottles) are launched. The latter is an un-peated cask strength from 1980.

2005 Serendipity is launched.

2006 Ardbeg 1965 and Still Young are launched. Almost There (9 years old) and Airigh Nam Beist are released.

2007 Ardbeg Mor, a 10 year old in 4.5 litre bottles is released.

2008 The new 10 year old, Corryvreckan, Rennaissance, Blasda and Mor II are released.

2009 Supernova is released, the peatiest expression from Ardbeg ever.

2010 Rollercoaster and Supernova 2010 are released.

2011 Ardbeg Alligator is released.

2012 Ardbeg Day and Galileo are released.

2013 Ardbog is released.

2014 Auriverdes and Kildalton are released.

2015 Perpetuum and Supernova 2015 are released.

2016 Dark Cove and a 21 year old are relased.

2017 An Oa, Kelpie and Twenty Something are released.

Tasting notes Ardbeg 10 year old:

GS – Quite sweet on the nose, with soft peat, carbolic soap and Arbroath smokies. Burning peats and dried fruit, followed by sweeter notes of malt and a touch of liquorice in the mouth. Extremely long and smoky in the finish, with a fine balance of cereal sweetness and dry peat notes.

Corryvreckan   Uigeadail   Kelpie

10 years old   An Oa

Ardmore

[ard•moor]

Owner:	**Region/district:**
Beam Suntory	Highland

Founded:	**Status:**	**Capacity:**
1898	Active	5 550 000 litres

Address: Kennethmont, Aberdeenshire AB54 4NH

Website:	**Tel:**
ardmorewhisky.com	01464 831213

There are many dedicated and experienced distillery managers in Scotland and then, there are the ones who show an extraordinary passion for their distillery and brand. Alistair Longwell at Ardmore is one.

Alistair began his career at Teachers in 1987 and has been with the company through various takeovers (Allied, Beam Inc and Beam Suntory). He became distillery manager at Ardmore in 2004 and since 2015, he is responsible for the company's five malt distilleries as well as the maturation sites. Ardmore distillery is kind of off the beaten whisky track but over the last 6-7 years there has been talk about opening up the distillery to visitors. Recently, Alistair declared that "We are actively developing plans for a small scale, high quality, visitor centre at Ardmore." He comes well prepared. Over the years, he has gathered and preserved old equipment, production records and ledgers, ads and photos – all of which will serve as a unique basis for a visitor centre.

The distillery is equipped with a 12.5 ton, cast iron, semi-lauter mash tun with a copper dome, 14 Douglas fir washbacks (4 large and 10 smaller ones) with a fermentation time of 55 hours, as well as four pairs of stills. At the moment, Ardmore is working a 7-day week with 23 mashes per week resulting in 4.5 million litres of alcohol. Traditionally, Ardmore has been the only distillery in the region consistently producing peated whisky with a phenol specification in the barley of 12-14 ppm. The earthy Highland peat is locally sourced from St Fergus. For blending purposes, they also produce the unpeated Ardlair (around 40% of the yearly output).

Ardmore serves as the backbone of Teacher's blended Scotch but is also released as a single malt. The core expression is **Legacy**, a mix of 80% peated and 20% unpeated malt. In 2015, **Tradition** was released as a duty free exclusive. Simultaneously, **Triple Wood** with no age statement and matured in bourbon barrels, quarter casks and sherry puncheons, was launched together with a **12 year old port finish** with 7 years in puncheons, previously used to mature Ardmore spirit and a second maturation of 5 years in port pipes. A new release in 2017 was a **20 year old**, double matured in a mix of first- and second-fill bourbon casks.

History:

1898 Adam Teacher, son of William Teacher, starts the construction of Ardmore Distillery which eventually becomes William Teacher & Sons' first distillery. Adam Teacher passes away before it is completed.

1955 Stills are increased from two to four.

1974 Another four stills are added, increasing the total to eight.

1976 Allied Breweries takes over William Teacher & Sons and thereby also Ardmore. The own maltings (Saladin box) is terminated.

1999 A 12 year old is released to commemorate the distillery's 100th anniversary. A 21 year old is launched in a limited edition.

2002 Ardmore is one of the last distilleries to abandon direct heating (by coal) of the stills in favour of indirect heating through steam.

2005 Jim Beam Brands becomes new owner when it takes over some 20 spirits and wine brands from Allied Domecq for five billion dollars.

2007 Ardmore Traditional Cask is launched.

2008 A 25 and a 30 year old are launched.

2014 Beam and Suntory merge. Legacy is released.

2015 Traditional is re-launched as Tradition and a Triple Wood and a 12 year old port finish are released.

2017 A 20 year old, double matured is released.

Legacy

Tasting notes Ardmore Legacy:

GS – Vanilla, caramel and sweet peat smoke on the nose, while on the palate vanilla and honey contrast with quite dry peat notes, plus ginger and dark berries. The finish is medium to long, spicy, with persistently drying smoke.

Arran

[ar•ran]

Owner: | **Region/district:**
Isle of Arran Distillers | Islands (Arran)

Founded: | **Status:** | **Capacity:**
1993 | Active (vc) | 1 200 000 litres

Address: Lochranza, Isle of Arran KA27 8HJ

Website: | **Tel:**
arranwhisky.com | 01770 830264

It's doubtful that the owners, when Arran distillery opened in 1993, could have predicted how incredibly quick development would have been for both the distillery and the brand during the first 20 years.

More than 100,000 people made the journey to the distillery in 2016 – an increase by 18% compared to the year before. No other distillery in Scotland is close to these figures. The broad range of whiskies is now sold in 50 countries and in February 2017, the capacity of the distillery was increased through a £1m investment (which included renovation and expansion of the visitor centre as well). But it doesn't stop at that. The owner's are now in full swing, building yet another distillery in the south part of the island, at Lagg, which will open in 2018. The idea is to move the peated production to the £10m Lagg distillery and focus on unpeated at the "old" distillery in Lochranza.

The distillery is equipped with a 2.5 ton semi-lauter mash tun, six Oregon pine washbacks with an average fermentation time of 60 hours and four brand new stills. Since 2004, the distillery has been producing a share of peated spirit every year, usually around 100,000 litres, from malt peated to either 20ppm or 50ppm.

The core range consists of **10, 14** and **18 year old, Robert Burns Malt** and **Lochranza Reserve**. Also included in the core range is the peated expression **Machrie Moor** (8th edition launched in September 2017) and **Machrie Moor Cask Strength**. The 12 year old cask strength which used to be a part of the range has now been discontinued. A range of wood finishes include **Amarone**, **Port** and **Sauternes** and every year a number of single casks, matured either in ex-bourbon or ex-sherry are released. The second release in the limited Smuggler's Edition range was launched in July 2017 – **The Exciseman** – and one month later, the 3rd edition of **The Bothy** appeared. Finally, in October 2017, a special bottling was released to celebrate the distillery manager's **James MacTaggart** 10th anniversary with the distillery.

History:

1993 Harold Currie founds the distillery.

1995 Production starts in full on 17th August.

1998 The first release is a 3 year old.

1999 The Arran 4 years old is released.

2002 Single Cask 1995 is launched.

2003 Single Cask 1997, non-chill filtered and Calvados finish is launched.

2004 Cognac finish, Marsala finish, Port finish and Arran First Distillation 1995 are launched.

2005 Arran 1996 and two finishes, Ch. Margaux and Grand Cru Champagne, are launched.

2006 After an unofficial launch in 2005, Arran 10 years old is released as well as a couple of new wood finishes.

2007 Four new wood finishes and Gordon's Dram are released.

2008 The first 12 year old is released as well as four new wood finishes.

2009 Peated single casks, two wood finishes and 1996 Vintage are released.

2010 A 14 year old, Rowan Tree, three cask finishes and Machrie Moor (peated) are released.

2011 The Westie, Sleeping Warrior and a 12 year old cask strength are released.

2012 The Eagle and The Devil's Punch Bowl are released.

2013 A 16 year old and a new edition of Machrie Moor and released.

2014 A 17 year old and Machrie Moor cask strength are released.

2015 A 18 year old and The Illicit Stills are released.

2017 The Exciseman is released.

14 years old

Tasting notes Arran 14 year old:

GS – Very fragrant and perfumed on the nose, with peaches, brandy and ginger snaps. Smooth and creamy on the palate, with spicy summer fruits, apricots and nuts. The lingering finish is nutty and slowly drying.

Auchentoshan

[ock•en•**tosh**•en]

Owner:
Morrison Bowmore (Suntory)

Region/district:
Lowlands

Founded: 1823
Status: Active (vc)
Capacity: 2 000 000 litres

Address: Dalmuir, Clydebank, Glasgow G81 4SJ

Website:
auchentoshan.com

Tel:
01389 878561

When the entire range from Auchentoshan was re-launched in 2007, the primary focus was on the domestic market and not that much attention was put to the duty free range. This changed however in 2012 when no less than six different bottlings appeared.

The owners at the same time recognised the importance of being present in the travel retail market and the rapidly increasing sales figures in recent years was largely due to action in that particular market. Therefore it was surprising when it was announced in late 2015, that all six bottlings were to be replaced by two new ones, Noble Oak and Blood Oak, both of them considerably more expensive than some of the previous ones. Almost two years later, two of the "old" and lower-priced expressions can still be found in airports and border-shops and it remains to be seen whether or not they will continue to be a part of the range

Auchentoshan is the only distillery in the entire Scotland doing 100% triple distillation. This means, among other things, having a very narrow spirit cut. They start collecting the middle cut at 82% and stop at 80%, long before any other distillery starts collecting. The equipment consists of a semilauter mash tun with a 6.8 ton mash charge, four Oregon pine washbacks and three made of stainless steel, all with a fermentation time of 50 to 120 hours, and three stills. On site are also three dunnage and two racked warehouses which can hold about 20,000 casks. The plan for 2017 is to do a mixture of 10 to 15 mashes per week and 1.5 million litres of alcohol.

The core range consists of **American Oak**, a first fill bourbon maturation without age statement, **12 years, Three Woods, 18 years** and **21 years**. The former duty free range of six expressions, was replaced in 2015 by **Blood Oak**, without age statement and matured in a combination of bourbon and red wine casks and the 24 year old **Noble Oak**, a vatting of bourbon and oloroso casks. A limited version named **Bartender´s Malt** was launched in summer 2017. Designed to be used in cocktails, it is a vatting of malt from five decades including whiskies matured in ex-Laphroaig casks, rum casks, red wine barriques, German oak and American oak.

History:

1817 First mention of the distillery Duntocher, which may be identical to Auchentoshan.

1823 The distillery is founded by John Bulloch.

1823 The distillery is sold to Alexander Filshie.

1878 C.H. Curtis & Co. takes over.

1903 The distillery is purchased by John Maclachlan.

1941 The distillery is severely damaged by a German bomb raid.

1960 Maclachlans Ltd is purchased by the brewery J. & R. Tennant Brewers.

1969 Auchentoshan is bought by Eadie Cairns Ltd who starts major modernizations.

1984 Stanley P. Morrison, eventually becoming Morrison Bowmore, becomes new owner.

1994 Suntory buys Morrison Bowmore.

2002 Auchentoshan Three Wood is launched.

2004 More than a £1 million is spent on a new, refurbished visitor centre. The oldest Auchentoshan ever, 42 years, is released.

2006 Auchentoshan 18 year old is released.

2007 A 40 year old and a 1976 30 year old are released.

2008 New packaging as well as new expressions - Classic, 18 year old and 1988.

2010 Two vintages, 1977 and 1998, are released.

2011 Two vintages, 1975 and 1999, and Valinch are released.

2012 Six new expressions are launched for the Duty Free market.

2013 Virgin Oak is released.

2014 American Oak replaces Classic.

2015 Blood Oak and Noble Oak are released for duty free.

2017 Bartender´s Malt is launched.

American Oak

Tasting notes Auchentoshan American Oak:
GS – An initial note of rose water, then Madeira, vanilla, developing musky peaches and icing sugar. Spicy fresh fruit on the palate, chilli notes and more Madeira and vanilla. The finish is medium in length, and spicy to the end.

Auchroisk

[ar•thrusk]

Owner: Diageo

Region/district: Speyside

Founded: 1974

Status: Active

Capacity: 5 900 000 litres

Address: Mulben, Banffshire AB55 6XS

Website: malts.com

Tel: 01542 885000

When Auchroisk started production in 1974, it was a time of great optimism in the Scotch whisky industry. For three decades after the Second World War, Scotch had become the favourite spirit in Europe and, not least, America.

The producers had a hard time keeping up with the demand and from 1970-75, seven new distilleries were built and another 15 were sizably expanded. Historically there had been two similar 5-year periods. One was 1895-1900 when close to 20 new distilleries opened, but the happy days ended with the Pattison crash. A much larger expansion happened between 1823 and 1828 when no less than 203 new distilleries were registered. The amazing figure is easily explained though. The Excise Act of 1823 called for whisky distilleries to obtain a license and the vast majority of these more than 200 distilleries, which had previously been working as illicit stills, were now entered into the rolls. Of the 203, only 14 are still working today.

Auchroisk is a big distillery with an unusually large number of warehouses. The equipment consists of a 12 ton stainless steel semilauter mash tun, eight stainless steel washbacks with a fermentation time of 53 hours and four pairs of stills. The spacious still house was a role model for the still house of Diageo´s latest distillery, Roseisle. Auchroisk produces 5.8 million litres of alcohol per year, currently with a nutty/malty character. This has changed over the years though and not so long ago, the style was green/grassy. This is not unusual for distilleries that produce malt mainly for blends. It all depends on what the owner predicts they will need for the coming 5 years.

The first, widely available release of Auchroisk single malt was in 1986 under the name Singleton, as the Scottish name was deemed unpronounceable by the consumers. In 2001, it was replaced by a **10 year old** in the Flora & Fauna range. Recent, limited bottlings include a **20 year old** from 1990 and a **30 year old**, both launched as part of the Special Releases. In October 2016, it was time for the next limited Auchroisk in the Special Releases series; a **25 year old**, distilled in 1990 and bottled at 51.2%.

History:

1972 Building of the distillery commences by Justerini & Brooks (which, together with W. A. Gilbey, make up the group IDV) in order to produce blending whisky. In February the same year IDV is purchased by the brewery Watney Mann which, in July, merges into Grand Metropolitan.

1974 The distillery is completed and, despite the intention of producing malt for blending, the first year's production is sold 12 years later as single malt thanks to the high quality.

1986 The first whisky is marketed under the name Singleton.

1997 Grand Metropolitan and Guinness merge into the conglomerate Diageo. Simultaneously, the subsidiaries United Distillers (to Guinness) and International Distillers & Vintners (to Grand Metropolitan) form the new company United Distillers & Vintners (UDV).

2001 The name Singleton is abandoned and the whisky is now marketed under the name of Auchroisk in the Flora & Fauna series.

2003 Apart from the 10 year old in the Flora & Fauna series, a 28 year old from 1974, the distillery's first year, is launched in the Rare Malt series.

2010 A Manager´s Choice single cask and a limited 20 year old are released.

2012 A 30 year old from 1982 is released.

2016 A 25 year old from 1990 is released.

10 years old

Tasting notes Auchroisk 10 year old:

GS – Malt and spice on the light nose, with developing nuts and floral notes. Quite voluptuous on the palate, with fresh fruit and milk chocolate. Raisins in the finish.

Aultmore

[ault•moor]

Owner:		Region/district:
John Dewar & Sons (Bacardi)		Speyside

Founded:	Status:	Capacity:
1896	Active	3 200 000 litres

Address: Keith, Banffshire AB55 6QY

Website:	Tel:
aultmore.com	01542 881800

Aultmore was founded by Alexander "Sandy" Edward – one of the most dynamic entrepreneurs in Scotland during the late 19th century. Today his name has faded behind better known names of the industry such as Walker, Dewar and Bell.

At the age of 31 he took over the ownership of Benrinnes after his father's death, but five years prior to this he had founded Craigellachie distillery. The small town was close to his heart and he believed he could contribute greatly in order to make the town prosper. At this point in time, it was popular for the English upper class to visit Scotland and hunting, amongst other pastimes, was a main attraction and Craigellachie sat conveniently beside the Strathspey railway line. In 1896 he built what would eventually become the whisky world's most legendary hotel, The Craigellachie Hotel, and he managed to do this whilst also building Aultmore. Two years earlier he founded Dallas Dhu and over time he gained ownership of Oban and Yoker distilleries. When he died in 1946 at the age of 81 at his Sanquhar Estate in Forres, the obituary in the Elgin Courant and Courier referred to him as "one of the oldest and best-known distillers in Scotland".

Aultmore was completely rebuilt at the beginning of the 1970s and nothing is left of the old buildings from 1896. The distillery is equipped with a 10 ton Steinecker full lauter mash tun, six washbacks made of larch with a minimum fermentation time of 56 hours and two pairs of stills. Since 2008 production has been running seven days a week, which for 2017, means 16 mashes per week and just over 3 million litres of alcohol.

Until 2014, a 12 year old which was released in 2004 was the only official bottling available. Through the launch of the Last Great Malts in 2014 there is now a new **12 year old**, as well a **25 year old** for domestic markets. At the same time a **21 year old** has been reserved for duty free. The range was further expanded to include an **18 year old** in 2015. All the new bottlings are un chill-filtered, without colouring and bottled at 46%.

History:

1896 Alexander Edward, owner of Benrinnes and co-founder of Craigellachie Distillery, builds Aultmore.

1897 Production starts.

1898 Production is doubled; the company Oban & Aultmore Glenlivet Distilleries Ltd manages Aultmore.

1923 Alexander Edward sells Aultmore for £20,000 to John Dewar & Sons.

1925 Dewar's becomes part of Distillers Company Limited (DCL).

1930 The administration is transferred to Scottish Malt Distillers (SMD).

1971 The stills are increased from two to four.

1991 United Distillers launches a 12-year old Aultmore in the Flora & Fauna series.

1996 A 21 year old cask strength is marketed as a Rare Malt.

1998 Diageo sells Dewar's and Bombay Gin to Bacardi for £1,150 million.

2004 A new official bottling is launched (12 years old).

2014 Three new expression are released – 12, 25 and 21 year old for duty free.

2015 An 18 year old is released.

12 years old

Aultmore 12 years old:

GS – A nose of peaches and lemonade, freshly-mown grass, linseed and milky coffee. Very fruity on the palate, mildly herbal, with toffee and light spices. The finish is medium in length, with lingering spices, fudge, and finally more milky coffee.

Balblair

[bal•blair]

Owner:
Inver House Distillers
(Thai Beverages plc)

Region/district:
Northern Highlands

Founded: 1790

Status: Active (vc)

Capacity: 1 800 000 litres

Address: Edderton, Tain, Ross-shire IV19 1LB

Website: balblair.com

Tel: 01862 821273

The visitor centre at Balblair wasn't opened until 2012 but five years later it has become obvious that this was something that fans of one of the oldest distilleries in Scotland had been waiting for.

A contemporary centre and shop combined with an excellent tour of a compact and traditional distillery is a winning combination. The fact that Balblair was part of the set in Ken Loach's movie The Angels' Share in 2012 is also evident during the tour.

The distillery is equipped with a stainless steel, 4.4 ton semi lauter mash tun, six Oregon pine washbacks with a fermentation time of 72 hours (up from the previous 56 hours) and one pair of stills. There used to be a third still which hadn't been used for many years but this can now be seen outside the Station Hotel in Rothes. The production target for 2017 is 19 mashes per week which translates to 1.5 million litres of alcohol. In 2011 and 2012, part of the production was heavily peated spirit with a phenol specification of 52ppm in the barley. Since then, however, there has been no peated production and unlike at Knockdhu (also owned by Inver House) there was never any plan for a peated Balblair single malt release. In 2015 the distillery converted from using heavy fuel oil to gas, thereby reducing the emission of greenhouse gases significantly.

In 2007, the entire range of Balblair single malt was relaunched when they decided to build on vintages rather than age statements in the same way that Glenrothes do. Sales have increased over the years in a slow but steady pace but it seems that many consumers are still not accustomed to think about whisky in a vintage context. The current core range consists of four vintages – **1983, 1990, 1999** and **2005**. For the duty free market, three expressions were released in 2014; a **1999** and two versions of **2004** matured in **bourbon** and **sherry** casks respectively. The oldest vintage available from the distillery at the moment is **1969**. For visitors to the distillery there is also the opportunity to bottle a **single cask** Balblair, from a selected cask which is replaced as it becomes depleted.

History:

1790 The distillery is founded by James McKeddy.

1790 John Ross takes over

1836 John Ross dies and his son Andrew Ross takes over with the help of his sons.

1872 New buildings replace the old.

1873 Andrew Ross dies and his son James takes over.

1894 Alexander Cowan builds a new distillery, a few kilometres from the old.

1911 Cowan is forced to cease payments and the distillery closes.

1941 The distillery is put up for sale.

1948 Robert Cumming buys Balblair for £48,000.

1949 Production restarts.

1970 Cumming sells Balblair to Hiram Walker.

1988 Allied Distillers becomes the new owner through the merger between Hiram Walker and Allied Vintners.

1996 The distillery is sold to Inver House Distillers.

2000 Balblair Elements and the first version of Balblair 33 years are launched.

2001 Thai company Pacific Spirits (part of the Great Oriole Group) takes over Inver House.

2004 Balblair 38 years is launched.

2005 12 year old Peaty Cask, 1979 (26 years) and 1970 (35 years) are launched.

2006 International Beverage Holdings acquires Pacific Spirits UK.

2007 Three new vintages replace the former range.

2008 Vintage 1975 and 1965 are released.

2009 Vintage 1991 and 1990 are released.

2010 Vintage 1978 and 2000 are released.

2011 Vintage 1995 and 1993 are released.

2012 Vintage 1975, 2001 and 2002 are released. A visitor centre is opened.

2013 Vintage 1983, 1990 and 2003 are released.

2014 Vintage 1999 and 2004 are released for duty free.

2016 Vintage 2005 is released.

Tasting notes Balblair 2005:

GS – Chocolate-flavoured ice cream, vanilla and a hint of ozone on the nose. The palate is full and oily, with big spice notes, honey, soft toffee and citrus fruit. The finish is medium in length, with malt and enduring spice.

Vintage 2005

Balmenach

[bal•may•nack]

Owner:	**Region/district:**
Inver House Distillers	Speyside
(Thai Beverages plc)	

Founded:	**Status:**	**Capacity:**
1824	Active	2 800 000 litres

Address: Cromdale, Moray PH26 3PF

Website:	**Tel:**
inverhouse.com	01479 872569

Balmenach was the last of five distilleries that Inver House bought and it is the only one that is not represented by an official bottling. Actually, there has been one, very limited expression which was released in 2002.

It was a 25 year old, launched to celebrate Queen Elizabeth´s Golden Jubilee. The whisky had been distilled in 1977 when the Queen had been on the throne for 25 years. And not only that. During the celebrations, one of the wash stills was brought to London to be displayed in Hyde Park. After the festivities, the still was transported to Scotland and installed at the distillery.

The distillery´s old cast iron mash tun was replaced in 2014 with an 8 ton stainless steel semi-lauter tun, but the old copper canopy was fitted to the new tun. There are six washbacks made of Douglas fir with a 52 hour fermentation period, and three pairs of stills connected to worm tubs where each worm is 94 metres long. In 2017, the distillery will be doing 15 mashes per week which translates to 1.8 million litres of alcohol for the year. Since 2012, a part of the production (of up to 400,000 litres) has been heavily peated (50ppm), but during 2016 and 2017 they are taking a break and there will be no peated production. The three dunnage warehouses currently hold 9,500 casks.

For the past eight years, gin has also been part of the production at Balmenach. Purchased neutral spirit is pumped through a vaporiser and then to a copper berry chamber where the vapours travel upwards passing five trays with different kinds of botanicals and finally end up in the condenser. From the initial 6,000 litres produced in 2009, Caorunn gin has become the third biggest super-premium gin in the UK.

There is no official bottling of Balmenach single malt. Aberko in Glasgow though, has been working with the distillery for a long time and, over the years, has released Balmenach under the name Deerstalker. The current expression is a 12 year old.

History:

1824 The distillery is licensed to James MacGregor who operated a small farm distillery by the name of Balminoch.

1897 Balmenach Glenlivet Distillery Company is founded.

1922 The MacGregor family sells to a consortium consisting of MacDonald Green, Peter Dawson and James Watson.

1925 The consortium becomes part of Distillers Company Limited (DCL).

1930 Production is transferred to Scottish Malt Distillers (SMD).

1962 The number of stills is increased to six.

1964 Floor maltings replaced with Saladin box.

1992 The first official bottling is a 12 year old.

1993 The distillery is mothballed in May.

1997 Inver House Distillers buys Balmenach from United Distillers.

1998 Production recommences.

2001 Thai company Pacific Spirits takes over Inver House at the price of £56 million. The new owner launches a 27 and a 28 year old.

2002 To commemorate the Queen's Golden Jubilee a 25-year old Balmenach is launched.

2006 International Beverage Holdings acquires Pacific Spirits UK.

2009 Gin production commences.

Tasting notes Deerstalker 12 years old:

GS – The nose is sweet and fruity, with sherry and chilli. Faintly savoury. Fruity and very spicy on the palate, with black pepper and hints of sherry. More chilli in the finish, plus plain chocolate-coated raisins.

Deerstalker 12 years old

Balvenie

[bal•ven•ee]

Owner:
William Grant & Sons

Region/district:
Speyside

Founded: 1892
Status: Active (vc)

Capacity:
7 000 000 litres

Address: Dufftown, Keith, Banffshire AB55 4DH

Website:
thebalvenie.com

Tel:
01340 820373

The Balvenie single malt of modern days has always been unpeated but on two previous occasions the owners have released bottlings that in one way or another involved smoky notes and peat.

The first one was Balvenie Islay Cask where unpeated Balvenie malt received a finish in ex-Islay casks. The second attempt, The Balvenie Peated Cask, was a vatting of 17 year old finished in virgin oak and a 17 year old finished in casks that had held peated Balvenie. Now, for the first time, there are two expressions that are made from 100% peated Balvenie malt, i.e. the smokiness comes from the whisky itself and not from the casks. The first one, a triple cask, was released for travel retail in July 2017 and then in October, we saw the launch of Balvenie Peat Week 2002, a 14 year old peated Balvenie matured in American oak

The distillery is equipped with an 11.8 ton full lauter mash tun, nine wooden and five stainless steel washbacks with a fermentation time of 68 hours, five wash stills and six spirit stills. Balvenie is one of few distilleries still doing some of their own maltings and there is also a coppersmith and a cooperage on site. For 2017, the production plan is the same as for 2016 – 30 mashes per week and 7 million litres of alcohol which is a new production record for the distillery. The main part is unpeated but each year one week of production comes from peated barley (20-40 ppm).

The core range consists of **Doublewood 12 years, Doublewood 17 years, Caribbean Cask 14 years, Single Barrel 12 years First Fill, Single Barrel 15 years Sherry Cask, Single Barrel 25 years Traditional Oak, Portwood 21 years, 30 years, 40 years** and the rare **50 years old**. Recent limited releases include batch 3 of **Tun 1509** and **Tun 1858** which has been reserved for Asia. Chapter three of **The Balvenie DCS Compendium** was launched in October 2017 and at the same time, **The Balvenie Peat Week 2002** was released For Duty Free there is the **Triple Cask** series (**12, 16 and 25 years old**). In spring 2016, a **21 year old madeira finish** was included in the Triple Cask range and in July 2017 the range was complemented by the 14 year old **Peated Triple Cask**.

History:

1892 William Grant rebuilds Balvenie New House to Balvenie Distillery (Glen Gordon was the name originally intended). Part of the equipment is brought in from Lagavulin and Glen Albyn.

1893 The first distillation takes place in May.

1957 The two stills are increased by another two.

1965 Two new stills are installed.

1971 Another two stills are installed and eight stills are now running.

1973 The first official bottling appears.

1982 Founder's Reserve is launched.

1996 Two vintage bottlings and a Port wood finish are launched.

2001 The Balvenie Islay Cask, with 17 years in bourbon casks and six months in Islay casks, is released.

2002 A 50 year old is released.

2004 The Balvenie Thirty is released.

2005 The Balvenie Rum Wood Finish 14 years old is released.

2006 The Balvenie New Wood 17 years old, Roasted Malt 14 years old and Portwood 1993 are released.

2007 Vintage Cask 1974 and Sherry Oak 17 years old are released.

2008 Signature, Vintage 1976, Balvenie Rose and Rum Cask 17 years old are released.

2009 Vintage 1978, 17 year old Madeira finish, 14 year old rum finish and Golden Cask 14 years old are released.

2010 A 40 year old, Peated Cask and Carribean Cask are released.

2011 Second batch of Tun 1401 is released.

2012 A 50 year old and Doublewood 17 years old are released.

2013 Triple Cask 12, 16 and 25 years are launched for duty free.

2014 Single Barrel 15 and 25 years, Tun 1509 and two new 50 year olds are launched.

2015 The Balvenie DCS Compendium is launched.

2016 A 21 year old madeira finish is released.

2017 The Balvenie Peat Week 2002 and Peated Triple Cask are released.

Doublewood 12 years old

Tasting notes Balvenie Doublewood 12 years:

GS – Nuts and spicy malt on the nose, full-bodied, with soft fruit, vanilla, sherry and a hint of peat. Dry and spicy in a luxurious, lengthy finish.

Ben Nevis

[ben nev•iss]

Owner:
Ben Nevis Distillery Ltd
(Nikka, Asahi Breweries)

Region/district:
Western Highlands

Founded: **Status:** **Capacity:**
1825 Active (vc) 2 000 000 litres

Address: Lochy Bridge, Fort William PH33 6TJ

Website: **Tel:**
bennevisdistillery.com 01397 702476

Ben Nevis is managed by one of the true veterans of the Scotch whisky trade – Colin Ross, born in 1948. Aside from a short spell with Laphroaig 1989-1991, Colin has been with the distillery since 1983.

He was there in 1989 when the Japanese company Nikka bought the distillery and over the years he has developed countless expressions of Ben Nevis single malt. In 2015 he was inducted in the Whisky Hall of Fame together with other celebrities such as Michael Urquhart and Jim Beveridge.

Ben Nevis has a colourful history, being founded by the legendary Long John Macdonald it remained in the family until 1941. It was then taken over by the eccentric Joseph Hobbs who bought several distilleries in Scotland. He installed both a Coffey still and concrete washbacks as well as experimenting with blending grain and malt spirit and let them mature as a blend ("blended at birth"). With Nikka as the owner since 1989, as much as 75% of the production (new make, not matured whisky) is shipped every year to Japan to become part of their whiskies, not least the popular blend Black Nikka.

Ben Nevis is equipped with one lauter mash tun, six stainless steel washbacks and two made of Oregon as well as two pairs of stills. Fermentation used to be 48 hours in the steel washbacks and 96 hours in the wooden ones. From 2014, however, when 24/7 production was introduced, fermentation is 48 hours in all washbacks. The plan for 2017 is to do 2 million litres. Around 50,000 litres of this will be heavily peated.

The core range consists of the recently repackaged **MacDonald´s Ben Nevis 10 year old** and the peated **MacDonald´s Traditional Ben Nevis**. The latter, which is an attempt to replicate the style of Ben Nevis single malt from the 1880s, was introduced as a limited expression but has now become a part of the core range. There is also an 8 year old blended malt, MacDonald´s Glencoe. A range of limited releases, called Forgotten Bottlings, was introduced in 2014 but they have now sold out.

History:

1825 The distillery is founded by 'Long' John McDonald.

1856 Long John dies and his son Donald P. McDonald takes over.

1878 Demand is so great that another distillery, Nevis Distillery, is built nearby.

1908 Both distilleries merge into one.

1941 D. P. McDonald & Sons sells the distillery to Ben Nevis Distillery Ltd headed by the Canadian millionaire Joseph W. Hobbs.

1955 Hobbs installs a Coffey still which makes it possible to produce both grain and malt whisky.

1964 Joseph Hobbs dies.

1978 Production is stopped.

1981 Joseph Hobbs Jr sells the distillery back to Long John Distillers and Whitbread.

1984 After restoration and reconstruction totalling £2 million, Ben Nevis opens up again.

1986 The distillery closes again.

1989 Whitbread sells the distillery to Nikka Whisky Distilling Company Ltd.

1990 The distillery opens up again.

1991 A visitor centre is inaugurated.

1996 Ben Nevis 10 years old is launched.

2006 A 13 year old port finish is released.

2010 A 25 year old is released.

2011 McDonald´s Traditional Ben Nevis is released.

2014 Forgotten Bottlings are introduced.

2015 A 40 year old "Blended at Birth" single blend is released.

Tasting notes Ben Nevis 10 years old:

GS – The nose is initially quite green, with developing nutty, orange notes. Coffee, brittle toffee and peat are present on the slightly oily palate, along with chewy oak, which persists to the finish, together with more coffee and a hint of dark chocolate.

10 years old

Benriach

[ben•ree•ack]

Owner:
BenRiach Distillery Company
(Brown Forman)

Region/district:
Speyside

Founded: 1897   **Status:** Active   **Capacity:** 2 800 000 litres

Address: Longmorn, Elgin, Morayshire IV30 8SJ

Website:
benriachdistillery.co.uk

Tel:
01343 862888

When Brown Forman bought BenRiach distillery, as well as GlenDronach and Glenglassaugh, in 2016 it marked the ending of a 12 year long success story led by the former Burn Stewart director, Billy Walker.

He agreed to stay in the company during a transition period but when Rachel Barrie took over as master blender for the company in March 2017, Billy Walker decided to step down. He can look back at three succesful distillery take-overs and having re-launched three brands that are now sold globally. The new master blender, Rachel Barrie, has had a carreer with Glenmorangie and, more recently, Morrison Bowmore.

BenRiach distillery is equipped with a traditional cast iron mash tun with a stainless steel shell, eight washbacks made of stainless steel with both short (48 hours) and long fermentations (66 hours) and two pairs of stills. The production for 2017 will be 2.35 million litres of alcohol which includes 500,000 litres of peated spirit at 35ppm. Peated production has increased substantially compared to 2016 when it was only 150,000 litres. In 2013, the owners revamped the malting floor which hadn't been used since 1998 but it has only been used sporadically. In 2016 there were two mashes and the plan is to use it again in September 2017.

The core range of BenRiach is **Heart of Speyside** (no age), **Cask Strength, 10, 16, 20, 25** and **35** years old in what the distillery calls Classic Speyside style. Peated varieties include **Birnie Moss, Curiositas 10 year old, Septendecim 17 year old, Authenticus 25 year old** and **Peated Quarter Cask**. The latter, without age statement, has been matured in quarter casks for around 8 years. A new addition to the peated range appeared in spring 2017 by way of **Peated Cask Strength**. There are three different wood finishes in the Classic Speyside style - **21 year old Tawny Port, 17 year old PX Sherry** and **22 year old Moscatel** as well as a **12 year old,** fully matured in **Sherry Wood**. In June 2017, the brand made its debut in the travel retail segment with **10 year old Triple Distilled** as well as duty-free versions of **Classic Quarter Cask** and **Peated Quarter Cask**. Finally, every year a number of **single cask** bottlings are released and **batch number 14** was launched in August 2017.

History:

1897 John Duff & Co founds the distillery.

1900 The distillery is closed.

1965 The distillery is reopened by the new owner, The Glenlivet Distillers Ltd.

1978 Seagram Distillers takes over.

1983 Production of peated Benriach starts.

1985 The number of stills is increased to four.

1998 The maltings is decommissioned.

2002 The distillery is mothballed in October.

2004 Intra Trading, buys Benriach together with the former Director at Burn Stewart, Billy Walker.

2004 Standard, Curiositas and 12, 16 and 20 year olds are released.

2005 Four different vintages are released.

2006 Sixteen new releases, i.a. a 25 year old, a 30 year old and 8 different vintages.

2007 A 40 year old and three new heavily peated expressions are released.

2008 New expressions include a peated Madeira finish, a 15 year old Sauternes finish and nine single casks.

2009 Two wood finishes (Moscatel and Gaja Barolo) and nine single casks are released.

2010 Triple distilled Horizons and heavily peated Solstice are released.

2011 A 45 year old and 12 vintages are released.

2012 Septendecim 17 years is released.

2013 Vestige 46 years is released. The maltings are working again.

2015 Dunder, Albariza, Latada and a 10 year old are released.

2016 Brown Forman buys the company for £285m. BenRiach cask strength and Peated Quarter Cask are launched.

2017 10 year old Triple Distilled and Peated Cask Strength are released.

10 years old

Tasting notes BenRiach 10 year old:
GS – Earthy and nutty on the early nose, with apples, ginger and vanilla. Smooth and rounded on the palate, with oranges, apricots, mild spice and hazelnuts. The finish is medium in length, nutty and spicy.

Benrinnes

[ben rin•ess]

Owner: **Region/district:**
Diageo   Speyside

Founded: **Status:**   **Capacity:**
1826   Active   3 500 000 litres

Address: Aberlour, Banffshire AB38 9NN

Website: **Tel:**
malts.com   01340 872600

The whisky from Benrinnes has never been famous as a stand alone single malt but over the years it has contributed to several blended whiskies - not least Crawford's.

Launched around 1900 by A&A Crawford, a Leith blending company founded in 1860, Crawford's blend was hugely popular in the 1960s when it sold more than 1 million bottles in Scotland alone. That particular version was (and still is) called Crawford's 3 Star and for a time there was also a deluxe 5 Star version. A&A Crawford was absorbed into the DCL in 1944 and when Guinness took over in 1986, the brand was sold to Whyte & Mackay with Diageo still maintaining the overseas right for the brand.

Benrinnes was completely rebuilt in the 1950s and none of the original buildings remain. A major upgrade was made in autumn 2012 which included a full automation of the process, as well as a new control room where one operator can handle all the work. The equipment consists of an 8.5 ton semilauter mash tun, eight washbacks made of Oregon pine with short a fermentation time of 65 hours and long of 100 hours. There are also two wash stills and four spirit stills and from 1966 until a few years ago, they were run three and three with a partial triple distillation. This system has since been abandoned and one wash still will now serve two spirit stills. The spirit vapours are cooled using cast iron worm tubs which contribute to the character of Benrinnes newmake, which is light sulphury. The wide spirit cut (73%-58%) also plays its part in creating a robust and meaty spirit. For 2017, the distillery will be doing 15 mashes per week which translates to 2.3 million litres of alcohol for the entire year.

Most of the production goes into blended whiskies – J&B, Johnnie Walker and Crawford's 3 Star – and there is currently only one official single malt, the **Flora & Fauna 15 year old**. In 2010 a **Manager's Choice** from **1996** was released and in autumn 2014 it was time for a **21 year old** Special Release bottled at 57%.

History:

1826   Lyne of Ruthrie distillery is built at Whitehouse Farm by Peter McKenzie.

1829   A flood destroys the distillery and a new distillery is constructed by John Innes a few kilometres from the first one.

1834   John Innes files for bankruptcy and William Smith & Co takes over.

1864   William Smith & Co goes bankrupt and David Edward becomes the new owner.

1896   Benrinnes is ravaged by fire which prompts major refurbishment. Alexander Edward takes over.

1922   John Dewar & Sons takes over ownership.

1925   John Dewar & Sons becomes part of Distillers Company Limited (DCL).

1956   The distillery is completely rebuilt.

1964   Floor maltings is replaced by a Saladin box.

1966   The number of stills doubles to six.

1984   The Saladin box is taken out of service and the malt is purchased centrally.

1991   The first official bottling from Benrinnes is a 15 year old in the Flora & Fauna series.

1996   United Distillers releases a 21 year old cask strength in their Rare Malts series.

2009   A 23 year old is launched as a part of this year's Special Releases.

2010   A Manager's Choice 1996 is released.

2014   A limited 21 year old is released.

Tasting notes Benrinnes 15 years old:

GS – A brief flash of caramel shortcake on the initial nose, soon becoming more peppery and leathery, with some sherry. Ultimately savoury and burnt rubber notes. Big-bodied, viscous, with gravy, dark chocolate and more pepper. A medium-length finish features mild smoke and lively spices.

15 years old

Benromach

[ben•ro•mack]

Owner:
Gordon & MacPhail

Region/district:
Speyside

Founded: 1898

Status: Active (vc)

Capacity: 700 000 litres

Address: Invererne Road, Forres, Morayshire IV36 3EB

Website: benromach.com

Tel: 01309 675968

The distillery itself may be the third smallest in Speyside but the single malt has really made a big impact during the past few years. Not only in terms of quality but also volumes.

The result of patient and methodical work by the owner since 1993, Gordon & MacPhail, begin to emerge. Benromach single malt is now exported to more than 40 countries and last year's sales increased by 23%. Benromach has recently had a massive expansion on the fermentation side with nine new washbacks made of larch being installed in late 2016. That makes a total of 13 washbacks with a fermentation time between 72 and 120 hours. There is also a 1.5 ton semi-lauter mash tun with a copper dome and one pair of stills with the condensers outside. An unusual feature are the spirit receiver and feints receiver which are both made of oak. In 2017 the production will be 14 mashes per week and 400,000 litres of pure alcohol. The goal at Benromach is to produce a Speyside whisky, just like it used to taste back in the 1950s. This is achieved by predominantly using medium peated barley (12ppm). New warehouses have lately been added, all dunnage and holding 18,000 casks.

The core range consists of **10** and **15 year old** and the **100 Proof** (bottled at 57%). The 5 year old, introduced in 2014 to replace Benromach Traditional, has been discontinued. Recent limited releases include a **35 year old**, a **1975 single cask**, a **1976 single cask** for the Speyside Festival and **a 2009 Triple Distilled** released in September 2017. There are also special editions; **Organic**, the first single malt to be fully certified organic by the Soil Association and **Peatsmoke**, produced by using heavily peated barley and distilled in 2008. Every year wood finishes are released in limited quantities with **Sassicaia 2009** (March 2017) and **Chateau Cissac 2009** (September 2017) being the latest. Three exclusives have been released in select markets; **Imperial Proof** (USA), **Vintage 1973** (UK) and **Vintage 1975** (China). Finally, a duty free bottling called **Traveller's Edition**, was introduced in 2014.

History:
1898 Benromach Distillery Company starts the distillery.
1911 Harvey McNair & Co buys the distillery.
1919 John Joseph Calder buys Benromach and sells it to recently founded Benromach Distillery Ltd owned by several breweries.
1931 Benromach is mothballed.
1937 The distillery reopens.
1938 Joseph Hobbs buys Benromach and sells it on to National Distillers of America (NDA).
1953 NDA sells Benromach to Distillers Company Limited (DCL).
1966 The distillery is refurbished.
1968 Floor maltings is abolished.
1983 Benromach is mothballed.
1993 Gordon & McPhail buys Benromach from United Distillers.
1998 The distillery is once again in operation.
1999 A visitor centre is opened.
2004 The first bottle distilled by the new owner is released under the name 'Benromach Traditional'.
2005 A Port Wood finish (22 years old) and a Vintage 1968 are released together with the Benromach Classic 55 years.
2006 Benromach Organic is released.
2007 Peat Smoke, the first heavily peated whisky from the distillery, is released.
2008 Benromach Origins Golden Promise is released.
2009 Benromach 10 years old is released.
2011 New edition of Peatsmoke, a 2001 Hermitage finish and a 30 year old are released.
2013 A Sassicaia Wood Finish is released.
2014 Three new bottlings are launched; a 5 year old, 100 Proof and Traveller's Edition.
2015 A 15 year old and two wood finishes (Hermitage and Sassicaia) are released.
2016 A 35 year old and 1974 single cask are released.
2017 A 1976 single cask and a 2009 Triple Distilled are released.

Tasting notes Benromach 10 year old:
GS – A nose that is initially quite smoky, with wet grass, butter, ginger and brittle toffee. Mouth-coating, spicy, malty and nutty on the palate, with developing citrus fruits, raisins and soft wood smoke. The finish is warming, with lingering barbecue notes.

10 years old

Bladnoch

[blad•nock]

Owner:
David Prior

Region/district:
Lowlands

Founded: 1817
Status: Mothballed
Capacity: 1 500 000 litres

Address: Bladnoch, Wigtown, Wigtonshire DG8 9AB

Website: bladnoch.com
Tel: 01988 402605

To celebrate a 200th anniversary for a closed distillery is hardly something one would do. However, thanks to an Australian entrepreneur in the dairy business, Bladnoch escaped that fate.

It was another enterprising man who saved it the last time it was closed. Raymond Armstrong bought the mothballed distillery in 1994 but the intermittent production stopped again in 2009 and five years later, Armstrong's company was liquidated when he and his brother could not agree on the future of the business. The distillery went up for sale and David Prior, who had sold his successful yoghurt company five:am, stepped in. He also managed to involve the Master Blender from Burn Stewart, Ian MacMillan, who joined the team as distillery manager.

When the new owners took over, they found that the distillery was in a poor condition. The only piece of equipment that could be used was the mill – everything else was replaced. The distillery is now equipped with a 5 ton stainless steel semi-lauter mash tun, six Douglas fir washbacks with a minimum fermentation time of 48 hours and two pairs of stills. Production started in summer 2017 and the plan is to make 350-400,000 litres the first year. Focus will be on unpeated whisky but at least 12 weeks every year, a heavily peated spirit will be produced.

When the new owners took over, the deal included several thousand casks of whisky dating back to the 1980s. Where needed, MacMillan re-filled whiskies from inferior casks into quality casks and in November 2016, the first new whiskies were released, initially in Australia but later rolled out into other markets as well. The range includes **Samsara** with no age statement and matured in ex-bourbon and casks that had contained Californian red wine, the 15 year old **Adela** matured in ex-oloroso casks and the 25 year old **Talia**. The latter had been matured in a mix of bourbon and sherry casks and finished in new American oak. It was later replaced by one that had received a finish in port pipes. For the 200th anniversary, a **Vintage 1988** finished in moscatel casks was released in autumn 2017. The owners have also launched a blended Scotch under the name Pure Scot.

History:

1817 Founded by Thomas and John McClelland.

1878 John McClelland's son Charlie reconstructs and refurbishes the distillery.

1905 Production stops.

1911 Dunville & Co. buys T. & A. McClelland Ltd. Production is intermittent until 1936.

1937 Dunville & Co. is liquidated and Bladnoch is wound up. Ross & Coulter from Glasgow buys the distillery after the war. The equipment is dismantled and shipped to Sweden.

1956 A. B. Grant (Bladnoch Distillery Ltd.) takes over and restarts production with four new stills.

1964 McGown and Cameron becomes new owners.

1973 Inver House Distillers buys Bladnoch.

1983 Arthur Bell and Sons take over.

1985 Guiness Group buys Arthur Bell & Sons which, from 1989, are included in United Distillers.

1988 A visitor centre is built.

1993 United Distillers mothballs Bladnoch in June.

1994 Raymond Armstrong buys Bladnoch in October.

2000 Production commences in December.

2003 The first bottles from Armstrong are launched, a 15 year old cask strength from UD casks.

2008 First release of whisky produced after the take-over in 2000 - three 6 year olds.

2009 An 8 year old of own production and a 19 year old are released.

2014 The distillery is liquidated.

2015 The distillery is bought by David Prior.

2016 Samsara, Adela and Talia are released.

2017 Production starts again and a Vintage 1988 is released.

Tasting notes Bladnoch Samsara:

GS – The nose is slightly savoury, with soft spices and tinned peaches with cream. Sweet on the palate, with passion fruit and vanilla. Long in the finish with ripe pears, and increasingly dry spices, plus a suggestion of tannins.

Samsara

Blair Athol

[blair ath•ull]

Owner:	**Region/district:**
Diageo	Eastern Highlands
Founded: **Status:**	**Capacity:**
1798 Active (vc)	2 800 000 litres

Address: Perth Road, Pitlochry, Perthshire PH16 5LY

Website:	**Tel:**
malts.com	01796 482003

A handful of distilleries in Scotland are known as the spiritual home of a certain blended whisky in which that particular single malt plays a significant part. Sometimes that connection is a bit far fetched but not so when it comes to Blair Athol and Bell's.

The brand Bell's was introduced in 1896 and from the very start, single malt from Blair Athol was a vital component. The connection became stronger when Bell's acquired the distillery in 1933. The independence of Arthur Bell & Sons lasted much longer than most of the old family companies and it wasn't until 1985 that they were sold to Guinness and later became a part of Diageo. There was a time in the 1970s when every third bottle of blended whisky that was sold in the UK was Bell's. Such dominance is unlikely to occur again with a much fiercer competition. Today, Famous Grouse has taken over the number one position in the UK with a market share of 21% with Bell's being second at 16%.

Blair Athol has an excellent visitor centre and with the perfect location close to the A9 heading from Edinburgh to Inverness, they have more than 70,000 people coming to the distillery each year. Only Arran distillery beats these figures. The equipment of Blair Athol distillery consists of an 8 ton semi-lauter mash tun, six washbacks made of stainless steel and two pairs of stills. The part of the spirit which goes into Bell's is matured mainly in bourbon casks, while the rest is matured in sherry casks. The last couple of years, the distillery has been working a 5-day week with 12 mashes per week and 1.9 million litres of alcohol. This also means a scheme of short (46 hours) and long (104 hours) fermentations. A very cloudy wort gives Blair Athol newmake a nutty and malty character.

The output today is still used for Bell's whisky and the only official bottling is the **12 year old Flora & Fauna**. In autumn 2017, however, a **23 year old**, matured in ex-bodega European oak butts was released as part of the Special Releases.

History:

1798 John Stewart and Robert Robertson found Aldour Distillery, the predecessor to Blair Athol. The name is taken from the adjacent river Allt Dour.

1825 The distillery is expanded by John Robertson and takes the name Blair Athol Distillery.

1826 The Duke of Atholl leases the distillery to Alexander Connacher & Co.

1860 Elizabeth Connacher runs the distillery.

1882 Peter Mackenzie & Company Distillers Ltd of Edinburgh (future founder of Dufftown Distillery) buys Blair Athol and expands it.

1932 The distillery is mothballed.

1933 Arthur Bell & Sons takes over by acquiring Peter Mackenzie & Company.

1949 Production restarts.

1973 Stills are expanded from two to four.

1985 Guinness Group buys Arthur Bell & Sons.

1987 A visitor centre is built.

2003 A 27 year old cask strength from 1975 is launched in Diageo's Rare Malts series.

2010 A distillery exclusive with no age statement and a single cask from 1995 are released.

2016 A distillery exclusive without age statement is released.

2017 A 23 year old is released as part of the Special Releases.

23 years old

Tasting notes Blair Athol 12 years old:

GS – The nose is mellow and sherried, with brittle toffee. Sweet and fragrant. Relatively rich on the palate, with malt, raisins, sultanas and sherry. The finish is lengthy, elegant and slowly drying.

Bowmore

[bow•<u>moor</u>]

Owner: **Region/district:**
Morrison Bowmore (Suntory)   Islay

Founded: **Status:**   **Capacity:**
1779   Active (vc)   2 000 000 litres

Address: School Street, Bowmore, Islay,
Argyll PA43 7GS

Website: **Tel:**
bowmore.com   01496 810441

With a complete overhaul of the core range packaging, including some new releases, Bowmore are preparing themselves to take the next step to increase sales.

During the past few years, sales figures have remained stable at 2 million bottles per annum. Lagavulin, on the other hand, has been increasing their numbers during the same period and have now surpassed Bowmore to become the second best-selling Islay whisky. To compliment the new packaging, the owners of Bowmore have also launched a global campaign called Unlock Hidden Depths, which ties into the distillery´s heritage as well as the historic No. 1 Vaults. In these days of releases of no age statement on the labels, it is interesting to see Bowmore largely sticking to age statements, also for their new releases.

The distillery is one of only a few Scottish distilleries with its own floor maltings, with 30% of the malt requirement being produced inhouse. The remaining part is bought from Simpson's. Both parts have a phenol specification of 25 ppm and are always mixed on a 1:3 ratio, with 2 tons in house malt and 6 tons of malt from Simpsons before mashing. The distillery has an eight ton stainless steel semi-lauter mash tun, six washbacks of Oregon pine, with both short (48 hours) and long (100 hours) fermentations and two pairs of stills. The 27,000 casks are stored in two dunnage and one racked warehouse. Vault No. 1, closest to the sea and dating back to the 1700s, is probably the oldest whisky warehouse still in use in Scotland. In 2017, they will be doing 13 mashes per week, which amounts to 1.6 million litres of alcohol.

The core range for domestic markets includes the new **No. 1**, (which replaces Small Batch Reserve), **12 years, 15 years** (with the name Darkest having been dropped), **18 years** and **25 years**. It is uncertain if the **9 year old**, which was released in autumn 2016, will continue to be a part of the range. The duty free line-up has been completely revamped and all the old varieties are gone (Springtide, Black Rock, Gold Reef, White Sands and Vintage 1984). They were replaced in spring 2017 by **10 year old** (Dark and Intense), **15 year old** (Golden and Elegant) and **18 year old** (Deep and Complex). A limited release was made in autumn 2016, highlighting the influence from Vault No. 1 where some of the warehouse walls are actually found below sea level. The new expression, bottled at 51.5% is called **Bowmore Vault Edition** with the added "Atlantic Sea Salt". Two limited releases of impressive age appeared in late 2016. First was the fifth and final edition of the famous **Black Bowmore** distilled in 1964. The first release was in 1993 as a 29 year old and it was then relaunched in 1994, 1995 and 2007. There are 159 bottles in the final release. Shortly after, the final 50 bottles of the **50 year old**, distilled in 1961 were also released. There were two bottlings for Feis Ile 2017; an **11 year old** (53.8%) matured in a combination of oloroso sherry casks and Bordeaux red wine casks and a very limited **27 year old** (52.4%) that had been fully matured in port pipes.

History:

1779 Bowmore Distillery is founded by David Simpson and becomes the oldest Islay distillery.

1837 The distillery is sold to James and William Mutter of Glasgow.

1892 After additional construction, the distillery is sold to Bowmore Distillery Company Ltd, a consortium of English businessmen.

1925 J. B. Sheriff and Company takes over.

1929 Distillers Company Limited (DCL) takes over.

1950 William Grigor & Son takes over.

1963 Stanley P. Morrison buys the distillery and forms Morrison Bowmore Distillers Ltd.

1989 Japanese Suntory buys a 35% stake in Morrison Bowmore.

1993 The legendary Black Bowmore is launched.

1994 Suntory now controls all of Morrison Bowmore.

1996 A Bowmore 1957 (38 years) is bottled at 40.1% but is not released until 2000.

1999 Bowmore Darkest with three years finish on Oloroso barrels is launched.

2000 Bowmore Dusk with two years finish in Bordeaux barrels is launched.

2001 Bowmore Dawn with two years finish on Port pipes is launched.

2002 A 37 year old Bowmore from 1964 and matured in fino casks is launched in a limited edition of 300 bottles (recommended price £1,500).

2003 Another two expressions complete the wood trilogy which started with 1964 Fino - 1964 Bourbon and 1964 Oloroso.

2004 Morrison Bowmore buys one of the most outstanding collections of Bowmore Single Malt from the private collector Hans Sommer. It totals more than 200 bottles and includes a number of Black Bowmore.

History continued:

2005 Bowmore 1989 Bourbon (16 years) and 1971 (34 years) are launched.

2006 Bowmore 1990 Oloroso (16 years) and 1968 (37 years) are launched. A new and upgraded visitor centre is opened.

2007 An 18 year old is introduced. New packaging for the whole range. 1991 (16yo) Port and Black Bowmore are released.

2008 White Bowmore and a 1992 Vintage with Bordeaux finish are launched.

2009 Gold Bowmore, Maltmen´s Selection, Laimrig and Bowmore Tempest are released.

2010 A 40 year old and Vintage 1981 are released.

2011 Vintage 1982 and new batches of Tempest and Laimrig are released.

2012 100 Degrees Proof, Springtide and Vintage 1983 are released for duty free.

2013 The Devil´s Casks, a 23 year old Port Cask Matured and Vintage 1984 are released.

2014 Black Rock, Gold Reef and White Sands are released for duty free.

2015 New editions of Devil´s Cask, Tempest and the 50 year old are released as well as Mizunara Cask Finish.

2016 A 9 year old, a 10 year old travel retail exclusive and Bowmore Vault Edit1on are released as well as the final batch of Black Bowmore.

2017 No. 1 is released together with three new expressions for travel retail.

Tasting notes Bowmore 12 year old:

GS – An enticing nose of lemon and gentle brine leads into a smoky, citric palate, with notes of cocoa and boiled sweets appearing in the lengthy, complex finish.

10 years old
Travel Retail

18 years old
Travel Retail

Vault Edition
Atlantic Sea Salt

No. 1

12 years old

25 years old

Braeval

[bre•vaal]

Owner: **Region/district:**
Chivas Brothers (Pernod Ricard)   Speyside

Founded: **Status:**   **Capacity:**
1973   Active   4 200 000 litres

Address: Chapeltown of Glenlivet, Ballindalloch,
Banffshire AB37 9JS

Website: **Tel:**
-                             01542 783042

Nearly all the distilleries in Scotland have at least at one time or another been blessed with an official bottling by the owners but never Braeval. At least not until now.

In 2017, for the first time since the distillery was founded in 1973, there is the possibility to buy a Braeval single malt, bottled by the owners Chivas Brothers. However, you can only find it at any of Chivas Bros visitor centres. It is a 16 year old single cask from a second fill hogshead and it is a part of the new Distillery Reserve Collection.

The 1960s and 1970s were golden years for Scotch whisky with booming sales. During those years, a total of 16 distilleries were founded and one of them was Braeval. Seagram's, the owners of Chivas Brothers at the time, only owned two distilleries (Strathisla and Glen Keith) and a higher capacity for production was needed. The legendary Sam Bronfman had successfully established Chivas Regal as a premium blend in USA by launching a 12 year-old version and the demand had sky-rocketed. A failed attempt to purchase Glenlivet forced the Bronfman family to build their own distilleries, first Braeval and the following year Allt-a-Bhainne. These were the first two of a "five distilleries in five years"-plan, but in 1977, they finally managed to acquire Glenlivet, Glen Grant and even Longmorn, thus fulfilling their quota.

The equipment consists of a 9 ton stainless steel mash tun with traditional rakes, but this may be converted to a more modern full lauter tun in keeping with Allt-a-Bhainne which was converted two years ago. Furthermore, there are 13 stainless steel washbacks with a fermentation time of 70 hours and six stills. There are two wash stills with aftercoolers and four spirit stills, and with the possibility of doing 26 mashes per week, the distillery can now produce 4 million litres per year.

The new **16 year old single cask** is the only offical bottling of Braeval. From time to time independent bottlers have made releases and it has also been used for the bottling of Deerstalker from Aberko.

History:

1973 The distillery is founded by Chivas Brothers (Seagram's) and production starts in October.

1975 Three stills are increased to five.

1978 Five stills are further expanded to six.

1994 The distillery changes name to Braeval.

2001 Pernod Ricard takes over Chivas Brothers.

2002 Braeval is mothballed in October.

2008 The distillery starts producing again in July.

2017 The first official bottling, a 16 year old single cask, is released.

16 years old

Tasting notes Braeval 16 year old:
GS – Marzipan, milk chocolate-coated Turkish Delight and orange peel on the nose. The palate is sweet and fruity, with stewed apples, sugared almonds, nutmeg and ginger. Medium to long in the finish, consistently sugary and spicy.

The formation of
Pernod Ricard

The seed, in a double sense of the word, essential to the foundation of the second largest spirits producer is in fact aniseed (*Pimpinella anisum*). The conglomerate of today is a merger between two companies, Pernod and Ricard, both of which built their success on the production of pastis, a French national spirit which takes its flavour from the fruits of the aniseed plant as well as liquorice root.

The oldest of the companies, Maison Pernod Fils, was founded by Henri-Louis Perrenoud (he later changed his last name to Pernod) in 1805 in the French-Swiss border village of Pontarlie. Just a few years earlier, a retired physician by the name Pierre Ordinaire, had developed an elixir for medicinal purposes which was based on wormwood (Artemisia absinthium). Following Ordinaire´s death, the recipe fell into Perrenoud´s hands and he started producing absinthe on a commercial scale. The spirit became hugely popular in France. Towards the end of the century close to 40 million litres were consumed yearly. But absinthe also acquired a bad reputation and was supposed to cause hysteria, hallucinations and mental illness. The spirit was formally banned in France in 1915 and it wasn´t until 2011 that the law was repealed. By then, it had been known for quite some time, that it was not the absinthe or the wormwood which was the problem but rather excessive drinking of the popular spirit. Nevertheless, for Pernod as a company the ban was a huge problem and in order to remain in business, they (as well as other producers) had to change the recipe. Wormwood was replaced with aniseed and pastis was born. More producers were established and among them were Paul Ricard, the son of a wine merchant in Marseille. In 1932, at the age of 23, he created his own version of pastis and founded the company Ricard. Today Ricard is by far the world´s most popular pastis with 55 million bottles sold in 2016.

The two companies carried on through the decades, focusing on pastis and the French market until they joined forces in 1974 when Pernod Ricard was created. They soon realised that growth must now come from a more diversified portfolio of spirits and also diversification into the export market. That same year, 1974, the new company made their first move into the Scotch whisky sector when they bought Campbell Distillers including several blends and, not least, Aberlour distillery. During the seventies and eighties, several other brands and spirit producers were acquired including two smaller distilleries, Edradour (1982) and Glenallachie (1989). When they took over Irish Distillers in 1989 they came into possesion of the world's most popular Irish whiskey - Jameson – which today sells more than 65 million bottles per year. In 2001, Pernod Ricard and their rival Diageo bought the Canadian Seagram´s wine and spirits division and split the assets between them. Among the brand were Chivas Regal, Glenlivet and Glen Grant that went to Pernod Ricard which in turn meant they doubled in size. Included in the deal were also five other distilleries in Scotland (All-a-Bhainne, Braeval, Glen Keith, Longmorn and Strathisla). Only four years later, the company doubled in size once again. This time it was also a joint take-over when they, together with Fortune Brands, took over Allied Domecq. Added to the company´s portfolio was Ballantine´s blend but there were also a number of distilleries, including BenRiach, Glenburgie, GlenDronach, Glentauchers, Miltonduff, Scapa and Tormore.

The two most important brands in these two deals were undoubtedly Glenlivet and Ballantine´s. In 2001, Glenlivet was the third biggest single malt in the world with Glenfiddich and Glen Grant in the top. Three years later, the owners set up a goal that Glenlivet should eventually become the number one. At the time, it seemed highly unlikely as Glenfiddich outsold their brand more than two to one but in 2014 it became a reality. It lasted just a year though and Glenlivet is now back as number two. The same spot on the blended Scotch list is occupied by Ballantine´s which is the only of the leading blended Scotch brands that has managed to increase volumes since 2012.

After the Allied take-over in 2005, Pernod Ricard had become the second biggest producer of wine and spirits in the world after Diageo. But the acquisitions didn´t stop there, in 2008 Pernod Ricard paid €5.7 billion for the Swedish group Vin & Sprit, owner of Absolut - the second biggest vodka brand in the world after Smirnoff. When Patrick Ricard, son of the founder Paul Ricard and long time chairman and CEO of Pernod Ricard, died in 2012, his role was eventually taken over by his nephew Alexandre Ricard. In an interview just after assuming leadership of the company in 2015, Alexandre Ricard stated that the goal for the company is to overtake Diageo one day, to become the world´s biggest spirits company.

Bruichladdich

[brook•lad•dee]

Owner:	**Region/district:**
Rémy Cointreau	Islay

Founded:	**Status:**	**Capacity:**
1881	Active (vc)	1 500 000 litres

Address: Bruichladdich, Islay, Argyll PA49 7UN

Website:	**Tel:**
bruichladdich.com	01496 850221

The purchase of Bruichladdich in 2012 by drinks giant Rèmy Cointreau proved not to be a solitary move into whisky territory for the cognac focused company. Recent acquisitions indicate a well thoughtout plan to grow within the new category.

In November 2016, Rèmy bought the French whisky producer Domaine des Hautes Glaces and shorly after, Westland Distillers in Seattle became part of the group. This effectively mirrors other major spirits companies strive to gain a foothold in an industry being influenced by smaller producers. The dedication from Rèmy is also evidenced by the fact that Simon Coughlin, who was one of the individuals influencial in the resurrection of Bruichladdich in 2000, recently changed jobs from CEO of Brucihladdich to take up the management of a new whisky business unit within Rèmy.

The distillery is equipped with a 7 ton cast iron, open mash tun with rakes, dating back to 1881 when the distillery was founded. There are six washbacks of Oregon pine with a fermentation time between 70 and 105 hours and two pairs of stills. All whisky produced is based on Scottish barley, 30% of which comes from Islay and with 5% being organically grown. During 2017, they will be doing on average 10 mashes per week, resulting in 1.3 million litres of alcohol per year. The breakdown of the three whisky varieties during 2017 are 60% Bruichladdich, 30% Port Charlotte and 10% Octomore.

The malting floors at Bruichladdich were closed in 1961 but there are now definite plans to start their own malting again. The idea is to move the bottling facility to a new location on site and build a malting plant where the current bottling plant is located. No time table for commencement of the work has yet been presented.

Bruichladdich single malt was unpeated between 1962 and 1994 but, today, there are three main lines in the distillery´s production; unpeated **Bruichladdich**, heavily peated **Port Charlotte** and the ultra-heavily peated **Octomore**. The core expressions for each of the three varieties are **Scottish Barley** and **Islay Barley**. For Bruichladdich there are two duty free exclusives – **The Laddie Eight** and the newly introduced **25 year old** sherry cask from 1990. Organic Barley, Bere Barley and Black Art 4 have been discontinued but a **Black Art 5 1992** was introduced in spring 2017 in the core range. The duty free expressions for Port Charlotte are **PC12**, bottled at cask strength and **2007 CC: 01** with a full maturation in Eau de Vie casks. For Octomore it is **7.2 Cask Evolution**, which is a vatting of whiskies matured in American oak and syrah casks. A **10 year old** version of all three varieties have been available in the distillery shop together with **Octomore OBA/C_0.1** and several **Micro Provenance** single casks. Finally, there were three special bottlings for Feis Ile 2017; a multi-vintage **Port Charlotte** called **Transparency**, a **2006 Organic Bruichladdich** and a **2007 Bruichladdich Bere Barley**.

History:

1881 Barnett Harvey builds the distillery with money left by his brother William III to his three sons William IV, Robert and John Gourlay.

1886 Bruichladdich Distillery Company Ltd is founded and reconstruction commences.

1889 William Harvey becomes Manager and remains on that post until his death in 1937.

1929 Temporary closure.

1936 The distillery reopens.

1938 Joseph Hobbs, Hatim Attari and Alexander Tolmie purchase the distillery through the company Train & McIntyre.

1938 Operations are moved to Associated Scottish Distillers.

1952 The distillery is sold to Ross & Coulter from Glasgow.

1960 A. B. Grant buys Ross & Coulter.

1961 Own maltings ceases and malt is brought in from Port Ellen.

1968 Invergordon Distillers take over.

1975 The number of stills increases to four.

1983 Temporary closure.

1993 Whyte & Mackay buys Invergordon Distillers.

1995 The distillery is mothballed in January.

1998 In production again for a few months, and then mothballed.

2000 Murray McDavid buys the distillery from JBB Greater Europe for £6.5 million.

2001 The first distillation (Port Charlotte) is on 29th May and the first distillation of Bruichladdich starts in July. In September the owners' first bottlings from the old casks are released, 10, 15 and 20 years old.

2002 The world's most heavily peated whisky is produced on 23rd October when Octomore (80ppm) is distilled.

History continued:

2004 Second edition of the 20 year old (nick-named Flirtation) and 3D are launched.

2005 Infinity, Rocks, Legacy Series IV, The Yellow Submarine and The Twenty 'Islands' are launched.

2006 The first official bottling of Port Charlotte; PC5.

2007 New releases include Redder Still, Legacy 6, PC6 and an 18 year old.

2008 New expressions include the first Octomore, Bruichladdich 2001, PC7 and Golder Still.

2009 New releases include Classic, Organic, Black Art, Infinity 3, PC8, Octomore 2 and X4+3 - the first quadruple distilled single malt.

2010 PC Multi Vintage, Organic MV, Octomore/3_152, Bruichladdich 40 year old are released.

2011 The first 10 year old from own production is released as well as PC9 and Octomore 4_167.

2012 Ten year old versions of Port Charlotte and Octomore are released as well as Laddie 16 and 22, Bere Barley 2006, Black Art 3 and DNA4. Rémy Cointreau buys the distillery.

2013 Scottish Barley, Islay Barley Rockside Farm, Bere Barley 2nd edition, Black Art 4, Port Charlotte Scottish Barley, Octomore 06.1 and 06.2 are released.

2014 PC11 and Octomore Scottish Barley are released.

2015 PC12, Octomore 7.1 and High Noon 134 are released.

2016 The Laddie Eight, Octomore 7.4 and Port Charlotte 2007 CC:01 are released.

2017 Black Art 5 and 25 year old sherry cask are launched.

Tasting notes Bruichladdich Scottish Barley:

GS – Mildly metallic on the early nose, then cooked apple aromas develop, with a touch of linseed. Initially very fruity on the gently oily palate. Ripe peaches and apricots, with vanilla, brittle toffee, lots of spice and sea salt. The finish is drying, with breakfast tea.

Tasting notes Port Charlotte Scottish Barley:

GS – Wood smoke and contrasting bonbons on the nose. Warm Tarmac develops, with white pepper. Finally, fragrant pipe tobacco. Peppery peat and treacle toffee on the palate, with a maritime note. Long in the finish, with black pepper and oak.

Tasting notes Octomore Scottish Barley:

GS – A big hit of sweet peat on the nose; ozone and rock pools, supple leather, damp tweed. Peat on the palate is balanced by allspice, vanilla and fruitiness. Very long in the finish, with chilli, dry roasted nuts and bonfire smoke.

Bruichladdich 25 yo Vintage 1990

Bruichladdich Islay Barley 2010

Black Art 5

Port Charlotte PC12

The Classic Laddie Scottish Barley

Port Charlotte 2007 CC:01

Bunnahabhain

[buh•nah•hav•enn]

Owner: Distell International Ltd.
Region/district: Islay

Founded: 1881
Status: Active (vc)
Capacity: 2 700 000 litres

Address: Port Askaig, Islay, Argyll PA46 7RP

Website: bunnahabhain.com
Tel: 01496 840646

The interest in Bunnahabhain single malt has certainly increased in the last decade. Until 2005, a 12 year old was all you could find. This year, if you include limited releases, the number of bottlings is close to twenty!

The increased range has also shown value through the sales figures. In 2016, around 420,000 bottles were sold. More and more of the production is now being saved for future single malts rather than going into blends.

The distillery is equipped with a 12.5 ton traditional stainless steel mash tun, six washbacks made of Oregon pine and two pairs of stills. The fermentation time varies between 48 and 110 hours. The production for 2017 will be 2 million litres, split between 35% peated and 65% unpeated. The peated volume has more than doubled compared to last year and the peating level has also increased slightly to 35-45ppm.

The core range consists of **12, 18, 25** and **40 year old**, as well as two peated versions – the 10 year old **Toiteach** (a blend of young peated and older unpeated whisky) and **Ceobanach** (at least 10 years old and peated). A no age statement addition to the range appeared in June 2017 in the shape of **Stiùireadair**, matured in first and re-fill sherry casks. Recent limited releases include the 46 year old **Eich Bhana Lìr**, the oldest malt ever released from the distillery. This was followed up in February 2017 with a peated **Moine Oloroso** and, later in the year, a **1980 vintage**, a **14 year old PX finish** and a **12 year old Moine brandy finish**. For Feis Ile 2017, there were two releases; the peated **Moine 13 year old** with a finish in port pipes and a **1997 bourbonmatured** with a finish in virgin American oak. There are three travel retail exclusives – **Cruach-Mhòna** which comprises of young, heavily peated Bunnahabhain, **Eirigh Na Greine**, a vatting of whisky from bourbon, sherry and red wine casks and, released in August 2017, **An Cladach**. Finally, there are two distillery exclusives – an **11 year old** with a PX finish and a **13 year old Moine** finished in Marsala casks.

History:

1881 William Robertson of Robertson & Baxter, founds the distillery together with the brothers William and James Greenless, owners of Islay Distillers Company Ltd.

1883 Production starts in earnest in January.

1887 Islay Distillers Company Ltd merges with William Grant & Co. in order to form Highland Distilleries Company Limited.

1963 The two stills are augmented by two more.

1982 The distillery closes.

1984 The distillery reopens. A 21 year old is released to commemorate the 100th anniversary.

1999 Edrington takes over Highland Distillers and mothballs Bunnahabhain but allows for a few weeks of production a year.

2001 A 35 year old from 1965 is released during Islay Whisky Festival.

2002 A 35 year old from 1965 is released during Islay Whisky Festival. Auld Acquaintance 1968 is launched at the Islay Jazz Festival.

2003 Edrington sells Bunnahabhain and Black Bottle to Burn Stewart Distilleries for £10 million. A 40 year old from 1963 is launched.

2004 The first limited edition of the peated version is a 6 year old called Moine.

2005 Three limited editions are released - 34 years old, 18 years old and 25 years old.

2006 14 year old Pedro Ximenez and 35 years old are launched.

2008 Darach Ur is released for the travel retail market and Toiteach (a peated 10 year old) is launched on a few selected markets.

2009 Moine Cask Strength is released.

2010 The peated Cruach-Mhòna and a limited 30 year old are released.

2013 A 40 year old is released.

2014 Eirigh Na Greine and Ceobanach are released.

2017 Moine Oloroso, Stiùireadair and An Cladach are released.

Tasting notes Bunnahabhain 12 years old:

GS – The nose is fresh, with light peat and discreet smoke. More overt peat on the nutty and fruity palate, but still restrained for an Islay. The finish is full-bodied and lingering, with a hint of vanilla and some smoke.

12 years old

Caol Ila

[cull <u>eel</u>•a]

Owner: **Region/district:**
Diageo   Islay

Founded: **Status:**   **Capacity:**
1846   Active (vc)   6 500 000 litres

Address: Port Askaig, Islay, Argyll PA46 7RL

Website: **Tel:**
malts.com   01496 302760

Twenty years after the foundation of Caol Ila, new owners entered the scene which would have a great influence on the future development of the distillery.

Bulloch Lade & Co was a collaboration of two companies, when combined represented lots of experience in whisky production and sales. The Bulloch family had opened Duntocher distillery (predecessor of Auchentoshan) already in 1817 and they were also running Camlachie in the Lowlands before the two brothers Archibald and Matthew Bulloch joined forces with Daniel Lade and his son William in 1855. In 1863, they took over Caol Ila and in 1867, they purchased another Islay distillery, Lossit, then the following year built Benmore distillery in Campbeltown. The owners extended and rebuilt Caol Ila in 1879 and managed to expand the reach of the single malt to England and abroad.

A decade ago, just a couple of thousand visitors per year came to see Caol Ila. Things have changed though, and last year 13,000 people followed the road to Port Askaig on the northern part of Islay. Four different tours are available, one of them being an unusual whisky and chocolate pairing.

Caol Ila is equipped with a 13.5 ton full lauter mash tun, eight wooden washbacks and two made of stainless steel and three pairs of stills. The fermentation time is 60 hours, except for the unpeated version when it is increased to 80 hours. In recent years, the distillery has been doing 26 mashes per week which amounts to 6.5 million litres of alcohol. Caol Ila is known for its peated whisky but, since 1999, an increasingly bigger part of unpeated, nutty new-make has been produced.

The core range consists of **Moch** without age statement, **12, 18** and **25 year old**, **Distiller's Edition** with a moscatel finish and **Cask Strength**. The release for Islay Festival 2017 was an unusual **12 year old** that had been matured in ex-bourbon barrels and then given a finish in amoroso sherry casks that had previously been used to mature Talisker Distiller's Edition. As tradition prescribes, the unpeated version of Caol Ila was represented in the Special Releases that appeared in autumn 2017. This time it was an **18 year old** which had been bottled at 59.8%.

History:

1846 Hector Henderson founds Caol Ila.

1852 Henderson, Lamont & Co. is subjected to financial difficulties and Henderson is forced to sell Caol Ila to Norman Buchanan.

1863 Norman Buchanan sells to the blending company Bulloch, Lade & Co. from Glasgow.

1879 The distillery is rebuilt and expanded.

1920 Bulloch, Lade & Co. is liquidated and the distillery is taken over by Caol Ila Distillery.

1927 DCL becomes sole owners.

1972 All the buildings, except for the warehouses, are demolished and rebuilt.

1974 The renovation, which totals £1 million, is complete and six new stills are installed.

1999 Experiments with unpeated malt.

2002 The first official bottlings since Flora & Fauna/ Rare Malt appear; 12 years, 18 years and Cask Strength (c. 10 years).

2003 A 25 year old cask strength is released.

2006 Unpeated 8 year old and 1993 Moscatel finish are released.

2007 Second edition of unpeated 8 year old.

2009 The fourth edition of the unpeated version (10 year old) is released.

2010 A 25 year old, a 1999 Feis Isle bottling and a 1997 Manager's Choice are released.

2011 An unpeated 12 year old and the unaged Moch are released.

2012 An unpeated 14 year old is released.

2013 Unpeated Stitchell Reserve is released.

2014 A 15 year old unpeated and a a 30 year old are released.

2016 A 15 year old unpeated is released.

2017 An 18 year old unpeated is released.

Tasting notes Caol Ila 12 year old:

GS – Iodine, fresh fish and smoked bacon feature on the nose, along with more delicate, floral notes. Smoke, malt, lemon and peat on the slightly oily palate. Peppery peat in the drying finish.

12 years old

Cardhu

[car•doo]

Owner:	**Region/district:**
Diageo	Speyside
Founded:	**Status:**	**Capacity:**
1824	Active (vc)	3 400 000 litres

Address: Knockando, Aberlour, Moray AB38 7RY

Website:	**Tel:**
malts.com	01479 874635

It would hardly be an overstatement to claim that Cardhu has a very special place within Diageos 28 malt distilleries. Not only due to historical reasons but also for the high position in terms of sales that the single malt achieved early on.

Cardhu was the first of only two malt distilleries that was acquired by John Walker & Sons. It was bought from the Cummings family in 1893 and three years later, the company took over Annandale in the Lowlands. This long connection with the Walker family is still apparent today with Cardhu being a key malt in most Johnnie Walker expressions and for a long time the distillery has been the brand home of Johnnie Walker whisky. Cardhu single malt was commercially launched for the first time in 1965, only two years after Glenfiddich Straight Malt had ignited the interest in single malt. A marketing budget of £15,000 was allocated to promote the Cardhu 8 year old. Two years after the launch, the brand was reported to sell well in Italy while only 5,000 bottles were sold in the UK. The brands best performance was in 2003 with 3.5 million bottles sold. Since then, sales have slipped and in 2016, around 2.3 million bottles were sold.

Cardhu distillery is equipped with an 8 ton stainless steel full lauter mash tun, ten washbacks (eight made of Douglas fir and two of stainless steel), all with a fermentation time of 75 hours and three pairs of stills. Four of the wooden washbacks are brand new having replaced four old ones made of larch. In 2017, Cardhu will be working a 7-day week with 21 mashes per week and a production of 3.4 million litres of alcohol. In 2016, Cardhu and three nearby distilleries (Dalmunach, Tamdhu and Knockando) were connected to Scotland´s gas network by way of an eight-mile pipeline. A similar construction was made in 2014 when another four Speyside distilleries shifted from fuel oil to gas.

The core range from the distillery is **12, 15** and **18 year old** and two expressions without age statement – **Amber Rock** and **Gold Reserve**, both bottled at 40%. There is also a **Special Cask Reserve** matured in rejuvenated bourbon casks and in 2016, a **distillery exclusive** was released.

History:

1824 John Cumming applies for and obtains a licence for Cardhu Distillery.

1846 John Cumming dies and his wife Helen and son Lewis takes over.

1872 Lewis dies and his wife Elizabeth takes over.

1884 A new distillery is built to replace the old.

1893 John Walker & Sons purchases Cardhu for £20,500.

1908 The name reverts to Cardow.

1960 Reconstruction and expansion of stills from four to six.

1981 The name changes to Cardhu.

1998 A visitor centre is constructed.

2002 Diageo changes Cardhu single malt to a vatted malt with contributions from other distilleries in it.

2003 The whisky industry protests sharply against Diageo's plans.

2004 Diageo withdraws Cardhu Pure Malt.

2005 The 12 year old Cardhu Single Malt is relaunched and a 22 year old is released.

2009 Cardhu 1997, a single cask in the new Manager´s Choice range is released.

2011 A 15 year old and an 18 year old are released.

2013 A 21 year old is released.

2014 Amber Rock and Gold Reserve are launched.

2016 A distillery exclusive is released.

Amber Rock

Tasting notes Cardhu 12 years old:

GS – The nose is relatively light and floral, quite sweet, with pears, nuts and a whiff of distant peat. Medium-bodied, malty and sweet in the mouth. Medium-length in the finish, with sweet smoke, malt and a hint of peat.

Websites to watch

scotchwhisky.com
Without a doubt the best whiskysite there is! It covers every possible angle of the subject in an absolutely brilliant way.

whiskyfun.com
Serge Valentin, one of the Malt Maniacs, is almost always first with well written tasting notes on new releases.

whiskyreviews.blogspot.com
Ralfy does this video blog with tastings and field reports in an educational yet easy-going and entertaining way.

maltmadness.com
Our all-time favourite with something for everyone. Managed by the founder of Malt Maniacs, Johannes van den Heuvel.

edinburghwhiskyblog.com
Lucas, Chris and company review new releases, interview industry people and cover news from the whisky world.

whiskycast.com
The best whisky-related podcast on the internet and one that sets the standard for podcasts in other genres as well.

nonjatta.com
An excellent blog with a wealth of interesting information on Japanese whisky and Japanese culture.

whiskyintelligence.com
The best site on all kinds of whisky news. The first whisky website you should log into every morning!

whisky-news.com
Apart from daily news, this site contains tasting notes, distillery portraits, lists of retailers, events etc.

thewhiskylady.net
Anne-Sophie Bigot´s mission is "to remove the dusty cliché that whisky is only an old man´s drink" and she does it so well!

whisky-emporium.com
Keith Wood has created a treasure trove for whisky geeks with more than 1,000 tasting notes.

meleklerinpayi.com
I don´t read Turkish but, since Burkay Adalig´s blog is the 7th most visited whisky blog in the world (!), a lot of people do.

whiskynotes.be
This blog is almost entirely about tasting notes (and lots of them, not least independent bottlings) plus some news.

whiskyforeveryone.com
Educational site, perfect for beginners, with a blog where both new releases and affordable standards are reviewed.

blog.thewhiskyexchange.com
A knowledgeable team from The Whisky Exchange write about new bottlings and the whisky industry in general.

whisky-distilleries.net
Ernie Scheiner describes more than 130 distilleries in both text and photos and we are talking lots of great images!

connosr.com
This whisky social networking community is a virtual smorgasbord for any whisky lover!

canadianwhisky.org
Davin de Kergommeaux presents reviews, news and views on all things Canadian whisky. High quality content.

whiskyisrael.co.il
Gal Granov is definitely one of the most active of all bloggers. Well worth checking out daily!

spiritsjournal.klwines.com
Reviews about whiskies and the whisky industry in general by David Driscoll from the US retailer K&L Wines.

thewhiskywire.com
Steve Rush mixes reviews of the latest bottlings with presentations of classics plus news, interviews etc.

bestshotwhiskyreviews.com
Jan van den Ende presents his honest opinions on everything from cheap blends to rare single cask bottlings.

scotch-whisky.org.uk
The official site of SWA (Scotch Whisky Association) with i.a. press releases and publications about the industry.

whiskysaga.com
Brilliant blog by Norwegian whisky enthusiast Thomas Öhrbom - not least on every detail relating to Nordic whiskies.

whiskysponge.com
The brilliantly sarcastic blog by Angus Macraild is where everyone in the business secretely wants to be mentioned.

speller.nl
Thomas and Ansgar Speller explore the world of whisky and they´ve been to more distilleries than most people.

thewhiskeywash.com
Since 2015, this great team of whisky writers has brought us initiated reviews and recently they started a podcast as well.

whiskeyreviewer.com
This is a web magazine covering the world of whisky through news, reviews (more than 800), features and interviews.

thewhiskyphiles.com
An incredibly comprehensive blog filled no just with well written reviews but also news, comments, distillery profiles...

spiritedmatters.com
When Billy Abbott, known from The Whisky Exchange website, writes something it´s always thoughtful and interesting.

whiskywaffle.com
Enjoy the no-nonsense reviews and comments about affordable whiskies and not just the latest unobtainable single cask.

allthingswhisky.com
Even though postings sometimes occur intermittently, these reviews and musings are always an interesting read.

Clynelish

[cline•leash]

Owner: Diageo

Region/district: Northern Highlands

Founded: 1967

Status: Active (vc)

Capacity: 4 800 000 litres

Address: Brora, Sutherland KW9 6LR

Website: malts.com

Tel: 01408 623003 (vc)

In 1896, Clynelish was described in Harper's Weekly as "a singularly valuable property, as the make has always obtained the highest price of any single Scotch whisky".

That same year, James Ainslie took ownership of the distillery. He was a brewer who in 1888 made the transition from beer to become a whisky broker based in Leith. The company gained early success and Ainslie soon realised that he would need his own distillery to keep up with the growing number of orders. Clynelish was in great need of renovation and Ainslie invested substantial capital to increase capacity. He also introduced steam power to the distillery. James Ainslie was a good owner but it didnt take long before his company also fell foul to the crisis of the Pattison crash and so an efficient modern distillery again swapped hands.

It was this distillery that changed its name to Brora and closed in 1983. On the same site today, stands the modern Clynelish distillery. It was closed for refurbishing in May 2016 and started production again in June 2017. Among the renovation and instillations a new and efficient mash tun was included. The distillery is now equipped with a 12.5 ton full lauter mash tun, 8 wooden washbacks and two made of stainless steel. The still room, with its three pairs of stills, has stunning views towards the village of Brora and the North Sea. When in production, Clynelish will be working a 7-day week, producing some 4.8 million litres of alcohol. Approximately 6,000 casks of Clynelish are stored in the two old Brora warehouses next door, but most of the production is matured elsewhere. There are also two casks of Brora single malt (1977 and 1982). Some of the old Brora equipment (stills, feints receiver, spirit receiver and spirit safe) is still left in the listed buildings.

The main part of the production is used for blends, mainly Johnnie Walker Gold Label. Official bottlings include a **14 year old** and a **Distiller's Edition**, with an Oloroso Seco finish. Recent limited bottlings include **Clynelish Select Reserve** which has been launched two years in a row as part of the annual Special Releases.

History:

1819 The 1st Duke of Sutherland founds a distillery called Clynelish Distillery.

1827 The first licensed distiller, James Harper, files for bankruptcy and John Matheson takes over.

1846 George Lawson & Sons become new licensees.

1896 James Ainslie & Heilbron takes over.

1912 James Ainslie & Co. narrowly escapes bankruptcy and Distillers Company Limited (DCL) takes over together with James Risk.

1916 John Walker & Sons buys a stake of James Risk's stocks.

1931 The distillery is mothballed.

1939 Production restarts.

1960 The distillery becomes electrified.

1967 A new distillery, also named Clynelish, is built adjacent to the first one.

1968 'Old' Clynelish is mothballed in August.

1969 'Old' Clynelish is reopened as Brora and starts using a very peaty malt.

1983 Brora is closed in March.

2002 A 14 year old is released.

2006 A Distiller's Edition 1991 finished in Oloroso casks is released.

2009 A 12 year old is released for Friends of the Classic Malts.

2010 A 1997 Manager's Choice single cask is released.

2014 Clynelish Select Reserve is released.

2015 Second version of Clynelish Select Reserve is released.

2017 The distillery produces again after a year long closure for refurbishing.

14 years old

Tasting notes Clynelish 14 year old:

GS – A nose that is fragrant, spicy and complex, with candle wax, malt and a whiff of smoke. Notably smooth in the mouth, with honey and contrasting citric notes, plus spicy peat, before a brine and tropical fruit finish.

Cragganmore

[crag•an•moor]

Owner: **Region/district:**
Diageo   Speyside

Founded: **Status:**   **Capacity:**
1869   Active (vc)   2 200 000 litres

Address: Ballindalloch, Moray AB37 9AB

Website: **Tel:**
malts.com   01479 874700

The first actively promoted single malt on a global scale was Glenfiddich Straight Malt in 1963. Most competitors were slow to follow but with time many jumped on the bandwagon – Macallan in 1978 and Glenmorangie in 1981.

The company with the biggest number of distilleries, Diageo or at that time known as DCL, however were not sure how to handle this "new" category. Cardhu, admittedly, was being promoted but the company directors felt the full focus should be placed on the blends. When Guinness and DCL merged in 1987 to form United Distillers, perceptions changed. Mike Collings and Roy MacMillan were given the task to increase the company´s presence in the single malt segment and they came up with the six Classic Malts. Six different malts were chosen to represent six whisky regions in Scotland with Cragganmore chosen as the Speyside whisky. The idea had a huge impact on the interest in malt whiskies and Mike Collings, who worked as the company´s marketing director from 1987 to 2005, also developed the Rare Malts selection in 1995 and was involved in the creation of Johnnie Walker Blue Label. He now works as an independentt bottler of exclusive malts.

Cragganmore is equipped with a 6.8 ton stainless steel full lauter mash tun with a copper canopy and six washbacks made of Oregon pine with a 60 hour fermentation time. There are two large wash stills with sharply descending lyne arms and two considerably smaller spirit stills with boil balls and long, slightly descending lyne arms. In 2017, the distillery will be working a 5-day week which translates to 1.65 million litres of alcohol.

Cragganmore single malt is a key contributor to the Old Parr blend, first launched in 1909 and popular in Latin America, but there is also a core range of single malts made up of a **12 year old** and a **Distiller's Edition** with a finish in Port pipes. In 2014, a **25 year old** appeared as a Special Release and in 2015, the oldest Cragganmore ever, a **43 year old**, was released as an exclusive to Dubai Duty Free with only 474 bottles available. Finally, in autumn 2016, a **special vatting** appeared as part of the Special Releases.

History:

1869 John Smith, who already runs Glenfarclas distillery, founds Cragganmore.

1886 John Smith dies and his brother George takes over operations.

1893 John's son Gordon, at 21, is old enough to assume responsibility for operations.

1901 The distillery is refurbished and modernized with help of the famous architect Charles Doig.

1912 Gordon Smith dies and his widow Mary Jane supervises operations.

1917 The distillery closes.

1918 The distillery reopens and Mary Jane installs electric lighting.

1923 The distillery is sold to the newly formed Cragganmore-Glenlivet Distillery Co. where Mackie & Co. and Sir George Macpherson-Grant of Ballindalloch Estate share ownership.

1927 White Horse Distillers is bought by DCL which thus obtains 50% of Cragganmore.

1964 The number of stills is increased from two to four.

1965 DCL buys the remainder of Cragganmore.

1988 Cragganmore 12 years becomes one of six selected for United Distillers' Classic Malts.

1998 Cragganmore Distillers Edition Double Matured (port) is launched for the first time.

2002 A visitor centre opens in May.

2006 A 17 year old from 1988 is released.

2010 Manager´s Choice single cask 1997 and a limited 21 year old are released.

2014 A 25 year old is released.

2016 A Special Releases vatting without age statement and a distillery exclusive are released.

Tasting notes Cragganmore 12 years old:

GS – A nose of sherry, brittle toffee, nuts, mild wood smoke, angelica and mixed peel. Elegant on the malty palate, with herbal and fruit notes, notably orange. Medium in length, with a drying, slightly smoky finish.

12 years old

Craigellachie

[craig•ell•ack•ee]

Owner: **Region/district:**
John Dewar & Sons   Speyside
(Bacardi)

Founded: **Status:**   **Capacity:**
1891   Active   4 100 000 litres

Address: Aberlour, Banffshire AB38 9ST

Website: **Tel:**
craigellachie.com   01340 872971

As with Dewar's four other distilleries it's full speed ahead at Craigellachie during 2017 – at least in terms of production. A slightly shorter silent season compared to last year, brings the production to almost 4 million litres.

Even though all five distilleries provided us with brand new and expanded ranges of single malts in 2014, the lions share of the whisky will go into Dewar's own blends as well as being sold to other producers. The one blend which is mostly associated with Craigellachie is naturally White Horse. After all, it was the creator of the brand, Peter Mackie, who founded the distillery in the late 1800s. White Horse now belongs to Diageo (who still use Craigellachie single malt in the blend) but a lot of the malt these days land in Dewar's White Label and William Lawson's. In terms of sales figures, the latter used to play second fiddle to the well established Dewar's blend but since 2012, Lawson's is the biggest blend, in terms of volume, in the Bacardi/Dewar's range.

Craigellachie was refurbished in 1964 under the supervision of Leslie Darge who was Chief Architect of Scottish Malt Distilleries (SMD). During 28 years, he was in charge of the building or re-furbishing of no less than 46 distilleries. The distillery is equipped with a modern Steinecker full lauter mash tun, installed in 2001, which replaced the old, open cast iron mash tun. There are also eight washbacks made of larch with a fermentation time of 56-60 hours and two pairs of stills. Both stills are attached to worm tubs. The old cast iron tubs were exchanged for stainless steel in 2014 and the existing copper worms were moved to the new tubs. Production during 2017 will be 21 mashes per week and 3.9 million litres of alcohol.

Apart from a 14 year old, which at times could be hard to get hold of, there was no official bottling of Craigellachie until 2014, when the brand was completely re-launched. No less than three new expressions (**13, 17** and **23 year old**) were released for selected domestic markets and a **19 year old** was launched for duty free. This was later followed by a **31** and a **33 year old** as well as a limited **1994 Madeira single cask.**

History:

1890 The distillery is built by Craigellachie–Glenlivet Distillery Company which has Alexander Edward and Peter Mackie as part-owners.

1891 Production starts.

1916 Mackie & Company Distillers Ltd takes over.

1924 Peter Mackie dies and Mackie & Company changes name to White Horse Distillers.

1927 White Horse Distillers are bought by Distillers Company Limited (DCL).

1930 Administration is transferred to Scottish Malt Distillers (SMD), a subsidiary of DCL.

1964 Refurbishing takes place and two new stills are bought, increasing the number to four.

1998 United Distillers & Vintners (UDV) sells Craigellachie together with Aberfeldy, Brackla and Aultmore and the blending company John Dewar & Sons to Bacardi Martini.

2004 The first bottlings from the new owners are a new 14 year old which replaces UDV's Flora & Fauna and a 21 year old cask strength from 1982 produced for Craigellachie Hotel.

2014 Three new bottlings for domestic markets (13, 17 and 23 years) and one for duty free (19 years) are released.

2015 A 31 year old is released.

2016 A 33 year old and a 1994 Madeira single cask are released.

13 years old

Tasting notes Craigellachie 13 years old:

GS – Savoury on the early nose, with spent matches, green apples and mixed nuts. Malt join the nuts and apples on the palate, with sawdust and very faint smoke. Drying, with cranberries, spice and more subtle smoke.

Dailuaine

[dall•yoo•an]

Owner:	**Region/district:**
Diageo	Speyside
Founded: **Status:**	**Capacity:**
1852 Active	5 200 000 litres

Address: Carron, Banffshire AB38 7RE

Website:	**Tel:**
malts.com	01340 872500

The flavour of a malt whisky, or any whisky for that matter, depends on a multitude of factors which individually have an effect on the final outcome of the profile.

It is often said that the casks used for maturation and the maturation itself has the biggest influence and that is most probably true. However, the final flavour can´t be altered as you please. It is the character of the newmake that will define the parameters within which you will be able to work. For the sake of clarity, the character of various new makes can be split into a several groups; fruity, oily, green/grassy, sulphury etc. One of the rarer styles is waxy and I know of only three distilleries in Scotland that achieve that character; Clynelish, Deanston and, at least at the moment, Dailuaine. Exactly how this style is achieved can depend on several factors where clear worts and the length of fermentation plays a part. At least at Clynelish, there is also a contribution from the oily residue in the feints receiver – something which is usually cleaned away at other distilleries.

Dailuaine distillery is equipped with a stainless steel, 11.2 ton full lauter mash tun, eight washbacks made of larch, plus two stainless steel ones placed outside and three pairs of stills. In 2015, the fermentation time was changed to help achieve a more waxy character to the spirit. The reason for the change was that Clynelish distillery has been closed for refurbishing. That is the only Diageo distillery so far that has accounted for this style which is so important for some blends. During 2017 they will be doing four short fermentations (85 hours) per week and eight long (110 hours) amounting to 2.6 million litres of pure alcohol. On site also lies a dark grains plant processing draff and pot ale into cattle feed. To help power the plant and the distillery, Diageo recently invested £6m in a ground breaking bio-energy plant. Through anaerobic digestion, spent lees and waste water from the distillation are converted into biogas.

The only core bottling is the **16 year old Flora & Fauna** release. In autumn 2015, a **34 year old** from 1980 was launched as part of the Special Releases.

History:

1852 The distillery is founded by William Mackenzie.

1865 William Mackenzie dies and his widow leases the distillery to James Fleming, a banker from Aberlour.

1879 William Mackenzie's son forms Mackenzie and Company with Fleming.

1891 Dailuaine-Glenlivet Distillery Ltd is founded.

1898 Dailuaine-Glenlivet Distillery Ltd merges with Talisker Distillery Ltd and forms Dailuaine-Talisker Distilleries Ltd.

1915 Thomas Mackenzie dies without heirs.

1916 Dailuaine-Talisker Company Ltd is bought by the previous customers John Dewar & Sons, John Walker & Sons and James Buchanan & Co.

1917 A fire rages and the pagoda roof collapses. The distillery is forced to close.

1920 The distillery reopens.

1925 Distillers Company Limited (DCL) takes over.

1960 Refurbishing. The stills increase from four to six and a Saladin box replaces the floor maltings.

1965 Indirect still heating through steam is installed.

1983 On site maltings is closed down and malt is purchased centrally.

1991 The first official bottling, a 16 year old, is launched in the Flora & Fauna series.

1996 A 22 year old cask strength from 1973 is released as a Rare Malt.

1997 A cask strength version of the 16 year old is launched.

2000 A 17 year old Manager´s Dram matured in sherry casks is launched.

2010 A single cask from 1997 is released.

2012 The production capacity is increased by 25%.

2015 A 34 year old is launched as part of the Special Releases.

Tasting notes Dailuaine 16 years old:

GS – Barley, sherry and nuts on the substan-tial nose, developing into maple syrup. Medium-bodied, rich and malty in the mouth, with more sherry and nuts, plus ripe oranges, fruitcake, spice and a little smoke. The finish is lengthy and slightly oily, with almonds, cedar and slightly smoky oak.

16 years old

Dalmore

[dal•moor]

Owner:
Whyte & Mackay Ltd
(Emperador Inc)

Region/district:
Northern Highlands

Founded: 1839

Status: Active (vc)

Capacity: 4 300 000 litres

Address: Alness, Ross-shire IV17 0UT

Website:
thedalmore.com

Tel:
01349 882362

The whisky from Dalmore was exported to Australia as single malt, or self whisky as it was called at that time, already in the early 1870s. The success prompted the owners to employ agents in Shanghai, Karachi, Yokohama and many other places as well.

At this time, the distillery was owned by the founder, Alexander Matheson but it was run by the Mackenzie brothers whose impact and development of the distillery should be recognised. They bought the distillery in 1891, expanded it and increased the good reputation of the whisky. Over time the distillery was purchased by Whyte & Mackay, most of the production went into their blends and the Dalmore brand moved into the background. It is only in the last 15 years that Dalmore has once again caught the eye of the consumer. A lot of the credit for this revival should be given to Master Blender Richard Patterson. In 2016 he celebrated his 50th anniversary working in the Scotch whisky industry.

The distillery is equipped with a 10.4 ton stainless steel, semi-lauter mash tun, eight washbacks made of Oregon pine with a fermentation time of 50 hours and four pairs of stills. All the wash stills have peculiar flat tops while the spirit stills are equipped with water jackets, which allow cold water to circulate between the reflux bowl and the neck of the stills, thus increasing the reflux. The owners expect to do 23 mashes per week during 2017, producing 4 million litres.

The core range consists of **12, 15, 18** and **25 year old, 1263 King Alexander III** and **Cigar Malt**. **Valour**, exclusive to travel retail, was joined in the summer of 2016 by **Regalis** with a finish in Amoroso casks, **Luceo** with a final maturation in Apostoles casks and **Dominium** finished in Matusalem casks. Recent limited bottlings include new versions of the **21** and **30 year old** and, in autumn 2016, a **35 year old** and **Quintessence** with a finish in five different red wine casks. The pièce de résistance appeared in early 2017 in the shape of a **50 year old** to celebrate Richard Patterson´s 50 years in the industry. The current distillery exclusive is a **Vintage 2000**, finished for 5 years in Califonian Merlot barriques. A new range, **Vintage Port Collection**, has been announced for release later in 2017.

History:

1839 Alexander Matheson founds the distillery.

1867 Three Mackenzie brothers run the distillery.

1891 Sir Kenneth Matheson sells the distillery for £14,500 to the Mackenzie brothers.

1917 The Royal Navy moves in to start manufacturing American mines.

1920 The Royal Navy moves out and leaves behind a distillery damaged by an explosion.

1922 The distillery is in production again.

1956 Floor malting replaced by Saladin box.

1960 Mackenzie Brothers (Dalmore) Ltd merges with Whyte & Mackay.

1966 Number of stills is increased to eight.

1982 The Saladin box is abandoned.

1990 American Brands buys Whyte & Mackay.

1996 Whyte & Mackay changes name to JBB (Greater Europe).

2001 Through management buy-out, JBB (Greater Europe) is bought from Fortune Brands and changes name to Kyndal Spirits.

2002 Kyndal Spirits changes name to Whyte & Mackay.

2007 United Spirits buys Whyte & Mackay. A 15 year old, and a 40 year old are released.

2008 1263 King Alexander III is released.

2009 New releases include an 18 year old, a 58 year old and a Vintage 1951.

2010 The Dalmore Mackenzie 1992 is released.

2011 More expressions in the River Collection and 1995 Castle Leod are released.

2012 The visitor centre is upgraded and Constellaton Collection is launched.

2013 Valour is released for duty free.

2014 Emperador Inc buys Whyte & Mackay.

2016 Three new travel retail bottlings are released as well as a 35 year old and Quintessence.

2017 Vintage Port Collection is launched.

Tasting notes Dalmore 12 years old:

GS – The nose offers sweet malt, orange marmalade, sherry and a hint of leather. Full-bodied, with a dry sherry taste though sweeter sherry develops in the mouth along with spice and citrus notes. Lengthy finish with more spices, ginger, Seville oranges and vanilla.

12 years old

Dalwhinnie

[dal•whin•nay]

Owner: Diageo

Region/district: Speyside

Founded: 1897

Status: Active (vc)

Capacity: 2 200 000 litres

Address: Dalwhinnie, Inverness-shire PH19 1AB

Website: malts.com

Tel: 01540 672219 (vc)

When the Classic Malts were launched in 1988, Cragganmore got to represent Speyside and Dalwhinnie the Highlands but is that entirely correct?

Admittedly, these regions have stopped playing their part when it comes to the character of the whisky which is produced there. Today you can find a heavily peated Lowlander like Ailsa Bay as well as a non-peated Islay like some Bunnahabhain. But if you want to go by the book, the Scotch Whisky Association recognises five different regions or localities - Highlands, Lowlands, Campbeltown, Islay and Speyside. The geographical boundaries of Campbeltown and Islay are clear to establish and essentially the Highland/Lowland line stretches from the Southern foreshore of the Firth of Clyde towards the North East to the Southern foreshore of the Firth of Tay. Speyside on the other hand has been debated. Here's how it is according to the SWA; it consists of the entire Moray Council and the Badenoch and Strathspey ward of the Highland Council and it is in the latter that Dalwhinnie is situated, a few kilometres east of Loch Spey where the source of the river can be found. Hence, Dalwhinnie is a Speyside whisky.

The distillery is equipped with a 7.3 ton full lauter mash tun and six wooden washbacks with the fermentation split into four short sessions at 60 hours and six long, fermenting over the weekend, at 110 hours. There is one pair of stills (planned to be replaced in 2018) attached to worm tubs which were replaced with new ones in 2015. The 5-day production week for 2017 means 10 mashes per week which gives 1.4 million litres of alcohol in the year. Dalwhinnie is one of Diageo's best selling single malts and comes in at sixth place with more than 1 million bottles sold in 2016. It is also the signature malt in one of the fastest increasing Scotch blends in the world right now – Buchanan's – with its main markets in USA, Mexico and Venezuela.

The core range is made up of a **15 year old** and a **Distiller's Edition** with a finish in oloroso casks. A new addition, **Dalwhinnie Winter's Gold**, was released in July 2015. Autumn 2015 saw the release of a limited **25 year old** and in 2016, a **distillery exclusive** was launched.

History:

1897 John Grant, George Sellar and Alexander Mackenzie commence building the facilities. The first name is Strathspey.

1898 The owner encounters financial troubles and John Somerville & Co and A P Blyth & Sons take over and change the name to Dalwhinnie.

1905 Cook & Bernheimer in New York, buys Dalwhinnie for £1,250 at an auction. The administration of Dalwhinnie is placed in the newly formed company James Munro & Sons.

1919 Macdonald Greenlees & Willliams Ltd headed by Sir James Calder buys Dalwhinnie.

1926 Macdonald Greenlees & Williams Ltd is bought by Distillers Company Ltd (DCL) which licences Dalwhinnie to James Buchanan & Co.

1930 Operations are transferred to Scottish Malt Distilleries (SMD).

1934 The distillery is closed after a fire in February.

1938 The distillery opens again.

1968 The maltings is decommissioned.

1987 Dalwhinnie 15 years becomes one of the selected six in United Distillers' Classic Malts.

1991 A visitor centre is constructed.

1992 The distillery closes and goes through a major refurbishment costing £3.2 million.

1995 The distillery opens in March.

2002 A 36 year old is released.

2006 A 20 year old is released.

2010 A Manager's Choice 1992 is released.

2012 A 25 year old is released.

2014 A triple matured bottling without age statement is released for The Friends of the Classic Malts.

2015 Dalwhinnie Winter's Gold and a 25 year old are released.

2016 A distillery exclusive without age statement is released.

15 years old

Tasting notes Dalwhinnie 15 years old:

GS – The nose is fresh, with pine needles, heather and vanilla. Sweet and balanced on the fruity palate, with honey, malt and a very subtle note of peat. The medium length finish dries elegantly.

Deanston

[deen•stun]

Owner:
Distell International Ltd.

Region/district:
Southern Highlands

Founded:
1965

Status:
Active (vc)

Capacity:
3 000 000 litres

Address: Deanston, Perthshire FK16 6AG

Website:
deanstonmalt.com

Tel:
01786 843010

Once a cotton mill, built in the 18th century, Deanston was remade into a distillery in 1965. The transformation was the brainchild of Brodie Hepburn, a whisky broker from Glasgow.

Born in the late 19th century, Hepburn became one of the first whisky brokers, a link between the producers that hadn´t existed before. Protecting their company secrets but at the same time depending on the exchange of casks for their blends, the broker became an integral and vital link for the whisky producers. But Brodie Hepburn did not stop at that. He bought Tullibardine distillery in 1953, was part of the founding of Macduff in 1960 and eventually co-founded Deanston in 1965. After more than 50 years in the business, his company was bought by Invergordon Distillers in 1971.

The distillery is equipped with a red 11 ton traditional open top, cast iron mash tun, eight stainless steel washbacks and two pairs of stills with ascending lyne arms. The average fermentation time is 80 hours but two mashes per week are allowed to ferment for 130 hours! Together with Clynelish and Dailuaine, Deanston is the only distillery in Scotland producing a waxy new make. One way to obtain that character is a long fermentation. The distillery is doing 10 mashes per week and producing 1.9 million litres of alcohol. Having started in 2000, organic spirit (40,000 litres) is being produced one week per year. As late as in 2012, a visitor centre was opened which today is one of the best in the industry.

The core range is **12** and **18 year old, Virgin Oak** matured in first fill bourbon and with a 1-3 months finish in virgin oak casks and **Organic**. The latter, a 15 year old, is certified as organic by the Organic Food Federation. Recent limited releases include a **40 year old**, the oldest expression so far from the distillery. There is also a **Vintage 2008** that has matured in red wine casks. For those who travel to the distillery, there is a reward in the form of some exclusive bottlings – **Spanish Oak 14 years, Sauternes 15 years, Port finish 20 years** and **Palo Cortado 12 years old**.

History:

1965 A weavery from 1785 is transformed into Deanston Distillery by James Finlay & Co. and Brodie Hepburn Ltd Brodie Hepburn also runs Tullibardine Distillery.

1966 Production commences in October.

1971 The first single malt is named Old Bannockburn.

1972 Invergordon Distillers takes over.

1974 The first single malt bearing the name Deanston is produced.

1982 The distillery closes.

1990 Burn Stewart Distillers from Glasgow buys the distillery for £2.1 million.

1991 The distillery resumes production.

1999 C L Financial buys an 18% stake of Burn Stewart.

2002 C L Financial acquires the remaining stake.

2006 Deanston 30 years old is released.

2009 A new version of the 12 year old is released.

2010 Virgin Oak is released.

2012 A visitor centre is opened.

2013 Burn Stewart Distillers is bought by South African Distell Group for £160m

2014 An 18 year old cognac finish is released in the USA.

2015 An 18 year old is released.

2016 Organic Deanston is released.

2017 A 40 year old and Vintage 2008 are released.

12 years old

Tasting notes Deanston 12 years old:
GS – A fresh, fruity nose with malt and honey. The palate displays cloves, ginger, honey and malt, while the finish is long, quite dry and pleasantly herbal.

Dufftown

[duff•town]

Owner: Diageo

Region/district: Speyside

Founded: 1896

Status: Active

Capacity: 6 000 000 litres

Address: Dufftown, Keith, Banffshire AB55 4BR

Website:
malts.com
thesingleton.com

Tel:
01340 822100

Dufftown in Speyside is sometimes referred to as the whisky capital of the world or at least of Scotland and it is hard to disagree with that. With 1600 inhabitants and six distilleries it deserves the title.

Additionally, one can still see two distilleries which were closed long ago, Parkmore and Convalmore, and the location of one that has been demolished, Pittyvaich. The town was established in 1817 and the first distillery, Mortlach, was founded six years later. It would take more than 60 years until the next distillery came on stream, Glenfiddich, but it wasn´t until the 1890s that the town saw whisky production becoming the number one industry. Today, apart from the distilleries and being the epicentre of the world famous Speyside Whisky Festival, Dufftown is also home to Joseph Brown Vats, suppliers of wooden washbacks to many distilleries in the area.

Dufftown distillery is equipped with a 13 ton full lauter mash tun, 12 stainless steel washbacks and three pairs of stills. All stills furthermore have sub coolers. The style of Dufftown single malt is green and grassy which is achieved by a clear wort and long fermentation (75 hours minimum). Add to that, a slow distillation and the fact that the stills are filled with small volumes, to allow as much copper contact as possible and you have what gives it its real character. Dufftown has been working 24/7 since 2007 and during 2017 they will be producing 6 million litres of alcohol.

The core range consists of **The Singleton of Dufftown 12, 15** and **18 year old**. In 2013 a new sub-range exclusive to duty free was launched. The first two releases were **Trinité** and **Liberté** and yet a third release, **Artisan**, was added in spring of 2014. New releases, however, didn´t stop there. March 2014 saw the launch of two new bottlings for domestic markets in Western Europe; **Tailfire** and **Sunray** and the two were followed in autumn 2014 by a new entry level bottling called **Spey Cascade**. Limited releases appear from time to time. The two latest, released in April 2016 were exclusive to Hong Kong – a **21 year old** matured in sherry casks and a **25 year old** from ex bourbon casks.

History:

1895 Peter Mackenzie, Richard Stackpole, John Symon and Charles MacPherson build the distillery Dufftown-Glenlivet in an old mill.

1896 Production starts in November.

1897 The distillery is owned by P. Mackenzie & Co., who also owns Blair Athol in Pitlochry.

1933 P. Mackenzie & Co. is bought by Arthur Bell & Sons for £56,000.

1968 The floor maltings is discontinued and malt is bought from outside suppliers. The number of stills is increased from two to four.

1974 The number of stills is increased from four to six.

1979 The stills are increased by a further two to eight.

1985 Guinness buys Arthur Bell & Sons.

1997 Guinness and Grand Metropolitan merge to form Diageo.

2006 The Singleton of Dufftown 12 year old is launched as a special duty free bottling.

2008 The Singleton of Dufftown is made available also in the UK.

2010 A Manager´s Choice 1997 is released.

2013 A 28 year old cask strength and two expressions for duty free - Unité and Trinité - are released.

2014 Tailfire, Sunray and Spey Cascade are released.

2016 Two limited releases are made - a 21 year old and a 25 year old.

Tasting notes Dufftown 12 years old:

GS – The nose is sweet, almost violet-like, with underlying malt. Big and bold on the palate, this is an upfront yet very drinkable whisky. The finish is medium to long, warming, spicy, with slowly fading notes of sherry and fudge.

Singleton of Dufftown 12 year

Edradour

[ed•ra•<u>dow</u>•er]

Owner:
Signatory Vintage
Scotch Whisky Co. Ltd

Region/district:
Southern Highland

Founded: 1825

Status: Active (vc)

Capacity: 130 000 litres

Address: Pitlochry, Perthshire PH16 5JP

Website: edradour.com

Tel: 01796 472095

It may be the case that Edradour has used the title of "smallest distillery in Scotland" a little too long. It's been a while since it was true and now there are more than 10 distilleries which are smaller.

On the other hand, it's doubtful if the owners are concerned about this fact. The problem instead, is that demand has outweighed supply and being small is actually more of a burden. For this reason Andrew Symington took the decision to increase capacity, more or less by mirroring the current distillery. The plan is to commission the stills before Christmas and start producing in January 2018. The new distillery (Edradour 2) will be equipped with two stills connected to a worm tub and four Oregon pine washbacks. With space for another two, it means that the distillery in the long term could run double shift and reach a total capacity of 500,000 litres of pure alcohol. When the new distillery is on stream, all peated production will remain in the old plant. At the same time, six new distillery warehouses have been erected, holding an additional 19,000 casks.

The current distillery is equipped with an open, traditional cast iron mash tun with a mash size of 1.1 tons. The two washbacks are made of Oregon pine and two stills are connected to a worm tub which is over 100 years old. In 2017 they will be doing 6 mashes per week and producing 130,000 litres of alcohol of which 26,000 litres will be heavily peated.

The core range consists of **10 year old, 12 year old Caledonia Selection** (oloroso finish), **Cask Strength Sherry 14 year old,** and **Cask Strength Bourbon 10 year old.** The 15 year old Fairy Flag has been discontinued. There is also the peated **Ballechin 10 year old.** The Straight From The Cask range is made up of six expressions, all fully matured in different casks; **Edradour 2006 Madeira, 2006 Sherry** and **2003 Chardonnay** and **Ballechin 2004 Burgundy, 2004 Port** and **2005 Bordeaux.** Recent limited releases include three Edradour finishes; **16 year old Barolo, 17 year old Bordeaux** and **21 year old Oloroso** as well as the interesting **8 year old vatting** of sherrymatured Edradour and bourbon-matured Ballechin.

History:

1825 Probably the year when a distillery called Glenforres is founded by farmers in Perthshire.

1837 The first year Edradour is mentioned.

1841 The farmers form a proprietary company, John MacGlashan & Co.

1886 John McIntosh & Co. acquires Edradour.

1933 William Whiteley & Co. buys the distillery.

1982 Campbell Distilleries (Pernod Ricard) buys Edradour and builds a visitor centre.

1986 The first single malt is released.

2002 Edradour is bought by Andrew Symington from Signatory for £5.4 million. The product range is expanded with a 10 year old and a 13 year old cask strength.

2003 A 30 year old and a 10 year old are released.

2004 A number of wood finishes are launched as cask strength.

2006 The first bottling of peated Ballechin is released.

2007 A Madeira matured Ballechin is released.

2008 A Ballechin matured in Port pipes and a 10 year old Edradour with a Sauternes finish are released.

2009 Fourth edition of Ballechin (Oloroso) is released.

2010 Ballechin #5 Marsala is released.

2011 Ballechin #6 Bourbon and a 26 year old PX sherry finish are relased.

2012 A 1993 Oloroso and a 1993 Sauternes finish as well as the 7th edition of Ballechin (Bordeaux) are released.

2013 Ballechin Sauternes is released.

2014 The first release of a 10 year old Ballechin.

2015 Fairy Flag is released.

2017 New releases include an 8 year old vatting of Edradour and Ballechin.

12 years old

Tasting notes Edradour 10 years old:

GS – Cider apples, malt, almonds, vanilla and honey ar present on the nose, along with a hint of smoke and sherry. The palate is rich, creamy and malty, with a persistent nuttiness and quite a pronounced kick of slightly leathery sherry. Spices and sherry dominate the medium to long finish.

Fettercairn

[fett•er•cairn]

Owner: **Region/district:**
Whyte & Mackay (Emperador)   Eastern Highlands

Founded:	**Status:**	**Capacity:**
1824	Active (vc)	3 200 000 litres

Address: Fettercairn, Laurencekirk, Kincardineshire AB30 1YB

Website: **Tel:**
fettercairndistillery.co.uk   01561 340205

Distillation of malt whisky in Scotland has been a very traditional process for hundreds of years, generally using two copper pot stills working in pair.

This is also the way most distilleries operate today but over the years there has been experimentation with other types of stills. A well known example is that of the Lomond stills that were installed in the 1950s and 1960s at distilleries including Glenburgie and Miltonduff. A relatively unknown still was designed by William Shand and was used at Fettercairn in 1833. It was constructed so that between the head of an ordinary still and the worm tub, were a series of two or more rectifying vessels. The spirit they obtained was strong and pure and the character was depending on where in the process you drew off the spirit. This reminds us of another experimental still patented by Jean Jacques Saintmarc in 1825. Apparently the quality was good, or as one spirit merchant in Edinburgh writes; "we are of the opinion that this aqua is as good as any malt aqua in the market." Despite the positive reviews the Shand still was only used for a short time.

Fettercairn distillery is equipped with a traditional, 5 ton cast iron mash tun with a copper canopy and eleven washbacks with a fermentation time of 60 hours. There are two pairs of stills with a feature making Fettercairn unique among Scottish distilleries (although a similar technique is used at Dalmore). When collecting the middle cut, cooling water is allowed to trickle along the outside of the spirit still necks and is collected at the base for circulation towards the top again. This is done in order to increase reflux and thereby produce a lighter and cleaner spirit. For some time, the owners have also produced a portion of heavily peated spirit (55ppm), but there has been no peated production for the last couple of years. The producion goal for 2017 is 24 mashes per week and 2.2 million litres of alcohol.

The vast majority of the production goes into the owner's blends. Currently, there is only one official bottling, the lightly peated **Fior** without age statement. Fasque, which was launched in 2011, has been discontinued and the owners have also stopped bottling the 24, 30 and 40 year olds that existed previously.

History:

1824 Sir Alexander Ramsay founds the distillery.

1830 Sir John Gladstone buys the distillery.

1887 A fire erupts and the distillery is forced to close for repairs.

1890 Thomas Gladstone dies and his son John Robert takes over. The distillery reopens.

1912 The company is close to liquidation and John Gladstone buys out the other investors.

1926 The distillery is mothballed.

1939 The distillery is bought by Associated Scottish Distillers Ltd. Production restarts.

1960 The maltings discontinues.

1966 The stills are increased from two to four.

1971 The distillery is bought by Tomintoul-Glenlivet Distillery Co. Ltd.

1973 Tomintoul-Glenlivet Distillery Co. Ltd is bought by Whyte & Mackay Distillers Ltd.

1974 The mega group of companies Lonrho buys Whyte & Mackay.

1988 Lonrho sells to Brent Walker Group plc.

1989 A visitor centre opens.

1990 American Brands Inc. buys Whyte & Mackay for £160 million.

1996 Whyte & Mackay and Jim Beam Brands merge to become JBB Worldwide.

2001 Kyndal Spirits buys Whyte & Mackay from JBB Worldwide.

2002 The whisky changes name to Fettercairn 1824.

2003 Kyndal Spirits changes name to Whyte & Mackay.

2007 United Spirits buys Whyte & Mackay. A 23 year old single cask is released.

2009 24, 30 and 40 year olds are released.

2010 Fettercairn Fior is launched.

2012 Fettercairn Fasque is released.

Fior

Tasting notes Fettercairn Fior:

GS – A complex, weighty nose of toffee, sherry, ginger, orange and smoke. More orange and smoke on the palate, with a sherried nuttiness and hints of treacle toffee. Mild, spicy oak and a touch of liquorice in the lengthy finish.

Glenallachie

[glen•alla•key]

Owner:
The Glenallachie Consortium

Region/district:
Speyside

Founded: 1967
Status: Active
Capacity: 4 000 000 litres

Address: Aberlour, Banffshire AB38 9LR

Website: -
Tel: 01542 783042

Just a year after Billy Walker sold his BenRiach Distillery Company with its three distilleries, he returned to the whisky business through the acquisition of Chivas Brothers' Glenallachie distillery.

The deal may have come as a surprise for many but according to Pernod Ricard it is in line with their strategy to focus on its priority brands. No sum was disclosed but the takeover includes the distillery, the Glenallachie brand, two blended Scotch brands (MacNair's and White Heather) and sufficient stock, "to support the future development of those brands". The two blends may not belong to the best known, but MacNair's has a presence in the French and Polish markets, while White Heather is very popular in Australia. The new owners, The Glenallachie Consortium, consists of Billy Walker, Trisha Savage, who had been working with Walker for many years and Graham Stevenson, who recently left the position as managing director of Inver House.

The process structure of Glenallachie was designed by the famous whisky architect, William Delmé Evans and it also became his last distillery project. With Glenallachie, he finally managed to design the gravity-fed distillery that he had been planning since the 1940s. The distillery is now equipped with a 9.4 ton semi-lauter mash tun, six washbacks made of mild steel, but lined with stainless steel, plus another two washbacks which have been brought in from Caperdonich which was demolished in 2011. There are also two pairs of unusually wide stills.

Glenallachie single malt is a key ingredient in one of the top selling blends in France – Clan Campbell. Until recently, the only official bottling from the distillery has been a cask strength from 2000, which was released in 2014. This was an exclusive for Chivas' visitor centres but has now been withdrawn. However, in June 2017, a new official bottling, **Glenallachie Distillery Edition**, was launched in the UK market. A rather surprising move considering the brand changed hands shortly afterwards.

History:

1967 The distillery is founded by Mackinlay, McPherson & Co., a subsidiary of Scottish & Newcastle Breweries Ltd. William Delmé Evans is architect.

1985 Scottish & Newcastle Breweries Ltd sells Charles Mackinlay Ltd to Invergordon Distillers which acquires both Glenallachie and Isle of Jura.

1987 The distillery is decommissioned.

1989 Campbell Distillers (Pernod Ricard) buys the distillery, increases the number of stills from two to four and takes up production again.

2005 The first official bottling for many years is a Cask Strength Edition from 1989.

2017 Glenallachie Distillery Edition is released and the distillery is sold to The Glenallachie Consortium.

Distillery Edition

Tasting notes Glenallachie Distillery Edition:

GS – Warm toffee, milk chocolate and ripe apples on the nose. The palate is smooth, with vanilla fudge, chocolate orange notes, and light spice. The spices linger through the sweet, fruity, medium-length finish.

Glenburgie

[glen•bur•gee]

Owner:
Chivas Brothers
(Pernod Ricard)

Region/district:
Speyside

Founded: 1810   **Status:** Active   **Capacity:** 4 200 000 litres

Address: Glenburgie, Forres, Morayshire IV36 2QY

Website: -

Tel: 01343 850258

Despite its size, producing more than 4 million litres per year, Glenburgie is a distillery that goes relatively unmentioned. You can clearly see the chimney from the A96 between Forres and Elgin.

However, if you decide to go there (which actually you shouldn't because it's not open to the public), you need to choose the correct junction exit. Coming from Forres, don't take the first right when you've spotted the chimney. It will take you to the distillery but the road is narrow and winding. Take the next right and you will end up at a distillery which was founded in the early 1800s but looks perfectly modern. The reason for this is that the whole distillery, with the exception of the customs house, was demolished in 2003 and a new distillery was built.

But it's not just the distillery itself whose existence is rather unknown. The single malt is essentially 100% intended for use in various blends and most notably Ballantines. One detail though is worth noting for malt whisky buffs. For slightly more than two decades, 1958-1981, two Lomond stills were operative at Glenburgie. Instead of the traditional swan neck, they had columns with a number of plates inside. The plates were adjustable and the thinking was to be able to produce different kinds of newmake from the same still. The idea however, was short-lived, but the whisky that the Lomond stills produced got its own name - Glencraig. With a bit of luck bottles of Glencraig can still be found from independent bottlers. Two of these were released in 2012 and 2013 by Gordon & MacPhail and Signatory.

Glenburgie is equipped with a 7.5 ton full lauter mash tun, 12 stainless steel washbacks with a fermentation time of 52 hours and three pairs of stills. The majority of the production is filled into bourbon casks and a part thereof is matured in four dunnage, two racked and two palletised warehouses.

The only current, official bottling is a **17 year old** cask strength, distilled in 1999, matured in first fill ex-bourbon barrels and bottled in 2016 in the new range The Distillery Reserve Collection which can be found at Chivas' visitor centres.

History:

1810 William Paul founds Kilnflat Distillery. Official production starts in 1829.

1870 Kilnflat distillery closes.

1878 The distillery reopens under the name Glenburgie-Glenlivet, Charles Hay is licensee.

1884 Alexander Fraser & Co. takes over.

1925 Alexander Fraser & Co. files for bankruptcy and the receiver Donald Mustad assumes control of operations.

1927 James & George Stodart Ltd (owned by James Barclay and R A McKinlay since 1922) buys the distillery which by this time is inactive.

1930 Hiram Walker buys 60% of James & George Stodart Ltd.

1936 Hiram Walker buys Glenburgie Distillery in October. Production restarts.

1958 Lomond stills are installed producing a single malt, Glencraig. Floor malting ceases.

1981 The Lomond stills are replaced by conventional stills.

1987 Allied Lyons buys Hiram Walker.

2002 A 15 year old is released.

2004 A £4.3 million refurbishment and reconstruction takes place.

2005 Chivas Brothers (Pernod Ricard) becomes the new owner through the acquisition of Allied Domecq.

2006 The number of stills are increased from four to six in May.

17 year old cask strength

Tasting notes Glenburgie 20 years old:

GS – The nose is very floral, sweet and fruity. Peaches, apricots and nougat. Silky palate texture, with deep fruit notes that become more citric, with cream and hazelnuts. Nutty in the finish, drying slightly with mild oak.

Glencadam

[glen•ka•dam]

Owner:
Angus Dundee Distillers

Region/district:
Eastern Highlands

Founded: **Status:**
1825   Active

Capacity:
1 300 000 litres

Address: Brechin, Angus DD9 7PA

Website:
glencadamdistillery.co.uk

Tel:
01356 622217

In this day and age of NAS (bottlings with No Age Statement) there are a handful of companies that stand out, working against the current trend. One of them is Angus Dundee Distillers – owners of Glencadam and Tomintoul distilleries.

If you ask the producers, the reason for the increase in releases without an age on the label, is the current (and supposedly temporary) lack of "old" whisky in the warehouses in Scotland. The brand owners claim they need the freedom of not being tied to a certain age when they create new whiskies. From the consumer side, on the other hand, you often hear of conspiracy theories talking about the owners trying to push out inferior whisky to the market. Be that as it may, with the current legislation, a whisky containing predominantly 15 year old whiskies and a minor share of a 5 year old, must be labelled a 5 year old. Angus Dundee however, are firm in their belief that a whisky should carry an age statement and of the 16 core releases currently available from their two distilleries, only two are NAS.

Glencadam distillery is equipped with a traditional, 4.9 ton cast iron mash tun, six stainless steel washbacks with a fermentation time of 52 hours and one pair of stills. The distillery is currently working seven days a week, which enables 16 mashes per week and 1.3 million litres of alcohol per year. Glencadam is not only a busy distillery, but also hosts a huge filling and bottling plant with 16 large tanks for blending malt and grain whisky. Angus Dundee has a wide range of blended Scotch brands in its portfolio and is represented in more than 70 countries, not least of all China, where The Angus blend was recently launched.

Six new bottlings last year, increased an already substantial range. The core range now consists of **Origin 1825, 10, 13, 15, 21** and **25 year old**. Also in the core range are two wood finishes; a **17 year old port finish** and a **19 year old oloroso finish**. The 13 year old was released in spring 2017 and is made from the very first production in autumn of 2003 when the distillery was acquired by Angus Dundee. Recent limited editions include a **33 year old single cask** from 1982.

History:

1825 George Cooper founds the distillery.

1827 David Scott takes over.

1837 The distillery is sold by David Scott.

1852 Alexander Miln Thompson becomes the owner.

1857 Glencadam Distillery Company is formed.

1891 Gilmour, Thompson & Co Ltd takes over.

1954 Hiram Walker takes over.

1959 Refurbishing of the distillery.

1987 Allied Lyons buys Hiram Walker Gooderham & Worts.

1994 Allied Lyons changes name to Allied Domecq.

2000 The distillery is mothballed.

2003 Allied Domecq sells the distillery to Angus Dundee Distillers.

2005 The new owner releases a 15 year old.

2008 A re-designed 15 year old and a new 10 year old are introduced.

2009 A 25 and a 30 year old are released in limited numbers.

2010 A 12 year old port finish, a 14 year old sherry finish, a 21 year old and a 32 year old are released.

2012 A 30 year old is released.

2015 A 25 year old is launched.

2016 Origin 1825, 17 year old port finish, 19 year old oloroso finish, an 18 year old and a 25 year old are released.

2017 A 13 year old is released.

10 years old

Tasting notes Glencadam 10 years old:

GS – A light and delicate, floral nose, with tinned pears and fondant cream. Medium-bodied, smooth, with citrus fruits and gently-spiced oak on the palate. The finish is quite long and fruity, with a hint of barley.

GlenDronach

[glen•dro•nack]

Owner:	**Region/district:**
Benriach Distillery Co	Highlands
(Brown Forman)	

Founded:	**Status:**	**Capacity:**
1826	Active (vc)	1 400 000 litres

Address: Forgue, Aberdeenshire AB54 6DB

Website:	**Tel:**
glendronachdistillery.co.uk	01466 730202

When Billy Walker and his associates took over GlenDronach in 2008, sales volumes of BenRiach and GlenDronach were more or less equal. Since then GlenDronach has increased with 150% while BenRiach managed "only" 65%.

The most credible explanation is that when Teachers took over Glendronach in 1960, they were already familiar with the whisky as they had been using it in their blend for some time. They also saw the possibility to launch Glendronach single malt and the first release came as early as 1968. That explains one of the reasons behind the success of Glendronach – the brand had a solid fanbase even before later changes in ownership, whereas BenRiach´s reputation was essentially built from scratch.

The equipment consists of a 3.7 ton cast iron mash tun with rakes, nine washbacks made of larch with a fermentation time of 60 to 90 hours and two pairs of stills. The plan is to produce 1.2 million litres of alcohol in 2017. The distillery has made increasingly larger volumes of peated spirit, and for 2017 it will be 150,000 litres with a phenol specification of 38ppm.

The core range is **The Hielan 8 years, Original 12 years, Allardice 18 years, Parliament 21 years** and **Grandeur 25 years** where the 8th release was made in November 2016. A new addition to the core range appeared in 2015 with the first (at least in modern times) **Peated GlenDronach**. Without age statement, the whisky has been matured in bourbon casks and then finished in a combination of oloroso and PX sherry. There are four wood finishes; **12 year old Sauternes, 14 year old Virgin Oak, 18 year old Tawny Port** and **19 year old Madeira** plus a very limited **14 year old Marsala**. Batch number 6 of the **cask strength** expression was launched in November 2016 and batch 15 of the **single casks** appeared in June 2017, The limited **20 year old GlenDronach Octaves** released in autumn 2015, represents the first GlenDronach that has been finished in the smaller octave casks. Younger versions have since been released – **Octaves Classic** and **Octaves Peated**. Finally, the owners declare that a range is being prepared for the travel retail segment in the near future.

History:

1826 The distillery is founded by a consortium with James Allardes as one of the owners.

1837 Parts of the distillery is destroyed in a fire.

1852 Walter Scott (from Teaninich) takes over.

1887 Walter Scott dies and Glendronach is taken over by a consortium from Leith.

1920 Charles Grant buys Glendronach for £9,000.

1960 William Teacher & Sons buys the distillery.

1966 The number of stills is increased to four.

1976 Allied Breweries takes over William Teacher & Sons.

1996 The distillery is mothballed.

2002 Production is resumed on 14th May.

2005 The distillery closes to rebuild from coal to indirect firing by steam. Reopens in September. Chivas Brothers (Pernod Ricard) becomes new owner through the acquisition of Allied Domecq.

2008 Pernod Ricard sells the distillery to the owners of BenRiach distillery.

2009 Relaunch of the whole range including 12, 15 and 18 year old.

2010 A 31 year old, a 1996 single cask and a total of 11 vintages and four wood finishes are released. A visitor centre is opened.

2011 The 21 year old Parliament and 11 vintages are released.

2012 A number of vintages are released.

2013 Recherché 44 years and a number of new vintages are released.

2014 Nine different single casks are released.

2015 The Hielan, 8 years old, is released.

2016 Brown Forman buys the distillery. Peated GlenDronach and Octaves Classic are released.

2017 A range of new single casks is released.

12 years old Original

Tasting notes GlenDronach 12 years old:

GS – A sweet nose of Christmas cake fresh from the oven. Smooth on the palate, with sherry, soft oak, fruit, almonds and spices. The finish is comparatively dry and nutty, ending with bitter chocolate.

Glendullan

[glen•dull•an]

Owner: Diageo

Region/district: Speyside

Founded: 1897

Status: Active

Capacity: 5 000 000 litres

Address: Dufftown, Keith, Banffshire AB55 4DJ

Website: www.malts.com

Tel: 01340 822100

Glendullan is one of three Diageo distilleries working under the brand name The Singleton. Glen Ord and Dufftown are the other two.

During the last decade, The Singleton of Glendullan could only be found in the American market and sometimes in Duty Free. Recently though, the brand was rolled out to the rest of the world.

Glendullan distillery is situated just one minute's drive east of Glenfiddich and was built in 1897 by William Williams – a blender from Aberdeen. Williams was well acquainted with the owners of Glenfiddich, the Grant family, and when Glenfiddich started producing in 1888, an agreement was made where Williams bought the entire volume coming from the distillery. This contract was dissolved in 1890, when the two parties had differing opinions about the terms and conditions. Two years later, when the Grants founded Balvenie, Williams approached them again, looking for a new agreement but was rejected. Finlly he had no alternative other than to build his own distillery, Glendullan. The working distillery we see today is of a much later date, built in 1972 and the two plants operated simultaneously until 1985 when the old distillery was closed. The buildings are now used by Diageo's distillery engineering team. The old distillery, with one pair of stills, had a capacity of one million litres a year.

The distillery is equipped with a 12 ton full lauter stainless steel mash tun, 8 washbacks made of larch and two made of stainless steel with a fermentation time of 75 hours to promote a green/grassy character of the whisky, as well as three pairs of stills. In 2017 the distillery will be doing 21 mashes per week, producing 5 million litres of alcohol.

The core range of Singleton of Glendullan is **12, 15** and **18 year old**. There is also a subrange exclusive to duty free, The Singleton Reserve Collection with **Classic** (matured in American oak), **Double Matured** (matured separately in American and European oak and then married together) and **Master's Art** (with a finish in Muscat casks). In 2014, a Glendullan single malt was launched as part of the Special Releases – a **38 year old** distilled in 1975.

History:

1896 William Williams & Sons, a blending company with Three Stars and Strahdon among its brands, founds the distillery.

1902 Glendullan is delivered to the Royal Court and becomes the favourite whisky of Edward VII.

1919 Macdonald Greenlees buys a share of the company and Macdonald Greenlees & Williams Distillers is formed.

1926 Distillers Company Limited (DCL) buys Glendullan.

1930 Glendullan is transferred to Scottish Malt Distillers (SMD).

1962 Major refurbishing and reconstruction.

1972 A brand new distillery is constructed next to the old one and both operate simultaneously during a few years.

1985 The oldest of the two distilleries is mothballed.

1995 The first launch of Glendullan in the Rare Malts series is a 22 year old from 1972.

2005 A 26 year old from 1978 is launched in the Rare Malts series.

2007 Singleton of Glendullan is launched in the USA.

2013 Singleton of Glendullan Liberty and Trinity are released for duty free.

2014 A 38 year old is released.

2015 Classic, Double Matured and Master's Art are released.

12 years old

Tasting notes Singleton of Glendullan 12 years:

GS – The nose is spicy, with brittle toffee, vanilla, new leather and hazelnuts. Spicy and sweet on the smooth palate, with citrus fruits, more vanilla and fresh oak. Drying and pleasingly peppery in the finish.

Glen Elgin

[glen el•gin]

Owner:
Diageo

Region/district:
Speyside

Founded:
1898

Status:
Active

Capacity:
2 700 000 litres

Address: Longmorn, Morayshire IV30 8SL

Website:
malts.com

Tel:
01343 862100

With 28 operating distilleries, and many more some decades ago, Diageo (and their predecessors) have over the years grouped their brands after how they are promoted and marketed.

The most famous constellation is of course the six Classic Malts introduced in 1988. This was an approach that meant a lot for the rising interest in single malt whiskies. Glen Elgin was never one of the six but it was actually sold as a single malt already in 1977. It has always had a solid reputation amongst the blenders and apparently the owners saw a potential with the consumers as well. Briefly it appeared as one of many in the Flora & Fauna range but in 2002, Diageo decided to give four of their brands some more attention and the Hidden Malts range was launched comprised of Glen Elgin, Caol Ila, Clynelish and Glen Ord. Hidden Malts ex- isted for several years but today three of the whiskies are included in the extended Classic Malts range while Glen Ord has become part of the hugely succesful Singleton family.

The distillery is equipped with an 8.4 ton Steinecker full lauter mash tun from 2001, nine washbacks made of larch and six small stills. Three of the washbacks were installed as late as 2012 in the extended tun room, which meant that the production capacity had increased by 50%. Having moved recently from a 7 day operation to 5 days, the distillery is now working with a combination of short and long fermentations between 80 and 120 hours. The stills are connected to six wooden worm tubs where the spirit vapours are condensed. A new boiler was installed in 2014, replacing the two, old existing ones. During 2017, they will be doing 12 mashes per week which translates to a production of 1.6 million litres.

Glen Elgin single malt is an integral part of the White Horse blended Scotch which sells around 20 million bottles every year in key markets spread across the world: i. a. Japan, Greece, Bra- zil and South Africa. The only official bottling is a **12 year old**, but a limited **18 year old**, matured in ex-bodega European oak butts was one of the Special Releases in 2017.

History:

1898 The former manager of Glenfarclas, William Simpson and banker James Carle found Glen Elgin.

1900 Production starts in May but the distillery closes just five months later.

1901 The distillery is auctioned for £4,000 to the Glen Elgin-Glenlivet Distillery Co. and is mothballed.

1906 The wine producer J. J. Blanche & Co. buys the distillery for £7,000 and production resumes.

1929 J. J. Blanche dies and the distillery is put up for sale again.

1930 Scottish Malt Distillers (SMD) buys it and the license goes to White Horse Distillers.

1964 Expansion from two to six stills plus other refurbishing takes place.

1992 The distillery closes for refurbishing and installation of new stills.

1995 Production resumes in September.

2001 A 12 year old is launched in the Flora & Fauna series.

2002 The Flora & Fauna series malt is replaced by Hidden Malt 12 years.

2003 A 32 year old cask strength from 1971 is released.

2008 A 16 year old is launched as a Special Release.

2009 Glen Elgin 1998, a single cask in the new Manager´s Choice range is released.

2017 An 18 year old is launched as part of the Special Releases.

18 years old

Tasting notes Glen Elgin 12 years old:

GS – A nose of rich, fruity sherry, figs and fragrant spice. Full-bodied, soft, malty and honeyed in the mouth. The finish is lengthy, slightly perfumed, with spicy oak.

Glenfarclas

[glen•fark•lass]

Owner:
J. & G. Grant

Region/district:
Speyside

Founded: 1836
Status: Active (vc)
Capacity: 3 500 000 litres

Address: Ballindalloch, Banffshire AB37 9BD

Website:
glenfarclas.com

Tel:
01807 500257

When Alfred Barnard published his ground-breaking book on distilleries in the UK in 1887, he devoted but one page to Glenfarclas and he did not seem overwhelmed by what he saw.

At that time, the distillery had been owned by George Grant for 20 years and his interest was devoted more to the farm than the distillery. A few years after he died in 1890 his two sons soon decided to go into partnership with the Pattison brothers who, with their fraudelent actions, initiated a disaster for the entire whisky industry. From 1905, however, the entire ownership of the distillery was safely back in the hands of the Grant family and has remained so with the 6th generation currently working the business.

The distillery is equipped with a 16.5 ton semi-lauter mash tun and twelve stainless steel washbacks with a minimum fermentation time of 60 hours but on average it is currently 102 hours. There are three pairs of directly fired stills (very rarely seen these days) and the wash stills are equipped with rummagers. This is a copper chain rotating at the bottom of the still to prevent solids from sticking to the copper. At the time of writing, there are 34 dunnage warehouses on-site, with a vintage 1953 as the oldest cask, but come October 2017 there will be another ten warehouses. In 2017, the distillery will produce 8 to 9 mashes per week, resulting in 2.5 million litres of pure alcohol. Glenfarclas single malt has always been highly ranked among whisky aficionados and close to 800,000 bottles is sold annually.

The Glenfarclas core range consists of the **8, 10, 12, 15, 21** and **25 year old**, as well as the **105 Cask Strength**. There is also a **17 year old** destined for the USA, Japan and Sweden. Also in the core range, is the lightly sherried **Glenfarclas Heritage** which comes without an age statement. The **30 and 40 year olds** are limited but new editions occur regularly. An **18 year old** exclusive to travel retail was launched in 2014.

The owners quite often make spectacular limited releases and the rarity of the expressions clearly show the impressive selection that they have available in their warehouses. In 2014, the first of six releases in a new range named The Generations Range appeared. It was a **1966 Fino** maturation, followed in 2015 by the **1956 Sherry cask**. The third bottling, a **50 year old** matured in oloroso casks, appeared in spring 2016 and later in the year the final three expressions were launched; a **1981** matured in port pipes, a **1986 cask strength** and a **40 year old** from 1976. Few, if any other producer, have the opportunity to offer six such whiskies in just two years! Another limited release in 2015 was a bottling to celebrate the 150th anniversary of the Grants taking over Glenfarclas. It was named **£511.19s.0d Family Reserve**, being the amount paid for the distillery by John Grant on 8 June 1865. The owners also continue to release bottlings in their **Family Casks** series with vintages ranging from 1954 to 2002. Finally, every year the owners produce special limited bottlings for their biggest markets.

History:

- **1836** Robert Hay founds the distillery on the original site since 1797.
- **1865** Robert Hay passes away and John Grant and his son George buy the distillery. They lease it to John Smith at The Glenlivet Distillery.
- **1870** John Smith resigns in order to start Cragganmore and J. & G. Grant Ltd takes over.
- **1889** John Grant dies and George Grant takes over.
- **1890** George Grant dies and his widow Elsie takes over the license while sons John and George control operations.
- **1895** John and George Grant take over and form The Glenfarclas-Glenlivet Distillery Co. Ltd with the infamous Pattison, Elder & Co.
- **1898** Pattison becomes bankrupt. Glenfarclas encounters financial problems after a major overhaul of the distillery but survives by mortgaging and selling stored whisky to R. I. Cameron, a whisky broker from Elgin.
- **1914** John Grant leaves due to ill health and George continues alone.
- **1948** The Grant family celebrates the distillery's 100th anniversary, a century of active licensing. It is 9 years late, as the actual anniversary coincided with WW2.
- **1949** George Grant senior dies and sons George Scott and John Peter inherit the distillery.
- **1960** Stills are increased from two to four.
- **1968** Glenfarclas is first to launch a cask-strength single malt. It is later named Glenfarclas 105.
- **1972** Floor maltings is abandoned and malt is purchased centrally.
- **1973** A visitor centre is opened.
- **1976** Enlargement from four stills to six.

History continued:

2001 Glenfarclas launches its first Flower of Scotland gift tin which becomes a great success and increases sales by 30%.

2002 George S Grant dies and is succeeded as company chairman by his son John L S Grant

2003 Two new gift tins are released (10 years old and 105 cask strength).

2005 A 50 year old is released to commemorate the bi-centenary of John Grant´s birth.

2006 Ten new vintages are released.

2007 Family Casks, a series of single cask bottlings from 43 consecutive years, is released.

2008 New releases in the Family Cask range. Glenfarclas 105 40 years old is released.

2009 A third release in the Family Casks series.

2010 A 40 year old and new vintages from Family Casks are released.

2011 Chairman´s Reserve and 175th Anniversary are released.

2012 A 58 year old and a 43 year old are released.

2013 An 18 year old for duty free is released as well as a 25 year old quarter cask.

2014 A 60 year old and a 1966 single fino sherry cask are released.

2015 A 1956 Sherry Cask and Family Reserve are released.

2016 40 year old, 50 year old, 1981 Port and 1986 cask strength are released.

Tasting notes Glenfarclas 10 year old:

GS – Full and richly sherried on the nose, with nuts, fruit cake and a hint of citrus fruit. The palate is big, with ripe fruit, brittle toffee, some peat and oak. Medium length and gingery in the finish.

105 Cask Strength

50 years old

18 years old

Family Cask 1959

12 years old

21 years old

40 years old

Glenfiddich

[glen•fidd•ick]

Owner:
William Grant & Sons

Region/district:
Speyside

Founded: 1886

Status: Active (vc)

Capacity: 13 700 000 litres

Address: Dufftown, Keith, Banffshire AB55 4DH

Website:
glenfiddich.com

Tel:
01340 820373 (vc)

When William Grant Gordon, the third generation of the owners, died in 1953 the responsibility of taking over the company fell on his two young sons – Charles and Sandy.

They were only 26 and 22 years old respectively but they would soon show that they were more than capable of bearing the responsibility of running the business. Charles made sure the company got its own grain distillery in Girvan while Sandy saw the possibilities of releasing their Glenfiddich single malt and not just using it for their blends. In 1963 he became the first to systematically promote a single malt around the world including television commercials. This gave Glenfiddich the position of the world's best-selling single malt, a position it still maintains today despite Glenlivet sneaking in for one year (2014). In 2016, Glenfiddich sold 14.3 million bottles which was an increase by 9% compared to the year before. Due to the increased demand, a whole new distillery is being built on the grounds and, if everything goes according to plan, it will start producing in spring 2019. The new unit will be equipped with one mash tun, 16 washbacks, 5 wash stills and 10 spirit stills. When the expansion is finished, the combined capacity of the two distilleries will be 18-20 million litres. Currently, Glenfiddich is equipped with two, stainless steel, full lauter mash tuns – both with a 10 ton mash. In May 2017, eight stainless steel washbacks were replaced by wooden ones which means there are now a total of 32 washbacks made of Douglas fir – all with a fermentation time of 72 hours. There are two still rooms with a total of 11 wash stills and 20 spirit stills. All the stills in still house number 2 are directly fired using gas. The production for 2017 will be 68 mashes per week and 13.65 million litres of pure alcohol.

The core range consists of **12, 15, 18** and **21 year old, Rich Oak 14 year old** and **15 year old Distillery Edition**. Included in the core range, although in limited quantities, is also the **26 year old Glenfiddich Excellence** while Malt Master's Edition has been discontinued. Some older expressions have also been released over the years – which include **30, 40** and **50 year old** as well as the **38 year old Glenfiddich Ultimate**. In 2014, **Glenfiddich The Original** was released, created to replicate the flavour profile of the legendary Straight Malt from the early 1960s. The same year, **Glenfiddich Gallery** was introduced where Malt Master, Brian Kinsman, has selected 36 different casks from 1958 to 1996. In 2015 an exclusive to the US market was released by way of a **14 year old** matured in bourbon casks. Two bottlings in the Experimental Series were released in September 2016; **IPA Experiment** with a finish in IPA beer casks and **Project XX** where the casks were selected by 20 brand ambassadors. Included in the duty free range are three Age of Discovery bottlings; **Madeira cask, Bourbon cask** and **Red Wine cask** finish as well as the Cask Collection with **Select Cask, Reserve Cask, Vintage Cask** and **Finest Solera**. Another duty free exclusive is **Glenfiddich Rare Oak 25 years**, which was launched in 2014.

History:

1886 The distillery is founded by William Grant, 47 years old, who had learned the trade at Mortlach Distillery. The equipment is bought from Mrs. Cummings of Cardow Distillery. The construction totals £800.

1887 The first distilling takes place on Christmas Day.

1892 William Grant builds Balvenie.

1898 The blending company Pattisons, largest customer of Glenfiddich, files for bankruptcy and Grant decides to blend their own whisky. Standfast becomes one of their major brands.

1903 William Grant & Sons is formed.

1957 The famous, three-cornered bottle is introduced.

1958 The floor maltings is closed.

1963 Glennfiddich becomes the first whisky to be marketed as single malt in the UK and the rest of the world.

1964 A version of Standfast's three-cornered bottle is launched for Glenfiddich in green glass.

1969 Glenfiddich becomes the first distillery in Scotland to open a visitor centre.

1974 16 new stills are installed.

2001 1965 Vintage Reserve is launched in a limited edition of 480 bottles. Glenfiddich 1937 is bottled (61 bottles).

2002 Glenfiddich Gran Reserva 21 years old, finished in Cuban rum casks is launched. Caoran Reserve 12 years is released. Glenfiddich Rare Collection 1937 (61 bottles) is launched and becomes the oldest Scotch whisky on the market.

2003 1973 Vintage Reserve (440 bottles) is launched.

2004 1991 Vintage Reserve (13 years) and 1972 Vintage Reserve (519 bottles) are launched.

History continued:

2005 Circa £1.7 million is invested in a new visitor centre.

2006 1973 Vintage Reserve, 33 years (861 bottles) and 12 year old Toasted Oak are released.

2007 1976 Vintage Reserve, 31 years is released in September.

2008 1977 Vintage Reserve is released.

2009 A 50 year old and 1975 Vintage Reserve are released.

2010 Rich Oak, 1978 Vintage Reserve, the 6th edition of 40 year old and Snow Phoenix are released.

2011 1974 Vintage Reserve and a 19 year old Madeira finish are released.

2012 Cask of Dreams and Millenium Vintage are released.

2013 A 19 year old red wine finish and 1987 Anniversary Vintage are released. Cask Collection with three different expressions is released for duty free.

2014 The 26 year old Glenfiddich Excellence, Rare Oak 25 years and Glenfiddich The Original are released.

2015 A 14 year old for the US market is released.

2016 Finest Solera is released for travel retail. Two expressions in the Experimental Series are launched; Project XX and IPA Experiment.

Tasting notes Glenfiddich 12 year old:

GS – Delicate, floral and slightly fruity on the nose. Well mannered in the mouth, malty, elegant and soft. Rich, fruit flavours dominate the palate, with a developing nuttiness and an elusive whiff of peat smoke in the fragrant finish.

Project XX   18 years old   IPA Experiment

Reserve Cask   Vintage Cask

12 years old

Rich Oak   The Original

Glen Garioch

[glen gee•ree]

Owner:
Morrison Bowmore (Suntory)

Region/district:
Eastern Highlands

Founded: 1797

Status: Active (vc)

Capacity: 1 370 000 litres

Address: Oldmeldrum, Inverurie, Aberdeenshire AB51 0ES

Website: glengarioch.com

Tel: 01651 873450

Even though Glen Garioch was founded in 1797, it was not until a 100 years later that the distillery took a more prominent place in the industry. This was all the doing of William Sanderson.

Sanderson, who became part-owner in 1886, was a wine and spirit merchant who set up his business in Leith in 1863. The Spirits Act which was passed three years earlier allowed for grain- and malt whiskies to be blended under bond and Sanderson saw the huge business opportunities in blending whisky. Among many of the brands he created was Vat 69 in 1882, which today sells over 15 milion bottles per year. Sanderson realised that he needed a distillery to secure the required volume of malt spirit, so together with J G Thomson & Co, he increased the capacity of Glen Garioch. However a blend also needs grain whisky and to avoid being dependant on the mighty Distillers Company Limited, he decided, together with other blenders, to build North British grain distillery in Edinburgh in 1885. North British is today jointly owned by Diageo and Edrington.

Glen Garioch single malt is typically unpeated, but smoky notes can easily be detected in expressions distilled before 1994 when their own floor maltings closed. Until then, the malt was peated with a phenol specification of 8-10ppm. The distillery is equipped with a 4 ton full lauter mash tun, eight stainless steel washbacks with a fermentation time of 48 hours, one wash still and one spirit still (replaced in 2016). There is also a third still, which has not been used for a long time. The spirit is tankered to Glasgow, filled into casks and returned to the distillery´s four warehouses. During 2017 the production will be 7 mashes per week and around 450,000 litres in the year.

The core range is the **1797 Founder´s Reserve** (without age statement) and a **12 year old**, both of them bottled at 48%. Recent limited releases include **Virgin Oak** – the first Glen Garioch fully matured in virgin American white oak – and the first two chapters of a new range of cask strength bottlings called **Glen Garioch Renaissance Collection** – **15** and **16 years** respectively.

History:

1797 John Manson founds the distillery.

1798 Thomas Simpson becomes licensee.

1825 Ingram, Lamb & Co. bcome new owners.

1837 The distillery is bought by John Manson & Co.

1884 The distillery is sold to J. G. Thomson & Co.

1908 William Sanderson buys the distillery.

1933 Sanderson & Son merges with the gin maker Booth's Distilleries Ltd.

1937 Booth´s Distilleries Ltd is acquired by Distillers Company Limited (DCL).

1968 Glen Garioch is decommissioned.

1970 It is sold to Stanley P. Morrison Ltd.

1973 Production starts again.

1978 Stills are increased from two to three.

1994 Suntory controls all of Morrison Bowmore Distillers Ltd.

1995 The distillery is mothballed in October.

1997 The distillery reopens in August and from now on, it is using unpeated malt.

2004 Glen Garioch 46 year old is released.

2005 15 year old Bordeaux Cask Finish is launched. A visitor centre opens in October.

2006 An 8 year old is released.

2009 Complete revamp of the range - 1979 Founders Reserve (unaged), 12 year old, Vintage 1978 and 1990 are released.

2010 1991 vintage is released.

2011 Vintage 1986 and 1994 are released.

2012 Vintage 1995 and 1997 are released.

2013 Virgin Oak, Vintage 1999 and 11 single casks are released.

2014 Glen Garioch Renaissance Collection 15 years is released.

SPIRIT Nº2   SAMPLE SAFE

GLENGARIOCH DISTILLERY

12 years old

Tasting notes Glen Garioch 12 years old:

GS – Luscious and sweet on the nose, peaches and pineapple, vanilla, malt and a hint of sherry. Full-bodied and nicely textured, with more fresh fruit on the palate, along with spice, brittle toffee and finally dry oak notes.

The formation of *Beam Suntory*

The world's third largest producer of premium spirits, Beam Suntory, was the result of a merger in 2014 between Suntory and Beam. However the path to the forming of the new conglomerate included two other companies that no longer exist. Their history is both important and interesting, so let's start with those two.

In 1951, Stanley Pringle Morrison, by then already a veteran in the Scotch whisky business, founded Stanley P Morrison together with James Howatt. The company acted as a whisky broker, a position in the whisky industry that has more or less vanished in modern days. In the 1950s, blended Scotch was becoming increasingly popular. The big producers needed a variety of malts and grains for their blends. Being competitors and not keen on exposing company secrets to each other, it was a good idea to have a middleman - a broker - who could buy and sell whisky on behalf of the companies. But Stanley P wasn't satisfied with that. He wanted a distillery of his own. And so in 1963, Bowmore Distillery became available after the owner had died and Stanley bought it instantly. Over the years, he would add another two distilleries to his group - Glen Garioch and Auchentoshan and in 1988 the company changed its name to Morrison Bowmore. Their business idea was no longer acting as a broker but as a producer of blended Scotch and single malt Scotch but also as a seller of bulk whisky to other companies. A huge part of that went to Japan and the biggest whisky company in the country - Suntory. In 1989 Suntory purchased 35% of the company and in 1994 the Japanese distilling giant acquired the rest of the shares and Morrison Bowmore became a subsidiary.

Let's move on to the other company that no longer exists. Allied Breweries was the result of a 1961 merger between three of the biggest brewers in the UK. In 1978 they merged with a catering group to form Allied Lyons. At that time, the company still didn't have any interests in the spirits business but this changed in 1987 when they purchased the UK operations of Canadian distiller Hiram Walker and a handful of Scottish distilleries became part of the group. Another merger in 1994, this time with the Spanish producer of brandy and sherry, Pedro Domecq, saw the formation of Allied Domecq - a giant corporation, which despite its size was swallowed up by Pernod Ricard in 2005. The new French owner kept most of the distilleries but sold off Laphroaig and Ardmore to Fortune Brands, owner of top-selling bourbon Jim Beam.

With the background explained, we can now focus on to the main event which when brokered in 2014 created one of the current giants in the whisky business. The foundation of what would become Suntory Limited in 1963, was laid already in 1899 when Shinjiro Torii established his company Torii Shoten and started to produce wine. Over the years he added other products such as tea, spices and soy sauce. It wasn't until 1923 that whisky was added to the range. In that year the Yamazaki distillery was founded which was the start of the Japanese whisky wonder that we see today. In 1937 the hugely popular blend Kakubin was introduced and in 1962, when Shinjiro Torii died, the control of the company went to his son Keizo Saji. A second distillery, Hakushu, the largest in the world at the time, was built in 1973. As mentioned, Suntory took over Morrison Bowmore in 1989 but this wasn't the company's first encounter with the Scotch whisky industry. Only three years earlier the company had acquired 25% of the prestigeous single malt Macallan. In 2009, Suntory Holdings was created as an umbrella for a large number of companies which were not only involved in spirits, but also beer, wine, soft drinks, food, health food and restaurants.

The background of Beam Inc can be traced back to 1795 when Jacob Beam sold his first barrels of whisky. Seven generations of this family that emigrated from Germany have since been involved in the business. The modern part of the company's history starts in 1935, two years after prohibition had been repealed, when James Beauregard Beam rebuilt the family's distillery in Clermont, Kentucky. James B. Beam Distilling Company was founded in 1935 and from that moment on, the number one selling bourbon in the world became known as Jim Beam after James Beauregard. After World War II, Harry Blum took over the business but even though that ended the Beam family's ownership, members of the family have ever since been deeply involved in running the company. Blum owned the company until 1967 when it was taken over by Fortune Brands (or American Brands as it was called at the time). Over the years, Fortune Brands became a diversified company. Apart from being in the spirits business, they also had divisions working in the golf sector and home and hardware. Eventually, everything apart from spirits were sold off and Beam Inc was formed in 2011. Finally, in 2014 Suntory Holdings acquired Beam Inc for the sum of $16 billion. A new company named Beam Suntory, combining Beam and the spirits part of Suntory, was formed.

Glenglassaugh

[glen•glass•ock]

Owner: **Region/district:**
Glenglassaugh Distillery Co   Highlands
(BenRiach Distillery Co.)

Founded: **Status:**   **Capacity:**
1875   Active (vc)   1 100 000 litres

Address: Portsoy, Banffshire AB45 2SQ

Website: **Tel:**
glenglassaugh.com   01261 842367

It can hardly be said that Glenglassaugh has had the most glamorous history among the Scottish distilleries. During the 106 years that it was owned by Highland Distillers/Edrington, it was closed on several occassions which totalled no less than 69 years.

The distillery was surprisingly re-opened in 2008 and is now under its third ownership since then. When Brown Forman bought BenRiach Distillery Company with its three distilleries in 2016, their primary goal was to have a presence within the Scotch whisky market. It was also important to gain access to good brands and GlenDronach together with BenRiach are both quite well-known with good sales figures. Glenglassaugh on the other hand will require some work. It has never been known as a single malt and since the distillery didn´t produce anything between 1986 and 2008, there is very little stock of old whisky with which to play around.

The equipment of the distillery consists of a 5.2 ton Porteus cast iron mash tun with rakes, four wooden washbacks and two stainless steel ones with a fermentation time between 54 and 80 hours and one pair of stills. The production is 800,000 litres of pure alcohol, of which 40,000 litres is peated (30ppm). The main part (85%) is filled to be used as single malt while the rest is sold externally.

The core range is **Revival**, a 3 year old with a 6 month Oloroso finish, followed by **Evolution**, slightly older, matured in American oak and bottled at 50%. Then there is **Torfa** which is peated (20ppm), matured in bourbon casks, bottled at 50% and without age statement. Limited releases include **30, 40** and **51 year old**, as well as single casks in the **Rare Cask Series** where batch two was released in September. Two new limited releases also appeared in June 2016 – **Octaves Classic** and **Octaves Peated**. Both have been matured for around seven years in octaves (which are small casks holding approximately 60 litres) and are bottled at 48%.

History:

1873   The distillery is founded by James Moir.

1887   Alexander Morrison embarks on renovation work.

1892   Morrison sells the distillery to Robertson & Baxter. They in turn sell it on to Highland Distilleries Company for £15,000.

1908   The distillery closes.

1931   The distillery reopens.

1936   The distillery closes.

1957   Reconstruction takes place.

1960   The distillery reopens.

1986   Glenglassaugh is mothballed.

2005   A 22 year old is released.

2006   Three limited editions are released - 19 years old, 38 years old and 44 years old.

2008   The distillery is bought by the Scaent Group for £5m. Three bottlings are released - 21, 30 and 40 year old.

2009   New make spirit and 6 months old are released.

2010   A 26 year old replaces the 21 year old.

2011   A 35 year old and the first bottling from the new owners production, a 3 year old, are released.

2012   A visitor centre is inaugurated and Glenglassaugh Revival is released.

2013   BenRiach Distillery Co buys the distillery and Glenglassaugh Evolution and a 30 year old are released.

2014   The peated Torfa is released as well as eight different single casks and Massandra Connection (35 and 41 years old).

2015   The second batch of single casks is released.

2016   Octaves Classic and Octaves Peated are released.

Torfa

Tasting notes Glenglassaugh Evolution:

GS – Peaches and gingerbread on the nose, with brittle toffee, icing sugar, and vanilla. Luscious soft fruits dipped in caramel figure on the palate, with coconut and background stem ginger. The finish is medium in length, with spicy toffee.

Glengoyne

[glen•goyn]

Owner:
Ian Macleod Distillers

Region/district:
Southern Highlands

Founded: | **Status:** | **Capacity:**
1833 | Active (vc) | 1 100 000 litres

Address: Dumgoyne by Killearn, Glasgow G63 9LB

Website: | **Tel:**
glengoyne.com | 01360 550254 (vc)

Whisky broker Peter Russel bought Ian Macleod & Co in 1963. Over the next 40 years, the Russel family built a stable and successful company as blenders and bottlers.

They were among the first to provide own-label spirits to supermarkets all over Europe while simultaneously developing a well-regarded range of brands such as Isle of Skye and Robert II. But something was missing – they did not have a distillery of their own. The outlook of continuing to be dependent on other producers for their whisky didn't sit well with the family. In April 2003, Glengoyne distillery came up for sale together with large stocks of maturing whisky and the Russel family snapped it up. They increased the production and began to promote Glengoyne single malt actively. Eight years later they acquired Tamdhu, also from Edrington, and in 2016, they took over Spencerfield Spirits and their flagship brand, Edinburgh Gin. Included were also whisky brands such as Pig´s Nose and Sheep Dip.

Glengoyne, with a magnificent location in the scenic region of the Trossarchs, is situated at the base of Dumgoyne Hill and right on the border between the Lowlands and the Highlands. Every year, around 60,000 visitors come to the distillery which offers no less than seven different tours and tastings.The distillery is equipped with a 3.8 ton semi lauter mash tun. There are also six Oregon pine washbacks, as well as the rather unusual combination of one wash still and two spirit stills. Both short (56 hours) and long (110 hours) fermentations are practised. To achieve a smooth and fruity character, they perform a very slow distillation, allowing the spirit to have as much copper contact as possible. In 2017, the production will be 920,000 litres of alcohol.

The core range consists of **10, 12, 15, 18, 21** and **25 year old**. There is also a **cask strength** (currently at 58.7%) without age statement. Recent limited releases include batch 4 of **The Teapot Dram**. The line-up for duty free is a **15 year old Distiller´s Gold** and a **First Fill 25 year old**. A distillery exclusive bottling is available, currently a **15 year old single cask**. The owners have also anounced that in the near future they will be releasing a 30 year old as well as a new range for duty free.

History:

1833 The distillery is licensed under the name Burnfoot Distilleries by the Edmonstone family.

1876 Lang Brothers buys the distillery and changes the name to Glenguin.

1905 The name changes to Glengoyne.

1965 Robertson & Baxter takes over Lang Brothers and the distillery is refurbished. The stills are increased from two to three.

2001 Glengoyne Scottish Oak Finish (16 years old) is launched.

2003 Ian MacLeod Distillers Ltd buys the distillery plus the brand Langs from the Edrington Group for £7.2 million.

2005 A 19 year old, a 32 year old and a 37 year old cask strength are launched.

2006 Nine "choices" from Stillmen, Mashmen and Manager are released.

2007 A new version of the 21 year old, two Warehousemen´s Choice, Vintage 1972 and two single casks are released.

2008 A 16 year old Shiraz cask finish, three single casks and Heritage Gold are released.

2009 A 40 year old, two single casks and a new 12 year old are launched.

2010 Two single casks, 1987 and 1997, released.

2011 A 24 year old single cask is released.

2012 A 15 and an 18 year old are released as well as a Cask Strength with no age statement.

2013 A limited 35 year old is launched.

2014 A 25 year old is released.

Tasting notes Glengoyne 12 years old:

GS – Slightly earthy on the nose, with nutty malt, ripe apples, and a hint of honey. The palate is full and fruity, with milk chocolate, ginger and vanilla. The finish is medium in length, with milky coffee and soft spices.

12 years old

Glen Grant

[glen grant]

Owner: Campari Group   **Region/district:** Speyside

Founded: 1840	**Status:** Active (vc)	**Capacity:** 6 200 000 litres

Address: Elgin Road, Rothes, Banffshire AB38 7BS

Website: glengrant.com   **Tel:** 01340 832118

Today it may seem odd that Pernod Ricard in 2005 let go of such an iconic brand as Glen Grant and not only that – the distillery itself was of a considerable size and was well visited.

But 12 years ago, there were two main reasons for their actions. A short time prior to the sale of Glen Grant, Pernod Ricard had aquired Allied Domecq, the third largest spirits company at the time. This merger alarmed the European Commission. The company was growing too big and competition was threatened. Pernod Ricard had already agreed to sell on Teacher´s and Laphroaig to Fortune Brands but the EU authorities were still not satisfied. Another sacrifice was needed. So, the French company decided to put up Glen Grant, the fourth best selling single malt in the world, for sale as well and there was no shortage of potential buyers. The lucky winner was Campari who took over Glen Grant for the sum of 115 million Euros. Glen Grant had, during a long period, an Italian connection and was by far the best selling single malt in the country. Since the late 1990s, the new Italian owner had been on a shopping spree in an effort to grow from a local company to a world player. In just a few years time, brands such as SKYY vodka, Ouzo 12, Cinzano and Aperol were bought and with Glen Grant in early 2006, they finally had a foot in the door of the Scotch whisky market. The second reason for letting go of Glen Grant was plain and simple, Pernod Ricard had to reduce their debts after many expensive acquisitions.

The distillery is equipped with a 12.3 ton semi-lauter mash tun, ten Oregon pine washbacks with a minimum fermentation time of 48 hours and four pairs of stills. The wash stills are peculiar in that they have vertical sides at the base of the neck and all eight stills are fitted with purifiers. This gives an increased reflux and creates a light and delicate whisky. A new, extremely efficient £5m bottling hall was inaugurated in 2013. It has a capacity of 12,000 bottles an hour and Glen Grant is the only one of the larger distillers bottling the entire production on site. In 2015 a second bottling line for the premium range was installed. During 2017, whisky will be produced for two thirds of the year, while the same operators will be working in the bottling hall for the remainder of the year. In litres of alcohol, this translates to 2.5 million.

The Glen Grant core range consists of **Major´s Reserve** with no age statement, a **5 year old** sold in Italy only and a **10 year old**. Two additions to the core range were made in 2016 – a **12 year old** matured in both bourbon and sherry casks and an **18 year old** bourbonmatured. Summer 2016 also saw the introduction of a **12 year old non chill-filtered** expression for the duty free market. Recent limited editions include **Glen Grant Fiodh**, 43 years old and exclusive to Singapore. Without further details, the owners have announced a **15 year old** to be released for the American market as well as duty free in late 2017 together with a **no age statement bottling** for duty free only. The latest bottling exclusively available at the distillery is a **lightly peated** from **2004**.

History:

- **1840** The brothers James and John Grant, managers of Dandelaith Distillery, found the distillery.
- **1861** The distillery becomes the first to install electric lighting.
- **1864** John Grant dies.
- **1872** James Grant passes away and the distillery is inherited by his son, James junior (Major James Grant).
- **1897** James Grant decides to build another distillery across the road; it is named Glen Grant No. 2.
- **1902** Glen Grant No. 2 is mothballed.
- **1931** Major Grant dies and is succeeded by his grandson Major Douglas Mackessack.
- **1953** J. & J. Grant merges with George & J. G. Smith who runs Glenlivet distillery, forming The Glenlivet & Glen Grant Distillers Ltd.
- **1961** Armando Giovinetti and Douglas Mackessak found a friendship that eventually leads to Glen Grant becoming the most sold malt whisky in Italy.
- **1965** Glen Grant No. 2 is back in production, but renamed Caperdonich.
- **1972** The Glenlivet & Glen Grant Distillers merges with Hill Thompson & Co. and Longmorn-Glenlivet Ltd to form The Glenlivet Distillers. The drum maltings ceases.
- **1973** Stills are increased from four to six.
- **1977** The Chivas & Glenlivet Group (Seagrams) buys Glen Grant Distillery. Stills are increased from six to ten.

History continued:

2001 Pernod Ricard and Diageo buy Seagrams Spirits and Wine, with Pernod acquiring the Chivas Group.

2006 Campari buys Glen Grant for €115m.

2007 The entire range is re-packaged and re-launched and a 15 year old single cask is released. Reconstruction of the visitor centre.

2008 Two limited cask strengths - a 16 year old and a 27 year old - are released.

2009 Cellar Reserve 1992 is released.

2010 A 170th Anniversary bottling is released.

2011 A 25 year old is released.

2012 A 19 year old Distillery Edition is released.

2013 Five Decades is released and a bottling hall is built.

2014 A 50 year old and the Rothes Edition 10 years old is released.

2015 Glen Grant Fiodh is launched.

2016 A 12 year old and an 18 year old are launched and a 12 year old non chill-filtered is released for travel retail.

2017 A 15 year old is released for the American market.

Tasting notes Glen Grant 12 year old:

GS – A blast of fresh fruit – oranges, pears and lemons – on the initial nose, before vanilla and fudge notes develop. The fruit carries over on to the palate, with honey, caramel and sweet spices. Medium in length, with cinnamon and soft oak in the finish.

12 years old

12 years old
non chill-filtered

18 years old

10 years old

The Major's Reserve

Glengyle

[glen•gajl]

Owner:
Mitchell´s Glengyle Ltd

Region/district:
Campbeltown

Founded: **Status:**
2004 Active

Capacity:
750 000 litres

Address: Glengyle Road, Campbeltown, Argyll PA28 6LR

Website:
kilkerran.com

Tel:
01586 551710

Founded by William Mitchell in 1872, the distillery was dormant for 79 years until Hedley Wright, owner of Springbank and related to the founder, brought it back to life.

One of the reasons for Wright´s interest in reviving the old distillery, was that the Scotch Whisky Association in 1998 had decided to stop referring to Campbeltown as a whisky region. Two distilleries (Springbank and Glen Scotia) were simply not enough. Hedley Wright noted that with only three distilleries, Lowland was still considered a region and so he decided to resurrect Glengyle. In 2004, Campbeltown once again became a region of its own.

The distillery is equipped with a 4.5 ton semi-lauter mash tun, three washbacks made of larch and one made of Douglas fir with a fermentation time between 72 and 110 hours and one pair of stills. Malt is obtained from the neighbouring Springbank and the same staff also runs operations. The capacity is 750,000 litres, but considerably smaller amounts have been produced over the years. The plan for 2017 is an increase from the previous year, but it shouldn´t involve more than 60,000 litres of alcohol. The production in 2017 will take place in August and September.

Although the bottlings so far haven´t revealed it, there is a lot of experimentation going on at Glengyle where different wood maturations, peated barley, triple- and even quadruple distillations are being used. The idea is to make limited releases from these experiments in the future.

After many years of Work in Progress releases where the customers could follow how the whisky was developing, the first core **12 year old** was launched in August 2016. It was a vatting of bourbon- (70%) and sherry-matured (30%) whisky. The owners had plans for only one bottling but due to demand, they made another two and more is to be expected. In spring 2017, an **8 year old**, matured in bourbon casks and bottled at 56.2%, was launched with another batch planned for late 2017.

History:

1872 The original Glengyle Distillery is built by William Mitchell.

1919 The distillery is bought by West Highland Malt Distilleries Ltd.

1925 The distillery is closed.

1929 The warehouses (but no stock) are purchased by the Craig Brothers and rebuilt into a petrol station and garage.

1941 The distillery is acquired by the Bloch Brothers.

1957 Campbell Henderson applies for planning permission with the intention of reopening the distillery.

2000 Hedley Wright, owner of Springbank Distillery and related to founder William Mitchell, acquires the distillery.

2004 The first distillation after reconstruction takes place in March.

2007 The first limited release - a 3 year old.

2009 Kilkerran "Work in progress" is released.

2010 "Work in progress 2" is released.

2011 "Work in progress 3" is released.

2012 "Work in progress 4" is released.

2013 "Work in progress 5" is released and this time in two versions - bourbon and sherry.

2014 "Work in progress 6" is released in two versions - bourbon and sherry.

2015 "Work in progress 7" is released in two versions - bourbon and sherry.

2016 Kilkerran 12 years old is released.

2017 Kilkerran 8 year old cask strength is released

Tasting notes Kilkerran 12 year old:

GS – Initially, quite reticent on the nose, then peaty fruit notes develop. Oily and full on the palate, with peaches and more overt smoke, plus an earthy quality. Castor oil and liquorice sticks. Slick in the medium-length finish, with slightly drying oak and enduring liquorice.

12 years old

The formation of *William Grant*

There are only a handful family-owned whisky companies left in Scotland and William Grant & Sons is by far the biggest with a turnover of close to £900 million. Not only do they have the third largest malt distilling capacity in the industry – they are also the owners of some of the biggest and most iconic brands with single malts such as Glenfiddich, Balvenie and Grants blended Scotch.

It all started in Dufftown where William Grant was born in 1839. In his youth he worked as a shoemaker and in a limeworks but William had a head for figures and at the age of 26 he was hired as a bookkeeper at Mortlach distillery, also in Dufftown. He soon advanced to become the manager and worked there for 20 years. Meanwhile he had married Elizabeth and the couple had nine children. With a large family to feed and with a burning ambition, William decided it was time to build his own distillery. In 1886 he left his position at Mortlach and in one year, with the aid of his family and with some of the equipment being bought from Cardow distillery, he had built Glenfiddich distillery with the first distillation on Christmas Day 1887. Business was good and only five years later he built a second distillery, Balvenie, and two years after that, Convalmore – both of them just a stones throw from the first.

In 1899 the first blended whiskies from the company were offered to the market. William Grant´s son in law, Charles Gordon, was the first salesman and in 1909 he spent a year in Australia and the Far East securing new markets for their products. Before that, one of William´s sons, John Grant, had introduced Grant´s whisky to the western part of the world when he closed a deal with the Hudson Bay Company of Canada. Charles Gordon died in 1929 and William Grant Gordon took the business further until he died at the early age of 53 in 1953. He left two sons – Charles and Alexander (Sandy), now the fourth generation of the family. When they took over the company they were just 26 and 22 years old respectively but they would soon prove themselves worthy of the huge responsibility.

Their most important product at the time was the Grants Stand Fast blend which later on would be known as Family Reserve. In order to make a blend you need both malt whisky and grain whisky and while on the malt side, Grant´s were well supplied from their own distilleries, they did not have a grain distillery and therefore relied on other companies for their supply. The grain whisky came mainly from Cambus and Caledonian – two distilleries owned by DCL. In 1962, Charles Grant Gordon decided to use the new television media to promote the company´s products. DCL, at the time a highly conservative company, had in previous discussions, communicated their aversion to advertising whisky via television commercials. DCL therefore decided to demonstrate their disapproval with the Grant family´s decision and they essentially notified them that they would cease supplying grain whisky to Wm Grant & Sons. Aside from being a matter of survival for the company, Charles Gordon refused to accept that a market competitor could dictate conditions for his company. He purchased a plot of land in Girvan situated on the West coast and within nine months successfully built Girvan grain distillery. From that point forward all aspects of production were entirely in their hands.

Whilst Charles was occupied with the construction of Girvan, Sandy focused on developing another side of the business. Up until the beginning of the 1960's, single malt Scotch had been available to purchase but had never been promoted or marketed in a major way. It was simply used to make blended whisky. Sandy decided to change that. In 1961 he packaged the 5 year old straight malt (the term single malt didn´t exist at the time) in the same triangular bottle as the blend and offered it to the consumers on a small scale. He noticed there was an interest and in 1963 he started promoting Glenfiddich Straight Malt in a worldwide advertising campaign and the bottle for the malt changed from clear to green. These were the first steps towards the huge interest in single malt we see today and the other big companies followed suit soon after. The fact that Glenfiddich got a headstart gave them a unique position and until 2014, their brand was the biggest selling single malt in the world. That year, Glenlivet took over and the two brands have taken turns occupying the top spot since then.

Another two malt distilleries were built; Kininvie in Dufftown in 1990 and Ailsa Bay on the Girvan site in 2007. A premium gin, Hendrick´s which is also produced at Girvan, was introduced in 1999 and in 2010, the company took a position in the thriving Irish whiskey business when they bought the Tullamore Dew brand, the second biggest Irish whiskey in the world. At that time, Tullamore Dew was produced at Midleton but in 2014 a brand new Tullamore Dew distillery was opened at Clonminch.

Glen Keith

[glen <u>keeth</u>]

Owner: **Region/district:**
Chivas Brothers   Speyside
(Pernod Ricard)

Founded: **Status:**   **Capacity:**
1957   Active   5 800 000 litres

Address: Station Road, Keith, Banffshire AB55 3BU

Website: **Tel:**
-                      01542 783042

The 1960's was truly a golden age for Scotch and this was before single malt had become fashionable so the blends were still at the forefront. The majority of the larger brands saw the light of day by the beginning of the 1900's but new brands were being launched now as well.

Two of them, 100 Pipers and Passport, were created by Seagrams which at the time also owned Chivas Bros. Sam Bronfman, the owner of the company, wanted something light in style that would suit the American palate and could compete with established brands like Cutty Sark and J&B. Glen Keith distillery became a cornerstone of the production, not least through the unusual process of triple distillation which gave a lighter spirit. Glen Keith single malt is still a major component used today to bolster the characteristics in both these blends, especially Passport. With 16 million bottles sold yearly, 100 Pipers has its largest market in Asia where it was introduced in Korea in 1992. Passport, which sold 21 million bottles during 2016, can mostly be found in Brazil, Mexico, Angola and Eastern Europe.

Following 13 years of no production, Chivas Brothers started to reignite the work at the distillery in spring 2012. The old Saladin maltings were demolished and part of that area now holds a new building with a Briggs 8 ton full lauter mash tun and six stainless steel washbacks. In the old building there are nine new washbacks made of Oregon pine and six, old but refurbished stills. The distillery was re-opened in April 2013 and now has the capacity to do 5.8 million litres with the possibility of producing 40 mashes per week.

For a short period in the 1970s, Glen Keith produced two unusual single malts named Craigduff and Glenisla. They were never released by the owners but the independent bottler Signatory, has bottled them both.

The only current, official bottling is a **17 year old** cask strength bottled in 2016 in the new range The Distillery Reserve Collection which can be found at Chivas' visitor centres.

History:

1957 The Distillery is founded by Chivas Brothers (Seagrams).

1958 Production starts.

1970 The first gas-fuelled still in Scotland is installed, the number of stills increases from three to five.

1976 Own maltings (Saladin box) ceases.

1983 A sixth still is installed.

1994 The first official bottling, a 10 year old, is released as part of Seagram's Heritage Selection.

1999 The distillery is mothballed.

2001 Pernod Ricard takes over Chivas Brothers from Seagrams.

2012 The reconstruction and refurbishing of the distillery begins.

2013 Production starts again.

17 year old cask strength

Tasting notes Glen Keith 19 years old:

GS – Malt, cereal, figs and gingery banana on the nose. Smooth and viscous on the palate, white pepper, sweet sherry, fudge, and Madeira cake. Slighlty drying in the lengthy finish.

Glenkinchie

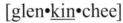

Owner: **Region/district:**
Diageo   Lowlands

Founded: **Status:**   **Capacity:**
1837   Active (vc)   2 500 000 litres

Address: Pencaitland, Tranent,
East Lothian EH34 5ET

Website: **Tel:**
malts.com   01875 342004

In the year 2000, there were only two malt distilleries left in the Lowlands – Auchentoshan and Glenkinchie. When the latter was founded in 1825, there were 115! Things have changed though and today there are 12 distilleries operating.

There are two reasons for Glenkinchie having survived as a distillery when so many others were decommissioned. One was the formation of Scottish Malt Distillers with four other distilleries which took it through the hard years after the First World War. The other is the proximity to Edinburgh which obviously makes it an attractive distillery to visit and which also perhaps contributed to Glenkinchie being selected as one of six Classic Malts. More than 40,000 visitors find their way to the distillery and its excellent visitor centre each year. Nowadays there´s even a shuttle bus that takes you straight from Edinburgh city centre to the distillery.

Unlike many of the distilleries in the Highlands, there´s nothing wild and rugged about Glenkinchie´s surroundings. A mere 15 miles from Edinburgh, it is situated within well kept farming landscape which has been cultivated this way for nearly 2000 years with some of the best barley in Britain. This part of Scotland is called Lothian after Lot, the brother-in-law of King Arthur, who reigned over this region.

Glenkinchie is equipped with a full lauter mash tun (9 tons) and six wooden washbacks with a fermentation time of 60 hours. There are only two stills but they, on the other hand, are very big – in fact, the wash still (30,963 litres) is the biggest in Scotland. Steeply descending lyne arms give very little reflux and condensation of the spirit vapours take place in a cast iron worm tub. In 2017, the distillery will be working a 5-day week with 10 mashes, producing around 2 million litres of alcohol.

The core range consists of a **12 year old** and a **Distiller´s Edition** with a finish in amontillado sherry casks. There is also a new **distillery exclusive** without age statement. In October 2016, a **24 year old**, distilled in 1991 and bottled at 57.2% was launched as part of the Special Releases.

History:

1825 A distillery known as Milton is founded by John and George Rate.

1837 The Rate brothers are registered as licensees of a distillery named Glenkinchie.

1853 John Rate sells the distillery to a farmer by the name of Christie who converts it to a sawmill.

1881 The buildings are bought by a consortium from Edinburgh.

1890 Glenkinchie Distillery Company is founded. Reconstruction and refurbishment is on-going for the next few years.

1914 Glenkinchie forms Scottish Malt Distillers (SMD) with four other Lowland distilleries.

1939-
1945 Glenkinchie is one of few distilleries allowed to maintain production during the war.

1968 Floor maltings is decommissioned.

1969 The maltings is converted into a museum.

1988 Glenkinchie 10 years becomes one of selected six in the Classic Malt series.

1998 A Distiller's Edition with Amontillado finish is launched.

2007 A 12 year old and a 20 year old cask strength are released.

2010 A cask strength exclusive for the visitor centre, a 1992 single cask and a 20 year old are released.

2016 A 24 year old and a distillery exclusive without age statement are released.

Tasting notes Glenkinchie 12 years old:

GS – The nose is fresh and floral, with spices and citrus fruits, plus a hint of marshmallow. Notably elegant. Water releases cut grass and lemon notes. Medium-bodied, smooth, sweet and fruity, with malt, butter and cheesecake. The finish is comparatively long and drying, initially rather herbal.

12 years old

Glenlivet

[glen•liv•it]

Owner: **Region/district:**
Chivas Brothers   Speyside
(Pernod Ricard)

Founded: **Status:**   **Capacity:**
1824   Active (vc)   10 500 000 litres

Address: Ballindalloch, Banffshire AB37 9DB

Website: **Tel:**
theglenlivet.com   01340 821720 (vc)

It is not always the founders of a distillery that manage to make the product into a well-known and prosperous brand. It often takes a generation or two before that happens.

That was also the story with Glenlivet. Without taking any credit away from previous generations it was Captain Bill Smith Grant that started the process that enabled Glenlivet to become one of the world's most popular single malts. Born in 1896, he was the great grandson of the founder, George Smith, and after having served in the First World War he left the army and in 1921 took over the responsibility of running Glenlivet. With prohibition having just been enforced in the USA these were troublesome times for the whisky industry. Still, the Glenlivet brand already had a good reputation in America and when prohibition was repealed in 1933, Bill Smith Grant was quick to strengthen their position in the country. When the train operator Pullman Company decided to have miniatures of Glenlivet single malt in their restaurant cars, popularity grew even quicker and Glenlivet is still the most sold malt whisky in the USA. Later on Bill Smith Grant joined forces with other distillers to avoid Glenlivet being bought by any multinational company and Glenlivet remained independent until Bill Smith Grant died in 1975. Only three years later, the distillery was taken over by Seagrams. Today, Glenlivet is the second biggest Scotch malt in the world with 12.8 million bottles sold in 2016.

The distillery is equipped with a Briggs mash tun (13.5 ton capacity) and 16 wooden washbacks. There are seven pairs of stills, three of which are lined up in a still house with a stunning view of Glen of the Livet. The plan for 2017 is to do 43 mashes per week which equates to 10.5 million litres of alcohol. A substantial expansion of the distillery is now underway. With no time frame announced, the plan is to construct two new distillery units towards the back of the existing warehouses. Construction of the first unit started in 2015 and when completed, it will be equipped with one mash tun, 16 washbacks and seven pairs of stills.

The core range of Glenlivet is made up of **Founder's Reserve, 12 year old, 12 year old Excellence** (for Asia and Russia), **15 year old French Oak Reserve, 18 year old, 21 year old Archive** and **Glenlivet XXV**. A special range of non-chill filtered whiskies called Nàdurra include: **Nàdurra Oloroso Cask Strength** and **Nàdurra First Fill Selection Cask Strength** for domestic markets which are also available in duty free, bottled at 48%. Two new expressions were released in autumn 2015 - the **Nàdurra Peated Whisky Cask Finish**, available at both cask strength and at 48% for duty free. The smoky notes come from a finish in casks that had previously held peated Scotch whisky. The travel retail range also includes **Master Distiller's Reserve, Master Distiller's Reserve Solera Vatted**, as well as **Master Distiller's Reserve Small Batch**, all without age statement. In 2014 a **50 year old** became the inaugural bottling in a new range, The Winchester Collection with a second edition being released in September 2016.

History:

1817 George Smith inherits the farm distillery Upper Drummin from his father Andrew Smith who has been distilling on the site since 1774.

1840 George Smith buys Delnabo farm near Tomintoul and leases Cairngorm Distillery.

1845 George Smith leases three other farms, one of which is situated on the river Livet and is called Minmore.

1846 William Smith develops tuberculosis and his brother John Gordon moves back home to assist his father.

1858 George Smith buys Minmore farm and obtains permission to build a distillery.

1859 Upper Drummin and Cairngorm close and all equipment is brought to Minmore which is renamed The Glenlivet Distillery.

1864 George Smith cooperates with the whisky agent Andrew P. Usher and exports the whisky with great success.

1871 George Smith dies and his son John Gordon takes over.

1880 John Gordon Smith applies for and is granted sole rights to the name The Glenlivet.

1890 A fire breaks out and some of the buildings are replaced.

1896 Another two stills are installed.

1901 John Gordon Smith dies.

1904 John Gordon's nephew George Smith Grant takes over.

1921 Captain Bill Smith Grant, son of George Smith Grant, takes over.

1953 George & J. G. Smith Ltd merges with J. & J. Grant of Glen Grant Distillery and forms the company Glenlivet & Glen Grant Distillers.

1966 Floor maltings closes.

1970 Glenlivet & Glen Grant Distillers Ltd merges with Longmorn-Glenlivet Distilleries Ltd and Hill Thomson & Co. Ltd to form The Glenlivet Distillers Ltd.

History continued:

1978 Seagrams buys The Glenlivet Distillers Ltd. A visitor centre opens.

1996 The visitor centre is expanded, and a multimedia facility installed.

2000 French Oak 12 years and American Oak 12 years are launched

2001 Pernod Ricard and Diageo buy Seagram Spirits & Wine. Pernod Ricard thereby gains control of the Chivas group.

2004 This year sees a lavish relaunch of Glenlivet. French Oak 15 years replaces the previous 12 year old.

2005 Two new duty-free versions are introduced – The Glenlivet 12 year old First Fill and Nadurra. The 1972 Cellar Collection (2,015 bottles) is launched.

2006 Nadurra 16 year old cask strength and 1969 Cellar Collection are released. Glenlivet sells more than 500,000 cases for the first time in one year.

2007 Glenlivet XXV is released.

2009 Four more stills are installed and Nadurra Triumph 1991 is released.

2010 Another two stills are commissioned and capacity increases to 10.5 million litres. Glenlivet Founder's Reserve is released.

2011 Glenlivet Master Distiller's Reserve is released for the duty free market.

2012 1980 Cellar Collection is released.

2013 The 18 year old Batch Reserve and Glenlivet Alpha are released.

2014 Nadurra Oloroso, Nadurra First Fill Selection, The Glenlivet Guardian's Chapter and a 50 year old are released.

2015 Founder's Reserve is released as well as two new expressions for duty free; Solera Vatted and Small Batch.

2016 The Glenlivet Cipher and the second edition of the 50 year old are launched.

Tasting notes Glenlivet 12 year old:

GS – A lovely, honeyed, floral, fragrant nose. Medium-bodied, smooth and malty on the palate, with vanilla sweetness. Not as sweet, however, as the nose might suggest. The finish is pleasantly lengthy and sophisticated.

Tasting notes Glenlivet Founder's Reserve:

GS – The nose is fresh and floral, with ripe pears, pineapple, tangerines, honey and vanilla. Medium-bodied, with ginger nuts, soft toffee and tropical fruit on the smooth palate. Soft spices and lingering fruitiness in the finish.

Master Distiller's Reserve Solera Vatted   Master Distiller's Reserve   The Glenlivet Cipher

21 years old Archive   Nàdurra Peated

Founder's Reserve   15 years old   12 years old

Glenlossie

[glen•loss•ay]

Owner: **Region/district:**
Diageo   Speyside

Founded: **Status:**   **Capacity:**
1876   Active   3 700 000 litres

Address: Birnie, Elgin, Morayshire IV30 8SS

Website: **Tel:**
malts.com   01343 862000

Glenlossie is located just south of Elgin in an area that is like a veritable bee's nest of distilleries. No less than seven other distilleries are situated within a radius of merely 4 kilometres.

To the west lies Miltonduff, to the north Glen Moray and Linkwood, to the south BenRiach, Longmorn and Glen Elgin and on the same site as Glenlossie, there is Mannochmore, built as late as 1971. Glenlossie was founded almost 100 years before that and the malt whisky has, over the years, earned a reputation amongst blenders to be one of the best there is to work with when creating a blended Scotch. Glenlossie has always been an integral part of Haig´s and Dimple, both brands emanating from the Haig family which could probably be called Scotland´s oldest whisky dynasty. Already in 1667, Robert Haig was rebuked for distilling on the Sabbath! The golden years of Haig whisky were from 1930-1970 when it was the brand leader in the UK. It was actually the first Scotch to sell one million cases (12 million bottles) in a year in the UK alone! The slogan that was used is still a classic, "Don't be vague - ask for Haig". Ever since the 1970's sales have decreased but, despite that, around 4 million bottles are still being sold every year.

The distillery is equipped with an 8 ton stainless steel full lauter mash tun and eight washbacks made of larch with a mix of short and long fermentations, 65 and 106 hours respectively. There are three pairs of stills with the spirit stills equipped with purifiers between the lyne arms and the condensers, thus increasing the reflux which gives Glenlossie newmake its light and green/grassy character. A 5-day production is planned for 2017 with 12 mashes per week and 2 million litres for the year. Next to Glenlossie lies the much younger Mannochmore distillery and except for the two distilleries, a dark grains plant and a newly constructed bio-plant, the site also holds fourteen warehouses that can store 250,000 casks of maturing whisky.

The only official bottling of Glenlossie available today is a **10 year old.**

History:

1876   John Duff, former manager at Glendronach Distillery, founds the distillery. Alexander Grigor Allan (to become part-owner of Talisker Distillery), the whisky trader George Thomson and Charles Shirres (both will co-found Longmorn Distillery some 20 years later with John Duff) and H. Mackay are also involved in the company.

1895   The company Glenlossie-Glenlivet Distillery Co. is formed. Alexander Grigor Allan passes away.

1896   John Duff becomes more involved in Longmorn and Mackay takes over management of Glenlossie.

1919   Distillers Company Limited (DCL) takes over the company.

1929   A fire breaks out and causes considerable damage.

1930   DCL transfers operations to Scottish Malt Distillers (SMD).

1962   Stills are increased from four to six.

1971   Another distillery, Mannochmore, is constructed by SMD on the premises. A dark grains plant is installed.

1990   A 10 year old is launched in the Flora & Fauna series.

2010   A Manager´s Choice single cask from 1999 is released.

10 years old

Tasting notes Glenlossie 10 years old:

GS – Cereal, silage and vanilla notes on the relatively light nose, with a voluptuous, sweet palate, offering plums, ginger and barley sugar, plus a hint of oak. The finish is medium in length, with grist and slightly peppery oak.

The formation of
Diageo

Diageo is the biggest spirits producer in the world with net sales in 2016 of more than £10 billion. Their versatile product range includes mega brands such as Johnnie Walker Scotch, Smirnoff vodka, Guinness beer, Captain Morgan rum and Baileys liqueur.

The formation of today's company is the story of mergers and take-overs and can be traced back to 1865. At this time, the large grain distilleries in the Lowlands, using the new patent still technique, were fierce competitors and able to produce large quantities of spirit, larger than what was required by demand. The outcome was overproduction and lower prices. In order to control the output, limit the competition and increase the profits, eight Lowland distilleries formed an alliance in 1865 called Scotch Distillers Association. The co-operation had little effect and it became obvious that a much tighter structure had to be constructed. And so in 1877 six grain spirit producers amalgamated to form the Distillers Company Limited (DCL).

The ten years leading up to 1900 were some of the best for Scotch whisky. The demand exploded and the number of distilleries nearly doubled. Then in 1898/1899 the bubble burst due to economic turmoil, high taxes and temperance movements. The result was huge stocks of maturing whisky and the closure of many distilleries. DCL survived the crisis relatively well. They didn´t have stocks of unsaleable whisky and they could also switch their production into making industrial alcohol something which was impossible for the pot still distilleries. Meanwhile they took the opportunity to exploit the market conditions of the crisis and purchased several companies and distilleries. When DCL was founded, they controlled 70% of the patent still capacity in Scotland. By 1922, they owned all but one patent still in Scotland and could therefore dictate pricing and conditions. The main blenders at the time, known as the Big Five (Haig, Buchanan, Dewar, Walker and Mackie), started to get nervous and eventually followed the old adage of "If you can't beat them, join them" and so they made the move to DCL. Haig was bought in 1919 while John Walker and the merged Buchanan-Dewars joined in 1925. The last one to yield was Mackies (White Horse Distillers) but they finally joined the group in 1927 after Peter Mackie had died. DCL was now at the peak of its greatness, controlling 80% of the domestic whisky market and 75% of the global Scotch whisky market.

With two World Wars, a global depression and a 13 year long alcohol prohibition in the USA, the first four decades of the 20th century would be quite challenging, not only for Scotch whisky but also for many other businesses and companies. However, in many ways thanks to the influence of the DCL, the Scotch whisky industry managed to weather the storm and immediately after 1945 started to build on their position as producers of the most succesful spirit in the world. The individual credited with having the most influence on the company's development was William Ross. He was appointed general manager of DCL in 1897 and chairman from 1925 to 1935. He saw the need for the rationalisation of whisky production but also the importance of blending and marketing. With high morals in business he was known as "the Abraham Lincoln of the trade" and Tommy Dewar referred to him as "our new Moses to take us out of the wilderness of strenuous competition and lead us into the land flowing with respectable dividends".

The 1950s, 1960s and 1970s were golden decades for Scotch whisky – this was the era of the blends and demand was growing all across the globe. DCL, although still succesful in the beginning of this period, found it hard to hold on to its position as the industry leader. The old fashioned management style of the company and the inability to adopt to new consumer behaviour and new ways of doing business quickly made the company a target for a take-over. At the same time, a new generation lost interest in brown spirits and turned to vodka and white wine. In 1983, DCL had to close 11 of its 45 malt distilleries. In 1985, the Argyll Group headed by Jimmy Gulliver made an offer to purchase DCL for £1.9 billion. The board of DCL refused and turned to Guinness and their manager Ernest Saunders as their white knight. Eventually it turned out that Saunders hadn´t been as white as expected. Guinness did win the battle and took over DCL but by way of several fraudulent moves and Saunders, together with some of his colleagues were later sent to prison. The new company after the Guinness take-over in 1987 was named United Distillers. It took only a decade before the newly formed company was again part of a giant merger. This time it was between Guinness and Grand Metropolitan. Starting as a hotel group, Grand Met later moved into food and restaurants and when they joined forces with Guinness in 1997, they were also involved in beer and spirits production. The new company, today by far the biggest spirits producer in the world, was named Diageo – a peculiar mix of latin and Greek. Every day (Dia) the company operates all around the world (Geo).

Glenmorangie

[glen•mor•run•jee]

Owner:
The Glenmorangie Co
(Moët Hennessy)

Region/district:
Northern Highlands

Founded: 1843
Status: Active (vc)

Capacity: 6 000 000 litres

Address: Tain, Ross-shire IV19 1PZ

Website: glenmorangie.com

Tel: 01862 892477 (vc)

Since a few years back, the Scotch whisky industry has strenuously increased its efforts to reduce the carbon footprint that whisky production leaves on the environment.

In 2017 Glenmorangie took a significant step towards a more sustainable production. By-products such as pot ale and spent lees used to be pumped out in the Dornoch Firth but in May, an anaerobic digestion plant was installed, where microorganisms break down the waste in the absence of oxygen into methane gas. This is then used as fuel for the boiler. But the company has also, together with the Marine Conservation Society and Heriot-Watt University, embarked on a plan to re-introduce the European flat oyster to the Dornoch Firth. Common until the mid 19th century, the species has now disappeared in most of Europe.

Since 2007 Glenmorangie has held the 4th spot among the worlds most sold single malts and over that time they have increased sales volumes with 60%. In 2016, 6.4 million bottles were sold with USA as one of the brand's fastest growing markets.

The distillery is equipped with a full lauter mash tun with a charge of 10 tons, 12 stainless steel washbacks with a fermentation time of 52 hours and six pairs of stills. They are the tallest in Scotland and the still room is one of the most magnificent to be seen. Production for 2017 will be 28 mashes per week which equates to 5.5 million litres in the year. Almost the entire production starts its maturation in first fill ex-bourbon casks.

The core range consists of **Original** (10 year old), **18 year old** and three 12 year old wood finishes: **Quinta Ruban** (port), **Nectar D'Or** (Sauternes) and **Lasanta** (sherry). Included in the core range is also **Signet**. The 25 year old which used to be a part of the range has been discontinued. A series of bottlings, called Private Edition, started in 2009 with the release of the sherried **Sonnalta PX**. This has been followed up once a year with **Finealta**, **Artein**, **Ealanta**, **Companta**, **Tùsail** and **Milsean**. The new release for 2017 was **Bacalta**. American oak casks were seasoned with malmsey madeira and left to bake in the Madeira sun. Once emptied, they were filled with Glenmorangie that had been matured in ex-bourbon barrels. For the travel retail market, there is **Dornoch**, **Duthac**, **Tayne** and **Tarlogan**. A **19 year old** was added to the range in September 2017. At the same time, there was the re-launch of **Astar** which first appeared in 2008. It has been maturing in what is called designer casks made from slow growth Missouri oak that has been air seasoned, heavily toasted and lightly charred before being filled with bourbon. A new collection of vintage malts was launched in late 2016. The first bottling in the Bond House No. 1 collection was **Grand Vintage Malt 1990** – a mix of ex-bourbon and ex-sherry. In spring 2017, **Glenmorangie Pride 1974** was released as the oldest Glenmorangie whisky so far. Previous Pride releases were from 1978 and 1981. Finally, the third edition of **A Midwinter Night's Dram**, a vatting of ex-bourbon and ex-oloroso casks, was released in 2017.

History:

1843 William Mathesen applies for a license for a farm distillery called Morangie, which is rebuilt by them. Production took place here in 1738, and possibly since 1703.

1849 Production starts in November.

1880 Exports to foreign destinations such as Rome and San Francisco commence.

1887 The distillery is rebuilt and Glenmorangie Distillery Company Ltd is formed.

1918 40% of the distillery is sold to Macdonald & Muir Ltd and 60 % to the whisky dealer Durham. Macdonald & Muir takes over Durham's share by the late thirties.

1931 The distillery closes.

1936 Production restarts in November.

1980 Number of stills increases from two to four and own maltings ceases.

1990 The number of stills is doubled to eight.

1994 A visitor centre opens. September sees the launch of Glenmorangie Port Wood Finish which marks the start of a number of different wood finishes.

1995 Glenmorangie's Tain l'Hermitage (Rhone wine) is launched.

1996 Two different wood finishes are launched, Madeira and Sherry. Glenmorangie plc is formed.

1997 A museum opens.

2001 A limited edition of a cask strength port wood finish is released in July, Cote de Beaune Wood Finish is launched in September and Three Cask (ex-Bourbon, charred oak and ex-Rioja) is launched in October for Sainsbury's.

2002 A Sauternes finish, a 20 year Glenmorangie with two and a half years in Sauternes casks, is launched.

History continued:

2003 Burgundy Wood Finish is launched in July and a limited edition of cask strength Madeira-matured (i. e. not just finished) in August.

2004 Glenmorangie buys the Scotch Malt Whisky Society. The Macdonald family decides to sell Glenmorangie plc (including the distilleries Glenmorangie, Glen Moray and Ardbeg) to Moët Hennessy at £300 million. A new version of Glenmorangie Tain l´Hermitage (28 years) is released and Glenmorangie Artisan Cask is launched in November.

2005 A 30 year old is launched.

2007 The entire range gets a complete makeover with 15 and 30 year olds being discontinued and the rest given new names as well as new packaging.

2008 An expansion of production capacity is started. Astar and Signet are launched.

2009 The expansion is finished and Sonnalta PX is released for duty free.

2010 Glenmorangie Finealta is released.

2011 28 year old Glenmorangie Pride is released.

2012 Glenmorangie Artein is released.

2013 Glenmorangie Ealanta is released.

2014 Companta, Taghta and Dornoch are released.

2015 Túsail and Duthac are released.

2016 Milsean, Tayne and Tarlogan are released.

2017 Bacalta, Astar and Pride 1974 are released.

Tasting notes Glenmorangie Original 10 year old:

GS – The nose offers fresh fruits, butterscotch and toffee. Silky smooth in the mouth, mild spice, vanilla, and well-defined toffee. The fruity finish has a final flourish of ginger.

Bacalta   19 years old   Tarlogan

Original 10 years old   Astar   Nectar D´Or

Glen Moray

[glen mur•ree]

Owner:
La Martiniquaise (COFEPP)

Region/district:
Speyside

Founded: 1897

Status: Active (vc)

Capacity: 5 700 000 litres

Address: Bruceland Road, Elgin, Morayshire IV30 1YE

Website:
glenmoray.com

Tel:
01343 542577

Celebrating its 120th anniversary this year, Glen Moray is one of the most expansive distilleries right now. Production capacity has steadily increased and the range of single malts has been expanded.

Having been built in the final years of the 19th century, the first years were difficult. The distillery had to close and the owners eventually went bankrupt. Since 1920 the distillery has had two owners which both utilised Glen Moray single malt as the backbone for their blended whiskies however their approach towards the brand has been different. Macdonald & Muir took over in 1920 and until they sold it on to the French company La Martiniquaise, very little attention was given to bottling single malts. The French also use it for blending (including Label 5) but they soon discovered the huge potential Glen Moray had as a single malt and the core range is now made up of no less than 8 expressions.

Since 2016, the distillery is equipped with an 11 ton full lauter mash tun. There are 14 stainless steel washbacks placed outside with a fermentation time of 50-60 hours and nine stills. The three old wash stills were converted to spirit stills which make it a total of six and three new wash stills were constructed by Frilli in Italy. The current capacity is 5.7 million litres of alcohol, but the owners have the option of reintroducing the old mash tun, adding a few more washbacks and two more wash stills which would increase the capacity to 8.9 million litres. In 2017, the distillery will be producing 4.5 million litres, of which 200,000 litres will be heavily peated (50ppm) spirit. Peated production is fairly new to the distillery and did not start until 2009.

The core range consists of **Classic, Classic Port Finish, Classic Chardonnay Finish, Classic Sherry Finish** and **Classic Peated**. Furthermore, we can also find a **12, 15** and **18 year old**. Recent limited releases include batch 4 of the **25 year old Port finish** and, to celebrate the 120th anniversary, **Glen Moray Mastery**, a vatting of five different vintages from a variety of wine casks. Finally, a collection of **1994 vintage** cask strength bottlings can be found exclusively at the visitor centre.

History:

1897 Elgin West Brewery, dated 1830, is reconstructed as Glen Moray Distillery.

1910 The distillery closes.

1920 Financial troubles force the distillery to be put up for sale. Buyer is Macdonald & Muir.

1923 Production restarts.

1958 A reconstruction takes place and the floor maltings are replaced by a Saladin box.

1978 Own maltings are terminated.

1979 Number of stills is increased to four.

1996 Macdonald & Muir Ltd changes name to Glenmorangie plc.

1999 Three wood finishes are introduced - Chardonnay (no age) and Chenin Blanc (12 and 16 years respectively).

2004 Louis Vuitton Moët Hennessy buys Glenmorangie plc and a 1986 cask strength, a 20 and a 30 year old are released.

2006 Two vintages, 1963 and 1964, and a new Manager's Choice are released.

2007 New edition of Mountain Oak is released.

2008 The distillery is sold to La Martiniquaise.

2009 A 14 year old Port finish and an 8 year old matured in red wines casks are released.

2011 Two cask finishes and a 10 year old Chardonnay maturation are released.

2012 A 2003 Chenin Blanc is released.

2013 A 25 year old port finish is released.

2014 Glen Moray Classic Port Finish is released.

2015 Glen Moray Classic Peated is released.

2016 Classic Chardonnay Finish and Classic Sherry Finish are released as well as a 15 and an 18 year old.

2017 Glen Moray Mastery is launched.

Classic Peated

Tasting notes Glen Moray 12 years old:

GS – Mellow on the nose, with vanilla, pear drops and some oak. Smooth in the mouth, with spicy malt, vanilla and summer fruits. The finish is relatively short, with spicy fruit.

Glen Ord

[glen ord]

Owner:	**Region/district:**
Diageo	Northern Highlands
Founded: **Status:**	**Capacity:**
1838 Active (vc)	11 000 000 litres

Address: Muir of Ord, Ross-shire IV6 7UJ

Website:	**Tel:**
malts.com	01463 872004 (vc)

The huge success for the Singleton brand in the last ten years made it essential for the owners to increase the capacity of the Glen Ord distillery in a major way. It is now the second biggest in the Diageo group after Roseisle.

The Singleton brand is made up of whiskies from three distilleries with Glen Ord as the biggest seller (Glendullan and Dufftown being the other two). Since 2011, Glen Ord distillery has been expanded rapidly in several stages and with the latest expansion in 2015, the distillery now has a capacity of 11 million litres. The complete set of equipment comprises of two stainless steel mashtuns, each with a 12.5 ton mash. There are 22 wooden washbacks with a fermentation time of 75 hours and no less than 14 stills. The expansion has been carried out in such a way that the buildings, being more than a century old (the old kiln and malt storage, as well as the Saladin maltings), have been elegantly utilized to house the new equipment.

Glen Ord is probably the only distillery in Scotland which over the years has had three types of maltings on site – from the traditional floor maltings via Saladin boxes to the drum maltings which are used today. The barley is soaked for two days in 18 steeping vessels and then germinated for four days in the 18 drums. There are four kilns to dry the malt – two that are always used for unpeated production and two where they exchange between using peat and hot air. The total capacity is 45,000 tons per year and, apart for their own need, they produce malt mainly for Talisker but also for a few other Diageo distilleries. Recently, with Port Ellen maltings closed for maintenance, they also deliver malt to Caol Ila and Lagavulin. The peat used for drying comes from Aberdeenshire.

The core range is the **Singleton of Glen Ord 12, 15** and **18 year old**. A sub-range, The Singleton Reserve Collection, is exclusive to duty free and consists of **Signature**, **Trinité**, **Liberté** and **Artisan**. Limited releases appear from time to time and the latest, in September 2017, was a **41 year old**, the oldest whisky ever released from the distillery.

History:

1838 Thomas Mackenzie founds the distillery.

1855 Alexander MacLennan and Thomas McGregor buy the distillery.

1870 Alexander MacLennan dies and the distillery is taken over by his widow who marries the banker Alexander Mackenzie.

1877 Alexander Mackenzie leases the distillery.

1878 Alexander Mackenzie builds a new still house and barely manages to start production before a fire destroys it.

1896 Alexander Mackenzie dies and the distillery is sold to James Watson & Co. for £15,800.

1923 John Jabez Watson, James Watson's son, dies and the distillery is sold to John Dewar & Sons. The name changes from Glen Oran to Glen Ord.

1961 A Saladin box is installed.

1966 The two stills are increased to six.

1968 Drum maltings is built.

1983 Malting in the Saladin box ceases.

1988 A visitor centre is opened.

2002 A 12 year old is launched.

2003 A 28 year old cask strength is released.

2004 A 25 year old is launched.

2005 A 30 year old is launched as a Special Release from Diageo.

2006 A 12 year old Singleton of Glen Ord is launched.

2010 A Singleton of Glen Ord 15 year old is released in Taiwan.

2011 Two more washbacks are installed, increasing the capacity by 25%.

2012 Singleton of Glen Ord cask strength is released.

2013 Singleton of Glen Ord Signature, Trinité, Liberté and Artisan are launched.

2015 The Master´s Casks 40 years old is released.

2017 A 41 year old reserved for Asia is released.

Tasting notes Glen Ord 12 years old:

GS – Honeyed malt and milk chocolate on the nose, with a hint of orange. These characteristics carry over onto the sweet, easy-drinking palate, along with a biscuity note. Subtly drying, with a medium-length, spicy finish.

12 years old

Glenrothes

[glen•roth•iss]

Owner:	**Region/district:**
The Edrington Group	Speyside
(the brand is owned by Berry Bros)	
Founded: **Status:**	**Capacity:**
1878 Active	5 600 000 litres

Address: Rothes, Morayshire AB38 7AA

Website:	**Tel:**
theglenrothes.com	01340 872300

Glenrothes distillery has been in the hands of Edrington or its predecessor Highland Distilleries for 130 years. The story of Glenrothes single malt on the other hand is much younger - around 30 years.

Ever since the start, the legendary wine and spirits company Berry Brothers & Rudd have been deeply involved in the brand. They have been using the malt for their blend Cutty Sark since the 1930s and in 2010 they took over the ownership from Edrintgon who in turn got Cutty Sark. Seven years on and the brand is now back in the Edrington family. No sum has been mentioned but according to the Berry Bros CEO Dan Jago, Edrington made them "an offer we simply couldn't refuse". Berry Bros will continue to distribute Glenrothes in the UK.

Glenrothes distillery is equipped with a 5.5 ton stainless steel full lauter mash tun. Twelve washbacks made of Oregon pine are in one room, whilst an adjacent modern tun room houses eight new stainless steel washbacks – all of them with a 58 hour fermentation time. The magnificent, cathedral-like still house has five pairs of stills performing a very slow distillation. In 2017, the distillery will be doing 44 mashes per week, producing just over 4 million litres of alcohol.

How the recent takeover by Edrington will affect the Glenrothes range in the long run remains to be seen but this is the current non-vintage core range; **Select Reserve, Bourbon Cask Reserve, Sherry Cask Reserve, Vintage Reserve** (made up of ten different vintages from 1989 to 2007), **Peated Cask Reserve** (with additional maturation in casks that have formerly held Islay malt) and a **12 year old** for selected markets only (mainly Japan). Recent vintages include the second releases of **1988** and **1995** and the new **2004**. The duty free range consists of **Robur Reserve, Manse Reserve, Elder's Reserve, Minister's Reserve** and the 25 year old **Ancestor's Reserve**. Limited releases include single casks from **1968, 1969** and **1970** as well as a new range called **The Glenrothes Wine Merchant's Collection**. Whisky distilled in 1992 has received a two year finish in casks that have held either wine, port, rum or sherry.

History:

1878 James Stuart & Co. begins planning the new distillery with Robert Dick, William Grant and John Cruickshank as partners.

1879 Production starts in December.

1884 The distillery changes name to Glenrothes-Glenlivet.

1887 William Grant & Co. joins forces with Islay Distillery Co. and forms Highland Distillers Company.

1897 A fire ravages the distillery.

1903 An explosion causes substantial damage.

1963 Expansion from four to six stills.

1980 Expansion from six to eight stills.

1989 Expansion from eight to ten stills.

1999 Edrington and William Grant & Sons buy Highland Distillers.

2002 Four single casks from 1966/1967 are launched.

2005 A 30 year old is launched together with Select Reserve and Vintage 1985.

2007 A 25 year old is released as a duty free item.

2008 1978 Vintage and Robur Reserve are launched.

2009 The Glenrothes John Ramsay, Alba Reserve and Three Decades are released.

2010 Berry Brothers takes over the brand.

2011 Editor's Casks are released.

2013 2001 Vintage and the Manse Brae range are released.

2014 Sherry Cask Reserve and 1969 Extraordinary Cask are released.

2015 Glenrothes Vintage Single Malt is released.

2016 Peated Cask Reserve and Ancestor's Reserve are released.

2017 The brand returns to Edrington and The Glenrothes Wine Merchant's Collection is introduced.

Select Reserve

Tasting notes Glenrothes Select Reserve:

GS – The nose offers ripe fruits, spice and toffee, with a whiff of Golden Syrup. Faint wood polish in the mouth, vanilla, spicy and slightly citric. Creamy and complex. Slightly nutty, with some orange, in the drying finish.

The formation of *Edrington*

The story of Edrington is a fascinating one of crossowning, take-overs and fighting off hostile bids and it all starts in 1855. That was when William Alexander Robertson started his first business as a whisky and wine merchant. In 1861 he took in John Baxter as a partner and even though Baxter left 12 years later, the company continued to be known as Robertson & Baxter. William Robertson became an influential player on the Scotch whisky scene and members of later whisky dynasties such as Walker and Dewar, would serve their apprenticeship in his firm.

He became involved in the formation of yet another company in 1887, Highland Distilleries, and also became the company's first chairman. The two companies shared offices in Glasgow and for many years R&B would focus on blending and distribution while Highland Distilleries were concentrating on production as distillery owners. The first distilleries to be integrated in the company were Bunnahabhain and Glenrothes. During the 1890s, Glenglassaugh and Tamdhu were acquired and in 1937 it was Highland Park's turn to join the company. When William Robertson died in 1897 he had 10 children and he left the control of the company to his two eldest sons, James and Alexander. They continued to grow the business and Robertson & Baxter and Highland Distilleries became more and more intertwined through cross-shareholding. James died in 1944 and his three daughters, Agnes, Elspeth and Ethel were now the majority owners with Ethel (Babs) taking on the role as chairman.

With the increasing demand for Scotch whisky after the war, the interest from companies across the Atlantic to buy Scottish whisky producers was high and Robertson & Baxter was no exception. The legendary Sam Bronfman of Canadian Seagram's sent a message to Miss Ethel in 1947 saying, "I want to buy your company." The answer, "The company is not for sale." was ignored by Bronfman who replied,"You have not yet asked what price I would pay." and Miss Ethel dismissed him by stating "The company is not for sale at any price." But Seagram's hadn't given up hope. Eight years later, a new bid and now for Highland Distilleries was delivered by way of a middleman, the well-known Stanley P Morrison. A white knight in the shape of DCL appeared, stating that they would counter any offer to buy the company and Seagram's withdrew. It became clear that further attempts to buy the company would be made and the three Robertson sisters, who were all spinsters with no heirs, decided to take precautionary actions to guarantee

the survival of the company. They put all their interest in the whisky business into a new company, The Edrington Group and at the same time established The Robertson Trust, a charitable trust which owned all the voting shares in the company. Since then, every year the Trust uses the dividends from Edrington to support various charitable organisations in Scotland.

Until now, Highland Distilleries and Robertson & Baxter had built their fame and fortune on producing and supplying whiskies for blending to Scotland's whisky industry but they did not own any major brands themselves. This was about to change in 1970 when Highland Distilleries bought Famous Grouse from Matthew Gloag & Sons. All of a sudden, one of the big brands were in their hands. Their next move came in 1996 when they bought 75% of Macallan (with Japanese Suntory already having acquired 25% in 1986). In spite of the cross share holding, Edrington and Highland Distilleries were still two separate companies but this changed in 1999 when Edrington and William Grant & Sons in a joint venture acquired Highland Distilleries for £601 million. The 1887 Company was formed to operate the assets, with Edrington holding 70% of the shares and William Grant & Sons the remaining 30%. This means that Suntory is still a part of the picture but only as a 25% owner of Macallan - they have no interests in the other brands.

Since 1999, Tamdhu and Glenglassaugh have been sold and The Glenrothes single malt brand was sold to Berry Brothers in 2010 in exchange for Cutty Sark but just recently, Glenrothes was bought back. When it comes to grain distillation, Edrington share a 50/50 ownership of North British Distillery in Edinburgh together with Diageo. Their mutual company is called Lothian Distillers which was formed in 1993. Unlike some of the other big companies, Edrington has few engagements in other spirits. One is Brugal, the Dominican rum producer which Edrington acquired in 2008. The other is Snow Leopard vodka, created in 2006 by Stephen Sparrow and in 2013, Edrington took a majority stake in the brand. In line with the groups other charitable donations, every year 15% of the profits from the vodka goes to the Snow Leopard Trust to help save the endangered animal.

Glen Scotia

[glen sko•sha]

Owner:
Loch Lomond Group
(majority owner Exponent)

Region/district:
Campbeltown

Founded: **Status:** **Capacity:**
1832 Active (vc) 800 000 litres

Address: High Street, Campbeltown, Argyll PA28 6DS

Website: **Tel:**
glenscotia.com 01586 552288

It takes a lot of money to bring back a distillery from the nearly dead to one with increased production and ten new whiskies in the range that are sold globally. Exponent Private Equity, who took over Glen Scotia in 2014, have made a huge difference.

But you also need dedicated people like Iain McAllister, the distillery manager for the past 10 years. Campbeltown born and bred, Iain´s passion for the distillery and the brand has been vital to the success. Apart from the day-to-day work, his engagement in establishing a visitor centre and the distillery becoming a part of the Campbeltown Whisky Festival has meant a lot to promote the brand.

Glen Scotia is equipped with a traditional 2.8 ton cast iron mash tun, nine washbacks made of stainless steel and one pair of stills. The shortest fermentation time is 70 hours but can reach over 100 hours. For some years, the distillery had a very short middle cut (possibly the shortest in the industry), starting to collect the spirit at 71% and stopping at 68%. This has now changed and they come off spirit at 63%, at least for the unpeated distillations. The production in 2017 will be 10 mashes per week resulting in 540,000 litres of pure alcohol, of which 10% is a combination of lightly peated (15ppm) and heavily peated (58ppm) spirit.

Since spring 2015, the core range consists of three expressions; **Double Cask** (matured in bourbon casks and with a 3-4 months finish in PX sherry), **15 year old** (American oak and a short finish in oloroso casks) and the gently peated **Victoriana** which has been bottled at cask strength. In 2017, another two expressions were added to the range – a **25 year old** matured in ex-bourbon casks and married for 12 months in first fill bourbon and an **18 year old**. The owners also released the first bottlings for duty free in 2017; the **Glen Scotia Campbeltown 1832** and a **16 year old**. A number of **single cask** bottlings available only at the distillery, have been released, most of them in connection with the open day of the distillery in May every year.

History:

1832 The families of Stewart and Galbraith start Scotia Distillery.

1895 The distillery is sold to Duncan McCallum.

1919 Sold to West Highland Malt Distillers.

1924 West Highland Malt Distillers goes bankrupt and Duncan MacCallum buys back the distillery.

1928 The distillery closes.

1930 Duncan MacCallum commits suicide and the Bloch brothers take over.

1933 Production restarts.

1954 Hiram Walker takes over.

1955 A. Gillies & Co. becomes new owner.

1970 A. Gillies & Co. becomes part of Amalgated Distillers Products.

1979 Reconstruction takes place.

1984 The distillery closes.

1989 Amalgated Distillers Products is taken over by Gibson International and production restarts.

1994 Glen Catrine Bonded Warehouse Ltd takes over and the distillery is mothballed.

1999 The distillery re-starts under Loch Lomond Distillery supervision using labour from Springbank.

2000 Loch Lomond Distillers runs operations with its own staff from May onwards.

2005 A 12 year old is released.

2006 A peated version is released.

2012 A new range (10, 12, 16, 18 and 21 year old) is launched.

2014 A 10 year old and one without age statement are released - both heavily peated.

2015 A new range is released; Double Cask, 15 year old and Victoriana.

2017 A 25 year old and an 18 year old as well as two bottlings for duty-free are released.

Tasting notes Glen Scotia Double Cask:

GS – The nose is sweet, with bramble and redcurrant aromas, plus caramel and vanilla. Smooth mouth-feel, with ginger, sherry and more vanilla. The finish is quite long, with spicy sherry and a final hint of brine.

Double Cask

Glen Spey

Photo: © Raymond MacDonald

[glen spey]

Owner:
Diageo

Region/district:
Speyside

Founded: **Status:**   **Capacity:**
1878   Active   1 400 000 litres

Address: Rothes, Morayshire AB38 7AU

Website: **Tel:**
malts.com   01340 831215

Until a few years ago, the sign in front of Glen Spey distillery in Rothes read Glen Spey Distillery and (in larger type) Spey Royal. Today, Spey Royal has been exchanged for J&B Rare.

In both cases they tell the story about the blended whiskies where Glen Spey malt whisky plays a significant role. Spey Royal, introduced as a brand by W&A Gilbey in the early 20th century, has had its strongest market in Thailand over the past 20 years. In the late 1990s it was the leader in the country in the standard Scotch segment with an 80% share. Just a few years later it was down to 20% having not only been surpassed by 100 Pipers, but also by some of Diageo's other brands like Benmore and Johnnie Walker Red Label. J&B on the other hand, plays in a different division. When W&A Gilbey joined IDV and Justerini & Brooks in 1962, they brought with them three Speyside distilleries (Glen Spey, Knockando and Strathmill). Single malt from these three distilleries are still an important part of the J&B blend. Even if the brand has struggled over the last couple of years, it still remains the fifth most popular Scotch in the world with more than 40 million bottles sold in 2016.

The distillery is equipped with a 4.4 ton semi-lauter mash tun, eight stainless steel washbacks with both short (46 hours) and long (100 hours) fermentations and two pairs of stills, where the spirit stills are equipped with purifiers. Even though a new control room was installed in 2017, Glen Spey is still run largely as a manual distillery. The cut points (coming on spirit at 76% and off at 66%) together with a cloudy wort results in a nutty new make. In 2017, the distillery will be doing 18 mashes per week and 1.5 million litres of pure alcohol in the year.

The single malt from Glen Spey has its biggest importance in the blend J&B, where it is one of the signature malts and the only official single malt is the **12 year old** Flora & Fauna bottling. In 2010, two limited releases were made – a **1996 single cask** from new American Oak and a **21 year old** with maturation in ex-sherry American oak.

History:

1878 James Stuart & Co. founds the distillery which becomes known by the name Mill of Rothes.

1886 James Stuart buys Macallan.

1887 W. & A. Gilbey buys the distillery for £11,000 thus becoming the first English company to buy a Scottish malt distillery.

1920 A fire breaks out and the main part of the distillery is re-built.

1962 W. & A. Gilbey combines forces with United Wine Traders and forms International Distillers & Vintners (IDV).

1970 The stills are increased from two to four.

1972 IDV is bought by Watney Mann which is then acquired by Grand Metropolitan.

1997 Guiness and Grand Metropolitan merge to form Diageo.

2001 A 12 year old is launched in the Flora & Fauna series.

2010 A 21 year old is released as part of the Special Releases and a 1996 Manager's Choice single cask is launched.

12 years old

Tasting notes Glen Spey 12 years old:

GS – Tropical fruits and malt on the comparatively delicate nose. Medium-bodied with fresh fruits and vanilla toffee on the palate, becoming steadily nuttier and drier in a gently oaky, mildly smoky finish.

Glentauchers

[glen•tock•ers]

Owner: **Region/district:**
Chivas Brothers   Speyside
(Pernod Ricard)

Founded: **Status:**   **Capacity:**
1897   Active   4 200 000 litres

Address: Mulben, Keith, Banffshire AB55 6YL

Website: **Tel:**
-                            01542 860272

A few years ago, Chivas Brothers decided they should offer the whisky enthusiasts something special from a number of their distilleries and the Cask Strength Edition range was introduced.

They were sold exclusively at Chivas's visitor centres and both well established distilleries, such as Glenlivet, and lesser known, Glenallachie for instance, were represented in the range. But there were also a handful which never gained a place in the range with Glentauchers being one of them. The range was replaced in 2016 by The Distillery Reserve Collection and in 2017, Glentauchers, finally got its spot in the sun by way of a 15 year old single first fill barrel. For the first time in more than 10 years there is an official bottling from the owners.

From the first days until today, Glentauchers role has been to produce malt whisky for blends. Founded by whisky baron, James Buchanan, Black & White was obviously the first to rely on Glentauchers for its character. As owners changed hands over the years it became a signature malt for Teacher's and today it is an integral part of Ballantine's.

The distillery is equipped with a 12 ton stainless steel full lauter mash tun. There are six washbacks made of Oregon pine and three pairs of stills. The distillery is now doing 18 mashes per week and a total of 4 million litres per year. Most of the process at Glentaucher's is done mechanically using traditional methods. The thought behind this is that new employees and trainees from Chivas Brothers will be able to work here for a while to learn the basic techniques of whisky production. In 1910, trials with continuous distillation of malt whisky using column stills were carried out at Glentauchers.

Apart from the new **15 year old single cask**, Chivas Brothers have also made attempts to lift the whisky from obscurity. A range called Ballantine's 17 year old Signature Distillery Editions was launched to highlight the four signature malts of the famous blend. The Glentaucher's version was released in 2014.

History:

1897 James Buchanan and W. P. Lowrie, a whisky merchant from Glasgow, found the distillery.

1898 Production starts.

1906 James Buchanan & Co. takes over the whole distillery and acquires an 80% share in W. P. Lowrie & Co.

1915 James Buchanan & Co. merges with Dewars.

1923 Mashing house and maltings are rebuilt.

1925 Buchanan-Dewars joins Distillers Company Limited (DCL).

1930 Glentauchers is transferred to Scottish Malt Distillers (SMD).

1965 The number of stills is increased from two to six.

1969 Floor maltings is decommissioned.

1985 DCL mothballs the distillery.

1989 United Distillers (formerly DCL) sells the distillery to Caledonian Malt Whisky Distillers, a subsidiary of Allied Distillers.

1992 Production recommences in August.

2000 A 15 year old Glentauchers is released.

2005 Chivas Brothers (Pernod Ricard) become the new owner through the acquisition of Allied Domecq.

2017 A 15 year old single cask is released.

15 years old

Tasting notes Glentauchers 15 years old:

GS – Ripe tropical fruit, soft toffee and barley sugar on the nose. Initially fruity on the palate, with orange peel and a squeeze of lemon, then malt, nutmeg and ginger. Relatively long in the finish, with lingering citrus and allspice.

Glenturret

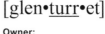
[glen•turr•et]

Owner: **Region/district:**
The Edrington Group   Southern Highlands

Founded: **Status:**   **Capacity:**
1775   Active (vc)   340 000 litres

Address: The Hosh, Crieff, Perthshire PH7 4HA

Website: **Tel:**
theglenturret.com   01764 656565

There are only nine distilleries in Scotland founded in the 18th century that are still producing whisky today. Some years ago there was a debate about which one was the oldest. Today most people seem to agree that the honour goes to Glenturret.

The distillery today has a very traditional and manual way of producing whisky, including stirring the mash tun by hand. However, if you look at the report by the famous Alfred Barnard when he was here in 1886, the mash tun actually had automatic stirring rakes and the production was at least twice as much as the current one. Today, apart from producing whisky to be bottled as single malt, Glenturret acts as the stage for the excellent Famous Grouse Experience - the spiritual home to the popular blend, receiving more than 70,000 visitors every year.

Glenturret is equipped with a stainless steel, open mash tun, the only one left in Scotland where the mash is stirred by hand and where the draff at the end of the process must be removed manually. Furthermore, there are eight Douglas fir washbacks with a fermentation time of up to 120 hours and one pair of stills with vertical condensers. From April 2017 to March 2018, the distillery will be producing 170,000 litres of alcohol. The main part of this, 140,000 litres, will be unpeated Glenturret, while the remaining part is made up of the heavily peated (80ppm in the barley) Ruadh Maor, which has been produced at the distillery since 2009 and is used mainly for blended whisky. The distillery manager for the past 20 years, Neil Cameron, retired in 2017.

The **10 year old** is still available but, since 2015, it has been joined by **Glenturret Sherry** (a combination of American and European oak seasoned with sherry), **Glenturret Triple Wood** (where ex bourbon casks complement the sherry casks) and **Glenturret Peated**. Recent limited releases include the 29 year old **Cameron´s Cut** to celebrate the distillery manager Neil Cameron´s 40 years in the industry and **Jamieson´s Jigger Edition**, also 29 years old, released in March 2017. The oldest bottling so far from the distillery, was the 32 year old **James Fairlie** launched in 2015.

History:

1775 Whisky smugglers establish a small illicit farm distillery named Hosh Distillery.

1818 John Drummond is licensee until 1837.

1826 A distillery in the vicinity is named Glenturret, but is decommissioned before 1852.

1852 John McCallum is licensee until 1874.

1875 Hosh Distillery takes over the name Glenturret Distillery and is managed by Thomas Stewart.

1903 Mitchell Bros Ltd takes over.

1921 Production ceases and the buildings are used for whisky storage only.

1929 Mitchell Bros Ltd is liquidated, the distillery dismantled and the facilities are used as storage for agricultural needs.

1957 James Fairlie buys the distillery and re-equips it.

1959 Production restarts.

1981 Remy-Cointreau buys the distillery and invests in a visitor centre.

1990 Highland Distillers takes over.

1999 Edrington and William Grant & Sons buy Highland Distillers for £601 million. The purchasing company, 1887 Company, is a joint venture between Edrington (70%) and William Grant (30%).

2002 The Famous Grouse Experience, a visitor centre costing £2.5 million, is inaugurated.

2003 A 10 year old Glenturret replaces the 12 year old as the distillery´s standard release.

2007 Three new single casks are released.

2013 An 18 year old bottled at cask strength is released as a distillery exclusive.

2014 A 1986 single cask is released.

2015 Sherry, Triple Wood and Peated are released.

2016 Fly´s 16 Masters is released.

2017 Cameron´s Cut and Jamieson´s Jigger Edition are launched.

10 years old

Tasting notes Glenturret 10 years old:

GS – Nutty and slightly oily on the nose, with barley and citrus fruits. Sweet and honeyed on the full, fruity palate, with a balancing note of oak. Medium length in the sweet finish.

Highland Park

[hi•land park]

Owner:	**Region/district:**
The Edrington Group	Highlands (Orkney)
Founded: **Status:**	**Capacity:**
1798 Active (vc)	2 500 000 litres

Address: Holm Road, Kirkwall, Orkney KW15 1SU

Website:	**Tel:**
highlandpark.co.uk	01856 874619

The Viking influence on Orkney over the centuries, has been a part of Highland Park marketing for quite some time now but recently it has become even more evident.

The Vikings settled in the late 8th century but believed to have taken ownership and ruled the islands from the late 9th century. Controlled by their descendants the Orkneys belonged to the Kingdom of Norway and Denmark until 1468 before the islands became a part of Scotland once again. A large part of the population living on Orkney have a strong sense of affinity with Scandinavia and these ties were emphasized in spring/summer 2017 when the entire Highland Park core range was re-launched. A key message was "The Orkney Single Malt with Viking Soul". In 2016, Highland Park sold a total of 1.4 million bottles.

The distillery is equipped with a semi-lauter mash tun, twelve Oregon pine washbacks with a fermentation time between 50 and 80 hours, and two pairs of stills. The mash tun has a capacity of 12 tons but is only filled to 50%. The plan for 2017 is to produce 2 million litres of alcohol. Highland Park is malting 30% of its malt themselves and there are five malting floors with a capacity of almost 36 tonnes of barley. The phenol content is 30-40 ppm in its own malt and the malt which has been bought from Simpson's is unpeated. The two varieties are always mixed before mashing.

The core range of Highland Park consists of **10 year old Viking Scars, 12 year old Viking Honour, 18 year old Viking Pride** as well as **25, 30** and **40 year olds**. The duty free range, called the Warrior Series, will be reviewed in 2018 but currently it consists of **Svein, Einar, Harald, Sigurd, Ragnvald, Thorfinn, King Christian I** and **Ingvar**. The latest release aimed for duty free is **Voyage of the Raven** with a high proportion of first fill sherry, launched in autumn 2017.

The whisky makers of Highland Park have been extremely busy this year and a large number of limited and special editions have been released. **Valkyrie** (the first of three in the Viking Legend series with Valknut and Valhalla coming next) was matured in a combination of American oak sherry, American oak bourbon and European oak sherry casks while **Full Volume**, distilled in 1999, is the result of a 100% first fill bourbon maturation. A limited range was introduced in 2016 when **Ice** was launched followed by **Fire** in 2017. They were replaced in late 2017 by two new expressions, both 17 years old and bottled at 52.9%. **The Dark** has been matured in sherry seasoned European oak while **The Light** takes its flavour from refill American oak. A second range, also launched in 2016, is based on the distillery's five keystones (hand-turned malt, aromatic peat, cool maturation, sherry oak casks and harmonisation). The first release was **Hobbister** and it was then followed in 2017 by **Shiel**, distilled from 100% floor malted malt. Finally, there is the extra smoky **Dragon Legend**, at least initially exclusive to the UK, which has been matured entirely in sherry casks, both American and European oak.

History:

1798 David Robertson founds the distillery. The local smuggler and businessman Magnus Eunson previously operated an illicit whisky production on the site.

1816 John Robertson, an Excise Officer who arrested Magnus Eunson, takes over production.

1826 Highland Park obtains a license and the distillery is taken over by Robert Borwick.

1840 Robert's son George Borwick takes over but the distillery deteriorates.

1869 The younger brother James Borwick inherits Highland Park and attempts to sell it as he does not consider the distillation of spirits as compatible with his priesthood.

1895 James Grant (of Glenlivet Distillery) buys Highland Park.

1898 James Grant expands capacity from two to four stills.

1937 Highland Distilleries buys Highland Park.

1979 Highland Distilleries invests considerably in marketing Highland Park as single malt which increases sales markedly.

1986 A visitor centre, considered one of Scotland's finest, is opened.

1997 Two new Highland Park are launched, an 18 year old and a 25 year old.

1999 Highland Distillers are acquired by Edrington Group and William Grant & Sons.

2000 Visit Scotland awards Highland Park "Five Star Visitor Attraction".

2005 Highland Park 30 years old is released. A 16 year old for the Duty Free market and Ambassador's Cask 1984 are released.

History continued:

2006 The second edition of Ambassador´s Cask, a 10 year old from 1996, is released. New packaging is introduced.

2007 The Rebus 20, a 21 year old duty free exclusive, a 38 year old and a 39 year old are released.

2008 A 40 year old and the third and fourth editions of Ambassador´s Cask are released.

2009 Two vintages and Earl Magnus 15 year are released.

2010 A 50 year old, Saint Magnus 12 year old, Orcadian Vintage 1970 and four duty free vintages are released.

2011 Vintage 1978, Leif Eriksson and 18 year old Earl Haakon are released.

2012 Thor and a 21 year old are released.

2013 Loki and a new range for duty free, The Warriors, are released.

2014 Freya and Dark Origins are released.

2015 Odin is released.

2016 Hobbister, Ice Edition, Ingvar and King Christian I are released.

2017 Valkyrie, Dragon Legend, Voyage of the Raven, Shiel, Full Volume, The Dark and The Light are released.

Tasting notes Highland Park 12 year old:

GS – The nose is fragrant and floral, with hints of heather and some spice. Smooth and honeyed on the palate, with citric fruits, malt and distinctive tones of wood smoke in the warm, lengthy, slightly peaty finish.

Dragon Legend   Valkyrie   Voyage of the Raven

10 years old

12 years old

Shiel

Inchgower

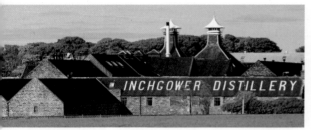

[inch•gow•er]

Owner:	**Region/district:**
Diageo	Speyside
Founded: **Status:**	**Capacity:**
1871 Active	3 200 000 litres

Address: Buckie, Banffshire AB56 5AB

Website:	**Tel:**
malts.com	01542 836700

Over the years, there have been close to 800 legal distilleries operating in Scotland. The vast majority of the ones that were closed have also been torn down and there is nothing left to see. Tochineal is an exception.

Founded by John Wilson in 1825, it operated until 1867. The link to Inchgower is that John Wilson, who founded Tochineal, was the uncle of Alexander Wilson who later started Inchgower. When the owner of the land doubled the rent, it became obvious to Alexander (who had taken over Tochineal when his uncle died) that he had to take his business elsewhere. He simply packed up all the equipment and moved to a new site (Inchgower) 10 kilometres to the west. Alexander Wilson died in 1913 and his company went bankrupt in 1936. Some of the old Tochineal buildings are still left to see in Lintmill, just south of Cullen.

After an extensive upgrade in 2012, the distillery is now equipped with an 8.4 ton stainless steel semilauter mash tun and six washbacks made of Oregon pine. Recently, the production has been a 5-day operation which means short (40-45 hours) and long (90-92 hours) fermentation. There are also 2 pairs of stills with a fairly unusual middle cut. Starting at 70% to avoid the fruity esters and cutting at 55% to catch the more robust flavours. This, together with a cloudy wort, gives a robust and nutty/spicy flavour to the newmake which makes Inchgower a perfect signature malt in Bell´s blended Scotch. In 2017, the distillery was closed from June-September to replace the five existing malt bins with three larger ones.

Inchgower is situated on the south side of Moray Firth and is difficult to miss as it is situated just at the A98 near the small fishing port of Buckie. If one is driving from Elgin towards Banff, it is even easier to spot the distillery as the name appears on the roof. Besides the official **Flora & Fauna 14 year old**, there have also been a few limited bottlings of Inchgower single malt. In 2010, for example, a **single sherry cask** distilled in **1993**, was released.

History:

1871 Alexander Wilson & Co. founds the distillery. Equipment from the disused Tochineal Distillery, also owned by Alexander Wilson, is installed.

1936 Alexander Wilson & Co. becomes bankrupt and Buckie Town Council buys the distillery and the family's home for £1,600.

1938 The distillery is sold on to Arthur Bell & Sons for £3,000.

1966 Capacity doubles to four stills.

1985 Guinness acquires Arthur Bell & Sons.

1987 United Distillers is formed by a merger between Arthur Bell & Sons and DCL.

1997 Inchgower 1974 (22 years) is released as a Rare Malt.

2004 Inchgower 1976 (27 years) is released as a Rare Malt.

2010 A single cask from 1993 is released.

14 years old

Tasting notes Inchgower 14 years old:

GS – Ripe pears and a hint of brine on the light nose. Grassy and gingery in the mouth, with some acidity. The finish is spicy, dry and relatively short.

Jura

[joo•rah]

Owner:
Whyte & Mackay
(Emperador Inc)

Region/district:
Highlands (Jura)

Founded: **Status:**
1810   Active (vc)

Capacity:
2 400 000 litres

Address: Craighouse, Isle of Jura PA60 7XT

Website:
isleofjura.com

Tel:
01496 820240

Some fifteen years ago, Jura single malt was selling reasonably well (around 300,000 bottles) but the quality was inconsistent and the brand never seemed to take off in a major way.

Around 2010 something happened and sales figures climbed dramatically and one year later it was the third biggest single malt in the UK after Glenfiddich and Glenmorangie. The increase has slowed down a bit in recent years and it is now number five in the UK with total global sales close to 2 million bottles. The reason for the turn-around is thoughtful marketing of the brand and, more important, an increase in the quality of the whisky. This was initiated in 1999, when a re-racking programme led to huge volumes of maturing whisky being filled into high quality bourbon casks.

Jura distillery is equipped with a 5 ton semi-lauter mash tun, six stainless steel washbacks with a fermentation time of 54 hours and two pairs of stills – the second tallest in Scotland. Working a 7-day week since 2011, they will be doing 28 mashes per week during 2017, which will include around 7% of peated production (at 50ppm). The production in 2016 (2.39 million litres of pure alcohol) was the largest ever in the histroy of the distillery. Although nothing has been decided, the increase in sales may trigger the construction of a second distillery on site which could be operational within five years.

The core range consists of **Origin** (10 years), **Diurach's Own** (16 years), **Superstition** (lightly peated), the peated **Prophecy** and **Jura Elixir**, a 12 year old matured in both American and European oak. **Turas-Mara**, a duty free exclusive with no age statement, was released in 2013 and yet another bottling aimed for travel retail appeared in spring 2017 - an **18 year old** with a finish in Bordeaux barriques. This year's **Jura Tastival** whisky had been matured in ex-bourbon barrels with a finish in both first fill bourbon and port pipes from Graham's. In April a **10 year old** was released exclusively for the US market and in September, **One And All** was released - a 20 year old with a maturation in ex-bourbon, ex-sherry and three different ex-wine casks.

History:

1810   Archibald Campbell founds a distillery named Small Isles Distillery.

1853   Richard Campbell leases the distillery to Norman Buchanan from Glasgow.

1867   Buchanan files for bankruptcy and J. & K. Orr takes over the distillery.

1876   Licence transferred to James Ferguson & Sons.

1901   Ferguson dismantles the distillery.

1960   Charles Mackinlay & Co. extends the distillery. Newly formed Scottish & Newcastle Breweries acquires Charles Mackinlay & Co.

1963   The first distilling takes place.

1985   Invergordon Distilleries acquires Charles Mackinlay & Co., Isle of Jura and Glenallachie from Scottish & Newcastle Breweries.

1993   Whyte & Mackay (Fortune Brands) buys Invergordon Distillers.

1996   Whyte & Mackay changes name to JBB (Greater Europe).

2001   The management buys out the company and changes the name to Kyndal.

2002   Isle of Jura Superstition is launched.

2003   Kyndal reverts back to its old name, Whyte & Mackay. Isle of Jura 1984 is launched.

2004   Two cask strengths (15 and 30 years old) are released in limited numbers.

2006   The 40 year old Jura is released.

2007   United Spirits buys Whyte & Mackay. The 18 year old Delmé-Evans and an 8 year old heavily peated expression are released.

2008   A series of four different vintages, called Elements, is released.

2009   The peated Prophecy and three new vintages called Paps of Jura are released.

2010   Boutique Barrels and a 21 year old Anniversary bottling are released.

2012   The 12 year old Jura Elixir is released.

2013   Camas an Staca, 1977 Juar and Turas-Mara are released.

2014   Whyte & Mackay is sold to Emperador Inc.

2016   The 22 year old "One For The Road" is released.

2017   The limited One and All is released..

Tasting notes Jura 10 years old:

GS – Resin, oil and pine notes on the delicate nose. Light-bodied in the mouth, with malt and drying saltiness. The finish is malty, nutty, with more salt, plus just a wisp of smoke.

10 years old

Kilchoman

[kil•ho•man]

Owner:
Kilchoman Distillery Co.

Region/district:
Islay

Founded: **Status:** **Capacity:**
2005 Active (vc) 200 000 litres

Address: Rockside farm, Bruichladdich,
Islay PA49 7UT

Website: **Tel:**
kilchomandistillery.com 01496 850011

Establishing a new distillery is never an easy task. Especially if you do it on Islay where you inevitably will be compared to a group of 200 year old, iconic distilleries. But Anthony Wills and his family did it and they seem to have come through as winners.

Critics have been positive and sales have increased steadily since the first release back in 2009. The initial two washbacks were expanded to four in 2007 and another two were installed in 2016. It has now become evident that this will not be sufficient for future demand. The plan now is to build a new still/mash house which will be a mirror image of the existing one. This means another pair of stills and six more washbacks with a total capacity of 450,000 litres of pure alcohol. If everything goes according to plan, the new part of the distillery could be operational by autumn 2018. Already in late 2017, a new malting floor and a new kiln will enable the owners to double their own malting which means 25-30% of their future malt requirement.

The distillery has its own floor maltings with a quarter of the barley requirements coming from fields that surround the distillery. At present, 20% of the malt requirement (peated to 20ppm) comes from own maltings, while the balance comes from Port Ellen (at 50ppm). Other equipment include a 1.2 tonne stainless steel semi-lauter mash tun, six stainless steel washbacks with an average fermentation time of 90 hours and one pair of stills. The distillery is currently doing 9 mashes per week which translates to 200,000 litres of alcohol.

The core range consists of **Machir Bay** and **Sanaig**. The latter was released in 2016 and has been matured in a combination of ex-bourbon and ex-oloroso sherry casks. Limited, but regular releases are the sherry matured **Loch Gorm** and **100% Islay**. Recent, limited releases include a **Sauternes cask maturation**, the **Original Cask Strength**, a **Portugese red wine cask** maturation and the **2009 Vintage**. The special Feis Ile 2017 bottling was a **9 year old** cask strength version of the 100% Islay. For the UK duty free market there is **Coull Point** and for global duty free, **Saligo Bay** is available.

History:

2002 Plans are formed for a new distillery at Rockside Farm on western Islay.

2005 Production starts in June.

2006 A fire breaks out in the kiln causing a few weeks' production stop but malting has to cease for the rest of the year.

2007 The distillery is expanded with two new washbacks.

2009 The first single malt, a 3 year old, is released on 9th September followed by a second release.

2010 Three new releases and an introduction to the US market. John Maclellan from Bunnahabhain joins the team as General Manager.

2011 Kilchoman 100% Islay is released as well as a 4 year old and a 5 year old.

2012 Machir Bay, the first core expression, is released together with Kilchoman Sherry Cask Release and the second edition of 100% Islay.

2013 Loch Gorm and Vintage 2007 are released.

2014 A 3 year old port cask matured and the first duty free exclusive, Coull Point, are released.

2015 A Madeira cask maturation is released and the distillery celebrates its 10th anniversary.

2016 Sanaig and a Sauternes cask maturation are released.

2017 A Portugese red wine maturation and Vintage 2009 are released.

Machir Bay

Tasting notes Kilchoman Machir Bay:

GS – A nose of sweet peat and vanilla, undercut by brine, kelp and black pepper. Filled ashtrays in time. A smooth mouth-feel, with lots of nicely-balanced citrus fruit, peat smoke and Germolene on the palate. The finish is relatively long and sweet, with building spice, chili and a final nuttiness.

Kininvie

[kin•in•vee]

Owner:	**Region/district:**
William Grant & Sons	Speyside
Founded: **Status:**	**Capacity:**
1990 Active	4 800 000 litres

Address: Dufftown, Keith, Banffshire AB55 4DH

Website:	**Tel:**
-	01340 820373

Until recently, when the first official bottlings of Kininvie single malt were released, the distillery was seen as something secret and almost mythical by many whisky drinkers

It is hard to say why but perhaps it had something to do with the fact that the stillhouse was more or less hidden in a "shed" behind Balvenie and it was difficult to get any access to it. At some time it was rumoured it had been closed for good when the owners opened up Ailsa Bay and that they were never really satisfied with the spirit. William Grants were always surprised to hear these stories as they themselves had never taken part in the mythbuilding. To them it was just another working distillery, providing malt for their blends, especially Clan MacGregor, and of no or little interest to the general whisky drinker. In all honesty, however, the marketing and packaging of the recent Kininvie single malts display in depth the imagery of Kininvie as a "secret" distillery.

Kininvie distillery consists of one still house with three wash stills and six spirit stills, tucked away behind Balvenie. There is one 9.6 ton stainless steel full lauter mash tun which is placed next to Balvenie's in the Balvenie distillery and ten Douglas fir washbacks with a minimum fermentation time of 75 hours can be found in two separate rooms next to the Balvenie washbacks. Production in 2017 will be 18 mashes per week for the first six months and 20 mashes for the remainder of the year which means a total of 2.35 million litres of pure alcohol.

The first time that Kininvie appeared as an official single malt bottling was in 2006, when a Hazelwood 15 year old was launched to celebrate the 105th birthday of Janet Sheed Roberts, the last, surviving grand-daughter of William Grant. It wasn't until autumn 2013 that Kininvie single malt was launched under its own name for the first time as a **23 year old**. The first batch was exclusive to Taiwan and was then followed by batch 2 for UK, USA and selected European markets. Batch 3 was offered globally. The end of 2015 saw the release of a **23 year old** core bottling. A **17 year old** is available in duty free and three, limited **25 year old single casks** named First Drops, were launched in November 2015.

History:

1990 Kininvie distillery is inaugurated and the first distillation takes place on 25th June.

1994 Another three stills are installed.

2006 The first expression of a Kininvie single malt is released as a 15 year old under the name Hazelwood.

2008 In February a 17 year old Hazelwood Reserve is launched at Heathrow's Terminal 5.

2013 A 23 year old Kininvie is launched in Taiwan.

2014 A 17 year old and batch 2 of the 23 year old are released.

2015 Batch 3 of the 23 year old is released and later in the year, the batches are replaced by a 23 year old signature bottling. Three 25 year old single casks are launched.

23 years old

Tasting notes Kininvie 17 years old:

GS – The nose offers tropical fruits, coconut and vanilla custard, with a hint of milk chocolate. Pineapple and mango on the palate, accompanied by linseed oil, ginger, and developing nuttiness. The finish dries slowly, with more linseed, plenty of spice, and soft oak.

Knockando

[nock•an•doo]

Owner: | **Region/district:**
Diageo. | Speyside

Founded: | **Status:** | **Capacity:**
1898 | Active | 1 400 000 litres

Address: Knockando, Morayshire AB38 7RT

Website: | **Tel:**
malts.com | 01340 882000

There are 50 distilleries in what is known as the Speyside region which in whisky terms consists of the entire Moray Council and the Badenoch and Strathspey ward of the Highland Council.

Many of them are easily found and can often be spotted from the main roads with the pagoda roofs giving them away. Knockando is different. It is one that you have to actively seek to find. A narrow road from the B9102 leads you down towards the river Spey and once you've passed its neighbour, Tamdhu, you have to make a choice between two roads. Take left and the road leads you to Knockando, beautifully situated on the river Spey. No need continuing because a few hundred metres further, the road ends.

The hidden location doesn't tell the whole story about the whisky though. It is Diageo's 8th most sold single malt (600,000 bottles in 2016) and has for many years been especially popular in France, Spain and Greece. It is also one of the most important malts in the top-selling blend J&B which in 2016 sold more than 43 million bottles.

The distillery is equipped with a small (4.4 ton), semi-lauter mash tun, eight Douglas fir washbacks and two pairs of stills. Knockando has always worked a five-day week with 16 mashes per week, 8 short fermentations (50 hours) and 8 long (100 hours). In 2017 this will mean a production of 1.4 million litres of alcohol. The following year though, volumes will be considerably lower due to a planned closure for six months (December to May). The distillery's control systems will undergo a substantial upgrade. Knockando's nutty character, a result of the cloudy worts coming from the mash tun, has given it its fame. However, in order to balance the taste, the distillers also wish to create the typical Speyside floral notes by using boiling balls on the spirit stills to increase reflux.

The core range consists of **12 year old, 15 year old Richly Matured, 18 year old Slow Matured** and the **21 year old Master Reserve**. In 2011 a **25 year old** matured in first fill European oak was released as part of the Special Releases.

History:

1898 John Thompson founds the distillery. The architect is Charles Doig.

1899 Production starts in May.

1900 The distillery closes in March and J. Thompson & Co. takes over administration.

1903 W. & A. Gilbey purchases the distillery for £3,500 and production restarts in October.

1962 W. & A. Gilbey merges with United Wine Traders (including Justerini & Brooks) and forms International Distillers & Vintners (IDV).

1968 Floor maltings is decommissioned.

1969 The number of stills is increased to four.

1972 IDV is acquired by Watney Mann who, in its turn, is taken over by Grand Metropolitan.

1978 Justerini & Brooks launches a 12 year old Knockando.

1997 Grand Metropolitan and Guinness merge and form Diageo; simultaneously IDV and United Distillers merge to United Distillers & Vintners.

2010 A Manager's Choice 1996 is released.

2011 A 25 year old is released.

12 years old

Tasting notes Knockando 12 years old:

GS – Delicate and fragrant on the nose, with hints of malt, worn leather, and hay. Quite full in the mouth, smooth and honeyed, with gingery malt and a suggestion of white rum. Medium length in the finish, with cereal and more ginger.

Knockdhu

[nock•doo]

Owner:
Inver House Distillers
(Thai Beverages plc)

Region/district:
Highland

Founded: 1893
Status: Active (vc)
Capacity: 2 000 000 litres

Address: Knock, By Huntly, Aberdeenshire AB54 7LJ

Website:
ancnoc.com

Tel:
01466 771223

The basics of malt whisky production in Scotland have been the same for hundreds of years; malting, milling, mashing, fermentation and a double distillation in pot stills.

But there are always small details that can be added or changed to improve either the efficiency or the quality or both. Knockdhu distillery manager Gordon Bruce is a master of seeking out and testing these improvements. Just recently he installed hydro cyclones which basically is a filter used to remove solids from the mash. Gordon is hoping to get a better fermentation with more esters and more alcohol while at the same time lowering the acidity feed to the surrounding wetlands. Cyclones are sometimes being used in grain distilleries but this is probably a first for a malt distillery.

Knockdhu distillery is equipped with a 5 ton stainless steel lauter mash tun, eight washbacks made of Oregon pine, with fermentation time now increased to 65 hours and one pair of stills with worm tubs. For 2017 they plan to run 7 days until October and then 5 days for the rest of the year. This means a total of 1.6 million litres of alcohol. Around 20% of that will be heavily peated (45ppm). The spirit is filled mainly into bourbon casks with an additional 15% of sherry butts.

The core range consists of **12, 18, 24** (which has replaced the 22 year old), **35 years old** and the limited **Vintage 1975** where the stock is almost depleted. The latter, released in 2015, is the oldest expression yet to be released by the owner. In addition to that there is the peated range where almost ten different expressions have replaced each other over the past few years. The current bottlings are **Rascan** (11.1ppm) and **Stack** (20ppm). The phenol specification (ppm) for these two refer to the content in the bottle and not, which is more common, to the malted barley that has been used. Every year a new vintage is released and in spring 2017 it was a **2002** which replaced the **2000**. In 2015, two new expressions were released for duty-free; **Black Hill Reserve** and the peated (13.5ppm) **Barrow**. Both have matured in bourbon casks and they were complemented by **Rùdhan** in autumn 2016.

History:

1893 Distillers Company Limited (DCL) starts construction of the distillery.

1894 Production starts in October.

1930 Scottish Malt Distillers (SMD) takes over production.

1983 The distillery closes in March.

1988 Inver House buys the distillery from United Distillers.

1989 Production restarts on 6th February.

1990 First official bottling of Knockdhu.

1993 First official bottling of anCnoc.

2001 Pacific Spirits purchases Inver House Distillers at a price of $85 million.

2003 Reintroduction of anCnoc 12 years.

2004 A 14 year old from 1990 is launched.

2005 A 30 year old from 1975 and a 14 year old from 1991 are launched.

2006 International Beverage Holdings acquires Pacific Spirits UK.

2007 anCnoc 1993 is released.

2008 anCnoc 16 year old is released.

2011 A Vintage 1996 is released.

2012 A 35 year old is launched.

2013 A 22 year old and Vintage 1999 are released.

2014 A peated range with Rutter, Flaughter, Tushkar and Cutter is introduced.

2015 A 24 year old, Vintage 1975 and Peatlands are released as well as Black Hill Reserve and Barrow for duty free.

2016 Vintage 2001, Blas and Rùdhan are released.

2017 Vintage 2002 is released.

Tasting notes anCnoc 12 years old:

GS – A pretty, sweet, floral nose, with barley notes. Medium bodied, with a whiff of delicate smoke, spices and boiled sweets on the palate. Drier in the mouth than the nose suggests. The finish is quite short and drying.

12 years old

Lagavulin

[lah•gah•<u>voo</u>•lin]

Owner: Diageo
Region/district: Islay

Founded: 1816
Status: Active (vc)
Capacity: 2 530 000 litres

Address: Port Ellen, Islay, Argyll PA42 7DZ

Website: malts.com
Tel: 01496 302749 (vc)

When the capacity to produce more spirit is restricted there are different paths to take. One obvious option is to install more equipment in terms of washbacks or stills. Another is to cut down on the silent season and make every step of the production more efficient.

The third is to shorten the fermentation time or do a more rapid distillation. This last road could prove dangerous to distilleries whose production is earmarked for single malt releases and not to become a part of a blend as this could seriously affect the character of their new make. For Lagavulin the choice was simple when demand outstripped the supply. The lion's share of the production is destined to end up in a single malt bottling and they chose the second way. During 2017, they have increased from 28 mashes to 29 and it took 12 months to plan this change. A more efficient cleaning system in the stillhouse gave space for one more mash per week without interfering with fermentation times or run times in the still.

At one time the number one Islay single malt in terms of sales, Lagavulin was later surpassed by both Laphroaig and Bowmore, partly because of lack of mature whisky due to low production in the 1980s. Laphroaig is still number one but in 2016, Lagavulin managed to pass Bowmore with an increase in volumes by 18% to 2.2 million bottles.

The distillery is equipped with a 4.4 ton stainless steel full lauter mash tun, ten washbacks made of larch with a 55 hour fermentation cycle and two pairs of stills. The spirit stills are actually larger than the wash stills and are filled almost to the brim. This diminishes the copper contact and that, together with a slow distillation, creates the rich and pungent character of Lagavulin single malt. Bourbon hogsheads are used, almost without exception, for maturation and all of the new production is stored on the mainland. The distillery is working 24/7 and the volume for 2017 will be around 2.53 million litres of alcohol.

The core range of Lagavulin is unusually limited and only consists of a **12 year old cask strength** (which actually forms part of the Special Releases but new bottlings appear every year), a **16 year old** and the **Distiller's Edition**, a Pedro Ximenez sherry finish. Two limited bottlings to celebrate the recent bicentenary were released in 2016. The first, in March, was an **8 year old** bottled at 48% and more bottles were released in the autumn. At the beginning of summer, a **25 year old** bottled at cask strength and matured in sherry casks was launched. It was released in honour of the 21 distillery managers that have overseen the distillery since its inception and their names can all be seen on the bottle. Finally, in December, a single cask **Lagavulin 1991** was released with all proceeds being split between seven Islay charities. The Islay Festival special release for 2017, bottled at 55.8%, was a **16 year old** finished in **Moscatel** casks.

History:

1816 John Johnston founds the distillery.

1825 John Johnston takes over the adjacent distillery Ardmore founded in 1817 by Archibald Campbell and closed in 1821.

1836 John Johnston dies and the two distilleries are merged and operated under the name Lagavulin. Alexander Graham, a wine and spirits dealer from Glasgow, buys the distillery.

1861 James Logan Mackie becomes a partner.

1867 The distillery is acquired by James Logan Mackie & Co. and refurbishment starts.

1878 Peter Mackie is employed.

1889 James Logan Mackie passes away and nephew Peter Mackie inherits the distillery.

1890 J. L. Mackie & Co. changes name to Mackie & Co. Peter Mackie launches White Horse onto the export market with Lagavulin included in the blend. White Horse blended is not available on the domestic market until 1901.

1908 Peter Mackie uses the old distillery buildings to build a new distillery, Malt Mill, on the site.

1924 Peter Mackie passes away and Mackie & Co. changes name to White Horse Distillers.

1927 White Horse Distillers becomes part of Distillers Company Limited (DCL).

1930 The distillery is administered under Scottish Malt Distillers (SMD).

1952 An explosive fire breaks out and causes considerable damage.

1962 Malt Mills distillery closes and today it houses Lagavulin's visitor centre.

1974 Floor maltings are decommisioned and malt is bought from Port Ellen instead.

1988 Lagavulin 16 years becomes one of six Classic Malts.

History continued:

1998 A Pedro Ximenez sherry finish is launched as a Distillers Edition.

2002 Two cask strengths (12 years and 25 years) are launched.

2006 A 30 year old is released.

2007 A 21 year old from 1985 and the sixth edition of the 12 year old are released.

2008 A new 12 year old is released.

2009 A new 12 year old appears as a Special Release.

2010 A new edition of the 12 year old, a single cask exclusive for the distillery and a Manager's Choice single cask are released.

2011 The 10th edition of the 12 year old cask strength is released.

2012 The 11th edition of the 12 year old cask strength and a 21 year old are released.

2013 A 37 year old and the 12th edition of the 12 year old cask strength are released.

2014 A triple matured for Friends of the Classic Malts and the 13th edition of the 12 year old cask strength are released.

2015 The 14th edition of the 12 year old cask strength is released.

2016 An 8 year old and a 25 year old are launched as well as the yearly 12 year old cask strength.

2017 A new edition of the 12 year old cask strength is released.

Tasting notes Lagavulin 16 year old:

GS – Peat, iodine, sherry and vanilla merge on the rich nose. The peat and iodine continue on to the expansive, spicy, sherried palate, with brine, prunes and raisins. Peat embers feature in the lengthy, spicy finish.

Distiller's Edition 25 years old 8 years old

16 years old 12 years old cask strength

Laphroaig

[lah•froyg]

Owner: **Region/district:**
Beam Suntory   Islay

Founded: **Status:**   **Capacity:**
1815   Active (vc)   3 300 000 litres

Address: Port Ellen, Islay, Argyll PA42 7DU

Website: **Tel:**
laphroaig.com   01496 302418

It was in 2001 that Laphroaig surpassed Lagvulin as the most sold Islay malt and since then there has been no looking back. In 2016, the brand sold 3.7 million bottles – almost as much as Lagavulin and Bowmore combined.

A doubling of sales volumes over the past decade has given Laphroaig a 7th place among the Top 10 selling single malts. Laphroaig stands with the same problem as one of their nearest neighbours – Ardbeg. They both run at full capacity and with the current increase in demand, that simply won´t be enough for the future. An expansion of the production at Laphroaig is being discussed but as of yet the owners have not revealed or confirmed any plans. There are many stories of distillery managers on Islay that were born and bred on the island but the current manager of Laphroaig, John Campbell, is actually the first Ileach in the history of the distillery to run the place. He started there in 1994 and became the manager in 2006.

Laphroaig is equipped with a 5.5 ton stainless steel full lauter mash tun and six stainless steel washbacks with an average fermentation time of 50-55 hours. The distillery uses an unusual combination of three wash stills and four spirit stills, all fitted with ascending lyne arms. It is one of very few distilleries with its own maltings which produces 20% of its requirements. The barley is steeped in three waters for 51 hours and then spread out on two malting floors for 6 days. It is dried for 15 hours using peat smoke and then for a further 19 hours with hot air. The own malt has a phenol specification of 40-60ppm, while the remaining malt from Port Ellen or the mainland lies between 35 and 45ppm. The distillery is running at full capacity which means 34 mashes per week and 3.3 million litres in the year. Around 70% of the production is reserved for single malts while the remaining 30% is used for blends. Laphroaig has one of the best visitor centres in the industry with tours at a variety of levels.

The core range consists of **Select** without age statement, **10 year old, 10 year old cask strength, Quarter Cask, Triple Wood** and a **25 year old**. A new addition to the range, **Lore**, was launched in 2016. With no age statement, the whisky has been matured in a combination of first fill bourbon barrels, quarter casks and oloroso hogsheads. The travel retail range was recently modified with the old varieties being replaced by **Four Oak** and **The 1815 Edition**. Four Oak, is a vatting from four different casks – bourbon, quarter casks, virgin American oak and European oak hogsheads, while The 1815 Edition is a mix of first-fill, heavily charred bourbon barrels and new European oak hogsheads. Recent limited releases include three bottlings that were launched in 2015; **15 year old, 21 year old** and **32 year old**. A limited **30 year old** was released in late 2016 and was followed in autumn 2017 by a **27 year old** with a maturation in first-fill ex-bourbon barrels and refill quarter casks. The Feis Ile bottling for 2017 was a cask strength quarter cask **Cairdeas**.

History:

1815 Brothers Alexander and Donald Johnston found Laphroaig.

1836 Donald buys out Alexander and takes over operations.

1837 James and Andrew Gairdner found Ardenistiel a stone's throw from Laphroaig.

1847 Donald Johnston is killed in an accident in the distillery when he falls into a kettle of boiling hot burnt ale. The Manager of neigh-bouring Lagavulin, Walter Graham, takes over.

1857 Operation is back in the hands of the Johnston family when Donald's son Dougald takes over.

1860 Ardenistiel Distillery merges with Laphroaig.

1877 Dougald, being without heirs, passes away and his sister Isabella, married to their cousin Alexander takes over.

1907 Alexander Johnston dies and the distillery is inherited by his two sisters Catherine Johnston and Mrs. William Hunter (Isabella Johnston).

1908 Ian Hunter arrives in Islay to assist his mother and aunt with the distillery.

1924 The two stills are increased to four.

1927 Catherine Johnston dies and Ian Hunter takes over.

1928 Isabella Johnston dies and Ian Hunter becomes sole owner.

1950 Ian Hunter forms D. Johnston & Company

1954 Ian Hunter passes away and management of the distillery is taken over by Elisabeth "Bessie" Williamson, who was previously Ian Hunters PA and secretary.

1967 Seager Evans & Company buys the distillery through Long John Distillery, having already acquired part of Laphroaig in 1962. The number of stills is increased from four to five.

1972 Bessie Williamson retires. Another two stills are installed bringing the total to seven.

History continued:

1975 Whitbread & Co. buys Seager Evans (now renamed Long John International) from Schenley International.

1989 The spirits division of Whitbread is sold to Allied Distillers.

1991 Allied Distillers launches Caledonian Malts. Laphroaig is one of the four malts included.

1994 HRH Prince Charles gives his Royal Warrant to Laphroaig. Friends of Laphroaig is founded.

1995 A 10 year old cask strength is launched.

2001 A 40 year old is released.

2004 Quarter Cask is launched.

2005 Fortune Brands becomes new owner.

2007 A vintage 1980 (27 years old) and a 25 year old are released.

2008 Cairdeas, Cairdeas 30 year old and Triple Wood are released.

2009 An 18 year old is released.

2010 A 20 year old for French Duty Free and Cairdeas Master Edition are launched.

2011 Laphroaig PX and Cairdeas - The Ileach Edition are released. Triple Wood is moved to the core range and replaced in duty free by Laphroaig PX.

2012 Brodir and Cairdeas Origin are launched.

2013 QA Cask, An Cuan Mor, 25 year old cask strength and Cairdeas Port Wood Edition are released.

2014 Laphroaig Select and a new version of Cairdeas are released.

2015 A 21 year old, a 32 year old sherry cask and a new Cairdeas are released and the 15 year old is re-launched.

2016 Lore, Cairdeas 2016 and a 30 year old are released.

2017 Four Oak, The 1815 Edition and a 27 year old are released.

Tasting notes Laphroaig Select:

GS – The nose offers chocolate and malt notes set against peat, citrus fruit and iodine. Citrus fruit is most apparent on the relatively light palate, along with ginger, cinnamon and dried fruits. The peat is muted. The finish offers bright spices, new oak and medicinal notes.

Tasting notes Laphroaig 10 year old:

GS – Old-fashioned sticking plaster, peat smoke and seaweed leap off the nose, followed by something a little sweeter and fruitier. Massive on the palate, with fish oil, salt and plankton, though the finish is quite tight and increasingly drying

Select

Quarter Cask

Lore

27 years old

The 1815 Edition

10 years old

Triple Wood

Four Oak

Linkwood

[link•wood]

Owner:	**Region/district:**
Diageo	Speyside

Founded:	**Status:**	**Capacity:**
1821	Active	5 600 000 litres

Address: Elgin, Morayshire IV30 8RD

Website:	**Tel:**
malts.com	01343 862000

For more than hundred years, single malt from Linkwood has played a vital part in whisky from many different producers. Blenders have all agreed that Linkwood contributes both flavour and body to a blend.

A common way to view single malts and their ability to influence a blend is to place them into three groups. Packers (or fillers) combine well with other malts but add little to the flavour. They balance the sweetness from the grain whisky and provide texture. Next are the core malts with the task of defining the overall flavour character of the blend. Finally, and here is where Linkwood comes in, we have the top dressing malts. They contribute with depth, complexity and elegant top notes. Whiskies from all three categories play their part in the blend but the top dressers are the ones which are hardest to replace.

In 1962, a major refurbishment and expansion of the distillery took place. The old part of the distillery, which stopped producing in 1996, was equipped with worm tubs and had a slightly different character than the Linkwood of today. On two occasions during 2011-2013, the distillery has been expanded. The old distillery buildings facing Linkwood Road were demolished and an extension of the current still house, which houses two of the stills and the tunroom, was constructed. The only original buildings from 1872 left standing are No. 6 warehouse and the redundant, old kiln with the pagoda roof. The set up of equipment now is one 12.5 ton full lauter mash tun, 11 wooden washbacks and three pairs of stills. The fermentation time during 5-day week production varies between 65 and 105 hours. The long hours (and the clear wort) are a requirement to get the green/grassy character of the newmake. Production during the last couple of years has varied between 3.6 and 5.6 million litres of alcohol, depending on having a 5 or 7 day production week.

The only official core bottling is a **12 year old** Flora & Fauna. In October 2016, a **37 year old** distilled in 1978 and bottled at 50.3%, was launched as part of the Special Releases.

History:

1821 Peter Brown founds the distillery.

1868 Peter Brown passes away and his son William inherits the distillery.

1872 William demolishes the distillery and builds a new one.

1897 Linkwood Glenlivet Distillery Company Ltd takes over operations.

1902 Innes Cameron, a whisky trader from Elgin, joins the Board and eventually becomes the major shareholder and Director.

1932 Innes Cameron dies and Scottish Malt Distillers takes over in 1933.

1962 Major refurbishment takes place.

1971 The two stills are increased by four. Technically, the four new stills belong to a new distillery referred to as Linkwood B.

1985 Linkwood A (the two original stills) closes.

1990 Linkwood A is in production again for a few months each year until 1996.

2002 A 26 year old from 1975 is launched as a Rare Malt.

2005 A 30 year old from 1974 is launched as a Rare Malt.

2008 Three different wood finishes (all 26 year old) are released.

2009 A Manager´s Choice 1996 is released.

2013 Expansion of the distillery including two more stills.

2016 A 37 year old is released.

12 years old

Tasting notes Linkwood 12 years old:

GS – Floral, grassy and fragrant on the nutty nose, while the slightly oily palate becomes increasingly sweet, ending up at marzipan and almonds. The relatively lengthy finish is quite dry and citric.

The formation of
Dewars/Bacardi

The founding stone for what would become one of the most successful Scotch whisky brands was laid by John Dewar in 1846. After almost 20 years in the business as an employee, John decided it was time to set up his own business as a wine and spirits merchant in Perthshire. He soon started to master the art of blending and by 1880 when he died, he left a prosperous legacy to his sons, John Alexander and Tommy.

They continued in their father's footsteps and eventually developed the business into a global enterprise. The two brothers displayed completely different personality traits, with John Alexander being the analytical and responsible, while the younger Tommy was more enigmatic but showing great social skills. In 1891, the firm was renamed John Dewar & Sons and also received a very special order from a country that, in time, would become their largest market – the USA. The order was sent by the famous industrialist, Andrew Carnegie, and the whisky should be sent to President Benjamin Harrison. This ignited Tommy's interest for export and the next year he embarked on his first of two world tours promoting Dewar's whisky to all corners of the world. Demand was on the increase and the brothers had now started looking for a distillery of their own. Instead of buying one, they decided to build and so, Aberfeldy was completed in 1898. Aberfeldy was the only distillery that Dewers commissioned, however they successfully acquired a further nine; Glentauchers (1915), Royal Lochnagar (1916), Benrinnes (1922), Aultmore (1923), Oban (1923), Glen Ord (1923) and finally, as a part of the Bacardi takeover in 1998, Craigellachie, Macduff and Royal Brackla. Today, the last three, together with Aberfeldy and Aultmore are the ones that are now controlled by Dewars.

In 1899 Dewars launched White Label which remains their core expression even to this day. The company grew with offices being opened in Sydney, Calcutta and Johannesburg but rougher times were to follow with the advent of the First World War which was followed by Prohibition in the USA. This was a time for consolidation and mergers and Dewar's and Buchanan joined forces. A few years later, the company, teamed up with John Walker & Sons and were absorbed into Distillers Company Ltd (DCL) which formed the nucleus of today's giant, Diageo. The market for Scotch whisky grew rapidly after World War II and by 1980, Dewars White Label had taken over the top position as best selling Scotch in America from J&B Rare and it is still number one. During all these years, Dewars was an integral part of DCL, a company which over time became a dominant player that for the main part relied heavily on old tradtions. Multiple potential purchasers of the company

stepped forward, but eventually it was the giant brewer Guinness, that, in dubious circumstances, took control in 1987 and merged DCL with Bells. The new company was named United Distillers. Ten years later another merger occurred, this time between Guiness and Grand Metropolitan. The latter company had a very diverse portfolio of businesses within food, alcohol and hospitality and amongst the spirit brands that they brought with them into the deal were J&B Scotch, Gilbey's gin, Smirnoff vodka and Baileys Irish Cream. Together with the brands that had belonged to Guinness/United Spirits, the new company (known as Diageo) had a powerful foothold within the spirits industry. To preserve a balanced competition within the liquor industry, regulatory authorities demanded that Diageo were to sell off some of their brands to other companies and in 1998, Diageo complied and sold Dewar's and Bombay gin to their rival Bacardi for the staggering sum of $1.93 billion.

There were others in the race to snap up the brands, including Allied Domecq, Seagram and Pernod-Ricard but it was the biggest privately owned spirits company in the world which had the winning bid. Bacardi was founded in Cuba in 1862 by Facundo Bacardi Masso, a Spanish wine merchant who emmigrated to Cuba in 1830. When Don Facundo started his distillery, rum was considered a fiery spirit with very little finesse. Don Facundo started filtering his rum through charcoal and also aged it in barrels made of white oak with a much more mellow spirit as the result. The company prospered until the late 1950s when the Cuban revolution began. Following the victory of Fidel Castro and his revolutionary army, all Bacardi's assets in Cuba were confiscated. This could have been the end for Bacardi, however, they had had the vision to create branches and start production plants in neighbouring countries such as Bahamas, Puerto Rico and Mexico and opened a new company headquarter in 1964 in Florida. When they bought Martini & Rossi, in 1993, this initiated Bacardi's entrance into the Scotch whisky market as the Italian company owned Macduff Distillery and the growing blend William Lawson's. When Dewar's was acquired 5 years later this meant that Bacardi suddenly had become, and still remains, a very important player in the Scotch whisky industry.

Loch Lomond

[lock low•mund]

Owner: **Region/district:**
Loch Lomond Group   Western Highlands
(majority owner Exponent Private Equity)

Founded: **Status:**   **Capacity:**
1965   Active   5 000 000 litres

Address: Lomond Estate, Alexandria G83 0TL

Website: **Tel:**
lochlomonddistillery.com   01389 752781

Loch Lomond Group was established in 2014 when Exponent Private Equity acquired Loch Lomond and Glen Scotia distilleries and Glen Catrine bottling plant with all its brands, including big sellers like High Commissioner whisky and Glen vodka

The former owner, Sandy Bulloch, was an entrepreneur with a solid family background in the whisky business. The same can't be said for the new owner. It is a private equity company with interests in a wide range of businesses; food, newspapers, mortgage financing, handbags, shipping, sightseeing bus tours and including a theatre group. What they may lack in whisky knowledge they make up for with a good insight in marketing, distribution and, not least, brandbuilding. In just three years they have launched ranges of whisky that are present in more than 100 markets.

Loch Lomond distillery is equipped with one full lauter mash tun complemented by ten 25,000 litres and eleven 50,000 litres washbacks, all of which are made of stainless steel. The set-up of stills differs completely from any other distillery in Scotland. There are two, traditional, copper pot stills and six copper stills where the swan necks have been exchanged with rectifying columns. Furthermore, there is one Coffey still used for continuous distillation. And if this was not enough, an additional distillery with column stills producing grain whisky is housed in the same building. For the grain side of production there are twelve 100,000 litres and eight 200,000 litres washbacks. Its total capacity is 5 million litres of malt spirit and 18 million litres of grain.

The core range is divided between two brands; **Loch Lomond** with **Original**, a **12** and an **18 year old** and **Inchmurrin**, also with a **12** and an **18 year old** but a **Madeira wood finish** as well. Previously, more brand names were used. One of these, **Inchmoan**, has now been re-introduced in a new range called Loch Lomond Island Collection. In 2017 a **12 year old** and a **1992 vintage** were released. Both were made using heavily peated malt (50ppm) and have matured in American oak but whereas the 1992 vintage was distilled in stills with the rectifying column, the 12 year old is a combination of that and spirit distilled in traditional pot stills.

History:

1965 The distillery is built by Littlemill Distillery Company Ltd owned by Duncan Thomas and American Barton Brands.

1966 Production commences.

1971 Duncan Thomas is bought out.

1984 The distillery closes.

1985 Glen Catrine Bonded Warehouse Ltd buys Loch Lomond Distillery.

1987 The distillery resumes production.

1993 Grain spirits are also distilled.

1997 A fire destroys 300,000 litres of maturing whisky.

1999 Two more stills are installed.

2005 Inchmoan and Craiglodge as well as Inchmurrin 12 years are launched.

2006 Inchmurrin 4 years, Croftengea 1996 (9 years), Glen Douglas 2001 (4 years) and Inchfad 2002 (5 years) are launched.

2010 A peated Loch Lomond with no age statement is released as well as a Vintage 1966.

2012 New range for Inchmurrin released – 12, 15, 18 and 21 years.

2014 The distillery is sold to Exponent Private Equity. Organic versions of 12 year old single malt and single blend are released.

2015 Loch Lomond Original Single Malt is released together with a single grain and two blends, Reserve and Signature.

2016 A 12 year old and an 18 year old are launched.

2017 This year´s releases include Inchmoan 12 year old and Inchmurrin 12 and 18 year old.

Loch Lomond Original

Tasting notes Loch Lomond Original:

GS – Initially earthy on the nose, with malt and subtle oak. The palate is rounded, with allspice, orange, lime, toffee, and a little smokiness. Barley, citrus fruits and substantial spiciness in the finish.

Longmorn

[long•morn]

Owner:
Chivas Brothers
(Pernod Ricard)

Region/district:
Speyside

Founded: 1894
Status: Active
Capacity: 4 500 000 litres

Address: Longmorn, Morayshire IV30 8SJ

Website: -
Tel: 01343 554139

Longmorn was founded by John Duff and had he not been caught up in the aftermath of the great Pattison whisky scandal in 1898, he might well have been better remembered as one of the most prolific whisky entrepreneurs of the 1800s.

Duff was the owner of Fife Arms Hotel in Llhanbryde, just east of Elgin, when be became manager of Glendronach distillery. In 1876, he founded, together with partners, his own distillery – Glenlossie. After 12 years, he moved to Transvaal in South Africa with his entire family with the aim to build a distillery. When it didn't go as planned the journey continued to Kentucky, with the same goal of building a distillery. Alas, the outcome was the same as before. Back in Scotland in 1892, he took up a position as manager of Bon Accord distillery near Aberdeen. The desire of owning his own distillery lead to the founding of Longmorn in 1893 and five years later, the sister distillery Benriach. Unfortunately for him and his company, was their affiliation and connection to the Pattison brothers and their inflated whisky business and when the bubble burst, John Duff went bankrupt.

Longmorn distillery is equipped with a modern 8.5 ton Briggs full lauter mash tun which replaced the old, traditional tun in 2012. There are ten stainless steel washbacks and four pairs of stills, all fitted with sub-coolers and the wash stills have external heat exchangers. The production capacity was also increased in 2012 by 30% to 4.5 million litres.

Longmorn single malt is often referred to as a hidden gem, and to the owners, Chivas Brothers, the whisky has become an integral part of several of their blends, especially Chivas Regal 18 year old and Royal Salute. In 2015, **The Distiller's Choice** (with no age statement) replaced the 16 year old as the only core bottling. Or at least so it was said. A year later though, the **16 year old** was back with a higher proportion of first fill casks. At the same time, a **23 year old** was released. The **16 year old cask strength** in the new range, The Distillery Reserve Collection, that was released last year has now been discontinued.

History:

1893 John Duff & Company, which founded Glenlossie already in 1876, starts construction. John Duff, George Thomson and Charles Shirres are involved in the company. The total cost amounts to £20,000.

1894 First production in December.

1897 John Duff buys out the other partners.

1898 John Duff builds another distillery next to Longmorn which is called Benriach (at times aka Longmorn no. 2). Duff declares bankruptcy and the shares are sold by the bank to James R. Grant.

1970 The distillery company is merged with The Glenlivet & Glen Grant Distilleries and Hill Thomson & Co. Ltd. Own floor maltings ceases.

1972 The number of stills is increased from four to six. Spirit stills are converted to steam firing.

1974 Another two stills are added.

1978 Seagrams takes over through The Chivas & Glenlivet Group.

1994 Wash stills are converted to steam firing.

2001 Pernod Ricard buys Seagram Spirits & Wine together with Diageo and Pernod Ricard takes over the Chivas group.

2004 A 17 year old cask strength is released.

2007 A 16 year old is released replacing the 15 year old.

2012 Production capacity is expanded.

2015 The Distiller's Choice is released.

2016 A 16 year old and a 23 year old are released.

The Distiller's Choice

Tasting notes Longmorn Distiller's Choice:

GS – Barley sugar, ginger, toffee and malt on the sweet nose. The palate reveals caramel and milk chocolate, with peppery Jaffa orange. Toffee, barley and a hint of spicy oak in the medium-length finish.

Macallan

[mack•al•un]

Owner:
Edrington Group

Region/district:
Speyside

Founded: **Status:** **Capacity:**
1824 Active (vc) 11.000 000 litres

Address: Easter Elchies, Craigellachie, Morayshire
AB38 9RX

Website: **Tel:**
themacallan.com 01340 871471

In autumn 2013, Edrington revealed their plans to build a new, state of the art Macallan distillery. Four years later the new plant was commissioned and the old distillery was closed.

Shaped like five hills with meadow grass on the roof, the distillery resembles no other in Scotland. The total cost of the project will be a staggering £120m but that includes a new cooperage, more warehouses and, not least, a new visitor centre with an art gallery and six different rooms representing each of the six pillars that define the character of Macallan single malt. The visitor centre will be opened in summer 2018. The distillery, with a capacity of 15 million litres, will be equipped with 24 wash stills and 12 spirit stills, all supplied by Forsyths in Rothes. Until the new distillery is ready in November 2017, production continues in two separate plants. The number one plant holds an 8.3 ton full lauter mash tun, 19 stainless steel washbacks, five wash stills and ten spirit stills. The number two plant comprises of a 6.7 ton semi-lauter mash tun, six wooden washbacks and three made of stainless steel, two wash stills and four spirit stills. In 2016, 11 million litres of alcohol were produced while the figures for 2017 depend on the phasing in of the new distillery.

Starting in 2012, the core range for Macallan was revamped in a way which caused lively discussion among the fans of the whisky. Four new expressions were released (**Gold, Amber, Sienna** and **Ruby**) with the intention that they should gradually replace the sherry oak and fine oak ranges. The reason for the debate was that the new expressions were without age statements. Five years on, production of Ruby has stopped and the other three will be discontinued in summer 2018. This means that the core range going forward will be a return of sherry oak and fine oak with age statements although these have been available in some markets the whole time. The ages will be; **Sherry oak 12, 18, 25** and **30 year old** and **Fine Oak 10, 12, 15, 17, 18, 21, 25** and **30 year old**. One further core bottling was introduced in spring 2016, the **12 year old Double Cask**, which has been matured in a mix of sherry casks from both American and European oak. At the same time, the first in a new series of limited bottlings, **Edition No 1** was launched and this was followed by **Edition No 2** and **Edition No 3**. In 2014, an extension of the range called 1824 Masters Series was launched. Four prestige expressions, all sherry matured with the last two bottled in Lalique decanters, have been included – **Rare Cask, Reflexion, No.6** and **M**. The Macallan duty free range holds five expressions; **Select Oak, Whisky Maker's Edition, Estate Reserve, Oscuro** and **Rare Cask Black**. The latter, released in autumn 2015, was made up of 100 sherry-seasoned casks but what is unusual is that it is lightly peated. A series of bottlings called Folio was introduced in 2015. It highlights the Macallan advertising campaigns of the 1970s, 80s and 90s and the bottles are accompanied by a book. **Folio 2**, available only from the distillery, was launched in May 2017. Finally, **The Fine & Rare** range showcases vintages from 1926 to 1991.

History:

1824 The distillery is licensed to Alexander Reid under the name Elchies Distillery.

1847 Alexander Reid passes away and James Shearer Priest and James Davidson take over.

1868 James Stuart takes over the licence. He founds Glen Spey distillery a decade later.

1886 James Stuart buys the distillery.

1892 Stuart sells the distillery to Roderick Kemp from Elgin. Kemp expands the distillery and names it Macallan-Glenlivet.

1909 Roderick Kemp passes away and the Roderick Kemp Trust is established to secure the family's future ownership.

1965 The number of stills is increased from six to twelve.

1966 The trust is reformed as a private limited company.

1968 The company is introduced on the London Stock Exchange.

1974 The number of stills is increased to 18.

1975 Another three stills are added, now making the total 21.

1984 The first official 18 year old single malt is launched.

1986 Japanese Suntory buys 25% of Macallan-Glenlivet plc stocks.

1996 Highland Distilleries buys the remaining stocks. 1874 Replica is launched.

1999 Edrington and William Grant & Sons buys Highland Distilleries for £601 million through The 1887 Company with 70% held by Edrington and 30% by William Grant & Sons. Suntory still holds 25% in Macallan.

2000 The first single cask from Macallan (1981) is named Exceptional 1.

No.17
WASHBACK

History continued:

2001 A new visitor centre is opened.

2002 Elegancia replaces 12 year old in the duty-free range. 1841 Replica, Exceptional II and Exceptional III are also launched.

2003 1876 Replica and Exceptional IV, single cask from 1990 are released.

2004 Exceptional V, single cask from 1989 is released as well as Exceptional VI, single cask from 1990. The Fine Oak series is launched.

2005 New expressions are Macallan Woodland Estate, Winter Edition and the 50 year old.

2006 Fine Oak 17 years old and Vintage 1975 are launched.

2007 1851 Inspiration and Whisky Maker´s Selection are released as a part of the Travel Retail range. 12 year old Gran Reserva is launched in Taiwan and Japan.

2008 Estate Oak and 55 year old Lalique are released.

2009 Capacity increased by another six stills. The Macallan 1824 Collection and a 57 year old Lalique bottling is released.

2010 Oscuro is released for Duty Free.

2011 Macallan MMXI is released for duty free.

2012 Macallan Gold, the first in the new 1824 series, is launched.

2013 Amber, Sienna and Ruby are released.

2014 1824 Masters Series (with Rare Cask, Reflexion and No. 6) is released.

2015 Rare Cask Black is released.

2016 Edition No. 1 and 12 year old Double Cask are released.

2017 Folio 2 is released.

Amber   Sienna   Ruby

15 years old Fine Oak   12 years old Double Cask   12 years old Sherry Cask

Tasting notes Macallan 12 year old Sherry oak:

GS – The nose is luscious, with buttery sherry and Christmas cake characteristics. Rich and firm on the palate, with sherry, elegant oak and Jaffa oranges. The finish is long and malty, with slightly smoky spice.

Tasting notes Macallan 12 year old Fine oak:

GS – The nose is perfumed and quite complex, with marzipan and malty toffee. Expansive on the palate, with oranges, marmalade, milk chocolate and oak. Meidum in length, balanced and comparatively sweet.

Gold   Rare Cask Black   Reflexion   Rare Cask

Macduff

[mack•duff]

Owner:
John Dewar & Sons Ltd
(Bacardi)

Region/district:
Highlands

Founded: 1960
Status: Active
Capacity: 3 400 000 litres

Address: Banff, Aberdeenshire AB45 3JT

Website:
lastgreatmalts.com

Tel:
01261 812612

Until 2010, Glen Deveron, as the official single malt from Macduff was called, was the best-selling malt in the Dewar´s/Bacardi range but since then Aberfeldy has taken over the pole position.

The biggest market for the Deveron brand was (and still is) France but even though it is selling around 300,000 bottles per year, that is nothing compared to the blend where the single malt plays a key part. William Lawson´s sold 35 million bottles during 2016 which means it places 8th on the best/selling list. The brand has however dropped a couple of places in the past year, (to Famous Grouse and William Peel) but the past decade, despite everything, has been an amazing journey, not least in Eastern Europe. Since 2014 it is the most sold Scotch in Russia and also the fastest growing brand in the Ukraine. In autumn 2014, William Lawson took the same route as several brands have done recently. They produced a flavoured spirit drink based on whisky and launched William Lawson´s Super Spiced which is infused with vanilla and spices.

The distillery is equipped with a 6.8 ton stainless steel semi-lauter mash tun and nine washbacks made of stainless steel with a fermentation time of 55 hours. There is also a rather unusual set-up of five stills – two wash stills and three spirit stills. In order to fit the stills into the still room, the lyne arms on four of the stills are bent in a peculiar way and on one of the wash stills it is U-shaped. In 2017 the distillery will be doing 26 mashes per week for 48 weeks, producing 3.4 million litres of alcohol.

Official bottlings from Macduff have always been made under the name Glen Deveron. When a completely new range of bottlings was launched in September 2015, the name had changed to The Deveron. The core range now consists of a **10 year old**, exclusive to France, as well as a **12** and **18 year old**. For duty free, a new range was launched in 2013 under the name The Royal Burgh Collection encompassing a **16**, a **20** and a **30 year old**.

History:

1960 The distillery is founded by Marty Dyke, George Crawford, James Stirrat and Brodie Hepburn (who is also involved in Tullibardine and Deanston). Macduff Distillers Ltd is the name of the company.

1964 The number of stills is increased from two to three.

1967 Stills now total four.

1972 William Lawson Distillers, part of General Beverage Corporation which is owned by Martini & Rossi, buys the distillery from Glendeveron Distilleries.

1990 A fifth still is installed.

1993 Bacardi buys Martini Rossi (including William Lawson) and eventually transfered Macduff to the subsidiary John Dewar & Sons.

2013 The Royal Burgh Collection (16, 20 and 30 years old) is launched for duty free.

2015 A new range is launched - 10, 12 and 18 years old.

12 years old

Tasting notes The Deveron 12 years old:

GS – Soft, sweet and fruity on the nose, with vanilla, ginger, and apple blossom. Medium-bodied, gently spicy, with butterscotch and Brazil nuts. Caramel contrasts with quite dry spicy oak in the finish.

Mannochmore

[man•och•moor]

Owner:
Diageo

Region/district:
Speyside

Founded: | **Status:** | **Capacity:**
1971 | Active | 6 000 000 litres

Address: Elgin, Morayshire IV30 8SS

Website:
malts.com

Tel:
01343 862000

Within five miles from Mannochmore in Speyside, lies a further seven distilleries, but while they were built in the 1800s, Mannochmore is a relative newcomer.

The distillery was constructed during a time when interest in whisky was booming. The demand had increased steadily every decade since the end of WWII. Exports of Scotch whisky tripled from 1960 to 1971 and the lions share went to the US. But towards the end of the seventies, the oil crisis hit the world economy hard and people started to change their drinking habits from expensive, imported Scotch to cheaper, domestic vodka or to wine and beer. Mannochmore managed to survive the closings of several distilleries in 1983 but was mothballed in 1985 only to be re-opened again in 1989. Today the distillery is mainly a reliable supplier of malt whisky for Diageo´s blended brands.

The Glenlossie/Mannochmore complex, south of Elgin, is a busy site with 14 warehouses holding 250,000 casks from many of Diageo´s 28 distilleries. There is also a dark grains plant which converts pot ale into cattle feed, as well as a newly installed biomass burner which generates draff into steam which will power the entire site. And, of course, there are two distilleries with Glenlossie having been built almost a hundred years before its younger sister, Mannochmore. Six years ago, the two distilleries produced a combined total of 5 million litres – a figure which today, thanks largely to a powerful expansion, has almost doubled to 9 million litres. Mannochmore has now outgrown its older sibling and accounts for two thirds of the capacity. Since summer 2013 the distillery is equipped with an 11.1 ton Briggs full lauter mash tun, eight wooden washbacks and another eight external made of stainless steel and four pairs of stills. Clear wort and long fermentations creates a new-make spirit with a fruity character.

The only current official bottling of Mannochmore is a **12 year old** Flora & Fauna. In October 2016, a **25 year old** distilled in 1990 and bottled at 53.4%, was launched as part of the Special Releases.

History:

1971 Distillers Company Limited (DCL) founds the distillery on the site of their sister distillery Glenlossie. It is managed by John Haig & Co. Ltd.

1985 The distillery is mothballed.

1989 In production again.

1992 A Flora & Fauna series 12 years old becomes the first official bottling.

2009 An 18 year old is released.

2010 A Manager´s Choice 1998 is released.

2013 The number of stills is increased to four.

2016 A 25 year old cask strength is released.

Tasting notes Mannochmore 12 years old:

GS – Perfumed and fresh on the light, citric nose, with a sweet, floral, fragrant palate, featuring vanilla, ginger and even a hint of mint. Medium length in the finish, with a note of lingering almonds.

12 years old

Miltonduff

[mill•ton•duff]

Owner:
Chivas Brothers
(Pernod Ricard)

Region/district:
Speyside

Founded: | **Status:** | **Capacity:**
1824 | Active | 5 800 000 litres

Address: Miltonduff, Elgin, Morayshire IV30 8TQ

Website:
-

Tel:
01343 547433

Miltonduff single malt, is one of the main components of Ballantine´s – the second largest Scotch in the world after Johnnie Walker. Even though the top spot seems unattainable, Ballantine´s is doing remarkably well at the moment.

In 2016, when five of the Top 10 blended Scotch had reduced sales volumes and four of them managed a 2-3% increase Ballantines stood out. With an increase of 8%, the brand sold no less than 77 million bottles worldwide. Ballantines is known for its wide range of bottlings, but out of the total sales in 2016, well over 90% were Ballantines Finest without age statement. The Ballantines Master Blender for many years, Sandy Hyslop, was promoted last year when the entire Chivas Brothers blending team was reorganised. With 30 years in the industry, he is now Director of Blending with an overall responsibility for all the company´s blends. Colin Scott, who has been with the company for 44 years will act as mentor to the entire blending team with the title Chivas Regal Custodian Master Blender.

Miltonduff distillery is equipped with an 8 ton full lauter mash tun with a copper dome, 16 stainless steel washbacks with a fermentation time of 56 hours and six, large stills. The lyne arms are all sharply descending which allows for very little reflux. This makes for a rather robust and oily new make in contrast to the lighter and more floral Glenburgie – another key malt in Ballantines. In 1964, two Lomond stills were installed at Miltonduff. They were equipped with columns with adjustable plates with the intention of distilling different styles of whisky from the same still. They were dismantled in 1981 but the special whisky produced in the still, Mosstowie, can still, with a bit of luck, be found.

The most recent, and currently only, official bottling of Miltonduff is a **19 year old**, matured in first fill bourbon barrels which was released in Chivas Brothers´ new Distillery Reserve Collection and is available only at Chivas´ visitor centres.

History:

1824 Andrew Peary and Robert Bain obtain a licence for Miltonduff Distillery. It has previously operated as an illicit farm distillery called Milton Distillery but changes name when the Duff family buys the site it is operating on.

1866 William Stuart buys the distillery.

1895 Thomas Yool & Co. becomes new part-owner.

1936 Thomas Yool & Co. sells the distillery to Hiram Walker Gooderham & Worts. The latter transfers administration to the newly acquired subsidiary George Ballantine & Son.

1964 A pair of Lomond stills is installed to produce the rare Mosstowie.

1974 Major reconstruction of the distillery.

1981 The Lomond stills are decommissioned and replaced by two ordinary pot stills, the number of stills now totalling six.

1986 Allied Lyons buys 51% of Hiram Walker.

1987 Allied Lyons acquires the rest of Hiram Walker.

1991 Allied Distillers follow United Distillers´ example of Classic Malts and introduce Caledonian Malts in which Tormore, Glendro-nach and Laphroaig are included in addition to Miltonduff. Tormore is later replaced by Scapa.

2005 Chivas Brothers (Pernod Ricard) becomes the new owner through the acquisition of Allied Domecq.

19 years old

Tasting notes Miltonduff 19 years old:

GS – The nose offers fragrant ginger and light malt, with developing caramel and greengages. Creamy and soft on the palate, with milk chocolate and big orchard fruit flavours. The finish is gently spicy, with cocoa powder and a hint of lime.

Mortlach

[mort•lack]

Owner: Diageo

Region/district: Speyside

Founded: 1823

Status: Active

Capacity: 3 800 000 litres

Address: Dufftown, Keith, Banffshire AB55 4AQ

Website: mortlach.com, malts.com

Tel: 01340 822100

Mortlach was the first distillery to be founded in Dufftown however during the initial 30 years the distillery failed to make an impact in whisky history.

Many owners replaced each other, including the brothers James and John Grant who later founded Glen Grant, and at times there was no production at all. Not until George Cowie joined the company as part owner in 1853, did the situation start to change. Cowie was an engineer and a railway surveyor who had worked with the expansion of the railway in Banffshire. He streamlined production and made sure that Mortlach single malt was to be sold beyond Scotland's borders. Eventually he also became provost of Dufftown. His son, Alexander, joined the company in 1896, expanded the distillery and introduced the 2.81 distillation that is still in use today.

The distillery is equipped with a 12 ton full lauter mash tun and six washbacks made of larch, currently with 6 short fermentations (54 hours) and 6 long (108 hours). There are six stills of various sizes, all of them being attached to worm tubs for cooling the spirit vapours. There are three wash stills and three spirit stills where the No. 3 pair acts as a traditional double distillation. The low wines from wash stills No. 1 and 2 are directed to the remaining two spirit stills according to a certain distribution. In one of the spirit stills, called Wee Witchie, the charge is redistilled twice and, with all the various distillations taken into account, it could be said that Mortlach is distilled 2.81 times. In recent years, production has shifted between 12 and 16 mashes per week but from July 2017, the distillery is operating a 5-day week with a target of making 2.6 million litres in 2017.

The core range consists of **Rare Old** with no age statement and matured mostly in first fill bourbon casks, but also in ex sherry casks, **Special Strength**, which is exclusive to duty free, similar to Rare Old but bottled at 49%. Then there is an **18 year old** matured in a combination of first fill sherry casks and re-fill American oak, as well as a **25 year old**, which is predominantly matured in re-fill American oak.

History:

1823 The distillery is founded by James Findlater.

1824 Donald Macintosh and Alexander Gordon become part-owners.

1831 The distillery is sold to John Robertson for £270.

1832 A. & T. Gregory buys Mortlach.

1837 James and John Grant of Aberlour become part-owners. No production takes place.

1842 The distillery is now owned by John Alexander Gordon and the Grant brothers.

1851 Mortlach is producing again after having been used as a church and a brewery for some years.

1853 George Cowie joins and becomes part-owner.

1867 John Alexander Gordon dies and Cowie becomes sole owner.

1896 Alexander Cowie joins the company.

1897 The number of stills is increased from three to six.

1923 Alexander Cowie sells the distillery to John Walker & Sons.

1925 John Walker becomes part of Distillers Company Limited (DCL).

1964 Major refurbishment.

1968 Floor maltings ceases.

1996 Mortlach 1972 is released as a Rare Malt.

1998 Mortlach 1978 is released as a Rare Malt.

2004 Mortlach 1971, a 32 year old cask strength is released.

2014 Four new bottlings are released - Rare Old, Special Strength, 18 year old and 25 year old.

Rare Old

Tasting notes Mortlach Rare Old:

GS – Fresh and fruity on the nose, majoring in peaches and apricots. Parma violets, milk chocolate, and finally caramel. Fruit carries over from the nose to the nutty palate, with cinnamon spice. The finish is relatively long and spicy.

Oban

[oa•bun]

Owner: Diageo

Region/district: Western Highlands

Founded: 1794

Status: Active (vc)

Capacity: 870 000 litres

Address: Stafford Street, Oban, Argyll PA34 5NH

Website: malts.com

Tel: 01631 572004 (vc)

There are at least two connections between Oban and America. The first is a very physical one. It was between Gallanach Bay, just south of Oban, and Clarenville in Newfoundland that the world's first transatlantic telephone cable was connected 1956.

Before that, telephone services across the Atlantic were radio-based. The TAT-1 (Transatlantic No. 1) was used among other things to establish the famous Moscow-Washington hotline in the 1960s and the cable was finally retired in 1978. The other connection is that Oban single malt is hugely popular in the USA, an important and growing market for Scotch single malt overall. There are no signs of the demand slowing down and so the owners have done everything in their power to increase production at the distillery. The obvious thing would be to install more washbacks or stills but there is simply no space to expand the distillery, since it is situated right in the middle of the town centre surrounded by other buildings. They have, instead, managed to increase the charge in the mash tun to 7 tons and at the same time, all the necessary maintenance work is carried out during weekends throughout the year.

Oban distillery is one of Scotland's oldest distilleries as well as one of the few remaining urban distilleries. The equipment consists of a 7 ton traditional stainless steel mash tun with rakes, four washbacks made of European larch and one pair of stills. Attached to the stills is a rectangular, stainless steel, double worm tub to condense the spirit vapours. One washback will fill the wash still twice. However, the character of Oban single malt is dependent on long fermentations (110 hours), hence they can only manage six mashes per week, giving it five long fermentations and one short one. The production for 2017 will be slightly more than 800,000 litres.

The core range consists of **Little Bay**, a **14 year old**, an **18 year old** exclusive for USA and a **Distiller's Edition** with a montilla fino sherry finish. In 2013 a **21 year old** was launched as part of the Special Releases and in autumn 2016, a **distillery exclusive** without age statement was released.

History:

1793 John and Hugh Stevenson found the distillery.

1820 Hugh Stevenson dies.

1821 Hugh Stevenson's son Thomas takes over.

1829 Bad investments force Thomas Stevenson into bankruptcy. His eldest son John takes over.

1830 John buys the distillery from his father's creditors for £1,500.

1866 Peter Cumstie buys the distillery.

1883 Cumstie sells Oban to James Walter Higgins who refurbishes and modernizes it.

1898 The Oban & Aultmore-Glenlivet Co. takes over with Alexander Edwards at the helm.

1923 The Oban Distillery Co. owned by Buchanan-Dewar takes over.

1925 Buchanan-Dewar becomes part of Distillers Company Limited (DCL).

1931 Production ceases.

1937 In production again.

1968 Floor maltings ceases and the distillery closes for reconstruction.

1972 Reopening of the distillery.

1979 Oban 12 years is on sale.

1988 United Distillers launches Classic Malts and Oban 14 year old is included.

1998 A Distillers' Edition is launched.

2002 The oldest Oban (32 years) so far is launched.

2004 A 1984 cask strength is released.

2009 Oban 2000, a single cask, is released.

2010 A no age distillery exclusive is released.

2013 A limited 21 year old is released.

2015 Oban Little Bay is released.

2016 A distillery exclusive without age statement is released.

Tasting notes Oban 14 years old:

GS – Lightly smoky on the honeyed, floral nose. Toffee, cereal and a hint of peat. The palate offers initial cooked fruits, becoming spicier. Complex, bittersweet, oak and more gentle smoke. The finish is quite lengthy, with spicy oak, toffee and new leather.

14 year old

Pulteney

[poolt•ni]

Owner:
Inver House Distillers
(Thai Beverages plc)

Region/district:
Northern Highlands

Founded: 1826
Status: Active (vc)
Capacity: 1 800 000 litres

Address: Huddart St, Wick, Caithness KW1 5BA

Website: oldpulteney.com
Tel: 01955 602371

The take-over of Pulteney distillery in 1995 by Inver House turned out to be a blessing for the brand. During the 30 or so years that the distillery was owned by Allied Domecq almost all the production went into blends.

If you wanted to get your hands on an Old Pulteney single malt, you had turn to the independent bottlers, primarily Gordon & MacPhail. Inver House introduced a 12 year old in 1997 and soon followed up with a 17 and a 21 year old. Success for what was called "The Maritime Malt" came quickly and today it is the second biggest malt in the Inver House portfolio efter Speyburn.

The distillery is equipped with a stainless steel semi-lauter mash tun clad with wood and with a copper canopy. There used to be five Corten steel washbacks and one made of stainless steel but since 2016 there are seven washbacks all made of stainless steel. Fermentation time is a mix of short cycles (50 hours) and long ones (110 hours). The wash still, equipped with a huge boil ball and a very thick lye pipe, is quaintly chopped off at the top. Both stills use stainless steel worm tubs for condensing the spirit. Around 1.6 million litres of alcohol are produced yearly.

The core range of Old Pulteney used to comprise of **12, 17, 21** and **35 year old**. In summer 2017 it was revealed that the future of the popular 17 and 21 year olds was under scrutiny. A couple of months later, the 21 year old was replaced by a **25 year old** with an extra maturation in ex-sherry Spanish oak. As to whether the 17 year old may be due for retirement, had not been announced at the time of writing. To complement the bottlings with age statements, there is also **Navigator**. The duty free range is made up of three bottlings named after lighthouses; **Noss Head** is matured in ex-bourbon American oak, while **Duncansby Head** and **Dunnet Head** are a mix of ex-bourbon and ex-sherry. They were complemented by two vintages in autumn 2017 – **1990** and **2006**. A limited Vintage 1989 was replaced by a **1983 Vintage** in August 2017. In 2017, the second edition of **Flotilla 2005** was released exclusively to France.

History:
1826 James Henderson founds the distillery.
1920 The distillery is bought by James Watson.
1923 Buchanan-Dewar takes over.
1930 Production ceases.
1951 In production again after being acquired by the solicitor Robert Cumming.
1955 Cumming sells to James & George Stodart, a subsidiary to Hiram Walker & Sons.
1958 The distillery is rebuilt.
1959 The floor maltings close.
1961 Allied Breweries buys James & George Stodart Ltd.
1981 Allied Breweries changes name to Allied Lyons.
1995 Allied Domecq sells Pulteney to Inver House Distillers.
1997 Old Pulteney 12 years is launched.
2001 Pacific Spirits (Great Oriole Group) buys Inver House at a price of $85 million.
2004 A 17 year old is launched.
2005 A 21 year old is launched.
2006 International Beverage Holdings acquires Pacific Spirits UK.
2010 WK499 Isabella Fortuna is released.
2012 A 40 year old and WK217 Spectrum are released.
2013 Old Pulteney Navigator, The Lighthouse range (3 expressions) and Vintage 1990 are released.
2014 A 35 year old is released.
2015 Dunnet Head and Vintage 1989 are released.
2017 Three vintages (1983, 1990 and 2006) are released together with a 25 year old.

12 years old

Tasting notes Old Pulteney 12 years old:
GS – The nose presents pleasingly fresh malt and floral notes, with a touch of pine. The palate is comparatively sweet, with malt, spices, fresh fruit and a suggestion of salt. The finish is medium in length, drying and decidedly nutty.

Royal Brackla

[royal brack•lah]

Owner:	**Region/district:**
John Dewar & Sons	Highlands
(Bacardi)	

Founded:	**Status:**	**Capacity:**
1812	Active	4 100 000 litres

Address: Cawdor, Nairn, Nairnshire IV12 5QY

Website:	**Tel:**
lastgreatmalts.com	01667 402002

The last couple of years, with sales of Scotch whisky slowing down around the world, has made some of the producers a bit cautious. Many distilleries have cut down their production, at least temporarily.

The most recent figures, however, show that this decrease in sales may have been shortlived. Scotch is on the move again but many producers are not ready yet to increase production. They follow the development thoroughly, still preferring a 5-day week to a full weeks distillation. This is not the tactics of Dewar´s. All five of their distilleries will be producing at full capacity during 2017 and in some cases even exceeding capacity, like at Royal Brackla. At this time it must be said that a capacity figure is not always written in stone. Sometimes small tweeks in the mashing stage can increase the yield as can fermentation times. When Royal Brackla in 2017 will reach their largest volume ever, it is simply because they have had a shorter silent season and have been working through Christmas and New Year.

It is no wonder that production at Brackla is running at full speed. Sales of the single malt may be comparatively low but the malt is highly regarded and vital for many blends, not least the two owned by Bacardi – Dewar´s and William Lawson..

Royal Brackla is equipped with a 12.5 ton full lauter mash tun. There are six wooden washbacks and another two made of stainless steel which have been placed outside. Finally, there are also two pairs of stills. In 2017, the distillery will be doing 17 mashes per week which translates to 4.13 million litres of alcohol per year. In 2015 a biomass boiler (fired with wood-chips) replaced the old, heavy fuel oil boiler. Not only will this contribute to a 5,000 ton reduction of CO^2 emissions, but it will also be 50% more energy efficient.

The new core range introduced in 2015 and replacing the 10 year old, consists of a **12, 16** and **21 year old**. There are also plans for a possible release of a **30 year old** in the near future. Recent, limited releases include a **25 year old**.

History:

1812 The distillery is founded by Captain William Fraser.

1833 Brackla becomes the first of three distilleries allowed to use 'Royal' in the name.

1852 Robert Fraser & Co. takes over the distillery.

1897 The distillery is rebuilt and Royal Brackla Distillery Company Limited is founded.

1919 John Mitchell and James Leict from Aberdeen purchase Royal Brackla.

1926 John Bisset & Company Ltd takes over.

1943 Scottish Malt Distillers (SMD) buys John Bisset & Company Ltd and thereby acquires Royal Brackla.

1964 The distillery closes for a big refurbishment -1966 and the number of stills is increased to four. The maltings closes.

1970 Two stills are increased to four.

1985 The distillery is mothballed.

1991 Production resumes.

1993 A 10 year old Royal Brackla is launched in United Distillers´ Flora & Fauna series.

1997 UDV spends more than £2 million on improvements and refurbishing.

1998 Bacardi–Martini buys Dewar´s from Diageo.

2004 A new 10 year old is launched.

2014 A 35 year old is released for Changi airport in Singapore.

2015 A new range is released; 12, 16 and 21 year old.

12 years old

Tasting notes Royal Brackla 12 years old:

GS – Warm spices, malt and peaches in cream on the nose. The palate is robust, with spice and mildly smoky soft fruit. Quite lengthy in the finish, with citrus fruit, mild spice and cocoa powder.

Royal Lochnagar

[royal loch•nah•gar]

Owner:
Diageo

Region/district:
Eastern Highlands

Founded:
1845

Status:
Active (vc)

Capacity:
500 000 litres

Address: Crathie, Ballater, Aberdeenshire AB35 5TB

Website:
malts.com

Tel:
01339 742700

When Lochnagar distillery came into the hands of DCL in 1925, a well known blend at the time was part of the deal – John Begg Blue Cap. The new owners kept on producing it until the 1990s when it was taken off the list.

John Begg was the blender who took over the "old" distillery and built a new Lochnagar in 1846. A succesful man and friends with the royals he was also haunted by terrible circumstances which unfortunately meant that he outlived 6 of his 9 children. In 1847, the first-born son drowned off the coast of Brazil, a year later his second son drowned in the river Dee – both were aged 15. In 1852, another son died of the flu at the age of 17 and in 1865, a fourth son was found dead of unknown reasons in the distillery manager's house. Three years later, a fifth son died followed the next year by the death of his youngest daughter, aged 17. John Begg died in 1882 at the age of 79.

The distillery is one of two operating distilleries which can boast a Royal Warrant, the other being Royal Brackla. There was a third distillery, Glenury Royal, just south of Aberdeen, but it closed in 1983 and was later demolished.

The distillery is equipped with a 5.4 ton open, traditional stainless steel mash tun. There are three wooden washbacks, with short fermentations of 70 hours and long ones of 110 hours. The two stills are quite small with a charge in the wash still of 6,100 litres and 4,000 litres in the spirit still and the spirit vapours are condensed in cast iron worm tubs. The whole production is filled on site with around 1,000 casks being stored in its only warehouse, while the rest is sent to Glenlossie. Four mashes per week during 2017 will result in 450,000 litres of pure alcohol.

Royal Lochnagar is the signature malt of the best selling Scotch blend in Korea – Windsor. The core range of single malts consists of the **12 year old** and **Selected Reserve**. The latter is a vatting of casks, usually around 18-20 years of age. In autumn 2015 one of the oldest bottlings from the distillery was launched, a **36 year old single cask**.

History:

1823 James Robertson founds a distillery in Glen Feardan on the north bank of River Dee.

1826 The distillery is burnt down by competitors but Robertson decides to establish a new distillery near the mountain Lochnagar.

1841 This distillery is also burnt down.

1845 A new distillery is built by John Begg, this time on the south bank of River Dee. It is named New Lochnagar.

1848 Lochnagar obtains a Royal Warrant.

1882 John Begg passes away and his son Henry Farquharson Begg inherits the distillery.

1896 Henry Farquharson Begg dies.

1906 The children of Henry Begg rebuild the distillery.

1916 The distillery is sold to John Dewar & Sons.

1925 John Dewar & Sons becomes part of Distillers Company Limited (DCL).

1963 A major reconstruction takes place.

2004 A 30 year old cask strength from 1974 is launched in the Rare Malts series (6,000 bottles).

2008 A Distiller's Edition with a Moscatel finish is released.

2010 A Manager's Choice 1994 is released.

2013 A triple matured expression for Friends of the Classic Malts is released.

2016 A distillery exclusive without age statement is released.

Tasting notes Royal Lochnagar 12 years old:

GS – Light toffee on the nose, along with some green notes of freshly-sawn timber. The palate offers a pleasing and quite complex blend of caramel, dry sherry and spice, followed by a hint of liquorice before the slightly scented finish develops.

12 years old

Scapa

[ska•pa]

Owner:
Chivas Brothers
(Pernod Ricard)

Region/district:
Highlands (Orkney)

Founded: 1885
Status: Active
Capacity: 1 300 000 litres

Address: Scapa, St Ola, Kirkwall, Orkney KW15 1SE

Website:
scapawhisky.com

Tel:
01856 876585

There is something about Scottish islands and peated whisky. Admittedly, in the 1800s, most of the whisky produced in Scotland, regardless of the location, had a peaty touch due to the fact that peat was the most accessible fuel available to dry the barley.

But over the years, we have grown accustomed to mainly island whiskies being smoky. For a long time there was one exception and that was Scapa. On the rare occasions when it was marketed and promoted it was described as smooth and unpeated. This changed in 2016 when Glansa was launched. First matured in American oak, it had then been given a finish in casks that had previously contained peated whisky.

Scapa distillery has long lived in the shadows of Highland Park. In spring 2015, however, things started to change. A visitor centre was opened, a new expression was released and production increased. Ever since Pernod Ricard assumed ownership in 2005, the distillery has only been working 3-4 days per week. From 2015 the production has been increased to 7 days, which means one million litres of alcohol per year including a small part of peated production as well.

The equipment consists of a 2.9 ton semi-lauter mash tun with a copper dome, eight washbacks (four made of Corten steel and four of stainless steel) and two stills. Due to the increased production, fermentation time is down to 52 hours from the previous 160. The wash still, sourced from Glenburgie distillery, is only one of two surviving Lomond stills in the industry but on the Scapa still, the adjustable plates have been removed.

The previous 16 year old has been replaced by **Scapa Skiren**, which was introduced in 2015. Matured in first fill bourbon, it doesn´t carry an age statement. This was followed up in autumn 2016 with **Scapa Glansa**, matured in American oak and then finished in casks that previously held peated whisky. The two cask strength distillery exclusives from last year were replaced by two new ones in 2017 – a **10 year old first fill sherry** and a **15 year old first fill bourbon**. These two can also be found at the other Chivas visitor centres.

History:

- **1885** Macfarlane & Townsend founds the distillery with John Townsend at the helm.
- **1919** Scapa Distillery Company Ltd takes over.
- **1934** Scapa Distillery Company goes into voluntary liquidation and production ceases.
- **1936** Production resumes.
- **1936** Bloch Brothers Ltd (John and Sir Maurice) takes over.
- **1954** Hiram Walker & Sons takes over.
- **1959** A Lomond still is installed.
- **1978** The distillery is modernized.
- **1994** The distillery is mothballed.
- **1997** Production takes place a few months each year using staff from Highland Park.
- **2004** Extensive refurbishing takes place at a cost of £2.1 million. Scapa 14 years is launched.
- **2005** Production ceases in April and phase two of the refurbishment programme starts. Chivas Brothers becomes the new owner.
- **2006** Scapa 1992 (14 years) is launched.
- **2008** Scapa 16 years is launched.
- **2015** The distillery opens for visitors and Scapa Skiren is launched.
- **2016** The peated Glansa is released.

Tasting notes Scapa Skiren:

GS – Lime is apparent on the early nose, followed by musty peaches, almonds, cinnamon, and salt. More peaches on the palate, with tinned pear and honey. Tingling spices in the drying finish, which soon becomes slightly astringent.

Scapa Skiren

Speyburn

[spey•burn]

Owner:
Inver House Distillers
(Thai Beverages plc)

Region/district:
Speyside

Founded: **Status:** **Capacity:**
1897 Active 4 500 000 litres

Address: Rothes, Aberlour, Morayshire AB38 7AG

Website: **Tel:**
speyburn.com 01340 831213

Partly for historic reasons, including having an American owner in the past, Speyburn single malt has been popular in the USA for many years. The range however, consisted of just a 10 year old, apart from a few limited releases, for a long time.

In 2009, Bradan Orach without age statement was introduced and in the summer of 2017 it was time for a third addition. A 15 year old matured in a combination of American and Spanish oak was released. Non-chill filtered and bottled at 46% it will be part of the core range although limited to 20,000 bottles per year. The key markets are USA, the UK and the rest of Europe.

In 1900, Speyburn was the first distillery to abandon floor maltings in favour of a new method – drum malting. In the late sixties, the maltings closed and ready malt was bought instead, but the drum maltings are still there to see, protected by Historic Scotland.

An impressive expansion of the distillery commenced during 2014 and was completed during the spring of 2015. The expansion had cost £4m and included a new 6.25 ton stainless steel mash tun. Four of the six wooden washbacks were kept but they have also expanded with no less than 15 washbacks made of stainless steel. Finally, the existing wash still was converted to a spirit still of exactly the same shape as the other one, while a new and much larger wash still was installed. The two spirit stills are connected to a worm tub while the wash still is fitted with a shell and tube condenser. The fermentation time has also been lengthened from the original 48 hours to a minimum of 72 hours. The production in 2017 will be 40 mashes per week and 4.1 million litres of alcohol.

The core range of Speyburn single malt is the **10 year old**, **Bradan Orach** without age statement and the recently introduced **15 year old**. In September 2015, **Arranta Casks** was released as a limited USA exclusive. A second release was made in 2016.

History:

1897 Brothers John and Edward Hopkin and their cousin Edward Broughton found the distillery through John Hopkin & Co. They already own Tobermory. The architect is Charles Doig. Building the distillery costs £17,000 and the distillery is transferred to Speyburn-Glenlivet Distillery Company.

1916 Distillers Company Limited (DCL) acquires John Hopkin & Co. and the distillery.

1930 Production stops.

1934 Productions restarts.

1962 Speyburn is transferred to Scottish Malt Distillers (SMD).

1968 Drum maltings closes.

1991 Inver House Distillers buys Speyburn.

1992 A 10 year old is launched as a replacement for the 12 year old in the Flora & Fauna series.

2001 Pacific Spirits (Great Oriole Group) buys Inver House for $85 million.

2005 A 25 year old Solera is released.

2006 Inver House changes owner when International Beverage Holdings acquires Pacific Spirits UK.

2009 The un-aged Bradan Orach is introduced for the American market.

2012 Clan Speyburn is formed.

2014 The distillery is expanded.

2015 Arranta Casks is released.

2017 A 15 year old is launched.

15 years old

Tasting notes Speyburn 10 years old:

GS – Soft and elegant on the spicy, nutty nose. Smooth in the mouth, with vanilla, spice and more nuts. The finish is medium, spicy and drying.

Speyside

[spey•side]

Owner:
Speyside Distillers Co.

Region/district:
Speyside

Founded: 1976

Status: Active

Capacity: 600 000 litres

Address: Glen Tromie, Kingussie, Inverness-shire
PH21 1NS

Website:
speysidedistillery.co.uk

Tel:
01540 661060

The foundation of Speyside distillery is a story of determination and patience and of one man´s dream to build a dedicated, small scale malt distillery.

The former submarine captain George Christie started a distillery with partners in 1957. North of Scotland distillery was first and foremost a grain distillery but two pot stills also produced malt whisky for a while. Speyside distillery would become something completely different though. Christie commissioned a drystone dyker to build a distillery in beautiful surroundings in Drumguish, near Kingussie on land that Christie had acquired already in 1956. It would take 28 years before the distillery started production and by that time George Christie had already sold the company. For many years though, he lived just up the road from the distillery and he was a frequent guest until he passed away in 2012. Speyside is one of the most romantic distilleries in Scotland and it was no wonder that BBC chose it to be Lagganmore distillery in their television series Monarch of the Glen from the early 2000.

The distillery is equipped with a 4.2 ton semi-lauter mash tun, four stainless steel washbacks with a 70-120 hour fermentation time and one pair of stills. For the last couple of years they have been working a 6 day week with a total production of 600,000 litres of alcohol. There are also plans to build a second distillery in Rothiemurches near Aviemore.

The core range of Spey single malt is made up of **Tenné** (with a 6 months port finish), **12 year old** (6 months finish in new American oak), **18 year old** (sherry matured), **Chairman´s Choice** and **Royal Choice**. The latter two are multi-vintage marriages from both American and European oak. Two new core bottlings were added in early 2017; **Trutina** which is a 100% bourbon maturation and **Fumare**, similar to Trutina but distilled from peated barley. Also part of the core range is **Beinn Dubh** which replaced the black whisky Cu Duhb. Destined for export markets is **Black Burn** without age statement. Recent limited releases include **Flying Scotsman** in collaboration with national Rail Museum in York and **Thunder in the Glens** to mark the 20th anniversary of the largest gathering of Harley owners in Europe.

History:

1956 George Christie buys a piece of land at Drumguish near Kingussie.

1957 George Christie starts a grain distillery near Alloa.

1962 George Christie (founder of Speyside Distillery Group in the fifties) commissions the drystone dyker Alex Fairlie to build a distillery in Drumguish.

1986 Scowis assumes ownership.

1987 The distillery is completed.

1990 The distillery is on stream in December.

1993 The first single malt, Drumguish, is launched.

1999 Speyside 8 years is launched.

2000 Speyside Distilleries is sold to a group of private investors including Ricky Christie, Ian Jerman and Sir James Ackroyd.

2001 Speyside 10 years is launched.

2012 Speyside Distillers is sold to Harvey´s of Edinburgh.

2014 A new range, Spey from Speyside Distillery, is launched (NAS, 12 and 18 year old).

2015 The range is revamped again. New expressions include Tenné, 12 years old and 18 years old.

2016 "Byron´s Choice - The Marriage" and Spey Cask 27 are released.

2017 Trutina and Fumare are released.

12 years old

Tasting notes Spey 12 years old:

GS – Malt and white pepper on the nose, with a mildly savoury background. The palate features vanilla, orange, hazelnuts and cloves. Black pepper and lively oak in the medium-length finish.

The formation of Inver House

With the highly acclaimed single malts coming from Inver House today, it is a noteworthy coincidence that somewhere in the misty past, it´s founders wealth was built on industrial alcohol. Harry Publicker, a Ukrainian immigrant started his company, Publicker Industries in 1912 in Philadelphia. His business concept was to produce industrial alcohol from molasses with the US Government as one of his biggest customers. Success came quickly and in the early 1920's he produced 60 million gallons each year. The lack of oil and gasoline during World War II meant the need for industrial alcohol increased dramatically which saw massive growth for Publicker Industries.

By the end of the war, Harry Publicker owned a company with 5,000 employees. Harry died in 1951 and Si Neuman, his son-in-law took over the running of business. He decided that the company would expand into potable alcohol as well. Without any production facility (matured stock of whisky was bought), the company launched Inver House Rare, a blend of Scotch whisky in 1956. The brand was a success and after a few years, Si Neuman realised that they would have to start their own production to keep up with demand. Inver House Distillers was established in 1964 and almost instantly Garnheath grain distillery was built on the site of the disused Moffat Paper Mill in Airdrie east of Glasgow. On the same site, two small malt distilleries (Killyloch and Glen Flagler) were added in 1965. Three years later they opened Moffat maltings which would eventually grow to become the largest commercial malting plant in Europe. They also bought Bladnoch distillery in 1973 and for a short time in the mid 1980s, they were also the owners of Loch Lomond distillery.

However, just as the future looked promising, the interest in whisky began to wain across global markets. A new generation preferred vodka and white wine and ́in the beginning of the 1980s there was an over production of whisky due to the increased capacities in many of the Scottish distilleries. Several distilleries were mothballed and Inver House was no exception. Bladnoch was sold to Bells in 1983, Glen Flagler closed in 1985 (by then, Killyloch had long been out of production) and Garnheath ceased production in 1986. By that time, Inver House was already under new ownership when Standard Brands bought the company in 1979 after Si Neuman´s death three years earlier. In 1988, Inver House changed hands again when the company was sold by Standard Brands to the company´s four UK directors for £8.2m. The following decade brought more stability and structure for Inver House as the new owners methodically acquired five established distilleries throughout Scotland; Knockdhu (1988), Speyburn (1991), Pulteney (1995), Balblair (1996) and Balmenach (1997). Their efforts payed off and in 2000 the companies past turmoils were put behind them as they recorded a profit of £6.8 million. The owners felt that this was the right time to sell and in October 2001 Pacific Spirits from Thailand took the reigns of Inver House at a cost of £56m.

The driving force behind Pacific Spirits is the founder and owner Charoen Sirivadhanabhakdi. Born in 1944, the sixth of eleven children, of a Chinese street vendor in Bangkok, Charoen left school at the age of nine to work. Eventually he started a business supplying distilleries producing Thai whisky. At this time (in the 1980s) all liquor production in Thailand was state owned but after a while Charoen managed to acquire a license, covering 15% of the market, to produce his own spirits. In 1985 the remaining 85% were opened to bids and through a loan of $200m, Charoen took over the entire alcohol production in Thailand. To comprehend the enormity of this situation, in 1987 the combined fees that Charoen paid to the Thai state equated to 5% of the national budget! Together with Carlsberg, Charoen created the Chang beer brand in order to compete with the well established Singha beer. The 73 year old Charoen is one of the richest men in the world and the estimated value of his assets is $16bn. The company today is called Thai Beverage (or ThaiBev for short) and Inver House is a part of International Beverage Holdings (InterBev) - the international arm of ThaiBev.

Inver House still occupies the same site in Airdrie where they have their headquarters, warehouses holding 500,000 barrels, blending and a bottling plant. Apart from single malts from four of their five distilleries (Balmenach being the exception), the company also produces blends such as Hankey Bannister, McArthur´s and Catto's as well as selling whisky to third parties. Lately, the company has also entered the gin business with premium gin Caorunn which is produced at Balmenach.

PULTENEY DISTILLERY

Springbank

[spring•bank]

Owner: **Region/district:**
Springbank Distillers   Campbeltown
(J & A Mitchell)

Founded: **Status:**   **Capacity:**
1828   Active (vc)   750 000 litres

Address: Well Close, Campbeltown, Argyll PA28 6ET

Website: **Tel:**
springbankdistillers.com   01586 551710

Many whisky drinkers believe that Springbank has always been the one distillery which walks its own path, always relying on sales of their single malts for their success.

But this was not always the case. In the 1960s and 1970s, part of the whisky produced was sold to blenders and that is also why Springbank, like many others, were hit by the crash in the 1980s. They were forced to close the distillery from 1979 to 1987 and when they reopened, Hedley Wright, the owner and the great-great-grandson of one of the founders, made a decision. Never again should they sell their whisky to third parties but instead build their fortune on single malts. Springbank has also been famous for being the only Scottish distillery malting all their barley themselves but from 1960 to 1992, the maltings were closed. Today, however, Springbank is widely considered as a producer of high quality malts with a style of its own. They are also being recognised for their dedication to the Campbeltown community. The hands-on production without very much automation brings jobs to more than 70 people in the town.

The distillery is equipped with a 3.5 ton open cast iron mash tun, six washbacks made of Scandinavian larch with a fermentation time of up to 110 hours, one wash still and two spirit stills. The wash still is unique in Scotland, as it is fired by both an open oil-fire and internal steam coils. Ordinary condensers are used to cool the spirit vapours, except in the first of the two spirit stills, where a worm tub is used. Springbank is also the only distillery in Scotland that malts its entire need of barley using own floor maltings. A lot of investment went into the distillery in 2017 including an additional bottling line, renewing the malting floors and a new boiler.

Springbank produces three distinctive single malts with different phenol contents in the malted barley. Springbank is distilled two and a half times (12-15ppm), Longrow is distilled twice (50-55 ppm) and Hazelburn is distilled three times and unpeated. When Springbank is produced, the malted barley is dried using 6 hours of peat smoke and 30 hours of hot air, while Longrow requires 48 hours of peat smoke to achieve its character. In 2017 a total of 150,000 litres will be produced of which 10% is Longrow and 10% Hazelburn.

The core range is **Springbank 10, 15** and **18 year old**, as well as **12 year old cask strength**. There are also limited but yearly releases of a **21 year old** and a **25 year old**. Longrow is represented by **Longrow** without age statement, the **18 year old** and the **Longrow Red**. The latest edition of the latter was a 13 year old malbec finish. Finally, there is **Hazelburn** where the core range consists of a **10 year old** and the new Hazelburn **Sherry Wood 13 year old**, bottled at cask strength and replacing the 12 year old. Recent, limited editions include **Springbank Local Barley 11 year old, Hazelburn 9 year old Barolo finish** and a **14 year old Springbank** matured in bourbon casks.

History:

1828   The Reid family, in-laws of the Mitchells (see below), founds the distillery.

1837   The Reid family encounters financial difficulties and John and William Mitchell buy the distillery.

1897   J. & A. Mitchell Co Ltd is founded.

1926   The depression forces the distillery to close.

1933   The distillery is back in production.

1960   Own maltings ceases.

1969   J. & A. Mitchell buys the independent bottler Cadenhead.

1979   The distillery closes.

1985   A 10 year old Longrow is launched.

1987   Limited production restarts.

1989   Production restarts.

1992   Springbank takes up its maltings again.

1997   First distillation of Hazelburn.

1998   Springbank 12 years is launched.

1999   Dha Mhile (7 years), the world's first organic single

2000   A 10 year old is launched.

2001   Springbank 1965 'Local barley' (36 years), 741 bottles, is launched.

2002   Number one in the series Wood Expressions is a 12 year old with five years on Demerara rum casks.

2004   Springbank 10 years 100 proof is launched as well as Springbank Wood Expression bourbon, Longrow 14 years old, Springbank 32 years old and Springbank 14 years Port Wood.

2005   Springbank 21 years, the first version of Hazelburn (8 years) and Longrow Tokaji Wood Expression are launched.

2006   Longrow 10 years 100 proof, Springbank 25 years, Springbank 9 years Marsala finish, Springbank 11 years Madeira finish and a new Hazelburn 8 year old are released.

History continued:

2007 Springbank Vintage 1997 and a 16 year old rum wood are released.

2008 The distillery closes temporarily. Three new releases of Longrow - CV, 18 year old and 7 year old Gaja Barolo.

2009 Springbank Madeira 11 year old, Springbank 18 year old, Springbank Vintage 2001 and Hazelburn 12 year old are released.

2010 Springbank 12 year old cask strength and a 12 year old claret expression together with new editions of the CV and 18 year old are released. Longrow 10 year old cask strength and Hazelburn CV are also new.

2011 Longrow 18 year old and Hazelburn 8 year old Sauternes wood expression are released.

2012 New releases include Springbank Rundlets & Kilderkins, Springbank 21 year old and Longrow Red.

2013 Longrow Rundlets & Kilderkins, a new edition of Longrow Red and Springbank 9 year old Gaja Barolo finish are released.

2014 Hazelburn Rundlets & Kilderkins, Hazelburn 10 year old and Springbank 25 years old are launched.

2015 New releases include Springbank Green 12 years old and a new edition of the Longrow Red.

2016 Springbank Local Barley and a 9 year old Hazelburn barolo finish are released.

2017 Springbank 14 year old bourbon cask and Hazelburn 13 year old sherrywood are released.

12 years old c.s.   18 years old   21 years old

Local Barley   Longrow Red

Tasting notes Springbank 10 years old:

GS – Fresh and briny on the nose, with citrus fruit, oak and barley, plus a note of damp earth. Sweet on the palate, with developing brine, nuttiness and vanilla toffee. Long and spicy in the finish, coconut oil and drying peat.

Tasting notes Longrow NAS:

GS – Initially slightly gummy on the nose, but then brine and fat peat notes develop. Vanilla and malt also emerge. The smoky palate offers lively brine and is quite dry and spicy, with some vanilla and lots of ginger. The finish is peaty with persistent, oaky ginger.

Tasting notes Hazelburn 10 years old:

GS – Pear drops, soft toffee and malt on the mildly floral nose. Oiliness develops in time, along with a green, herbal note and ultimately brine. Full-bodied and supple on the smoky palate, with barley and ripe, peppery orchard fruits. Developing cocoa and ginger in the lengthy finish.

Springbank 10 years   Hazelburn 10 years   Longrow

Strathisla

[strath•eye•la]

Owner:
Chivas Bros (Pernod Ricard)

Region/district:
Speyside

Founded:
1786

Status:
Active (vc)

Capacity:
2 200 000 litres

Address: Seafield Avenue, Keith,
Banffshire AB55 5BS

Website:
maltwhiskydistilleries.com

Tel:
01542 783044

James "Jimmy" Barclay, one of the most adventurous and enigmatic profiles of the 20th century whisky industry, has played an important part in the history of Chivas Brothers and Strathisla.

At the age of 16 he started working at Benrinnes distillery as a clerk and later joined Mackie & Co. to work for the legendary Peter Mackie. In 1919 he bought George Ballantine & Son together with R A McKinlay and expanded the brand to be an international player. They sold the company to Hiram Walker in 1938, Barclay joined the board of the Canadian company but soon moved on. In 1949, he was asked by Hiram Walker's fierce competitor, Seagram's, to help them establish a foothold in the Scotch whisky market. He acquired Chivas Brothers, became the managing director and in 1950 bought Strathisla which has been an important part of the Chivas Regal brand both before and after.

Strathisla is the spiritual home to Chivas Regal and is also the signature malt of the blend. With 54 million bottles sold in 2016, the brand places 3rd on the best-selling list. The core range is made up of 12, 18 and 25 year old with several limited editions having been launched over the years. The most recent is Chivas Regal Ultis from 2016, which is the first blended malt in the portfolio. The blend of five malts – Allt-a-Bhainne, Braeval, Longmorn, Strathisla and Tormore – has been made in honour of the five master blenders that have been custodians of the brand since 1909 – Charles Howard, Charles Julian, Allan Baillie, Jimmy Lang and the current Master Blender, Colin Scott

The distillery is equipped with a 5 ton traditional mash tun with a raised copper canopy, seven washbacks made of Oregon pine and three of larch – all with a 54 hour fermentation cycle. There are two pairs of stills in a cramped, but very charming still room. Most of the spirit produced at Strathisla is piped to nearby Glen Keith distillery for filling or to be tankered away.

The core expression is the **12 year old** but there is also one cask strength bottling in the new range The Distillery Reserve Collection which can be found at Chivas´ visitor centres; a **17 year old** bottled at 57.9%.

History:

1786 Alexander Milne and George Taylor found the distillery under the name Milltown, but soon change it to Milton.

1823 MacDonald Ingram & Co. purchases the distillery.

1830 William Longmore acquires the distillery.

1870 The distillery name changes to Strathisla.

1880 William Longmore retires and hands operations to his son-in-law John Geddes-Brown. William Longmore & Co. is formed.

1890 The distillery changes name to Milton.

1940 Jay (George) Pomeroy acquires majority shares in William Longmore & Co. Pomeroy is jailed as a result of dubious business transactions and the distillery goes bankrupt in 1949.

1950 Chivas Brothers buys the run-down distillery at a compulsory auction for £71,000 and starts restoration.

1951 The name reverts to Strathisla.

1965 The number of stills is increased from two to four.

1970 A heavily peated whisky, Craigduff, is produced but production stops later.

2001 The Chivas Group is acquired by Pernod Ricard.

12 years old

Tasting notes Strathisla 12 years old:

GS – Rich on the nose, with sherry, stewed fruits, spices and lots of malt. Full-bodied and almost syrupy on the palate. Toffee, honey, nuts, a whiff of peat and a suggestion of oak. The finish is medium in length, slightly smoky and a with a final flash of ginger.

Strathmill

[strath•mill]

Owner:	Region/district:
Diageo	Speyside

Founded:	Status:	Capacity:
1891	Active	2 600 000 litres

Address: Keith, Banffshire AB55 5DQ

Website:	Tel:
malts.com	01542 883000

Those of you who have visited a couple of Scottish distilleries, will probably, at the beginning of the tour, have encountered a red mill (or, very rarely, green) grinding the malted barley into grist.

In most cases this will have been a Porteus mill (occasionally a Boby). One of these was installed at Strathmill in September 2016, replacing a 6-roller Buhler mill. No big news it would seem apart from the fact that a Swissmade Buhler mill is from the 1970s or later and a Porteus mill can very well have been made in the early 1900s, apart from the fact that the company closed down in the 1970s. So why exchange a later model for an older one and from where did they manage to obtain a Porteus mill? First of all, a Porteus mill is one of the most reliable and durable machines within mechanical engineering that exists. Some of the mills running in Scotland today are more than 100 years old. Secondly, the mill was brought in from Glen Ord which recently went through a total renovation and expansion.

The equipment at Strathmill consists of a 9 ton stainless steel semi-lauter mash tun and six stainless steel washbacks with an average fermentation time of 83 hours. There are two pairs of stills and Strathmill is one of few distilleries still using purifiers on the spirit stills. This device is mounted between the lyne arm and the condenser and acts as a mini-condenser, allowing the lighter alcohols to travel towards the condenser and forcing the heavier alcohols to go back into the still for another distillation. The result is a lighter spirit. The distillery is working a 5-day week with 10 mashes resulting in almost 2 million litres of pure alcohol.

The whisky from Strathmill has always been an important component in J&B blended whisky. Until 2005, the brand was the second best-selling blend in the world after Johnnie Walker, but has since been surpassed by Ballantine's, Chivas Regal and Grant's. In 2016, 43 million bottles were sold with the largest markets being France, Spain and the USA.

The only official bottling is the **12 year old Flora & Fauna**, but a limited **25 year old** was launched in 2014 as part of the Special Releases.

History:

1891 The distillery is founded in an old mill from 1823 and is named Glenisla-Glenlivet Distillery.

1892 The inauguration takes place in June.

1895 The gin company W. & A. Gilbey buys the distillery for £9,500 and names it Strathmill.

1962 W. & A. Gilbey merges with United Wine Traders (including Justerini & Brooks) and forms International Distillers & Vintners (IDV).

1968 The number of stills is increased from two to four and purifiers are added.

1972 IDV is bought by Watney Mann which later the same year is acquired by Grand Metropolitan.

1993 Strathmill becomes available as a single malt for the first time since 1909 as a result of a bottling (1980) from Oddbins.

1997 Guinness and Grand Metropolitan merge and form Diageo.

2001 The first official bottling is a 12 year old in the Flora & Fauna series.

2010 A Manager's Choice single cask from 1996 is released.

2014 A 25 year old is released.

12 years old

Tasting notes Strathmill 12 years old:

GS – Quite reticent on the nose, with nuts, grass and a hint of ginger. Spicy vanilla and nuts dominate the palate. The finish is drying, with peppery oak.

Talisker

[tal•iss•kur]

Owner: Diageo
Region/district: Highlands (Skye)

Founded: 1830
Status: Active (vc)
Capacity: 3 300 000 litres

Address: Carbost, Isle of Skye, Inverness-shire IV47 8SR

Website: malts.com
Tel: 01478 614308 (vc)

To say that it is full steam ahead at Talisker is certainly no exaggeration. The demand for the single malt has been growing constantly during the past decade and to keep up with demand, the owners are doing their utmost to increase production.

Through reduced shutdowns and by introducing one extra mash per week, the goal is to produce 3.3 million litres of alcohol during 2017 – a new record for the distillery! It seems viable that if the distillery continues its development, it'd be likely that the distillery should be up for an expansion in the not too distant future. Some years ago, Diageo set a target that Talisker should break into the Top 10 single malt list in terms of sales and this was achieved in 2014. In 2016 the brand sold 2,680,000 bottles however further progress up the table would take some time as Glen Grant, in 9th place currently, is close to 1 million bottles ahead.

With a phenol specification of 18-20 ppm in the barley, which gives it a phenol content of 5-7 ppm in the new make, Talisker is not as heavily peated as some of its cousins on Islay. Herein lies a part of the success for Talisker as it appeals to the consumers who enjoy smoky whisky but find the Islay malts too overpowering. Together with Blair Athol, Talisker is the most visited Diageo distillery with 75,000 people showing up in 2016. The Isle of Skye is a popular destination and the fact that Talisker up until recently was the only distillery on the island has definitely played its part. Since January 2017 though, they have gained some competition from Torabhaig distillery.

The distillery is equipped with a stainless steel lauter mash tun with a capacity of 8 ton, eight washbacks made of Oregon pine and five stills (two wash stills and three spirit stills), all of which are connected to wooden worm tubs. The wash stills are equipped with a special type of purifiers, which use the colder outside air, and have a u-bend in the lyne arm. The purifiers and the peculiar bend of the lyne arms allow for more copper contact and increase the reflux during distillation. The fermentation time is quite long (65-75 hours) and the middle cut from the spirit still is collected between 76% and 65% which, together with the phenol specification, gives a medium peated spirit. Production in 2017 will be 20 mashes per week which accounts for 3.3 million litres of alcohol.

The range of Talisker single malts has been given plenty of attention in recent years. Talisker's core range now consists of **Skye** and **Storm**, both without age statement, **10, 18, 25** and **30 year old, Distiller's Edition** with an Amoroso sherry finish, **Talisker 57° North** which is released in small batches, and **Port Ruighe**. The latter, which is pronounced Portree after the main town on Isle of Skye, has a finish in ruby port casks. There is also **Dark Storm**, the peatiest Talisker so far, which is exclusive to duty free. A second bottling for duty free, **Neist Point**, was launched in 2015. There is also a **distillery exclusive** without age statement with the latest batch being released in spring 2017.

History:

1830 Hugh and Kenneth MacAskill, sons of the local doctor, found the distillery.

1848 The brothers transfer the lease to North of Scotland Bank and Jack Westland from the bank runs the operations.

1854 Kenneth MacAskill dies.

1857 North of Scotland Bank sells the distillery to Donald MacLennan for £500.

1863 MacLennan experiences difficulties in making operations viable and puts the distillery up for sale.

1865 MacLennan, still working at the distillery, nominates John Anderson as agent in Glasgow.

1867 Anderson & Co. from Glasgow takes over.

1879 John Anderson is imprisoned after having sold non-existing casks of whisky.

1880 New owners are now Alexander Grigor Allan and Roderick Kemp.

1892 Kemp sells his share and buys Macallan Distillery instead.

1894 The Talisker Distillery Ltd is founded.

1895 Allan dies and Thomas Mackenzie, who has been his partner, takes over.

1898 Talisker Distillery merges with Dailuaine-Glenlivet Distillers and Imperial Distillers to form Dailuaine-Talisker Distillers Company.

1916 Thomas Mackenzie dies and the distillery is taken over by a consortium consisting of, among others, John Walker, John Dewar, W. P. Lowrie and Distillers Company Limited (DCL).

1928 The distillery abandons triple distillation.

1960 On 22nd November the distillery catches fire and substantial damage occurs.

1962 The distillery reopens after the fire.

History continued:

1972 Own malting ceases.

1988 Classic Malts are introduced, Talisker 10 years included. A visitor centre is opened.

1998 A new stainless steel/copper mash tun and five new worm tubs are installed. Talisker is launched as a Distillers Edition with an amoroso sherry finish.

2004 Two new bottlings appear, an 18 year old and a 25 year old.

2005 To celebrate the 175th birthday of the distillery, Talisker 175th Anniversary is released. The third edition of the 25 year old cask strength is released.

2006 A 30 year old and the fourth edition of the 25 year old are released.

2007 The second edition of the 30 year old and the fifth edition of the 25 year old are released.

2008 Talisker 57° North, sixth edition of the 25 year old and third edition of the 30 year old are launched.

2009 New editions of the 25 and 30 year old are released.

2010 A 1994 Manager´s Choice single cask and a new edition of the 30 year old are released.

2011 Three limited releases - 25, 30 and 34 year old.

2012 A limited 35 year old is released.

2013 Four new expressions are released – Storm, Dark Storm, Port Ruighe and a 27 year old.

2014 A bottling for the Friends of the Classic Malts is released.

2015 Skye and Neist Point are released.

2016 A distillery exclusive without age statement is released.

Tasting notes Talisker 10 years old:

GS – Quite dense and smoky on the nose, with smoked fish, bladderwrack, sweet fruit and peat. Full-bodied and peaty in the mouthy; complex, with ginger, ozone, dark chocolate, black pepper and a kick of chilli in the long, smoky tail.

Tasting notes Talisker Storm:

GS – The nose offers brine, burning wood embers, vanilla, and honey. The palate is sweet and spicy, with cranberries and blackcurrants, while peat-smoke and black pepper are ever-present. The finish is spicy, with walnuts, and fruity peat.

Port Ruighe

Storm

Skye

Neist Point

Dark Storm

10 years old

18 years

Distiller´s Edition

Tamdhu

[tam•doo]

Owner:
Ian Macleod Distillers

Region/district:
Speyside

Founded: 1897

Status: Active

Capacity: 4 000 000 litres

Address: Knockando, Aberlour, Morayshire AB38 7RP

Website: tamdhu.com

Tel: 01340 872200

When Tamdhu celebrated its 120th anniversary this year it was not in a shy way. In fact, they released the oldest ever bottling from the distillery – a 50 year old that had matured in a first fill European oak sherry butt!

Only 100 decanters were launched in March at a price of £16,000 each. When Edrington, the previous owners for more than a hundred years, sold the distillery to Ian Macleod in 2011, it came as a surprise to many. It was always thought that Edrington would need Tamdhu to fill their need of malt for their blends (Famous Grouse and Cutty Sark). Be that as it may, the shift in ownership proved to be a blessing for malt whisky aficionados. Edrington never showed any greater interest in single malt releases from the distillery while Ian Macleod re-launched the brand just two years after the take-over.

The distillery is equipped with an 11.8 ton semilauter mash tun, nine Oregon pine washbacks with a fermentation time of 59 hours and three pairs of stills. There are a total of 14 warehouses (a mix of dunnage, racked and palletized) and the owners are awaiting permission to build another 11. Production for 2017 will be 16 mashes per week which translates to 3.1 million litres for the entire year. There are plans to build a cooperage on site for cask repairs as well as a fish ladder on the cooling water dam to comply with environmental aspects.

The owners, Ian Macleod, are committed to maturing Tamdhu single malt in sherry casks but the flavour is further enhanced by the fact that they are using both American and European oak. The core range consists of a **10 year old** matured in first and second fill sherry casks and the un chill-filtered **Tamdhu Batch Strength**. Batch two of the latter was released in November 2016 and like the first one, it is a vatting of first- and secondfill sherry casks made of American oak and European oak. Limited releases include the aforementioned **50 year old** and the owners have also announced that we can expect limited Tamdhu single cask releases as well as 12 and 15 year olds in the core range sometime during 2018.

History:

1896 The distillery is founded by Tamdhu Distillery Company, a consortium of whisky blenders with William Grant as the main promoter. Charles Doig is the architect.

1897 The first casks are filled in July.

1898 Highland Distillers Company, which has several of the 1896 consortium members in managerial positions, buys Tamdhu Distillery Company.

1911 The distillery closes.

1913 The distillery reopens.

1928 The distillery is mothballed.

1948 The distillery is in full production again in July.

1950 The floor maltings is replaced by Saladin boxes when the distillery is rebuilt.

1972 The number of stills is increased from two to four.

1975 Two stills augment the previous four.

1976 Tamdhu 8 years is launched as single malt.

2005 An 18 year old and a 25 year old are released.

2009 The distillery is motballed.

2011 The Edrington Group sells the distillery to Ian Macleod Distillers.

2012 Production is resumed.

2013 The first official release from the new owners – a 10 year old.

2015 Tamdhu Batch Strength is released.

2017 A 50 year old is released.

Tasting notes Tamdhu 10 years old:

GS – Soft sherry notes, new leather, almonds, marzipan and a hint of peat on the nose. Very smooth and drinkable, with citrus fruit, gentle spice and more sweet sherry on the palate. Persistent spicy leather, with a sprinkling of black pepper in the finish.

10 years old

Tamnavulin

[tam•na•voo•lin]

Owner: Whyte & Mackay (Emperador)
Region/district: Speyside

Founded: 1966
Status: Active
Capacity: 4 000 000 litres

Address: Tomnavoulin, Ballindalloch, Banffshire AB3 9JA

Website: -
Tel: 01807 590285

Tamnavulin is often described as one of the most anonymous distilleries in Scotland. It is true that almost the entire production is reserved for blending but that doesn´t stop the crew from constantly striving to improve both efficiency and quality.

In 2015, the remaining old Corten steel washbacks were replaced by ones made of stainless steel. A year later the 20,000 litre intermediate spirits receiver was replaced by one twice its original size which allows them to continue to produce all through the week without any interruptions. In 2017, the milling system was replaced in order to get a better control of the grist and at the same time, a lot of maturing whisky was re-racked from poorer quality wood into first fill bourbon.

Tamnavulin distillery is equipped with a full lauter mash tun with an 11 ton capacity, nine washbacks made of stainless steel with a fermentation time of 60 hours (an increase from the previous 48) and three pairs of stills. During 2017, the owners will be doing 18 mashes per week but due to a prolonged silent season (to replace the mill and install a new boiler), the total production will remain at 3.5 million litres of alcohol. From 2010 to 2013, part of the yearly production (around 5%) was heavily peated with a phenol specification in the barley of 55ppm. There has been no peated production since but they have retained the feints from the last run which means they can go straight into peated production should they choose to do so.

The character of Tamnavulin new make is slightly grassy with a 25 minute foreshot and a middle cut running from 75% down to 60%. The spirit always goes into first fill bourbon and part of it is then finished in sherry casks.

There used to be an official 12 year old bottling but this was discontinued years ago. In autumn 2016, however, a new **Tamnavulin Double Cask** with a sherry finish, was released as an exclsuive for the UK market to celebrate the distillery´s 50th anniversary. Since then it has been launched in Spain, Belgium and France as well.

History:

1966 Tamnavulin-Glenlivet Distillery Company, a subsidiary of Invergordon Distillers Ltd, founds Tamnavulin.

1993 Whyte & Mackay buys Invergordon Distillers.

1995 The distillery closes in May.

1996 Whyte & Mackay changes name to JBB (Greater Europe).

2000 Distillation takes place for six weeks.

2001 Company management buy out operations for £208 million and rename the company Kyndal.

2003 Kyndal changes name to Whyte & Mackay.

2007 United Spirits buys Whyte & Mackay. Tamnavulin is opened again in July after having been mothballed for 12 years.

2014 Whyte & Mackay is sold to Emperador Inc.

2016 Tamnavulin Double Cask is released.

Double Cask

Tasting notes Tamnavulin Double Cask:

GS – The nose offers malt, soft toffee, almonds and tangerines. Finally, background earthiness. Smooth on the palate, with ginger nut biscuits, vanilla and orchard fruits, plus walnuts. The finish is medium in length, with lingering fruity spice.

Teaninich

[tee•ni•nick]

Owner: Diageo
Region/district: Northern Highlands

Founded: 1817
Status: Active
Capacity: 10 200 000 litres

Address: Alness, Ross-shire IV17 0XB

Website: malts.com
Tel: 01349 885001

There are two pieces of equipment that differentiate Teaninich from all other Scottish distilleries except the newly created Inchdairnie – a hammer mill and a mash filter.

Both are commonly used in breweries for grinding and mashing the barley but extremely unusual in the distilling industry. The process in essence is as follows: The malt is ground into fine flour without husks in an Asnong hammer mill. The grist is mixed with water in a conversion vessel. Once the conversion from starch to sugar is done, the mash passes through a Meura 2001 mash filter which consists of a number of mesh bags. The filter compresses the bags and the wort is collected for the next step – fermentation. The advantages with a hammer mill and a mash filter is the efficiency, the high yield and also that you get a very clear wort. The drawbacks, and the reasons this technicue hasn´t been implemented at other distilleries, is that it is significantly more expensive to install than a traditional mash tun. The clear wort would also be negative for distilleries that rely on a cloudy wort for the character of their newmake, like Knockando and Strathmill for instance. And of course, there is always the fear of changing the flavour of your whisky if you make radical changes to any of the three main steps in production – mashing, fermentation and distillation.

A huge expansion of the distillery was conducted in 2015 which lead to a doubled capacity. The equipment now consists of a new filter with a 14 ton mash to cope with the larger volumes. There are also 18 wooden washbacks and two made of stainless steel – all with a fermentation time of 75 hours. Three of the original wash stills have been altered into spirit stills so that the old still house now houses all six spirit stills, while a new house has been built for the six, new wash stills. At the moment, the distillery is doing 16 mashes per week. There were also plans to build a completely new distillery on the same grounds as Teaninich but these plans have been postponed.

The only official core bottling is a **10 year old** in the Flora & Fauna series but a limited **17 year old** matured in refill American oak was launched in autumn 2017 as part of the Special Releases.

History:

1817 Captain Hugh Monro, owner of the estate Teaninich, founds the distillery.
1831 Captain Munro sells the estate to his younger brother John.
1850 John Munro, who spends most of his time in India, leases Teaninich to the infamous Robert Pattison from Leith.
1869 John McGilchrist Ross takes over the licence.
1895 Munro & Cameron takes over the licence.
1898 Munro & Cameron buys the distillery.
1904 Robert Innes Cameron becomes sole owner of Teaninich.
1932 Robert Innes Cameron dies.
1933 The estate of Robert Innes Cameron sells the distillery to Distillers Company Limited.
1970 A new distillation unit with six stills is commissioned and becomes known as the A side.
1975 A dark grains plant is built.
1984 The B side of the distillery is mothballed.
1985 The A side is also mothballed.
1991 The A side is in production again.
1992 United Distillers launches a 10 year old Teaninich in the Flora & Fauna series.
1999 The B side is decommissioned.
2000 A mash filter is installed.
2009 Teaninich 1996, a single cask in the new Manager´s Choice range is released.
2014 Another six stills and eight washbacks are installed and the capacity is doubled.
2015 The distillery is expanded with six new stills and the capacity is doubled.
2017 A 17 year old is launched as part of the Special Releases.

Tasting notes Teaninich 10 years old:

GS – The nose is initially fresh and grassy, quite light, with vanilla and hints of tinned pineapple. Mediumbodied, smooth, slightly oily, with cereal and spice in the mouth. Nutty and slowly drying in the finish, with pepper and a suggestion of cocoa powder notes.

17 years old

Tobermory

[tow•bur•mo•ray]

Owner:
Distell International Ltd.

Region/district:
Highland (Mull)

Founded: 1798

Status: Active (vc)

Capacity: 1 000 000 litres

Address: Tobermory, Isle of Mull, Argyllsh. PA75 6NR

Website: tobermorydistillery.com

Tel: 01688 302647

Tobermory is closed but it is not as alarming as it may sound. It will stay closed at least until late 2018 due to a substantial upgrade of both the distillery and the visitor centre.

The distillery was known as Tobermory from 1798 until its closure in 1930. In 1972, when the distillery was re-opened, the new owners decided to name the distillery Ledaig Distillery. Seven years later it was time for yet another change of ownership when Stewart Jowett took over. During the sporadic production years of his ownership, he continued to use the name Ledaig. However, to confuse matters even further, he also launched both a blended whisky and a vatted malt under the name Tobermory. Nine years after Burn Stewart´s take-over in 1993, a decision was taken to use Tobermory as the brand for unpeated malts and Ledaig was reserved for all peated expressions with a phenol content of 30-40 ppm.

The distillery is equipped with a traditional 5 ton cast iron mash tun, four wooden washbacks with a fermentation time of 50 to 90 hours and two pairs of stills. Two of the stills were replaced in August 2014 with the other two being replaced during the current upgrade. Before the temporary closure, the production was 8 mashes per week and 750,000 litres of alcohol with a 50/50 split between Ledaig and Tobermory.

The core range from Tobermory distillery is the **10 and 18 year old Ledaig** with **10 year old Tobermory** now being sold only (at least temporarily) in the distillery shop. Also available at the distillery are **Tobermory 14 year old** with a port finish, a **12 year old Tobermory** matured in palo cortado sherry casks, a **Ledaig 16 year old** American oak and a **20 year old Ledaig** with a moscatel finish. In 2017, several limited bottlings were launched – a **Tobermory 21 year old** manzanilla finish, a **15 year old Tobermory** marsala finish, a **13 year old Ledaig** matured in amontillado sherry casks and a **19 year old Ledaig** with an extra maturation in marsala casks.

History:

1798 John Sinclair founds the distillery.

1837 The distillery closes.

1878 The distillery reopens.

1890 John Hopkins & Company buys the distillery.

1916 Distillers Company Limited (DCL) takes over John Hopkins & Company.

1930 The distillery closes.

1972 A shipping company in Liverpool and the sherrymaker Domecq buy the buildings and embark on refurbishment. When work is completed it is named Ledaig Distillery Ltd.

1975 Ledaig Distillery Ltd files for bankruptcy and the distillery closes again.

1979 The estate agent Kirkleavington Property buys the distillery, forms a new company, Tobermory Distillers Ltd and starts production.

1982 No production. Some of the buildings are converted into flats and some are rented to a dairy company for cheese storage.

1989 Production resumes.

1993 Burn Stewart Distillers buys Tobermory for £600,000 and pays an additional £200,000 for the whisky supply.

2002 Trinidad-based venture capitalists CL Financial buys Burn Stewart Distillers for £50m.

2005 A 32 year old from 1972 is launched.

2007 A Ledaig 10 year old is released.

2008 A limited edition Tobermory 15 year old is released.

2013 Burn Stewart Distillers is sold to Distell Group Ltd. A 40 year old Ledaig is released.

2015 Ledaig 18 years and 42 years are released together with Tobermory 42 years.

2017 The distillery is closed for refurbishing.

Tasting notes Tobermory 10 years old:
GS – Fresh and nutty on the nose, with citrus fruit and brittle toffee. A whiff of peat. Medium-bodied, quite dry on the palate with delicate peat, malt and nuts. Medium finish with a hint of mint and a slight citric tang.

Tasting notes Ledaig 10 years old:
GS – The nose is profoundly peaty, sweet and full, with notes of butter and smoked fish. Bold, yet sweet on the palate, with iodine, soft peat and heather. Developing spices. The finish is medium to long, with pepper, ginger, liquorice and peat.

10 years old

Tomatin

[to•mat•in]

Owner: **Region/district:**
Tomatin Distillery Co   Highland
(Takara Shuzo Co., Kokubu & Co., Marubeni Corp.)

Founded:	Status:	Capacity:
1897	Active (vc)	5 000 000 litres

Address: Tomatin, Inverness-shire IV13 7YT

Website: **Tel:**
tomatin.com   01463 248144 (vc)

As a consumer you are really spoilt for choice when it comes to Tomatin single malt. Currently there are around 30 different expressions to choose from. Looking back at the first edition of the Malt Whisky Yearbook in 2006 – there were two!

The owners have begun an incredible journey which is apparent in the number of visitors to the distillery, more than 40,000 per year, and sales, with 530,000 bottles sold in 2016. This journey has taken the distillery from being a provider of tanks of young whisky to third parties to a producer of high class single malts.

The distillery is equipped with one 8 ton stainless steel mash tun, 12 stainless steel washbacks with a fermentation time from 54 to 108 hours and six pairs of stills (only four of the spirit stills are still in use). The goal is to produce 1.7 million litres in 2017, including a couple of weeks of peated production at 30-35ppm. Recently, the owners have prepared nine water beds with 28,000 plants through which effluents, especially spent lees containing copper, are pumped. This biological way of reducing toxic waste can also be seen at Glengoyne and Knockdhu.

The core range consists of **Legacy** (without age statement), **12**, **18** and **36 year old**. Included are also **Cask Strength, 14 year old port finish** and a **Vintage 1988**. Recent limited releases include a new range focusing on the effect of different cask maturations called Five Virtues with **Wood, Fire** and **Earth** released so far. There are also a number of vintages; **1981, 1995, 2002 Cabernet Sauvignon** and **2007 Carribean rum** as well as **Contrast**, a pack of two bottles (bourbon and sherry matured) with whiskies from six vintages. **Warehouse 6 Collection**, a new range of 40-year-old-plus whiskies, was introduced in July 2016. Two expressions have been released so far – **1971** and **1972**. In 2016, the distillery´s first range for duty-free was launched including **8, 12, 15** and **40 year olds**. The smoky side of Tomatin is represented by **Cù Bòcan** without age statement, **Cù Bòcan Sherry, Cù Bòcan Virgin Oak, Cù Bòcan Bourbon** and four vintages; **1988, 1989, 2005** and, released in September 2017, **2006**.

History:

1897 The distillery is founded by Tomatin Spey Distillery Company.

1906 Production ceases.

1909 Production resumes through Tomatin Distillers.

1956 Stills are increased from two to four.

1958 Another two stills are added.

1961 The six stills are increased to ten.

1974 The stills now total 23 and the maltings closes.

1985 The distillery company goes into liquidation.

1986 Takara Shuzo Co. and Okara & Co., buy Tomatin through Tomatin Distillery Co.

1998 Okara & Co is liquidated and Marubeni buys out part of their shareholding.

2004 Tomatin 12 years is launched.

2005 A 25 year old and a 1973 Vintage are released.

2006 An 18 year old and a 1962 Vintage are launched.

2008 A 30 and a 40 year old as well as several vintages from 1975 and 1995 are released.

2009 A 15 year old, a 21 year old and four single casks (1973, 1982, 1997 and 1999) are released.

2010 The first peated release - a 4 year old exclusive for Japan.

2011 A 30 year old and Tomatin Decades are released.

2013 Cù Bòcan, the first peated Tomatin, is released.

2014 14 year old port finish, 36 year old, Vintage 1988, Tomatin Cuatro, Cù Bòcan Sherry Cask and Cù Bòcan 1989 are released.

2015 Cask Strength and Cù Bòcan Virgin Oak are released.

2016 A 44 year old Tomatin and two Cù Bòcan vintages (1988 and 2005) are released.

2017 New releases include Wood, Fire and Earth as well as a 2006 Cù Bòcan.

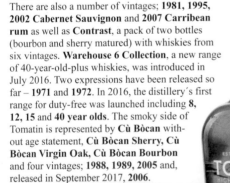

12 years old

Tasting notes Tomatin 12 years old:

GS – Barley, spice, buttery oak and a floral note on the nose. Sweet and medium-bodied, with toffee apples, spice and herbs in the mouth. Medium-length in the finish, with sweet fruitiness.

Tomintoul

[tom•in•towel]

Owner: **Region/district:**
Angus Dundee Distillers   Speyside

Founded: **Status:**   **Capacity:**
1965   Active   3 300 000 litres

Address: Ballindalloch, Banffshire AB37 9AQ

Website: **Tel:**
tomintouldistillery.co.uk   01807 590274

The owners of Tomintoul and Glencadam distilleries, Angus Dundee, keep a low profile and may be anonymous to the average whisky lover but they account for 5% of Scotland's whisky exports.

Founded by Terry Hillman, the company is still family-owned and is run today by his children Tania and Aaron. Apart from owning the two distilleries, the company also runs a blending business creating brands such as The Dundee, Scottish Royal and Big Ben and the company has a turnover of £55m per year. An instrumental part of the company's success has been Robert Fleming who is the Distillery Director. After spending the first years of his career with Chivas Bothers, he took up the role as manager at Tomintoul in 1990 and was appointed a director of Angus Dundee after they had taken over the distillery in 2000.

Tomintoul distillery is equipped with a 12 ton semi lauter mash tun, six stainless steel washbacks with a fermentation time of 54-60 hours and two pairs of stills. There are currently 15 mashes per week, which means that capacity is used to its maximum, and a number of racked and palletised warehouses have a storage capacity of 120,000 casks. The malt used for mashing is unpeated, but every year since 2001, heavily peated (55ppm) spirit is also produced. In 2017, 850 tons of peated malt will be processed in June and December which amounts to 360,000 litres of pure alcohol. On the site there is also a blend centre with 14 large blending vats.

The core range consists of **Tlàth** without age statement, **10, 14, 16, 21** and **25 year old**. There are also two finishes; a **12 year old** with an extra maturation in **oloroso sherry** casks and a **15 year old port finish**. The peaty side of Tomintoul is represented by **Peaty Tang** and, as a standalone range, **Old Ballantruan** and **Old Ballantruan 10 year old**. Two new expressions were released in July 2017 – the **15 year old Peaty Tang** (40%) and a **15 year old Old Ballantruan** (50%). Recent limited releases include a **1976 Vintage** (the latest bottling from 2013), a **Single Sherry Cask** (the most recent distilled in 1977), **Five Decades** and, launched in 2016, a **40 year old**. Only 500 bottles were filled of the latter.

History:

1965 The distillery is founded by Tomintoul Distillery Ltd, which is owned by Hay & MacLeod & Co. and W. & S. Strong & Co.

1973 Scottish & Universal Investment Trust, owned by the Fraser family, buys the distillery. It buys Whyte & Mackay the same year and transfers Tomintoul to that company.

1974 The two stills are increased to four and Tomintoul 12 years is launched.

1978 Lonhro buys Scottish & Universal Investment Trust.

1989 Lonhro sells Whyte & Mackay to Brent Walker.

1990 American Brands buys Whyte & Mackay.

1996 Whyte & Mackay changes name to JBB (Greater Europe).

2000 Angus Dundee plc buys Tomintoul.

2002 Tomintoul 10 year is launched.

2003 Tomintoul 16 years is launched.

2004 Tomintoul 27 years is launched.

2005 A young, peated version called Old Ballantruan is launched.

2008 1976 Vintage and Peaty Tang are released.

2009 A 14 year old and a 33 year old are released.

2010 A 12 year old Port wood finish is released.

2011 A 21 year old, a 10 year old Ballantruan and Vintage 1966 are released.

2012 Old Ballantruan 10 years old is released.

2013 A 31 year old single cask is released.

2015 Five Decades and a 40 year old are released.

2016 A 40 year old and Tlàth without age statement are launched.

2017 15 year old Peaty Tang and 15 year old Old Ballantruan are launched.

Tasting notes Tomintoul 10 years old:

GS – A light, fresh and fruity nose, with ripe peaches and pineapple cheesecake, delicate spice and background malt. Medium-bodied, fruity and fudgy on the palate. The finish offers wine gums, mild, gently spiced oak, malt and a suggestion of smoke.

10 years old

Tormore

[tor•more]

Owner:	**Region/district:**
Chivas Bros (Pernod Ricard)	Speyside
Founded: **Status:**	**Capacity:**
1958 Active	4 800 000 litres

Address: Tormore, Advie, Grantown-on-Spey, Morayshire PH26 3LR

Website:	**Tel:**
tormoredistillery.com	01807 510244

Among the previous owners of Tormore Distillery there have been a couple of controversial characters that stick out. Less so for their knowledge of the production of whisky but more for their unorthodox and sometimes dubious ways of conducting business.

First was Lewis Rosenstiel, owner of the company that founded Tormore – Schenley Industries. He made it big during prohibition as a dealer in spirits and wines and was indicted but never convicted for bootlegging. It wasn't until after his death in 1976, that the truth about Rosenstiel´s connections with Mafia members such as Frank Costello and Meyer Lansky really became known. Schenley Industries (including Tormore) was sold to Rapid American in 1968. The owner of that company, Meshulam Riklis, became known as the "inventor" of junk bond transactions and leveraged buyouts. When his company went bankrupt it had debts up to $3 billion. He was also suspected of manipulating the share price of Guinness which helped to beat off competitors when Guinness took over DCL in 1986.

From the outside, Tormore is without competition the most unusual looking distillery in Scotland, at least until the new Macallan has been opened. When it was built in the 1950s it was decided by the owners that it should become a showpiece. The famous architect Sir Albert Richardson was called in and the result is magnificent from the green copper roofs to the elegant, barred windows. You can enjoy it from the A95 in the middle of Speyside but unfortunately they do not accept visitors. Following an upgrade in 2012, Tormore is now equipped with a stainless steel full lauter mash tun, 11 stainless steel washbacks and four pairs of stills. Tormore single malt is known for its fruity and light character which is achieved by a clear wort, a slow distillation and by using purifiers on all the stills.

Nearly everything that is produced at Tormore is used for blended Scotch but there is a **14 year old** bottled at 43% and a **16 year old**, non chill-filtered, bottled at 48%. Both have been matured in American oak.

History:

- **1958** Schenley International, owners of Long John, founds the distillery.
- **1960** The distillery is ready for production.
- **1972** The number of stills is increased from four to eight.
- **1975** Schenley sells Long John and its distilleries (including Tormore) to Whitbread.
- **1989** Allied Lyons (to become Allied Domecq) buys the spirits division of Whitbread.
- **1991** Allied Distillers introduce Caledonian Malts where Miltonduff, Glendronach and Laphroaig are represented besides Tormore. Tormore is later replaced by Scapa.
- **2004** Tormore 12 year old is launched as an official bottling.
- **2005** Chivas Brothers (Pernod Ricard) becomes new owners through the acquisition of Allied Domecq.
- **2012** Production capacity is increased by 20%.
- **2014** The 12 year old is replaced by two new expressions - 14 and 16 year old.

Tasting notes Tormore 14 years old:

GS – Vanilla, butterscotch, summer berries and light spice on the nose. Milk chocolate and tropical fruit on the smooth palate, with soft toffee. Lengthy in the finish, with a sprinkling of black pepper.

14 years old

Tullibardine

[tully•bar•din]

Owner:	**Region/district:**
Terroir Distillers	Highlands
(Picard Vins & Spiritueux)	
Founded: **Status:**	**Capacity:**
1949 Active (vc)	3 000 000 litres

Address: Blackford, Perthshire PH4 1QG

Website:	**Tel:**
tullibardine.com	01764 682252

When the wine producer Picard bought Tullibardine distillery in 2011 they set up a company to handle their growing distillery side of operations. Apart from Tullibardine, Terroir Distillers now include two distilleries in France and four bottling plants.

Through the company, they produce and distribute Scotch whisky, pastis, bitters, rhum agricole and eau de vie. In 2015 they also added cognac to the portfolio when they acquired the Louis Royer brand from Suntory. The new owners have invested heavily in Tullibardine which has resulted in a new visitor centre, a bottling line, a vatting hall, more warehouses and even a small cooperage used for repairing casks.

Tullibardine is also the spiritual home to the famous brand, Highland Queen. First launched in 1893 the brand had its heyday in the 1970s when it was popularly sold all over the world. In 2008, it was taken over by the Picard family. The range, with Tullibardine single malt as a key component, now consists of three blends and six single malts, the oldest being a 40 year old.

Tightly fitted into a very cramped production area, the equipment consists of a 6 ton stainless steel semi-lauter mash tun, nine stainless steel washbacks with a fermentation of 52-70 hours and two pairs of stills. After a couple of years with reduced production, the distillery is on maximum capacity since 2016 which means 26 mashes per week, producing 3 million litres of alcohol.

The core range of Tullibardine single malts consists of **Sovereign**, bourbon matured and without age statement, three wood finishes; **225 Sauternes finish**, **228 Burgundy finish** and **500 Sherry finish** and two older bottlings – a **20 year old** and a **25 year old**. A new range called Custodian's Collection was introduced in 2015 with a **50 year old** as the first release. This was followed up in 2016 with a **Vintage 1970** and yet again in September 2017 with a **Vintage 1962**. The first cask strength Tullibardine made this century was **The Murray 2004 vintage**, launched in 2016. A new edition, **The Murray Chateauneuf-du-Pape**, was released in 2017.

History:

- **1949** The architect William Delmé-Evans founds the distillery.
- **1953** The distillery is sold to Brodie Hepburn.
- **1971** Invergordon Distillers buys Brodie Hepburn Ltd.
- **1973** The number of stills increases to four.
- **1993** Whyte & Mackay (owned by Fortune Brands) buys Invergordon Distillers.
- **1994** Tullibardine is mothballed.
- **1996** Whyte & Mackay changes name to JBB (Greater Europe).
- **2001** JBB (Greater Europe) is bought out from Fortune Brands by management and changes name to Kyndal (Whyte & Mackay from 2003).
- **2003** A consortium buys Tullibardine for £1.1 million. The distillery is in production again by December.
- **2005** Three wood finishes from 1993, Port, Moscatel and Marsala, are launched together with a 1986 John Black selection.
- **2006** Vintage 1966, Sherry Wood 1993 and a new John Black selection are launched.
- **2007** Five different wood finishes and a couple of single cask vintages are released.
- **2008** A Vintage 1968 40 year old is released.
- **2009** Aged Oak is released.
- **2011** Three vintages and a wood finish are released. Picard buys the distillery.
- **2013** A completely new range is launched – Sovereign, 225 Sauternes, 228 Burgundy, 500 Sherry, 20 year old and 25 year old.
- **2015** A 60 year old Custodian Collection is released.
- **2016** A Vintage 1970 and The Murray from 2004 are released.
- **2017** Vintage 1962 and The Murray Chateauneuf-du-Pape are released.

Tasting notes Tullibardine Sovereign:

GS – Floral on the nose, with new-mown hay, vanilla and fudge. Fruity on the palate, with milk chocolate, brazil nuts, marzipan, malt, and a hint of cinnamon. Cocoa, vanilla, a squeeze of lemon and more spice in the finish.

Sovereign

Ncn`ean Distillery stillhouse

New
distilleries

New distilleries are being opened in Scotland
at a rate we haven´t experienced since the great whisky boom
of the late 19th century. In the first twelve years of the new millennium,
six new malt whisky distilleries opened up in Scotland. In the next four
years, another fourteen distilleries came on stream and in 2017 alone,
six more distilleries were added! There are at least another
22 distilleries in different stages of construction or planning.
In theory, this means that in a couple of years there could be a
total of 140 malt whisky distilleries operating in Scotland.

Wolfburn

[wolf•burn]

Owner: Aurora Brewing Ltd.

Region/district: Northern Highlands

Founded: 2013

Status: Active

Capacity: 135 000 litres

Address: Henderson Park, Thurso, Caithness KW14 7XW

Website: wolfburn.com

Tel: 01847 891051

The most northerly distillery on the Scottish mainland, Wolfburn, is situated in an industrial area on the outskirts of Thurso.

There are four, large, newly constructed buildings of which one is the distillery, while the other three are warehouses and a bottling plant. The owners have chosen a site that is situated 350 metres from the ruins of the old Wolfburn Distillery. Construction work commenced in August 2012 and the first newmake came off the stills at the end of January 2013. From the very onset, before the equipment was ordered, the company hired Shane Fraser as the distillery manager. Shane had previously managed Glenfarclas.

The distillery is equipped with a 1.1 ton semi-lauter stainless steel mash tun with a copper canopy, four stainless steel washbacks with a fermentation time of 70-92 hours, holding 5,500 litres each, one wash still (5,500 litres) and one spirit still (3,600 litres). Each mash takes about 6 hours

and the run in the spirit still is 10 minutes of foreshots, 2 hours of spirit cut and 2 hours on feints. Wolfburn uses a mix of casks: approximately one third of the spirit is laid down in ex-bourbon quarter casks, a further third is in ex-bourbon hogsheads as well as barrels, and the final third is laid down in ex-sherry butts.

The main part of the malt is unpeated and the intention is to create a smooth whisky. However, since 2014, a lightly peated (10 ppm) spirit has also been produced. The inaugural bottling from the distillery appeared in early 2016 and had a smoky profile due to the fact that it had partly been matured in quarter casks from Islay. This limited release was followed by a more widely available bourbon matured whisky which in September 2016 was re-named Northland. At the same time a second bottling appeared, Aurora, which had been partly matured in oloroso sherry casks. A range of limited releases named Kylver started in summer 2016 and so far two varieties have been launched.

Kingsbarns

[kings•barns]

Owner: Wemyss family

Region/district: Lowlands

Founded: 2014

Status: Active (vc)

Capacity: 600 000 litres

Address: East Newhall Farm, Kingsbarns, St Andrews KY16 8QE

Website: kingsbarnsdistillery.com

Tel: 01333 451300

The plans for this distillery near St Andrews in Fife, were drafted in 2008 and came to fruition in 2014 when the distillery was opened.

The idea, initiated by Doug Clement, was to restore a dilapidated farmhouse from the late 18th century and turn it into a modern distillery. Planning permission was received in March 2011 and in September 2012, the Scottish government awarded a grant of £670,000. This, in turn, led to the Wemyss family agreeing to inject £3m into the project and becoming the new owners. The family-owned company owns and operates the independent bottling company, Wemyss Malts, and also owns other companies in the field of wine and gin.

Construction began in June 2013 and the distillery was officially opened on 30th November 2014 on St Andrew's Day. Commissioning of the distillery began in January

2015 with the first casks being filled early in March. The distillery is equipped with a 1.5 ton stainless steel mash tun, four 7,500 litre stainless steel washbacks with a fermentation time of 65-80 hours, one 7,500 litre wash still and one 4,500 litre spirit still. First fill bourbon barrels are used for maturation, together with some sherry butts. Production was increased in October 2016 to 7 mashes per week, with annual production increasing from 140,000 to 200,000 litres of alcohol. Further expansion is being considered.

There are several different types of tours for visitors to choose from. New make spirit is available, both for tasting on the tour and in the shop. Also, a limited bottling of 2 year old spirit was released at the distillery in June 2017. The first bottling of Kingsbarns Single Malt is expected in summer 2018 and will be exclusively available to members of the Kingsbarns Founders' Club.

Ballindalloch

[bal•lin•da•lock]

Owner:
The Macpherson-Grant family

Region/district:
Speyside

Founded: 2014
Status: Active (vc)
Capacity: 100 000 litres

Address: Ballindalloch, Banffshire AB37 9AA

Website:
ballindallochdistillery.com

Tel:
01807 500 331

In the heart of Speyside, the owners of Ballindalloch Castle, the Macpherson-Grant family, decided in 2012 to turn a steading from 1820 into a whisky distillery.

Previous generations of the family had been involved in distilling from the 1860s and from 1923 to 1965, they owned part of Cragganmore distillery, not far away from the castle. The old farm building was meticulously renovated with attention given to every little detail and the result is an amazingly beautiful distillery which can be seen from the A95 between Aberlour and Grantown-on-Spey.

Ballindalloch distillery takes its water from the nearby Garline Springs and all the barley (currently Concerto) is grown on the Estate. All of the distillery equipment are gathered on the second floor which makes it easy for visitors to get a good view of the production. The equipment consists of an extraordinary 1 ton semi lauter,

copper clad mash tun with a copper dome. There are four washbacks made of Oregon pine with two short (66 hours) fermentations per week and three long (114 hours). Finally there is a 5,000 litre lantern-shaped wash still and a 3,600 litre spirit still with a reflux ball. Both stills are connected to two wooden worm tubs for cooling the spirit vapours. The distillery is run by three persons only and, with no automation or computers. The distillery came on stream in September 2014 and was officially opened 16th April 2015 by Prince Charles. The distillery is working 5 days a week, making 100,000 litres of alcohol. The idea is to produce a robust and bold whisky, enhanced not least by the use of worm tubs. The one warehouse on site, filled up quickly and in May 2015 they started to move casks into a second warehouse close to Glenfarclas distillery.

The distillery is open for visitors by appointment and there is also the opportunity to take part in The Art of Whisky Making, which means spending a day with the crew and learning about whisky from mashing to warehousing.

Ardnamurchan

[ard•ne•mur•ken]

Owner:
Adelphi Distillery Ltd

Region/district:
Western Highlands

Founded: 2014
Status: Active (vc)
Capacity: 500 000 litres

Address: Glenbeg, Ardnamurchan, Argyll PH36 4JG

Website:
adelphidistillery.com

Tel:
01972 500 285

The success for the independent bottler, Adelphi Distillery, has forced the owners to build their own distillery.

The chosen site is Glenbeg on the Ardnamurchan peninsula, just north of Isle of Mull, which makes it the most westerly distillery on mainland Scotland. It is a stunning location, on the shores of Loch Sunart, overlooking the Atlantic. Most of the buildings were completed by August 2013, the equipment started to arrive in the autumn and, on 11th July 2014, the distillery came on stream. The distillery was officially opened two weeks later by Princess Anne.

The distillery is equipped with a 2 tonne semi lauter mash tun made of stainless steel with a copper canopy, four oak washbacks and three made of stainless steel, a wash still (10,000 litres) and a spirit still (6,000 litres). The four wooden washbacks are very special because they were retrieved in France, where they had been used as cognac

vats, were dismantled and then rebuilt at Ardnamurchan. Minimum fermentation time is 72 hours. The production started with 2 mashes per week and has now increased to five, which means around 180,000 litres per year with the intention of moving to 400,000 litres sometime soon. Two different styles of whisky are produced; peated for six months of the year and unpeated for the rest. For the peated spirit, the barley has a phenol specification of 30-35ppm. The ultimate goal is to have the ability to floor malt a high proportion of their own barley as well.

The owners have put in a lot of effort into creating a distillery whose environmental footprint is as small as possible and all the power and heat requirements for the distillery come from local renewables. Adelphi Distillery is named after a distillery which closed in 1902. The company is owned by Keith Falconer and Donald Houston, with Alex Bruce as Managing Director.

Annandale

[ann•an•dail]

Owner: Annandale Distillery Co.	**Region/district:** Lowlands

Founded:	**Status:**	**Capacity:**
2014	Active (vc)	500 000 litres

Address: Northfield, Annan, Dumfriesshire DG12 5LL

Website: annandaledistillery.com	**Tel:** 01461 207817

In 2010 Professor David Thomson and his wife, Teresa Church, obtained consent from the local council for the building of the new Annandale Distillery in Dumfries and Galloway in the south-west of Scotland.

The old one had been producing since 1836 and was owned by Johnnie Walker from 1895 until it closed down in 1918. From 1924 to 2007, the site was owned by the Robinson family, who were famous for their Provost brand of porridge oats. David Thomson began the restoration of the site in June 2011 with the two, old sandstone warehouses being restored to function as two-level dunnage warehouses. The distillery was in a poor condition and the mash house and the tun room was largely reconstructed while the other buildings were refurbished substantially. The old maltings, with the kiln and original pagoda roof, have been turned into an excellent visitor centre. The total cost, including restoration, construction and new equipment amounted to £10.5m.

Entering the production area of the new distillery is like walking into a beautiful village church. First you run into the 2.5 ton semi-lauter mash tun with an elegant copper dome. Then, with three wooden washbacks (a fermentation time of 72-96 hours) on each side, you are guided up to the two spirit stills (4,000 litres). Once you have reached them, you find the wash still (12,000 litres) slightly hidden behind a wall. The capacity is 500,000 litres per annum but so far they have been working one shift, which means 6 mashes per week and 250,000 litres. The casks used for maturation are first fill and second fill bourbon barrels but sherry butts have also been filled.

The first cask was filled on 15 November 2014 and both unpeated and peated (45ppm) whisky is distilled. New make of the two styles has been released under the name Rascally Liquor.

Inchdairnie

[inch•dairnie]

Owner: John Fergus & Co. Ltd	**Region/district:** Lowlands

Founded:	**Status:**	**Capacity:**
2015	Active	2 000 000 litres

Address: Whitecraigs Rd, Glenrothes, Fife KY6 2RX

Website: inchdairniedistillery.com	**Tel:** 01595 510010

The majority of new and planned distilleries in Scotland (except the ones built by the biggest companies) are quite small with a capacity of 50-500,000 litres.

A rare exception is Inchdairnie, which was officially opened in May 2016, a few miles west of Glenrothes in Fife. The distillery will be able to distil 2 million litres per year with a possibility of expanding to 4 million litres. The distillery is owned by John Fergus & Co. which was founded by Ian Palmer in 2011. Palmer has 40 years of experience in the Scotch whisky industry and his latest position was general manager for Glen Turner. He is a minority share holder, with CES Whisky holding the rest of the shares.

With an investment of £10m, it took only 18 months to build and the distillery is equipped with a Meura mash filter, instead of a traditional mash tun. There is only one distillery in Scotland, Teaninich, that already uses this technique. Working with a mash filter also means a hammer mill must be used to create a finer grist compared to, for example, a Porteus mill. There are four washbacks with a fermentation time of 72 hours and one pair of traditional pot stills with double condensers and aftercoolers to increase the copper to spirit ratio. The two stills are complemented by a Lomond still with six plates to provide the opportunity for triple distillation and experimental distillation. A unique yeast recipe combining beer-, wine- and distiller's yeast is used and high gravity fermentation will create a fruitier character of the newmake.

Two main styles of whisky will be produced. Strathenry (80% of the production both unpeated and peated) will be used for blended whisky, not least by Macduff International (producers of Islay Mist and Lauder's) while Inchdairnie will be matured to be sold as a single malt in the future.

Daftmill

[daf•mil]

Owner:	**Region/district:**
Francis Cuthbert	Lowlands
Founded: **Status:**	**Capacity:**
2005 Active	c 65 000 litres
Address: By Cupar, Fife KY15 5RF	
Website:	**Tel:**
daftmill.com	01337 830303

Permission was granted in 2003 for a steading at Daftmill Farmhouse in Fife, just a few miles west of Cupar and dating back to 1655, to be converted into a distillery.

The first distillation was on 16th December 2005 and around 20,000 litres are distilled in a year. A little less was produced in 2013 when a new boiler was fitted. It is run as a typical farmhouse distillery. The barley is grown on the farm and they also supply other distilleries. Of the total 800 tonnes that Francis Cuthbert harvests in a year, around 100 tonnes are used for his own whisky. The malting is done without peat at Crisp´s in Alloa. The equipment consists of a one tonne semi-lauter mash tun with a copper dome, two stainless steel washbacks with a fermentation between 72 and 100 hours and one pair of stills with slightly ascending lyne arms. The equipment is designed to give a lot of copper contact, a lot of reflux. The wash still has a capacity of 3,000 litres and the spirit still 2,000 litres.

Francis Cuthbert´s aim is to do a light, Lowland style whisky similar to Rosebank. In order to achieve this they have very short foreshots (five minutes) and the spirit run starts at 78% to capture all of the fruity esters and already comes off at 73%. The spirit is filled mainly into ex-bourbon casks, always first fill, but there are also a few sherry butts in the two dunnage warehouses.

Taking care of the farm obviously prohibits Francis from producing whisky full time. His silent season is during spring and autumn when work in the fields take all of his time. Whisky distillation is therefore reserved for June-August and November-February. The whisky in the warehouse is now close to 12 years old and whisky enthusiasts have been asking for years when the first bottling is due. Francis however doesn´t seem to be in a hurry or as he himself puts it "patience is a virtue".

Abhainn Dearg

[aveen jar•rek]

Owner:	**Region/district:**
Mark Tayburn	Islands (Isle of Lewis)
Founded: **Status:**	**Capacity:**
2008 Active	c 20 000 litres
Address: Carnish, Isle of Lewis,	
Na h-Eileanan an Iar HS2 9EX	
Website:	**Tel:**
abhainndearg.co.uk	01851 672429

In September 2008, spirit flowed from a newly constructed distillery in Uig on the island of Lewis in the Outer Hebrides.

This was the first distillery on the island since 1840 when Stornoway distillery was closed. The conditions for new distilleries being built at that time were not improved when James Matheson, a Scottish tradesman, bought the entire island in 1844. Even though he had made his fortune in the opium trade, he was an abstainer and a prohibitionist and did not look kindly on the production or use of alcohol.

The Gaelic name of the new distillery is Abhainn Dearg which means Red River, and the founder and owner is Mark "Marko" Tayburn who was born and raised on the island. Part of the distillery was converted from an old fish farm while some of the buildings are new. There are two 500 kg mash tuns made of stainless steel and two 7,500 litre washbacks made of Douglas fir with a fermentation time of 4 days. The wash still has a capacity of 2,112 litres and the spirit still 2,057 litres. Both have very long necks and steeply descending lye pipes leading out into two wooden worm tubs. Both bourbon and sherry casks are used for maturation. The plan is to use 100% barley grown on Lewis and in 2013 the first 6 tonnes of Golden Promise (15% of the total requirement) were harvested. In 2015, the owner reported that all the barley needed for the production, now came from the island. Over the years, production has been limited to around 10,000 litres of pure alcohol yearly even though the distillery has the capacity to do more.

The first release from the distillery was The Spirit of Lewis (matured for a short time in sherry casks) in 2010 and the first single malt was a limited release (2,011 bottles) of a 3 year old in October 2011, followed up by a cask strength version (58%) in 2012. The owners currently still sell Spirit of St Lewis and the 3 year old single malt. The goal is to offer a 10 year old single malt some time in 2018.

Ailsa Bay

[ail•sah bey]

Owner:
William Grant & Sons

Region/district:
Lowlands

Founded: **Status:**
2007   Active

Capacity:
12 000 000 litres

Address: Girvan, Ayrshire KA26 9PT

Website:
-

Tel:
01465 713091

Commisioned in September 2007, it only took nine months to build this distillery on the same site as Girvan Distillery near Ayr on Scotland´s west coast.

Until recently, it was equipped with a 12,1 tonne full lauter mash tun, 12 washbacks made of stainless steel and eight stills. In August 2013 however, it was time for a major expansion when yet another mash tun, 12 more washbacks and eight more stills were commissioned, doubling the capacity to 12 million litres of alcohol.

Each washback will hold 50,000 litres and fermentation time is 60 hours for the heavier styles and 72 hours for the lighter "Balveniestyle". The stills are made according to the same standards as Balvenie's and two of the wash stills and two of the spirit stills have stainless steel condensers instead of copper. That way, they have the possibility

of making batches of a more sulphury spirit if desired. A unique feature is the octangular spirit safe which sits between the two rows of stills. Each side corresponds to one specific still. To increase efficiency and to get more alcohol, high gravity distillation is used. The wash stills are heated using external heat exchangers but they also have interior steam coils. The spirit stills are heated by steam coils. In 2017, the distillery will be producing 11.7 million litres of alcohol.

Five different types of spirit are produced. The most common is a light and rather sweet spirit. Then there is a heavy, sulphury style and three peated with the peatiest having a malt specification of 50ppm. The production is destined to become a part of Grant´s blended Scotch which is currently the fourth most popular Scotch in the world with 53 million bottles sold in 2015. However, a peated single malt Ailsa Bay has also been released, in spring 2016, with more batches to follow.

Roseisle

[rose•eyel]

Owner:
Diageo

Region/district:
Highlands

Founded: **Status:**
2009   Active

Capacity:
12 500 000 litres

Address: Roseisle, Morayshire IV30 5YP

Website:
-

Tel:
01343 832100

Roseisle distillery is located on the same site as the already existing Roseisle maltings just west of Elgin. The distillery has won several awards for its ambition towards sustainable production.

The distillery is equipped with two stainless steel mash tuns with a 12.5 tonne charge each. There are 14 huge (115,500 litres) stainless steel washbacks and 14 stills with the wash stills being heated by external heat exchangers while the spirit stills are heated using steam coils. The spirit vapours are cooled through copper condensers but on three spirit stills and three wash stills there are also stainless steel condensers attached, that you can switch to for a more sulphury spirit. The fermentation time for a Speyside style of whisky is 90-100 hours and for a heavier style it is 50-60 hours. The plan for 2017 is to do 21 mashes per week and a total of 10,7 million litres of alcohol.

The total cost for the distillery was £40m and how to use the hot water in an efficient way was very much a focal point from the beginning. For example, Roseisle is connected by means of two long pipes with Burghead maltings, 3 km north of the distillery. Hot water is pumped from Roseisle and then used in the seven kilns at Burghead and cold water is then pumped back to Roseisle. The pot ale from the distillation will be piped into anaerobic fermenters to be transformed into biogas and the dried solids will act as a biomass fuel source. The biomass burner on the site, producing steam for the distillery, covers 72% of the total requirement. Furthermore, green technology has reduced the emission of carbon dioxide to only 15% of an ordinary, same-sized distillery.

Destined to be used for blends, Roseisle single malt was in autumn 2017, for the first time used in a different role. It was part of the blended malt Collectivum XXVIII where Diageo has used whiskies from all 28 malt distilleries.

Strathearn

[strath•earn]

Owner:	**Region/district:**
Tony Reeman-Clark	Southern Highlands
Founded: **Status:**	**Capacity:**
2013 Active	c 30 000 litres
Address: Bachilton Farm Steading, Methven PH1 3QX	
Website:	**Tel:**
strathearndistillery.com	01738 840 100

This is something as unique as Scotland´s first micro-distillery. Abhainn Dearg on the Isle of Lewis has the same capacity, but the stills at Strathearn are considerably smaller.

The brainchild of Tony Reeman-Clark, it is situated a couple of miles west of Methven near Perth. Gin production was started in August 2013 and the first whisky was filled into casks in October. The distillery uses the Maris Otter barley which was abandoned by other distillers years ago due to the low yield. Reeman-Clark prefers it though, because of the flavours that it contributes. All the equipment is fitted into one room and consists of a stainless steel mash tun, two stainless steel washbacks with a fermentation time of 4-5 days, one 1,000 litre wash still and a 500 litre spirit still. Both stills are of the Alambic type with vertical tube copper condensers. When they are producing gin, they simply detach the lyne arm and mount a copper basket

to the still to hold the botanicals. On the whisky side, both peated (35ppm) and un-peated whisky is produced and for maturation a variety of 50-100 litre casks are used; virgin French oak, virgin American oak and ex-sherry casks.

Reeman-Clark has also been experimenting with other types of wood like chestnut, mullberry and cherry. According to the rules, spirit matured in anything other than oak, cannot be called Scotch whisky. This problem is solved by labelling the content Uisge Beatha – the ancient name for Scotch. In early 2017, the Uisge was discontinued due to a controversy with the authorities whether or not the name Uisge was in accordance with the EU regulations. The first single malt Scotch from the distillery was released in December 2016. One hundred 50cl bottles were put up for auction and they were sold for a median price of £333. More bottles will follow in 2017. Gin is currently the big seller with several varieties having been released including Heather Rose, Citrus, Oaked Highland and Juniper.

Eden Mill

[eden mill]

Owner:	**Region/district:**
Paul Miller	Lowlands
Founded: **Status:**	**Capacity:**
2014 Active (vc)	80 000 litres
Address: St Andrews, Fife, KY16 0UU	
Website:	**Tel:**
edenmill.com	01334 834038

In 2012, Paul Miller, the former Molson Coors sales director, with a background in the whisky industry (Diageo and Glenmorangie), opened up the successful Eden Brewery in Guardbridge 3 miles west of St Andrews.

The site was an old paper mill and only 50 metres away, there was a distillery called Seggie which was operative between 1810 and 1860 and owned by the Haig family. As an extension of the brewery, Paul decided to build a distillery called Eden Mill Distillery. The distillery, with a capacity of 80,000 litres per year, mainly produces malt whisky, but gin is also on the map. The distillery is equipped with two wash stills and one spirit still of the alambic type. Made by Hoga in Portugal, all three stills are of the same size – 1,000 litres. Eden Mill is the first combined brewery and distillery in Scotland – a combination which

has proven so successful, especially in the USA. The brewery/distillery also has a visitor centre which already attracts 20,000 visitors a year.

Whisky production started in November 2014 and, waiting for the first whisky to be launched in January 2018, Miller has already released several, young malt spirits – St Andrews Day, Hogmanay and Robert Burns Day. Recently, sourced Scotch malt and grain whisky has been blended by the team and released under the name Art of the Blend. Different varieties of gin have been launched continuously since the start, which include Hop, Love, Golf and Oak Gin. In 2016, the gin was launched in the USA and later in the year also in China. A new product category for the company has also been introduced – ready-to-drink gin cocktails. Of the whisky production, around 10,000 litres a year will be reserved for the distillery´s Private Cask Owners' Club, where customers can buy anything from octaves to hogsheads of whisky.

Dalmunach

[dal•moo•nack]

Owner: Chivas Brothers

Region/district: Speyside

Founded: 2015

Status: Active

Capacity: 10 000 000 litres

Address: Carron, Banffshire AB38 7QP

Website: -

Tel: -

One of the newest distilleries in Scotland, and one of the most beautiful, has been built on the site of the former Imperial distillery.

Imperial distillery was built in 1897, the year of Queen Victoria´s Diamond Jubilee so no surprise where the distillery got its name. On the top of the roof there was even a large cast iron crown to mark the occasion. The founder was Thomas Mackenzie who at the time already owned Dailuaine and Talisker. The timing was not the best though. One year after the opening, the Pattison crash brought the whisky industry to its knees and the distillery was forced to close. Eventually it came into the hands of DCL (later to become Diageo) who owned it from 1916 until 2005, when Chivas Brothers took over. It was out of production for 60% of the time until 1998 when it was mothballed. The owners probably never planned to use it for distillation again as it was put up for sale in 2005 to become available

as residential flats. Soon after, it was withdrawn from the market and, in 2012, a decision was taken to tear down the old distillery and build a new. Demolition of the old distillery began in 2013 and by the end of that year, nothing was left, except for the old warehouses.

Construction on the new Dalmunach distillery started in 2013 and it was commissioned in October 2014. The exceptional and stunning distillery is equipped with a 12 ton Briggs full lauter mash tun, 16 stainless steel washbacks with a fermentation time of 54 hours and 4 pairs of stills of a considerable size - 30,000 litres. The stills are positioned in a circle with a hexagonal spirit safe in the middle. The distillery, which cost £25m to build, has a capacity of 10 million litres and was officially opened in 2015 by Nicola Sturgeon, First Minister of Scotland. One interesting and quite spectacular feature is the use of part of an old Imperial washback in the main entrance.

Glasgow

[glas•go]

Owner: Liam Hughes, Ian McDougall

Region/district: Lowlands

Founded: 2015

Status: Active

Capacity: 270 000 litres

Address: Deanside Rd, Hillington, Glasgow G52 4XB

Website: glasgowdistillery.com

Tel: 0141 4047191

When Glasgow Distillery was opened in Hillington Business Park, it became the first new whisky distillery in Glasgow in modern times.

There were stills within the Strathclyde grain distillery producing the malt whisky Kinclaith from 1958-1975 but Liam Hughes, Mike Hayward and Ian McDougall had the intention of building the first proper malt distillery in Glasgow in more than hundred years. Backed up by Asian investors, the distillery was ready to start production in February 2015.

The distillery is equipped with a one ton mash tun, seven wash backs (5,400 litres each) with a minimum fermentation of 72 hours, one 2,500 litre wash still, one 1,400 litre spirit still and one 450 litre gin still - all from Firma Carl in Germany. Starting with 75,000 litres, since 2017 they are more or less on full production and an already planned

expansion is due to take place within the next couple of years. This means yet another pair of stills, seven more washbacks and a total capacity of 500,000 litres. The first distillation of whisky was unpeated but since then peated spirit (50ppm) is also part of the production and since January 2017, triple distillation is also practised one month per year. The distillery is located in an industrial area and the owners have no plans for a visitor centre.

Their big seller now is Makar gin in several versions including two that were aged for 10 weeks in mulberry casks and oak barrels. The first release (5,000 bottles) of their malt whisky is due in October 2018 with a peated version planned for 2019. Whisky, however, has already been offered by the company. Prometheus, a sourced 26 year old single malt where the distillery was not revealed, was released in April 2015. The second release, a 27 year old, appeared in 2016 and a 28 year old is planned.

Harris

[har•ris]

Owner:
Isle of Harris Distillers Ltd.

Region/district:
Islands (Isle of Harris)

Founded: 2015   **Status:** Active (vc)

Capacity: 230 000 litres

Address: Tarbert, Isle of Harris,
Na h-Eileanan an Iar HS3 3DJ

Website: harrisdistillery.com

Tel: 01859 502212

Almost ten years ago, Anderson Bakewell had conjured up an idea that has now resulted in a distillery which has come to fruition on the Isle of Harris.

Bakewell, who has been connected to the island for more than 40 years, acquired the services of Simon Erlanger for the company's benefit at an early stage. Erlanger, a former marketing director for Glenmorangie, is now MD of the new distillery, while Bakewell is chairman of the company. Construction started in 2014 and the distillery came into production in September 2015. The total cost for the whole project is £11.4m, but this sum probably also covers the cost for barley and casks until the first whisky is ready to be bottled. The distillery, located in Tarbert, is the second distillery after Abhainn Dearg on Lewis to be located in the Outer Hebrides.

The equipment consists of a 1.2 tonne semi lauter mash tun made of stainless steel but clad with American oak, 5 washbacks made of Oregon pine and with a fermentation time of 3-4 days, one 7,000 litre wash still and a 5,000 litre spirit still - both with descending lyne arms and made in Italy. Currently the distillery is doing 5 mashes per week. The style of the whisky, which will be called Hearach (the Gaelic word for a person living on Harris), will be medium peated with a phenol specification in the barley of 12-14ppm. The first spirit to be distilled in September 2015 was gin and this was followed by whisky in December. The gin has already been released and apart from traditional gin botanicals, local ingredients are also used such as sugar kelp.

With the new distillery, 20 new jobs have been created on the island, some of whom are working in the distillery visitor centre with around 40,000 guests per year.

Lone Wolf

[loan wolf]

Owner:
Brewdog plc.

Region/district:
Highlands

Founded: 2016   **Status:** Active

Capacity: 450 000 litres

Address: Balmacassie Commercial Park, Ellon,
Aberdeenshire AB41 8BX

Website: brewdog.com

Tel: 01358 724924

Founded in 2007 by James Watt and Martin Dickie, Brew Dog has grown to become the biggest independent brewery in the UK and is also the fastest-growing drinks producer in the country.

A decision was made in 2014 to also open a distillery on the premises in Fellon, outside of Aberdeen. To manage the distillery, Steven Kearsley who has a background at several Diageo distilleries, was called in. Early on, Steven was determined that this should not be "just another" whisky distillery. To use his own words, it is multi-faceted and by that he means they will not limit themselves to just a few styles of spirits. Apart from malt whisky, there will also be grain and rye, bourbon style whiskey, vodka, gin, rum and fruit brandies on offer.

The adjacent brew house provides the wash for the distil-lery which has the following equipment; one 3,000 litre pot still with an 8 plate rectification column which will be used for stripping the wash for vodka, whisky and rum, another 3,000 litre still with a 60-plate column is used for the final distillation of vodka and whisky, a 600 litre pot still is dedicated to gin and brandy production, while a 50 litre pot still is used for research and experimentation. The idea is to have an innovative distillery where, for example, cherry or apple wood may be used for drying the barley or other types of wood, other than just oak, may be used for maturation. First production was gin and vodka and following a few prototype releases, the first bottles were launched in spring 2017. Whisky production has also started but so far it has been mainly experimentation with grain bills (mostly wheat and rye) and wood. Steven Kersley has also distilled a spirit from 100% malted barley in the pot still but using the rectification column to give a better control of the cut points.

Arbikie

[ar•bi•ki]

Owner:
The Stirling family

Region/district:
Eastern Highlands

Founded: 2015   **Status:** Active

Capacity:
200 000 litres

Address: Inverkeilor, Arbroath, Angus DD11 4UZ

Website:
arbikie.com

Tel:
01241 830770

The Stirling family has been farming since the 17th century and the 2000-acre Arbikie Highland Estate in Angus has now been in their possession for four generations.

The three brothers (John, Iain and David) started their careers within other fields but have now returned to the family lands to open up a single-estate distillery. The definition of a single-estate distillery is that, not only does the whole chain of production take place on site, but all the ingredients are also grown on the farm. Ballindalloch is one example but Arbikie is the first to produce both brown and white spirits.

The first vodka from potatoes was distilled in October 2014 which was followed by gin in May 2015. Trials with malt whisky started in March 2015, has gone over to full production since October 2015.

The barley is grown in fields of their own and then sent to Boorts malt in Montrose, 7 miles away. The distillery, which is based in an old barn at the farm, is equipped with a stainless steel, semi-lauter mash tun with a 0.75 ton charge, four washbacks (two 4,400 litre and two 9,000 litre), one 4,000 litre wash still and one 2,400 litre spirit still. For the final stage of vodka and gin production, there is also a 40 plate rectification column. The whisky is mainly matured in ex bourbon barrels and ex sherry hogsheads.

The products released so far are Arbikie Potato Vodka, Arbikie Chilli Vodka made with chipotle chilli, Arbikie Kirsty's Gin named after the master distiller, Kirsty Black, AK's Gin and, most recently, a strawberry flavoured vodka. According to the owners, the style of their malt whisky will be unpeated Highland with a coastal influence. At the moment the Stirlings don't intend to launch their first whisky any time soon. The plan is to release it at the age of 14 in 2030.

Dornoch

[dor•nock]

Owner:
Phil and Simon Thompson

Region/district:
Northern Highlands

Founded: 2016   **Status:** Active

Capacity:
30 000 litres

Address: Castle Street, Dornoch, Sutherland, IV25 3 SD

Website:
dornochdistillery.com

Tel:
01862 810 216

Along with their parents, Phil and Simon Thompson have been running the Dornoch Castle Hotel in Sutherland for fifteen years.

The hotel is famous for its outstanding whisky bar and the two brothers are passionate about whisky and other spirits. So passionate in fact that they decided to convert a 135-year old fire station into a distillery. The building is only 47 square metres and the brothers have struggled to fit all the equipment into the limited space. The distillery is equipped with a 300 kg stainless steel, semi-lauter mash tun from China, seven washbacks made of oak from Eastern Europe, a 1,000 litre wash still and a 600 litre spirit still. Both stills, made by Hoga in Portugal, have shell and tube condensers, but the brothers are no strangers when it comes to installing worm tubs in the future. The stills are directly fired using gas but they are also equipped with steam coils as an alternative heating method. There is also a 2,000 litre still

with a column from Holland for the production of gin and other spirits. The distillery has a yearly capacity of 30,000 litres of pure alcohol of which approximately 15,000 litres are dedicated to whisky. The first distillation was gin in October 2016 and whisky production commenced in January 2017. A range of experimental batches of the gin has been released during spring 2017 and they were followed by Thompson Brothers Highland Gin in August.

Their interest in "old-style" whiskies produced in the 1960s and earlier also affects the production. All the barley is floor malted, oftn using old heritage varieties, while brewer's yeast is used instead of distiller's yeast. They are currently working on their own yeast and most of the production is organic. For maturation, they will be using different ex-sherry casks as well as casks that have previously held bourbon and rye. Initially, the whisky will be unpeated but the key word for this distillery is experimentation, so production in the future may involve peat.

Torabhaig

[tor•a•<u>v</u>aig]

Owner:	**Region/district:**
Mossburn Distillers	Islands (Skye)
Founded: **Status:**	**Capacity:**
2016 Active (vc)	500 000 litres

Address: Teangue, Sleat, Isle of Skye IV44 8RE

Website:	**Tel:**
www.torabhaig.com	01471 833337

The idea to build a second distillery on Skye (with Talisker being the first) was presented several years ago by the late Sir Iain Noble.

He had chosen a 19th century listed farm building near Torabhaig on the southeast coast as a suitable location, but the plans were never realized until after Sir Iain had died in 2010. A new company, Mossburn Distillers, took over the plans and after a planning consent was granted, the first phase of restoration was completed in December 2014. Chris Anderson, a former head of distilling for Dewar's blend was responsible for the construction of the distillery. By June 2016, most of the equipment had been installed and production started in January 2017.

The distillery is equipped with a 1.5 ton stainless steel mash tun with a copper top. There are eight washbacks made of Douglas fir with a fermentation time of around 72 hours, one 8,000 litre wash still and one 5,000 litre spirit still, made by Forsyth in Rothes. In 2017, 250,000 litres will be produced, rising to 500,000 litres in 2018. The owners aim to produce a heavily peated whisky with a phenol specification of 30ppm in the malted barley. The cost to build the distillery is estimated to be around £5m and this also includes a visitor centre which will probably open in March 2018.

Mossburn Distillers was founded in 2013 and apart from Torabhaig, they have plans to build another two distilleries, one considerably larger, in the Borders near Jedburgh. Mossburn is owned by Marussia Beverages, a Dutch company specialising in spirits and fine wine. That company in turn is actually a part of the privately owned Swedish group Haydn Holding. So, for the first time in history, we now have a Swedish owned malt distillery in Scotland!

Isle of Raasay

[ajl ov r<u>a</u>ssay]

Owner:	**Region/district:**
R&B Distillers	Highlands (Raasay)
Founded: **Status:**	**Capacity:**
2017 Active (vc)	200 000 litres

Address: Borodale House, Raasay, By Kyle IV40 8PB

Website:	**Tel:**
rbdistillers.com	01478 470177

This new Island distillery on Raasay, east of the Isle of Skye, could be defined as a "bi-product" coming from the plans to build a distillery in the Borders.

Since 2010 Alasdair Day has planned for a new distillery in the south of Scotland. The funding, however, became an issue but was resolved when Alasdair teamed up with Bill Dobbie, entrepreneur and co-founder of online dating site Cupid. As the new company was formed, the plans for yet another distillery took shape. The idea was to turn Borodale House, a derelict Victorian hotel on the island of Raasay, into a distillery or at the least the distillery visitor's centre. Planning approval was granted in February 2016 and the company was named R&B Distillers (Raasay and Borders). When work on the distillery got underway, the owners also decided that the project in the Borders should be put on hold until the distillery on Raasay had been built.

The Raasay Distillery, which was commissioned in early autumn 2017, is equipped with a 1 ton mash tun, six stainless steel washbacks, temperature controlled and with a 90 hour fermentation, one 5,000 litre wash still and a 3,600 litre spirit still equipped with a separate purifier. Both stills were made by Frilli in Italy. The source for all the water (process, cooling and reduction) comes from a well with high mineral content which the owners hope will come through in the lightly peated (15ppm) whisky. The intention is to start with one shift, 5 days a week for 48 weeks which would result in 95,000 litres of pure alcohol. The actual capacity on 7 days and two shifts will be 200,000 litres.

A visitor's centre opened in summer 2017 and the view from the distillery is one of Scotland's most spectacular. In anticipation of their own whisky, a sourced single malt Scotch named Raasay While We Wait, will be offered to the visitors.

Lindores Abbey

[linn•doors aebi]

Owner:
The Lindores Distilling Co.

Region/district:
Lowlands

Founded: **Status:** **Capacity:**
2017 Active (vc) 150 000 litres

Address: Lindores Abbey House, Abbey Road, Newburgh, Fife KY14 6HH

Website:
lindoresabbeydistillery.com

Tel:
01337 842547

The famous, first written record of whisky was a letter to Friar John Cor, a monk at the Abbey of Lindores, dated 1494 where, by order of King James IV, he was instructed to make "aqua vitae, VIII bolls of malt".

More than five hundred years later, whisky is again produced at Lindores Abbey in Fife. Drew McKenzie Smith, whose family for a century has owned the land on which the ruins of the abbey stands, has attracted investors in order to build a distillery. In his work, he had also been assisted by the well-known whisky consultant, the late Dr. Jim Swan, Planning permission was granted already in 2013 however the council required McKenzie Smith to carry out a full excavation of the ancient area before the distillery could be constructed. An 18-metre abbey wall was discovered as well as several bits of medieval pottery.

The distillery was finally commissioned in autumn 2017.

All the barley used in the production comes from the owners own farm which makes Lindores Abbey Distillery one of few producers in Scotland of single estate whisky (others being Ballindalloch and Arbikie). The equipment consists of a 2 ton semi lauter mash tun with a copper lid, four Oregon pine washbacks with a minimum fermentation time of 72 hours, one 10,000 litre wash still and two 3,500 litre spirit stills. The idea behind having two spirit stills is to allow for more copper contact during distillation. One unique feature is that part of the warehouse will be a heated area for experimenting with temperature and evaporation. The style of the whisky will be light and fruity and they will also produce Aqua Vitae as it was made during the 15th century, which they will infuse with herbs and plants growing around the Abbey. A visitor centre with a wide range of activities, including whisky and champagne afternoon teas (!), is also a part of the distillery.

The Clydeside

[klajdsajd]

Owner:
Morrison Glasgow Distillers

Region/district:
Lowlands

Founded: **Status:** **Capacity:**
2017 Active (vc) 500 000 litres

Address: 100 Stobcross Road, Glasgow G3 8QQ

Website:
theclydeside.com

Tel:

Since 2012, Tim Morrison had been working on the idea of building a whisky distillery in Glasgow and it would be difficult to find a person better suited for the task.

Morrison represents the fourth generation of one of Scotland's best known whisky families. Originally a whisky broker, Tim Morrison's father, Stanley P Morrison eventually created Morrison Bowmore Distillers and acquired three distilleries - Bowmore, Glen Garioch and Auchentoshan. The company is today owned by Beam Suntory and Tim Morrison has long left the company. Instead he took over the independent bottler AD Rattray and expanded that business by opening up a first class shop and whisky centre in Kirkoswald in Ayrshire. The Clydeside Distillery though, is run from a different company - Morrison Glasgow Distillers.

The distillery is beautifully situated on the river Clyde with well-known attractions such as the Riverside Museum, Glasgow Science Centre and the SEC Centre as its closest neighbours. A visitor centre, expected to attract 65,000 guests a year has been constructed within the old Pump House building from 1877 while an adjacent, modern building houses the distillery. The equipment consists of a 1.5 ton semi lauter mash tun, 8 stainless steel washbacks, a 7,500 litre wash still and a 5,000 litre spirit still. Production started in autumn 2017 and the aim is to produce a light, Lowland style whisky. In June 2017, the former distillery manager of Auchentoshan, Alistair McDonald joined the team. As mentioned, the location is stunning but that was not the only reason for choosing this site. Tim Morrison's great grandfather built the Pump House which was used to power the hydraulic gates allowing ships in and out of the Queens Dock and thereby controlling the important whisky export going out from Glasgow.

Ncn´ean

[nook•knee•anne]

Owner:
Ncn´ean Distillery Ltd.

Region/district:
Western Highlands

Founded: 2017
Status: Active (vc)
Capacity: 100 000 litres

Address: Drimnin, By Lochaline PA80 5XZ

Website: ncnean.com
Tel: 01967 421698

Drimnin Estate, which overlooks the Isle of Mull in the west, is located on the Morvern peninsula in the Western Highlands. The 7,000 acre estate was bought by Derek and Louise Lewis in 2001.

Their daughter Annabel Thomas, a former strategy consultant in London, is the initiator to this new distillery which, when it was in the planning stage, was called Drimnin but later changed name to Ncn´ean after a witch-queen according to Gaelic folk tales. In early 2016, the company received a £513,000 grant from the Scottish government and construction work began later that year. The late Dr. Jim Swan acted as consultant and in March 2017, the distillery came on stream.

It is equipped with a one ton semi lauter mash tun, four stainless steel washbacks with a fermentation time between 65 and 115 hours. Furthermore there is a 5,000 litre wash still and a 3,500 litre spirit still. All the malted barley used is organic and the owners strive to make all aspects of production as environmentally friendly as possible including a wood chip boiler and recycling waste heat through the temperature controlled warehouses.

Thomas intends to produce a light and fruity whisky with maturation predominantly in ex-bourbon and red wine casks. There will also be plenty of space for experimentation, including trials with different yeast strains. The first bottling is planned for spring 2020. A visitor centre opened in July 2017 and customers also have the possibility of buying a full cask already now.

Ncn´ean is one of the most remote distilleries in Scotland, competing with Ardnamurchan which isn´t far away, but on the opposite side of Loch Sunart.

The Borders

[boar•ders]

Owner:
The Three Stills Co. Ltd.

Region/district:
Lowlands

Founded: 2017
Status: Active (vc)
Capacity: 2 000 000 litres

Address: Commercial Road, Hawick TD9 7AQ

Website: -
Tel: 01450 374330

A race to build the first legal whisky distillery in The Borders in 180 years has been going on for a few years now, but in 2017 we had a winner.

The distillery is situated in Hawick and owned by The Three Stills Company which was founded in 2013. Behind the company are four men who had all previously worked for William Grant & Sons – George Tait, Tony Roberts, John Fordyce and Tim Carton. Unlike some other new distillery projects, a sum of £10m had been secured before they applied for a planning permission. The owners include private investors as well as companies in the UK and abroad. In 2015, the company purchased a site in Hawick which had been occupied by an electric company and then by an engineering firm. Construction started in August 2016 and the distillery was commissioned in autumn 2017 with a visitor centre to open soon after. It is equipped with a 5 ton mash tun, eight stainless steel washbacks, two wash stills and two spirit stills with all equipment provided by Forsyths in Rothes. The capacity is quite large, 2 million litres, and the aim is to produce an un-peated, floral whisky. Other spirits will also be produced, including gin using local botanicals.

Since construction of the distillery started, the owners also applied for planning permission (which was granted in May 2017) to install a bio plant on the site. Using anaerobic digestion technique, by-products from the distillation will be converted into biogas which will help to power the distillery. Another £3m is required to build the plant which brings the total investment to £13m.

The owners have already released a blended Scotch from sourced whisky called Clan Fraser with its core markets in the Middle East and southern Africa.

Distilleries per owner

c = closed, d = demolished, mb = mothballed, dm = dismantled

Diageo
Auchroisk
Banff (d)
Benrinnes
Blair Athol
Brora (c)
Caol Ila
Cardhu
Clynelish
Coleburn (dm)
Convalmore (dm)
Cragganmore
Dailuaine
Dallas Dhu (c)
Dalwhinnie
Dufftown
Glen Albyn (d)
Glendullan
Glen Elgin
Glenesk (dm)
Glenkinchie
Glenlochy (d)
Glenlossie
Glen Mhor (d)
Glen Ord
Glen Spey
Glenury Royal (d)
Inchgower
Knockando
Lagavulin
Linkwood
Mannochmore
Millburn (dm)
Mortlach
North Port (d)
Oban
Pittyvaich (d)
Port Ellen (dm)
Rosebank (c)
Roseisle
Royal Lochnagar
St Magdalene (dm)
Strathmill
Talisker
Teaninich

Pernod Ricard
Aberlour
Allt-a-Bhainne
Braeval
Caperdonich (d)
Dalmunach
Glenburgie
Glen Keith
Glenlivet
Glentauchers
Glenugie (dm)
Imperial (d)
Inverleven (d)
Kinclaith (d)
Lochside (d)
Longmorn
Miltonduff
Scapa
Strathisla
Tormore

Edrington Group
Glenrothes
Glenturret
Highland Park
Macallan

Inver House (Thai Beverage)
Balblair
Balmenach
Glen Flagler (d)
Knockdhu
Pulteney
Speyburn

John Dewar & Sons (Bacardi)
Aberfeldy
Aultmore
Craigellachie
Macduff
Royal Brackla

William Grant & Sons
Ailsa Bay
Balvenie
Glenfiddich
Kininvie
Ladyburn (dm)

Whyte & Mackay (Emperador)
Dalmore
Fettercairn
Jura
Tamnavulin

Morrison Bowmore (Beam Suntory)
Auchentoshan
Bowmore
Glen Garioch

Burn Stewart Distillers (Distell)
Bunnahabhain
Deanston
Tobermory

Benriach Dist. Co. (Brown Forman)
Benriach
Glendronach
Glenglassaugh

Loch Lomond Group
Glen Scotia
Littlemill (d)
Loch Lomond

Beam Suntory
Ardmore
Laphroaig

J & A Mitchell
Glengyle
Springbank

Glenmorangie Co. (LVMH)
Ardbeg
Glenmorangie

Angus Dundee Distillers
Glencadam
Tomintoul

Ian Macleod Distillers
Glengoyne
Tamdhu

Campari Group
Glen Grant

Isle of Arran Distillers
Arran

Signatory
Edradour

Tomatin Distillery Co.
Tomatin

J & G Grant
Glenfarclas

Rémy Cointreau
Bruichladdich

David Prior
Bladnoch (c)

Gordon & MacPhail
Benromach

La Martiniquaise
Glen Moray

Ben Nevis Distillery Ltd (Nikka)
Ben Nevis

Picard Vins & Spiritueux
Tullibardine

Harvey's of Edinburgh
Speyside

Kilchoman Distillery Co.
Kilchoman

Cuthbert family
Daftmill

Mark Tayburn
Abhainn Dearg

Aurora Brewing Ltd
Wolfburn

Strathearn Distillery Ltd
Strathearn

Annandale Distillery Co.
Annandale

Adelphi Distillery Co.
Ardnamurchan

Wemyss
Kingsbarns

Mcpherson-Grant family
Ballindalloch

Paul Miller
Eden Mill

Isle of Harris Distillers
Harris

The Glasgow Distillery Company
Glasgow Distillery

John Fegus & Co. Ltd
Inchdairnie

Stirling family
Arbikie

Brewdog plc
Lone Wolf

Thompson family
Dornoch

Mossburn Distillers
Torabhaig

R & B Distillers
Isle of Raasay

The Lindores Distilling Company
Lindores Abbey

Morrison Glasgow Distillers
Clydeside

Ncn'ean Distillery Ltd.
Ncn'ean

The Three Stills Co.
The Borders

The Glenallachie Consortium
Glenallachie

Closed
distilleries

The distilleries on the following pages
have all been closed and some of them even demolished.
New releases from a few of them appear on a regular basis
but for most of them chances are very slim
of ever finding another bottling.

Banff

Owner:	Region:	Founded:	Status:
Diageo	Speyside	1824	Demolished

Banff's tragic history of numerous fires, explosions and bombings have contributed to its fame. The most spectacular incident was when a lone Junkers Ju-88 bombed one of the warehouses in 1941. Hundreds of casks exploded and several thousand litres of whisky were destroyed. The distillery was closed in 1983 and the buildings were destroyed in a fire in 1991. The distillery was owned for 80 years by the Simpson family but when their company filed for bankruptcy in 1932, it was sold to Scottish Malt Distillers which later would be a part of Diageo. When the distillery was at its largest it produced 1 million litres per year in three pairs of stills.

Bottlings:

There has only been one official Rare Malts bottling from 2004. A 49 year old from Gordon & MacPhail (distilled in 1966) was released in 2015 while Cadenheads launched a 40 year old (1976) in 2017.

Ben Wyvis

Owner:	Region:	Founded:	Status:
Whyte & Mackay	N Highlands	1965	Dismantled

The large grain distillery, Invergordon, today producing 36 million litres of grain whisky per year, was established in 1959 on the Cromarty Firth, east of Alness. Six years later a small malt distillery, Ben Wyvis, was built on the same site with the purpose of producing malt whisky for Invergordon Distiller's blends. The distillery was equipped with one mash tun, six washbacks and one pair of stills. Funnily enough the stills are still in use today at Glengyle distillery. Production at Ben Wyvis stopped in 1976 and in 1977 the distillery was closed and dismantled.

Bottlings:

There have been only a few releases of Ben Wyvis. The first, a 27 year old, was released by Invergordon in 1999, followed by a 31 year old from Signatory in 2000 and finally a 37 year old from Kyndal (later Whyte & Mackay) in 2002. It is highly unlikely that there will be more Ben Wyvis single malt to bottle.

Brora

[bro•rah]

Owner:
Diageo

Region/district:
Northern Highlands

Founded: **Status:** **Capacity:**
1819 Closed -

Although founded under the name Clynelish distillery in 1819, it is under the name Brora that the single malt has enjoyed its newfound fame during the past two decades.

The whisky has mostly appealed to peat freaks around the world but, for the first 140 years (and the final decade), it actually wasn't that peated. In 1967 DCL decided to build a new, modern distillery on the same site. This was given the name Clynelish and it was decided the old distillery, with a capacity of 1 million litres of alcohol, should be closed. Shortly after, the demand for peated whisky, especially for the blend Johnnie Walker, increased and the old site re-opened but now under the name Brora and the "recipe" for the whisky was changed to a heavily peated malt. This continued from 1969 to 1973 when production levels at Lagavulin and Talisker had increased to a sufficient level and after that the peatiness was reduced, even if single peated batches turned up until the late seventies. Brora closed permanently in 1983 but the buildings still stand next to the new Clynelish. The two stills, the feints receiver, the spirit receiver and the brass safe remain, while the warehouses are used for storage of spirit from Clynelish.

The first distillery was built in the time referred to as the Highland Clearances. Many land-owners wished to increase the yield of their lands and consequently went into large-scale sheep farming. Thousands of families were ruthlessly forced away and the most infamous of the large landowners was the Marquis of Stafford who founded Clynelish (Brora) in 1819.

Since 1995 Diageo has regularly released different expressions of Brora in the Rare Malts series. The latest, which also became the last, appeared in 2003. In 2002 a new range was created, called Special Releases and bottlings of Brora have appeared ever since. In September 2017, it was time for the 16th release. This time it was a 34 year old distilled in 1982 and bottled at 51.9%. A total of 3000 bottles were launched.

History:

1819 The Marquis of Stafford, 1st Duke of Sutherland, founds the distillery as Clynelish Distillery.

1827 The first licensed distiller, James Harper, files for bankruptcy and John Matheson takes over.

1828 James Harper is back as licensee.

1833 Andrew Ross takes over the license.

1846 George Lawson & Sons takes over.

1896 James Ainslie & Heilbron takes over and rebuilds the facilities.

1912 Distillers Company Limited (DCL) takes over together with James Risk.

1925 DCL buys out Risk.

1930 Scottish Malt Distillers takes over.

1931 The distillery is mothballed.

1938 Production restarts.

1960 The distillery becomes electrified (until now it has been using locally mined coal from Brora).

1967 A new distillery is built adjacent to the first one, it is also named Clynelish and both operate in parallel from August with the new distillery named Clynelish A and the old Clynelish B.

1969 Clynelish B is closed in April but reopened shortly after as Brora and starts using a heavily peated malt until 1973.

1975 A new mashtun is installed.

1983 Brora is closed in March.

1995 Brora 1972 (20 years) and Brora 1972 (22 years) are launched as Rare Malts.

2002 A 30 year old is the first bottling in the Special Releases.

2014 The 13th release of Brora – a 35 year old.

2015 The 14th release of Brora – a 37 year old.

2016 The 15th release of Brora – a 38 year old.

2017 The 16th release of Brora - a 34 year old.

34 years old

Caperdonich

Owner:	Region:	Founded:	Status:
Chivas Bros.	Speyside	1897	Demolished

The distillery was founded by James Grant, owner of Glen Grant which was located in Rothes just a few hundred metres away. Five years after the opening, the distillery was shut down and was re-opened again in 1965 under the name Caperdonich. In 2002 it was mothballed yet again, never to be re-opened. Parts of the equipment were dismantled to be used in other distilleries within the company. In 2010 the distillery was sold to the manufacturer of copper pot stills, Forsyth´s in Rothes, and the buildings were demolished. In the old days a pipe connected Caperdonich and Glen Grant for easy transport of spirit, ready to be filled.

Bottlings:

An official cask strength was released in 2005. Recent independent bottlings are a 21 year old distilled in 1994 from Douglas Laing and a 22 year old from 1995 by Ian Macleod, released in 2017.

Coleburn

Owner:	Region:	Founded:	Status:
Diageo	Speyside	1897	Dismantled

Like so many other distilleries, Coleburn was taken over by DCL (the predecessor of Diageo) in the 1930s. Although the single malt never became well known, Coleburn was used as an experimental workshop where new production techniques were tested. In 1985 the distillery was mothballed and never opened again. Two brothers, Dale and Mark Winchester, bought the buildings in 2004 with the intention of transforming the site into an entertainment centre - a plan that never materialised. Since 2014, the warehouses are used by Aceo Ltd, who bought independent bottler Murray McDavid in 2013, for storing their own whiskies as well as stock belonging to clients.

Bottlings:

There has been one official Rare Malts bottling from 2000, and Independent bottlings are also rare. Two recent releases from Gordon & MacPhail are a 1972 bottled in 2013 and a 1981 bottled in 2015.

Convalmore

Owner:	Region:	Founded:	Status:
Diageo	Speyside	1894	Dismantled

This distillery is still intact and can be seen in Dufftown next to Balvenie distillery. The buildings were sold to William Grant´s in 1990 and they now use it for storage. Diageo, however, still holds the rights to the brand. In the early 20th century, experimental distilling of malt whisky in continuous stills (the same method used for producing grain whisky) took place at Convalmore. The distillery closed in 1985. One of the more famous owners of this distillery was James Buchanan who used Convalmore single malt as a part of his famous blend Black & White. He later sold the distillery to DCL (later Diageo).

Bottlings:

A 28 year old was released by the owners in 2005. The latest independent bottling was a 40 year old from 1975 released by Gordon & MacPhail in 2015. In autumn 2013, as part of the Special Releases, Diageo released a 36 year old from 1977 and this was repeated in 2017 with a 32 year old from 1984.

Dallas Dhu

Owner:	Region:	Founded:	Status:
Diageo	Speyside	1898	Closed

Dallas Dhu distillery is located along the A96 between Elgin and Inverness and is still intact, equipment and all, but hasn´t produced since 1983. Three years later, Diageo sold the distillery to Historic Scotland and it became a museum which is open all year round. In spring 2013 a feasibility study was commissioned by Historic Environment Scotland to look at the possibilities of re-starting production again. One of the founders of the distillery, Alexander Edwards, belonged to the more energetic men in the 19th century Scotch whisky business. Not only did he start Dallas Dhu but also established Aultmore, Benromach and Craigellachie and owned Benrinnes and Oban.

Bottlings:

There are two Rare Malts bottlings from Diageo, the latest in 1997. The latest from independents is a 1980 bottled in 2014 by Gordon & MacPhail.

Glen Albyn

Owner:	Region:	Founded:	Status:
Diageo	N Highlands	1844	Demolished

Glen Albyn was one of three Inverness distilleries surviving into the 1980s. Today, there is no whisky production left in the city. The first forty years were not very productive for Glen Albyn. Fire and bankruptcy prevented the success and in 1866 the buildings were transformed into a flour mill. In 1884 it was converted back to a distillery and continued producing whisky until 1983 when it was closed by the owners at the time, Diageo. Three years later the distillery was demolished.

Bottlings:

Glen Albyn has been released as a Rare Malt by the owners on one occasion. It is rarely seen from independents as well. In 2010, Signatory released a 29 year old and in 2012 a 1976 was bottled by Gordon & MacPhail.

Glenesk

Owner:	Region:	Founded:	Status:
Diageo	E Highlands	1897	Demolished

Few distilleries, if any, have operated under as many names as Glenesk; Highland Esk, North Esk, Montrose and Hillside. The distillery was one of four operating close to Montrose between Aberdeen and Dundee. Today only Glencadam remains. At one stage the distillery was re-built for grain production but reverted to malt distilling. In 1968 a large drum maltings was built adjacent to the distillery and the Glenesk maltings still operate today under the ownership of Boortmalt, the fifth largest producer of malt in the world. The distillery building was demolished in 1996.

Bottlings:

The single malt from Glen Esk has been bottled on three occasions as a Rare Malts, the latest in 1997. It is also very rare with the independent bottlers. Last time it appeared was in 2014 when Gordon & MacPhail released a 34 year old distilled in 1980.

Glen Flagler

Owner:	Region:	Founded:	Status:
InverHouse	Lowlands	1965	Demolished

In 1964 Inver House Distillers was bought by the American company, Publicker Industries, and that same year they decided to expand the production side as well. Moffat Paper Mills in Airdrie was bought and rebuilt into one grain distillery (Garnheath) and two malt distilleries (Glen Flagler and Killyloch). A maltings was also built which, at the time, became the biggest in Europe. The American interest in the Scotch whisky industry faded rapidly and Killyloch was closed in the early 1970s, while Glen Flagler continued to produce until 1985. A year later, Garnheath was closed only to be demolished in 1988.

Bottlings:

Glen Flagler was bottled as an 8 year old by the owners in the 1970s. The next releases came in the mid 1990s when Signatory launched a handful of bottlings distilled in the early 1970s. In 2003, Inver House released a Glen Flagler 1973. A peated version (15ppm) of Glen Flagler, produced until 1970, was called Islebrae.

Glenlochy

Owner:	Region:	Founded:	Status:
Diageo	W Highlands	1898	Demolished

Glenlochy was one of three distilleries in Fort William at the beginning of the 1900s. In 1908 Nevis merged with Ben Nevis distillery (which exists to this day) and in 1983 (a disastrous year for Scotch whisky industry when eight distilleries were closed), the time had come for Glenlochy to close for good. Today, all the buildings have been demolished, with the exception of the kiln with its pagoda roof and the malt barn which both have been turned into flats. For a period of time, the distillery was owned by an energetic and somewhat eccentric Canadian gentleman by the name of Joseph Hobbs who, after having sold the distillery to DCL, bought the second distillery in town, Ben Nevis.

Bottlings:

Glenlochy has occurred twice in the Rare Malts series. The most recent independent bottling is a 35 year old, distilled in 1980 and released by Signatory in 2015.

Glen Mhor

Owner:	Region:	Founded:	Status:
Diageo	N Highlands	1892	Demolished

Glen Mhor is one of the last three Inverness distilleries and probably the one with the best reputation when it comes to the whisky that it produced. When the manager of nearby Glen Albyn, John Birnie, was refused to buy shares in the distillery he was mana-ging, he decided to build his own and founded Glen Mhor. Almost thirty years later he also bought Glen Albyn and both distilleries were owned by the Birnie family until 1972 when they were sold to DCL. Glen Mhor was closed in 1983 and three years later the buildings were demolished. Today there is a supermarket on the site.

Bottlings:

Glen Mhor has appeared on two ocasions as Rare Malts. The most recent independent bottling is a 50 year old distilled in 1965 and with 8 years extra maturation in a first fill sherry butt. It was released in 2016 by Signatory.

Glenugie

Owner:	Region:	Founded:	Status:
Chivas Bros	E Highlands	1831	Demolished

Glenugie, positioned in Peterhead, was the most Eastern distillery in Scotland, producing whisky for six years before it was converted into a brewery. In 1875 whisky distillation started again, but production was very intermittent until 1937 when Seager Evans & Co took over. Eventually they expanded the distillery to four stills and the capacity was around 1 million litres per year. After several ownership changes Glenugie became part of the brewery giant, Whitbread, in 1975. The final blow came in 1983 when Glenugie, together with seven other distilleries, was closed never to open again.

Bottlings:

The first official bottling of Glenugie came as late as in 2010 when Chivas Bros (the current owners of the brand) released a 32 year old single sherry cask in a new range called Deoch an Doras. Recent independent bottlings include a 33 year old with 8 years Oloroso finish from Signatory, released in 2011.

Glenury Royal

Owner:	Region:	Founded:	Status:
Diageo	E Highlands	1825	Demolished

Glenury Royal did not have a lucky start. Already a few weeks after inception in 1825, a fire destroyed the whole kiln, the greater part of the grain lofts and the malting barn, as well as the stock of barley and malt. Just two weeks later, distillery worker James Clark, fell into the boiler and died after a few hours.The founder of Glenury was the eccentric Captain Robert Barclay Allardyce, the first to walk 1000 miles in 1000 hours in 1809 and also an excellent middle-distance runner and boxer. The distillery closed in 1983 and part of the building was demolished a decade later with the rest converted into flats.

Bottlings:

Bottled as a Rare Malt on three occasions. Even more spectacular were three Diageo bottlings released 2003-2007; two 36 year olds and a 50 year old. In early 2012 a 40 year old was released. There are few independent bottlings, the latest being a 38 year old released in 2012 by Gordon & MacPhail.

Imperial

Owner:	Region:	Founded:	Status:
Chivas Bros	Speyside	1897	Demolished

Rumours of the resurrection of this closed distillery have flourished from time to time during the last decade. Eight years ago, the owner commissioned an estate agent to sell the buildings and convert them into flats. Shortly after that, Chivas Bros withdrew it from the market. In 2012, the owners announced that a new distillery would be built on the site, ready to start producing in 2015. Demolition of the old distillery began and in spring 2015 the new Dalmunach distillery was commissioned. In over a century, Imperial distillery was out of production for 60% of the time, but when it produced it had a capacity of 1,6 million litres per year.

Bottlings:

The 15 year old official bottling is long gone but independents are more frequent. The most recent (all from 2017) are a 27 year old from Carn Mor, a 21 year old by Signatory and a 20 year old released by Gordon & MacPhail.

Inverleven

Owner:	Region:	Founded:	Status:
Chivas Bros	Lowlands	1938	Demolished

Dumbarton was the largest grain distillery in Scotland when it was built in 1938. It was mothballed in 2002 and finally closed in 2003 when Allied Domecq moved all their grain production to Strathclyde. On the same site, Inverleven malt distillery was built, equipped with one pair of traditional pot stills. In 1956 a Lomond still was added and this still (with the aid of Inverleven's wash still), technically became a second distillery called Lomond. Inverleven was mothballed in 1991and finally closed. The Lomond still is now working again since 2010 at Bruichladdich.

Bottlings:

The first official bottling of Inverleven came in 2010 when Chivas Bros released a 36 year old in a range called Deoch an Doras. The latest independent was a 1986 released by Gordon & MacPhail in 2015. The same year, Wm Grant released Ghosted Reserve, a 26 year old vatting of Ladyburn and Inverleven.

Killyloch

Owner:	Region:	Founded:	Status:
InverHouse	Lowlands	1965	Demolished

When Publicker Industries launched the Inver House brand in the USA in the 1950s, it soon became a success and the company realised they had to invest in their own grain- and maltwhisky production. A paper mill in Airdrie was rebuilt into a grain distillery (Garnheath) and two malt distilleries (Glen Flagler and Killyloch). However, after the boom in the 1960s, the American interest in Scotch whisky faded and Killyloch (originally named Lillyloch after the water source) was closed in the early 1970s, while Glen Flagler continued to produce until 1985. Garnheath stopped production in 1986 and was demolished in 1988.

Bottlings:

While Glen Flagler was bottled regularly by the owners during the 1970s, Killyloch single malt seem to have been used solely for blends. Killyloch was released a couple of times in the mid 1990s by Signatory and then again in 2003 when Inver House bottled a Killyloch 1967 which is said to have been a vatting of the last six casks from the distillery.

Kinclaith

Owner:	Region:	Founded:	Status:
Chivas Bros	Lowlands	1957	Demolished

This was the last malt distillery to be built in Glasgow and was constructed on the grounds of Strathclyde grain distillery by Seager Evans (later Long John International). Strathclyde still exists today and produces 40 million litres of grain spirit per year. Kinclaith distillery was equipped with one pair of stills and produced malt whisky to become a part of the Long John blend. In 1975 it was dismantled to make room for an extension of the grain distillery. It was later demolished in 1982.

Bottlings:

There are no official bottlings of Kinclaith. The latest from independents came in 2009 when Signatory released a 40 year old distilled in 1969. In 2005, Duncan Taylor and Signatory both released 35 year old bottlings.

Ladyburn

Owner:	Region:	Founded:	Status:
W Grant & Sons	Lowlands	1966	Dismantled

In 1963 William Grant & Sons built their huge grain distillery in Girvan in Ayrshire. Three years later they also decided to build a malt distillery on the site which was given the name Ladyburn. The distillery was equipped with two pairs of stills and they also tested a new type of continuous mashing. The whole idea was to produce malt whisky to become a part of Grant's blended whisky. The distillery was closed in 1975 and finally dismantled during the 1980s. In 2008 a new malt distillery opened up at Girvan under the name Ailsa Bay.

Bottlings:

No less than three official bottlings (40, 41 and 42 years old) appeared in 2014/2015 while an independent 40 year old under the name Rare Ayrshire was released by Signatory in 2015. The year after, Blackadder released a 43 year old distilled in 1973.

Littlemill

Owner:	Region:	Founded:	Status:
Loch Lomond Co.	Lowlands	1772	Demolished

Until 1992 when production stopped, Littlemill was Scotland´s oldest working distillery and could trace its roots back to 1772, possibly even back to the 1750s! Triple distillation was practised at Littlemill until 1930 and after that some new equipment was installed, for example, stills with rectifying columns. The stills were also isolated with aluminium. The goal was to create whiskies that would mature faster. Two such experimental releases were Dunglas and Dumbuck. In 1996 the distillery was dismantled and part of the buildings demolished and in 2004 much of the remaining buildings were destroyed in a fire.

Bottlings:

Official bottlings still occur – in Summer 2017 a 27 year old was released. Several independent bottlings have been released lately, including a 24 year old Pearls of Scotland from 1991 and a 27 year old from 1988, released by Hunter Laing.

Lochside

Owner:	Region:	Founded:	Status:
Chivas Bros	E Highlands	1957	Demolished

Originally a brewery for two centuries, In the last 35 years of production Lochside was a whisky distillery. The Canadian, Joseph Hobbs, started distilling grain whisky and then added malt whisky production in the same way as he had done at Ben Nevis and Lochside. Most of the output was made for the blended whisky Sandy MacNab´s. In the early 1970s, the Spanish company DYC became the owner and the output was destined for Spanish blended whisky. In 1992 the distillery was mothballed and five years later all the equipment and stock were removed. All the distillery buildings were demolished in 2005.

Bottlings:

There are no recent official bottlings. In 2016, a 47 year old single malt was released by Cooper´s Choice and the same year saw a 52 year old single grain Lochside from Hunter Laing. Some years ago there was also an unusual single blend released by Adelphi Distillers.

Millburn

Owner:	Region:	Founded:	Status:
Diageo	N Highlands	1807	Dismantled

The distillery is the oldest of those Inverness distilleries that made it into modern times and it is also the only one where the buildings are still standing. It is now a hotel and restaurant owned by Premier Inn. With one pair of stills, the capacity was no more than 300,000 litres. The problem with Millburn distillery was that it could never be expanded due to its location, sandwiched in between the river, a hill and the surrounding streets. It was bought by the London-based gin producer Booth´s in the 1920s and shortly after that absorbed into the giant DCL. In 1985 it was closed and three years later all the equipment was removed.

Bottlings:

Three bottlings of Millburn have appeared as Rare Malts, the latest in 2005. Other bottlings are scarce. The most recent was a 33 year old distilled in 1974, released by Blackadder in 2007.

North Port

Owner:	Region:	Founded:	Status:
Diageo	E Highlands	1820	Demolished

The names North Port and Brechin are used interchangeably on the labels of this single malt. Brechin is the name of the city and North Port comes from a gate in the wall which surrounded the city. The distillery was run by members of the Guthrie family for more than a century until 1922 when DCL took over. Diageo then closed 21 of their 45 distilleries between 1983 and 1985 of which North Port was one. It was dismantled piece by piece and was finally demolished in 1994 to make room for a supermarket.The distillery had one pair of stills and produced 500,000 litres per year.

Bottlings:

North Port was released as a Rare Malt by Diageo twice and in 2005 also as part of the Special Releases (a 28 year old). Independent bottlings are very rare - the latest (distilled in 1977) was released by Cadenhead´s in 2016.

Port Ellen

[port ell•en]

Owner:	**Region/district:**
Diageo	Islay
Founded: **Status:**	**Capacity:**
1825 Dismantled	-

When Port Ellen closed in 1983 it was one of three Islay distilleries owned by Diageo (then DCL). The other two were Lagavulin and Caol Ila who had been operating uninterruptedly for many years.

Port Ellen, mothballed since 1930, had only been producing for 16 years since re-opening, which made it easy for the owners to single out which Islay distillery was to close when malt whisky demand decreased. It was also the smallest of the three, with an annual output of 1,7 million litres of alcohol.

The stills were shipped abroad early in the 1990s, possibly destined for India, and the distillery buildings were destroyed shortly afterwards. The whisky from Port Ellen is so popular, however, that rumours of distilling starting up again, do flourish from time to time.

Today, the site is associated with the huge drum maltings that was built in 1973. It supplies all Islay distilleries and a few others, with a large proportion of their malt. There are seven germination drums with a capacity of handling 51 tonnes of barley each. Three kilns are used to dry the barley and for every batch, an average of 6 tonnes of peat are required which means 2,000 tonnes per year. The peat was taken from Duich Moss until 1993 when conservationists managed to obtain national nature reserve status for the area in order to protect the thousands of Barnacle Geese that make a stop-over there during their migration. Nowadays the peat is taken from nearby Castlehill.

Besides a couple of versions in the Rare Malts series, Diageo began releasing one official bottling a year in 2001. The single malt soon became a target for collectors and whisky enthusiasts alike and prices have increased rapidly in the last years. In September 2017, it was time for the 17th bottling as part of the Special Releases. This year it was a 37 year old distilled in 1979 and bottled at 51%. A total of 2,988 bottles were launched and this is, together with last year´s bottling, the oldest Port Ellen ever to appear in the Special Releases series.

History:

1825 Alexander Kerr Mackay assisted by Walter Campbell founds the distillery. Mackay runs into financial troubles after a few months and his three relatives John Morrison, Patrick Thomson and George Maclennan take over.

1833 John Ramsay, a cousin to John Morrison, comes from Glasgow to take over.

1836 Ramsay is granted a lease on the distillery from the Laird of Islay.

1892 Ramsay dies and the distillery is inherited by his widow, Lucy.

1906 Lucy Ramsay dies and her son Captain Iain Ramsay takes over.

1920 Iain Ramsay sells to Buchanan-Dewar who transfers the administration to the company Port Ellen Distillery Co. Ltd.

1925 Buchanan-Dewar joins Distillers Company Limited (DCL).

1930 The distillery is mothballed.

1967 In production again after reconstruction and doubling of the number of stills from two to four.

1973 A large drum maltings is installed.

1980 Queen Elisabeth visits the distillery and a commemorative special bottling is made.

1983 The distillery is mothballed.

1987 The distillery closes permanently but the maltings continue to deliver malt to all Islay distilleries.

2001 Port Ellen cask strength first edition is released.

2014 The 14th release of Port Ellen - a 35 year old from 1978.

2015 The 15th release of Port Ellen - a 32 year old from 1983.

2016 The 16th release of Port Ellen - a 37 year old from 1978.

2017 The 17th release of Port Ellen - a 37 year old from 1979.

37 years old

Parkmore

Owner:	Region:	Founded:	Status:
Edrington	Speyside	1894	Dismantled

The distillery, located in Dufftown close to Glenfiddich, was built during the great whisky boom in the late 1890s. In 1900, it was taken over by James Watson & Co. which, in turn, was bought by John Dewar & Sons. From 1925 to the last distillation in 1931, the distillery was owned by Distiller's Company Limited. The whisky from Parkmore never maintained a high quality, apparently because of problems with the water source. The water was taken from an area that is now used as a limestone quarry. The beautiful buildings remain today and are used by Edrington for warehousing.

Bottlings:

No bottles of Parkmore single malt have been offered for sale since 1995 when one was auctioned by Christie's. It is not unlikely though, that the odd bottle may be hiding in private collections.

Pittyvaich

Owner:	Region:	Founded:	Status:
Diageo	Speyside	1974	Demolished

The life span for this relatively modern distillery was short. It was built by Arthur Bell & Sons on the same ground as Dufftown distillery which also belonged to them and the four stills were exact replicas of the Dufftown stills. Bells was bought by Guinness in 1985 and the distillery was eventually absorbed into DCL (later Diageo). For a few years in the 1990s, Pittyvaich was also a back up plant for gin distillation (in the same way that Auchroisk is today) in connection with the production of Gordon's gin having moved from Essex till Cameronbridge. The distillery was mothballed in 1993 and has now been demolished.

Bottlings:

An official 12 year old Flora & Fauna can no longer be found but the latest official bottling was a 25 year old, released in 2015 as a part of the yearly Special Releases.

Rosebank

Owner:	Region:	Founded:	Status:
Diageo	Lowlands	1798	Dismantled

When Rosebank in Falkirk was mothballed in 1993, there were only two working malt distilleries left in the Lowlands – Glenkinchie and Auchentoshan. The whisky from the distillery has always had a great amount of supporters and there was a glimmer of hope that a new company would start up the distillery again. At the beginning of 2009 though, most of the equipment was stolen and furthermore, Diageo has indicated that they are not interested in selling the brand. The buildings are still intact and most of them have been turned into restaurants, offices and flats. The whisky from Rosebank was triple distilled.

Bottlings:

The official 12 year old Flora & Fauna is now almost impossible to find but in 2014 a 21 year old Special Release appeared. The latest independent bottling was a 1990, bottled and released by Gordon & MacPhail in 2015.

St Magdalene

Owner:	Region:	Founded:	Status:
Diageo	Lowlands	1795	Dismantled

At one time, the small town of Linlithgow in East Lothian had no less than five distilleries. St Magdalene was one of them and also the last to close in 1983. The distillery came into ownership of the giant DCL quite early (1912) and was at the time a large distillery with 14 washbacks, five stills and with the possibility of producing more than 1 million litres of alcohol. Ten years after the closure the distillery was carefully re-built into flats, making it possible to still see most of the old buildings, including the pagoda roofs.

Bottlings:

These include two official bottlings in the Rare Malts series. In 2008/2009 a handful of independent releases appeared, all of them distilled in 1982 and released by Ian MacLeod, Douglas Laing, Blackadder, Signatory and Berry Brothers. The latest was a 33 year old, distilled in 1982 and released by Gordon & MacPhail in 2015.

Brora Distillery in the 1930s

Japanese Malt Whisky?
Please hold the line

by Stefan Van Eycken

Last year, we could report on the scarcity of malt whisky from Japan. The big producers turned to bottlings without age statement and prices for older versions were shooting through the roof. The trend seems to continue – at least in the short run.

We're all familiar with the situation. Even for the most patient among us, waiting in telephone queues is one of life's biggest bugbears. In spite of high hopes every year to be able to bring some good news to whisky fans thirsty for quality nectar from the land of the rising sun, the situation with Japanese whisky – and malt whisky, in particular – is starting to resemble looped Vivaldi interrupted every so often by a disembodied voice asking you to "please hold the line". It pains me to have to be that voice, but there's hope. After all, that's why we put up with the on-hold music.

Figures for 2015 – the most recent available – indicate that Japanese whisky makers are busier than ever trying to satisfy the demand, both at home and abroad. They bottled and sold around 140 million liters of whisky in 2015, and exports alone accounted for 10.4 billion yen in sales, an increase by 1,100% compared with 10 years ago (when there was plenty of whisky lying in the warehouses but no one wanted it). In spite of these impressive figures, it seems like there's hardly any quality Japanese whisky on the shelves of liquor retailers these days. Yes and no. There is Japanese whisky around, but almost all of it is blended and entry-level. That's where the big money is to be made.

The big boys, Suntory and Nikka, don't have time for releases in the malt category at the moment. Sure, there was the domestic-only, blink-and-you-miss-it annual Yamazaki Limited Release 2017 and a few (similarly NAS!) items for their respective distillery shops but other than that, nothing at all. The situation is so dire that it's getting harder for bars in Japan to even get hold of the NAS Yamazaki, and those who do want to keep it on their shelves often have to resort to paying as much as 50% more than the RRP to purchase it from 'specialized' websites.

One way in which producers are dealing with the stock-shortage pressure is by putting malt whisky on the disattend track. Grain whisky has been in the spotlight for a few years now. Nikka has their Coffey Grain and Coffey Malt. Suntory has their premium grain whisky The Chita, which was only available in Japan when it was released in September 2015, but since July 2016 in selected markets abroad, as well. At the Tokyo International Bar Show 2017, Suntory didn't have any new products at its booth, but they had brought along three product samples: two single grains (a Hakushu rye and a Chita wine cask finish) and one malt (a peated Yamazaki) – a sign of the times! The rye in particular was the talk of the show. Given a few more years – the sample was 4 years old – many people agreed Suntory would have a winner if they put that in the market. Whether they will, remains to be seen, but diversification in the grain category – in the portfolio, that is – seems to be on the horizon, not just at Suntory but also at Kirin, which has a long history of making different types of grain whisky for their blends, and at Nikka.

Japanese gin on the move

The other big story of 2017 was gin. Following The Kyoto Distillery's successful launch of their craft gin Ki No Bi in October 2016, both Nikka and Suntory came out with a 'craft gin' of their own, Roku and Coffey Gin respectively, ahead of the hot summer months. It's not hard to see the attraction. These premium gins retail for about the same price as the NAS single malts in their respective portfolios, but contrary to whisky it's a make-today-sell-tomorrow game.

So where does that leave Japanese single malt whisky, as far as immediate consumption is concerned? Mostly in the hands of the smaller producers, would be the answer to that, even though their stock is young and limited by the scale of their operations. Unfortunately, the single malt that is released by the likes of Venture Whisky (Chichibu distillery), Eigashima (Akashi) and Hombo Shuzo (Mars Shinshu) is getting pricier by the year. The average retail price for a 700ml single cask bottling is slowly but surely approaching 20,000 yen (£140) at home … if you can get it! Remember, this is for 5 year old whisky, give or take a year or two. One of the side effects of this price evolution is that limited edition Scotch whisky has started joining Japanese whisky in the elevator up. After all, selling a 15 year old single cask Tomatin in Japan for less than a 5 year old Japanese single cask bottling would be sending the wrong signal. Right?

It's not all doom and gloom, though. There are more distilleries making malt whisky in Japan than ever before. At the time of writing, we're at 16 and counting. You'll find all about them in the pages that follow. By the time you're holding next year's edition, chances are we'll have to make room for number 17. Kinryu is a shochu maker based in Sakata city, Yamagata prefecture. Unless you're a hardcore shochu fan, this won't ring a bell. Kinryu is a small company, founded in 1950, and they sell 95% of what they make in their home prefecture. Yamagata has one of the oldest populations in Japan (which is saying something!), so Kinryu figured it was time to branch out into something more lucrative and to cast their net a bit wider.

In May 2017, Kinryu announced their plan to set up a whisky distillery in the neigbouring town of Yuzamachi. The idea is to start construction in October 2017, to install the equipment – ordered from Forsyths in Scotland – in July 2018 by which time they hope to have received their distilling license and to start distilling towards the end of 2018. It's an ambitious project, not only in terms of the projected time line, but also in terms of the finances involved (a whopping 500 million yen, more than half of the company's annual sales).

Kinryu is aiming to produce a top-quality single malt whisky. Annual production is slated to be around 90,000 litres a year. In addition to the equipment, they're also planning to import their barley and casks from Scotland. Inspired by the success of Venture Whisky and Hombo Shuzo, from whom they will be getting technical support in calibrating the processes at their distillery, Kinryu is shooting for the stars. They're looking to establish their single malt brand nationwide and abroad. The first release is scheduled for 2021. By the time their first whisky is bottled, they won't be alone on the shelves of liquor stores in the Japanese single malt whisky department. In fact, it may be quite crowded by then. In terms of quality, we won't have anything to worry about as far as the new wave of distillers is concerned. We can only hope that the presence of more serious players and the increased availability of juice will bring the prices of single malt Japanese whisky down to reasonable levels again. Until then, and I hate to say it, please hold the line…

© pictures; Akkeshi, Kenten Co., Chichibu Peated, Venture Whisky and Mars Kohiganzakura, Hombo Shuzo

Stefan Van Eycken grew up in Belgium and Scotland and moved to Japan in 2000. Editor of Nonjatta, he is also the man behind the 'Ghost Series' bottlings and the charity event 'Spirits for Small Change'. He is regional editor (Japan) for Whisky Magazine UK, and a regular contributor to Whisky Magazine Japan and France. His book "Whisky Rising: The Definitive Guide to the Finest Whiskies and Distillers from Japan" was published by Cider Mill Press in April 2017.

Akkeshi

Owner:
Kenten Jitsugyo

Location:
Hokkaido

Founded:
2015

Capacity:
60,000 l

Malt whisky range:
none yet

Asaka

Owner:
Sasanokawa Shuzo

Location:
Fukushima P.

Founded:
2015

Capacity:
40,000 l

Malt whisky range:
none yet

Unlike most new distilleries in Japan, which are expansions of existing liquor operations, Akkeshi is one of two that was built from the ground up. The distillery is located in the town of the same name on the east coast of Hokkaido.

It's quite a remote area with particularly harsh winters, when temperatures can drop to -20°C, so the maintenance season here is in the winter, rather than in the summer. The distillery is located near the sea and surrounded by beautiful wetlands with an abundance of peat. Also, the town of Akkeshi is famous for a local delicacy that goes hand-in-glove with peated whisky: oysters.

Akkeshi is definitely a distillery to watch. They started producing around the time last year's issue of this book came out, and the first five and a half months of production have resulted in 264 casks maturing in the warehouse. They are on a 7-days-a-week production schedule and have increased their staff to 6. You've got to be a Jack of all trades to work at Akkeshi as everyone is involved in all stages of production.

The production target for 2016 was 30,000 litres. The goal for 2017 is to produce around 100,000 litres. This will include a second run of peated spirit from September 2017 onwards. The folks at Akkeshi will also start experimenting with different barley types this year, and have sourced some unorthodox cask types to carry out some maturation experiments. This may sound a bit vague, but watch this space!

Speaking of which: a second large storage house was built on the grounds directly opposite the distillery in 2017 and another site, closer to the sea, has been secured to build yet another warehouse in the near future. This will make it possible to explore the effect of micro-climate on the maturation process.

Most new distilleries in Japan have released some new-make (non-peated and/or peated), but the people at Akkeshi have deliberately steered away from that. However, they're very happy with the way the maturing spirit is developing and may consider putting out a "taster" product next year so that fans can get an idea of what the Akkeshi spirit is like.

Some Japanese whisky fans may know Sasanokawa Shuzo as the company that came to the rescue when Ichiro Akuto had purchased the remaining 400-odd casks of Hanyu and he was looking for a place to store them.

In fact, the people at Sasanokawa were so kind as to modify the racks in their warehouses so the larger-sized casks could be accommodated. However, there's much more to Sasanokawa Shuzo than that. The company was founded in 1765. They turned their hand to whisky making straight after World War II, when there was a scarcity of rice (throwing a spanner in the works of their sake business) but a huge demand for whisky (particularly from the side of the Allied occupation). Sasanokawa applied for a license to make whisky in 1945 and the year after they got to work. Their focus was on the lowest grade of blended whisky. Like others, they 'made' whisky by using industrial alcohol from the war effort that was coloured, flavoured and mixed with other types of booze to look and taste like 'whisky'.

As the economy recovered so did people's palates, so Sasanokawa – looking to up their game – started making whisky in makeshift stills (not made out of copper!) Sales weren't always great but the structure of the company kept their whisky business afloat. Sake making took up about 200 days of the year, so rather than having the staff while away the rest of the year, they were kept busy making whisky. During the 80s, Sasanokawa became one of the three big players of the 'ji whisky' boom (usually translated as 'craft whisky', but maybe 'crafty whisky' is a better way of putting it) along with Hombo Shuzo and Toa Shuzo.

With demand for Japanese whisky at an all-time high but supply pretty low, Sasanokawa decided to set up a proper malt whisky distillery in 2015, the 250th anniversary of the company. By December 2015, two small pot stills had been installed in a vacant warehouse, and by June 2016 the distillery was ready to start producing.

It is the most compact distillery in Japan, with all processes from milling to filling taking place under one roof. Most of the production is non-peated, but the weeks leading up to the summer break are reserved for some heavily-peated runs (50ppm). Interestingly, the distillery is run entirely by two young people, stillman Daisuke Taura and mash-woman Minami Sakakura. At the time of writing, the latter is not even of legal drinking age. How's that for handing the baton to the younger generation!

Chichibu

Owner:	Location:	Founded:	Capacity:
Venture Whisky	Saitama P.	2007	60,000 l

Malt whisky range:
Occasional limited releases

Fuji Gotemba

Owner:	Location:	Founded:	Capacity:
Kirin Holdings	Shizuoka P.	1973	2,000,000 l

Malt whisky range:
Fuji-Gotemba 17 year old Small Batch

Ichiro Akuto, founder of Chichibu distillery, is the rock star of the Japanese whisky scene. At whisky festivals, no booth draws bigger crowds than his.

When word spreads of a new release, people will queue in the hope of scoring a bottle. The new generation of Japanese distillers look to him for advice and guidance – and you'd be hard pressed to find someone who didn't spend some time observing his crew at Chichibu distillery – and the big dogs have come to respect him for his dedication to the craft of whisky making, which is second to none.

Ichiro set up his own distillery a few years after his grandfather's whisky distillery, Hanyu, was liquidated and this at a time when whisky consumption in Japan was at an all-time low. The distillery building is quite compact: a 2,400 litre mashtun (manually stirred with a wooden paddle!), 8 mizunara washbacks and a pair of 2,000 litre pot stills. Every year, about 10% of production is dedicated to local barley so there is an area for floor malting. There are 4 warehouses and a fully-operational cooperage, which is mostly used to make mizunara (i.e. Japanese oak) hogs-heads. Ichiro and his team have been going to Hokkaido several times a year since 2010 to buy mizunara logs at the hardwood auction there. His two young coopers, Masahi Watanabe and Kenta Nagae, have been perfecting their mizunara-barrel-making skills since 2016. It's a stubborn and porous wood, so it's far from easy.

Getting hold of Chichibu single malt is still not an easy thing to do. In fact, contrary to expectation, it seems to be getting harder by the year. The latest "general" release was "The Peated 2016" but those disappeared like snow before the sun. The mid-term goal is to release a 10 year old by the time of the Tokyo Olympics in 2020, so he's being careful with his stocks in the meantime.

Tasting note The Peated 2016:
Vegetal peat, fruit candy and potato peel on the nose. Beautifully balanced on the palate with the peat providing a bed for the fruit and sweetness. The peat crescendoes on the finish and brings out some nutty flavours.

Fuji Gotemba Distillery is on a roll. At the World Whiskies Awards 2016 in London, they won "Best Single Grain Whisky in the World" for their 25 old Small Batch Single Grain.

A year later, they got the same award for the same whisky, and their Chief Blender Jota Tanaka got crowned "Master Distiller/Blender of the Year" at the Icons of Whisky Awards 2017. These recognitions have energized the team at the distillery which is great for the consumer, as the company will be keen to spotlight the versatility of their whisky making in more products in the years to come.

Versatility is the key-word here. Fuji Gotemba Distillery was established in 1972 by Kirin Brewery Co. (Japan), J.E. Seagram & Sons (U.S.) and Chivas Brothers (U.K.). The idea was to set up a comprehensive whisky manufacturing plant where everything – from malt and grain whisky distilling to blending and bottling – could be done on site. Unlike most Japanese distilleries, which followed Scottish whisky-making practice, Fuji Gotemba adopted production techniques from all around the world. After Seagram started selling off its beverage assets worldwide, Kirin became the sole owner of Fuji Gotemba distillery.

In addition to malt whisky, three types of grain whisky are made at the distillery using a multi-column still, a kettle and a doubler in a modular way. This allows Jota Tanaka and his team to come up with innovative blends. Fans interested in trying the Fuji Gotemba malt should keep an eye out for the Blender's Choice Single Malt, or make a trip to the distillery where you may be able to pick up one of the Distiller's Select Single Malt bottlings (there is also a Single Grain) which is put together ever year in the spring by the team at the distillery, rather than by the Chief Blender and his team.

Tasting note Fuji Gotemba Single Malt 17yo Small Batch:

A smorgasbord of fruity delights (Poire belle Hélène, pineapple tarts and over-ripe mangoes). The fruity notes gain in intensity on the palate, accompanied by candied ginger and a gentle, peppery spiciness. The finish is long and lingering with a hint of burdock in the afterglow.

Hakushu

Owner: Beam Suntory
Location: Yamanashi P.
Founded: 1973
Capacity: 4,000,000 l

Malt whisky range:
NAS, 12, 18, 25 year old plus occasional limited releases

Miyagikyo

Owner: Nikka Whisky
Location: Miyagi P.
Founded: 1969
Capacity: 3,000,000 l

Malt whisky range:
NAS and occasional limited releases

Half a century after Shinjiro Torii had built Japan's first whisky distillery, Keizo Saji, the second president of Suntory, decided to build a second distillery to expand the company's palette of malt whisky components.

The site picked was a vast forest area at the foot of Mt Kaikomagatake in the Southern Alps. Hakushu is often referred to as "the forest distillery" and that's not just a PR spin. More than 80% of the site bought by Suntory is undeveloped and it includes a wild bird sanctuary.

Hakushu distillery has changed quite a bit over the years. The original distillery was equipped with 6 pairs of stills. In 1977, capacity was doubled and another 6 pairs of stills added in a building next to 'Hakushu 1'. With its 4 mashtuns, 44 washbacks and 24 stills, Hakushu (1+2) was the biggest distillery in the world at the time. In 1981, they decided to change this radically. Suntory built a new distillery, 'Hakushu 3' or 'Hakushu East' on the site, and decided to phase out production at '1+2' in favor of '3'. This may seem a bit silly, but if you know that '1+2' had big stills, all of the same shape and size, and '3' had a variety of stills with different shapes, sizes, lyne-arm orientations, heating methods and condenser types, you can hazard a guess as to why Suntory did what they did: quantity vs. diversity and quality. The distillery, as it's operative now, is Hakushu 3, albeit with the addition of two pairs of pot stills in 2014, bringing the total to 8 pairs. It's also worth noting that there is a small grain whisky facility at Hakushu since December 2010.

The range today is NAS, 12, 18 and 25 year old, at least on paper, because finding the age-statement expressions in the wild is becoming more and more unlikely. Hopefully, as stocks recover, we'll see a return of the much-celebrated sherry or peated limited editions.

Tasting note Hakushu NAS:

Green in all senses of the word. Cucumber and mint on the nose. On the palate, mossy twigs and citrus, with faint smoke emerging later on. The finish is long and woody.

It is said that it took Masataka Taketsuru three years to find the perfect site for his second distillery, settling on the valley that brings the Hirosegawa and Nikkagawa (no relation to the company name) rivers together.

The location was chosen for the quality of the water (which is very soft), the suitable humidity and the crisp air. Originally known as 'Sendai', the distillery was renamed 'Miyagikyo' when Asahi took control of Nikka in 2001.

Miyagikyo is equipped with 22 steel washbacks and 8 huge pot stills of the boil ball type with upward lyne arms, encouraging reflux which – given the slow distillation method (steam-heated) – results in a lighter, cleaner spirit. The site also houses two enormous Coffey stills imported by Taketsuru from Scotland. Moved from Nishinomiya in 1999, these are used to produce grain whisky (Coffey Grain) but, occasionally, also used to distil malted barley (Coffey Malt).

In September 2015, Nikka discontinued the entire Miyagikyo range – which included a no-age-statement expression, a 10 year old, 12 year old and 15 year old – because of stock shortages. It was replaced with a new NAS expression, which for the foreseeable future is meant to be the only permanently available expression of Miyagkiyo.

If you want a glimpse of the different facets of Miyagikyo, you have to make a trip out to the distillery where – on a good day – you can pick up three so-called 'Key Malt' bottlings: 'Fruity & Rich', 'Malty & Soft' and 'Sherry & Sweet'.

Tasting note Miyagikyo NAS (2015 release):

Apples and pears on the nose with grassy and light floral elements; dried fruits, vanilla and anise on the palate, with a tiny bit of bitterness and some milk chocolate on the finish.

Nagahama

Owner: **Location:** **Founded:** **Capacity:**
Nagahama Roman Beer Co.   Shiga P.   2016   15,000 l

Malt whisky range:
none yet

Nukada

Owner: **Location:**   **Founded:** **Capacity:**
Kiuchi Shuzo   Ibaraki P.   2016   12,000 l

Malt whisky range:
none yet

Nagahama Distillery is located in the picturesque town of the same name in Shiga and it is one of the smallest distilleries in Japan at the time of writing. It was set up in a record time of 7 months, but the owners didn't have to start from scratch.

Nagahama distillery is, in fact, an extension of Nagahama Roman (with the emphasis on the second syllable, as in romantic) Brewery, which was established in 1996 as a brewpub. The first half of the whisky-making process – mashing and fermentation – takes place in the equipment used for beer-making. For the second half of the process, a small 'still room' was created behind the bar counter.

Inspired by some of the new wave of craft distillers in Scotland (Strathearn and Eden Mill, in particular), the team at Nagahama decided to go for small stills (a 1,000 litre wash still and 500 litre spirit still) fitted with alembic heads of the type seen more often in calvados, cognac or pisco distillation than in whisky making. They were made by Hoga Stills in Portugal and delivered in a matter of months: they arrived in Nagahama on November 10th and the first distillation took place a week later.

For the time being, two types of barley are used: non-peated (imported from Germany) and medium-peated barley (20ppm, imported from the U.K.). For some mashes, a small proportion of peated barley is added to the non-peated barley, creating a sort of lightly-peated variation. The latter was the case for the first batch ever distilled at the distillery.

Nagahama Distillery follows a 'one batch = one barrel' policy. One mash consists of 400 kg barley, which results in 1,600 litres of wash. This is then sent to one of 6 stainless steel fermenters. After 60 hours' fermentation, half of the wort is pumped down into the wash still and distilled. In the afternoon, the remaining half is charged and distilled. After the second distillation, the result is around 100 litres of new make at about 68%. This is then reduced in strength to 59%and filled into an ex-bourbon barrel.

Keen to have whisky fans in Japan on board right from the start, Nagahama has bottled some of their new-make and sold it with an optional 1l mini-barrel for home-maturation purposes.

Nukada is possibly the most obscure distillery in Japan. It's not open to the public, hasn't released anything (not even new-make) and it doesn't self-advertise its efforts.

The company behind Nukada, however, is anything but obscure. If you've ever had a Japanese craft beer with an owl on the label, you know who's behind the whisky: the same people that make the acclaimed Hitachino Nest beer. The brewery dates from 1996, but the company can trace its roots to 1823, when they started making sake.

Local barley was the driving factor behind Kiuchi Shuzo's decision to expand into the field of whisky. Company director Toshiyuki Kiuchi insists the move was not motivated by a desire to jump on the bandwagon of the Japanese whisky boom that started in 2008. His plans predate that boom by several years. As a brewer, Kiuchi was keen to revive the first Japanese variety of beer barley but it soon became apparent that there was a lot of what he calls 'junk barley', i.e. barley that wasn't suitable for beer making. Kiuchi figured there was one way to avoid all that junk barley going to waste and that was to distill it. The investment in a bigger brewhouse delayed his distilling plans by several years, but by February 2016, a small hybrid still had been set up and they were ready to start making whisky.

The hybrid still is quite small (1,000 litres) so the folks at Kiuchi Shuzo are fairly limited at the moment, but there are bigger plans on the table. The company is in the process of ordering a set of pot stills from Forsyths in Scotland. The wash still will be 12,000 litres, so 12 times bigger than the kit used now. The idea is to set up a distillery on a completely different site, but still in Kiuchi Shuzo's home prefecture of Ibaraki. Until that is ready, production will continue at Nukada Distillery.

Sam Yoneda, who's half-Scottish, half-Japanese, is the man in charge of whisky production. Last business year he only managed to put 6,000 litres of new make into barrels because he was also brewing beer. This year, he is mainly distilling, and will be able to produce around 15,000 litres. For one of the batches made last year, rice polishings (a byproduct of making sake, and usually discarded) were added to the mash. Toshiyuki Kiuchi has a soft spot for sherried whiskies – Macallan in particular – so quite a bit of the new-make is filled into sherry butts. In June 2017, another 27 cream sherry butts were delivered from Spain, so lovers of sherried whisky are advised to keep their eyes peeled!

Okayama

Owner: Miyashita Shuzo

Location: Okayama P.

Founded: 2011

Capacity: 7,000 l

Malt whisky range: none yet

Saburomaru

Owner: Wakatsuru Shuzo

Location: Toyama P.

Founded: ca. 1990

Capacity: t.b.d.

Malt whisky range: occasional releases

Miyashita Shuzo is a multitasking liquor producer based in Okayama. The company was founded in 1915 as a sake brewery. In 1983, they started making shochu and in 1994, they became one of the pioneers on the Japanese craft beer scene.

They entered the whisky business in the wake of the highball boom. The brewing and distilling know-how was already there and much of the infrastructure to make whisky, too. All it took was a few extra steps.

In 2003, Miyashita started single-distilling some of their hoppy beer in a stainless steel shochu still. They filled this into American white oak and kept a close watch on it. Encouraged by the way this distilled beer was maturing, they started thinking about producing whisky.

They acquired their license in 2011 and immediately got to work, using the equipment that was already in place. Mashing and fermentation was done in the equipment for beer making; distillation was carried out under low pressure in their shochu still by running it twice. Stainless steel and whisky are awkward bedfellows and the folks at Miyashita must have realized this, too. By July 2015, a brand new copper hybrid still had been installed on the premises by German maker Holstein. This has been used to make whisky ever since.

Okayama is a traditional barley-growing region and Miyashita is keen on using local barley. They source a local variety known as 'Sky Golden' from farmers in the region and send it to a malting company 750km away before it is trucked back to the distillery. This comes at a considerable expense. All in all, this makes using the local barley about 5 times as expensive as using imported barley. Since they can't use enough locally, half of their malted barley is imported from Germany. Still, no other distillery in Japan uses as much local barley as Okayama distillery.

In 2017, a tiny stillhouse was erected on the premises and the hybrid still moved there. By mid-2017, there were about 50 casks maturing in a racked warehouse on site. In addition to the usual ex-bourbon and ex-sherry, there are also some ex-brandy and virgin oak mizunara casks slumbering in the warehouse.

In most whisky-making countries, Saburomaru wouldn't be considered a malt whisky distillery, but in Japan it is. The reason for this is that 'whisky' is a notoriously under-regulated category there.

At Saburomaru, distillation of malt whisky takes place in an alumite pot still of the type commonly used in shochu-making. Recently, after a successful crowdfunding campaign, enough money was raised to replace the top of the pot still with a copper swan neck. Again, in most countries, that wouldn't qualify the liquid running off the still as malt whisky but in Japan, it does.

As part of the crowdfunding campaign, the rickety old building that houses all the equipment was renovated and turned into a visitor-friendly attraction. A little mill was also installed, much to the delight of the staff who – until then – had to manually empty bags of milled barley straight into the mashtun from the second floor of the building, resulting in thick clouds of flour dust on that floor. The barley used is imported from Scotland and heavily peated (50ppm).

Wakatsuru Shuzo, the company behind the distillery, has always used the in-house produced whisky as part of cheap blends marketed under the brandname "Sunshine". In 2016, however, the decision was made to properly focus on single malt whisky in their portfolio. Henceforth, single malt expressions will all be under the 'Saburomaru' banner, to avoid confusion with 'Sunshine'.

The first Saburomaru release was launched on June 21, 2016. This was a 55 year old, making it the oldest single malt Japanese whisky bottled so far. Again, in Scotland, it wouldn't be considered a single malt whisky because it was distilled in a continuous still, but in Japan that doesn't matter. The casks used for this 55 year old were ex-red wine casks from the days when Wakatsuru Shuzo dabbled in port wine.

There are winds of change blowing at Saburomaru distillery, which can only be a good thing. It will be interesting to see what niche they manage to eke out in the Japanese single malt whisky landscape over the years to come.

Shinshu

Owner: Hombo Shuzo
Location: Nagano P.
Founded: 1985
Capacity: 70,000 l

Malt whisky range:
Komagatake (various limited edition releases)

Shizuoka

Owner: Gaia Flow Distilling
Location: Shizuoka P.
Founded: 2015
Capacity: t.b.d.

Malt whisky range:
none yeat

Strikes and gutters – that's the Mars whisky history summed up in three words.

Hombo Shuzo got a license to distil whisky in 1949, but for the first decade simply blended sourced components with neutral spirits produced in-house. In 1960 they set up a distillery in Yamanashi prefecture and began producing a heavy, smoky style of whisky. It didn't sell well and after nine years, they stopped. In 1978, the company was ready to give it another go, but they were using the old site for winemaking, so they started looking for a new one. They set up in Kagoshima, on the southern island of Kyushu. In 1985, they moved north to Shinshu and changed to a lighter style. They were forced to mothball that plant in 1992 but in 2011, they fired up the stills once more.

Production is limited to the winter months, but lately they've been stretching their whisky season to 7 and a half months. In November 2014, they replaced the old pot stills with brand new ones, built following the original blueprints. They now produce four types of distillate (non-peated and peated at 3.5, 20 and 50ppm). They're exploring the influence of climate on the maturation process by sending some casks to the old site in Kagoshima, and some to Yakushima island which is extremely humid.

In 2016, Hombo released Kohiganzakura where they are seeking to bridge the decades by combining malt from the new regime with malt from the pre-1992 era. Recently they also launched their oldest single malt to date, a 30 year old, in three different editions: American White Oak, Sherry Cask and Sherry Cask at vatting strength (53%). There are now just a handful of casks from the pre-1992 era left in the warehouse, so we're literally talking "liquid history" here. But the future is looking bright. The Komagatake 'Tsunuki Aging' release was one of the highlights of the year and that was only 3 years old. Stay tuned!

Tasting note Komagatake Kohiganzakura:

Fabulous nose with stewed orchard fruits, guava jam and apple peel. On the palate: soft oak, orchard fruits again, citrus and a touch of spice. The finish is long and lingering on cotton candy and caramel sauce.

Shizuoka distillery is the brainchild of Gaia Flow founder Taiko Nakamura. Inspired by a visit to Kilchoman distillery in 2012, Nakamura started thinking about setting up a distillery of his own back home.

He set up a liquor import company, Gaia Flow, to get a foot in the door of the drinks business, and kept working on his distillery project. Shizuoka distillery was officially opened on February 25, 2017.

The main distillery building is ingeniously designed. Inspired by Karuizawa distillery, everything from milling to filling (the barley and casks, resp.) takes place under one roof, but in different rooms. Another thing that's carefully considered is the way in which the landscape – small green tea farms and forested mountains – is visible from various points in the distillery building. Also, the visitor experience is integrated into the design of the distillery, which is unusual for whisky distilleries in Japan.

In the mashroom there is room for 12 washbacks, but for the time being there are five: four made from Oregon pine and one made from Shizuoka cedar which was installed in February 2017. The stillhouse has 3 pot stills: one from the old Karuizawa distillery and a new pair made by Forsyths in Scotland. Both of the new stills have a bulge (or boil ball). Interestingly, Nakamura opted for direct heating for the wash still. The old Karuizawa still and the new spirit still are steam heated.

Initially, the staff at the distillery used the indirectly-heated pot stills, as the process is easier to control. On March 23, 2017, the directly-fired wash still was used for the first one. According to Nakamura, they have had their share of teething problems, but they're figuring things out little by little.

The idea is to produce a "light, delicate spirit" at Shizuoka distillery. This will be a welcome contrast to the type of spirit made by most of the younger Japanese craft distilleries, which is on the heavier side of the spectrum.

Tsunuki

Owner:
Hombo Shuzo

Location:
Kagoshima P.

Founded:
2016

Capacity:
70,000 l

Malt whisky range:
none yet

White Oak

Owner:
Eigashima Shuzo

Location:
Hyogo P.

Founded:
1984

Capacity:
60,000 l

Malt whisky range:
Akashi NAS and occasional, limited releases

Up until last year, who could have conceived of a craft distillery in Japan having two distilleries? That it was Hombo Shuzo, who became the first craft producer to set up a second one, seems even more unlikely on the surface.

After all, their other distillery, Mars Shinshu, only makes whisky for about half the year. Surely, it makes more sense to just distill all year round at that one distillery, rather than have two distilleries working half-time? Yes and no. Yes, if your goal is volume. No, if what you're after is diversity. For Hombo Shuzo, it's all about the latter. They are raising the bar, and for that, deservedly won 'Craft Producer of the Year' at the 2017 Icons of Whisky awards organized by Whisky Magazine.

The folks at Hombo Shuzo are interested in exploring terroir and that's why they set up a second distillery in Kagoshima. They want a new malt whisky that is radically different, not by engineering such difference in one and the same place, but by allowing the natural environmental conditions to play their part. Reducing those conditions to a central image, if that of Mars Shinshu is the majestic mountains, that of Tsunuki is Sakurajima, the nearby, active volcano. At Mars Shinshu, distillation takes place at high altitude; at Mars Tsunuki, they are a stone's throw from the sea. Tsunuki is also the southernmost whisky distillery in Japan, and the only one on the island of Kyushu.

Like Mars Shinshu distillery, one season – which ordinarily runs from October to June – sees 180 tons of malted barley being turned into spirit. That means 180 batches of 1 ton per day. Like at Mars Shinshu distillery, four peating levels are used: non-peat (0ppm), lightly-peated (3.5ppm), heavily peated (20ppm) and super heavily peated (50ppm). The emphasis is on lightly peated malt, which accounts for 80 tons. The plan for next season is to increase production by a little over 25%.

The very first distillation was on October 27th (stripping run) and 28th (spirit run) 2016 so there's not much in the warehouses yet, but the quality of the new make is top notch so we're in for a treat in a few years' time. In the meantime, the distillery is well worth a visit. All processes can be observed and you can even have a peek at the old continuous still on site. The Hombo family home next door has been renovated in the most beautiful visitor centre in Japan with a well-stocked bar. It's a bit of a trek to get to, but you won't regret it.

The people at Eigashima don't like to be hurried. Even with demand at an all-time high, they keep taking it easy – just like they have for the past 100 years.

On paper, it's the oldest whisky distillery in Japan – having acquired a distilling license in 1919, four years before Yamazaki, but it took them four decades to get started. And it took them another four decades to release their first single malt – that was an 8 year old in 2007 – and it wasn't until 2013 that they released their first single cask bottling. That's almost a hundred years – talk about a slow start. But whisky production was never a priority for Eigashima: they make their money with sake and shochu. When they entered the single malt market, whisky accounted for less than 1% of their total sales. They've expanded production to 7 months in 2017, but we're still talking single digits in sales percentage. However, for the first time they've exhibited at a whisky festival in Japan so they may be ready to shift gears. Time will tell.

The current distillery was built in 1984. After a period of using malt with varying peat levels, they switched to using only lightly peated (5ppm) malt. All production is matured on site, in old single-story rickety warehouses. They mostly fill into ex-bourbon wood, but they also have sherry butts, cognac casks, wine and recharred ex-barley shochu casks, as well as domestically-made virgin oak.

The oldest stock in the warehouses is approaching 10 years at the time of writing, but there is very little of that. By the time you are reading this, a special 10 year old bottling will have been released. There are also plans to release a new 5 year old, matured in ex-bourbon casks.

Tasting note Akashi NAS:

The deep colours and surprisingly warm nose, tips you off that there's a sherry influence. There's a peach tea and autumn fruits when you sip, and a fairly short finish.

Yamazaki

Owner:	Location:	Founded:	Capacity:
Beam Suntory	Osaka P.	1923	6,000,000 l

Malt whisky range:
NAS, 12, 18, 25 years old and occasional limited releases.

Yoichi

Owner:	Location:	Founded:	Capacity:
Nikka Whisky	Hokkaido	1934	2,000,000 l

Malt whisky range:
NAS and occasional limited releases.

Yamazaki, conveniently located between Osaka and Kyoto, is considered the birthplace of Japanese whisky. It was here that Shinjiro Torii decided to build the first whisky distillery.

The construction of Yamazaki distillery began in late 1932 and was completed the following year. The distillery started out with two pot stills but has been reconfigured and expanded many times over the years, first in 1957, and most recently in 2013, when four pot stills were added bringing the count to 16. There's plenty of variety in terms of heating method, shape, size, lyne-arm orientation and condenser type. Since 1988, eight of the washbacks are wooden whereas the other nine are stainless steel. With different peating levels for the barley, different yeast strains and a plethora of cask types, the variety of whisky types created at Yamazaki distillery is quite staggering.

Yamazaki was the first generally available single malt in Japan. That was 1984. These days, 'generally available' has to be taken with a pinch of salt. Of the theoretical line-up of NAS, 12, 18 and 25 year old, the age-statement expressions are fast becoming like unicorns – reputed to exist but when was the last time you saw one?

In the past, Suntory released limited editions on a regular basis, but those days are gone. All we have to report on that front is the Yamazaki Limited Edition 2017, the latest in the annual, NAS limited edition series for the domestic market. Word on the street is that a Yamazaki 18yo Mizunara bottling may see the light of day before the year is over. There's little doubt the liquid will be top notch, but there's even less doubt that it'll cost a pretty penny… if it materializes and if you can manage to put your hands on a bottle.

Tasting note Yamazaki NAS:
Zesty nose, with some sawdust and strawberry. Lots of bourbon influences on the palate, with creamy vanilla, creme brulee, but also some spice. A relatively short, sharp finish. Superb for its price bracket.

Thanks to the 2015 TV series 'Massan', Masa-taka Taketsuru has become a household name in Japan. Before, only hardcore whisky fans would have known about the man's role in the development of Japanese whisky.

After leaving his previous employer in 1934, Taketsuru set up his own distillery. He settled on the town of Yoichi, up in Hokkaido, because the locale and climate conditions reminded him of Scotland, where he had studied whisky making. The first spirit ran off the stills in 1936.

Initially equipped with a single still that doubled as spirit and wash still, the distillery now houses 6 stills. Coal-heated and featuring straight heads and downward lyne arms, these produce a robust spirit. Although the house style is peaty and heavy, people tend to forget that Yoichi is set up to create a wide range of distillates. Between various peating levels, yeast strains, fermentation times, distillation methods and maturation types, it is said that Yoichi is capable of producing 3,000 different types of malt whisky.

Though the importance of this sort of flavour palate for in-house blending is obvious, it is a pity that we are much less likely to be able to appreciate that variety as consumers. In September 2015, the entire Yoichi range (which included a no-age statement expression as well as a 10, 12, 15 and 20 year old) was axed and replaced with a single option: a new NAS.

The only way to get your hands on something special is to visit the distillery where a selection of so-called 'key malts' (NAS) is available for purchase – if you're lucky, that is. There's a choice of three: Woody & Vanillic, Peaty & Salty and Sherry & Sweet.

Tasting note Yoichi NAS, (2015 release):
Barley sweetness, pencil shavings, over-ripe orchard fruits and soft smoke on the nose; oak and peat lead the dance on the palate with some candied orange peel thrown in; the finish is earthy and vegetal, with some tea on the side.

Colin Spoelman and David Haskell from Kings County Distillery in Brooklyn, New York

Distilleries
around the globe

Including the subsections:
Europe
North America | Australia & New Zealand
Asia | Africa | South America

During the last ten years new malt whisky distilleries have been opening around the world at an incredible rate and the number has increased more than tenfold. This era has been characterized by the curiosity and inquisitiveness of the new producers, a time where old rules have been challenged and untried methods have been put to the test, sometimes with mixed results. But the possibility to meet similar minded producers, to discuss methodology and gain advice for future development and growth is also an important part of the game. This was something that Box Distillery and their Brand Ambassador Jan Groth took into account when they launched and hosted the inaugural World Whisky Forum at the distillery in Northern

Sweden in February 2017. Moderated by Dave Broom, speakers from all corners of the world joined to share their own experiences and it wasn't just from newly established distilleries. Representatives from Kirin and William Grant & Sons were also present. There is no doubt that many of the traditional companies find the ideas and methods of this new generation of whisky makers interesting. This is evidenced not least by several big producers buying into small distilleries around the world, to be a part of something that may impact the whisky industry in the future. The next World Whisky Forum will be held in June 2018 and will be hosted by Cotswolds Distillery in England.

Europe

Austria

Distillery: Whiskydistillery J. Haider, Roggenreith
Founded: 1995
Owner: Johann, Monika & Jasmin Haider
whiskyerlebniswelt.at

In the small village of Roggenreith in northern Austria, the Haider family has been distilling whisky since 1995 and three years later, the first Austrian whisky was released. In 2005, they opened up a Whisky Experience World with guided tours, a video show, whisky tasting and exhibitions. Roggenhof was the first whisky distillery in Austria and, over the years, production has steadily increased to 35,000 litres. The capacity currently stands at 100,000 litres per annum. The wash is allowed to ferment for 72 hours before it reaches either of the two 450 litre Christian Carl copper stills. The desired strength is reached in one single distillation, thanks to the attached column. The main part (70%) of the production are rye whiskies – Original Rye Whisky J.H., Pure Rye Malt J.H., Special Rye Malt J.H. and (since 2012) Special Rye Malt Peated J.H. The last three are made from 100% rye. A 10 year old Original Rye Selection was released recently. The current range of single malts made from barley is Single Malt J.H, Special Single Malt J.H. and Special Single Malt Peated J.H. In addition to that, some of these whiskies are also available as 9 year olds and bottled at a higher strength (46% instead of 41%). From time to time releases are also made in the Rare Selection range. Recent limited bottlings include Rare Selection Dark Rye Malt J.H., matured fot 6 years in eiswein barrels and a 3 year old Single Malt J.H. with a finish in Laphroaig casks.

Distillery: Broger Privatbrennerei, Klaus
Founded: 1976 (whisky since 2008)
Owner: Broger family
broger.info

The production of whisky is supplementing the distillation and production of eau de vie from apples and pears. For their whisky, Broger buys peated malt in the UK and unpeated malt from Germany but also floor malted barley from Bohemia. The distillery is equipped with a 150 litre Christian Carl still. The total volume of whisky produced in a year is 2,500 litres. The current range of whiskies consists of five expressions; Triple Cask which is a blend of whiskies matured in bourbon, sherry and madeira casks, Medium Smoked which has been smoked using beech wood, Burn Out, a heavily peated whisky, Riebelmais, a corn whisky and the limited Distiller's Edition which has been maturing in madeira casks and is bottled at cask strength (60,7%).

Other distilleries in Austria

Reisetbauer

Kirchberg-Thening, founded in 1994 (whisky since 1995)

www.reisetbauer.at

This is a family-owned farm distillery near Linz in northern Austria specialising in brandies and fruit schnapps. Since 1995, a range of malt whiskies are also produced. The distillery is equipped with five 350 litre stills. The 70 hour-long fermentation takes place in stainless steel washbacks. Local barley is used for the unpeated malt and casks are sourced locally from Austrian wine producers. The current range of whiskies have all been matured in casks that have previously contained Chardonnay and Trockenbeerenauslese and include a 7, a 12 and a 15 year old.

Destillerie Rogner

Rappottenstein, founded in 1997

www.destillerie-rogner.at

Originally a producer of spirits from fruits and berries. Recently, Hermann Rogner has also added whisky to the range. Two of them are called Rogner Waldviertel Whisky 3/3 with the last figures referring to barley, wheat and rye being used for one of the expressions and three different kinds of malted barley for the other. There is also a whisky from 100% rye called Rye Whisky No. 13 and a single malt, Whisky No. 2.

Destillerie Weutz

St. Nikolai im Sausal, founded in 2002

www.weutz.at

A family distillery with a history of producing schnapps and liqueur from fruits and berries. In 2004 Michael Weutz started cooperation with the brewer Michael Löscher and since then Weutz has added whisky to the range, based on the wash from the brewery. Some of the whiskies are produced in the traditional Scottish style such as the peated Black Peat. Others are more unorthodox, for example Franziska - based on elderflower. For maturation casks made of French Limousin and Alliere oak are used.

Old Raven

Neustift, founded in 2004

www.oldraven.at

In 2004, a distillery was added to the Rabenbräu brewery by Andreas Schmidt. More than 250,000 litres of beer are produced yearly and the wash from the brewery is used for distillation of the 2,000 litres of single malt whisky. The triple distilled Old Raven comes in three expressions – Old Raven, Old Raven Smoky and the limited Old Raven R1 Smoky. The last one was filled into a PX sherry cask which had been used to mature Islay whisky.

Jasmin Haider, CEO of Destilleri Haider

Waldviertler Granit Destillerie

Waidhofen/Thaya, founded in 1995

www.granitdestillerie.at

The distillery has from 1995 established a comprehensive product portfolio of liquers and schnapps from all kinds of berries and fruit. Whisky production started in 2006 and the owner, Günther Mayer, has not only released two different smoked single malts, but is also working with rye and dinkel.

Destillerie Hermann Pfanner

Lauterach, founded in 1854

www.pfanner-weine.com

Founded as a brewery more than 150 years ago, the production soon turned to distillation of eau de vie and schnapps. In 2005, the current owner, Walter Pfanner, started whisky production and today 10,000 litres per year are filled into casks used for maturing sherry and sweet wines. The two core expressions are Pfanner Single Malt Classic and Single Malt Red Wood with a maturation in red wine casks. There are also two recent limited releases; the smoky Pfanner Whisky X-peated and a 4 year old matured in Austrian oak.

Keckeis Destillerie

Rankweil, founded in 2003

www.destillerie-keckeis.at

Like so many Austrian distilleries, it started with schnapps and eau de vie from fruit, in Keckeis´ case, mostly pears and apples. Whisky production started in 2008 and today one expression, Keckeis Single Malt is for sale as well as the new make Keckeis Baby Malt. Part of the barley has been smoked with beech and maturation takes place in small ex-sherry casks made of Limousin oak.

Dachstein Destillerie

Radstadt, founded in 2007

www.mandlberggut.com

In 2007, Doris and Bernhard Warter added a distillery to their farm Mandlberggut. Apart from production of various spirits from berries, malt whisky is also produced. Maturation takes place in a mix of different casks – new Austrian oak, ex-sherry casks and red wine casks. Their only release so far is the five year old Rock-Whisky which is distilled 2,5 times.

Edelbrennerei Franz Kostenzer

Maurach/Achensee, founded in 1998, whisky since 2006

www.schnaps-achensee.at

The Kostenzer family is working on a huge range of different spirits, mainly from fruits and berries but whisky is also in the portfolio. Three expressions under the name Whisky Alpin have been released; a 6 year old single malt with a sherry cask finish, a 6 year old 100% single malt rye and a 3 year old single malt with smoky notes from beech wood.

Brennerei Ebner

Absam, founded in 1930

www.brennereiebner.at

A fourth generation brewer and distiller, Arno Pauli, began to make whisky at his combination of a guesthouse, brewery and distillery in 2005. The whisky production is just a small component of the business but, besides a single malt from barley, Pauli has also released whiskies made from maize, dinkel and wheat.

Belgium

Distillery:	The Owl Distillery, Grâce Hollogne
Founded:	1997
Owner:	Etienne Bouillon, Christian Polis, Pierre Roberti
	belgianwhisky.com

In October 2007, Belgium's first single malt, 'The Belgian Owl', was released. The next bottling came in 2008 but was exclusively reserved for private customers. The first commercial bottling was introduced in November 2008 and the core expression today is the un-chillfiltered Belgian Owl, a 3 year old bottled at 46%. There have been limited releases over the years. The latest, in spring 2017, was 42 months old, bottled at cask strength and there is a 4 year old due for release later in the year. The distillery is equipped with a 2.1 ton mash tun, four washbacks with a fermentation time of 60-100 hours and two stills (11,000 and 8,000 litres respectively) that had previously been used at Caperdonich distillery in Speyside. All the barley used for production comes from farms close to the distillery. The yearly production is around 50,000 litres of pure alcohol.

Distillery:	Het Anker Distillery, Blaasveld
Founded:	1471 (whisky since 2003)
Owner:	Charles Leclef
	hetanker.be

Charles Leclef started out as a brewer and currently maintains this role at Brouwerij Het Anker. He also experimented with distillation of his own beer into whisky with some assistance from a nearby

Etienne Bouillon, one of the owners of The Owl Distillery

genever distiller. The first bottles under the name Gouden Carolus Singe Malt, appeared on the market in 2008. In 2010, he started a distillery of his own at the Leclef family estate, Molenberg, at Blaasveld. The wash still has a capacity of 3,000 litres and the spirit still 2,000 litres. The wash for the distillation is made at their own brewery in Mechelen and it is basically a Gouden Carolus Tripel beer without hops and spices and with a fermentation time of four to five days. The core expression is the 3 year old Gouden Carolus Single Malt. In November 2016, the limited 12 year old Sola Jerez, finished for 3 years in sherry butts was released and there is also a 3 year old Distillery Edition matured in oloroso sherry casks.

Other distilleries in Belgium

Kempisch Vuur
Zandhoven, founded in 2011
www.kempisch-vuur.be

After having had brewing as a hobby for many years, Guy Pirlot became a fulltime brewer and started whisky distillation as well in 2013. The distillery is equipped with a German continuous still and the spirit is matured for 18 months in ex-bourbon casks and then another 18 months in quarter casks from Laphroaig. The first batch was released in March 2016 and several releases have followed. The annual production is around 1.000 litres of pure alcohol.

Czech Republic

Distillery:	Gold Cock Distillery
Founded:	1877
Owner:	Rudolf Jelinek a.s.
	rjelinek.cz

The distilling of Gold Cock whisky started already in 1877. Today it is produced in three versions – a 3 year old blended whisky, a 12 year old single malt and the 22 year old Small Batch 1992 single malt. Production was stopped for a while but after the brand and distillery were acquired by R. Jelinek a.s., the leading Czech producer of plum brandy, the whisky began life anew. The malt whisky is double distilled in 500 litre traditional pot stills. The new owner has created a small whisky museum which is also home to the club Friends of Gold Cock Whisky.

Denmark

Distillery:	Braunstein, Köge
Founded:	2005 (whisky since 2007)
Owner:	Michael & Claus Braunstein
	braunstein.dk

Denmark's first micro-distillery was built in an already existing brewery in Køge, just south of Copenhagen. The wash comes from the own brewery. A Holstein type of still, with four plates in the rectification column, is used for distillation and the spirit is distilled once. Peated malt is bought from Port Ellen, unpeated from Simpsons, but as much as 40% is from ecologically grown Danish barley. The lion's share of the whisky is stored in ex-bourbon (peated version) and first fill Oloroso casks (unpeated) from 190 up to 500 litres. The Braunstein brothers filled their first casks in 2007 and have since produced 50,000 litres annually. Their first release and the first release of a malt whisky produced in Denmark was in 2010 – a 3 year old single oloroso sherry cask called Edition No. 1 which was followed the same year by Library Collection 10:1, bottled at 46%. The most recent releases are Library Collection 17:1, a sherry maturation and Edition E7, peated and matured in an ex-bourbon cask. For duty free, there is a special version called Danica.

Distillery:	Stauning Whisky, Stauning
Founded:	2006
Owner:	Stauning Whisky A/S
	stauningwhisky.dk

The first Danish purpose-built malt whisky distillery entered a more adolescent phase in 2009, after having experimented with two small pilot stills bought from Spain. More stills were installed in 2012 and the yearly production reached 15,000 litres. The preconditions, however, were completely changed in December 2015 when it was announced that Diageo's incubator fund project, Distil Ventures, would spend £10m to increase the capacity of Stauning. This means that in spring 2018, there will be a completely new, 4,000 m² distillery with 16 wash stills and 8 spirit stills. The floor maltings will increase to 1,000 m² and the total production capacity will be 900,000 litres of pure alcohol! The aim has always been to be self-sustaining and Danish barley is bought and turned into malt on an own malting floor. The germinating barley usually has to be turned 6-8 times a day, but Stauning has constructed an automatic "grain turner" to do the job. Two core expressions are produced – Peated Reserve and Traditional Reserve. A variety of the smoked whisky, where heather has been used to dry the malted barley, is due for release in late 2017. There is also a rye whisky in the range together with several limited bottlings.

Other distilleries in Denmark

Fary Lochan Destilleri
Give, founded in 2009
www.farylochan.dk

This distillery in Jutland, was founded by Jens Erik Jørgensen who passed away in 2016. Fary Lochan is now run by his wife and their three children. The main part of the malted barley is imported from the UK but they also malt some of the barley themselves. A part of that is dried using nettles instead of peat to create a special flavour. The five day fermentation takes place in stainless steel washbacks and distillation is performed in traditional copper pot stills – two smaller ones (300 and 200 litres) and a newly installed 1,200 litre still. The first whisky, lightly smoked, was released in 2013 and a number of bottlings have been released since then. One of the latest (spring 2017) is the second batch of Forår, bourbonmatured and with a finish in Laphroaig casks.

One of Staunings big sellers - the malted rye

Trolden Distillery

Kolding, founded in 2011

www.trolden.com

The distillery is a part of the Trolden Brewery which started in 2005. Michael Svendsen uses the wash from the brewery and ferments it for 4-5 days before a double distillation in a 325 litre alembic pot still. The spirit is filled in bourbon casks and production is quite small as brewing beer is the main task. The first release of a single malt called Nimbus, came in November 2014 and was followed by Old No. 2 with a mixed mash bill and later by a single malt (bourbon/sherry) distilled in 2012.

Nordisk Brænderi/Thy Whisky

Fjerritslev, founded in 2009 (whisky since 2011)

www.nordiskbraenderi.dk, www.thy-whisky.dk

The production at this distillery is focused on gin, rum and aquavit. In 2011 however, the owner, Anders Bilgram, and a local ecological farmer, Nicolaj Nicolajsen, decided to join forces and also produce a small amount of whisky from the barley grown in Nicolajsen's fields. Within five years they have managed to fill 25 small casks of which three have been released under the name Thy Whisky, the first in 2014 and the latest one, a sherry maturation, in spring 2017.

Nyborg Destilleri

Nyborg, founded in 1997 (whisky since 2009)

www.oerbaek-bryggeri.nu

Niels Rømer and his son, Nicolai, have since 1997 run Ørbæk Brewery on the Danish island of Fyn. After ten years they added a distillery to the production line where the wash from the brewery is used to produce whisky. In 2009 the first barrels of Isle of Fionia single malt were filled and the first release was made three years later with further expressions the year after. The spirit production has been small and intermittent over the years. In 2014, however, the owners bought an old railway workshop in Nyborg with the intention of converting it into a new and bigger distillery. The new distillery, equipped with washbacks made of oak and two copper pot stills with attached columns, was officially opened in June 2017.

Braenderiet Limfjorden

Sillerslev Havn, founded in 2013

www.braenderiet.dk

Founded by Ole Mark, the distillery started production in June 2013. Mashing and fermentation is carried out at a local brewery while distillation takes place in alambic type stills. Both peated and unpeated single malt as well as rye is produced. Two releases have been made so far (including a peated) and the whisky is also available in 2 litre casks.

Ærø Whisky

Ærøskøbing, founded in 2013

www.ærøwhisky.dk

This microdistillery has been working on the small island of Ærø since 2013 using stills from Portugal. In 2016, new and larger stills made in Germany were installed and the production increased. The first bottling (made from the pilot still) was a bourbonmatured single cask released in March 2017.

Mosgaard Whisky

Oure, founded in 2015

www.mosgaardwhisky.dk

Founded by Gitte and Jes Mosgaard, this distillery on the island of Fionia is focusing on whisky but they also have a gin in their range. Alembic stills made in Portugal are used for the distillation and the aim is to produce 20,000 bottles per year. The first whisky release isn't due until 2019 but the owners have already released malt spirit under the name Young Malt.

England

Distillery:	St. George's Distillery, Roudham, Norfolk
Founded:	2006
Owner:	The English Whisky Co.
	englishwhisky.co.uk

St. George's Distillery near Thetford in Norfolk was started by father and son, James and Andrew Nelstrop, and came on stream in December 2006. This made it the first English malt whisky distillery for over a hundred years. In December 2009, it was time for the release of the first legal whisky called Chapter 5 (the first four chapters had been young malt spirit). This has been followed by several more chapters with the big sellers being 6, 9 and 11. The production includes peated and un-peated versions as well as triple distilled whisky. The latter was first released in 2015 (Chapter 17).

In summer 2013 a new series was introduced called The Black Range. The rationale behind the thinking was to have a more consistent product, predominantly for export and retail chains. Two expressions became available – Classic and Peated, both bourbon matured and bottled at 43%. In autumn 2016, they got a new look and were renamed Original and Smokey. In between the Chapter releases there are also very limited bottlings of the so called Founder's Private Cellar. These are unique casks chosen by the founding chairman, James Nelstrop who died in September 2014. The last cask by his hand was released as The Final Signature in May 2015. In 2017 a new and innovative sub range was introduced – The Norfolk. Two expressions have been bottled so far, Malt 'n' Rye made with malted barley and rye, matured in bourbon casks and Farmers where no less than eight different grains were used. A third variety, Parched, has also been announced but not yet released.

The distillery is equipped with a stainless steel semi-lauter mash tun with a copper top and three stainless steel washbacks with a fermentation time of 85 hours. There is one pair of stills, the wash still with a capacity of 2,800 litres and the spirit still of 1,800 litre capacity. First fill bourbon barrels are mainly used for maturation but the odd sherry, madeira and port casks have also been filled. Around 60% of production is unpeated and the rest is peated. The distillery capacity is 104,000 litres and all the whiskies from the distillery are un chill-filtered and without colouring. The distillery also has an excellent, newly expanded visitor centre, including a shop with more than 300 different whiskies. More than 50,000 people travel here every year.

Andrew Nelstrop - owner of The English Company

Other distilleries in England

The London Distillery Company

London, founded in 2012

www.londondistillery.com

The London Distillery Company is London's first whisky distillery since Lea Valley closed its doors for the final time, more than a century ago. Founded in 2012 by whisky expert, Darren Rook, and former microbrewery owner, Nick Taylor, the distillery started distilling gin at the beginning of 2013. The owners have one still designated for gin while a second still is used exclusively for whisky production. The first release in March 2013 was Dodd's Gin. In December 2013 they got the licence to produce whisky and production started shortly thereafter. Both single malt and rye are produced and the ratio between whisky and gin is 50:50. In September 2015, an unaged rye spirit was released under the name Spring-heeled Jack. Darren and his colleagues experiment with a huge variety of brewer's yeast strains and also use rare barley varieties. In December 2015, the distillery moved to a larger site in Bermondsey, close to Tower Bridge. In the near future, gin production will move to Battersea Power Station while whisky will continue to be produced in the current distillery.

Lakes Distillery

Bassenthwaite Lake, founded in 2014

www.lakesdistillery.com

Headed by Paul Currie, who was the co-founder of Isle of Arran distillery, a consortium of private investors founded the distillery which is housed in a converted Victorian farm near Bassenthwaite Lake. Production started in autumn 2014 and a visitor centre was opened a couple of months later. The £2,5m distillery is equipped with two stills for the whisky production, each with both copper and stainless steel condensers, and a third still for the distillation of gin. The capacity is 240,000 litres of pure alcohol and to help create a cash flow, the company launched a British Isles blended whisky called The One in autumn 2013, where whisky had been sourced from a variety of producers around the UK. Also gin and vodka are being distilled. The first single malt, The Lakes Malt Genesis, will be offered to members of the distillery's founders club end of 2017 with a general release planned for May 2018.

Adnams Copper House Distillery

Southwold, founded in 2010

www.adnams.co.uk

Famous for their beer since 1872, the owners of Adnams Brewery in Suffolk installed a new brewhouse in their Sole Bay Brewery in 2008. Left with a redundant, old building, they decided to convert it into a distillery. Distillation began in December 2010 and, apart from whisky – gin, vodka and absinthe are also produced. Two more stills, tripling the capacity, were installed in early 2016. The first two whiskies from the distillery were released in 2013 – Single Malt No. 1, a 3 year old matured in new French oak and Triple Grain No. 2 from malted barley, oats and wheat and matured in new American oak. Several whiskies have been added to the range since then, one of the latest being a Triple Malt, similar to the Triple Grain.

Cotswolds Distillery

Stourton, founded in 2014

www.cotswoldsdistillery.com

The distillery is the brainchild of Dan Szor, who acquired an estate with two stone buildings and started to convert them into a distillery as well as a visitor centre. Production of both whisky and gin started in September 2014. There are three stills; one wash still (2,400 litres), one spirit still (1,600 litres) and a Holstein still (500 litres) for production of gin and other spirits. The rest of the equipment includes a 0.5 ton mash tun and eight stainless steel wash backs with a capacity of producing 300,000 bottles per year. The first product for sale was their Cotswolds Dry Gin in September 2014 while the first single malt, the 3 year old Odyssey, was launched in September 2017. The limited, inaugural release of 4,000 bottles was a vatting of 70% reconditioned red wine casks and 30% first fill ex-bourbon. A widely available bottling is due in early November.

Chase Distillery

Rosemaund Farm, Hereford, founded in 2008

www.chasedistillery.co.uk

William Chase, who founded Tyrrell's Crisps, sold the company in 2008 and instead started a distillery on his farm in Hereford. Chase's main product is Chase Vodka made from potatoes and gin

Cotswolds Distillery   Casks being filled at Spirit of Yorkshire

has also become part of their range. By the end of 2011, the first whisky was distilled and since then around 40 casks are filled every year but no bottling has yet been released. The distillery is equipped with a copper still from Carl in Germany with a five plate column and an attached rectification column with another 42 plates. At 70 feet, the column is said to be the tallest of its kind in the world.

Spirit of Yorkshire Distillery
Hunmanby, founded in 2016

www.spiritofyorkshire.com

Plans for the distillery started in 2014 when Tom Mellor and David Thompson, the company directors, decided to make Yorkshire's first single malt whisky. The distillery is actually situated in two separate locations with a one ton mash tun and two 10,000 litre washbacks standing at Tom's farm which also houses a brewery while the 5,000 litre wash still and a 3,500 litre spirit still (both from Forsyths) are 2,5 miles down the road in Hunmanby. All the barley comes from the farm, is malted by Muntons and 20,000 litres of fermented wash is tankered to the distillery every week. The two pot stills are equipped with 4 plate columns and currently 50% of the production is distilled using the columns to achieve a lighter character of the new make. Around 90% of the production goes into first fill bourbon barrels and the remaining 10% is filled into a variety of sherry butts and hogsheads. The distillery was commissioned in May 2016. The current working schedule will result in 75,000 litres of pure alcohol a year but theoretically, they could go up to 900,000 litres. The distillery also has a visitor centre with daily tours.

Bimber Distillery
London, founded in 2015

www.bimberdistillery.co.uk

Founded by Dariusz Plazewski and Ewelina Chruszczyk, this is one of three distilleries in London currently producing whisky. The floor malted barley is bought from Warminster Maltings and the spirit is distilled in two copper stills made by Hoga in Spain – a 1,000 litre wash still and a 600 litre spirit still. Four different types of wood are used for maturation; bourbon, port, PX sherry and virgin American oak. The owners have already released a vodka but since the distillation of whisky did not commence until May 2016, the first bottled single malt can't be expected until mid 2019.

Copper Rivet Distillery
Chatham, founded in 2016

www.copperrivetdistillery.com

Situated in an old pump house in the Chatham Docks, this distillery founded and owned by the Russell family is the first in Kent to produce whisky. There is one copper pot still with a column attached as well as a special gin still. Dockyard Gin and Vela Vodka were released early on and in April 2017, Son of a Gun, an 8 week old grain spirit made from rye, wheat and barley, was released. The first single malt will be called Masthouse and is due for release in 2020.

Dartmoor Distillery
Bovey Tracey, founded in 2016

www.dartmoorwhiskydistillery.co.uk

The unusual start for this distillery was that the founders, Greg Millar and Simon Crow (later joined by Andrew Clough), first acquired a second hand still and then commenced building the distillery. Greg and Simon found a 50 year old alembic still in Cognac which hadn't been used since 1994. The brought it to England, refurbished it and attached a copper "wash warmer" to pre warm the wash and increase the copper contact. The distillery is situated in Devon, just north of Torquay and the first distillation was in February 2017. To assist in their work they have had help from the legendary Frank McHardy who recently retired from Springbank.

Isle of Wight Distillery
Newport, founded in 2015

www.isleofwightdistillery.com

The founders, Conrad Gauntlett and Xavier Baker, have years of combined experience in wine production and brewing but this is their first distillation venture. The fermented wash is bought from a local brewery and distilled in hybrid copper stills. The first whisky was distilled in December 2015 and the owners also produce gin and vodka.

Finland

Distillery:	Teerenpeli, Lahti
Founded:	2002
Owner:	Anssi Pyysing
	teerenpeli.com

The original distillery, located in the company's restaurant in central Lahti, is equipped with one wash still (1,500 litres) and one spirit still (900 litres). In 2010 a new mash tun was installed and a new visitor centre was opened. A completely new distillery, with one 3,000 litre wash still and two 900 litre spirit stills, was opened in October 2015 in the same house as the brewery and today the old distillery serves as a "laboratory" producing peated spirit, gin, brandy etc.. The expansion means that the two units will be able to produce 160,000 litres per year.

The first Teerenpeli Single Malt was sold as a 3 year old in 2005. Over the years more expressions have been made available, not only in Finland but also abroad. The core range now consists of a 10 year old matured in bourbon casks, Kaski which is a 100% sherry maturation and Portti which is a 3 year old with another 1.5 years in port casks. Recent limited releases include Rasi, a moscatel finish, Karhi (madeira finish), Aura which has been matured in the brewery's own porter casks and the smoky Suomi 100 to celebrate the 100th anniversary of Finland's declaration of independence from Russia in 1917.

Other distilleries in Finland

Helsinki Distilling Company
Helsinki, founded in 2014

www.hdco.fi

The first privately-owned distillery in Helsinki for over a hundred years, was opened in 2014 by two Finns, Mikko Mykkänen and Kai Kilpinen, and one Irishman, Séamus Holohan. Production started in August with gin and the first whisky was distilled one month later. The distillery is equipped with one mash tun and three washbacks made of stainless steel and one 300 litre pot still with a 7 plate column. Yet another still was added in spring 2017. The first gin was released in October 2014 and more gin and akvavit but also a 1 year old malt spirit has followed since. On the whisky side, the focus is on rye, either with a mash bill of 75% rye and 25% barley or 100% rye, but also single malt made from barley.

Valamo Distillery
Heinävesi, founded in 2014

www.valamodistillery.com

The Valamo Monastery in eastern Finland owns 51% of the distillery with the rest being divided among six private partners (Arttu Taponen, Samuli Taponen, Timo Kettunen, Arto Liimatta, Harri Turunen and Risto Toivanen). Experimental distillation started in 2011 in a small, 150 litre still. In 2015, production began in earnest when the distillery was equipped with a 5,000 litre mash tun, four stainless steel washbacks and a 1,000 litre Carl still which is used for both the wash and the spirit distillation. Around 30,000 litres, both peated and unpeated spirit, are produced yearly but the goal is to increase to 120,000 litres. A 5 year old, matured in first fill bourbon casks, from the early days of the distillery has already been released.

France

Distillery: Distillerie Warenghem, Lannion, Bretagne
Founded: 1900 (whisky since 1994)
Owner: Gilles Leizour
                distillerie-warenghem.com

Leon Warenghem founded the distillery at the beginning of the 20th century and in 1967 his grandson, Paul-Henri Warenghem, together with his associate, Yves Leizour, took over the reins. They moved the distillery to its current location on the outskirts of Lannion in Brittany. Today, the distillery is owned by the Leizour family and it was Gilles Leizour, taking over in 1983, who added whisky production to the repertoire. The first whisky, a blend called WB, was released in 1987 and in the ensuing year, the first single malt distilled in France, Armorik, was launched. The distillery is equipped with a 6,000 litres semilauter mash tun, four stainless steel washbacks and two, traditional copper pot stills (a 6,000 litre wash still and a 3,500 litre spirit still). Around 120,000 litres of pure alcohol (including 30% grain whisky) are produced yearly.

The single malt core range consists of Armorik Edition Originale and Armorik Sherry Finish. Both are around 4 years old, bottled at 40%, have matured in ex-bourbon casks plus a few months in sherry butts for the Sherry Finish and are sold in supermarkets in France. Armorik Classic, a mix of 4 to 8 year old whiskies from bourbon and sherry casks and the 7 year old Armorik Double Maturation which has spent time in both new French oak and sherry wood are earmarked for export as well as the Armorik Sherry cask. Armorik Millesime is a limited bottling released occasionally. The first French rye ever was released in 2015. Named Roof Rye, the 8 year old whisky is a collaboration between the distillery and the famous bartender Guillaume Ferroni. There are also three blended whiskies in the range; WB Whisky Breton, Galleg and Breizh.

Gilles Leizour (right) owner of Warenghem Distillery
and David Roussier, general manager.

Distillery: Glann ar Mor, Pleubian, Bretagne
Founded: 1999
Owner: Jean Donnay
                glannarmor.com

The owner of Glann ar Mor Distillery in Brittany, Jean Donnay, already started his first trials back in 1999. He then made some changes to the distillery and the process and regular production commenced in 2005. The distillery is very much about celebrating the traditional way of distilling malt whisky. The two small stills are directly fired and Donnay uses worm tubs for condensing the spirit. He practises a long fermentation in wooden washbacks and the distillation is very slow. For maturation, a variety of casks are used (first fill bourbon, ex-Sauternes casks, PX sherry etc.) and when the whisky is bottled, there is neither chill filtration nor caramel colouring. The full capacity is 50,000 bottles per year. There are two versions of the whisky – the unpeated Glann ar Mor and the peated Kornog. Core expressions are usually bottled at 46% but every year a number of limited releases are made including single casks and cask strength bottlings. In 2015, Donnay also released his first rye whisky - Only Rye, made from 100% malted rye.

Other distilleries in France

Distillerie Claeyssens de Wambrechies

Wambrechies, Hauts de France, founded in 1817
(whisky since 2000)
www.wambrechies.com

Owned by the Belgian company Grandes Distilleries de Charleroi, Claeyssens is one of the oldest in France. The distillery was originally famous for its genever, the traditional spirit consumed in the north of France, in Belgium and in Holland. The first whisky, a 3 year old, was released in 2003 followed by an 8 year old in 2009. In 2013, two 12 year old bottlings were released: one aged in madeira casks and another in sherry casks, and in September 2017 a limited 8 year old from sherry casks was launched to celebrate the distillery's 200th anniversary. Wambrechies whisky is also the heart of Bellevoye's triple malt whisky, launched by the independent bottler Sirech & Co at the end of 2015.

Domaine Mavela

Corsica, founded in 1991 (whisky since 2001)
www.domaine-mavela.com

Since 2001 whisky is produced in Corsica. The creators of P&M are the brewer Dominique Sialleli, also responsible for the creation of Pietra beer in 1996, and Jean-Claude Venturini who set up the Mavela distillery in 1991. They got some help from the Alsacian Jean-Claude Meyer from the distillery of the same name. Distilled in a Holstein still and aged in ex-Corsican muscat casks, the P&M single malt was sold for the first time in 2004 and its unique taste of the Corsican maquis surprised many whisky amateurs. Their first 12 year old is planned for a release by the end of 2017.

Distillerie Meyer

Hohwarth, Grand Est, founded in 1958 (whisky since 2004)
www.distilleriemeyer.fr

Founded by Fridolin Meyer in 1958, and joined by his son Jean-Claude in 1975, Meyer soon became one of the most awarded distillers in France. At the beginning of the 2000's, Jean-Claude together with his two sons, Arnaud and Lionel, decided to start whisky production as well. They launched two no-age statement whiskies in 2007, just one year before the sudden death of Jean-Claude. There are currently three different versions: Meyer's Pur Malt (a single malt), Meyer's Blend Supérieur and Oncle Meyer Blend Supérieur. The company refuses to be sold under the Protected Geographic Indications of Whisky d'Alsace because blend whiskies are not protected by this regulation. Meyer created a little buzz, in France, at the end of 2016 by releasing the most expensive French whisky ever: a limited 12 year old – Hommage à JC Meyer – at the staggering price of 1 000 euros.

Distillerie des Menhirs

Plomelin, Bretagne, founded in 1986 (whisky since 1998)

www.distillerie.bzh

Originally a portable column still distillery, Guy Le Lay and his wife Anne-Marie decided in 1986 to settle down for good and the first lambig with the name Distillerie des Menhirs was released in 1989. Shortly after, Guy Le Lay came up with the idea of producing a 100% buckwheat whisky. Eddu Silver was launched in 2002, followed by Eddu Gold in 2006, Eddu Silver Brocéliande in 2013 and Eddu Diamant in 2015. Today, the Menhirs distillery is managed by Anne-Marie and Guy's sons: Erwan, Kevin and Loïg. Ed Gwenn (white cereal in English), aged for 4 years in ex-cognac barrels, was released for the first time in June 2016 and in 2017, the third release in the Collector's Range (Eddu Dan Ar) appeared.

Distillerie Gilbert Holl

Ribeauvillé, Grand Est, founded in 1979 (whisky since 2000)

www.gilbertholl.com

In 1979, Gilbert Holl began to distill occasionally in the back of his wine and spirits shop but it wasn't until the beginning of 2000, that he finally started producing also whisky. His first bottling, Lac'Holl, was put on sale in 2004 and was followed by Lac'Holl Junior in 2007 and Lac'Holl Vieil Or in 2009. In 2015, Lac'Holl Junior was replaced by Lac'Holl Or. In 2016, Gilbert Holl sold his successful brewery to concentrate on distillation only but production of this light bodied whisky remains very limited.

Distillerie Hepp

Uberach, Grand Est, founded in 1972 (whisky since 2005)

www.distillerie-hepp.com

A family-owned distillery with a no-age statement core expression by the name Tharcis Hepp. Two limited editions have also been released, the first one aged in ex-plum cask, the second one under the name Johnny Hepp. As well as producing their own whisky, Hepp also supplies the independent bottler Denis Hanns with liquid for his Authentic Whisky Alsace. Hepp is also behind the brand Domus Cardinalis whose First Taste whisky is only available in Belgium.

Distillerie Rozelieures

Rozelieures, Grand Est, founded in 1860 (whisky since 2003)

www.whiskyrozelieures.com

Hubert Grallet and his son-in-law, Christophe Dupic started with whisky production in 2003 and launched the Glen Rozelieures brand in 2007. Four versions are currently available: the first two are aged in ex-fino sherry casks, the third is lightly peated and aged in Sauternes casks and the fourth is peated. Fully automated in 2017 and with a production of 200 000 litres, Rozelieures distillery is now the second biggest distillery in France and sales of their core expression exceeded 100 000 bottles in 2016. Rozelieures is also bottled under the brand name Lughnasadh for the Clair de Lorraine chainstore and supply single malt whisky to the new independent bottler Maison Benjamin Kuentz. The first two released – D'un Verre Printanier and Fin De Partie – were launched in June 2017.

Brûlerie du Revermont

Nevy sur Seille, Bourgogne-Franche Comté, founded in 1991 (whisky since 2003)

www.marielouisetissot-levin.com

For many years, the Tissot family were travelling distillers offering their services to the many wine producers in the Franche-Comté area. Relying upon a very unique distillation set-up, a Blavier still with three pots, designed and built in the early 1930's for the perfume industry, they have been producing single malt whisky since

2003. Pascal and Joseph Tissot launched their own whisky brand Prohibition in 2011. Aged in "feuillettes" (114 litres half-casks coopered specially for macvin and vin de paille french wines), the whisky is reduced to 41% or 42% and bottled uncoloured.

Rouget de Lisle

Bletterans, Bourgogne-Franche Comté, founded in 1994 (whisky since 2006),

www.brasserie-rouget-lisle.com

Rouget de Lisle is a micro-brewery created by Bruno Mangin and his wife. In 2006, they commissioned the Brûlerie du Revermont to distil whisky for them. The first Rouget De Lisle single malt whisky was released in 2009 and in 2012, Bruno Mangin bought his own still. Current bottlings are from the numerous casks he filled during his association with the Tissot family and which lie maturing in his own warehouse. The very first 100% Rouget de Lisle whisky won't be available until the end of 2017.

Distillerie Bertrand

Uberach, Grand Est, founded in 1874 (whisky since 2002)

www.distillerie-bertrand.com

Distillerie Bertrand is an independent affiliate of Wolfberger, the large wine and eau-de-vie producer. The manager, Jean Metzger, gets the malt from a local brewer and then distils it in Holstein type stills. Two different types of whisky are produced. One is a non-chill filtered single malt with a maturation in both new barrels and ex Banyuls barrels. The other is a single cask matured only in Banyuls barrels. Jean Metzger has also experimented with maturation and finishing whisky in a lot of other different ex-wine casks, and the new range became known as Cask Jaune. In 2017 the DRC, aged in a cask from the world famous wine estate in Burgundy, Domaine de la Romanée Conti, was released.

Distillerie de Northmaen

La Chapelle Saint-Ouen, Normandie, founded in 1997 (whisky since 2005)

www.northmaen.com

Northmaen is a craft brewery founded in 1997 by Dominique Camus and his wife. Every year since 2005, they have bottled and sold Thor Boyo, a 3 year old single malt, distilled in a small, mobile pot still. Several more releases have followed with the peated Fafnir from 2015 as one of the latest. The still is not portable anymore but now works in a real distillery.

Distillerie Lehmann

Obernai, Grand Est, founded in 1850 (whisky since 2001)

www.distillerielehmann.com

The story of Lehmann distillery starts in 1850 when the family of the actual owner set up a still in Bischoffsheim. Yves Lehmann inherited the facility in 1982 but decided to move all the equipment to a new distillery in 1993. The first regular bottling from the distillery, aged for seven years in Bordeaux casks, was launched in 2008 under the brand Elsass Whisky. An 8 year old from Sauternes casks followed soon after. The range now includes Elsass Origine (4-6 years) and Elsass Gold (6-8 years), both matured in ex-white wine casks, and Elsass Premium (8 years) matured in ex-Sauternes casks.

Distillerie Brunet

Cognac, Nouvelle Aquitaine, founded in 1920 (whisky since 2006)

www.drinkbrenne.com

In 2006, Stéphane Brunet made the bold move to start whisky production in the Poitou-Charentes region - famous for its cognac production. His whisky, Tradition Malt, was launched in 2009 and was launched in the USA by whisky enthusiast Allison Patel under the brand Brenne. Each version, bottled at 40% comes from a single cask. In September 2015 a 10 year old version was released in small quantities in the USA. Since 2015 Brenne Cuvée Spéciale is also available in France.

Distillerie de Paris

Paris, Ile de France, founded in 2014

www.distilleriedeparis.com

Sébastien and Nicolas Julhès – two brothers in charge of one of Paris's best groceries – set up a still in the heart of the French capital in 2014. The Distillerie de Paris is equipped with a 400 litre Holstein still configured to produce the equivalent of 50 litres of distillate at 65% per batch (double distillation). Distillation of gin and vodka started in January 2015, soon followed by brandy, rhum and grain spirit. The first single malt was distilled in June 2015 and versions of malt or aged spirits have already hit the shelves.

Distillerie Ninkasi

Tarare, Auvergne-Rhône Alpes, founded in 1998 (whisky since 2015)

www.ninkasi.fr

The Ninkasi brewery in Lyon had plans to produce whisky already in 2009 but it wasn´t until 2015 that they had the funds to make the plans a reality. The spirit is distilled in a 2,500 litres still made by Prulho Chalvignac, using wash produced on site, and then aged in different types of cask. Production began in September 2015 and should incresae in the coming years to reach 10,000 litres of pure alcohol. Ninkasi are planning to add a second still soon and are also looking to develop their own strain of yeasts.

Brasserie Michard

Limoges, Nouvelle Aquitaine, founded in 1987 (whisky since 2008)

www.bieres-michard.com

Started as a brewery, Jean Michard began to also produce whisky in 2008. Using their own unique yeast, the first batch of their whisky, released in 2011, was highly original and very fruity. Available in an 800 bottle limited edition, it was followed by a second batch in late 2013. Following issues with the French customs, Jean Michard was seriously considering stopping the production but ended up changing his mind and is now considering building a brand new distillery.

Bercloux

Bercloux, Nouvelle Aquitaine, founded in 2000 (whisky since 2014)

www.bercloise.fr

After many trials, Philippe Laclie opened his own brewery in 2000. In 2007 he decided to diversify by buying some Scotch whisky and finishing it for a few months in Pineau des Charentes barrels. At the beginning of 2014, Philippe took the next step and invested around 100,000 euros, buying an 800 litre column still. After the first trial runs in June 2014, regular whisky production started in September. The first bottlings of Bercloux (3 and 9 months old) were released at the end of 2015 and in 2017, a 9 months old peated version was launched.

Domaine des Hautes-Glaces

Saint Jean d´Hérans, Auvergne-Rhône Alpes, founded in 2009 (whisky since 2013)

www.hautesglaces.com

At an altitude of 900 metres in the middle of the French Alps, Jérémy Bricka and Frédéric Revol decided to produce whisky from barley to bottle. Apart from growing their own barley, all the parts of whisky production take place at the distillery – malting, brewing, distillation, maturation and bottling. Not only have they set out to create the first French single estate whisky, they are doing it organically. All of their cereal (mainly barley, but also rye) is harvested, malted, distilled and aged field by field and without any chemicals, in order to remain as faithful as possible to the expression of their unique terroir. Principium, the first whisky made at the distillery has been available since June 2014. Following the departure of Jérémy Bricka in 2015, Domaine des Hautes Glaces has been bought by Rémy Cointreau. For now, nothing has really changed as Frédéric Revol is still running the operation. The standard line-up includes two whiskies, Les Moissons Malt (100% malted barley) and Les Moissons Rye (ex-Vulson, 100% malted rye).

Dreumont

Neuville-en-Avesnois, Hauts de France, founded in 2005 (whisky since 2011)

www.ladreum.com

Passionate about beer, Jérôme Dreumont decided to open a distillery as well in 2005. In 2011 he built his own 300 litre still and ran it for the first time in November the same year. Since then, he has been filling only one cask per year, but intends to increase

The beautifully situated Domaine des Hautes-Glaces

production soon. His first whisky, distilled from a mix of peated and non-peated barley, was launched in March 2015 and was followed by more releases in 2016 and 2017.

Distillerie du Castor

Troisfontaines, Grand Est, founded in 1985 (whisky since 2011)

www.distillerie-du-castor.com

Founded by Patrick Bertin, the distillery produces both fruit and pomace brandies. It is equipped with two small stills which have been used since 2011 by Patrick's son to distill single malt whisky. The malt is brewed by a local brewery. The first distillation is carried out in the two stills whereas the low wines, mixed together, are re-distilled in the Carl still only. The distillate is then aged in ex-white wine casks and finished in ex-sherry casks. The first release appeared in June 2015 under the name St Patrick.

La Roche Aux Fées

Sainte-Colombe, Bretagne, founded in 1996 (whisky since 2010)

www.distillerie-larocheauxfees.com

Gonny Keizer installed a micro-brewery in the Roche aux Fées county in 1996. She is the first female master-brewer in France. In 2010, Gonny and her husband Henry bought a 400 litre portable automatic batch still. The still is wood-heated and equipped with a worm-tub condenser and the first spirit was put into cask in 2010. In 2014 a distillery was built to shelter the still. The first Roc'Elf bottling, distilled from three malted cereals (barley, wheat, oat), was released in January 2016 followed by a second in early 2017.

Distillerie Castan

Villeneuve Sur Vère, Occitanie, founded in 1946 (whisky since 2010)

www.distillerie-castan.com

In 2010, Sébastien Castan decided to permanently house the portable still that had been in the family for three generations in a proper distillery. The same year, he distilled his first whisky and aged the spirit in ex-Gaillac wine casks. Two bottlings of Vilanova Berbie were launched in 2013, with Vilanova Gost following in early 2014. These were the first in a series of two annual bottlings, some of them peated. The first smoky whisky, Vilanova Terrocita, was released towards the end of 2015. In 2017 Segala, the first rye whiskey, and Roja, a whisky aged in ex-red wine casks, were released.

Domaine de Bourjac

Broquiès, Occitanie, founded in 1994 (whisky since 2012)

www.domainedebourjac.com

With help from a local fruit eau-de-vie distiller, wine producer Olivier Toulouse produced a malt whisky in 2010. The first bottles of DDB were released in 2015 and that same year, Olivier bought an old Charentais type still which he refurbished in order to put it to its original use: direct distillation with smoke recuperation through a tube wrapped around the kettle to help the heat repartition. Around 400 bottles of organic whisky is produced yearly.

La Mine d'Or

Le Roc Saint-André, Bretagne, founded in 1990 (whisky since 2017)

www.brasserie-lancelot.bzh

Lancelot brewery was founded in 1990 by Bernard Lancelot, a beekeeper who was looking to diversify his business. When Lancelot retired in 2004, two of his employees, Stéphane Kerdodé and Eric Ollive bought the company. In 2015, they came up with the idea of adding spirit distillation as well and they bought an 800 litre Stupfler still. Production commenced in January 2017 and the new spirit is ageing in an old gold mine, located near the distillery.

Alp Spirits

Pontcharra, Auvergne-Rhône Alpes, founded in 2002 (whisky since 2012)

www.mandrin.eu

Vincent Gachet, opened the Brasserie Artisanale du Dauphiné brewery in 2002. The first beers were released the same year and in 2005, he joined forces with Gilles Gaudet, an ambulant brewer equipped with a four-kettle still. In 2012 they decided to produce whisky as well and every winter, Vincent Gachet goes to Pontcharra, where the ambulant still settles for the season, and distils his own brews. The first 400 bottles of Mandrin single malt were released end of 2015.

Miclo

Lapoutroie, Grand Est, founded in 1970 (whisky since 2012)

www.distillerie-miclo.com

Gilbert Miclo, the grandfather of Bertrand Lutt, the current manager, founded the distillery in 1970, specialising in fruit spirits. It is equipped with four Holstein waterbath pot stills and since 2012, wort from a local brewery is fermented and distilled into malt whisky. Under the brand name Welche's, three different whiskies were released in December 2016 - Welche, Welche Fine Tourbe, Welche Tourbé.

Ergaster

Passel, Hauts de France, founded in 2015 (whisky since 2016)

www.whisky-france.e-monsite.com

A couple of years ago, the founder of the brewery in Uberach, Eric Trossat, and his friend Hervé Grangeon, opened a small distillery in Picardy in Passel. The Noyon distillery was inaugurated in 2015 and production started in October 2016. A couple of weeks after the launch of its first malt spirit in May 2017, the owners were forced to change the distillery name to Ergaster. Their ambition is to produce a high-end malt whisky. At the moment, the first spirit - peated and not peated - matures in ex-cognac, ex-Pineau des Charentes, ex-vin jaune and ex-banyuls casks.

Distillerie d'Hautefeuille

Beaucourt En Santerre, Hauts de France, founded in 2016 (whisky since 2017)

www.distilleriedhautefeuille.com

In March 2017, the first drops of new make were made at Hautefeuille distillery. Behind the project are two whisky lovers: Étienne d'Hautefeuille took over a farm in 2013, surrounded by barley fields while Gaël Mordac is a well-respected wine merchant. The distillery is fitted with an 800 litre Stupfler still and in the future, the two men expect to carry out all the on-site production operations, including malting.

La Quintessence

Herrberg, Grand Est, founded in 2008 (whisky since 2013)

www.distillerie-quintessence.com

In 2008 Nicolas Schott took over the family distillery in Herrberg in order to continue the production of fruit spirits (raspberry, pear, plum, quetsche or quince) and also liqueurs (spices or asperule). End of 2016, the 34 year old distiller surprised everyone with the release of his first single malt whisky, Schott's, bottled at 42%.

Bows

Montauban, Occitanie, founded in 2008 (whisky since 2013)

https://www.bowsdistillerie.com

Benoit Garcia, a former climate engineer designed and built the Bows (Brave Occitan Wild Spirits) distillery on his own including a 900 litre still with a small rectification column which was manufactured by a local coppersmih. After two years the distillery came on stream in January 2017. The first malt spirit, Bestiut, aged in a cognac barrel, was released in September 2017.

Ouche Nanon

Ourouer Les Bourdelins, Centre-Val de Loire, founded in 2000 (whisky since 2015)

www.ouche-nanon.fr

This microbrewery has been producing artisanal beer since 2010. In 2015, Thomas Mousseau acquired a Guillaume still, removed the little column and made it into a pot still, heated by a wood fire. A first single malt spirit (3 months old) was offered to crowdfunding contributors allowing him to set up his own distillery.

La Distillerie du Vercors

Saint-Jean d'Hérans, Auvergne-Rhône-Alpes, founded in 2015 (whisky since 2016)

www.distillerie-vercors.com

At first, Éric Cordelle had set on building his distillery in Brittany but he then decided to move further south, and acquired an old silkworms farm in Saint-Jean d'Hérans in the heart of the Vercors mountains. The distillery is an atypical installation as it is equipped with a copper pot still (second still) and a steel boiler that operates under vacuum for the first distillation. This type of distillation is common in the perfume industry but not for whisky. Production started in September 2016 and the distillery also welcomes visitors.

La Piautre

Ménitré Sur Loire, Pays de Loire, founded in 2004 (whisky since 2014)

www.lapiautre.fr

In 2004, Yann Leroux and Vincent Lelièvre founded the Brasserie d'Anjou in La Ménitré on the banks of the Loire. Ten years later the

owners decided to take on two new challenges; to malt their own barley on site and to start experiments with distillation. For the last part they are assisted by a neighboring distiller, Gilles Boudier in Vihiers. Beginning of 2017, the first bottles of Loire Whisky, 40 months old, were for sale at the brewery only. La Piautre is now equipped with a Charentais direct fire-heating still to work on site.

Moutard-Diligent

Buxeuil, Pays de Loire, founded in 1642 (whisky since 2017)

www.champagne-moutard.fr

Buxeuil is the birthplace of the Moutard and Diligent families and by the end of the 19th century, Hyacinthe Diligent was famous for experiments on distilling champagne wines. Today, Alexandre and Benoit Moutard are still champagne producers but they have decided to produce whisky as well. The wort, brought in from a local brewery, is fermented and distilled at the estate. There are five pot stills and in April 2017 the first spirit was filled into casks that had previously held ratafia.

Moon Harbour

Bordeaux, Nouvelle Aquitaine, founded in 2015 (whisky since 2017)

www.moonharbour.fr

One of the largest French distilleries in operation today is located in Bordeaux. Moon Harbour is the brainchild of two local entrepreneurs, Jean-Philippe Ballanger and Yves Médina. Advised by the well-known whisky consultant John McDougall, the distillery and its visitor center has been constructed in an ultra-modern building on the banks of the Garonne river. The two men also bought a former submarine base which, once reconstructed, will serve as a warehouse. The distillery was inaugurated in September 2017 and is equipped with two 1,000 litre Stupfler stills. The idea is to distill malted barley but also malted corn and the new spirit will age mostly in ex-Sauternes casks.

Germany

Distillery:	Whisky-Destillerie Blaue Maus, Eggolsheim-Neuses
Founded:	1980
Owner:	Robert Fleischmann
	fleischmann-whisky.de

The oldest malt whisky distillery in Germany distilling their first whisky in 1983. It took, however, 15 years before the first whisky, Glen Mouse 1986, appeared. A completely new distillery became operational in April 2013. All whisky from Blaue Maus are single cask and there are around ten single malts in the range. Some of them are released at cask strength while others are reduced to 40%. An unusual experiment was made in 2016 when the owners transported some casks to the island of Sylt in the North Sea. They were lowered into the sea to continue the maturation process. Because of the tide, every six hours the casks were exposed to the air.

Distillery:	Slyrs Destillerie, Schliersee
Founded:	1928 (whisky since 1999)
Owner:	Stetter family
	slyrs.de

Lantenhammer Destillerie in Bavaria was founded in 1928 and was producing mainly brandy until 1999 when whisky took preference, and in 2003 Slyrs Destillerie was founded. The malt, smoked with beech, comes from locally grown grain and the spirit is distilled in 1,500 litre stills. Maturation takes place in charred 225-litre casks of new American white oak and they are

Thomas Mousseau, owner of Ouche Nanon

currently producing 150,000 bottles per year. The non chill-filtered whisky is called Slyrs after the original name of the surrounding area, Schliers. Around 40,000 bottles are sold annually. The core expressions are a 3 year old bottled at 43% and a cask strength version. In 2015, 1,000 bottles of the distillery´s first 12 year old whisky were released and other limited releases occur from time to time. One of the latest was Sild Crannog, released in late 2016, which had been distilled in Bavaria and then transported to the island of Sylt in northern Germany to be matured on a fishing boat named The Angel´s Share.

Distillery: Hammerschmiede, Zorge

Founded: 1984 (whisky since 2002)

Owner: Alexander Buchholz

hammerschmiede.de

In keeping with many other small whisky producers on mainland Europe, Hammerschmiede´s main products are spirits from fruit, berries and herbs and whisky distilling was only embarked on in 2002. In 2014, Alexander Buchholz, started the construction of a new still house with additional stills making it a total of five. The first bottles were released in 2006 under the name Glan Iarran. Today, all whisky produced has changed name to Glen Els. The core range consists of four expressions; Glen Els Journey with a blend of different maturations, Ember, which is woodsmoked, Unique Distillery Edition which is always from a sherry cask and Wayfare, bottled at cask strength. These whiskies are complemented by the Woodsmoked Malts, Four Seasons (non-woodsmoked) and Elements. Finally, there is the Alrik by Glen Els which, according to the owner, is the ultimate woodsmoked malt, usually matured in a PX sherry cask with an additional finish.

Bottlings from Hammerschmiede and Slyrs

Other distilleries in Germany

Spreewood Distillers

Schlepzig, founded in 2004 (whisky production)

www.stork-club-whisky.com

Founded by Torsten Römer, this distillery has since the opening had a wide range of products including beer, eau-de-vie, rum and whisky. The equipment consists of three stills and the annual production of whisky and rum is around 15,000 litres per year. Sloupisti, the first single malt, was released in 2007 as a 3 year old. In autumn 2016, the distillery was sold to a Berlin company, Spreewood Distillers. The company is owned by Steffen Lohr, Bastian Heuser and Sebastian Brack and they have decided to focus entirely on whisky and rum. The new range is called Stork Club with a single malt bottled at 47% and a Straight Rye bottled at 55%.

Obsthof am Berg

Kriftel, founded in 1983 (whisky since 2009)

www.obsthof-am-berg.de, www.gilors.de

Holger and Ralf Heinrich are the third generation running this distillery and their focal point is to produce spirits from fruits and berries. In 2009 the two brothers started whisky production and the first release of their 3 year old single malt Gilors was in 2012. The whisky is non chillfiltered and the majority of the production is unpeated. The two core expressions, Gilors fino sherry matured and Gilors port matured, are both 3 years old. Recent limited editions include Gilors Peated (made from peated malt and matured for three years in bourbon casks) and a 5 year old, finished in PX casks.

Bayerwald-Bärwurzerei und Spezialitäten-Brennerei Liebl

Kötzting, founded in 1970 (whisky since 2006)

www.coillmor.com

In 1970 Gerhard Liebl started spirit distillation from fruits and berries and in 2006 his son, Gerhard Liebl Jr., built a brand new whisky distillery. Around 30,000 litres of whisky are produced annually and in 2009 the first bottles bearing the name Coillmór were released. There is a wide range aged between 4 and 8 years currently available. The latest release was a peated 6 year old matured in a port cask, released in late 2016.

Brennerei Höhler

Aarbergen, founded in 1895 (whisky since 2001)

www.brennerei-hoehler.de

The main produce from this distillery in Hessen consists of different distillates from fruit and berries. The first whisky, a bourbon variety, was distilled in 2001 and released in 2004. Since then, Karl-Holger Höhler has experimented with different types of grain. A couple of the more recent releases of his Whesskey (so called since it is from the province Hessen) are a Cara-Aroma Single Malt and single malts made from smoked barley.

Stickum Brennerei (Uerige)

Düsseldorf, founded in 2007

www.stickum.de

Uerige Brewery, founded in 1862, was completed with a distillery in 2007. The wash comes from their own brewery and the distillation takes place in a 250 litre column still. The distillery produces around 700 bottles of their whisky BAAS per year and the first bottling (a 3 year old) was released in December 2010. In 2014 the owners released their first 5 year old whiskies – one matured in a sherry cask and the other in new oak.

Preussische Whiskydestillerie

Mark Landin, founded in 2009

www.preussischerwhisky.de

Cornelia Bohn purchased a closed-down distillery in 2009 in the Uckermark region, and installed a 550 litre copper still with a 4-plate rectification column attached. The spirit is distilled very slowly five to six times and is then matured in casks made of new, heavily toasted American white oak, German fine oak or German Spessart oak. Since 2013 only organic barley is used for the distillation. The first whisky was launched as a 3 year old in December 2012. From March 2015, all the whiskies from the distillery will be at least 5 years old.

Kleinbrennerei Fitzke

Herbolzheim-Broggingen, founded in 1874
(whisky since 2004)

www.kleinbrennerei-fitzke.de

The main commerce for the distillery is the production of eau de viex and vodka, but they also distill whisky from different grains. For the first six months of maturation they use virgin oak and, thereafter, the spirit is filled into used barrels for another two and a half years. The first release of the Derrina single malt was in 2007 and new batches have been launched ever since including a lightly peated. The different varieties of Derrina are either made from malted grains (barley, rye, wheat, oats etc.) or unmalted (barley, oats, buckwheat, rice, triticale, sorghum or maize).

Rieger & Hofmeister

Fellbach, founded in 1994 (whisky since 2006)

www.rieger-hofmeister.de

Marcus Hofmeister's stepfather, Albrecht Rieger, started the distillery and when Marcus entered the business in 2006 he expanded it to also include whisky production. The first release was in 2009 and currently there are two expressions in the range – a Single Malt matured in pinot noir casks and a Malt & Grain (50% wheat, 40% barley and 10% smoked barley) from chardonnay casks. The two most recent releases (October 2017) are Double Wood Single Malt (matured in a combination of sherry casks and white wine casks) and a malted rye whisky.

Kinzigbrennerei

Biberach, founded in 1937 (whisky since 2004)

www.biberacher-whisky.de

Martin Brosamer is the third generation in the family and he is also the one who expanded the production in 2004 to include whisky. The first release in 2008 was Badische Whisky, a blend made from wheat and barley. Two years later came the 4 year old Biberacher Whisky, the first single malt and in 2012, the range was expanded with Schwarzwälder Rye Whisky and the smoky single malt Kinzigtäler Whisky. The oldest whisky released so far is an 8 year old single cask.

Destillerie Kammer-Kirsch

Karlsruhe, founded in1961 (whisky since 2006)

www.kammer-kirsch.de

Like so many distilleries, production of spirits from various fruits and berries is the main focus for Kammer-Kirsch and they are especially known for their Kirschwasser from cherries. In 2006 they started a cooperation with the brewery, Landesbrauerei Rothaus, where the brewery delivers a fermented wash to the distillery and they continue distilling a whisky called Rothaus Black Forest Single Malt Whisky which matured in bourbon casks. The whisky was launched for the first time in 2009 and, every year in March, a new batch is released. Around 6,000 bottles are produced every year.

Alt Enderle Brennerei

Rosenberg/Sindolsheim, founded in 1991 (whisky since 1999)

www.alt-enderle-brennerei.de

While concentrating on the production of schnapps, gin, rum and

absinthe, Joachim Alt and Michael Enderle produced their first malt whisky in 2000. They now have a wide range of Neccarus Single Malt for sale from a 4 year old to an 18 year old! The latest limited release was the 7 year old, smoky Terrador with a finish in rum casks. In 2013 Neccarus was awarded as the best German whisky.

Brennerei Ziegler

Freudenberg, founded in 1865

www.brennerei-ziegler.de

Like so many other distilleries in Germany, Ziegler has distillation of spirits from fruits and berries as their main business, but has also added a small whisky production. One characteristic that distinguishes itself from most other distilleries is that the maturation takes place not only in oak casks, but also in casks made of chestnut! Their current bottling is a 5 year old called Aureum 1865 Single Malt and there is also a cask strength version. Limited releases occur yearly with a whisky finished in Taylor's Late Bottled Vintage port casks as one of the more recent.

AV Brennerei

Wincheringen, founded in 1824 (whisky since 2006)

www.avadisdistillery.de

For generations, the Vallendar family have been making schnapps and edelbrände but since 2006 the brothers Andreas and Carlo Vallendar, also produce malt whisky. Around 2,000 bottles per annum are available for purchase and the oak casks from France have previously been used for maturing white Mosel wine. Threeland Whisky is between 3 and 6 years old and the range also consists of finishes in oloroso and port casks.

Birkenhof-Brennerei

Nistertal, founded in 1848 (whisky since 2002)

www.birkenhof-brennerei.de

The traditional production of edelbrände made from a variety of fruits and berries was complemented with whisky production in 2002. The first release was a 5 year old rye whisky under the name Fading Hill in 2008. This was followed a year later by a single malt. The most recent bottling is a 4 year old single cask, launched in 2016. Since 2015, peated whisky is also produced.

Brennerei Faber

Ferschweiler, founded in 1949

www.faber-eifelbrand.de

Established as a producer of eau-de vie from fruits and berries, Ludwig Faber – the third generation of the owners – has included whisky production during the last few years. The only whisky so far is a single malt that has matured for 6 years in barrels made of American white oak.

Steinhauser Destillerie

Kressbronn, founded in 1828 (whisky since 2008)

www.weinkellerei-steinhauser.de

The distillery is situated in the very south of Germany, near Lake Constance, close to Austria. The main products are spirits which are derived from fruits, but whisky also has its own niche. The first release from Martin Steinhauser, was the single malt Brigantia which was released in 2011. It was triple distilled and more releases have followed since.

Weingut Simons

Alzenau-Michelbach, founded in 1879 (whisky since 1998)

www.feinbrenner.eu

The owner, Severin Simon, produces wine from his own vineyards, spirits from fruit as well as gin, vodka, rum and whisky.

Until recently all the whisky was produced in a 150 litre still but a new Holstein still was installed in 2013, raising the whisky production from 300 litres per year to 3-5,000 litres. A pure pot still whisky has since been released and the first whisky from 100% malted barley was distilled in January 2013. In March 2016, the first whisky from the new still was released – a 100% rye.

Nordpfälzer Edelobst & Whiskydestille

Winnweiler, founded in 2008

www.nordpfalz-brennerei.de

This distillery owned by Bernhard Höning is based on the production of spirits from fruits but also distilling whisky. The first release was in 2011, a 3 year old single malt by the name Taranis with a full maturation in a Sauternes cask and in 2013 a 4 year old from ex-bourbon casks with an Amarone finish was launched. Regular releases have occured since, the latest in September 2017. In 2013 a second distillery including a tasting room was opened.

Tecker Whisky-Destillerie

Owen, founded in 1979 (whisky since 1989)

www.tecker.eu

Founded by one of the German whisky pioneers, Christian Gruel, the distillery is now run by his grandchild Immanuel Gruel. Apart from a variety of eau de vie and other spirits, approximately 1,500 litres of whisky is produced annually. The core expression is the 10 year old Tecker Single Malt matured in port casks and a 5 year old Tecker Single Grain. Limited releases have included a cask strength 10 year old single malt and a cask strength 14 year old single grain.

Destillerie & Brennerei Heinrich Habbel

Sprockhövel, founded in 1878 (whisky since 1977)

www.habbel.com

Already in 1977, Michael Habbel produced his first whisky from 85% rye and 15% malted barley. After a 10 year maturation in bourbon casks, the whisky was transferred into stainless steel tanks and wasn't released until a few years ago as Habbel's Uralter Whisky. In spring of 2014 a designated whisky distillery called Hillock Park Distillery was opened on the premises. A sample of the product has already been released in the shape of a newmake – Hillock White Dog (78% rye and 22% malted barley).

Märkische Spezialitäten Brennerei

Hagen, whisky since 2010

www.msb-hagen.de

Under the brand name Bonum Bono, Klaus Wurm and Christian Vormann produce spirits and liqueurs from various fruits. In 2010 they added whisky to the range. The spirit is distilled four times, matured in ex-bourbon barrels for 12 months and then brought to a cave, with low temperature and high humidity, for further maturation. The first whisky, the 3 year old Tronje van Hagen, was released in 2013. The whisky has now been renamed DeCavo ("from the cave", in allusion to where the maturation takes place).

Sperbers Destillerie

Rentweinsdorf, founded in 1923 (whisky since 2002)

www.salmsdorf.de

Apart from distilling eau de vie and liqueurs from fruits, Helmut Sperber has also been producing whisky since 2002. At the moment, four different expressions have been released, all of them 7 years old – single malt matured in bourbon casks, single malt matured in a mix of sherry and bourbons casks, a sherrymatured single malt bottled at cask strength, as well as,a single grain whisky from a mix of bourbon, sherry and Spessart oak casks.

Brennerei Feller

Dietenheim-Regglisweiler, founded in 1820 (whisky since 2008)

www.brennerei-feller.de

Roland Feller, the owner of this old schnapps distillery, took up whisky production in 2008 and four years later he released his first single malt, the 3 year old Valerie (recent releases are 5 years old) matured in bourbon casks. It was recently followed by two 5 year olds, finished in sherry- and amarone-casks respectively and a 4 year old finished in a madeira cask.

Marder Edelbrände

Albbruck-Unteralpfen, founded in 1953 (whisky since 2009)

www.marder-edelbraende.de

Apart from a vast number of distillates from different fruits, Stefan Marder also produces whisky since 2009. The first release came in 2013 - the 3 year old Marder Single Malt matured in a combination of new American oak and sherry casks. One thousand bottles were released and the latest edition, a 5 year old matured in port pipes, was launched in July 2015.

Destillerie Drexler

Arrach, whisky since 2007

www.drexlers-whisky.de

The main business for Reinhard Drexler is the production of spirits from herbs, fruits and berries. In between he also finds the time to produce malt whisky and from 2013 also rye whisky. The first release was Bayerwoid in 2011 which was followed up by No. 1 Single Cask Malt Whisky and a 100% malted rye whisky. The latest edition of the No. 1 single cask (November 2016) was 4 years old.

Edelbrände Senft

Salem-Rickenbach, founded in 1988 (whisky since 2009)

www.edelbraende-senft.de

When Herbert Senft started whisky production, he experimented with a variety of different grains but, in future, he will be concentrating on whisky from 100% malted barley. The first 2,000 bottles of 3.5 year old Senft Bodensee Whisky were released in 2012 and they were later followed by a cask strength version (55%).

Dürr Edelbranntweine

Neubulach, founded in 2002

www.blackforest-whiskey.com

Third generation distillers, Nicolas and Sebastian Dürr, began producing whisky in 2002. It wasn't until 2012 when their first single malt (limited to 200 bottles) reached the market. Doinich Daal Batch 1 is a 4 year old matured in a combination of bourbon and cognac casks. The latest release (batch 3, Wolfsmähder and Teuchelwald) was released in December 2016.

Schwarzwaldbrennerei Walter Seger

Calw-Holzbronn, founded in 1952 (whisky since 1990)

www.krabba-nescht.de

Incorporated with a restaurant, this distillery which, apart from producing eau de vie from berries and fruit, also produces whisky. The first single malt was launched in 2009 and at the moment, Walter Seger has two expressions in the range; the 6 year old Black-Wood single malt matured in amontillado sherry casks and an 8 year old wheat whisky.

Landgasthof Gemmer

Rettert, founded in 1908 (whisky since 2008)

www.landgasthof-gemmer.de

The current owner, Klaus Gemmer, is the fourth generation

running this distillery, and he was also the one who introduced whisky production in 2008. Their only single malt is the 3 year old Georg IV which has matured for two years in toasted Spessart oak casks and finished for one year in casks that have contained Banyuls wine. Around 800 litres are produced per year.

Hausbrauerei Altstadthof

Nürnberg, founded in 1984

www.hausbrauerei-altstadthof.de

The owner, Reinhard Engel, was the first to produce a German organic single malt and the current range consists of the 4 year old Ayrer´s Red bottled at 43% and 58%, both matured in new American oak, Ayrer´s PX, bottled at 56% and finished in PX sherry casks, Ayrer´s Bourbon, bottled at 51% and matured in bourbon barrels, Ayrer´s Master Cut, bottled at an exceptional 74.2%, Ayrer´s White which is an 8 week old whisky spirit and, the most recent, Ayrer´s Ruby finished in port casks.

Destillerie Mösslein

Zeilitzheim, founded in 1984 (whisky since 1999)

www.frankenwhisky.de

Originally a winery but also producing a wide range of eau de vie from fruits, whisky production was brought on board in 1999. The first whisky was released in 2003 and at the moment, the owner, Reiner Mösslein, can offer two types of whisky – a single malt and a grain whisky, both 5 years old.

Brennerei Josef Druffel

Oelde-Stromberg, founded in 1792 (whisky since 2010)

www.brennerei-druffel.de

Jochen Druffel is the 7th generation to run this old family distillery where a variety of different spirits are distilled. The first single malt, Prum, was released in 2013 and had matured in a mix of different casks (bourbon, sherry, red wine and new Spessart oak) and was finished in small casks made of plum tree! In 2015, a 5 year old version was released.

Brauhaus am Lohberg

Wismar, whisky since 2010

brauhaus-wismar.de, hinricusnoyte.de

This unique combination of a guesthouse, brewery and distillery is situated at the centre of Wismar. Here Herbert Wenzel and Stefan Beck have been producing whisky since 2010. The first release of Baltach single malt was in December 2013. It was a 3 year old with a finish in sherry casks. The latest edition of Baltach was released in July 2016 and a peated version is due in 2019.

Wild Brennerei

Gengenbach, founded in 1855 (whisky since 2002)

www.wild-brennerei.de

The distillation of whisky constitutes only a small part of the production but Franz Wild has released two 5 year old whiskies – Wild Whisky Single Malt which has matured for three years in American white oak and another two in either sherry or port casks and Wild Whisky Grain, made from unmalted barley.

Brennerei Volker Theurer

Tübingen, founded in 1991

www.schwaebischer-whisky.de

Located in a guesthouse, this distillery which is run by Volker Theurer has been producing whisky since 1995. The first release was a 7 year old in 2003 and since then he has released Sankt Johann, an 8 year old single malt and the 9 year old Tammer which has been double matured in bourbon and sherry casks. Theurer is also selling a blended whisky called Original Ammertal Whisky.

Lübbehusen Malt Distillery

Emstek, founded in 2014

destill.de

Unlike most German producers, Jens Lübbehusen is focusing entirely on whisky. In one of the largest pot stills in the country, whisky made from peated Scottish malt is distilled. Lübbehusen doesn´t practise chill-filtration nor is the whisky coloured. The first release, a 3 year old, is due in autumn 2017. Rye whisky is also produced and attached to the distillery is a visitor centre, a tasting room and a shop.

Glina Whiskydestillerie

Werder a.d. Havel, founded in 2004

glina-whisky.de

After 12 years of production, Michael Schultz decided to move the distillery in 2016 to larger premises, thereby ten-folding the capacity. Around 1,000 casks are now filled yearly. The first Glina Single Malt was released in 2008. Most of the whiskies are between 3 and 5 years old and have matured in a variety of casks (bordeaux, burgundy, port and sherry). Around 80% of the production is malt whisky while the rest is made using rye.

Burger Hofbrennerei

Burg, founded in 2007 (whisky since 2012)

sagengeister.de

Apart from distillates from fruits and berries, Arno Ballaschk also produces whisky made from malted barley, smoked using beech wood. Maturation is in small (100 litres) casks made of American white oak. The first release of Der Kolonist single malt was in spring 2015.

Number Nine Spirituosen-Manufaktur

Leinefelde-Worbis, founded in 1999 (whisky since 2013)

ninesprings.de

The Ehbrecht family have been producing liquers for almost 20 years at this distillery situated in Thüringen in central Germany. Production was expanded in 2013 to also include rum, gin and whisky. The first single malt was launched in summer 2016 while one of the latest, a Madeira finish, appeared in April 2017.

Edelbrennerei Schloss Neuenburg

Freyburg, founded in 2012

schlossbrennerei.eu

While making spirits from fruits and berries, Matthias Hempel also continuously produces small volumes of single malt whisky. The spirit is matured for two years in new, German oak and then for another year in French pinot noir casks. The first Schlosswhisky was released in August 2016.

Gutsbrennerei Joh. B. Geuting

Bocholt Spork, founded in 1837 (whisky since 2010)

muensterland-whisky.de

Magnus Geuting is the 6th generation of this distilling family and he was also the one who expanded the business to include whisky production as well. The first releases, two single malts and two single grain, appeared in September 2013. More releases of the J.B.G. Münsterländer Single Malt have followed, the latest a 4 year old matured in sherry casks.

Sauerländer Edelbrennerei

Kallenhardt, founded in 2000 (whisky since 2004)

sauerlaender-edelbrennerei.de

The wide range of spirits produced was expanded by Ulrich Wolfkühler and Walter Mülheims in 2004 to also include whisky.

The first release of the Thousand Mountains McRaven appeared in 2007 as a 3 year old. The recipe was changed in 2011 from peated to unpeated and the first bottlings from the new era were launched in 2014. In 2016, the distillery was expanded when they moved the production to an old sawmill.

Destillerie Ralf Hauer

Bad Dürkheim, founded in 1989 (whisky since 2012)

sailltmor.de

Distillates from fruits and berries were expanded in 2012 to include whisky. The first release from Ralf Hauer appeared in 2015 with the 3 year old Saillt Mor single malt. Recent bottlings include a 4 year old matured in ex-bourbon casks as well as a PX sherry cask finish bottled at 59.3%. Produced, although not yet released is also a peated whisky (45ppm).

Destillerie Thomas Sippel

Weisenheim am Berg, founded in 1992 (whisky since 2011)

destillerie-sippel.de

Thomas Sippel is one of the many "Jack of all Trades" to be found in the German distillery community. Wines as well as distillates of all kinds are on the menu with whisky being introduced in 2011. The first release of the Palatinatus Single Malt came in 2014. It had been matured for 2.5 years in German wine casks before a final year in port casks.

St Kilian Distillers

Rüdenau, founded in 2015

stkiliandistillers.com

Founded and owned by Andreas Thümmler, St Kilian is one of few German distilleries designated to make whisky and nothing else. With the aid of David Hyne of Cooley and Great Northern Distillery fame, Thümmler built the distillery including stills from Forsyths in Scotland. The first whisky will not be ready to launch until 2018 but two new make spirits have been released - White Dog and the peated Turf Dog. The distillery has a capacity of 200,000 litres of alcohol.

Steinwälder Hausbrennerei

Erbendorf, founded in 1818 (whisky since 1920)

brennerei-schraml.de

The Schraml family have been working this distillery for 6 generations and Gregor Schraml is now the current owner. What can be described as a whisky was being made here already in the early 1900s but was then sold as "Kornbrand". It wasn´t until Gregor Schraml took over that the spirit was relaunched as a 10 year old single grain whisky under the name Stonewood 1880. Other releases include Woaz, a wheat whisky as well as the two 3 year old single malts, Dra and Smokey Monk.

Finch Whiskydestillerie

Heroldstatt, founded in 2001

finch-whisky.de

Hans-Gerhard Fink founded the distillery in 2001 and since then it has moved twice, the last time in 2016. The distillery is one of Germany´s biggest with a yearly production of 250,000 litres and it is also equipped with one of the biggest pot stills in Germany - 3,000 litres. The range of whiskies is large and they are made from a variety of different grains. The age is between 5 and 8 years and included is a 6 year old single malt.

Mönchguter Hofbrennerei

Middelhagen, founded in 2006

ruegen-whisky.de

Located on the island of Rügen in northern Germany, this distillery, owned by the Kliesow family, produces spirits from fruits and berries as well as whisky. The main product is a blended whisky made from malted barley and wheat but there is also a 5 year old single malt, Pommerscher Greif, matured in a sherry butt.

Schaubrennerei Am Hartmannsberg

Freital, founded in 2011

hartmannsberger.de

Working on a huge range of various spirits, Sandos Schubert also finds time to produce small volumes of whisky. The first whisky was released in 2015 and the latest was a 5 year old single malt, matured in ex-sherry casks.

Old Sandhill Whisky

Bad Belzig, founded in 2012

sandhill-whisky.com

Norbert and Tim Eggenstein released their first whisky as a 3 year old single malt, in 2015. Since then a wide range of bottlings have been launched. The most recent are two single malts matured in port pipes and Bordeaux barriques respectively.

Bellerhof Brennerei

Owen, founded in 1925 (whisky since 1990)

bellerhof-brennerei.com

Owned and operated by Susanne and Thomas Dannemann, it was Susanne´s grandfather August Beller who founded this distillery focused on spirits from fruits and berries. The production of whisky made from barley, wheat and rye started in 1990 and today there is one single malt in the range - a 5 year old matured in a combination of German oak and ex-bourbon casks.

Eifel Destillate

Koblenz, founded in 2009

eifel-destillate.de

Even though other spirits are produced at this distillery, Stephan Mohr´s main interest lies in whisky of all sorts. Located in Koblenz, circa 100 kilometres south of Cologne, the distillery currently has more than 200 barrels maturing in the warehouse. A fair amount of bottlings have already been released including rye, malt and blended whiskies (rye/barley/wheat). Single malts include Cask 99 (single cask bottled at cask strength) and Eifel 746.9 (at 8 years old, the oldest whisky so far). No whiskies are chill-filtered or coloured.

Hans-Gerhard Fink, owner of Finch Distillery

Iceland

Distillery: Eimverk Distillery, Reykjavik

Founded: 2012

Owner: Thorkelsson family

flokiwhisky.is

The country´s first whisky distillery emanated from an idea in 2008 when the three Thorkelsson brothers discussed the possibility of producing whisky in Iceland. In 2011 a company was formed, the first distillation was made in the ensuing year and full scale production started in August 2013. Only organic barley grown in Iceland is used for the production and everything is malted on site. Both peat and sheep dung is used to dry the malted barley. The distillery has a capacity of 100,000 litres where 50% is reserved for gin and aquavite and the rest for whisky. The first, limited whisky release will be in November 2017. Currently, the distillery is offering Flóki young malt and also a version called Sheep Dung Smoked Reserve. The owners also have Vor Gin and Víti Aquavit for sale.

Republic of Ireland

Distillery: Midleton Distillery, Midleton, Co. Cork

Founded: 1975

Owner: Irish Distillers (Pernod Ricard)

irishdistillers.ie

Midleton is by far the biggest distillery in Ireland and the home of Jameson´s Irish Whiskey. The distillery that we see today is barely 40 years old, but Jameson´s as a brand dates back much further. John Jameson, the founder, moved from Scotland to Ireland in 1777 and became part-owner in a distillery called Bow Street Distillery in Dublin. Some years later he became the sole owner and renamed the company John Jameson & Son. In 1966, John Jameson & Son with their distillery in Bow Street, merged with John Power & Son as well as Cork Distillery Company to form Irish Distillers Group. It was decided that the production of the three companies should move to Midleton Distillery in Cork. The result was that the Bow Street Distilllery was closed in 1971. Four years later an ultra modern distillery was built next to the old Midleton

distillery and this is what we can see today, while the old distillery has been refurbished as a visitor attraction. The production at Midleton comprises of two sections – grain whiskey and single pot still whiskey. The grain whiskey is needed for the blends, where Jameson´s is the biggest seller. Single pot still whiskey, on the other hand, is unique to Ireland. This part of the production is also used for the blends but is being bottled more and more on its own.

Midleton distillery is equipped with mash tuns both for the barley side and the grain side. Until recently, there were 14 washbacks for grain and 10 for barley, four, large copper pot stills and 5 column stills. The hugely increased demand for Irish whiskey, and for Jameson's in particular, has now forced the owners to greatly expand their capacitiy. The expansion, which was completed in autumn 2013, included a completely new brew house, another 24 washbacks, a new still house with three more pot stills (80,000 litres each) and six, new, larger columns replacing the existing ones. A new maturation facility with 40 warehouses has also been built in Dungourney, not far from Midleton. But it didn´t stop at that. In June 2017, yet another three stills were taken into production. In autumn 2015, a new micro distillery adjacent to the existing distillery, was opened. With a production capacity of 400 casks per year, it will be used for experiments and innovation.

Of all the brands produced at Midleton, Jameson´s blended Irish whiskey is by far the biggest. In 2016 the brand sold 75 million bottles. Apart from the core expression with no age statement, there are 12 and 18 year olds, Black Barrel, Gold Reserve and a Vintage. In autumn 2015 a new range, Deconstructed, was released for travel retail with three bottlings - Bold, Lively and Round. Other blended whiskey brands include Powers and the exclusive Midleton Very Rare. Another of their biggest sellers, Paddy, was sold in 2016 to the US group Sazerac. In recent years, Midleton has invested increasingly in their second category of whiskies, single pot still, and that range now includes Redbreast (12, 12 cask strength, 15, 21 year old and the sherrymatured Lustau Edition), Green Spot (no age and the 12 year old Leoville Barton bordeaux finish), Yellow Spot 12 years old, Powers (John´s Lane, Signature and Three Swallow) and Barry Crocket Legacy. In spring of 2015, the unique single pot still Midleton Dair Ghaelach was launched. It is the first ever Irish whiskey to be finished in virgin Irish oak. More innovation followed in 2017 when a range of experimental whiskeyes were released under the name Method and Madness. The range comprises four expressions; a single grain finished in virgin Spanish oak, a single pot still finished in French chestnut, a single malt finished in French Limousin oak and a 31 year old single grain single cask.

The new micro distillery at Midleton

Distillery: Tullamore Dew Distillery, Clonminch, Co. Offaly
Founded: 2014
Owner: Wm Grant & Sons
tullamoredew.com

Until 1954, Tullamore D.E.W. was distilled at Daly´s Distillery in Tullamore. When it closed, production was temporarily moved to Power´s Distillery in Dublin, and was later moved to Midleton Distillery and Bushmill´s Distillery. William Grant & Sons acquired Tullamore D.E.W. in 2010 and in March 2012, they announced that they were in the final stages of negotiations to acquire a site at Clonminch, situated on the outskirts of Tullamore. Construction of a new distillery began in May 2013 and in autumn 2014, the distillery was ready to start production. The four stills produce both malt whiskey and single pot still whiskey. The capacity is 1,8 million litres with plans to upgrade to 3,6 million in the near future. In May 2016, the company was seeking planning permission for a further development including a grain distillery with a capacity of doing 8 million litres of grain spirit. Construction started that same year and will be finished in late 2017. At the same location a new bottling plant is also being built.

Tullamore D.E.W. is the second biggest selling Irish whiskey in the world after Jameson with 12 million bottles sold in 2016, an increase by 8% from last year. The core range consists of Original (without age statement), 12 year old Special Reserve and 10, 14 and 18 year old Single Malts. Recent limited releases include Trilogy (a triple blend whiskey matured in three types of wood) and Phoenix. As an exclusive to duty free, the Tullamore D.E.W Cider Cask Finish was launched in summer 2015. The whiskey had been finished for three months in casks that had previously been used to produce apple cider.

Distillery: Cooley Distillery, Cooley, Co. Louth
Founded: 1987
Owner: Beam Suntory
kilbeggandistillingcompany.com

In 1987, the entrepreneur John Teeling bought the disused Ceimici Teo distillery and renamed it Cooley distillery. Two years later he installed two pot stills and in 1992 he released the first single malt from the distillery, called Locke´s Single Malt. Due to financial difficulties, the distillery was forced to close down but was re-opened in 1995. A number of brands were launched over the years and Teeling got several offers from companies wanting to buy Cooley. Finally, in December 2011 it was announced that Beam Inc. had acquired the distillery for $95m. In 2014, Suntory took over Beam in a $16bn deal and the new company was renamed Beam Suntory. Cooley distillery is equipped with one mash tun, four malt and six grain washbacks all made of stainless steel, two copper pot stills and two column stills. There is a production capacity of 650,000 litres of malt spirit and 2,6 million litres of grain spirit. Cooley´s master distiller Noel Sweeney, who has been with the distillery since 1987, recently changed job to become the master distiller for the new Powerscourt distillery. The range of whiskies is made up of several brands. Connemara single malts, which are all more or less peated, consist of a no age, a 12 year old, a 22 year old and the heavily peated Turf Mor. The other brand is Tyrconnel with a core expression bottled without age statement. Other Tyrconnel varieties include three 10 year old wood finishes and the recently launched 16 year old. The distillery also produces the single grain Kilbeggan (formerly known as Greenore) with a NAS bottling, a 6 year old, an 8 year old and a 18 year old.

Distillery: Teeling Distillery
Founded: 2015
Owner: Teeling Whiskey Co.
teelingwhiskey.com

After the Teeling family had sold Cooley and Kilbeggan distilleries to Beam in 2011, the family started a new company, Teeling Whiskey. A wide range of whiskeys have been released since then, all made from stock made at Cooley which the family kept while selling the distillery. In the meantime, the two sons, Jack and Stephen, opened a new distillery in Newmarket, Dublin in June 2015. This was the first new distillery in Dublin in 125 years. With the distillery in Dublin, the Teeling family are coming back to their roots. The family´s involvement in the whiskey industry started in 1782 when Walter Teeling owned a distillery in Marrowbone Lane in Dublin. One year after the opening, an amazing 60,000 people had been welcomed to the distillery! In summer 2017, Bacardi acquired a minority stake in Teeling Whiskey for an undisclosed sum. This is the first time Bacardi gets involved with Irish whiskey. It was also announced that Teeling Whiskey will be investing 500,000 euros in order to expand both the production area as well as the visitor centre.

The distillery is equipped with two wooden washbacks, four made of stainless steel and three stills made in Italy; wash still (15,000 litres), intermediate still (10,000 litres) and spirit still (9,000 litres) and the capacity is 500,000 litres of alcohol. Both pot still and malt whisky is produced and the total investment is 10 million euros. The core range from the distillery consists of the blend Small Batch which has been finished in rum casks, Single Grain which has been fully matured in Californian red wine barrels and Single Malt - a vatting of five different whiskies that have been finished in five different types of wine casks. Recent limited bottlings include The Revival Volume III, a 14 year old Pineau Des Charentes finish as well as a new range named the Brabazon Bottling where the first release focuses on the effect of ex-sherry casks.

Distillery: Walsh Whiskey Distillery, Carlow, Co. Carlow
Founded: 2016
Owner: Bernard Walsh, Illva Saronno
walshwhiskey.com

Bernard Walsh, CEO and owner of The Irishman Brands with whiskies like The Irishman and Writer´s Tears (both produced at Midleton), announced in autumn 2013 that he planned to build a distillery at Royal Oak, Carlow. It was later revealed that his company and thus the project in general, were backed up by the major Italian drinks company, Illva Saronno. Construction began in late 2014 and the distillery was commissioned in March 2016. It is one of the largest whiskey distilleries in Ireland with a capacity of 2.5 million litres of alcohol. All types of whiskey will be produced including grain- malt- and pot still whiskey. The equipment consists of a 3 ton semi-lauter mash tun, six washbacks, a 15,000 litre wash still, a 7,500 litre intermediate still and a 10,000 litre spirit still. There is also a column still for grain whiskey production. Apart from producing whiskey for its own brands, the distillery has allocated 15% of the output for a number of international partners.

Distillery: Great Northern Distillery, Dundalk, Co. Louth
Founded: 2015
Owner: The Irish Whiskey Co.
gndireland.com

The Irish Whiskey Company (IWC), with the Teeling family as the majority owners, signed an agreement with Diageo in August 2013, thus taking over the Great Northern Brewery in Dundalk. Diageo was about to move the brewing operation to Dublin and the IWC started restructuring the site into Great Northern Distillery at a cost of €35m. When it became operational in August 2015, it was the second biggest distillery in Ireland, with the capacity to produce 3.6 million litres of pot still whiskey and 8 million litres of grain spirit. The distillery is equipped with three columns for the grain spirit production and three pot stills for producing malt and single pot still whiskey. The distillery has been producing since September 2015 and the main part of the business will be to supply whiskey to private label brands. In autumn 2016, the company secured an additional €5m funding through the employment and investment incentive tax relief scheme (EIIS). Great Northern Distillery is owned by the Teeling family and two former directors of Cooley Distillery, Jim Finn and David Hynes.

Distillery: Waterford Distillery, Waterford, Co. Waterford
Founded: 2015
Owner: Renegade Spirits
               waterforddistillery.ie

The former co-owner of Bruichladdich distillery on Islay, Mark Reynier, has always been a man of action. When he, more or less against his will, was forced to sell the Islay distillery in 2012, he soon started to consider building a new distillery and this time in Ireland. In 2014 he bought the Diageo-owned Waterford Brewery in south east Ireland and only 16 months later, in December 2015, the first spirit was distilled. The distillery is equipped with two pot stills and one column still and, even though grain spirit will be produced, malt whiskey is the number one priority. The two pot stills have an interesting story. Built in 1972, they were used for 19 years at Inverleven distillery in Scotland until 1991 when the distillery closed. Later on, they were bought by Bruichladdich to be used in the planned Port Charlotte distillery. When that did not come to fruition, Reynier bought the pair of pot stills and shipped them to Waterford. The distillery also has a mash filter instead of a mash tun, in similar with Teaninich and Inchdairnie in Scotland. In keeping with the business at Bruichladdich, local barley is the main focus and Reynier is sourcing the barley from over 50 farms on 19 different soil types. The distillery has a capacity of 1 million litres but the owners have plans to go up to 3 million litres in the future. To aid the development, the owners managed in spring 2017 to raise an investment backing of 20 million Euros from Ulster Bank and the Business Growth Fund.

Other distilleries in Ireland

Kilbeggan Distillery

Kilbeggan, Co. Westmeath, founded in 1757

www.kilbegganwhiskey.com

The owners of Cooley distillery with John Teeling at the forefront, decided in 2007 to bring this distillery back to life and it is now the oldest producing whiskey distillery in the world. In 2011, Cooley Distillery was taken over by Beam Inc. and in spring 2014, Suntory bought Beam, which means that the current owners are the newly formed Beam Suntory. The distillery is equipped with a wooden mash tun, four Oregon pine washbacks and two stills with one of them being 180 years old. The first single malt whiskey release from the new production came in 2010 and limited batches have been released thereafter. The core blended expression of Kilbeggan is a no age statement bottling but limited releases of aged Kilbeggan blend (15, 18 and 21 year old) have occurred. To confuse matters, since 2015 there is also a Kilbeggan single grain, produced at Cooley, which used to be called Greenore.

West Cork Distillers

Skibbereen, Co. Cork, founded in 2004

www.westcorkdistillers.com

Started by John O´Connell, Denis McCarthy and Ger McCarthy in 2003 in Union Hall in West Cork, the distillery moved in 2013 to the present site. The distillery is equipped with four stills with the two wash stills coming from Sweden and the two spirit stills having been manufactured in Germany. The distillery is producing both malt whiskey and grain whiskey (from barley and wheat) and some of the malting is done on site. Apart from a range of vodka, gin and liqueurs, a 10 year old single malt and a blended whiskey are sold under the name West Cork. In autumn 2016, three new 12 year olds were launched - Sherry Cask, Port Cask and Rum Cask.

Connacht Whiskey Company

Ballina, Co. Mayo, founded in 2016

connachtwhiskey.com

The distillery, which nestles on the banks of the River Moy in northwest Ireland, was founded by three Americans - Robert

Cassell, Tom Jensen and PJ Stapleton - and one Irishman, David Stapleton. It is equipped with three pot stills which were made in Canada and has the capacity to produce 300,000 litres of pure alcohol per year and the first distillation of whiskey was made in April 2016. Apart from malt whiskey and single pot still whiskey, the owners also produce vodka, gin and poitin - all of which have already been launched. Sourced whiskies have been released with the most recent being the blend Brothership – a vatting of 10 year old Irish pot still and 10 year old American whiskey. Local barley is used and Robert Cassell, who is the Master Distiller, has decided to use a combination of several malts to create a special flavour.

The Dingle Whiskey Distillery

Milltown, Dingle, Co. Kerry, founded in 2012

www.dingledistillery.ie

When the intention of turning an old creamery into a distillery did not work out, Oliver Hughes, founder of the Porterhouse group of pubs, left his former business partners and found a new location. The old Fitzgerald sawmills was transformed into a distillery with three pot stills and a combined gin/vodka still and the first production of gin and vodka was in October 2012. Whiskey distillation began in December and the production is around 100,000 bottles per year. The first products that were launched were Dingle Original Gin and DD Vodka. The first whiskey, the limited Dingle Cask No. 2, was released in December 2015 and a general release of Dingle Whiskey and Dingle Whiskey Cask Strength was made in autumn 2016. In July 2016, co-founder Oliver Hughes died unexpectadly at the age of 57.

The Shed Distillery

Drumshanbo, Co. Leitrim, founded in 2015

www.thesheddistillery.com

One of the newest distilleries in Ireland, The Shed Distillery was founded by entrepreneur Pat Rigney who is a veteran in the drinks business, having worked with brands like Bailey´s, Gilbey´s and Grant´s. The distillery cost €2m to build and is equipped with three Holstein stills with columns attached. The focus for the owners will be single pot still whiskey but the product range also includes potato vodka, gin and liqueurs. The first whiskey distillation was in January 2015. In spring 2017, the owners received a planning permission to build a visitor centre which they hope will attract 10,000 visitors in 2018.

Boann Distillery

Drogheda, Co. Meath, founded in 2016

boanndistillery.ie

Boann Distillery is owned by the Cooney family. For forty years, Pat Cooney built the Gleeson Group from a small independent bottler to a leading supplier and distributor in the drinks business. In 2012, he sold most of the company and, together with his wife and children, he started planning a distillery of their own. Assisted by the well-known whisky consultant, John McDougall, the distillery has taken shape and production is likely to start up in autumn 2017 with a visitor centre planned for spring 2018. Three Italian-made copper pot stills (10,000, 7,500 and 5,000 litres respectively) were installed and they have been supplemented by a 500-litre Bennett gin still. On top of that, the distillery is equipped with a state of the art brewing equipment and will also produce craft beers under the name Boyne Brewhouse. Three bottlings of sourced whiskey under the name The Whistler have already been launched.

Glendalough Distillery

Newtown Mount Kennedy, Co. Wicklow, founded in 2012

glendaloughdistillery.com

The distillery was founded by five friends from Wicklow and Dublin in 2012. For the first three years, they acted as independent bottlers, sourcing their whisky mainly from Cooley distillery. A range of Glendalough whiskey was soon created with two single malts and a Double Barrel blend made from 90% corn and 10% malted barley. In 2015 Holstein stills were installed and gin production began. So far whiskey distillation has not started. In 2016, the Canadian drinks distribution group Mark Anthony Brands invested €5.5m in the distillery.

Slane Castle Distillery

Slane, Co. Meath, founded in 2017

www.slaneirishwhiskey.com

The Conyngham family, owners of the Slane Castle and Estate just north of Dublin, established a whiskey brand a few years ago which became popular not least in the USA. The whiskey was produced at Cooleys but the family decided to start a distillery of their own. They partnered with Camus Wine & Spirits to begin the construction but, eventually, Camus withdrew from the project. In June 2015, however, Brown-Forman, one of the biggest companies in the industry, announced that they were buying Slane Castle Irish Whiskey Ltd. for $50m, with the hope of having a distillery with a one million litre capacity ready by the end of 2016. The distillery will probably be ready in August/September 2017. Equipped with three copper pot stills, six column stills and washbacks made of wood, the distillery will also have a large visitor centre.

Italy

Distillery:	Puni Destillerie, Glurns, South Tyrol
Founded:	2012
Owner:	Ebensperger family
	puni.com

The lack of a whisky distillery in Italy was rectified in February 2012 when the first spirit was distilled at Puni distillery, situated in South Tyrol in the north of Italy. It is owned and run by the Ebensperger family with Albrecht, the father, and one of his sons, Jonas, as the dominant figures. There are at least two things that distinguish this project from most others. One characteristic is the design of the distillery – a 13-metre tall cube made of red brick. The other is the raw material that they are using. They are making malt whisky but malted barley is only one of three cereals in the recipe. The other two are malted rye and malted wheat. The family calls it Triple Malt and it is their intention to use this combination of cereals for their main line of whiskies. In 2016, however, they also started distilling 100% malted barley and anticipate to release their first whisky from that production in 2019. The distillery is equipped with five washbacks made of local larch and the fermentation time is 84 hours. There is one wash still (3,000 litres) and one spirit still (2,000 litres) and the capacity is 80,000 litres of alcohol per year.

In October 2015, it was time for the release of the first Italian single malt. Puni Nova was matured in American white oak for three years while Puni Alba had been matured for three years in Marsala casks and then finished in Islay casks. In 2017, a third addition to the range was made with Puni Sole, matured for two years in ex-bourbon barrels and another two in PX casks. There is also the limited Puni Nero where the latest edition had been matured for four years in Pinot Nero casks from nearby wineries.

Liechtenstein

Distillery:	Brennerei Telser, Triesen
Founded:	1880 (whisky since 2006)
Owner:	Telser family
	telserdistillery.com

The first distillery in Liechtenstein to produce whisky is not a new distillery. It has existed since 1880 and is now run by the fourth generation of the family. Telser is probably the only distillery in Europe still using a wood fire to heat the small stills (150 and 120 litres). Poduction mainly comprises spirits from fruits and berries, including grappa and vodka. For whisky, the distillery uses a mixture of three different malts (some peated) which are fermented and distilled separately. After a 10 day fermentation, the spirit is triple distilled and the three different spirits are blended and filled into pinot noir barriques and left to mature for a minimum of three years. The first bottling of Telsington was released in 2009 and in 2014, the name was changed from Telsington to Liechtenstein Whisky. The latest relase is X+1 which is also the first bottled at cask strength.

The Netherlands

Distillery:	Zuidam Distillers, Baarle Nassau
Founded:	1974 (whisky since 1998)
Owner:	Zuidam family
	zuidam.eu

Zuidam Distillers was started in 1974 as a traditional, family distillery producing liqueurs, genever, gin and vodka. The first release of a whisky, which goes by the name Millstone, was from the 2002 production and it was bottled in 2007 as a 5 year old. The current range is a 5 year old which comes in both peated and unpeated versions, American oak 10 years, French oak 10 years, Sherry oak 12 years and PX Cask 1999, a 14 year old bottled at 46%. Apart from single malts there is also a Millstone 100% Rye which is bottled at 50%. Recent limited releases include a 6 year old, triple distilled three grain whisky (equal parts of corn, rye and malted barley) and a 3 year old, triple distilled five grain whisky (wheat, corn, rye, spelt and malted barley).

The distillery has been expanded over the last years and the equipment now consists of one mash tun for malt whisky, one for rye and genever and 10 washbacks. Furthermore, there are a total of five stills with volumes ranging from 850 litres up to 5,000 litres. The total capacity is 280,000 litres of pure alcohol per year. But the expansion doesn't stop at that. Patrick van Zuidam has plans to build a second distillery at a farm where they will be growing their own barley and rye as well. The distillery will be equipped with four pot stills (5,000 litres each) with the possibility of adding another six.

Millstone 100 Rye
from Zuidam Distillers

Other distilleries in The Netherlands

Us Heit Distillery

Bolsward, founded in 2002

www.usheit.com

This is one of many examples where a beer brewery also contains a whisky distillery. Frysk Hynder was the first Dutch whisky and made its debut in 2005 at 3 years of age. The barley is grown in surrounding Friesland and malted at the distillery. Some 10,000 bottles are produced annually and the whisky (3 to 5 years old) is matured in various casks – sherry, bourbon, red wine, port and cognac. A cask strength version has also been released.

Kalkwijck Distillers

Vroomshoop, founded in 2009

www.kalkwijckdistillers.nl

Lisanne Benus and her father Bert opened their distillery in 2009. Kalkwijck is located in Vroomshoop, in the rural eastern part of the Netherlands. The distillery is equipped with a 300 litre pot still still with a column attached. The main part of the production is jenever, korenwijn and liqueurs but whisky has been distilled since 2010. In spring 2015, the first single malt was released. Eastmoor was 3 years old, made from barley grown on the estate and bottled at 40%. More releases have followed since.

Stokerij Sculte

Ootmarsum, founded in 2004 (whisky since 2011)

www.stokerijsculte.nl

Gerard Velthuis started the distillery in 2004, focusing on spirits made from fruit. From 2011, malt whisky is also on the agenda. The distillery is equipped with a 500 litre stainless steel mashtun, 4 stainless steel washbacks with a fermentation time of 4-5 days and two Austrian made stills. The first Sculte Twentse Whisky was released in October 2014 and this was followed by a 4 year old in May 2016. Velthuis is now working on new recipes, including a heavily peated, with the aim to start releasing them in 2019/2020.

Northern Ireland

Distillery:	Bushmill´s Distillery, Bushmills, Co. Antrim
Founded:	1784
Owner:	Casa Cuervo
	bushmills.com

Diageo took the market by surprise when they announced in 2014 that they were selling the distillery. This was Diageo´s only part of the increasing Irish whiskey segment and commentators struggled to see the reason for the sale. The buyer was the tequila maker Casa Cuervo, producer of José Cuervo. Diageo already owned 50% of the company´s other, upscale tequila brand, Don Julio and with the deal, they got the remaining 50% as well as $408m.

Bushmills is the second biggest of the Irish distilleries after Midleton, with a capacity to produce 4,5 million litres of alcohol a year. In 1972 the distillery became a part of Irish Distillers Group which thereby gained control over the entire whiskey production in Ireland. Irish Distillers were later (1988) purchased by Pernod Ricard who, in turn, resold Bushmill´s to Diageo in 2005 at a price tag of €295.5 million. Since the take-over, Diageo invested heavily into the distillery and it now has ten stills with a production running seven days a week, which means 4,5 million litres a year. In December 2015, the new owners announced that they had applied for a planning permission to build a £30 million addition to the current distillery which would effectively double the production capacity. Included in the application were also plans to build a new visitor´s centre. In March 2017, the owners also revealed that they were going to expand on to 62 acres of adjacent farmland with the intention of building another 29 warehouses. Two kinds of malt are used at Bushmills, one unpeated and one slightly peated.

Bushmill`s core range of single malts consists of a 10 year old, a 16 year old Triple Wood with a finish in Port pipes for 6-9 months and a 21 year old finished in Madeira casks for two years. There is also a 12 year old Distillery Reserve which is sold exclusively at the distillery and the 1608 Anniversary Edition. Black Bush and Bushmill´s Original are the two main blended whiskeys in the range. In spring 2016, Bushmill´s launched their first whiskey exclusive for duty free, The Steamship Collection, with three special cask matured whiskies plus a number of limited releases. The first part of the series was Sherry Cask Reserve which was followed up in autumn 2016 by Port Cask Reserve. Bushmill´s is the third most sold Irish whiskey after Jameson and Tullamore D.E.W.

Other distilleries in Northern Ireland

Echlinville Distillery

Kircubbin, Co. Down, founded in 2013

www.echlinville.com

After having relied on Cooley Distillery for his mature whiskey, Shane Braniff, who launched the Feckin Irish Whiskey brand in 2005, decided in 2012 to build his own distillery. Located near Kircubbin on the Ards Peninsula he started production in summer 2013. The distillery was further expanded with more equipment in 2015 and in April 2016, a visitor centre opened. The distillery also has its own floor maltings. Apart from single pot still and single malt whiskey, vodka and gin is also produced. Braniff recently revived the old Dunville´s brand of blended whiskey and has released a 10 year old single malt with a finish in PX sherry casks.

Rademon Estate Distillery

Downpatrick, Co. Down, founded in 2012

shortcrossgin.com

Fiona and David Boyd-Armstrong opened their distillery on the Rademon estate in 2012, which was owned by Frank Boyd, the father of Fiona. Since its inception, their main product has been Short Cross gin which quickly became a success story. In summer 2015 the production was expanded into whiskey and during the first year, around 100 barrels were filled. The couple are now planning to put in more stills to cope with the increased production of Irish malt whiskey.

Bushmill´s Distillery

Norway 🇳🇴

Distillery: Det Norske Brenneri, Grimstad
Founded: 1952 (whisky since 2009)
Owner: Norske Brenneri AS
detnorskebrenneri.no

The company was founded in 1952 by Karl Gustav Puntervold and for more than 50 years it mainly produced wine from apples and other fruits. The company was taken over by Karl Gustav´s son, Ole, in 1977. In July 2005 the state monopoly in terms of production of spirits in Norway was abolished and Ole decided to take advantage of that. He started to produce aquavit, among other products, and the first products were launched during autumn 2005. Whisky production started in 2009 and two Holstein stills are used for the distillation. In 2012, Audny, the first single malt produced in Norway was launched. This was followed by more releases and in 2015, Eiktyrne, a 3,5 year old, oloroso matured was released. In January 2014, K.G. Puntervold and the distillery were sold to the companies´ biggest customer – Norske Brenneri AS.

Other distilleries in Norway

Myken Distillery

Myken, founded in 2014
www.mykendestilleri.no

This distillery was built in the most unlikely place one can imagine. Myken is a group of islands in the Atlantic ocean, 32 kilometres from mainland Norway and 25 kilometres north of the Arctic Circle. The largest island has 13 people living the year round and this is where Myken distillery was opened in 2014. They distilled their first spirit in December 2014 and the equipment consists of one wash still (1,000 litres), one spirit still (700 litres) and one gin still (300 litres) – all alambic style, made in Spain and direct fired using propane gas burners. The fermentation time is 60-140 hours and the capacity is 20,000 litres per year.

The main part of the production is from unpeated malt but the first peated distillation (35ppm) was made in summer 2016. The production water is desalinated sea water, supplied by a municipal facility. The only spirit released so far is Myken Arctic Gin and the plan is to release the first whisky in autumn 2018. The distillery was in 2016 expanded with a small visitor centre.

Arcus

Gjelleråsen, founded in 1996 (whisky since 2009)
www.arcus.no

Arcus is the biggest supplier and producer of wine and spirits in Norway with subsidaries in Denmark, Finland and Sweden. They are also the largest aquavit producer in the world and are involved in cognac production in France. The first whisky produced by the distillery was released in 2013. Under the name Gjoleid, two whiskies made from malted barley and malted wheat were released – one matured in ex-bourbon American oak and the other in ex-oloroso American oak. In November 2016, another three Gjoleid expressions were launched.

Aurora Spirit

Tromsö, founded in 2016
www.auroraspirit.com

At 69.39°N, Aurora is the northernmost distillery in the world. The location, close to the Lyngen alps and well above the Arctic Circle, is nothing short of stunning. The mash is bought from a brewery, fermented at the distillery and distilled in the 1,200 litre Kothe pot still with an attached column. Co-founder and the main share holder, Tor Petter Christensen, has plans to produce both non-peated and peated whisky. The plan is to do 6,000 litres of whisky in 2017, increasing to at least 25,000 in 2020. Apart from single malt whisky, the owners also produce gin, vodka and aquavit. All their products, including the first whisky due for release in November 2019, are sold under the name Bivrost. The distillery also has a visitor centre with tours and tastings.

Spain 🇪🇸

Distillery: Distilerio Molino del Arco, Segovia
Founded: 1959
Owner: Distilerias y Crianza del Whisky (DYC)
dyc.es

Established by Nicomedes Garcia Lopez in 1959 (with whisky distilling commencing three years later), this is a distillery with capacity for producing eight million litres of grain whisky and two million litres of malt whisky per year. In addition to that, vodka and rum are produced and there are also in-house maltings.

Northern Lights over the Aurora Distillery in Norway

The distillery is equipped with six copper pot stills and there are 250,000 casks maturing on site.

The big seller when it comes to whiskies is a blend simply called DYC which is around 4 years old. It is supplemented by an 8 year old blend and, since 2007, also by DYC Pure Malt, i. e. a vatted malt consisting of malt from the distillery and from selected Scottish distilleries. To commemorate the distillery's 50th anniversary in 2009, they released a 10 year old single malt, the first from the distillery. A new extension of the range is DYC Red One which is a cherry infused whisky-based spirit, bottled at 30%.

Other distilleries in Spain

Destilerias Liber

Padul, Granada, founded in 2001

www.destileriasliber.com

This distillery is quite a bit younger than its competitor in Segovia, DYC. Destilerias Liber was founded in 2001 but did not start production until late 2002. Like so many other, newly established distilleries, they started distilling rum, marc and vodka – spirits that do not require maturation and can also instantaneously generate cash to the company. For the whisky production, the spirit is double distilled after a fermentation of 48-72 hours. Maturation takes place in sherry casks. The only available whisky on the market is a 5 year old single malt called Embrujo de Granada.

Sweden

Distillery:	Box Destilleri, Bjärtrå
Founded:	2010
Owner:	Box Destilleri AB
	boxwhisky.se

Set in buildings from the 19th century that had previously been used both as a box factory (hence the distillery name), as well as a power plant, Box distillery started production in November 2010. Initiated by a group of friends who shared the same interest in whisky, the company today has more than 1,500 share holders. Sales of their whisky, first released in 2014, has exceeded the owners' expectations and in summer 2017 it was decided that the distillery was due for a serious expansion. The equipment today consists of a four-roller Boby mill, a semilauter mash tun with a capacity of 1,5 tonnes, three 8,000 litre stainless steel washbacks, a wash still (3,800 litres) and a spirit still (2,500 litres). The proposed plans include adding two more stills, four new washbacks as well as a larger warehouse. When finished it means the capacity increases from the current 100,000 litres to 300,000.

The distillery is making two types of whisky – fruity/unpeated and peated. The distillery manager, Roger Melander, wants to create a new make which is as clean as possible by using a very slow distillation process with lots of copper contact in the still. The flavour of the spirit is also impacted by the effective condensation using what might be the coldest cooling water in the whisky world, namely 2-6°C, which is obtained from a nearby river. A fermentation time of 72-96 hours also affects the character. A majority of the casks (80%), from 500 litres down to 40 litres, are first fill bourbon but oloroso casks, virgin oak and casks made from Hungarian oak have also been filled. An interesting experiment was started in 2016 when 100 small casks made of Japanese oak (Quercus mongolica) were filled with new make.

The first whisky, The Pioneer, was released in June 2014 and all 5,000 bottles were sold out in less than 7 hours! Between 3 and 4 years old, it was a vatting of unpeated and lightly peated whisky, predominantly from bourbon casks but also a small amount of ex-sherry. The whisky was the first in a range of four called Early Days Collection with Challenger, Explorer and Messenger to follow. The next range, 2nd Step Collection was launched in 2016 with the third and final expression released in April 2017. By that time, the first core expression, Dålvve, had already been launched. This was instantly followed by a version finished in PX casks and reserved for the Asian market as well as one with a maturation in ex-bourbon casks and a finish in virgin oak. In June 2014 an excellent visitor centre was opened and this was also the location for the inaugural World Whisky Forum in February 2017, initiated by Box.

Box Distillery

Distillery: Mackmyra Svensk Whisky, Valbo
Founded: 1999
Owner: Mackmyra Svensk Whisky AB
mackmyra.se

Mackmyra´s first distillery was built in 1999 and, ten years later, the company revealed plans to build a brand new facility in Gävle, a few miles from the present distillery. In 2012, the distillery was ready and the first distillation took place in spring of that year. The total investment, which included a whisky village to be built within a ten year period, was expected to amount to approximately £50 million. The construction of the new distillery is quite extraordinary and with its 37 metre structure, it is perhaps one of the tallest distilleries in the world. Since April 2013, all the distillation takes place at the new gravitation distillery. In 2017 however, the old distillery was re-opened as the Lab Distillery where the company aim to develop innovative spirits in collaboration with craft distillers.

Mackmyra whisky is based on two basic recipes, one which produces a fruity and elegant whisky, while the other is smokier. The smoke does not stem from peat, but from the juniper wood and bog moss being used. The first release was in 2006 and the distillery now has four core expressions; Svensk Ek, Brukswhisky, the peated Svensk Rök and, new since 2015, MACK by Mackmyra which competes in the lower price segment. A range of limited editions called Moment was introduced in December 2010 and consists of exceptional casks selected by the Master Blender, Angela D´Orazio. The latest edition is Körsbär where the whisky was matured for more than eight years in casks that had previously held a sweet cherry wine. Seasonal expressions are also released regularly with the very first 10 year old Swedish whisky being one of the latest. In all honesty, Mackmyra themselves had a few months earlier launched a limited volume of an even older whisky, 12 years, In April 2017, Mackmyra was also the first Swedish distillery to release a bottling exclusively for the travel retail market. Expedition has been matured in ex-bourbon casks as well as in Swedish oak seasoned with cloudberry wine.

The Mackmyra gravitation distillery

Other distilleries in Sweden

Smögen Whisky
Hunnebostrand, founded in 2010
www.smogenwhisky.se

Pär Caldenby – a lawyer, whisky enthusiast and the author of Enjoying Malt Whisky - is the founder and owner of Smögen Whisky on the west coast of Sweden. The distillery is equipped with three washbacks (1,600 litres each), a wash still (900 litres) and a spirit still (600 litres) and the capacity is 35,000 litres of alcohol a year. Pär practices a slow distillation with unusually long foreshots (45 minutes) in order not to get a newmake with too many fruity esters. Heavily peated malt is imported from Scotland and the aim is to produce an Islay-type of whisky. The first release (1,600 bottles) from the distillery was the 3 year old Primör in March 2014. This has over the years been followed by many limited releases. The most recent include a 5 year old triple-distilled matured in Sauternes barriques, the 4 year old Sherry Project 2:1 and a 5 year old single cask matured in a bourbon barrel. Pär Caldenby has also released his own gin, Strane, in three versions – Merchant Strength, Navy Strength and Uncut Strength.

Spirit of Hven
Hven, founded in 2007
www.hven.com

The second Swedish distillery to come on stream, after Mackmyra, was Spirit of Hven, a distillery situated on the island of Hven right between Sweden and Denmark. The first distillation took place in May 2008. Henric Molin, founder and owner, is a trained chemist and very concerned about choosing the right oak for his casks. The distillery is equipped with a 0,5 ton mash tun, six washbacks made of stainless steel and three stills – a 2,000 litre wash still, a 1,500 litre spirit still and a designated gin still. Part of the barley is malted on site and for part of that they use Swedish peat, sometimes mixed with seaweed and sea-grass, for drying. Apart from whisky, other products include rum made from sugar beet, vodka, gin and aquavit. The plans for an expansion of the bottling plant was met by protests from some of the neighbours and the company had to move part of the bottling to the mainland in 2017. In the same year the distillery also started to export their products to the American market.

Their first whisky was the lightly peated Urania which was released in 2012. The second launch was the start of a new series of limited releases called The Seven Stars. The first expression was the 5 year old, lightly peated Dubhe, which was followed by Merak, Phecda, Megrez and, in 2017, the peated Alioth. Three different barley varities and four different types of casks had been involved to create the whisky. Other limited releases have occured but in autumn 2015 it was time for the distillery´s first core bottling - Tycho´s Star, named in honour of the famous astronomer Tycho Brahe, who lived and worked on the island in the 16th century.

Norrtelje Brenneri
Norrtälje, founded in 2002 (whisky since 2009)
www.norrteljebrenneri.se

This distillery, situated 70 kilometres north of Stockholm, was founded on a farm which has belonged to the owner´s family for five generations. The production consists mainly of spirits from ecologically grown fruits and berries. Since 2009, a single malt whisky from ecologically grown barley is also produced. The first bottling was released in summer 2015 and several limited editions have followed.

Gammelstilla Whisky
Torsåker, founded in 2005
www.gammelstilla.se

Less than 30 kilometres from the better known Mackmyra lies another distillery since 2011 – Gammelstilla. The company was already founded in 2005 by three friends but today there are more than 200 shareholders. Unlike most of the other Swedish whisky distilleries, they chose to design and build their pot stills themselves. The wash still has a capacity of 600 litres and the spirit still 300 litres and the annual capacity is 20,000 litres per year. The first, limited release for shareholders was in May 2017.

Gotland Whisky

Romakloster, founded in 2011

www.gotlandwhisky.se

This distillery, on the island of Gotland in the Baltic Sea, is situated in a decommissioned sugar works south of Visby. It is equipped with a wash still (1,600 litres) and a spirit still (900 litres) – both made by Forsyth´s in Scotland. The local barley is ecologically grown and malted on site. The floor malting is made easier through the use of a malting robot of their own construction which turns the barley. Both unpeated and peated whisky is produced and the capacity is 60,000 litres per year. The distillery came on stream in May 2012 and the first limited release of Isle of Lime single malt was in early 2017 with a general launch in August.

Uppsala Destilleri

Uppsala, founded in 2015

www.uppsladestilleri.se

Founded by Magnus Johansson, this is one of the smallest of the Swedish distilleries, currently with a yearly production of 1,500 litres but with a goal to increase production in the future. Production started in early 2016 with a 100 litre alambic still from Portugal but yet another still has already been installed. Apart from whisky, gin and rum are also produced.

Tevsjö Destilleri

Järvsö, founded in 2012

www.tevsjodestilleri.se

The owners of this combination of distillery and restaurang are primarily focused on distillation of aquavit and other white spirits and malt whisky production did not start until spring 2017. However, whisky has been produced earlier in the way of a "bourbon" with a mash bill of 70% corn, 10% malted barley, 10% unmalted barley, 5% wheat and 5% rye.

Switzerland

Distillery:	Whisky Castle, Elfingen, Aargau
Founded:	2002
Owner:	Ruedi Käser
	whisky-castle.com

The first whisky from this distillery in Elfingen, founded by Ruedi Käser, reached the market in 2004. It was a single malt under the name Castle Hill. Since then the range of malt whiskies has been expanded and today include Castle Hill Doublewood (3 years old matured both in casks made of chestnut and oak), Whisky Smoke Barley (at least 3 years old matured in new oak), Fullmoon (matured in casks from Hungary), Terroir (4 years old made from Swiss barley and matured in Swiss oak), Cask Strength (5 years old and bottled at 58%) and Edition Käser (71% matured in new oak casks from Bordeaux). Recent additions include Castle One (matured in Bordeaux casks) and Family Reserve (an 8 year old with a port finish). In 2010, new, open top fermenters were installed to add fresher and fruitier notes to the newmake. The owners have also cut down on the number of casks made from new oak and have added a variety of other casks. The yearly production is around 10,000 litres and on the premises one can have a complete visitor's experience, which includes a restaurant as well as a shop.

Distillery:	Brauerei Locher, Appenzell
Founded:	1886 (whisky since 1999)
Owner:	Locher family
	saentismalt.com

This old brewery started to produce whisky on a small scale in 1999 but from 2005, larger volumes have been produced. The equipment consists of a Steinecker mash tun, stainless steel wash backs and Holstein stills. Brauerei Locher is unique in using old beer casks for the maturation. The core range consists of three expressions; Himmelberg, bottled at 43%, Dreifaltigkeit which is slightly peated having matured in toasted casks and bottled at 52% and, finally, Sigel which has matured in very small casks and is bottled at 40%. A range of limited bottlings under the name Alpstein is also available. After a few years in a beer cask, these whiskies have received a further maturation in casks that previously held other spirits or wine. The most recent, Edition XIII, was released in July 2017 and had matured in beer casks for two years and then another five years in port casks. Snow White is another limitd range where the latest release was a 5 year old with one year´s finish in casks that had previously held Vieille Poire (a pear spirit).

Other distilleries in Switzerland

Langatun Distillery

Langenthal, Bern, founded in 2007

www.langatun.ch

The distillery was built in 2005 and under the same roof as the brewery Brau AG Langenthal. The casks used for maturation are all 225 litres and Swiss oak (Chardonnay), French oak (Chardonnay and red wine) and ex sherry casks are used. The two 5 year old core expressions are Old Deer and the peated Old Bear. Other bottlings include the single cask rye Old Eagle, a single cask "bourbon" Old Mustang, the triple matured Swiss Pipe andd the organic Old Woodpecker.

Bauernhofbrennerei Lüthy

Muhen, Aargau, founded in 1997 (whisky since 2005)

www.swiss-single-malt.ch

This farm distillery started in 1997 by producing distillates from fruit, as well as grappa, absinthe and schnapps. The range was expanded to include whisky in 2005 which was distilled in a mobile pot still distillery. The first single malt expression to be launched in 2008, was Insel-Whisky, matured in a Chardonnay cask and several releases have since followed. Starting in 2010, the yearly bottling was given the name Herr Lüthy and the 11th release from these had been matured in a combination o Swiss wine casks, ex-sherry casks and virgin American oak.

Brennerei Stadelmann

Altbüron, Luzern, founded in 1932 (whisky since 2003)

www.schnapsbrennen.ch

The distillery, founded by Hans Stadelmann in 2001, is equipped with three Holstein-type stills (150-250 litres) and the first whisky was distilled for a local whisky club in 2003. In 2006 it was bottled under the name Dorfbachwasser and finally, in 2010, the first official bottling from the distillery in the shape of a 3 year old single malt whisky was released. In autumn 2014, the sixth release was made, matured in a Bordeaux cask. The first whisky from smoked barley was distilled in 2012.

Etter Distillerie

Zug, founded in 1870 (whisky since 2007)

www.etter-distillerie.ch

This distillery was started in 1870 by Paul Etter and today it is the third and fourth generations who are running it. Their main produce is eau de vie from various fruits and berries. A sidetrack to the business was entered in 2007 when they decided to distil their first malt whisky. The malted barley was bought from a brewery, distilled at Etter, filled into wine casks and left to mature in moist caves for a minimum of three years. The first release was made in 2010 under the name Johnett Single Malt Whisky and this is currently sold as a 7 year old. In 2016, a limited Johnett with a 12 months finish in Caroni rum casks was released.

Spezialitätenbrennerei Zürcher

Port, Bern, founded in 1954 (whisky from 2000)

www.lakeland-whisky.ch

The first in the Zürcher family to distil whisky was Heinz Zürcher in 2000, who released the first 1,000 bottles of Lakeland single malt in 2003. Daniel and Ursula Zürcher took over in 2004 and continued their uncle's work. The main focus of the distillery is specialising in various distillates of fruit, absinth and liqueur but a Lakeland single malt is also in the range. The oldest version so far, appeared in August 2014. It was an 8 year old matured in an oloroso cask.

Whisky Brennerei Hollen

Lauwil, Baselland, founded in 1999

www.swiss-whisky.ch, www.single-malt.ch

The first Swiss whisky was distilled at Hollen in July 1999. The whisky from Brennerei Hollen is stored on French oak casks, which have been used for white wine (Chardonnay) or red wine (Pinot Noir). In the beginning most bottlings were 4-5 years old but in 2009 the first 10 year old was released and there has also been a 12 year old, the oldest expression from the distillery so far.

Brennerei Hagen

Hüttwilen, Thurgau, founded in 1999

www.distillerie-hagen.ch

A triple distilled malt whisky is produced by Ueli Hagen in the small village of Hüttwilen in the northernmost part of Switzerland. The spirit is matured in bourbon barrels and the first produce was sold in 2002 as a 3 year old. Ueli Hagen produces mainly schnapps and absinth and distills around 300 bottles of malt whisky a year.

Wales

Distillery: Penderyn Distillery, Penderyn
Founded: 2000
Owner: Welsh Whisky Company Ltd.
penderyn.wales

In 1998 four private individuals started The Welsh Whisky Company and two years later, the first Welsh distillery in more than a hundred years started distilling. A new type of still, developed by David Faraday for Penderyn Distillery, differs from the Scottish and Irish procedures in that the whole process from wash to new make takes place in one single still. But that is not the sole difference. Every distillery in Scotland is required by law, to do the mashing and fermenting on site. At Penderyn, though, the wash (until summer 2014) was bought from a regional beer brewer and transported to the distillery on a weekly basis. Even though the distillery had been working 24 hours a day to keep up with the increasing demand, it became obvious in 2012 that they had to do something to increase its capacity. In September 2013, a second still (almost a replica of the first still) was commissioned and in June 2014, two traditional pot stills, as well as their own mashing equipment was installed. The expansion, worth £1m, increased the production from 90,000 litres to 300,000 litres of alcohol per annum and also allowed the company to experiment with new styles and expressions of single malts.

The first single malt was launched in 2004. The core range today is divided into two groups. Dragon consists of the Madeira finished Legend, Myth which is fully bourbon matured and Celt with a peated finish. They are all bottled at 41%. The other range is Gold with Madeira, Peated, Portwood and Sherrywood bottled at 46%. Over the years, the company has released several single casks and limited releases and a new range of whiskies called Icons of Wales was introduced in 2012 with the fifth edition, Bryn Terfel, being released in 2016. The bottling is celebrating the famous Welsh opera singer Bryn Terfel and especially his favourite role as Falstaff. The main markets for Penderyn are UK, France and Germany and the brand sells around 250,000 bottles per year. The distillery also produces the popular Brecon Botanicals Gin. A visitor centre opened in 2008 which now attracts 40,000 visitors a year.

Penderyn Distillery - the first in Wales in more than a hundred years

North America

USA

Distillery: Westland Distillery, Seattle, Washington
Founded: 2011
Owner: Rémy Cointreau
westlanddistillery.com

Unlike most of the new craft distilleries in the USA producing whiskey, Westland Distillery did not distill other spirits to finance the early stages of production. Until November 2012, Westland was a medium sized craft distillery where they brought in the wash from a nearby brewery and had the capacity of doing 60,000 litres of whiskey per year. During the summer of 2013 the owners, the Lamb family, moved to another location which is equipped with a 6,000 litre brewhouse, five 10,000 litre fermenters and two Vendome stills (7,560 and 5,670 litres respectively). The capacity is now 260,000 litres per year. The malt for the production is sourced both locally, as well as from England, and the casks are predominantly heavy charred, new American oak. Trials are also being conducted with ex-bourbon, ex-sherry and ex-port casks.

The first 5,500 bottles of their core expression, Westland American Single Malt Whiskey, were released in autumn 2013 followed by a limited one-off release called Deacon Seat. Both were mashed with a 5-malt grain bill and matured in heavily charred American oak. Since then, the owners have released a core range which now consists of American Single Malt Whiskey, Peated Malt and Sherry Wood. In addition to this, the distillery also releases different single cask bottlings. The latest addition was Westland Garryana where 20% of the whiskey had matured in Garry oak while the rest had been filled into American white oak. Quercus garryana is a type of oak native to the Pacific Northwest and very rarely used for whiskey maturation. This was followed up by a second edition in June 2017.

In 2017, global spirits giant Remy Cointreau bought Westland Distillery. According to Westland master distiller and co-founder Matt Hoffman, the buyer´s views, not least on the influence of terroir, were very much in line with Westland´s way of working. The distillery has been focusing on local barley varieties and also local peat which differs hugely from peat used in for example Scotland. Five years before the French company took over Westland, they bought Bruichladdich, another believer in how terroir affects the product, and before starting Westland, the entire production team spent time at Bruichladdich studying their methods.

Distillery: Stranahans Whiskey Distillery, Denver, Colorado
Founded: 2003
Owner: Proximo Spirits
stranahans.com

Stranahan´s has always been a forerunner when it comes to focusing on what defines an American single malt whiskey. Founded by Jess Graber and George Stranahan, the distillery was bought by New York based Proximo Spirits (makers of Hangar 1 Vodka and Kraken Rum among others) in 2010. A surprising decision was soon made to withdraw Stranahans Colorado Whiskey from all other markets, but Colorado. The owners claimed that they wanted to build up a significant stock before delivering nationally again. Apparently the stock has grown as the whiskey is now sold across the USA.

Stranahans Colorado Whiskey is always made in batches aged from two to five years and since 2004, more than 200 batches have been released. Except for the core expression, a special version with different finishes is launched yearly under the name Snowflake. In the 19th edition (Crestone Peak), both red wine, madeira and rum casks were involved. Since spring 2015, there is also another limited version of Stranahans called Diamond Peak which is a vatting of casks that are around 4 years old. In spring 2014, a bourbon by the name Tincup American Whiskey was released by Proximo Spirit,s with a lot of references made to Stranahans. It turned out that the whiskey had been distilled in Indiana and shipped to Stranahans where it was cut with local water and bottled

Distillery: Balcones Distillery, Waco, Texas
Founded: 2008
Owner: Balcones Distilling Co.
balconesdistilling.com

The distillery was founded by Chip Tate but since end of 2014, he is no longer with the company. His exit was the result of a bitter feud between Tate and the company board, a feud which also included court hearings and restraining orders. A settlement was later made between the parties.

All of Balcones´ whisky is mashed, fermented and distilled on site and they were the first to use Hopi blue corn for distillation. Four different expressions of blue corn whiskey have been released so far – Baby Blue, bottled at 46%, True Blue which is a cask strength version, Brimstone Smoked Whiskey, a smoky version and True Blue 100, a 100 proof bottling of True Blue. The biggest

Westland´s Master Distiller, Matt Hoffman

seller, however, is the Texas Single Malt Whisky. Like the other whiskies it is un chill-filtered and without colouring. The most recent release, in June 2017, was a single barrel of the Single Malt. At 38 months this was the oldest single malt from the distillery so far. The demand for Balcones whiskies has grown rapidly and in January 2014, another four, small stills were installed. The big step though, was a completely new distillery which was built 5 blocks from the current site. Distillation started in February 2016 and the official opening was in April. The new distillery is equipped with one pair of stills and five fermenters with another set of stills going in during 2017.

Distillery:	Clear Creek Distillery, Portland, Oregon
Founded:	1985
Owner:	Hood River Distillers
	clearcreekdistillery.com

Steve McCarthy was one of the first to produce malt whiskey in the USA and, like many other, smaller distilleries, they started by distilling eau-de-vie from fruit, especially pears, and then expanded the product line into whiskey. They began making whiskey in 1996 and the first bottles were on the market three years later. McCarthy´s Oregon Single Malt 3 years old, is reminiscent of an Islay whisky and, in fact, the malt is purchased directly from Islay with a phenol specification of 30-40 ppm. It is only bottled twice a year and the next release is scheduled for October 2017. In early 2014, it was announced that Hood River Distillers was to take over the distillery with Steve McCarthy continuing as a consultant.

Distillery:	House Spirits, Portland, Oregon
Founded:	2004
Owner:	Christian Krogstad and Matt Mount
	housespirits.com

In September 2015, Christian Krogstad and Matt Mount moved their distillery a few blocks to bigger premises. The main products for House Spirits used to be Aviation Gin and Krogstad Aquavit but with their new equipment they drastically increased whiskey capacity from 150 barrels per year to 4,000 barrels! The first three whiskies were released in 2009 and in November 2012 it was time for the first, widely available single malt under the name of Westward Whiskey. It was a 2 year old, double pot distilled and matured in new American oak. Recent releases have been up to 5 years old and now each release is a single barrel.

Distillery:	Edgefield Distillery, Troutdale, Oregon
Founded:	1998
Owner:	Mike and Brian McMenamin
	mcmenamins.com

Mike and Brian McMenamin started their first pub in Portland, Oregon in 1983. It has now expanded to a chain of more than 60 pubs and hotels in Oregon and Washington. More than 20 of the pubs have adjoining microbreweries and the chain´s first distillery opened in 1998 at their huge Edgefield property in Troutdale with the first whiskey, Hogshead Whiskey, being bottled in 2002. Hogshead is still their number one seller. Another part of the range is the Devil´s Bit, a limited bottling released every year on St. Patrick´s Day, and for 2017 it was an 8 year old. A second distillery was opened in 2011 at the company´s Cornelius Pass Roadhouse location in Hillsboro.

Distillery:	High West Distillery, Park City, Utah
Founded:	2007
Owner:	Constellation Brands
	highwest.com

David Perkins has made a name for himself mainly because of the releases of several rye whiskies. None of these have been distilled at High West distillery. Perkins has instead, bought casks of mature

whiskies and blended them himself. The first (released in 2008) was Rendezvous Rye and today this is part of the core range together with Double Rye, American Prairie Bourbon and the unusual Campfire which is a blend of straight bourbon, straight rye and peated blended malt Scotch whisky. In autumn 2015, they opened another distillery at Blue Sky Ranch in Wanship, Utah. It started off with two 6,000 litre pot still with the capacity of doing 700,000 litres of pure alcohol per year. The plan, however, is to eventually have 18 washbacks and four pot stills (with rectification columns attached) with the possibility of producing 1,4 million litres! In autumn 2016, it was announced that Constellation Brands (makers of Corona beer and Svedka vodka) had bought High West Distillery for a sum of $160 million.

Distillery:	Prichard´s Distillery, Kelso, Tennessee
Founded:	1999
Owner:	Phil Prichard
	prichardsdistillery.com

When Phil Prichard started his business in 1999, it became the first legal distillery for 50 years in Tennessee. Today, it is the third largest in the state after giants Jack Daniel's and George Dickel. In 2012 the capacity was tripled with the installation of a new 1,500 gallon mash cooker and three additional fermenters. In spring 2014, a second distillery equipped with a new 400-gallon alembic copper still was opened at Fontanel in Nashville. Prichard produces around 20,000 cases per year with different kinds of rum as the main track. The first single malt was launched in 2010 and later releases usually have been vattings from barrels of different age (some up to 10 years old). The whiskey range also includes rye, two bourbons and a Tennessee whiskey.

Distillery:	Town Branch Distillery, Lexington, Kentucky
Founded:	1999
Owner:	Alltech Lexington Brewing & Distilling Co.
	lyonsspirits.com

The founder and owner, Dr Pearse Lyons has an interesting background. A native of Ireland, he used to work for Irish Distillers in the 1970s. In 1980 he changed direction and founded Alltech Inc, a biotechnology company specializing in animal nutrition and feed supplements. Alltech purchased Lexington Brewing Company in 1999 and in 2008, two traditional copper pot stills from Scotland were installed with the aim to produce Kentucky´s first malt whiskey. The first single malt whiskey was released in 2010 under the name Pearse Lyons Reserve and in 2011 it was time for a release of their Town Branch bourbon. It then took until 2014 before their third whiskey was released, the 4 year old Town Branch Rye. In 2012 the stills were relocated from the brewery to a new stand alone distillery building right across the street with a capacity of 450,000 litres of pure alcohol per year. In April 2015, Alltech started construction of a new brewery and distillery in Pikeville. Dueling Barrels Brewery and Distillery will cost $13m to build and the plan is to start production in late 2017.

Distillery:	Tuthilltown Spirits, Gardiner, New York
Founded:	2003
Owner:	William Grant & Sons
	tuthilltown.com

Just 80 miles north of New York City, Ralph Erenzo and Brian Lee produce bourbon, single malt whiskey, rye whiskey, rum, vodka and gin. The first products came onto the shelves in 2006 in New York and the whiskey range now consists of Hudson Baby Bourbon, a 2-4 year old bourbon made from 100% New York corn and the company´s biggest seller by far, Four Grain Bourbon (corn, rye, wheat and malted barley), Single Malt Whiskey (aged in small, new, charred American oak casks), Manhattan Rye, Maple Cask Rye and New York Corn Whiskey. A cooperative venture was announced between Tuthilltown and William Grant & Sons in 2010, in which W Grant acquired the Hudson Whiskey brand line in order to market and distribute it around the world. In spring 2017, William Grant followed up the deal by buying the entire company. In 2014, the distillery site was expanded with a new packaging building and a whole new R&D building.

Distillery:	RoughStock Distillery, Bozeman, Montana
Founded:	2008
Owner:	Kari and Bryan Schultz
	montanawhiskey.com

RoughStock buys its 100% Montana grown and malted barley and then mill and mash it themselves. The mash is not drained off into a wash, but brought directly from the mash tun into two 1,000 gallon open top wooden fermenters for a 72 hour fermentation before distillation in two Vendome copper pot stills. In 2009, the first bottles of RoughStock Montana Pure Malt Whiskey were released. Since then a single barrel bottled at cask strength has been added (Black Label Montana Whiskey) and apart from whiskey made from 100% malted barley, the product range also includes Spring Wheat Whiskey, Straight Rye Whiskey and Montana Bourbon Whiskey.

Distillery:	St. George Distillery, Alameda, California
Founded:	1982
Owner:	Jörg Rupf/Lance Winters
	stgeorgespirits.com

The distillery is situated in a hangar at Alameda Point, the old naval air station at San Fransisco Bay. It was founded by Jörg Rupf, who came to California in 1979 and who was to become one of the forerunners when it came to craft distilling in America. In 1996, Lance Winters joined him and today he is Distiller, as well as co-owner. In 2005, the two were joined by Dave Smith who now has the sole responsibility for the whisky production. The main produce is based on eau-de-vie which is produced from locally grown fruit, and vodka under the brand name Hangar One. Whiskey production was picked up in 1996 and the first single malt appeared on the market in 1999. St. George Single Malt used to be sold as a three year old but, nowadays, comes to the market as a blend of whiskeys aged from 4 to 16 years. The latest release was Lot 17 (October 2017) and every lot is around 3-4,000 bottles. A new addition to the range was released in April 2016. Baller is aged 3-4 years and the malt whiskey has been filtered through maple charcoal and then finished in casks that held house-made umeshu (a Japanese style of plum liqueur).

Distillery:	Corsair Distillery, Bowling Green, Kentucky and Nashville, Tennessee
Founded:	2008
Owner:	Darek Bell, Andrew Webber and Amy Lee Bell
	corsairdistillery.com

The two founders of Corsair, Darek Bell and Andrew Webber, first opened up a distillery in Bowling Green, Kentucky and two years later, another one in Nashville, Tennessee. Apart from producing around 20 different types of beer, the brewery is also where the wash for all the whisky production takes place. In spring 2015, the company established a malting facility in Nashville where they can floor malt their own grain and eventually there will also be a drum malting station. Corsair Distillery has a wide range of spirits – gin, vodka, absinthe, rum and whiskey. The number of different whiskies released is growing constantly and Corsair Artisan is most likely the distillery in the USA which experiments the most with different types of grain. The big sellers are Triple Smoke Single Malt Whiskey (made from three different types of smoked malt) and Ryemaggedon (made from malted rye and chocolate rye). Recent additions to the range include Hydra (made with malt that

has been dried with five different types of local wood), Green Malt (100% very lightly kilned barley malt) and Grainiac - a bourbon made with 9 different grains.

Distillery:	Virginia Distillery, Lovingston, Virginia
Founded:	2008 (production started 2015)
Owner:	Virginia Distillery Company
	vadistillery.com

The whole idea for this distillery was conceived by Chris Allwood in 2007, but he left the company in 2010 and several changes in ownership have occurred since then, the last one being in spring 2016. Even though the copper pot stills arrived from Turkey in 2008 (having been bought second hand from the Turkish government), the company was struggling with the financing and the first distillation didn´t take place until November 2015. The distillery has the capacity of making 1.1 million litres of alcohol and is equipped with a 3.75 ton mash tun, 8 washbacks, a 10,000 litre wash still and a 7,000 litre spirit still.

Other distilleries in USA

Dry Fly Distilling
Spokane, Washington, founded in 2007
www.dryflydistilling.com

Dry Fly Distilling was the first grain distillery to open in Washington since Prohibition. The first batch of malt whisky was distilled in 2008 but the first bottling will probably not be released until early 2018. However, several other types of whisky have been released recently – Bourbon 101, Straight Cask Strength Wheat Whiskey, Port Finish Wheat Whiskey, Peated Wheat Whiskey and Straight Triticale Whiskey (triticale is a hybrid of wheat and rye). A new limited bottling, released in November 2015, is the triple distilled O´Danaghers which is a mix of barley, wheat and oats.

Triple Eight Distillery
Nantucket, Massachusetts, founded in 2000
www.ciscobrewers.com

In 1995 Cisco Brewers was established and five years later it was expanded with Triple Eight Distillery. The Nantucket facility consists of a brewery, winery and distillery. Apart from whiskey, Triple Eight also produces vodka, rum and gin. Whiskey production was moved to a new distillery in May 2007. The first 888 bottles of single malt whiskey were released on 8th August 2008 as an 8 year old. To keep in line with its theme, the price of these first bottles was also $888. More releases of Notch (as in "not Scotch") have followed, the latest being a 12 year old in spring 2015.

Cedar Ridge Distillery
Swisher, Iowa, founded in 2003
www.crwine.com

Jeff Quint and his wife Laurie started Cedar Ridge Vineyards in 2003 and expanded the business soon afterwards to also include a distillery. Malt whiskey production started in 2005 and in 2013 the first single malt was launched. Four 15 gallon ex-bourbon barrels were bottled after having a finish in different secondary casks. More releases of the single malt have been made since then. A range of limited releases called Silver Label Single Malts has also been introduced. Other spirits in the range include both bourbon and rye.

Nashoba Valley Winery
Bolton, Massachusetts, founded in 1978
(whiskey since 2003)
www.nashobawinery.com

Nashoba Valley Winery is mainly about wines but over the last decade, the facilities have been expanded with a brewery and a distillery. The owner, Richard Pelletier, produces a wide range of spirits including vodka, brandy and grappa. Since 2003 malt whiskey is also being distilled. In autumn 2009, Stimulus, the first single malt was released. The second release of a 5 year old came in 2010 and it is Richard´s intention to release a 5 year old once a year. The first 10 year old single malt was released in autumn 2015 together with a 5 year old rye whiskey.

Woodstone Creek Distillery
Cincinnati, Ohio, founded in 1999
www.woodstonecreek.com

Don and Linda Outterson opened a farm winery in Lebanon, Ohio in 1999 and relocated to Evanston i Cincinnati in 2003 where a distillery was added to the business. In autumn 2014 they were forced to move again and the distillery/winery is now located a bit farther north in St. Bernard. The first whiskey, a five grain bourbon, was released in 2008. In 2010, the Outtersons released a peated 10 year old single malt from malted barley and in 2012 this was followed up by a 12 year old unpeated single malt whiskey, Ridge Runner (a five-grain bourbon white dog) and a blended whiskey. A 13 year old single malt matured in a sherry cask has also been recently released.

Cutwater Spirits (former spirit division of Ballast Point)
San Diego, California, founded in 2016
www.cutwaterspirits.com

Jack White and Yuseff Cherney founded Ballast Point Brewing Company in 1996. It soon became one of the most influential craft beer brewers in USA, with four production sites in the San Diego area and selling around 3 million cases per year. In December 2015, the company was bought by Constellation Brands (maker of Robert Mondavi wines and Svedka vodka) for the staggering sum of $1bn! The distilling side of Ballast Point, which started in 2008, was actually never a part of the deal and during 2016, a handful of executives and co-founders started a new company and distillery called Cutwater Spirits but still working with the same brands as

before; Devil´s Share Whiskey, Old Grove, Fugu Vodka and Three Sheets Rum. The Devil´s Share comes in two versions - single malt and bourbon.

Charbay Winery & Distillery
St. Helena, California, founded in 1983
www.charbay.com

Charbay was founded by Miles Karakasevic – a legend in American craft distilling – and the distillery is now run by his son Marko, the 13th generation in a winemaking and distilling family. With a wide range of products such as wine, vodka, grappa, pastis, rum and port, the owners decided in 1999 to also enter in to whiskey making. That year they took 20,000 gallons of Pilsner and double distilled it in their Charentais pot still. From this distillation, a 4 year old called Double-Barrel Release One was launched in 2002. It took six years before Release II appeared in 2008 and in 2013 it was time for the 14 year old Release III. This was followed by the 16 year old Release IV in autumn 2015. Other recent releases include Charbay R5 Whiskey matured in French oak for 29 months and S Whiskey Lot 211A. In spring 2017, the company was split in two with Marko and his wife Jenni focusing on the spirit side while Miles continues with the wine production.

New Holland Brewing Co.
Holland, Michigan, founded in 1996 (whiskey since 2005)
www.newhollandbrew.com

This company started as a beer brewery, but after a decade, it opened up a micro-distillery as well. Until 2011, the spirit was double distilled in a 225 litre, self-constructed pot still. At that time, the capacity increased tenfold, mainly as a result of the installation of a restored 3,000-litre still built in 1932. The first cases of New Holland Artisan Spirits were released in 2008 and among them were Zeppelin Bend, a 3 year old (minimum) straight malt whiskey which is now their flagship brand. Included in the range are also Zeppelin Bend Reserve, matured for four years and then finished for an additional 9 months in sherry casks and Beer Barrel Bourbon.

Lance Winters - distiller and co-owner of St George Distillery

DownSlope Distilling

Centennial, Colorado, founded in 2008

www.downslopedistilling.com

The three founders were brought together by their interest and passion for craft-brewing when they started the distillery in 2008. It is equipped with two stills – one copper pot still made by Copper Moonshine Stills in Arkansas and a vodka still of an in-house design. The first whiskey, Double-Diamond Whiskey, was released in 2010. It was made from 65% malted barley and 35% rye and is still the core whiskey. It was followed by a number of varieties of bourbon, rye and single malt. The most recent products include a 4 year old Double Diamond Whiskey finished in a cognac cask. All malt whiskies are made from floor malted Maris Otter barley.

Do Good Distillery

Modesto, California, founded in 2013

dogooddistillery.com

Founded in 2013 by six friends and family members, and headed by Jim Harrelson, the goal is to make whiskey and, in particular, single malt. First production was in autumn 2014 and since autumn 2015 a number of different releases have been made; Beechwood Smoked, Peat Smoked, Cherrywood Smoked - all of them single malts - and The Nighthawk bourbon. The latest addition to the range was The Benevolent Czar – a dark single malt from a combination of pale malt, crystal malt and chocolate malt. Due to a recent expansion of the distillery (including two more stills) the owners can now produce the equivalent of 200,000 bottles per year.

Copper Fox Distillery

Sperryville, Virginia, founded in 2000

www.copperfox.biz

Copper Fox Distillery was founded in 2000 by Rick Wasmund. In 2005 they moved to another site where they built a new distillery and began distilling in 2006. Rick Wasmund has become one of the most unorthodox producers of single malt. He does his own floor malting of barley and it is dried using smoke from selected fruitwood. After mashing, fermentation and distillation, the spirit is filled into oak barrels, together with plenty of hand chipped and toasted chips of apple and cherry trees, as well as oak wood. The first bottles of Wasmund's Single Malt (also known as Red Top) were just four months old but the current batches are more around 12-16 months. There is also an older version, Blue Top, which has matured for up to 42 months. Other expressions in the distillery range include Copper Fox Rye Whiskey with a mash bill of 2/3 Virginia rye and 1/3 malted barley and two unaged spirits – Rye Spirit and Single Malt Spirit. In summer 2016, Rick Wasmund opened up a second distillery in Williamsburg.

Bull Run Distillery

Portland, Oregon, founded in 2011

www.bullrundistillery.com

Founded by former brewer, Lee Medoff, the distillery made its first distillation in autumn of 2011. The distillery is equipped with two pot stills (800 gallons each) and the main focus is on 100% Oregon single malt whiskey. Waiting for their own whiskey to mature, the company has been selling bourbon under the label Temperance Trader sourced from other producers, but blended and sometimes matured for an additional period at Bull Run. The first release of a single malt under the name Bull Run was a 4 year old in October 2016. Shortly after that the Oregon Single Malt Whiskey was also released at cask strength (56%).

Rogue Ales & Spirits

Newport, Oregon, founded in 2009

www.rogue.com

The company has gradually expanded over the years and now consists of one brewery, two combined brewery/pubs, two distillery pubs and five pubs scattered over Oregon, Washington and California. The main business is still producing Rogue Ales, but apart from whiskey, rum and gin are also distilled. The first malt whiskey, Dead Guy Whiskey, was launched in 2009 and is based on five different types of barley. In April 2016, it was time for the first straight malt whiskey - Oregon Single Malt Whiskey, aged for at least two years. It is made from barley grown and floor malted on Rogue's own farm in Tygh Valley.

FEW Spirits

Evanston, Illinois, founded in 2010

fewspirits.com

Former attorney (and founder of a rock and roll band) Paul Hletko started this distillery in Evanston, a suburb in Chicago in 2010. It is equipped with three stills; a Vendome column still and two Kothe hybrid stills. Bourbon and rye have been on the market for a couple of years and the first single malt, with some of the malt being smoked with cherry wood, was released in 2015. In spring 2017, a limited vatting of bourbon, rye and single malt whiskies was released for the 23rd anniversary of legendary Chicago bar Delilah's.

Sons of Liberty Spirits Co.

South Kingstown, Rhode Island, founded in 2010

www.solspirits.com

Michael Reppucci started the distillery with the help of David Pickerell who was Master Distiller for Maker's Mark for 13 years. This distillery is equipped with a stainless steel mash tun, stainless steel, open top fermenters and one 950 litre combined pot and column still from Vendome. Sons of Liberty is first and foremost a whiskey distillery, but the first product launched was Loyal 9 Vodka. In 2011 the double distilled Uprising American Whiskey was launched, made from a stout beer and it was followed in early 2014 by Battle Cry made from a Belgian style ale. Both Uprising and Battle Cry have also been released as sherry finishes.

Cut Spike Distillery (formerly Solas Distillery)

La Vista, Nebraska, founded in 2009

www.cutspikedistillery.com

Originally opened as Solas distillery in 2009, Brian McGee and Jason Payne later renamed it Cut Spike distillery. The first product to hit the market in 2009 was Joss Vodka while the Cuban-style Chava Rum was released in 2011. In 2010 single malt whiskey was distilled and the first 140 bottles in a batch of 2,000 were launched in August 2013. New batches of the 2 year old whiskey have then appeared regularly.

Blue Ridge Distilling Co.

Bostic, North Carolina, founded in 2010

www.blueridgedistilling.com

After a career in commercial diving and salvage, Tim Ferris opted for a change and opened up a distillery in 2010. The equipment consists of a lauter mash tun, stainless steel fermenters and a modified Kothe still. The first distillation was in June 2012 and in December the first bottles of Defiant Single Malt Whisky were released. The maturation part is very unorthodox. The spirit is matured for 60 days in stainless steel tanks with oak spirals inserted. According to Ferris, this ensures a greater contact between the whisky and the wood which speeds up the maturation process.

Journeyman Distillery

Three Oaks, Michigan, founded in 2010

www.journeymandistillery.com

Before opening his own distillery, Bill Welter rented still time at Koval Distillery in Ravenswood to make sure he had an aged rye whiskey (Ravenswood Rye) available when his own distillery was opened. The range of whiskies distilled at his own premises now include Last Feather Rye, Featherbone Bourbon, Silver Cross Whiskey, W.R. Whiskey, Kissing Cousins and Federalist 12 Rye. The first release of Three Oaks Single Malt Whiskey was in October 2013 and the latest release (the 3 year old batch 5) appeared in October 2016. In December 2016, production capacity was expanded with another four fermenters.

Santa Fe Spirits

Santa Fe, New Mexico, founded in 2010

www.santafespirits.com

Colin Keegan, the owner of Santa Fe Spirits, is collaborating with Santa Fe Brewing Company which supplies the un-hopped beer that is fermented and distilled in a 1,000 litre copper still from Christian Carl in Germany. The whiskey gets a hint of smokiness from mesquite. The first product, Silver Coyote released in spring 2011, was an unaged malt whiskey. The first release of an aged (2 years) single malt whiskey, Colkegan, was in October 2013. By summer 2017 twelve batches had been released. Special releases have also occured, for example finished in brandy casks and bottled at cask strength.

Copperworks Distilling Company

Seattle, Washington, founded in 2013

www.copperworksdistilling.com

Jason Parker and Micah Nutt, both come from a brewing background and that is also where their whiskey comes from. They obtain their wash from a local brewery and then ferment it on site. The distillery is equipped with two, large copper pot stills for the whiskey production, one smaller pot still for the gin and one column still. The whiskey is matured in 53-gallon charred, American oak barrels. The first distillation was in 2014 and the first batch of the single malt was released in September 2016. The third batch in February 2017, was the first to be based on their "Five Malt" recipe including pale malt and caramel malt.

Wood's High Mountain Distillery

Salida, Colorado, founded in 2011

www.woodsdistillery.com

For the two brothers, PT and Lee Wood, whiskey is the main product. After a very long fermentation (9 days) the spirit is double-distilled in a 350 gallon stripping still and a 50 gallon pot-column hybrid still and then filled into small casks (25-30 gallons).Their first expression, Tenderfoot Whiskey released in 2013, is something as rare as a triple malt. The mash bill is 77% malted barley (a mix of chocolate malt and cherrywood smoked malt), 13% malted rye and 10% malted wheat. The next releases were Alpine Rye Whiskey, with a mash bill of 73% malted rye and 27% malted barley and a 16 months old whiskey made from local Oilman Imperial Stout.

Door County Distillery

Sturgeon Bay, Wisconsin, founded in 2011

www.doorcountydistillery.com

The Door Peninsula Winery was founded in 1974 and ten years later the current owners, the Pollman family, took over. It is a large facility including a shop and tasting rooms and attracts thousands of visitors every year. In 2011, the family decided to add a distillery to the site. The wash is brought in from a local brewery and distilled in a copper pot/column hybrid still. Gin, vodka and brandy are the main products but they also make single malt whiskey. The first Door County Single Malt was released as a one year old in 2013.

Immortal Spirits

Medford, Oregon, founded in 2008

www.immortalspirits.com

In the beginning, this distillery could be seen mainly as a labour of love by two home brewers, Jesse Gallagher and Enrico Carini, but they had their minds set on something bigger. The two stills (a 1,200 gallon pot still and an 88 gallon still for limited release runs) were designed and fabricated by themselves, and the wash used to

Journeyman Distillery

come from a local brewery. After some time, a 2,000 gallon mash tun and three 2,000 gallon fermenters were installed, so not only is all of the production handled at the distillery, but the volumes have increased substantially as well. A young single grain from unmalted barley, Early Whiskey, was released in spring 2015 and this was followed by a four year old Single Barrel made from malted barley, released when they opened their new tasting room in November 2015. The current version of the flagship Single Barrel is a five year old.

Deerhammer Distilling Company

Buena Vista, Colorado, founded in 2010

www.deerhammer.com

The location of the distillery at an altitude of 2,500 metres with drastic temperature fluctuations and virtually no humidity, have a huge impact on the maturation of the spirit. Owners Lenny and Amy Eckstein found that their first whiskey, based on five varieties of malted barley, was ready to be released after only 9 months´ maturation in December 2012. So far, they have released around 35 batches of the Down Time Single Malt (re-named Deerhammer Single Malt in autumn 2016). Recent bottlings have been matured between 2 and 3 years.

Hillrock Estate Distillery

Ancram, New York, founded in 2011

www.hillrockdistillery.com

What makes this distillery unusual, at least in the USA, is that they are not just malting their own barley – they are floor malting it. This a technique that has been abandoned even in Scotland, except for a handful of distilleries. Jeff Baker founded the distillery in 2011 and equipped it with a 250 gallon Vendome pot still and

five fermentation tanks. The first spirit was distilled in November 2011. The first release from the distillery was in 2012, the Solera Aged Bourbon. Today, the range has been expanded with a Single Malt and a Double Cask Rye. Over the years, limited bottlings have appeared such as the peated Single Malt and the rye with a finish in various casks (madeira, port and sauternes).

Painted Stave Distilling

Smyrna, Delaware, founded in 2013

paintedstave.com

Like for so many other new distilleries, production for Painted Stave started with vodka and gin. Whiskey production started in 2014, first with bourbon and rye, then followed by whiskey from malted barley. Most of the whiskey production is centered on bourbon and rye but the owners, Ron Gomes and Mike Rasmussen, have also released Ye Old Barley Whiskey made from 100% malted barley.

Long Island Spirits

Baiting Hollow, New York, founded in 2007

www.lispirits.com

Long Island Spirits, founded by Richard Stabile, is the first distillery on the island since the 1800s. The starting point for The Pine Barrens Whisky, the first single malt from the distillery, is a finished ale with hops and all. The beer is distilled twice in a potstill and matures for one year in a 10 gallon, new, American, white oak barrel. The whisky was first released in 2012 The range also includes Rough Rider straight bourbon, Happy Warrior cask strength bourbon and a cask strength rye called Rough Rider Big Stick.

Kings County Distillery in Brooklyn

Van Brunt Stillhouse

Brooklyn, New York, founded in 2012

www.vanbruntstillhouse.com

Part of the Brooklyn Spirits Trail in New York, Van Brunt Stillhouse is owned by Daric Schlesselman and located near the Red Hook waterfront. They made their first release of Van Brunts American Whiskey in December 2012, a mix of malted barley, wheat and a hint of corn and rye. This was followed by a malt whiskey from 100% malted barley, a wheated bourbon and a rye.

Kings County Distillery

Brooklyn, New York, founded in 2010

kingscountydistillery.com

The founders, Colin Spoelman and David Haskell, have made a name for themselves as being both experimental and yet at the same time true to traditional Scottish methods of distilling whiskey. The wash is fermented for four days in open-top, wooden fermenters and they practise a double distillation with a narrow middle cut in two copper pot stills made by Forsyths in Scotland. They use organic corn from upstate New York and malted barley from the UK. The first single malt (60% unpeated and 40% peated), matured in ex-bourbon barrels was distilled in 2012 but didn´t hit the market until 2016. In the product range is also bourbon with the unusual mash bill of 60% corn and 40% malted barley. Even more unusual is their peated bourbon! Apart from producing whiskey, Colin and David have shared their vision and knowledge in two books; The Guide to Urban Moonshining and Dead Distillers.

Civilized Spirits

Traverse City, Michigan, founded in 2009

www.civilizedspirits.com

Jon Carlson and Greg Lobdell developed a passion for craft beer and artisan spirits whilst they were attending the University of Michigan. Years later they founded Northern United Brewing Company which is the parent company of Civilized Spirits. The spirits are produced at a distillery on Old Mission Peninsula, just outside Traverse City in a 1,000 litre pot still with a 24-plate column attached. The whiskey side of the business includes Civilized Single Malt (at least 3 years old), Civilized Whiskey (made from locally grown rye), Civilized White Dog Whiskey (an unoaked wheat whiskey) and Civilized Bourbon.

Square One Brewery & Distillery

St. Louis, Missouri, founded in 2006

www.squareonebrewery.com

Steve Neukomm has been working with micro-breweries since 1999. In 2006 he opened a combined brewery and restaurant in St. Louis and two years later he was granted Missouri´s first micro-distilling licence. Apart from rum, gin, vodka and absinthe, Steve also produces J.J. Neukomm Whiskey, a malt whiskey made from toasted malt and cherry wood smoked malt.

Hamilton Distillers

Tucson, Arizona, founded in 2011

www.hamiltondistillers.com

Having worked as a manufacturer of furniture made from local mesquite wood, Stephen Paul came up with the idea of drying barley over mesquite, instead of peat. He started his distillery using a 40 gallon still but since 2014, a 500 gallon still is in place. In spring 2015, new malting equipment was installed which made it possible to malt the barley in 5,000 lbs batches, instead of the previous 70 lbs! Everything is done on site - from malting to maturation. The first bottlings appeared in 2013 and they now have three expressions – aged Mesquite smoked (Dorado), aged unsmoked (Classic) and unaged Mesquite smoked (Clear). In 2017, a cask strength version called Distiller´s Cut was released.

Cornelius Pass Roadhouse Distillery

Hillsboro, Oregon, founded in 2011

www.mcmenamins.com

The distillery is owned by the McMenamin brothers who also have a chain of more than 60 pubs and hotels, as well as the Edgefield Distillery in Troutdale. The Hillsboro distillery is equipped with a 19th century Charentais alambic still. The first release was an un-aged whiskey called The White Owl (72% malted wheat and 28% malted barley) in 2012 and it was followed by a gin in 2013. In September 2014, an aged version (3 years) of the White Owl was released under the name Billy Whiskey.

Great Wagon Road Distilling Co.

Charlotte, North Carolina, founded in 2014

gwrdistilling.com

For Ollie Mulligan, a native of Ireland, everything started with a 15 litre still and him taking classes under some of the country´s master distillers. Over time, he invested in bigger stills and in February he installed a 3,000 litres Kothe still in his new 15,000 sq foot facility. The mash comes from a neighbouring brewery and the fermentation is made in-house in four tanks. The first batch of his Rua Single Malt was launched at Christmas 2015 and several batches have since followed, including vodka and Drumlish poteen.

Maine Craft Distilling

Portland, Maine, founded in 2013

www.mainecraftdistilling.com

This distillery started production in January 2013 and the founder, Luke Davidson, built most of the equipment himself. Currently they are offering vodka, gin, rum and Chesuncook, which is a botanical spirit using barley and carrot distillates! Since March 2014 there is also a single malt whisky for sale – Fifty Stone. This is now released in limited batches. Luke Davidson is floor malting all the barley himself and due to a combustion of the kiln in November they had to postpone the whisky production until April 2014.

3 Howls Distillery

Seattle, Washington, founded in 2013

www.3howls.com

Inspired by Scotch whisky production, Will Maschmeier and Craig Phalen started distillation in 2013. All the malted barley is imported from Scotland including a small amount of peated malt. For the distillation they use a 300 gallon hybrid still with a stainless steel belly and a copper column. Their first whiskies were released at the end of 2013, a single malt and a hopped rye and these were followed in 2014 by a rye whiskey and a bourbon.

Montgomery Distillery

Missoula, Montana, founded in 2012

www.montgomerydistillery.com

In 2012, Ryan and Jenny Montgomery renovated the 19th century Pipestone Mountaineering building in Missoula and opened up a distillery. The barley and the rye is milled to a fine flour on site, using a hammer mill and the wash is then fermented on the grain. Distillation takes place in a 450 litre Christian Carl pot still with a 21 plate column attached. The first whiskey was Early Release rye in summer 2015 which was followed by the 2 year old straight rye Sudden Wisdom. The first release of the 3 year old Montgomery Single Malt was in November 2016 with a second release of a 4 year old planned for November 2017.

Ranger Creek Brewing & Distilling

San Antonio, Texas, founded in 2010

www.drinkrangercreek.com

The owners of Ranger Creek (TJ Miller, Mark McDavid and

Dennis Rylander) focus on beer brewing and whiskey production. They have their own brewhouse where they mash and ferment all their beers, as well as the beer going for distillation. The still is a 1,200 litre, 6-plate column still from Holstein. The first release was Ranger Creek .36 Texas Bourbon in 2011. Their first single malt, Rimfire, was launched early in 2013. Other expressions include Ranger Creek .44 Rye and the white dog, Ranger Creek .36 White.

Two James Spirits

Detroit, Michigan, founded in 2013

www.twojames.com

David Landrum and Peter Bailey named their distillery after their respective fathers, both named James. Equipped with a 500 gallon pot still with a rectification column attached, the distillery started production in September 2013. Vodka, gin, bourbon (even a peated version) and rye have already been released while a single malt is still maturing in the warehouse. Aged in ex-sherry casks the whiskey has been made from peated Scottish barley.

Brickway Brewery & Distillery (former Borgata)

Omaha, Nebraska, founded in 2013

www.drinkbrickway.com

Zac Triemert, who owns the distillery together with Holly Mulkins, was involved in founding Solas distillery (later re-named Cut Spike distillery) in 2009, and left a couple of years ago to start Borgata. All the wash for the distillation comes from their own brewery and distillation takes place in a 550 gallon Canadian wash still, while the 400 gallon spirit still comes from Forsyth´s in Scotland. The owners are focused on single malt whiskey but they will also produce smaller amounts of bourbon and rye. Their first whisky, Borgata American Single Malt White Whisky, was released in May 2014. End of 2014 the distillery´s name was changed to Brickway following a dispute with Borgata Casino and the whiskey now goes under the name Brickway Single Malt Whisky. Since August 2016 there is also a cask strength version in the range called Brickway Double Barrel.

Seven Stills Distillery

San Francisco, California, founded in 2013

www.sevenstillsofsf.com

Although already founded in 2013 by Tim Obert and Clint Potter, the first whiskies to be released from the Seven Stills distillery were all produced at Stillwater distillery in Petaluma. Not until March 2016, had the two owners managed to find the perfect spot for their own distillery – Bayview, an area in the San Francisco environs. Equipped with a 300 gallon copper pot still from Artisan Still Design, as well as brewing equipment, a range of unorthodox whiskies are now being produced in the new location. Their whiskies are made from different beers including oatmeal stout, peanut butter milk stout, sour dough sour and coffee porter. First releases of both vodka and whiskey appeared in 2016 and more have followed since.

Tualatin Valley Distilling

Hillsboro, Oregon, founded in 2013

www.tvdistilling.com

Founded by Jason O´Donnell and Corey Bowers, the distillery is equipped with a 26 gallon, 4-plate column still for the brandies and a 100 litre pot still for whiskey. Maturation takes place in small, charred American oak barrels but experiments have also been made with Hungarian oak. The owners concentrate on whiskey production and the first distillation was in 2013. The current range consists of two brands; Oregon Single Malt Whiskey and 50/50 American Whiskey (50% rye and 50% malted barley) - both of which have been aged for 6-8 months. A new range called Oregon Experimental Single Malt has also recently been introduced.

Vikre Distillery

Duluth, Minnesota, founded in 2012

www.vikredistillery.com

Joel and Emily Vikre fired up the still for their first distillation in November 2013. Gin and aquavit have already found their way to shops and bars in Minnesota and they also have three different kinds of whiskey maturing on site – Iron Range American Single Malt, Gunflint Bourbon and Temperance River Rye. The single malt was released in March 2017 while the other two will be matured for a little longer. The very first release, however, was Sugarbush, a young bourbon launched in November 2015. The distillery was expanded in April 2016 with six new fermentation tanks.

Rennaisance Artisan Distillers

Akron, Ohio, founded in 2013

renartisan.com

The distillery is an outgrowth of a homebrew supply shop run by brothers John and Jim Pastor. So far they have, apart from whiskey, produced gin, brandy, grappa and limoncello. The first whiskey release, The King´s Cut single malt, was made from a grain bill including special malts such as toasted and caramel malts. It was launched in 2014 and new batches appear every 6 months. Early 2016, a larger lauter mash tun was installed which increased production significantly.

Coppercraft Distillery

Holland, Michigan, founded in 2012

coppercraftdistillery.com

Located in Holland, close to Lake Michigan, this distillery is owned and operated by Walter Catton. He uses a stainless steel mash tun, six washbacks and two stills - one stripping still with stainless steel pot and copper column and a fractioning still with both pot and column made from copper. The first three whiskies - corn, wheat and malted rye - were released in summer 2014.

John Emerald Distilling Company

Opelika, Alabama, founded in 2014

www.johnemeralddistilling.com

Owned by John and Jimmy Sharp (father and son), the distillery started production in July 2014. The first distillations were made in a small, 26 gallon pilot still, but a larger pot/column hybrid still with four plates was now installed. The mashing is done in a lauter tun and the wash is fermented on the grain in stainless steel tanks. The main product is the Alabama Single Malt which gets its character from barley smoked with a blend of southern pecan and peach wood. The first release was made in March 2015. In spring 2017, the owners also started trial distillations using triticale.

11 Wells Distillery

St. Paul, Minnesota, founded in 2013

11wells.com

Located in the middle of St. Paul, close to the Flat Earth Brewing Company, this new distillery is run by Bob McManus and Lee Egbert. The distillery is equipped with a 650 gallon mash tun, stainless steel open-top fermentation tanks and two stills - a 250 gallon stripping still and a 100 gallon hybrid pot/column still. Whiskey is the main product and the first two releases, aged bourbon and rye, were released in November 2014 followed by a wheat whiskey in 2015, but the owners have still to release a whiskey made entirely from malted barley.

Blaum Bros. Distilling

Galena, Illinois, founded in 2012

blaumbros.com

Heavily influenced by Scotch whisky, the two brothers Matthew and Mike Blaum opened their distillery in 2012 and began distilling in early 2013. The equipment consists of a 2,000 litre mash tun, five 2,000 litre wash backs and a 2,000 litre Kothe hybrid still. Apart from gin and vodka, the first two releases were the sourced Knotter Bourbon and Knotter Rye. The first whiskey from their own production was a rye in 2015. It will probably be a couple of years before their first single malt is released.

Sugar House Distillery

Salt Lake City, Utah, founded in 2014

sugarhousedistillery.net

James Fowler's background as a dedicated home brewer for more than 20 years, led him to the decision to build a distillery. Assisted by Eric Robinson, an experienced distiller formerly based at High West distillery, he started production in 2014. The first release was a vodka, followed later that year by a single malt whisky. More releases of the single malt have followed and bourbon and rum have also been added to the range.

Venus Spirits

Santa Cruz, California, founded in 2014

venusspirits.com

After having worked in the brewing business and organic food industry, Sean Venus decided to build his own distillery. Production, which started in May 2014, is focused on whiskey, but he has also released gin and spirits from blue agave. The first single malt was Wayward Whiskey, made from crystal malt and released in January 2015. This was followed up by a rye and later a bourbon. The distillation takes place in a hand pounded alembic still from Spain.

Oak N' Harbor Distillery

Oak Harbor, Ohio, founded in 2014

oaknharbordistillery.com

Together with his wife Andrea, Joe Helle began distilling in December 2014 and only a week later his first single malt was on the shelves. Aptly named Six Days Seven Nights, it had been maturing for a week in small barrels made from Minnesota white oak. Since then, more releases have followed - the latest in December 2016, matured for two years. Other products include bourbon, gin, apple brandy, rum and vodka. Oak N'Harbor is probably the only distillery in the USA run by a mayor! Joe Helle was elected mayor of Oak Harbor end of 2015.

Bent Brewstillery

Roseville, Minnesota, founded in 2014

bentbrewstillery.com

After years of research and education in the arts of distilling and brewing, Bartley Blume decided to build a combined brewery and distillery. Production started in 2014 and apart from a range of beers, Blume is also producing gin and whiskey with plans for many other varieties. No whiskies have been released so far, but one called Kursed Single Malt is currently aging in a combination of charred oak and charred apple wood.

Orange County Distillery

Goshen, New York, founded in 2013

orangecountydistillery.com

This is a true farm distillery where the owners, Bryan Ensall and John Glebocki, grow every ingredient on the farm, including sugar beet, corn, rye, barley and even the botanicals needed for their gin. They malt their own barley and even use their own peat when needed. Production started in April 2014 and the first products, gin and vodka, were selling in October of the same year. Since then, they have also launched a wide range of whiskies, including corn, bourbon, rye and peated single malt. The first aged single malt was launched in summer 2015 and batch # 3 was released in April 2016.

Key West Distilling

Key West, Florida, founded in 2013

kwdistilling.com

The main track for Jeffrey Louchheim is to produce rum but he is also distilling whiskey. The mash is brought in from Bone Island Brewing, fermented, distilled and filled into new barrels or used rum barrels. The first release of Whiskey Tango Foxtrot was in July 2015 with more batches following in spring and summer 2016.

Thumb Butte Distillery

Prescott, Arizona, founded in 2013

thumbbuttedistillery.com

A variety of gin, dark rum and vodka, as well as whiskey are produced by the owners, Dana Murdock, James Bacigalupi and Scott Holderness. Rodeo Rye, Bloody Basin Bourbon and Central Highlands Single Malt have all now been released. Maris Otter barley is being used for the malt whiskies.

Seattle Distilling

Vashon, Washington, founded in 2013

seattledistilling.com

Paco Joyce and Tami Brockway Joyce produce gin, vodka, coffee liqueur, as well as a malt whiskey. The latter, named Idle Hour was first launched in 2013 with batch 9 being released in April 2017. The style is Irish with both malted and unmalted barley being used in the mashbill. A small amount of honey is also added during fermentation. The owners source used wine casks from a local winery and then re-cooper and char them on site.

Hewn Spirits

Pipersville, Pennsylvania, founded in 2013

hewnspirits.com

Using a 130 gallon copper still, Sean Tracy is producing a variety of spirits including rum, gin and vodka. On the whiskey side there is Dark Hollow Bourbon, Red Barn Rye and the Reclamation American Single Malt Whiskey which was released for the first time in summer 2014. After maturing the malt whiskey in barrels for 1-4 months, Tracy does a second maturation in stainless steel vats where he also puts in charred staves of either chestnut or hickory wood. The second maturation lasts for two weeks.

Damnation Alley Distillery

Belmont, Massachusetts, founded in 2013

damnationalleydistillery.com

A small distillery but with a wide range of whiskies. Founded in 2013 by Alison DeWolfe, Jeremy Gotsch, Jessica Gotsch, Alex Thurston and Emma Thurston. Among the varieties that can be mentioned are single malt, hopped single malt, smoked single malt (smoked with fruit wood), bourbon, rye and a house whiskey from barley, corn, rye and wheat. In June 2016, the first 2 year old whiskey from the distillery was launched and more releases of both single malt and rye followed in 2017.

Wright & Brown Distilling Co.

Oakland, California, founded in 2015

wbdistilling.com

Founded by Earl Brown and Daniel Wright, this distillery is focused on barrel aged spirits, i. e. whiskey, rum and brandy. The first whiskey was distilled in 2015 and the first product, a rye whiskey, was released in autumn of 2016 with the first single malt due for release in spring 2017. The equipment is made up of a 500 gallon mash tun, 500 gallon stainless steel fermenters and a 250 gallon copper pot still from Vendome.

Stark Spirits

Pasadena, California, founded in 2013

starkspirits.com

Greg Stark and Karen Robinson-Stark, co-founders of the distillery, obviously share the interest for distilled spirits but, while Karen is focused on gin, Greg tends to concentrate on whiskey and rum. The first single malt whiskey was distilled in July 2015 and the first release was a barrel of peated single malt in February 2016. The first official distillery release of single malt (both peated and un-peated) came in February 2017. They have two stills with one reserved for all the peated production and the whiskey is matured in a combination of new American oak and ex-bourbon barrels.

Cotherman Distilling

Dunedin, Florida, founded in 2015

cothermandistilling.com

All the whiskies made by Michael Cotherman and his wife, Tara Cupp, are from 100% malted barley. The mash is brought in from local breweries, fermented at the distillery and then distilled in a pot still and a 3-plate bubble-cap still. First launched in July 2016, the third batch was released in March 2017. Apart from whiskey – gin and vodka are also produced.

Quincy Street Distillery

Riverside, Illinois, founded in 2011

quincystreetdistillery.com

Derrick Mancini has built up an impressive range of spirits during the last couple of years which ranges from gin, vodka and absinth to bourbon, corn whiskey and rye. So far, single malt whiskey made from barley only forms a small part. The only single malt released so far is a 2 year old Golden Prairie which was in December 2015 and the next one isn´t due until the beginning of 2018.

Boston Harbor Distillery

Boston, Massachusetts, founded in 2015

bostonharbordistillery.com

This distillery was founded by a highly experienced "veteran" in the drinks business. In 1984, Rhona Kallman co-founded Boston Beer Company, famous worldwide for its Samuel Adams beer. The distillery started production in summer 2015 and while it concentrates mainly on whiskey, it is also making a variety of spirits based on different Samuel Adams´ beers. At the time of writing, Putnam New England Rye has been released but not the single malt version. Apart from the distillery with its 150-gallon Vendome copper pot still, the facility consists of a shop, tasting room and an event space.

Liquid Riot Bottling Co.

Portland, Maine, founded in 2013

liquidriot.com

When Liquid Riot opened its doors, it was Maine´s first brewery/ distillery/resto-bar. At the waterfront in the Old Port, Eric Michaud produces an extensive range of beers and spirits which include bourbon, rye, oat, single malt, rum, vodka and agave spirit. The Old Port single malt made from 80% cherry wood smoked malt was first released as a 16 month old in 2014, and more releases have followed. Distillation is made in a German hybrid still with a 5 plate rectification column.

Old Line Spirits

Baltimore, Maryland, founded in 2014

oldlinespirits.com

When the two former Naval Flight Officers, Mark McLaughlin

and Arch Watkins, decided to start producing whiskey, they happened to meet Bob Stilnovich at an American Distilling Institute conference. Bob was looking to sell his Golden Distillery in the Pacific Northwest and Mark and Arch seized the opportunity. They did an apprenticeship alongside Bob for a few months and then sent all the equipment to Baltimore and the maturing stock to Kentucky. During the summer of 2016, distilling started at their new location in Baltimore and a couple of months prior, the first Old Line single malt, two to three years old and obviously from the Golden Distillery production, was released. A peated version is planned for a 2017 release.

Cannon Beach Distillery

Cannon Beach, Oregon, founded in 2012

cannonbeachdistillery.com

Having been introduced to home brewing during his college days, Mike Selberg later decided to enter into distilling as well. His philosophy about whisky making is never to make the same spirit twice. So far 10 different whiskeys have been released, while the others are still maturing. Included in the releases are Embrued, a 2 year old made from malt smoked by using both applewood and cherrywood, New Branch with the starting point from a stout beer recipe and Strata which was made from 100% heavily peated malt from Baird´s. Distillation takes place in a 380 litre Vendome still with a 6-plate column.

Witherspoon Distillery

Lewisville, Texas, founded in 2011

witherspoondistillery.com

Two former US Marines, Quentin Witherspoon and Ryan DeHart, own and run the distillery together with Natasha DeHart. The main products are bourbon, rum and Bonfire (a cinnamon-infused rum), but they also make small runs of Witherspoon Single Malt which is generally aged between 1 and 2 years. The whiskey is distilled in two 1,110 litre stills and the single malt is matured in new American oak and finished in rum casks.

2nd Street Distilling Co

Kennewick, Washington, founded in 2011

2ndstreetdistillingco.com

Formerly known as River Sands Distillery, the company has been around since 1968 but the distillery only started in 2011. The principal owners are Paul and Deana Schiro and Russell and Ida Horn. Different types of gin and vodka are produced, as well as a single malt – R J Callaghan. It is aged for 1,5 years in charred American oak and then finished for 6 months in Hungarian oak. In summer of 2016 a 100% malted rye, Reser´s Rye, was also released.

Sound Spirits

Seattle, Washington, founded in 2010 (whiskey since 2012)

drinksoundspirits.com

When it opened, it was Seattle´s first craft distillery since prohibition. A number of different spirits are produced by the owner, Steven Stone, namely gin, vodka, aquavit, liqueurs and single malt whiskey. The first release of the 3 year old Madame Damnable single malt was in 2015 and more releases have since followed. The distillery closed temporarily in September 2016 only to re-open in a new location in spring 2017.

ASW Distillery

Atlanta, Georgia, founded in 2016

aswdistillery.com

Their interest in Scotch whisky, prompted Jim Chasteen and Charlie Thompson to start a distillery with the traditional Scottish equipment of two copper pot stills but with the American twist of fermenting and distilling on the grain. A year after opening the distillery, the owners have already decided to expand the business to a second location in West End Atlanta. Whiskies released so far are a bourbon and a malted rye (Resurgens). The latter has also been released as a port cask finish. Currently maturing are also a cherry-smoked single malt and a heavily peated version (35-40ppm), both made from 100% malted barley. The very latest release is a special bottling named Duality made from 50% malted barley and 50% malted rye.

Dallas Distilleries Inc.

Garland, Texas, founded in 2008

dallasdistilleries.com

The distillery which is run and owned by Herman Beckley and Marshall Louis, is primarily focused on whiskey alone. The first products in their Herman Marshall range were launched in 2013. It was a bourbon and a rye and was later followed by a single malt. The latest addition which was released in November 2015, was Temptress Single Malt – a collaboration with Lakewood Brewing Company where the whiskey has been flavoured with a milk stout. An unusual feature at the distillery is the open top fermenters which are made from cypress wood.

San Diego Distillery

San Diego, California, founded in 2015

sddistillery.com

Unlike many of the other new craft distilleries, Trent and Maria Tilton have decided to focus almost entirely on whiskey. For Trent, the inspiration came from tasting Lagavulin 16 year old for the first time in 2012. In March 2016 the first six whiskies were released; a bourbon, a rye and an Islay peated single malt – all three bottled at 90 proof and at cask strength. The next whiskey to appear was a single malt made from seven different types of brewing malt. Trent and Maria´s distillery model is based on small one-off batches that will be available in their tasting room only.

Alley 6 Craft Distillery

Healdsburg, California, founded in 2014

alley6.com

A small craft distillery in Sonoma county where everything from milling and mashing to distilling, barrelling and bottling is done by Jason and Krystle Jorgensen. The main product is rye whiskey and the first bottles were released in summer 2015 followed by a single malt in May 2016. The Jorgensen´s are experimenting with a range of different barley varieties, mainly from Germany and Belgium and the spirit is distilled in a 500 litre alembic copper still..

Gray Skies Distillery

Grand Rapids, Michigan, founded in 2014

grayskiesdistillery.com

In 2014, Brandon Voorhees and Steve Vander Pol bought an industrial building for their grain-to-glass distillery but, due to extensive refurbishing, it took more than a year before the first spirit was distilled. The equipment is made up of a 1,800 litre mash kettle, four fermenters and a 2,500 litre pot still with an attached column. After having released vodka and gin, the first bottle of Michigan Single Malt appeared in November 2016.

Hard Times Distillery

Monroe, Oregon, founded in 2009

hardtimesdistillery.com

James Stegall and Dudley Clark started off with just the one product, Sweet Baby Vodka, which was made from molasses. This was followed by a wasabi-flavoured vodka, moonshine from oats and barley and Appleshine made from apple juice. Eventually the two owners branched into the production of whiskey and the latest release is Eleventh Hour Whiskey, a single malt which is distilled twice in pot stills. In 2017, the owners have plans to move to a new location in Corvallis, 20 kilometres north of Monroe.

The new Duality bottling from ASW Distillery

Spirit Hound Distillers

Lyons, Colorado, founded in 2012

spirithounds.com

Craig Engelhorn and his four partners got off to a tough start when they opened up their distillery in 2012. Eight months after they had started production, the whole town of Lyons was devastated by flooding, which filled the distillery building with half a metre of flood water and mud. The distillery was shut down and between the first six barrels of whiskey and barrel #7, there was an 8 month gap. Rum, vodka and sambucca are on the production list, but their signature spirits are inherently gin and malt whiskey. The barley for the whiskey is grown, malted and peat-smoked in Alamosa by Colorado Malting and the whiskey released so far is straight, i.e. at least two years old. The first bottles (five single barrels) hit the shelves in summer 2015 and the most recent release came in spring 2017.

Arizona Distilling Company

Tempe Arizona, founded in 2012

azdistilling.com

When Jason Grossmiller and his partners released their first whiskey, it was a bourbon sourced from Indiana. The ensuing releases, which started with Desert Durum made from wheat, have all been produced in their distillery. Humphrey's – a single malt – was first released in late 2014 and more bottles became available in summer 2015. Other products include gin, vodka and rye whiskey.

Brothers Spirits

Buellton, California, founded in 2014

brothersspirits.com

Founded and owned by two brothers, Jeff and Jay Lockwood, the distillery started producing malt whisky on a small scale in March 2016. The barley is dried using mesquite smoke, fermentation is 72 hours and the triple distillation takes place in two reflux stills from Mile Hi Distilling. The releases so far have been unaged (White Hawk Malt Whiskey) but several barrels have been laid down for maturation.

Idlewild Spirits

Winter Park, Colorado, founded in 2015

idlewildspirits.com

Jeff Ruhle produced his first batch of malt whiskey in June 2016 and for maturation he has moved from 5 gallon barrels, via 10 and 30 gallons to the full-size 50 gallon barrels that he uses today. He also has plans to add staves of other hardwoods such as cherry, maple, peach etc., in hope of more complex flavours. Fermentation and distillation being on the grain will also add to the over-all character.

Timber Creek Distillery

Crestview, Florida, founded in 2014

timbercreekdistillery.com

Located on a family farm in northern Florida, this distillery is owned and operated by Camden Ford. Fermentation and distillation is off the grain and, surprisingly, they use a traditional worm tub to cool the spirits – a technique that has become rare even in Scotland. Currently they have whiskies maturing made from corn, wheat, rye, barley and oat. A small batch of their malt whiskey was released in autumn 2016 and another release is due for autumn 2017. According to Camden, the small, heavily charred Missouri oak barrels and the hot Florida summers make for a speedy maturation.

Lyon Distilling Co.

Saint Michaels, Maryland, founded in 2013

lyondistilling.com

Ben Lyon and Jaime Windon, both with a background in the spirits business, are focusing on whiskey and rum. They have a 2,000 litre mash tun, stainless steel fermenters and five small pot stills. Maturation takes place in small barrels (5 and 15 gallons). The first, unaged, malt whiskey was released in late 2015 and the first aged release came one year later.

Dirty Water Distillery

Plymouth, Massachusetts, founded in 2013

dirtywaterdistillery.com

Starting with vodka, gin and rum, Petras Avizonis expanded into malt whiskey in 2015. The first release, Bachelor Single Malt, came in 2016 and was followed by Boat For Sale Malt Whiskey which had been made using a beer from Independent Fermentations. One 200 gallon copper still is used for distillation and the whiskey matures in 15 gallon new oak barrels.

Long Road Distillers

Grand Rapids, Michigan, founded in 2015

longroaddistillers.com

Apart from vodka, gin and aquavit - owners Kyle Van Strein and Jon O´Connor have so far released three styles of whiskey - bourbon, wheat and a 6 month old whiskey made from 51% malted barley and 49% un-malted. The whiskey is distilled in a 500 gallon Vendome copper pot still and new American oak with a grade #3 char is used for maturation.

Motor City Gas

Royal Oak, Michigan, founded in 2014

motorcitygas.com

A small, family owned distillery where Rich Lockwood has managed to release no less than 30 different whiskies since the start. Rich has a very experimental approach to whiskey making and in the production he uses unusual and old grains (Maris Otter and Golden Promise), different yeast strains and unusual woods. The expressions so far have been both unpeated and heavily peated and the range has also included a bourbon from malted corn as well as whiskies finished in maple hard wood and IPA beer barrels.

Coppersea Distilling

New Paltz, New York, founded in 2011

coppersea.com

Founded by Michael Kinstlick, Coppersea is a true "farm-to-glass" distillery. Most of the grain is grown on their own farm and malted on site. The wash ferments in open-top wooden washbacks and the spirit is distilled using direct-fired alembic stills. One of the things that make Coppersea stand out is that they don´t dry the malted barley but instead produce a mash from green, unkilned barley, This is a technique sometimes used at grain distilleries in Scotland. The 1 year old Big Angus is made from 100% green barley and there is also a rye whiskey where the same method has been applied.

KyMar Farm Winery & Distillery

Charlotteville, New York, founded in 2011

kymarfarm.com

Since 2011, Ken and Lori Wortz have been producing primarily wine, liqeurs and apple brandy on their farm in the Catskill Mountains. Recently though, a whiskey made from 100% malted barley and distilled in a 300 gallon hybrid and an 80 gallon alembic still, was released. Ken and Lori mature their whiskey for 6 to 9 months in new American oak and then move it to a solera system for blending with older batches to ensure consistency.

Old Home Distillers

Lebanon, New York, founded in 2014

oldhomedistillers.com

Owned by the Carvell family, the distillery produces bourbon, corn whiskey and, since 2016, malt whiskey. The mash is fermented on the grain for 4-5 days, distillation takes place in a 100 gallon hybrid column still.and the spirit is matured in charred, new American oak for a minimum of seven months.

StilltheOne Distillery Two

Port Chester, New York, founded in 2010

stilltheonedistillery.com

Founded by Ed and Laura Tidge, the distillery was later taken over by Albert Savarese and Anthony Lanza. They have a 250 gallon pot column still from Arnold Holstein and for their single malts they use a beer wash from local breweries. The only single malt released so far is "287" from a pale ale. Upcoming releases are "9A" made from a stout and "Route.1" from a Belgian beer.

III Spirits

Talent, Oregon, founded in 2014

iiispirits.com

Whiskey production started in early 2015 and Todd Kemp and Alex Turner are focusing mainly on single malts. Currently there are two single malts in the range; Oregon Highlander made from a grain bill of brewer´s malt, Munich malt and crystal malt and Islay Style Peated Whisky produced from 100% heavily peated malt from Scotland. The whisky is neither coloured nor chill-filtered.

Telluride Distilling

Telluride, Colorado, founded in 2014

telluridedistilling.com

Four friends - Abbott Smith, Joanna Smith, James Jaeschke and Pete Jaeschke - produce vodka and malt whiskey in a distillery equipped with open top fermenters and a column still. Maturation is in new charred oak for two years followed by 6 months in port barrels. The first single malt was released in July 2016.

Canada

Distillery:	Shelter Point Distillery, Vancouver Island, British Columbia
Founded:	2009
Owner:	Patrick Evans
	shelterpointdistillery.com

In 2005, Patrick Evans and his family decided to switch from the dairy side of farming to growing crops and they bought the Shelter Point Farm just north of Comox on Vancouver Island. Eventually the idea to transform the farm into a distillery was raised and with the help of some Scottish investors, the construction work began. The buildings were completed in 2009 and in May 2010 all the equipment was in place. This includes a one tonne mash tun, five washbacks made of stainless steel (5,000 litres each) and one pair of stills (a 5,000 litre wash still and a 4,000 litre spirit still). To assist with the start up, Patrick Evans asked Mike Nicolson to join him and his operating manager, Jim Marinus. Mike is an experienced distiller having worked for many years at distilleries in Scotland. Distillation started in spring 2011 and the barley used for the distillation is grown on the farm. In May 2016, 7,000 bottles of the first single malt, 5 years old, were released. The plan for 2017, is to release another 17,000 bottles and the following year, increase to almost 30,000. Special, limited releases have also been made including a double grain blend of Shelter Point single malt and a Canadian rye, finished in port casks as well as a 6 year old single malt finished in barrels from a local winery.

Distillery:	Victoria Caledonian Distillery, Victoria, British Columbia
Founded:	2016
Owner:	Graeme Macaloney et al
	victoriacaledonian.com

The distillery was founded by the Scotsman Graeme Macaloney who had studied fermentation as well as biochemical engineering at the university before becoming a full time distiller. As a helping hand he had Mike Nicolson, who previously worked at 18 distilleries in Scotland. In addition, he had also acquired the services of the late Dr. Jim Swan, one of the foremost whisky consultants in the world. The distillery is equipped with a 1 ton semilauter mash tun, 7 stainless steel washbacks, a 5,500 litre wash still and a 3,600 litre spirit still from Forsyth. There is also a craft beer brewery on site. Distilling started in July 2016 and Macaloney is also planning for triple distilled pot still whiskey, as well as peated single malt once he has commissioned the planned traditional floor malting. A visitor centre has also been opened which offers tours on several levels of the distillery and the brewery, as well as tutored tastings..

Distillery:	Glenora Distillery, Glenville, Nova Scotia
Founded:	1990
Owner:	Lauchie MacLean
	glenoradistillery.com

Situated in Nova Scotia, Glenora was the first malt whisky distillery in Canada. The first launch of in-house produce came in 2000 but a whisky called Kenloch had been sold before that. This was a 5 year old vatting of some of Glenora's own malt whisky and whisky from Bowmore Distillery on Islay. The first expression, a 10 year old, came in 2000 and was named Glen Breton and this is still the core expression under the name Glen Breton Rare. Glen Breton Ice (10 years old), the world's first single malt aged in an ice wine barrel, was launched in 2006 and since then several expressions have been launched, among them single casks and sometimes under the name Glenora. To celebrate the distillery´s 25th anniversary, a 25

Graeme Macaloney, founder of Victoria Caledonian Distillery

year old single cask was released in 2015. This was complemented later in the year by yet another limited release, Jardine Specials.

Distillery: Still Waters Distillery, Concord, Ontario
Founded: 2009
Owner: Barry Bernstein and Barry Stein
stillwatersdistillery.com

In 2009, Barry Bernstein and Barry Stein opened Still Waters distillery in Concord, on the northern outskirts of Toronto. The distillery is equipped with a 3,000 litre mash tun, two 3,000 litre washbacks and a Christian Carl 450 litre pot still. The still also has rectification columns for brandy and vodka production. The focus is on whisky but they also produce vodka, brandy and gin. Their first release was a triple distilled, single malt vodka and they have also released a Canadian whisky with distillate sourced from other producers. Their first single malt, named Stalk & Barrel Single Malt, was released in April 2013 and it was followed in late 2014 by the first rye whisky, made from locally sourced Ontario rye.

Other distilleries in Canada

Victoria Spirits

Sidney, British Columbia, founded in 2008

www.victoriaspirits.com

This family-run distillery recently moved from Victoria on Vancouver Island to Sidney, 20 km to the north. Their best-selling product is Victoria Gin, which currently sells 10,000 bottles a year. Whisky production started in 2009 but has been very intermittent. The first and only single malt, Craigdarroch, was launched in early 2015. Only 250 bottles were released and more whisky can´t be expected for at least a couple of years.

Pemberton Distillery

Pemberton, British Columbia, founded in 2009

www.pembertondistillery.ca

Tyler Schramm started distilling in 2009, with vodka produced from potatoes as the first product. He used a copper pot still from Arnold Holstein and the first Schramm Vodka, was launched later that year. During the ensuing year, Tyler started his first trials, distilling a single malt whisky using organic malted barley. The first release was in 2013 when a limited 3 year old unpeated version was launched. Since autumn 2015, the owners have a regular expression called Pemberton Valley Organic Single Malt Whisky.

Yukon Spirits

Whitehorse, Yukon, founded in 2009

www.twobrewerswhisky.com

In 1997 Bob Baxter and Alan Hansen founded Yukon Brewing which more than 10 years later was expanded with also a small distillery. All of the whisky produced is made from malted grains but not only barley but also wheat and rye. The first 850 bottles of the 7 year old Two Brewer´s Yukon Single Malt Whisky were released in February 2016 and the portfolio is now based on four styles; Classic, Peated, Special Finishes and Innovative.

Okanagan Spirits

Vernon and Kelowna, British Columbia, founded in 2004

www.okanaganspirits.com

The first distillery named Okanagan was started in 1970 by Hiram Walker but it closed in 1995. The main part of the production was shipped to Japan to be used by Suntory for their whisky blending. In 2004, forestry engineer, Frank Deiter, decided to make a career change and established Okanagan Spirits. A distillery was opened in Vernon and, later on, a second one was built in Kelowna. A variety of spirits made from fruits and berries as well as gin, vodka,

absinthe and whisky ar being produced. Their core whisky is a blend of two 5 year old whiskies made from rye and corn with a small percentage of malted barley. Since 2013, there is also a 6 year old single malt in the range - The Laird of Fintry.

L B Distillers

Saskatoon, Saskatchewan, founded in 2012

www.lbdistillers.ca

The abbreviation for LB in the distillery name stands for Lucky Bastards and the luckiest bastard amongst the owners is Michael Goldney, who earned his nickname after winning the lottery in 2006. Joined by Cary Bowman and Lacey Crocker, he opened up the distillery in 2012. The first single malt whisky was released in summer 2016 but before that, the owners have released a fair amount of other spirits – vodka, gin and a variety of liqueurs.

Central City Brewers & Distillers

Surrey, British Columbia, founded in 2013

www.centralcitybrewing.com

What started as a brewpub in 2003 in downtown Surrey has now grown to one of Canada´s largest craft brewerys with Red Racer as their biggest seller. The success took off in 2005 when they started a canning line to sell their beer all over Canada. A much needed expansion followed in 2013 when they moved to a larger facility as well as adding a distillery. Apart from whisky they also produce gin and vodka. The only single malt released so far is Lohin McKinnon Single Malt but they also have a peated, malted rye in the range.

The Dubh Glas Distillery

Oliver, British Columbia, founded in 2015

www.thedubhglasdistillery.com

During his travels in Scotland, Grant Stevely fell in love with Scotch whisky and back in Canada he decided to build his own distillery at Gallagher Lake, north of Oliver. The whisky is double distilled in an Arnold Holstein still and even though malt whisky is Stevely´s main focus, gin is also produced. Apart from Noteworthy Gin, Virgin Spirits Barley (a newmake) has also been released.

The Dubh Glas Distillery

Australia & New Zealand

Australia

Distillery: Lark Distillery, Hobart, Tasmania
Founded: 1992
Owner: Lark Distillery Pty Ltd.
larkdistillery.com

In 1992, Bill Lark was the first person for 153 years to take out a distillation licence in Tasmania. Since then he has not just established himself as a producer of malt whiskies of high quality, but has also helped to off-set several new distilleries. The success of the distillery forced Bill and his wife Lyn to start thinking of how to generate future growth and in 2013 they took on board a group of Hobart based investors as majority owners of the company. The Lark couple, including their daughter Kristy, continued their work in the company. In January 2014, they acquired Old Hobart Distillery and the Overeem brand. Lark Distillery is situated on a farm at Mt Pleasant, 15 minutes' drive from Hobart. The whisky is double-distilled in a 1,800 litre wash still and a 600 litre spirit still and then matured in 100 litre "quarter casks". In 2015, more staff was hired and production was doubled compared to 2014 and in 2017, 50,000 litres were distilled. The old distillery site down in Hobart at the waterfront is now a cellar door and a showcase for Lark whisky.

In December 2016, Australian Whisky Holdings made an offer to buy Lark Distillery. At that time, Bill Lark and some of the other share holders had already sold their shares to AWH. Bill Lark's view was that the only way to grow the company would be to go public to attract more investment. The AWH attempt failed when the remaining share holders turned down the offer. AWH has already taken over Nant Distillery and also bought an equity interest in Redlands Estate Distillery last year.

The core product in the whisky range is the Classic Cask Single Malt Whisky at 43%, previously released as single casks but now a marriage of several casks. There is also the Distillers Selection at 46% and a Cask Strength at 58%, both of which are also single cask. To celebrate the distillery's 25th anniversary in 2017, an experimental series of 25 different 20 litre casks were released under the name Revolution Release.

Distillery: Bakery Hill Distillery, North Balwyn, Victoria
Founded: 1998
Owner: David Baker
bakeryhill.com

Since 2008, when Bakery Hill Distillery completed the installation of a 2,000 litre brewery, David Baker has had total control of all the processes from milling the grain to bottling the matured spirit. The first spirit at Bakery Hill Distillery was produced in 2000 and the first single malt was launched in autumn 2003. Three different versions are available – Classic and Peated (both matured in ex-bourbon casks) and Double Wood (ex-bourbon and a finish in French Oak). As Classic and Peated are also available as cask strength bottlings, they can be considered two more varieties. Limited releases also occur with one of the latest being A Wisp of Smoke - a 9 year old peated whisky bottled at 51.7%.

Distillery: Sullivans Cove Distillery, Cambridge, Tasmania
Founded: 1994
Owner: Sullivans Cove Distillery Pty Ltd.
sullivanscove.com

It wasn't until Patrick Maguire took over in 1999 that the Tasmania distillery started to show what it was capable of. The distillery obtains wash from Cascade Brewery in Hobart and the spirit is then double distilled. In September 2014 the distillery moved to a new building about four times the size of the current facility. Production was also escalated and they are now distilling 7 days a week. In December 2016, the distillery was taken over by a company led by Adam Sable who was general manager of Bladnoch distillery for two years. Patrick Maguire and the rest of the team will remain with the company. The range comprises of Sullivan's Cove Single Cask, bottled at 47,5% and matured in either bourbon casks or French oak port casks and Sullivan's Cove Double Cask (40%) which is a marriage of port and bourbon casks. The distillery has won several awards for its whiskies and to acknowledge that, a very limited (only 2 bottles) release was made in 2015 - The Sullivan's Cove Manifesto. Both decanters were sold on the same day that they were released at a staggering price of $10,000 each.

Patrick Maguire, distiller and former owner of Tasmania Distillery

Distillery: Old Hobart Distillery, Blackmans Bay, Tasmania
Founded: 2005
Owner: Lark Distillery Pty Ltd.

overeemwhisky.com

Inspired by his travels to Scotland, Casey Overeem, after several years of experimenting with different types of distillation, opened up his distillery in 2007. The mashing was done at Lark distillery where Overeem also had his own washbacks and the wash was made to his specific requirement. In every mash, a mix of 50% unpeated barley and 50% slightly peated is used. The wash is then transported to Old Hobart Distillery where the distillation takes place in two stills (wash still of 1,800 litres and spirit still of 600 litres). In January 2014, Old Hobart distillery was acquired by Lark Distillery Pty Ltd. Casey Overeem has now retired and his daugther, Jane, is the marketing manager for Overeem, as well as being the brand ambassador. The range consists of Overeem Port Cask Matured and Overeem Sherry Cask Matured, both varieties available at 43% and 60%. In 2013, Overeem Bourbon Cask Matured at 43% was released, followed by a 60% version in 2014.

Distillery: Hellyers Road Distillery, Burnie, Tasmania
Founded: 1999
Owner: Betta Milk Co-op

hellyersroaddistillery.com.au

Hellyer´s Road Distillery is the largest single malt whisky distillery in Australia with a capacity of doing 100,000 litres of pure alcohol per year. The distillery is equipped with a 6.5 ton mash tun and the wash is fermented for 65 hours. There is only one pair of stills but they compensate for numbers by size. The wash still has a capacity of 40,000 litres and the spirit still 20,000 litres. The foreshots take around 4-5 hours and the middle cut will last for 24 hours, which is six to seven times longer compared to what is common practice in Scotland. Another interesting fact is that the pots on both stills are made of stainless steel while heads, necks and lyne arms are made of copper. Maturation takes place in ex-bourbon casks but they also use Tasmanian red wine barrels for part of it. The first whisky was released in 2006 and there are now more than ten different expression in the range, including 10 and 12 year olds, peated as well as unpeated and various finishes. End of 2014, the

Henry´s Legacy Range was introduced. This is a new series of cask strength, single cask bottlings with Dismal Swamp as the fourth and latest release.

Distillery: Great Southern Distilling Company, Albany, Western Australia
Founded: 2004
Owner: Great Southern Distilling Company Pty Ltd./ Cameron Syme

limeburners.com.au

The distillery was built in Albany on the south-western tip of Australia in 2004 with whisky production commencing in late 2005. A move was made in 2007 to a new, custom-built distillery with a visitor centre at Princess Royal Harbour. In 2015, the company opened a second distillery in Margaret River which will be focsuing on gin production. End of 2016, the owners took over an old winery in Porongurup where the third and largest distillery in the group is now under construction. When Tiger Snake Whiskey distillery is operational, the total production will have increased from 12,000 cases per year to 130,000 cases! The current distillery in Albany is equipped with one pair of stills.

The first expression of the whisky, called Limeburners, was released in 2008 and this is still the core bottling. Included in the range are also American Oak, Port Cask and Sherry Cask, all bottled at 43% as well as Peated which is bottled at 48%. A limited, heavily peated whisky, Darkest Winter bottled at 65.1%, was released in August 2016.

Distillery: Starward Distillery, Melbourne, Victoria
Founded: 2008
Owner: David Vitale

starward.com.au

The distillery, founded by David Vitale, was until recently fitted into an old Qantas maintenance hangar at Essendon Fields, Melbourne´s original airport. The stills (an 1,800 litre wash still and a 600 litre spirit still) were bought from Joadja Creek Distillery in Mittagong and currently the yearly production is around 20,000 cases. At the end of October 2016, the distillery moved to a new

Single malt range from Old Hobart Distillery

and bigger site in Port Melbourne. The first whisky was released under the name Starward in 2013 and since then the range has been expanded. A range of limited releases called New World Projects has also been launched with a double maturation (re-fill and first fill port) as the latest addition. In 2015, the distillery was given a major financial injection when Diageo´s incubator fund project, Distill Ventures, announced that they would invest in the Australian company. The sum was not disclosed but it was said it would be used to boost production and help the company expand.

Other distilleries in Australia

Nant Distillery

Bothwell, Tasmania, founded in 2007

www.nant.com.au

Nant distillery, in the Central Highlands of Tasmania, started when Queensland businessman, Keith Batt, bought the property in 2004. He refurbished the Historic Sandstone Water Mill on the estate and converted it into a whisky distillery. The first distillation took place in 2008. The distillery is equipped with a 1,800 litre wash still, a 600 litre spirit still and wooden washbacks for the fermentation. The first bottlings were released in 2010 and the current core range consists of Sherry, Port, Bourbon and Pinot Noir - all bottled at 43%. In December 2015, Keith Batt filed for bankruptcy with debts of $16.2 million and after a long time of court proceedings, the distillery was taken over by Australian Whisky Holdings.

William McHenry and Sons Distillery

Port Arthur, Tasmania, founded in 2011

www.mchenrydistillery.com.au

In 2011, William McHenry and his family moved from Sydney to Tasmania to open their distillery. Equipped with a 500 litre copper pot still with a surrounding water jacket to get a lighter spirit, production started in 2012. To facilitate the cash flow, a range of different gins is also produced. The first whisky release made from Tasmanian Gairdner barley, aged in American oak casks from Maker´s Mark for four years and finished in Australian ex-apera (sherry) barrels, was released in May 2016 and a few more barrels have been bottled since.

Launceston Distillery

Western Junction (near Launceston), Tasmania, founded in 2013

www.launcestondistillery.com.au

The distillery was founded in 2013 by five friends and the first distillation was in October 2015. The equipment consists of a 1,100 litre stainless steel mash tun, stainless steel washbacks with a fermentation time of one week, a 1,600 litre wash still and a 700 litre spirit still – both with reflux balls. The newmake is filled into barrels which have previously held bourbon, sherry and port. The goal is to have the first whisky ready for release in early 2018.

Black Gate Distillery

Mendooran, New South Wales, founded in 2012

www.blackgatedistillery.com

The distillery was opened by Brian and Genise Hollingworth in January 2012. Both mashing and fermentation are done at the distillery and since autumn 2013 they have also started peatsmoking the barley on site. The first products were vodkas and liqueurs with rum following. The first release of a single malt came in the beginning of 2015 when a sherrymatured expression was launched. More bottlings have followed, some lightly peated, with the next one planned for September 2017.

Redlands Estate Distillery

Kempton, Tasmania, founded in 2013

www.redlandsestate.com.au

Redlands Estate in Derwent Valley dates back to the early 1800s and was run mainly as a hop and grain farm. A few years ago, Peter and Elizabeth Hope bought the rundown property, restored it into a working farm including a distillery. In spring 2016, the distillery re-located to Dysart House, an old coaching inn in Kempton. The first spirit was double distilled in March 2013 in a 900 litre copper pot still and in 2016, yet another and bigger still (2,000 litre) was installed. Two more stills have recently been ordered. The first whisky, from a 20 litre pinot noir cask, was released in September 2015 and this has been followed by several more releases. Since 2016, Australian Whisky Holdings own part of the distillery.

Starward Distillery and one of the owners - David Vitale

Archie Rose Distilling Company

Rosebery, New South Wales, founded in 2014

www.archierose.com.au

For many years brewing and spirit production was only a hobby for Will Edwards, but in 2014 he decided to go ahead and build Sydney´s first independent distillery. Archie Rose is situated just 5 km from the city centre and the first distillation was conducted in December 2014. Apart from producing single malt and rye whisky, Will has also produced and released gin and vodka. The whisky is still maturing but meanwhile a white rye has been released. Three copper pot stills (two for whisky and one for gin/vodka production) are all made in Tasmania. The single malt is both peated and unpeated and matures mainly in Australian ex-port and ex-sherry casks. By summer 2017, 500 casks had been filled.

Timboon Railway Shed Distillery

Timboon, Victoria, founded in 2007

www.timboondistillery.com.au

The small town of Timboon lies 200 kilometres southwest of Melbourne. Here, Tim Marwood established his combination of a distillery and a restaurant in 2007 in a renovated railway goods shed. Using a pilsner malted barley, Marwood obtains the wash (1,000 litres) from the local Red Duck microbrewery. The wash is then distilled twice in a 600 litre pot still. For maturation, resized (20 litres) and retoasted ex-port, tokay and bourbon barrels are used. The first release of a whisky, matured in port barrels, was made in 2010 and some of the latest expressions have been Tom´s Cut, bottled at 58% and Christie´s Cut at 60%.

Castle Glen Distillery

The Summit, Queensland, founded in 2009

www.castleglenaustralia.com.au

Established as a vineyard in 1990 by the current owner Cedric Millar, Castle Glen moved on to open up also a brewery and a distillery in 2009. Apart from wine and beer, a wide range of spirits are produced including rum, vodka, gin, absinthe and various eau de vies. Malted barley is imported and the first whiskey, Castle Glen Limited Edition, was released as a 2 year old in early 2012.

Joadja Distillery

Joadja, New South Wales, founded in 2014

www.joadjadistillery.com.au

In 2011, Valero Jimenez took over a distillery which had actually never started. There was no equipment and so Jimenez applied for an Excise Licence and consulted with Bill Lark on how to start up the production. The first distillation was in December 2014 when the distillery was equipped with just the one still (800 litres), used for both the wash and the spirit run. In 2015, a 2,400 litre wash still was installed together with another four washbacks. The owners plan to grow 30 acres of their own barley on the estate and also to malt it on site, using peat to dry it. The first whisky will be released in autumn 2017.

Shene Distillery

Pontville, Tasmania, founded in 2015

www.shene.com.au

Shene Distillery opened in 2015 but distillation actually began already in 2007 in a different location. That was the year when Damian Mackey built a minute distillery in a shed on his property in New Town outside Hobart. Over the years, Mackey has patiently been experimenting and learning the trade and in spring 2016 the opportunity came for him to move his production to the Shene Estate at Pontville, 30 minutes north of Hobart and owned by David and Anne Kemke. With four stills and a capacity of 300,000 litres this is one of the largest distilleries in Australia. The whisky is triple distilled and the first release from Mackey´s production at Shene was in August 2017.

Tin Shed Distilling Co.

Welland (Adelaide), South Australia, founded in 2013

www.iniquity.com.au

The first distillery founded by Ian Schmidt and Vic Orlow in

Archie Rose Distillery

2004 was Southern Coast Distillers. They made their first whisky release in 2010, but two years later the operation folded due to a disagreement with a third partner. Ian and Vic, however, kept going and started a new business, Tin Shed Distilling Company. Initially they used equipment from the first distillery, but in 2014 this was supplemented by a 2,200 litre wash still and a new mash tun. The first single malt, under the name, Iniquity, was launched as a 2 year old in 2015 and seven batches have so far been released.

Mt Uncle Distillery

Walkamin, North Queensland, founded in 2001

www.mtuncle.com

When Mark Watkins founded the distillery in 2001, he started out by producing gin, rum and vodka - all of which soon became established brands on the market. After a few years, Watkins decided to add whisky production as well. Their first single malt, The Big Black Cock, first released in April 2014, is produced using local Queensland barley and has been matured for five years in a combination of French and American oak.

Loch Distillery

Loch, Victoria, founded in 2014

www.lochbrewery.com.au

Situated in an old bank building, this combined brewery and distillery has been producing since summer 2014. The owner, Craig Johnson, learnt about distilling from Bill Lark (like so many others have) before ordering his stills from Portugal. Gin has already been released while whisky production didn´t start until March 2015. The wash used for the whisky production comes from their own brewery. In June 2016, the distillery was expanded with a new, 400 litre alembic still and a 1200 litre wash still was added in 2017.

Fanny´s Bay Distillery

Weymouth, Tasmania, founded in 2015

www.fannysbaydistillery.com.au

Built by Mathew and Julie Cooper in 2014 and with most of the equipment constructed by Mathew himself. The distillery is equipped with a 400 litre copper pot still, a 600 litre mash tun and a 300 litre washback with a 7-8 day fermentation. The whisky starts in 20 litre port barrels and is then finished in small bourbon casks. The first whisky was released in May 2017 and it is now available in two versions - sherry and port.

Applewood Distillery

Gumeracha, South Australia, founded in 2015

www.applewooddistillery.com.au

In their early twenties, Laura and Brendan Carter started Unico Zelo wines and, a few years later, expanded the business to include perfumes. In 2015, a further expansion led to the Carter´s opening a distillery in the Adelaide Hills. To start with, gin, eau de vie and liqueurs were on the menu, but in summer 2015, whisky production was added. In March 2016, a 3 months old single malt spirit that had matured in ex-tawny casks was released.

Killara Distillery

Hobart, Tasmania, founded in 2016

www.killaradistillery.com

When Kristy Booth opened her distillery in summer 2016, there was a lot of focus on her being a woman and also the daughter of the godfather of whisky, Bill Lark. What some people seemed to forget was that she had been working at Lark distillery for 17 years and in all aspects of the production, ending up as head distiller and then general manager. In other words, this is one experienced whisky professional. The first whisky distillation was in August 2016 but she has already released a gin.

New Zealand

Distillery:	New Zealand Malt Whisky Co., Oamary, South Island
Founded:	2000
Owner:	Extra Eight
	thenzwhisky.com, milfordwhisky.co.nz

In 2001, Warren Preston bought the entire stock of single malt and blended whisky from the decommissioned Wilsons Willowbank Distillery in Dunedin. The supplies that he acquired consisted of 400 casks of single malt whisky including production dating back to 1987. Before he bought it, the whisky was sold under the name Lammerlaw, but Preston renamed it Milford. Preston also had plans to build a distillery in Oamaru. In 2010, his company was placed in receivership and it was bought by a syndicate of investors led by Tasmanian-based businessman Greg Ramsay. Their capital injection revived the company and plans to build a distillery still exist. Since early 2015, the company has been distilling trial batches of whisky at Workshops Whisky, a small distillery owned by Doug and Anthony Lawry. The Milford range (10, 15, 18 and 20 years old) was released already when Warren Preston was the owner. With the new ownership, the range of expressions has increased rapidly. Among the most recent bottlings is the Otago 30 year old which was released in August 2017.

Distillery:	Thomson Whisky Distillery, Auckland, North Island
Founded:	2014
Owner:	Thomson Whisky New Zealand Ltd.
	thomsonwhisky.com

The company started out as an independent bottler, sourcing their whiskies from the closed Willowbank Distillery in Dunedin, New Zealand. In April 2014, Rachel and Mathew Thomson opened up a small distillery (basically just a copper pot still) based at Hallertau Brewery in North West Auckland. The wash for the distillation comes from the brewery. In summer 2014, trials were made producing a whisky where the malt had been kilned using New Zealand Manuka wood. "Work-in-progress" bottles of the Manuka spirit have been released but the first whisky isn´t expected until 2017 or 2018.

Distillery:	Cardrona Distillery, Cardrona (near Wanaka), South Island
Founded:	2015
Owner:	Desiree and Ash Whitaker
	cardronadistillery.com

The mastermind behind the distillery, Desiree Whitaker, sold her dairy farm in South Canterbury to pursue her dream of building a distillery. She found a site in Cardrona Valley and met her husband, Ash, at the same time. Building on the distillery started in January 2015 and in October the first distillation was made. The distillery is equipped with 1.4 ton mash tun, six metal washbacks, one 2,000 litre wash still and a 1,300 litre spirit still. For production of vodka there is also a Jacob Carl column still and for gin, a New Zealand built vapour infusion still. The two pot stills were made by the famous copper smiths in Scotland, Forsyth's. The production capacity is one barrel per day and the whisky will be matured in sherry casks and bourbon barrels. The owners have released a barrel-aged gin and a single malt vodka but the first single malt whisky will probably not be released until 2025.

Asia

India

Distillery: Amrut Distilleries Ltd., Bangalore
Founded: 1948
Owner: Jagdale Group

amrutwhisky.co.uk

The family-owned distillery, based in Bangalore, south India, started to distil malt whisky in the mid-eighties. The equivalent of 50 million bottles of spirits (including rum, gin and vodka) is manufactured a year, of which 1,4 million bottles is whisky. Most of the whisky goes to blended brands, but Amrut single malt was introduced in 2004. It was first launched in Scotland, but can now be found in more than 20 countries and has recently been introduced to the American market. The distillery, with a capacity of doing 200,000 litres of pure alcohol per year, is equipped with six washbacks with a fermentation time of 140 hours and two stills, each with a capacity of 5,000 litres. The barley is sourced from the north of India, malted in Jaipur and Delhi and finally distilled in Bangalore before the whisky is bottled without chill-filtering or colouring. The owners have had plans for a while now to build yet another distillery adjacent to the present. A new warehouse has already been built and it now looks like construction of the distillery will start in autumn 2017.

The Amrut core range consists of unpeated and peated versions bottled at 46%, a cask strength and a peated cask strength and Fusion which is based on 25% peated malt from Scotland and 75% unpeated Indian malt. Special releases over the years include Two Continents, where maturing casks have been brought from India to Scotland for their final period of maturation, Intermediate Sherry Matured where the new spirit has matured in ex-bourbon or virgin oak, then re-racked to sherry butts and with a third maturation in ex-bourbon casks, Kadhambam which is a peated Amrut matured in ex Oloroso butts, ex Bangalore Blue Brandy casks and ex rum casks and Portonova with a maturation in bourbon casks and port pipes. New editions of them all are released from time to time. A big surprise for 2013 was the release of Amrut Greedy Angels, an 8 year old and the oldest Amrut so far. That was an astonishing achievement in a country where the hot and humid climate causes major evaporation during maturation. In 2015 it was time for an even

older expression, 10 years old, and in 2016, a 12 year old, the oldest whisky from India so far, was released. In 2017, a second edition of the 8 year old was launched. The highly innovative Spectrum has now reached its fourth release, this time matured in casks made of four varieties of oak. Other limited releases include the second version of Double Cask, a 5 year old combination of ex-bourbon and port pipes, the 100% malted Amrut Rye Single Malt - the first rye whisky from the company, Amalgam comprising of Amrut as well as single malts from Scotland and Asia and Con-fusion - a special bottling for members of Amrut Fever.

Distillery: John Distilleries Jdl, Goa
Founded: 1992
Owner: Paul P John

pauljohnwhisky.com

Paul P John, who today is the chairman of the company, started in 1992 by making a variety of spirits including Indian whisky made from molasses. Their biggest seller today is Original Choice, a blend of extra neutral alcohol distilled from molasses and malt whisky from their own facilities. The brand, which was introduced in 1995/96 has since made an incredible journey. It is now one of the biggest whiskies in the world with sales of 130 million bottles in 2016. Another brand is Bangalore Malt which was the fastest growing spirit in the world in 2016. This is a simpler version of Original Choice and 24 million bottles were sold in 2016 - all in the state of Karnataka where the company has its head office!

John Distilleries owns three distilleries and produces its brands from 18 locations in India with its head office in Bangalore. The basis for their blended whiskies is distilled in column stills with a capacity of 500 million litres of extra neutral alcohol per year. In 2007 they set up their single malt distillery which was equipped with one pair of traditional copper pot stills but in 2017, another pair of stills were added, doubling the capacity to 1.5 million litres per year. The company released their first single malt in autumn 2012 and this was followed by several single casks. In 2013 it was time for two core expressions, both made from Indian malted barley. Brilliance is unpeated and bourbon-matured while Edited, also matured in bourbon

Amrut Distilleries´ master blender, Surrinder Khumar, and the latest edition of the 8 year old Greedy Angels casks, has a small portion of peated barley in the recipe. At the beginning of 2014, two cask strength bottlings were released; Select Cask Classic (55,2%) and Select Cask Peated (55,5%). In 2015, finally, the third core expression was released. It was a 100% peated bottling called Bold, bottled at 46%. Recent limited releases include three 7 year old single malts; Mars Orbiter, a peated whisky matured in American oak, Oloroso, unpeated and matured in oloroso butts and Kanya, unpeated from American oak.

Other distilleries in India

McDowell´s Distillery

Ponda, Goa, founded in 1988 (malt whisky)

unitedspirits.in

In 1826 the Scotsman, Angus McDowell, established himself as an importer of wines, spirits and cigars in Madras (Chennai) and the firm was incorporated in 1898. In the same town another Scotsman, Thomas Leishman, founded United Breweries in 1915. Both companies were bought by Vital Mallya around 1950 and eventually became the second largest producer of alcohol in the world after Diageo. Recently Diageo has taken control of United Spirits. The absolute majority of United Spirits´ whiskies are Indian whisky, made of molasses while single malt sales are negligible. McDowell´s Single Malt is made at the distillery in Ponda (Goa) and sells 20,000 cases each year.

Rampur Distillery

Rampur, Uttar Pradesh, founded in 1943

www.rampursinglemalt.com

This huge distillery is situated west of Delhi and around 100 kilometres from the Nepalese border. It was purchased in 1972 by G. N. Khaitan and is today owned by Radico Khaitan, the fourth biggest Indian liquor company. The distillery has a capacity of producing 75 million litres of whisky based on molasses, 30 million litres of grain whisky and 460,000 litres of malt whisky per year. The first whisky brand from Radico was 8PM, which in 2016 sold 68 million bottles. The first single malt release, un-chill filtered and without age statement, appeared in May 2016.

Israel

Distillery:	The Milk & Honey Distillery, Jaffa
Founded:	2013
Owner:	Gal Kalkshtein et al.
	mh-distillery.com

This is the first whisky distillery in Israel and the team behind the project comprises of Gal Kalkshtein, Simon Fried, Amit Dror and Nir Gilat. The distillery is equipped with a 1 ton stainless steel mash tun, two stainless steel washbacks and two copper stills (with a capacity of 9,000 and 3,500 litres each). The total capacity is 200,000 litres of pure alcohol. The first distillation was in March 2015 when the wash was brought in from a local brewery. In February 2016, the first in-house whisky production took place. Products released so far include Levantine gin, new make spirit and a couple of malt spirits of around 6-12 months old. The first 3 year old single malt, made before the final equipment was installed, was made available through Whisky Auctioneer in August 2017, similar to the first releases from Strathearn in Scotland.

Pakistan

Distillery:	Murree Brewery Ltd., Rawalpindi
Founded:	1860
Owner:	Bhandara family
	murreebrewery.com

Started as a beer brewery, the assortment was later expanded to include whisky, gin, rum, vodka and brandy. The core range of single malt holds two expressions – Murree´s Classic 8 years old and Murree´s Millenium Reserve 12 years old. In 2005 an 18 year old single malt was launched and the following year their oldest expression so far, a 21 year old, reached the market. There is also a Murree´s Islay Reserve, Vintage Gold, which is a blend of Scotch whisky and Murree single malt.

Michael John D´Souza - master distiller and blender at John Distilleries

Taiwan

Distillery: Kavalan Distillery, Yanshan, Yilan County
Founded: 2005
Owner: King Car Food Industrial Co.

kavalanwhisky.com

On the 11th of March 2006 at 3.30pm, the first spirit was produced at Kavalan distillery. This was celebrated in a major way a decade later when guests and journalists from all over the world were invited for the 10th anniversary. But it was not just to celebrate 10 years of whisky production but also to witness the recent expansion of the distillery which has made Kavalan one of the ten largest malt whisky distilleries in the world! This rapid development may even have surprised the founder, entrepreneur and business man Tien-Tsai Lee, and his son, the current CEO of the company Yu-Ting Lee. Early on, it was decided that expertise from Scotland was needed to get on the right track from the beginning. Dr. Jim Swan was consulted early on and he, together with the master blender, Ian Chang, developed a strategy including production as well as the future maturation. Jim Swan, involved in so many distillery projects around the worrld, sadly passed away in early 2017.

Kavalan distillery lies in the north-eastern part of the country, in Yilan County, just one hour's drive from Taipei. Following the expansion in 2016, the distillery is equipped with 4 mash tuns, 40 stainless steel washbacks with a 60-72 hour fermentation time and 10 pairs of lantern-shaped copper stills with descending lye pipes. The capacity of the wash stills is 12,000 litres and of the spirit stills 7,000 litres. After 10-15 minutes of foreshots, the heart of the spirit run takes 2-3 hours. The cut points for the spirit run are 65%-55% to accommodate a complex and rich flavour profile. The spirit vapours are cooled using tube condensers, but because of the hot climate, subcoolers are also used.

On site, there are two five-story high warehouses (with plans for a third) and the casks are tied together due to the earthquake risk. The climate in this part of Taiwan is hot and humid and on the top floors of the warehouses the temperature can easily reach 42°C. Hence the angel's share is quite dramatic – no less than 10-12% is lost every year. On the other hand, the heat speeds up the extraction of flavour from the casks which also makes the whisky mature quicker. The distillery has its own cooperage where the preparation of the wood plays a very important part for the final character of the whisky. Implemented by Dr. Swan, they use a shave-toast-rechar (STR)

process for some of the casks which, together with the subtropical climate, lends a very special character to the whisky.

The brand name, Kavalan, derives from the earliest tribe that inhabited Yilan, the county where the distillery is situated. Since the first bottling was released in 2008, the range has been expanded and now holds more than ten different expressions. The best seller globally is Classic Kavalan, bottled at either 40% or 43%. In 2011, an "upgraded" version of the Classic was launched in the shape of King Car Conductor – a mix of eight different types of casks, un chill-filtered and bottled at 46%. A port finished version called Concertmaster (currently the best selling Kavalan in the USA) was released in 2009 and, later that year, two different single cask bottlings were launched under the name Solist – one ex-bourbon and one ex-Oloroso sherry. It was the launch of these two expressions that made the rest of the world aware of Taiwanese whisky.

More expressions in the Solist series have been added and the range now consists of (apart from Bourbon and Sherry) Fino, Vinho Barrique (using Portuguese wine barriques), Manzanilla, Amontillado, PX, Moscatel and Port. All of these are bottled at cask strength but in 2012 two versions bottled at 46% were also introduced – Bourbon Oak and Sherry Oak. Other releases include Podium which is a vatting of whiskies from new American oak and a selection of re-fill casks and Distillery Reserve Peaty Cask. The latter, exclusively available at the distillery visitor centre, obtains its smoky flavour from maturation in ex-Islay casks. The distillery has produced whisky from peated barley (10ppm) as well, but this is still maturing. The latest release was the Distillery Reserve Rum Cask, also an exclusive for the visitor centre. Whisky is, of course, the main product for Kavalan but recently production of gin has also started with the first bottlings yet to be launched.

Kavalan is being exported to more than 60 countries including the USA, the UK, France, Belgium, Italy, The Netherlands, Russia, Israel and Hong Kong. Apart from Taiwan, Europe and the US are the most important markets. Their ambition to establish themselves on the American market was evidenced by the message on eleven of the electronic billboards on Times square during autumn 2016. There is an impressive visitor centre on site and it was awarded Whisky Visitor Attraction of the Year in 2011 by the Whisky Magazine. No less than one million visitors come here annually. The owning company, King Car Group, with 2,000 employees, was already founded in 1956 and runs businesses in several fields; biotechnology and aquaculture, among others. It is also famous for its ready-to-drink coffee, Mr. Brown.

Celebrating the expansion of Kavalan Distillery - (left to right) Ian Chang, Dr. Jim Swan, Mr. TT Lee and Mr. YT Lee

Africa

Other distilleries in Taiwan

Nantou Distillery

Nantou City, Nantou County, founded in 1978
(whisky since 2008)

en.ttl.com.tw

Nantou distillery is a part of the state-owned manufacturer and distributor of cigarettes and alcohol in Taiwan – Taiwan Tobacco and Liquor Corporation (TTL). Established as a government agency in the early 1900s, it was renamed Taiwan Tobacco and Wine Monopoly Bureau in 1947. Between 1947 and 1968 the Bureau exercised a monopoly over all alcohol, tobacco, and camphor products sold in Taiwan. It retained tobacco and alcohol monopolies until Taiwan's entry into the WTO in 2002.

There are seven distilleries and two breweries within the TTL group, but Nantou is the only with malt whisky production. The distillery is equipped with a full lauter Huppmann mash tun with a charge of 2.5 tonnes and eight washbacks made of stainless steel. The fermentation time is 60-72 hours and in order to regulate the fermentation, the washbacks are equipped with water-cooling jackets. There are two wash stills (9,000 and 5,000 litres) and two spirit stills (5,000 and 2,000 litres). All are equipped with shell and tube condensers, as well as aftercoolers. Malted barley is imported from Scotland and ex-sherry and ex-bourbon casks are used for maturation. Nantou Distillery also produces a variety of fruit wines and the casks that have stored lychee wine and plum wine are then used to give some whiskies an extra finish.

Due to extreme temperatures during summer, distillation only takes place from October to April. The hot and humid climate also increases the angle´s share which is around 6-7%. Until recently, the spirit from Nantou has been unpeated, but in 2014, trials with peated malt brought in from Scotland were made.

The main product from the distillery is a blended whisky which comprises of malt whisky from Nantou, grain whisky from Taichung distillery and imported blended Scotch. In October 2013, two cask strength single malt whiskies were launched – one from bourbon casks and the other from sherry casks. The next expressions were Omar single malt, where several versions have been released, matured in either sherry or bourbon casks. A very special variety of Omar (only 700 bottles) had been finished in a lychee liqueur barrel.

South Africa

Distillery:	James Sedgwick Distillery, Wellington, Western Cape
Founded:	1886 (whisky since 1990)
Owner:	Distell Group Ltd.
	threeshipswhisky.co.za

Distell Group Ltd. was formed in 2000 by a merger between Stellenbosch Farmers' Winery and Distillers Corporation, although the James Sedgwick Distillery was already established in 1886. The company produces a huge range of wines and spirits including the popular cream liqueur, Amarula Cream. James Sedgwick Distillery has been the home to South African whisky since 1990. The distillery has undergone a major expansion in the last years and is now equipped with one still with two columns for production of grain whisky, two pot stills for malt whisky and one still with six columns designated for neutral spirit. There are also two mash tuns and 23 washbacks. Grain whisky is distilled for nine months of the year, malt whisky for two months (always during the winter months July/August) and one month is devoted to maintenance. Three new warehouses have been built and a total of seven warehouses now hold 180,000 casks.

In Distell´s whisky portfolio, it is the Three Ships brand, introduced in 1977, that makes up for most of the sales. The range consists of Select and 5 year old Premium Select, both of which are a blend of South African and Scotch whiskies. Furthermore, there is Bourbon Cask Finish, the first 100% South African blended whisky and the 10 year old single malt. The latter was launched for the first time in 2003 and the release in 2016 was the fifth and the first to carry a vintage. A new range called Master´s Collection was introduced in 2015 with a 10 year old PX finish as the first release. This was followed in 2016 by a 15 year old pinotage cask finish. Apart from the Three Ships range, Distell also produces South Africa´s first single grain whisky, Bain´s Cape Mountain.

In 2013 the Distell Group acquired the Scottish whisky group, Burn Stewart Distillers, including Bunnahabhain, Tobermory and Deanston distilleries as well as the blended whisky, Scottish Leader. The man who tirelessly worked to bring the Three Ships single malt to the market, was Andy Watts. After 25 years as the distillery manager, he has now taken on a new role in the company where he will be responsible for overseeing Distell´s entire whisky portfolio.

Omar Single Malt from Nantou Distillery

Andy Watts, head of Distell´s whisky portfolio

South America

Argentina

Distillery: La Alazana Distillery, Golondrinas, Patagonia
Founded: 2011
Owner: Nestor Serenelli

laalazanawhisky.com

The first whisky distillery in Argentina concentrating solely on malt whisky production was founded in 2011 and the distillation started in December of that year. Located in the Patagonian Andes to the South of Argentina, it was Pablo Tognetti, an old time home brewer, and his son-in-law, Nestor Serenelli who started it but end of 2014, Pablo Tognetti withdrew from the company. Today it´s Nestor and his wife Lila who own and run the distillery. They are both big fans of Scotch whisky and before they built the distillery, they toured Scotland to visit distilleries and to get inspiration. Even though the Serenelli´s are producing their whisky according to Scottish tradition, they are also firm believers in the "terroir" concept where local barley and water and, not least, climate will affect the flavour of the whisky. The distillery is equipped with a lauter mash tun, four stainless steel 1,100 litre washbacks with a fermentation time of 4 to 6 days and two stills – one 500 litres and another, recently installed, 1,300 litres. The second still made it possible to double the production to 8,000 litres a year. The latest development is that the owners are now growing their own barley and also do the malting using local peat.

The owners are aiming for a light and fruity whisky but they have also filled several barrels with peated whisky. Maturation is mostly in ex-bourbon casks but fresh PX sherry casks and toasted Malbec casks are also used. A visitor centre has been built and a grand, official opening of the distillery was held in November 2014. The first, limited release was made in December 2013. The latest bottling appeared in September 2016, a "classic" La Alazana (70% ex bourbon and 30% ex sherry). The first peated bottling, the 4 year old Haidd Merlys, was also recently launched. Two versions

were presented - one chardonnay finish and one bourbon matured. Limited bottlings will continue to be released but the owners are planning for a core expression that is at least 8-10 years old.

Other distilleries in Argentina

Distillery Emilio Mignone & Cia

Luján, Buenos Aires province, founded in 2015

www.emiliomignoneycia.com.ar, www.emyc.com.ar

The distillery, founded and owned by the brothers Santiago and Carlos Mignone, became the second whisky distillery in Argentina. Inspired and mentored by Nestor and Lila Serenelli of La Alazana, the two brothers made their first distillation in November 2015. A number of tests followed and the first barrel was filled in July 2016. The distillery is equipped with a new, 300 litre open mash tun, a 250 litre washback with a 72-96 hour fermentation cycle and two stills, directly fired by natural gas. The plan for 2017 is to produce 1,000 litres and the first bottling will be released in 2019. End of 2016, the first batch of peated spirit (35-50ppm in the barley) was distilled. The Mignone brothers are working on a second and larger distillery (10,000 litres) in the near future in Lago Puelo, Patagonia, where the family owns a farm. The plan is to have it up and running by 2020 and also add a visitor centre.

Madoc Distillery

Dina Huapi, Rio Negro, founded in 2015

www.madocwhisky.com

In 2015 construction began on another whisky distillery in Patagonia. The founder, Pablo Tognetti, is no newcomer to whisky production as he was one of the founders of the Patagonian distillery, La Alazana. In 2015, he left the company and brought with him some of the equipment, as well as part of the maturing stock to build a new distillery in Dina Huapi, which is situated on the outskirts of the lake-side Andean ski resort, Bariloche. The existing equipment with a lauter mash tun, a washback and a copper pot still was complemented by a wash still and the first distillation took place in September 2016.

Brazil

Distillery: Union Distillery, Veranópolis
Founded: 1972
Owner: Union Distillery Maltwhisky Do Brasil Ltda

maltwhisky.com.br

The company was founded in 1948 as Union of Industries Ltd to produce wine. In 1972 they started to produce malt whisky and two years later the name of the company was changed to Union Distillery Maltwhisky do Brasil. In 1986 a co-operation with Morrison Bowmore Distillers was established in order to develop the technology at the Brazilian distillery. Most of the production is sold as bulk whisky to be part of different blends, but the company also has its own single malt called Union Club Whisky.

Distillery: Muraro Bebidas, Flores da Cunha
Founded: 1953
Owner: Muraro & Cia

muraro.com.br

This is a company with a wide range of products including wine, vodka, rum and cachaca and the total capacity is 10 million litres. Until recently, the blend Green Valley was the only whisky in the range. In November 2014, however, a new brand was introduced. It has the rather misleading name Blend Seven but it appears to be a malt whisky. The main market for the new whisky is The Carribean.

Nestor Serenelli, owner of La Alazana Distillery

The futuristic Puni Distillery in Italy

The Year
that was

Including the subsections:
The big players | The big brands | Changes in ownership
New distilleries | Bottling grapevine

Global alcohol consumption is on the decline and has been for the past five years with an average rate of -0.3%. In 2016, this downward trend became even more alarming as the decline for the year accelerated to -1.3%, at least according to the IWSR. Some other data companies reported smaller declines. Still, it is obvious that people around the world drink less alcohol every year. However, if you break down the figures into the different categories, it is largely beer and cider that is to blame for last year's disappointing figures. Beer volumes were down by -1.6% with many consumers changing their habits to drinking less by moving away from cheap budget brands and instead favouring craft beer producers.

Spirits on the other hand, does not seem to be affected by this trend of drinking less. Sales volumes grew in 2016 by 1.8% compared to a growth of 0.8% the year before. Most of the spirits subcategories increased their volumes with the exception of the continued downward trend for vodka (-0.7%). Whisky, on the other hand grew by 2.5% but were beaten by gin, tequila and cognac as all these spirits showed a volume increase of around 5-6%.

The question is, will this negative trend for alcohol consumption continue? If you ask the IWSR, it's a no. It will reverse in the next five years and the prediction is that volumes will rise by 0.8% until 2021, largely driven by whisky but also with beer bouncing back in Asian and sub-Saharan markets.

So, let's have a look at Scotch whisky. The industry has been through a couple of troublesome years with both volumes and value declining. In 2015, the decline was less noticeable but it was in 2016 that the negative trend significantly ended. For the entire category, volumes were up 4.8% and values by 4% with the continued success for single malt as the main driver. Values increased by almost 12% and for the first time, single malt Scotch broke the magic £1bn barrier. Single malt accounts for 9.3% of all exported Scotch in terms of volumes while its share of the values is an amazing 26% (an increase from 16% in 2006)!

SINGLE MALT SCOTCH - EXPORT

Value:	+11.8% to £1.02bn
Volume:	+10.0% to 113m bottles

OTHER BOTTLED SCOTCH* - EXPORT

Value:	+1.4% to £2,75bn
Volume:	+3.0% to 822m bottles

TOTAL SCOTCH - EXPORT

Value:	+4.0% to £4.01bn
Volume:	+4.8% to 1.21bn bottles

* Other bottled Scotch includes bottled blended malt, bottled blended Scotch and bottled grain Scotch whisky. Bulk expor is not included, except in the Total.

Whilst these figures seem reassuring, there is a cloud on the horizon. The Scotch whisky industry are naturally concerned about any possible negative impacts from Brexit and the 4% increase on spirits duty excise that was announced in spring 2017 didn't help either. On the other hand, in the short term, the Brexit decision has helped the industry by way of a weaker pound and it could also make growth in India easier in the future. For ten years now, India and the EU have been negotiating a free trade agreement with very little success. With the UK leaving the EU, the country will have the possibility of negotiating an agreement with India by themselves.

Even though Scotch whisky is exported to more than 200 countries, around 80% of the volumes and values are supplied to the top 25 markets. Of these 25 markets, 15 showed increasing values in 2016, while volumes grew in 16 of them. The most important export market for Scotch for a very long time has been the USA and with a value increase of no less than 14%, this had significant impact on the overall figures for 2016.

Looking at the detailed figures for each of the nine regions, five of them have shown both increasing volumes and values, two accounted for an increase in values only while the final two showed decreasing figures for both values and volumes.

The European Union

Since its inception, the European Union has always been the biggest export market for Scotch whisky. More than

Scotch whisky export got a boost in 2016 from the weaker pound caused by Brexit

every third bottle that is exported from Scotland goes here and if we focus on single malt it's almost every other. It is a mature and well established market and one would think there is little space for growth. This was not the case in 2016 though. Volumes increased by 8.6% while values climbed by 3.6%. This was a big improvement compared to the year before when both indicators dropped by 3%.

EU — Top 3

France	volumes	+8%	values	-2%
Spain	volumes	+10%	values	+10%
Germany	volumes	+13%	values	+13%

Unsurprisingly, France is still the biggest importer of Scotch whisky in the world in terms of volume - no less than 190 million bottles were sold last year. The Scotch interest in the country has always leaned towards the less expensive part of the range in contrast to the Americans where the revenue for each exported bottle is 220% higher compared to France. Another traditionally strong market comes in at second place - Spain. The 10% increase in 2016 was pleasant news for the producers but the volumes are still only 50% of that which was sold during the best years around 2003. Germany has over a period of time secured third place and in 2016 export volumes were at their highest ever. What one should remember regarding Germany is that a substantial part is re-directed to other countries,

not least Turkey and Belarus. In line with last year, there are two countries that continue to dramatically increase their import of Scotch; In Poland, volumes were up by 16% and values by 19% and The Netherlands increased volumes by 12% and values by 3%. One thing should be kept in mind though - both these countries also serve as a transit point where part of the volumes are transferred to other countries. Finally, Italy, which in the new millennium has shown decreasing interest in Scotch, surprised us with the highest imports since 2010.

North America

In 2013, North America passed Asia to become the second most important region in terms of values. Under 2016 the lead was extended due to an increase in volumes by 1.2% and values by 10.6%, surpassing £1bn. Not least the 17% increase in the value of single malts had considerable impact on the strong figures.

North America — Top 3

USA	volumes	+2%	values	+14%
Mexico	volumes	+1%	values	-3%
Canada	volumes	-5%	values	-4%

The region increased also during 2015 but while it was Mexico and Canada which helped drive the growth at that time and the USA stood still - in 2016 roles were reversed. USA is the biggest importer of Scotch in the world in terms of value and in 2016 the growth in volumes may have been small (+2%) but the increase in value (+14%) is all the more impressive. The difference between the two figures also show a continued premiumisation. Mexico and Canada however, went the other way. Volumes of Scotch imported to Mexico have gone up every year since 2006 and 2016 was no exception (+1%) but the value decreased (-3%). The situation in Canada was even worse in 2016 with both volumes (-5%) and values (-4%) down.

Asia

Asia, the third biggest region for Scotch whisky (and the second biggest in terms of volumes), has been going through some tough years since 2012 with both volumes and values decreasing every year. In 2016 one could see a slight improvement. Volumes were up 5.9% while values increased by 1.7%. This is a region that the producers of Scotch place great faith in, in the long term future but it is also a tricky one to predict where sales will be heading. A combination of fluctuating economies, legislative interference from politicians and high import duty make it a very difficult market to navigate.

Asia — Top 3

Singapore	volumes	+11%	values	+6%
Taiwan	volumes	-11%	values	-4%
India	volumes	+18%	values	+14%

In terms of values, Singapore is the third biggest market for Scotch and consumption has increased rapidly in the country. But with a little more than 5 million people, this cannot explain the volumes that come into the country. Actually, the vast majority of the whisky is re-exported to other markets in the region, not least to ASEAN countries and China. The positive numbers for 2016 from Singapore (volumes up 11% and values 6%) differ greatly to the latest figures from Taiwan, number two on the Asia list. For the second year in a row both volumes and sales were down. On the other hand, it was just two years ago that double digit increases were reported for the country. The reason for the recent downturn is a contracting Taiwanese economy but Taiwan is still the fourth biggest market for Scotch whisky, single malts in particular.

For the last couple of years we have been used to seeing South Korea in third place in the Asian region. Not so this year. India is on the move and is now the third biggest market in the world in terms of volume with a substantial share being exported in bulk to become a part of Indian blended whisky. This is a remarkable development. Just 15 years ago India was in 19th place and volumes have increased by more than 1000% since then. Even so, Scotch whisky's share of the total whisky market in India is just 1%. South Korea on the other hand moves in the opposite direction with almost 70% lost during the same period.

Central and South America

In 2016 a trend was broken in this region. For three consecutive years, both volumes and values had been dropping,

The economy in Taiwan is a cause of distress but this is still one of the most important markets, not least for single malt Scotch

sometimes dramatically, but last year both figures were positive. Volumes increased by 5.6% while values went up by 2%. Part of the improvement lies in the 58% increase in values for single malts while blended Scotch only managed a 1% increase. Single malts are only 1% of the total share but there might be a trend where more and more consumers aspire to drink more malt whisky.

Central & South America — Top 3

Brazil	volumes	-8%	values	-2%
Panama	volumes	+14%	values	+17%
Dom. Republic	volumes	+3%	values	+10%

The deep recession in Brazil still affects exports to this, the biggest market in the region, but while values have been down 20-30% per year over the past two years, the decline for 2016 stopped at a modest 2% while volumes dropped by 8%. Brazil is number eight on the top list in terms of volumes and was just one of two markets in 2016 (South Africa being the other) amongst the top ten to show red figures.

Numbers two and three on the list compensated for the declining numbers in Brazil. Panama turned the last couple of years of loss to a double digit increase in both volumes and values and so did the Dominican Republic. The former Scotch whisky giant in the region on the other hand, Venezuela, is completely in the dark. Since the top year in 2007, volumes have gone down by 95%!

Africa

The most under developed whisky region is Africa, at least if you consider how many people that live on the continent. Producers of Scotch are keen to explore the opportunities but so far it's been South Africa that has commanded the greatest interest. In terms of whisky export, the region has gone through a couple of bad years with volumes decreasing by 10% in 2016 and values down by 14% and those are pretty much the same figures as last year.

Africa — Top 3

South Africa	volumes	-12%	values	-22%
Nigeria	volumes	+148%	values	+110%
Morocco	volumes	+16%	values	+17%

The biggest drawback on the continent has recently been South Africa which during many years have stood for the lion's share of the import. The last three years though, the numbers have declined and even more dramatically in 2016 with volumes down by 12% and values by 22%. Things could have been even worse if it hadn't been for Nigeria where values increased by 110% and Morocco with a more moderate increase by 17%. Last year's number two, Angola, has on the other hand slipped behind.

Middle East

The Middle East becomes more and more important and makes up 5% of the total values. In 2016, volumes went down by 1% while values increased by 5% thanks in part to a strong increase, +38%, when it comes to malt whisky.

Middle East - Top 3

UAE*	volumes	+3%	values	+7%
Lebanon	volumes	-22%	values	-15%
Israel	volumes	+1%	values	+9%

* United Arab Emirates

The biggest market in the region by far is the United Arab Emirates with 55% of the volumes and 60% of the values. It occupies a seventh place on the top list ahead of larger nations such as Mexico, Australia and India. Most of the whisky, for religious reasons, is not consumed within the country. Instead, UAE acts as a distribution hub for parts of Africa, Asia and India. The break-through for Israel as a Scotch drinking nation came in 2009 and sales have continued to increase. Together with Lebanon the two countries represent 85% of the total values exported to the region.

European non EU-members

Following some good years, Scotch whisky export to non EU-members declined in 2016. Values were down by 11% and volumes by 12.5%. With 2% of the total Scotch export, this is the second smallest region (only Eastern Europe is smaller) and 93% of the whisky goes to three countries; Turkey, Switzerland and Norway.

Europe (non-EU) — Top 3

Turkey	volumes	-20%	values	-17%
Switzerland	volumes	+-0%	values	-6%
Norway	volumes	+2%	values	+2%

The sharp decline in 2016 is due to the weak economy in Turkey which stands for approximately 60% of the totals.

Australasia

Until 2016, Australasia was the second smallest Scotch export region but some good figures have made it possible to surpass non EU-members. In 2016, values were up 11.5% while volumes dropped by 3%. Clearly an indication of increased premiumisation and a detailed look at the figures gives clear evidence to that. Malt whisky values have surged by 38% and is now 28% of the total Scotch exports to the region.

Australasia — Top 3

Australia	volumes	-4%	values	+12%
New Zealand	volumes	+15%	values	+18%
N. Caledonia	volumes	-4%	values	-5%

Unsurprisingly, Australia is the dominating market with 92% of the value but New Zealand also showed some good numbers, making a comeback from the disappointing 2015.

Eastern Europe

The smallest of all regions is labelled Eastern Europe but with many countries in this geographical region being a part of the EU, these are in whisky export statistics a part of that larger group. Here, we are talking mainly about Russia and some of the surrounding countries. Export figures were down in 2014 and 2015, mainly because of the turmoil due to export restrictions against Russia but 2016 saw the numbers move in a positive direction. Values were up by 78% while volumes soared and increased by 210%.

Eastern Europe — Top 3

Georgia	volumes	+19%	values	+31%
Montenegro	volumes	+2370%	values	+10099%
Russia	volumes	+134905%	values	+415%

The individual figures are also extreme, not least for Russia and Montenegro, but first of all, they come from a very low starting level (only 11,000 litres were exported to Montenegro in 2015) and secondly it is likely that some of these volumes are re-exported to other markets.

The big players

Diageo

Before and during the fiscal year 2015/2016, Diageo sold off all of the wines business in order to focus on spirits and beer in the future. This softened the results which showed a fall in net sales and only a minor increase in profits. The following year, on the other hand, ending 30th June 2017, the company was back on track. Net sales were up by 15% to £12.05bn while operating profits soared 25% to £3.56bn. Impressive figures but one has to keep in mind that a weak pound throughout the year (due to Brexit) has played a large and positive role.

If we look at the regions, North America (35% of total Diageo sales) saw net sales increase by 3% with American whiskey as the biggest contributor with a sales rise of 12% while Scotch increased by 8%. Vodka, on the other hand, dropped by 8%. Europe plus Russia and Turkey (23% of the sales) is the second biggest market where net sales were up by 5% with Johnnie Walker, Baileys, Captain Morgan and Tanqueray as the main source of pleasure. Finally, Asia Pacific (20% of the sales), showed a 3% increase, mainly driven by strong growth in Greater China but also Australia and South East Asia.

Diageo has divided their brands into three groups; Global Giants where 5 of 6 brands showed increased or flat net sales in 2016/17; Johnnie Walker (+6%), Smirnoff (-1%), Captain Morgan (+6%), Baileys (+5%), Tanqueray (+9%) and Guinness (+–0%). A lot of attention is given by the company to Johnnie Walker, the best-selling Scotch in the world. Last year it was decided to return to the classic slogan 'Keep Walking' and abandon the 'Joy Will Take You Further' message that was introduced two years ago. Next level is Local Stars, a group which among others includes six Scotch whiskies; J&B (+–0%), Buchanans (+16%), Windsor (-12%), Old Parr (+5%) and Black & White (+16%). Scotch malts were up 2% and are included in a

Sales of Black & White increased by 16% in 2016

category with the rather disparaging name Reserve. Of the single malts, its top three sellers showed strong performances; The Singleton was up by 3% to 6 million bottles, Talisker had improved by 6% to 2.7 million and Cardhu impressed with a 16% increase to 2.6 million bottles.

Three years ago, Diageo sold off Bushmill's Irish whiskey, a deal which raised many eyebrows. Why exit a category which has increased considerably in the last decade? Admittedly, the deal included Diageo getting 100% control of the super-premium tequila brand Don Julio and tequila is also a segment in the spirits world that becomes more and more exciting. However, in spring 2017, Diageo declared that they were once again ready to have a go at Irish whiskey. A premium Irish blend by the name Roe & Co was released and while it currently is made by using sourced whiskey, the company will build a new distillery in The Liberties area in Dublin. St James's Gate Distillery will be ready to produce in 2019.

Pernod Ricard

When CEO Alexandre Ricard described the results for 2015/2016, he used the words "solid and encouraging". For the fiscal year ending 30 June 2017, he simply restricted himself to "a strong year" and 2016/2017 was indeed an improvement of the year before. Sales grew organically by 3.6% and for the first time, the company exceeded the €9bn barrier (€9.01bn to be exact). Net profits increased by an impressive 13% to €1.42bn

The company has divided the world into three markets; Americas, where sales were up 7% mainly thanks to a solid performance in the USA driven by premiumisation. Brazil

lantine´s is the second most sold blended Scotch in the world

on the other hand continues to decline (-2%). Europe was up by 3% and it was Spain (+5%) and the UK (+7%) which was the biggest pleasure beside Russia where sales leapt by 16%. Finally, Asia Rest of the World managed an increase but only by 1%. India disappointed with just a 1% increase and although China only increased by 2%, it was a huge step forward compared to the previous year when sales were down by 9%.

Eleven out of thirteen Strategic International Brands showed growth with Jameson being the star. Volumes of the Irish whiskey increased by 15% to 78 million bottles but also Ballantine´s volumes were more than satisfactory - up by 3% to 80 million bottles. Chivas Regal on the other hand saw volumes slipping by 2% while Glenlivet increased by 2% to 12.8 million bottles.

Since 2009, when the company sold Wild Turkey to Campari, Pernod Ricard hasn´t been represented in the American whiskey category. This changed in 2016 when the much smaller whiskey maker Smooth Ambler was acquired to fill the bourbon gap.

In summer 2017, another three stills were installed at the Midleton distillery in Ireland thereby increasing the total capacity to 100 million litres. According to the owners this is what is needed to bring Jameson's volumes from the current 6.5 million cases to 20 million in a decade. Considering the fact that the company sold off Paddy Irish whiskey to Sazerac, it is obvious that focus will be on Jameson.

During the year, Pernod Ricard also decided to close down their packaging and bottling plant in Paisley and move the operations to their other site in Kilmalid, Dumbarton, 12 miles to the north. The transition is expected to take place in 2019.

Edrington

Compared to the previous year, with flat sales and declining profits, the fiscal year ending March 2017 was a source of joy for the owners. Net sales were up by 6% to £668m while net profits soared, increasing by 32% to £91m. When profits fell the year before, it was partly due to the strength of the pound. This year it was the other way around with a weaker pound because of Brexit.

If we look at the key brands, the two single malts went in different directions in terms of volumes; Macallan was up 5% and Highland Park decreased by 5%. Major gains for Macallan could be found in the USA and travel retail. The owners view the latter channel as important for premium spirits such as Macallan. On the other hand, in recent years duty-free margins have dropped and the projected growth figures for Highland Park travel retail has therefore been revised. The Orkney malt recieved a complete revamp of the range in spring 2017 with a new design, new expressions and, not least, a new message - the whisky is for people with a Viking Soul where the company play on the strong, historic connections between Orkney and the Vikings.

As for the two major blends, Famous Grouse delivered a very healthy growth in volumes of 14%, delivering its highest ever market share in the UK. Cutty Sark, on the other hand, continued its decline with a volume loss of 8% but still managed to grow the profit.

Since 2015, the company has followed what they call the 2020 Strategy which can be summed up as "Perfect The Macallan, Accelerate Highland Park, Develop Super-Premium, Optimise Regional Power Brands". Recently, Edrington also moved its head quarter from Perth to Queen Street in Glasgow. The year 2017 also saw the return of ownership of The Glenrothes brand which has been in the hands of Berry Brothers for the past seven years

Gruppo Campari

With the sale of their remaining assets in the wine business, Campari are now completely focused on the spirits side. The figures for 2016, showed an increase in net sales of +4.2% to €1726m while the net profit went the other direction, -5.2%, landing on €175m. The reason for the drop in profits were transaction costs due to the takeover of Grand Marnier but also restructuring projects and debt refinancing. The agreement to acquire Grand Marnier and its parent company, states that the complete take-over should be completed by 2021. The company announced in July 2017, that the Irish cream whiskey liqueur Carolans and Irish Mist liqueur and whiskey had been sold to Heaven Hill Brands. At $165m, this was the largest disposal of brands ever completed by Campari.

The biggest brands in the group are called Global Priorities and include Campari, Aperol, Skyy, Wild Turkey and Grand Marnier, while their only Scotch single malt, Glen Grant, is labelled as a Regional Priorities brand. Sales figures for Campari and Aperol were particularly good in 2016, not least in the most important market, USA. Volumes of Glen Grant increased by 3% and 3.5 million bottles were sold. The whole ranged was re-launched in summer 2016 and includes two new expressions (12 and 18 year old).

Ian Macleod Distillers

The family-owned bottler and owner of Glengoyne and Tamdhu distilleries, is the tenth largest whisky firm in Scotland. The results for the financial year ending September 2016 followed the same strong trend as it had done during the previous few years. From a turnover of £64.8m, the company could present a pre-tax profit of £11.5m.

Apart from Tamdhu and Glengoyne single malts, the company also acts as an independent bottler by releasing malts from other distilleries under the name of Dun Bheagan and The Chieftain´s. Isle of Skye (with four different expressions) is a blended malt and there is also Smokehead, a peated single malt from Islay. In addition to this, it also produces gin and vodka, as well as selling bulk whisky to customers who wish to create their own brand, both within the UK and abroad. In September 2016, the company acquired Spencerfield Spirit which was created a few years ago by Alex and Jane Nicol. The deal included Edinburgh Gin with two distilleries as well as the blended malt Sheep Dip and Pig´s Nose blended Scotch.

Beam Suntory

When Suntory bought Beam Inc in May 2014 for $16bn, a new company called Beam Suntory was formed. It is now the third largest drinks group in the world after Diageo and Pernod Ricard. The new company is owned by Suntory Holdings. Before the merger, Suntory´s portfolio included Japanese brands such as Yamazaki, Hakushu, Hibiki and Kakubin. With the deal, a range of other spirit brands have been added to the list; Jim Beam bourbon, Teacher´s blended Scotch, the two single malts Laphroaig and Ardmore, as well as Canadian Club and Courvoisier cognac.

Beam Suntory Inc is a part of Suntory Holdings´ alcoholic beverage operations which also includes beer and wine. For 2016, sales for the entire division slipped by 3.6% while operating profits rose by 13%. The decline in sales was due to a bad year for beer. Wines increased marginally while the spirits division, Beam Suntory, posted "mid-single-digit" growth. Jim Beam and Maker´s Mark were the two brands which primarily contributed most value to the positive result. Looking at the Scotch whisky brands, Teacher´s was a disappointment and has lost nearly 15% of its volumes in the last two years. The three major single malt brands on the other hand, increased their volumes; Laphroaig (+2.3%), Bowmore (+4.6%) and Auchentoshan (+23%).

The merger of the two companies hasn't been problem free. Two different corporate cultures have been difficult to integrate and Suntory Holdings CEO Takeshi Niinami, stressed that "I have placed top priority on the integration of Beam Suntory".

Brown Forman

The backbone of Brown Forman´s business is Jack Daniel´s – the most sold American whiskey in the world and is in sixth place of all whiskies that are produced. No less than 149 million bottles were sold in 2016. The company has also announced that an extension of the range, Jack Daniel´s Tennessee Rye, will be launched in autumn 2017. Other brands in the portfolio include Finlandia vodka, Woodford Reserve bourbon, El Jimador tequila and, since spring 2016, BenRiach Distillery Company with BenRiach, GlenDronach and Glenglassaugh. The company also has an interest in Irish whiskey through the ownership of Slane Irish Whiskey.

The figures for the fiscal year ending April 2017, showed sales slipping by 3% to $3,857m while net profits dropped by 37% to $669m. The last figure is not as alarming as it looks. The large profit from the year before was due to the sale of Southern Comfort. If one compares the profit 2016/2017 to the ones for 2014/2015, it is still a decrease but only by 2%.

A rumour was floating around in May 2017, that Constellation Brands had made an offer to take over Brown Forman. The comment from Brown Forman CEO Paul Varga was that the company "is not for sale". Even though Brown Forman is listed on the New York Stock Exchange, 67.4% of its shares are held by members of the Brown family.

Inver House Distillers

Inver House Distillers is a part of International Beverage Holdings which is the international arm of ThaiBev and they own and operate five distilleries in Scotland. The last financial statement which was available at the time of going to press, is 2015. At first glance, the figures were nothing to be happy about. Turnover was down by 15% to £67.2m while pre-tax profits fell 19.5% to £9.5m. However, there is an explanation for the worsening results. The company´s current strategy is to move away from the sales of bulk whisky in order to focus on their core brands, especially the single malts but also the super-premium gin Caorunn which is produced at Balmenach distillery.

The company has invested heavily in the last couple of years, both in producion capacity at Speyburn and in maturation capacity with 12 new warehouses being built. With this in place, Inver House is now targeting new markets in Kazakhstan, Poland and India. In February 2017, Inver House secured a £45m loan to support the growth plans.

Rémy Cointreau

Not least thanks to a rebound for the cognac Rémy Martin in China and also in USA, Rémy Cointreau could report a sales growth of 4.2% to €1.09 billion for the financial year 2016/2017. Net profits were improved by 22.3% to €135m. The division Liqueurs & Spirits, which also includes Bruichladdich whisky and Botanist gin, was up 19.9% and without specifying any numbers, the company said both brands posted "double digit" gains. The company has also created a dedicated whisky division which apart from Bruichladdich also contains the French distillery Domaine des Hautes Glaces and Westland Distillery based in Seattle. Both distilleries were acquired in 2016. The new division will by headed by Simon Coughlin, former CEO of Bruichladdich.

The big brands

The biggest whisky market in the world is India. At least when we are using 'whisky' in the broad sense of the word. Most Indian whiskies cannot be sold for example in the EU as it has been made from molasses and not from any form of grain. But let's leave that aside for the moment and have a look at a market that is not only huge but also extremely competitive and exciting.

India is the world's third largest global spirits market by volume with China and Russia taking the top spots. However, it is also true that alcohol consumption in India is among the lowest in the world (0.9 litres compared to 4.5 litres which is the global average) but with 1.3 billion people, the market still becomes huge. The Indian alcohol market is growing and mainly due to three factors; urbanization, changing social norms and a rise in disposable income. But in spite of these positive factors, the drawback is that the market is highly regulated and difficult to navigate. The industry is subject to state laws and since the country has 29 states and another 7 territories with their own regulations and governments, there are few companies that can afford to be active on a national basis. To complicate things even further, there is a complete ban on liquor advertising in India. Moreover, a handful of states are so called dry states prohibiting sales of alcohol. Other states are considering imposing prohibition as well but then again there are states that have recently repealed a previous prohibition.

For the fifth year in a row, Officer's Choice is number one of the Indian whiskies and therefore also in the world. It managed to sell 395 million bottles in spite of 5% decrease in 2016. Of the 10 most sold whiskies in 2016, seven come from India and it's only Johnnie Walker, Jack Daniels and Jim Beam that have managed to prevent total domination.

If we look at the Top 30 whisky brands, the list contains 12 Indian whiskies, 10 Scotch, three from America, two from Canada, two from Japan and one from Ireland.

Blended Scotch

Still the category leader but fighting against a downward trend is Johnnie Walker. Last year it was the third most sold whisky in the world but due to a 1% decrease in 2016, the brand was surpassed by two Indian whiskies and is now in fifth place with total sales of 213 million bottles. However, looking at sales for the mega brand in fiscal 2016/17, it looks as though Johnnie Walker is back on track when Diageo reported an increase of 4% and a particularly good performance in India (+23%) but also in the US, Mexico and Europe. Ballantine's is still holding on to second place, a position it has maintained since 2007. Ballantine's is also the only of the leading blended Scotch brands that has managed to increase volumes since 2012 (+10.1%). The last two years have been remarkably good for the brand with an increase of 5% in 2015 and another 8% in 2016 with total sales of more than 77 million bottles. Similar to last year, it is a close call between Chivas Regal and Grant's on third and fourth place. Drinks International have Grant's as number three with 54 million bottles and Chivas Regal slightly behind with 52 million. The IWSR on the other hand declares Chivas as the winner but with the brand showing a downward trend while Grant's is moving upwards. There is no doubt about number five though - it's still J&B, which despite falling figures almost every year for the last

Officer's Choice - the most sold whisky in the world

decade managed to sell 41 million bottles. Last year we posed the question if William Lawson´s, which had quickly climbed the list over the last few years, would actually challenge J&B during 2016. This wasn't the case however, in fact, Lawson's dropped two places. New at number six is Famous Grouse which despite several years of falling sales, increased with 3% to 36 million bottles, closely followed by William Peel, owned by the French company Belvédère, which over the past three years increased with 13% and managed to sell 35 million. Not until eighth place with 34 million bottles do we find Lawsons, the biggest climber over the past decade, which for the first time in a while felt the effect of falling sales (-3%). Soon after in ninth place we find Lawson's stable mate Dewars (both owned by Bacardi) which with a positive increase of 2% sold 32 million bottles and in tenth place, just like last year, is Label 5 with 26 million bottles.

Single Malt Scotch

In the last few years the question has been which one of Glenfiddich and Glenlivet is the most sold single malt in the world. The former was the dominant from 1963 until 2014 when Glenlivet took over the leader's jersey. An impressive achievement by Chivas Bros flagship which as recently as 10 years ago sold "merely" 60% of Glenfiddich´s volumes. However, according to the IWSR, in 2015 Glenfiddich was back in pole position and in 2016, thanks to a 9% increase and more than 14 million bottles, they increased the gap to number two Glenlivet which sold just under 13 million. Together, the two account for almost one quarter of all Scotch single malt sold globally.

Amongst single malts there is a magic barrier of 1 million 9-litre cases sold in a year and with the two mentioned being the only ones that have succeeded, the next to make the attempt will be Macallan which is currently in third place with an increase of 4% in 2016 and 10 million bottles sold (equates to 833,000 cases). If the current trend continues, they may very well reach the 1 million limit in just a couple of years. Another brand which is definitely on the move is Glenmorangie in fourth place. With increasing sales figures every year since 2009, they sold 6.6 million bottles in 2016. Right behind Glenmorangie is The Singleton with sales of 6 million bottles in 2016. Diageo´s goal is to put the brand in the top spot in a not so distant future. With increasing sales every year since the launch in 2006, perhaps it can be achieved. On the other hand, The Singleton is actually made up of three sub-brands - which can come from either Glen Ord, Dufftown or Glendullan distilleries. So regardless of the very impressive sales records and intelligent branding, I prefer to look at The Singleton as three brands but since Diageo never make the respective sales volumes public but rather present a total, the brand now comes in at spot number five. In sixth place we find the most popular Scotch single malt in France, namely Aberlour. In just seven years, the whisky has more than doubled in sales volumes and passed brands like Laphroaig, Balvenie, Glen Grant and Cardhu. More than 4 million bottles were sold in 2016. The world´s best-selling Islay malt, and the only one in the Top 10, comes in at place number seven. Sales of Laphroaig increased by 3% and reached 3.7 million bottles. The new number eight (in place 9 last year) is Balvenie which displayed the greatest percentile increase among

the Top 10 during 2016. With volumes up by 12%, the number of bottles sold was 3.6 million. After a long time of declining sales figures, Glen Grant managed in 2013 to change the trend and they are continuing along that track. A 3% increase in 2016 gave them the number 9 spot with 3.5 million bottles. In tenth place, for the third consecutive year, following an impressive increase in the last decade is Talisker with 2.7 million bottles which was an increase of 6% compared to last year.

Finally, let´s have a look at the top whiskies in North America, India and Ireland.

In North America, Jack Daniel´s is the undisputed leader and the sixth most sold whisky in the world with 149 million bottles, followed by the bourbon Jim Beam (96 million), the Canadian Crown Royal (82 million and an impressive increase of 27% since last year), the bourbon Evan Williams (28 million) and in fifth place, Canadian Club (24 million).

We have already mentioned India, having the biggest whisky brands in the world. For 2016, Officer´s Choice still reigns supreme with 395 million bottles, followed by McDowell´s No. 1 (306 million), Imperial Blue and Royal Stag (216 million each) and Original Choice (130 million).

The Irish whiskey industry is dominated by three big brands with Jameson in top spot with 74 million bottles and a growth since last year of 17%. This is followed by Tullamore Dew (12 million bottles and for the first time over one million cases) and Bushmill´s (8.9 million bottles).

Changes in ownership

In the last three years we have seen three major take-overs or acquisitions being made in the Scotch whisky industry. The one which made the most noise was of course when Suntory took over Beam Inc in 2014 for the amazing price tag of $16bn, thus creating the third biggest drinks group in the world. That same year, Emperador bought Whyte & Mackay for £430m and two years later, Brown-Forman snapped up BenRiach Distillers with £281m changing hands. That last deal meant £95m for Billy Walker who acquired BenRiach in 2004 and then followed up by adding GlenDronach and Glenglassaugh as well.

It became apparent in early summer 2017 that Walker, with 40 years' experience in the industry, had no intention of putting the money idle in the bank and retire from the whisky business. Rather surprisingly, it was announced that Chivas Bros were to sell their Glenallachie Distillery to Glenallachie Consortium comprising Billy Walker, Trisha Savage who has been working with Walker for a long time and Graham Stevenson who recently left his job as managing director of Inver House Distilleries. No sum was disclosed but the deal includes the distillery itself, two blended Scotch whisky brands (MacNair´s and White Heather) as well as sufficient stock, "to support the future development of those brands."

Glenallachie has been in the hands of Pernod Ricard since 1989 and has been an important part of the blend Clan Campbell. Commenting the deal, Pernod Ricard said it was in line with its "strategy to focus on its priority spirits and wines brands and to adjust its industrial footprint

Glenallachie Distillery was taken over by the Glenallachie Consortium

to its needs." The brands serving as the backbone for Pernod Ricard are Absolut vodka, Jameson Irish whiskey, Ballantine's and Glenlivet. They probably have no intention of getting rid of Clan Campbell which sells 20 million bottles every year but single malt for that blend can easily come from other distilleries in the group in the future. It is also worth noting that even though the company loses a 4 million litre/year distillery by selling Glenallachie, they added 10 million litres in 2015 when Dalmunach was opened and will gain another 10 million soon when the first Glenlivet expansion is completed.

With the comment "adjust its industrial footprint to its needs" the question arises if there are more distilleries that the company deem surplus and would consider putting up for sale in the future. Most of their distilleries are either important brands in themselves or vital components of blends but a few come to mind; Glentauchers, Braeval and Allt-a-Bhainne. We will just have to wait and see.

New distilleries

Scotland

In the first twelve years of the new millennium, six new malt whisky distilleries opened up in Scotland. There were also a handful of closed ones that became operational again. In the next four years, another fourteen distilleries came on stream and in 2017 alone, six more distilleries were added which means no less than 20 new distilleries in the last five years! We haven't seen anything like this since the booming years in the late 19th century. But the new enterprises do not really constitute a homogenous group. The yearly capacity ranges from 30,000 litres to well over 2 million and while some of them are truly experimental distilleries, stretching the boundaries of Scotch whisky making as we know it, there are others solidly founded in old traditions. Then of course, we also have the imminent expansions of three of the biggest distilleries (Macallan,

Glenlivet and Glenfiddich) which effectively will mean yet another three new distilleries with a huge capacity.

Behind all the newcomers and expansions, a crowd of entrepreneurs are lining up with their distillery projects in different stages of progress. Let's start on Islay. The 8th distillery and the latest to start producing on the island was Kilchoman back in 2005. In 2014, Jean Donnay, the owner of Glann ar Mor distillery in Brittany, France, secured a planning permission for what seemed to become the ninth distillery on Islay. An old farm just south of Bowmore would be transformed into Gartbreck – a traditional distillery with directly fired stills connected to a wormtub. Construction work was delayed on several occasions and in summer 2017 news emerged indicating the project may not come through after all. The reason is a land dispute between Jean Donnay and independent bottler Hunter Laing. Apparently Hunter Laing became involved in the Gartbreck project in 2015 with the intention of buying Gartbreck and retaining Donnay as a consultant, at least temporarily. Before the final contract had been signed, Hunter Laing started the preparations to build the distillery, including demolishing the old farm house. As it looks, they also bought an adjoining patch of land from Islay Estates, land that was deemed necessary for warehousing for the new distillery. Donnay pulled out of the deal and wanted to buy back the land from Hunter Laing without success. The two parties have different views as to what happened but currently, it seems the plans for Gartbreck distillery have been put on ice. The next new distillery on Islay will instead be Ardnahoe on the northeast coast near Bunnahabhain. The owners, Hunter Laing, were granted planning permission in 2016 and construction work is now underway with the intention of starting production in summer 2018. The estimated cost for the distillery is £8m and it will have an annual capacity of 500,000 litres of alcohol, although 200,000 litres will be the initial target. In February 2017, the legendary Jim McEwan, who retired from Bruichladdich in 2015, joined the team as production director. The distillery will be equipped with worm tubs with the aim of producing a tra-

The artist´s impression of the future distillery at Lagg on Arran

ditional, heavily peated Islay malt. Rumours of yet another distillery on lslay emerged a year ago. The name is supposed to be Farkin distillery and apparently Sukhinder Singh from the Whisky Exchange could be involved. A company named Farkin Distillery Limited was incorporated in May 2016 with an address in Campbeltown. The proposed site for the distillery is just outside Port Ellen.

More news from the Islands, this time on Arran. The success for Arran Distillery in Lochranza has prompted the owners to build yet another distillery on the island, this time on the south part in Lagg. The construction cost is £10m and the idea is to move the peated production from Lochranza to the new distillery. It is due to open in 2018 and will have a capacity of 500,000 litres. When operational, the combined number of visitors to the two distilleries is expected to be around 165,000!

Plans to build a distillery in the Shetlands have been around since 2002 involving different people and companies. Behind the most recent plan is the whisky consultant, Stuart Nickerson, former distillery manager at Highland Park and Glenglassaugh. Together with Debbie and Frank Strang, he built a gin distillery at Saxa Vord on Unst, the most northerly of the islands. A range of different gins have been released but it still remains to be seen if also whisky will be a part of the range in the future. Meanwhile sourced whisky has been released under the name Shetland Reel.

Finally, plans for the first distillery on Barra were announced ten years ago but very little has happened so far. There are also rumours of a distillery about to be built on the island of Benbecula.

Over to the mainland and let´s start in the Lowlands. The race for the first whisky distillery in The Borders in modern times, was won by The Three Stills Company which opened The Borders Distillery in Hawick in autumn 2017. There are more projects in the loop though. R&B Distillers, which recently opened their first distillery on Raasay, will now be focusing on their second in The Borders. They recently joined forces with Alasdair Day who´s been nurtur-

ing plans for a distillery for a couple of years. Meanwhile, already in 2010, Day launched a blended whisky called The Tweeddale with the intention of recreating a brand from the late 1800s. Plans for a third, potential distillery in The Borders have been presented by Mossburn Distillers, owners of the second distillery on Skye, Torabhaig, which opened in 2017. Planning permission was granted in December 2016 for the building of, not one, but two distilleries on the site of Jedforest Hotel near Jedburgh. The first of the two, named Jedhart Distillery, to be built will be equipped with three stills and the intention according to the owners is to "focus on small production and educating visitors on the craft of making spirit." The next stage involves building Mossburn Distillery and visitor centre with the capacity of producing 2,5 million litres per year including also grain whisky. The goal is to have Jedhart distillery up and running by 2018 while Mossburn could be producing in 2021. Mossburn Distillers is owned by Marussia Beverages, a Dutch company specialising in spirits and fine wine and that company is a part of the privately owned Swedish group Haydn Holding.

Moving on to the west, The Ardgowan Distillery Company received planning permission in March 2017 to build a distillery on the Ardgowan Estate, 30 miles west of Glasgow. The goal is to have the distillery in production by 2019 and, while having a capacity of 800,000 litres of pure alcohol per year with the possibility of expanding to 1.6 million litres, the initial production will be around 200,000 litres of both peated and unpeated spirit. The company now hope to raise £17m through equity shares, loans and grant funding. That sum should also cover production costs for the first three years.

Two malt distilleries have opened in Glasgow in the last two years and now it seems there´s going to be three in a year or two. Douglas Laing & Co was established in 1948 and was for many years managed by Fred and Stewart, sons of the founder. In 2013, the brothers went separate ways with Stewart forming a new company, Hunter Laing while Fred continued with the present company. Being

David Robertson, founder of the Holyrood Distillery in Edinburgh

independent bottlers, which is a very contradictory name as these companies are very much depending on whisky from the producers, both companies felt they were in an exposed position without a distillery of their own. As mentioned, Hunter Laing are at the moment building Ardnahoe Distillery on Islay and in July 2017, it was announced that Douglas Laing would also become distillers. Their chosen site in Glasgow is on the banks of the river Clyde just opposite the new Clydeside Distillery which opened in 2017. The total cost for the distillery is £10.7m but this also includes a bottling complex, a new corporate head office, a visitor centre, whisky laboratory and archive. Initial capacity will be 100,000 litres of pure alcohol and the hope is that the distillery will be operational by the end of 2018.

From one of the big cities to the other, Edinburgh, where David Robertson has decided to bring back malt whisky distilling to the capital after almost 100 years (Glen Sciennes having closed in 1925). Robertson has more than 25 years of experience working for Diageo, Edrington and Whyte & Mackay. Planning permission was granted in August 2016 for Holyrood Distillery which will be built in the 180 year old, renovated Engine Shed building next to Holyrood Park. The distillery will be able to produce 100,000 litres annually. A funding drive was launched in June 2017 to secure the £5.5m needed for the project and if everything goes according to plans, the distillery could be ready to produce by the end of 2018. It will probably take a little longer for another Edinburgh distillery to start up. Patrick Fletcher and Ian Stirling haven´t applied for a planning permission yet but they have chosen the site in Leith beside Ocean Terminal Shopping Centre and the Royal Yacht Britannia. Once operational, the distillery will be producing 400,000 litres of pure alcohol per year and there will also be a visitor centre with a shop, restaurant and bar. And if that wasn´t enough, there are plans for a third distillery in Edinburgh. Family-owned Halewood Wines & Spirits have applied for planning permission to build a combined gin- and whisky distillery in Granton Harbour. The company currently exports wines and spirits to 90 countries around

the world and they also have a shareholding in West Cork Distillers in Ireland. The plan is to build a distillery with one pair of stills with a capacity of producing 165,000 litres of pure alcohol yearly.

Remaining in the Lowlands, there are another four projects in the works. The Falkirk Distillery Company is in the latter stages of constructing their distillery at Salmon Inn Road, Polmont and hopes to open it to the public by October 2017. The final approval was granted in 2010 and in 2013, the owners Fiona and Alan Stewart were awarded a grant of £444,000 by the Scottish Government.

A new farm distillery is also planned in Lochlea, Ayrshire just south of Kilmarnock. The man behind it, Neil McGeoch, had his planning application approved by the local council in autumn 2015 but construction has not yet started.

Bladnoch distillery in Wigtown might soon get a distillery neighbour situated just 20 kilometres to the north in Newton Stewart. Local businessman, Graham Taylor, managing director of Crafty Scottish Distillers, is building a combined gin, vodka and whisky distillery and the plan is to have the distillery up and running in autumn 2017.

Campbell Meyer & Co, blenders, bottlers and exporters of whisky, owns a 150,000 square ft bonded warehouse in East Kilbride, just south of Glasgow. In spring 2016, it was announced that the company had plans to add a distillery as well. Supposedly to be built in the former Rolls Royce factory, the owners have been advised by the experienced whisky consultant Harry Riffkin but as of yet no further news of the new Burnbrae distillery has been reported.

Let´s head north now. Morrison & MacKay owns and operates Scottish Liqueur Centre which is situated in Bankfoot, 5 miles north of Perth. In January 2015, Morrison & MacKay received £430,000 from the Scottish Government to build a distillery in Abergaire just south of Perth and their planning application was approved in May 2016. The distillery will be equipped with one pair of stills and four washbacks with a possibility of expanding to eight washbacks.

Alltech co-founders Deirdre and Pearse Lyons at the Pearse Lyons Distillery in Dublin.

Up in Speyside, The Cabrach Trust have plans to build a distillery in the village of Cabrach south of Dufftown. The idea is to convert the old Inverharroch Farm to a distillery and heritage centre and it will be operated as a social enterprise. A planning application was submitted to the council end of June 2017 and the forecast is to be operational by 2020.

North of Inverness we have five distillery projects so let´s start from the south with Glen Wyvis in Dingwall where local farmer and helicopter pilot, John McKenzie has initiated the building of Scotland's (and possibly the world's) very first community owned whisky distillery. A planning application was submitted in March 2016 and by summer more than £2.5 million had been raised via a community share offer. Construction started in January 2017 and production may start in late 2017. The Glen Wyvis distillery will be equipped with eight washbacks and two stills, which were being manufactured as I visited Forsyths in May, with a capacity of producing up to 200,000 litres of pure alcohol. The distillery is being built in classic whisky land. Just east of Dingwall, the oldest recorded whisky distillery in Scotland, namely Ferintosh, was established in 1690 and the town itself had a distillery until 1926 when Ben Wyvis closed.

Ardross Investments Ltd have plans to build a distillery in Ardross, just northwest of Alness. Planning approval was granted in February 2017 and the owners anticipate that the distillery will be producing by summer 2018. An old farm site will be transformed into a distillery with the unusually large capacity of 1 million litres of pure alcohol.

Quite possibly, Heather Nelson will be the first woman to found a Scotch whisky distillery. Co-owner of a film and TV production company, Nelson has studied at the Institute of Brewing and Distilling to gain the necessary qualification. Her planning application to build a distillery on the old World War II airbase at Fearn near Tain was submitted in March 2017 and was approved in just four weeks. The distillery will be equipped with two stills (1,000 and 600

litres respectively) and three washbacks with a capacity of producing 30,000 litres. Nelson will be making both peated and unpeated whisky and if everything goes according to plans, she will start production by the end of 2017.

A bit further north, just south of Brora, lies Dunrobin Castle which attracts 85,000 visitors each year. Here, Elizabeth Sunderland, a granddaughter of the former head of Clan Sutherland, and her husband Boban Costin will build a single estate distillery housed in an old powerhouse. Planning permission was granted in late 2016 and the owners hope to have the distillery up and running by summer 2018. Equipped with two stills and producing both gin and whisky, the distillery will have an initial capacity of 95,000 litres with the possibility of growing to 300,000 litres. Elizabeth Sunderland´s forefathers were the founders of Clynelish distillery in 1819.

The surroundings of Loch Eriboll in the northwest corner of the Highlands are one of the remotest parts of Scotland and subsequently have the lowest population density in the UK. This is now the most unlikely scene of a new distillery project. Construction tycoon David Morrison incorporated Loch Eriboll Distillery Ltd in March 2015. His plan is to build a whisky/gin/vodka distillery, as well as a microbrewery.

All in all, at least 22 new distilleries either being built as we speak or in a planning stage which, if they all succeed, would bring the total number of working Scotch malt whisky distilleries to a total of 140 in a couple of years.

Ireland & Northern Ireland

In Malt Whisky Yearbook 2017, we could report on six new distilleries in Ireland and Northern Ireland that had started to produce. One year later, there is only one more that has been moved from this chapter to "Distilleries around the world" – Slane Distillery. That means a total of twenty producing distilleries compared to just three a

Gerry Ginty (left) and Asley Gardiner (right) together with Sarah Slazenger, owner of Powerscourt Estate and Gardens.

decade ago. But it also means that many of the ongoing projects still haven´t been able to turn their plans into a working distillery, often due to lack of funds or delays relating to planning applications.

Let´s start in Dublin where in 2015, Jack and Stephen Teeling opened up the first whisky distillery in the city in 125 years. It won´t be long though before there are at least three more within walking distance from Teeling. The first one to open in autumn 2017, is Pearse Lyons Distillery in St James´ Street. The old St James´ Church has been meticulously restored and now houses the distillery equipped with copper pot stills from Vendome in Kentucky. Newly commissioned stained glass windows tell the story of brewing and distilling. The distillery sits 300 yards away from the Guinness Brewery, one of the most visited attractions in Dublin and the owner, Dr Pearse Lyons, hope to benefit from this for his own distillery. The Lyons family has strong connections with St James´ Church. His father was born near the church and his grandfather was one of the last people buried in the graveyard. After working for Irish Distillers, Dr Lyons moved to the US in 1977 and in 1999, he purchased the Lexington Brewing and Distilling Company in Kentucky.

Dublin Whiskey Company has plans to rebuild a former mill in Dublin´s Liberties less than 500 metres from St Patrick´s Cathedral and converting it into a whiskey distillery. The project came to a temporary halt in April 2014 but in March 2016, the company was bought by the UK-based drinks group, Quintessential Brands, and construction of the new distillery has now started. In summer 2017, Stock Spirits Group acquired 25% of Quintessential Brands and also agreed to invest another €18.3m in the new distillery.

Another company with a similar name, Dublin Whiskey Distillery Company Ltd, was founded in 2014 and more than €500,000 has been invested in the company by a number of businessmen including the former Diageo executive, Lorcan Rossi. Whether or not they will actually go ahead and build a distillery has not yet been decided. As Lorcan

Rossi says "Owning a distillery is not a prerequisite for making a great whiskey." The fourth proposed distillery in Dublin will be built by one of the heavyweights in the industry, namely Diageo. The company withdrew from the Irish whiskey scene in 2014 when they sold Bushmills. Three years later, they seemed ready for a comeback when they announced that not only were they about to release an Irish blend called Roe & Co but that they also have plans to build a distillery in the old Guinness power station in St James' gate. The distillery is expected to start production in the first half of 2019. The Roe & Co blend, which was released in spring 2017, takes its name from the George Roe & Co distillery in Dublin which closed in 1926.

Moving over to western Ireland, Jude and Paul Davis are working on the construction of their Nephin Distillery in County Mayo but a cooperage has already been opened. They have recently managed to secure funds for the project which is estimated to cost €5 million. The proposed capacity of the distillery is 500,000 litres and the use of local peat will add to the character of the whiskey. Unlike many other new distillers, Nephin will not source whiskey from other producers to sell under its own name, but prefers to wait until its own whiskey is ready to be bottled.

While still on the west coast, we can report on a few more projects. Planning permission was approved in 2014 for Burren Distillers to build a distillery in the coastal village, Ballyvaughan. The planned capacity is 100,000 litres. Software developer, David Raethorne, has recently bought Hazelwood House in Co. Sligo and plans to restore the mansion which was built in the early 1700s. Adjacent to the house lays a factory where Raethorne will establish a craft distillery called Lough Gill, as well as a visitor´s centre. Sliabh Liag Distillery in south west Donegal, received a planning permission in early 2017 and are hoping to start the construction by the end of the year to be able to start production in 2019. Meanwhile, a sourced blended whiskey named Silkie was released by the owners in summer 2016.

Moving down to the southeast in Co. Cork and Co.

Waterford, there are at least three distilleries which are being planned. Gortinore distillery, with Denis and Aidan Mehigan, has acquired The Old Mill in Kilmacthomas and plans to turn it into a distillery with three pot stills. Until the distillery has been built, a range of sourced whiskies under the name Natterjack has been launched.

The island co-op at Cape Clear, six kilometres off the Cork coast, received planning permission in August 2016 to build a €7m distillery on the island. Unfortunately along the way, one of their major investors pulled out and the owners are now looking for other ways of funding the project. Peter Mulryan is already producing gin and vodka at his Blackwater Distillery in Cappoquin in West Waterford. He is now planning an expansion with more stills in order to produce whiskey as well.

Tipperary Boutique Distillery was founded more than two years ago but a distillery has yet to be built. Local farmer, Liam Ahearn, and his wife, Jennifer Nickerson, have chosen the Ahearn Family farm between Clonmel and Tipperary as the designated spot for their distillery. Home-grown barley will be used for the future whiskey production. In addition to this, they have also included Jennifer´s father in the business. Stuart Nickerson is well-known to lovers of Scotch after having been the distillery manager at Glenmorangie and the mastermind behind the resurrection of Glenglassaugh. In March 2016, the company released a sourced 11 year old Irish single malt under the name The Rising and more bottlings have followed.

South of Dublin in Enniskerry, Co. Wicklow, lays the Powerscourt Estate and Gardens, a popular tourist attraction with 500,000 visitors per year and owned by the Slazenger family. Two local entrepreneurs, Gerry Ginty and Ashley Gardiner, have now teamed up with the family to build a distillery on the estate. The whole investment will cost €10m and once at full production, the distillery will have the capacity of producing 1 million bottles per year. The planning application was approved in March 2016 and the plan is to have the distillery ready by early 2018. By June 2017, the company had managed to secure €7m of the investment needed. Recently, Cooley Distillery´s master distiller, Noel Sweeney left Cooley (where he has been since 1987) to join the Powerscourt team.

Finally, in Northern Ireland, there are currently three proposed distilleries. In Derry, the producer of cream liqueurs, Niche Drinks, has been granted a permission to build a distillery in Ebrington Square. The total investment will amount to £12m with a capacity of 500,000 litres of alcohol per year and the plan is to start production in June 2018 and to open a visitor centre a couple of months later. In anticipation of its own whiskey, the company has released a blend called The Quiet Man based on whiskies from other sources.

Peter Lavery, lottery millionaire and founder of The Belfast Distillery Company, has started to transform the former Crumlin Road jail into a whiskey distillery. Three stills have been ordered from Forsyth´s in Rothes and its capacity will be 300,000 litres of alcohol. The whole investment is expected to be £6.8m, but construction came to a temporary halt in spring 2016 when it was discovered that additional repairs to the old building had to be undertaken.

Joe McGirr is the mastermind behind Boatyard Distillery in Enniskillen and he has taken on Darren Rook as his right hand, who's known as the founder and owner of London Distillery Company. The company received its planning permission in December 2015 and in spring of the ensuing year, the first still (of 250 litres) was installed. The beginning of May marked the first distillation and initially gin and potato vodka will be produced with whiskey to follow at a later stage

Bottling grapevine

Back in the days, the prize for the most prolific producer every year went to Bruichladdich (and sometimes BenRiach) for releasing numerous new expressions every year. Not so this year. Without comparison, the good people of Highland Park are the ones that most of all deserve a long vacation. Not only did they revamp the entire core range. They also found time to launch no less than eight new expressions. First out was Valkyrie, the first of three in the new Viking Legend series with Valknut and Valhalla coming next. This was followed by Voyage of the Raven, based on first fill sherry, for duty free. Next was Full Volume, distilled in 1999, and a 100% first fill bourbon maturation. The extra smoky Dragon Legend, matured entirely in sherry casks (both American and European oak) is initially a UK exclusive while Magnus was reserved for the American market. Shiel, the second in the keystone range was released and then The Dark (sherry matured) and The Light (from refill American oak) were launched.

With Highland Park resting on their laurels, let´s move on to another producer of peated whisky - Ardbeg. With only three core expressions in their range for the past ten years they enthused their followers with a fourth in the way of An Oa - a vatting of whiskies matured in several types of casks, i.a. PX sherry, ex-bourbon barrels and virgin oak and then married together in a 30,000 litre vat made of French oak. From Ardbeg we also had the new Kelpie and later in the year the 23 year old Twenty Something. Still on the smoky side but now in Speyside, Balvenie released The Balvenie Peat Week 2020 and Peated Triple Cask - their first expressions made from peated barley and not just matured in "smoky" casks.

Two distilleries celebrated their 120th anniversaries with commemorative releases. From Tamdhu came a 50 year old, the oldest ever bottling from the distillery while Glen Moray released their Mastery - a vatting of five different vintages from a variety of wine casks. As usual, Glenmorangie pleased their fans in February with a new whisky in the Private Edition range - the madeira influenced Bacalta and an old favourite made a comeback when a new edition of Astar, matured in casks made from slow growth Missouri oak was released. Also from Glenmorangie, we had the very rare Pride 1974.

Chivas Brothers gave some of their more unknown distilleries a well-deserved spot in the limelight when they launched the Distillery Reserve Collection with Braeval (16 years) and Glentauchers (15 years) being officially bottled for the first time. Laphroaig got rid of their old duty free expressions and replaced them with Four Oak and the 1815 Edition and they also followed up two oldies (30 and 32 year old) from the last years with a new 27 year old. Remaining on Islay, Bowmore also revamped their travel retail range and introduced 10 year old Dark & Intense, 15 year old Golden & Elegant and 18 year old Deep & Complex and they also made the final release of the very last bottles of the iconic Black Bowmore from 1964. Bruichladdich launched Black Art 5 and a 25 year old sherry cask while Kilchoman presented a Vintage 2009 and a whisky matured in Portuguese red wine casks. The owners of Bunnahabhain don't make life easy for their followers. The two new whiskies are superb but the names are as usual tongue wrecking - Stiùireadair and An Cladach! From BenRiach and GlenDronach we got more of their yearly single cask bottlings and BenRiach also released a 2009 Triple Distilled. Bladnoch in the south had two reasons to celebrate this year - it was a 200th anniversary of the foundation of the distillery but they also fired up the stills under the new owner. To mark the occasion four new bottlings were released - Samsara, Adela, Talia and a Vintage 1988.

Glen Scotia added another two expressions to their core range, an 18 year old and a 25 year old while at the same time entering the duty free category with Glen Scotia Campbeltown 1832 and a 16 year old. Loch Lomond, in the same group, revived an old brand name when they launched the heavily peated Inchmoan in two versions - a 12 year old and the Vintage 1992. Glengyle continued with more bottlings of the 12 year old Kilkerran but also managed to add a limited 8 year old to the range. With the Glenrothes brand back with Edrington, the new, exclusive The Glenrothes Wine Merchant's Collection was launched. Whisky distilled in 1992 has received a two year finish in casks that have held wine, port, rum and sherry from famous producers. Edradour came out with an interesting experiment when they launched an 8 year old vatting of sherry matured Edradour and bourbon matured, peated Ballechin. Speyside distillery added another two bottlings to an already extensive range - the bourbon matured

Trutina and the smoky Fumare while Speyburn added a new 15 year old to their range. Tullibardine continued their Custodian's Collection with a Vintage 1962 and also released The Murray Chateauneuf-du-Pape bottled at cask strength. Always with something rare and old in the warehouses, Benromach presented a 1976 single cask as well as a 2009 Triple Distilled. The oldest releases so far from two distilleries were a Deanston 40 year old and a Singleton of Glen Ord 41 year old. After 40 years in the industry, Neil Cameron left Tullibardine and to honour him the 29 year old Cameron's Cut was released. Three new vintages were launched by Pulteney - 1983, 1990 and 2006 - and Tomatin focused on the effect of different cask maturations with their new range called Five Virtues. Down in Campbeltown, Springbank bottled a Springbank 14 year old bourbon cask and the Hazelburn Sherry Wood 13 year old replaced the Hazelburn 12 year old.

Finally - the Special Releases from Diageo. The company has struggled in later years to keep the new bottlings in the series a secret until the launch in October, so this year, all but one were revealed already in spring. According to tradition there is always an unpeated Caol Ila, this year an 18 year old and the yearly Lagavulin 12 year old cask strength was also anticipated. Apparently there is more stock available from two distilleries that were closed long ago evidenced by the 34 year old Brora and the 37 year old Port Ellen but yet another "ghost" distillery was represented this year - Convalmore with a 32 year old from 1984. Furthermore, Blair Athol 24 year old, Glen Elgin 18 year old and Teaninich 17 year old were also released as well as a very old single grain, the 52 year old Port Dundas. Finally, a surprise and the only bottling that wasn't part of the press release in April - Collectivum XXVIII. This is nothing less than a vatting of malt whiskies from all of Diageo's 28 malt distilleries which means Roseisle is also included.

Laphroaig 27 years, Port Dundas 52 years, Convalmore 32 years, Ardbeg An Oa and Collectivum XXVIII

Independent
bottlers

The independent bottlers play an important role
in the whisky business. With their innovative bottlings, they increase
diversity. Single malts from distilleries where the owners' themselves
decide not to bottle also get a chance through the independents.
The following are a selection of the major companies.
Tasting notes have been prepared by Suzanne Redmond.

Gordon & MacPhail

www.gordonandmacphail.com

Established in 1895 the company, which is owned by the Urquhart family, still occupies the same premises in Elgin. Apart from being an independent bottler, there is also a legendary store in Elgin and, since 1993, an own distillery, Benromach. There is a wide variety of bottlings, for example Connoisseurs Choice (single malts bottled at either 43 or 46%), MacPhail's Collection (single malts bottled at 43%), Distillery Labels (a relic from a time when Gordon & MacPhail released more or less official bottlings for several producers. Currently 10 distilleries are represented in the range and the whisky is bottled at either 40 or 43%), Rare Old (exclusive whiskies from distilleries that are closed and sometimes even demolished, for example Glenugie, Glenury Royal, Coleburn, Glenesk and Glenlochy), Cask Strength (a range of single malts bottled at cask strength), Rare Vintage (single malts, including several Glen Grant and Glenlivet bottlings going back to the 1940s) and Speymalt (a series of single malts from Macallan from 1938 and onwards).

In 2010, a new range was launched under the name Generations. To say that these are rare and old whiskies is an understatement. The first release was a Mortlach 70 year old, which was followed the year after by a Glenlivet 70 year old. In September 2015, it was time for the third instalment in the series - a Mortlach 75 years old. This is the oldest single malt ever bottled and only 100 bottles were released. In 2017, they launched the Glen Grant Collection which comprises of six bottles ranging from 1950 to 1955. Only 75 collections were released.

Gordon & MacPhail rarely buy matured whisky from other producers. Instead, around 95% is bought as new make spirit and filled by the company. Some 7,000 casks are maturing in one racked and one dunnage warehouse in Elgin, another 7,000 casks are found at various distillers around Scotland and 20,000 casks are located in the warehouses at Benromach.

Macduff 2004, 46%
Nose: Creamed asparagus, melon, salty sea air, barley and fresh lemongrass.
Palate: Similar to the nose but with some ripe fruit notes such as fresh bananas and warm pineapple.
Finish: Long with a tickle of pepper.

Dufftown 2008, 46%
Nose: Fresh meadow flowers, sultanas, light honeycomb, lemon balm and soft malty tones.
Palate: A nutty biscuit note hits first followed by warm caramel, plump sultanas, a flicker of lemongrass and straw.
Finish: Soft with medium length.

Berry Bros. & Rudd

www.bbr.com

Britain's oldest wine and spirit merchant, founded in 1698 has recently opened a new shop in London. The famous address 3 St James's Street, where the company has been since the start, has now been returned to its appearance of 30 years ago and this will no be a space for consultations, meetings and events. The new, and much larger store, is just around the corner in 63 Pall Mall. Berry Brothers had been offering their customers private bottlings of malt whisky for years, but it was not until 2002 that they launched Berry's Own Selection of single malt whiskies. Under the supervision of Spirits Manager, Doug McIvor, some 30 expressions are on offer every year. Bottling is usually at 46% but expressions bottled at cask strength are also available. The super premium blended malt, Blue Hanger, is also included in the range. In autumn 2014 the Exceptional Casks Collection was launched. Handpicked by Doug McIvor a 50 year old North British single grain, two single casks of Glenlivet 1972 and a Jamaican rum from 1977 were the first bottles in the new range. In 2010, BBR sold Cutty Sark blended Scotch to Edrington and obtained The Glenrothes single malt in exchange but in 2017, BBR sold back The Glenrothes to Edrington.

Glen Garioch 1989 26 years old, 46%

Nose:	Mango, banana, apricot with a gentle charred note pop on the nose. Add some proven dough for interest.
Palate:	Carrageen moss enhances the smoky notes. With some milk chocolate and semi-dried fruits this layered whisky is ripe.
Finish:	Long, developing length.

Ardmore 2008 8 years old, 46%

Nose:	Lemongrass, honey, leather and salty nuances are wrapped gently in a blanket of peat.
Palate:	It has a warm honey texture with notes of pear, juicy melon and fresh leather wrapped up with peat.
Finish:	Long length.

Signatory

Founded in 1988 by Andrew and Brian Symington, Signatory Vintage Scotch Whisky lists at least 50 single malts at any one occasion. The most widely distributed range is Cask Strength Collection which sometimes contains spectacular bottlings from distilleries which have long since disappeared. One good example is a very rare Glencraig 1976, 38 years old. Another range is The Unchill Filtered Collection bottled at 46%. Some of the latest bottlings released are spectacular; Craigduff 1973 (an extremely rare, peated Strathisla), Mosstowie 1979 and Glen Mhor 1982. Finally there is also the Single Grain Collection. Andrew Symington bought Edradour Distillery from Pernod Ricard in 2002 and the entire operations, including Signatory, are now concentrated to the distillery.

Ian Macleod Distillers

www.ianmacleod.com

The company was founded in 1933 and is one of the largest independent family-owned companies within the spirits industry. Gin, rum, vodka and liqueurs, apart from whisky, are found within the range and they also own Glengoyne and Tamdhu distilleries. Their single malt ranges are single casks either bottled at cask strength or (more often) at reduced strength, always natural colour and un chill-filtered. The Chieftain´s cover a range of whiskies from 10 to 50 years old while Dun Bheagan is divided into two series – Regional Malts, 8 year old single malts expressing the character from 4 whisky regions in Scotland and Rare Vintage Single Malts, a selection of single cask bottlings from various distilleries. There are two As We Get It single malt expressions – Highland and Islay, both 8 year olds and bottled at cask strength. The Six Isles blended malt contains whisky from all the whisky-producing islands while one of the top sellers is the blended malt Isle of Skye with five

domestic expressions – 8, 12, 18, 21 and 50 years old. Finally, Smokehead, a heavily, peated single malt from Islay introduced in 2006, has become a huge success. There is also a Smokehead Extra Black 18 years old, Smokehead Extra Rare (basically a 1 litre duty free bottling of the 12 year old) and the limited Smokehead Rock Edition. In September 2016, the company acquired Spencerfield Spirit which was created a few years ago by Alex and Jane Nicol. The deal included Edinburgh Gin with two distilleries as well as the blended malt Sheep Dip and Pig´s Nose blended Scotch.

Pig´s Nose, 40%

Nose:	Slightly vegetal fruit notes hit first followed by dusty fruit spice and dried cigar leaves with a flicker of iodine.
Palate:	Dried apricots with a warming spice roll onto the palate with chunky fruit cake notes.
Finish:	Medium length.

Sheep Dip, 40%

Nose:	Youthful with some depth. Notes of dandelion honey, wild mint and lightly toasted crushed nuts.
Palate:	Malted milk biscuits with hints of dried orange peel, hay, raw fruit spice and gentle notes of wild flower.
Finish:	Malty, medium finish.

Blackadder International

www.blackadder.se

Blackadder is owned by Robin Tucek, one of the authors of The Malt Whisky File. Apart from the Blackadder and Blackadder Raw Cask, there are also a number of other ranges – Smoking Islay, Peat Reek, Aberdeen Distillers, Clydesdale Original and Caledonian Connections. The company has also been known for bottling unusual expressions of Amrut single malt. All bottlings are single cask, uncoloured and un chill-filtered. Most of the bottlings are diluted to 43-46% but Raw Cask (a range of completely unfiltered whiskies) is always bottled at cask strength. Around 100 different bottlings are launched each year.

Creative Whisky Company

www.creativewhisky.co.uk

David Stirk started the Creative Whisky Co in 2005 and the company exclusively bottles single casks, divided into three series: The Exclusive Malts are bottled at cask strength and vary in age between 8 and 40 years. Around 20 bottlings are made annually. This is followed by the Exclusive Range which comprises of somewhat younger whiskies, between 8 and 16 years, bottled at either 45% or 45.8%. Finally, Exclusive Casks are single casks, which have been 'finished' for three months in another type of cask, e. g. Madeira, Sherry, Port or different kinds of virgin oak. In 2015, the company´s 10th anniversary was celebrated with a range of 7 new bottlings and this was followed up by The Exclusive Malts Ireland – a 13 year old single cask from Cooley. The most recent releases include Cameronbridge 33 years old, Invergordon 43 years old, Highland Park 25 years old and Glen Elgin 21 years old. David also works with rum and has recently released Stirk´s Gin.

Duncan Taylor

www.duncantaylor.com

Duncan Taylor was founded in Glasgow in 1938 as a cask broker and trading company. Over the decades, the company built strong ties with distillers over Scotland, with the company bringing their own casks to the distilleries to be filled with new make spirit. This resulted in a collection of exceptionally rare casks, many from distilleries which are now closed. Duncan Taylor was acquired by Euan Shand in 2001 and operations were moved to Huntly.

Duncan Taylor´s flagship brand is the blended Scotch Black Bull, a brand with a history going back to 1864. The brand was trademarked in the US on the repeal of prohibition in 1933 and was rebranded in 2009 by Duncan Taylor. The range consists of three core releases – Kyloe, a 12 year old and a 21 year old. There are also three limited versions, 30 year old, 40 year old and Special Reserve. The Black Bull brand is complimented by Smokin' which is a blend of peated Speyside, Islay and grain whisky from the Lowlands.

The portfolio also includes Rarest (single cask, cask strength whiskies of great age from demolished distilleries), Dimensions (a collection of single malts and single grains aged up to 39 years), The Octave (single malt whiskies matured or 'Octavised' for a further period in small, 50 litre ex-sherry octave casks), The Tantalus (a selection of whiskies all aged in their 40s) and The Duncan Taylor Single Range (whiskies aged 30 years or more from closed distilleries). The blended malt category is represented by Big Smoke, a young peated whisky available in two strengths, 40% and 60%.

Octave North British 1991 25 years old, 52.7%

Nose:	Confected strawberries, nutmeg, hints of kerosene, mingle with gently salted caramel.
Palate:	Lively candied ginger kicks in along with banana bread, gingernuts and nutmeg. Add a drizzle of warm caramel sauce to the mix.
Finish:	Medium length.

Octave Glentauchers 2008 9 years old, 48.1%

Nose:	Inviting notes of plump raisins and sultanas with mixed peppercorns and elegant oak.
Palate:	Gingerbread drizzled with caramel and sultanas pop initially followed by fruit spice and baked lemons.
Finish:	Long, warming finish.

Scotch Malt Whisky Society

www.smws.com

The Scotch Malt Whisky Society, established in the mid 1980s and owned by Glenmorangie Co since 2003, has more than 25,000 members worldwide and apart from UK, there are 17 chapters around the world. The idea from the very beginning was to buy casks of single malts from the producers and bottle them at cask strength without colouring or chill filtration. The labels do not reveal the name of the distillery. Instead there is a number but also a short description which will give you a clue to which distillery it is. The SMWS also arranges tastings at their different venues but also at other locations. In recent years, the range has been expanded to also include single grain, whiskies from other countries as well as rum. In April 2015, Glenmorangie sold the SMWS to the HotHouse Club and a group of the managers. In July 2017, a sub-brand named Single Cask Spirits was launched for the non-malt whisky releases (rum, gin, cognac and bourbon) and in autumn 2017, the Society launched their first blended malt - the 10 year old Exotic Cargo.

Murray McDavid

www.murray-mcdavid.com

The company was founded in 1996 by Mark Reynier, Simon Coughlin and Gordon Wright and in 2000, they also acquired Bruichladdich distillery. In 2013 Murray McDavid was taken over by Aceo Ltd. and a year later they signed a lease for the warehouses at the closed Coleburn distillery for storing their own whiskies as well as stock belonging to clients. The bottlings are divided into six different ranges; Mission Gold (exceptionally rare whiskies bottled at cask strength), Benchmark (mature single malts bottled at 46%), Mystery Malt (single malts where the distillery is not revealed), Select Grain (single grains), The Vatting (vatted malts) and Crafted Blend (blended Scotch from their own blending). The vast majority of the releases are single casks.

Compass Box Whisky Co

www.compassboxwhisky.com

John Glaser, founder and co-owner of the company, has a philosophy which is strongly influenced by meticulous selection of oak for the casks, clearly inspired by his time in the wine business. But he also has a lust for experimenting to test the limits, which was clearly shown when Spice Tree was launched in 2005. For an additional maturation, Glaser filled malt whisky in casks prepared with extra staves of toasted French oak suspended within the cask. In spring 2016, Compass Box launched a campaign for more transparency in the Scotch whisky industry. where a producer would be allowed to give "complete, unbiased and clear" information on the components of their whiskies. Today, under EU law, a producer is only allowed to disclose the age of the youngest whisky in a blend. Glaser wants to have a change where it is optional (but not compulsory) for a producer to give as much information as they desire.

The company divides its ranges into a Signature Range and a Limited Range. Spice Tree (a blended malt), The Peat Monster (a combination of peated islay whiskies and Highland malts), Oak Cross (American oak casks fitted with heads of French oak), Asyla (a blended whisky matured in first-fill ex-bourbon American oak) and Hedonism (a vatted grain whisky) are included in the former.

In the Limited range, whiskies are regularly replaced and at times only to resurface a couple of years later in new variations. Recent limited releases include 15th anniversary expressions of Hedonism and Flaming Heart and This Is Not A Luxury Whisky - a blend of 19 year old Glen Ord and 40 year old grain from Strathclyde and Girvan. In summer 2016 the releases were Enlightenment, which is a blend of four different single malts and bottled at 46% and Circus, an unusual vatting of two blended malts, a blended grain and Benrinnes single malt - all matured in sherry casks and bottled at 49%. These were followed up by Three Year Old Deluxe which contained less than 1% of 3 year old malt whisky while 90% was a considerably older malt from Clynelish and 9% was malt from Talisker. Finally theere was The Double Single which is a combination of Glen Elgin malt whisky and grain whisky from Girvan. A third range, Great King Street, offers blended Scotch with a 50% proportion of malt whisky and using new French oak for complexity. The first expression was called Artist's Blend and in autumn 2014 Glasgow Blend was released.

In autumn 2014, Compass Box made a long-term agreement with John Dewar & Sons where the Bacardi-owned company would supply Compass Box with stocks of whisky for future bottlings. In spring 2015 it was further announced that Bacardi had aqcuired a minority share of the independent bottler.

The Double Single, 46%

Nose:	Zingy lemongrass, melon, daisies, light caramel and white pepper.
Palate:	Caramel and spice hit first, with a flicker of lemongrass breaking the sweetness. Vanilla and cinnamon finish it off.
Finish:	Medium length.

Hedonism, 43%

Nose:	Black cherries, cloves and cardamom hit first then polished wood, lemon-thyme and fresh leather.
Palate:	The leather and black cherries hit first followed by a peppery note with a liquorice tang.
Finish:	Spicy, long length.

Master of Malt

www.masterofmalt.com

Master of Malt is one of the biggest and most innovative whisky retailers in the UK. The company also has its own ranges of award-winning bottled whiskies. One range is called the Secret Bottlings Series, where no distillery names appear on the labels. Although many of the competitively priced well-aged releases are now blended whiskies (30, 40 and 50 year olds), the range of no age statement regional single malt bottlings at 40% (Highland, Speyside, Lowland, Islay and Island) is continuing. They also bottled a 60 year old Speyside single malt. Their Single Cask Series, meanwhile, contains natural cask strength bottlings from various distilleries. Some of the latest are a 23 year old Glenrothes, a 14 year old Port Charlotte and a peated 5 year old from the English Whisky Co. You can also Blend Your Own whisky on the site. Another feature is that they stock thousands of Drinks by the Dram's 30ml bottles, allow customers to personalise the contents of Drinks by the Dram Tasting Sets as they order and now also offer a Dram Club whisky subscription service.

English Whisky Co. Heavily Peated 5 years old 2010, 67.4%

Nose: Lemon-thyme, proven dough, honeycomb with gentle earthy tones and a kiss of peat.

Palate: Quite bold on the palate with the peat notes being upfront. Herbal and citrus notes follow slowly with a flicker of cigar leaf and cocoa on the finish.

Finish: Long length.

Atom Brands

Part of the same Atom Drinks group as retailer Master of Malt, Atom Brands includes a number of independent bottlers. They're distributed by Maverick Drinks who also import many American craft whiskeys, including malts, from the likes of St. George Spirits, Balcones and FEW Spirits.

That Boutique-y Whisky Company

www.thatboutiqueywhiskycompany.com

Established in 2012, That Boutique-y Whisky Company's releases have all carried age statements since 2016. (Previously, the age difference between the whiskies in a single NAS batch had been as much as 30 years, but this is much less the case now.) TBWC has made it clear that they believe flavour is still the most important aspect, but are aware that customers are nonetheless interested in ages of the constituent parts. They have also offered their support to Compass Box's Campaign for Scotch Whisky. Over 250 different bottlings have now been released from more than 90 different distilleries including Springbank, Ardbeg, Mortlach, Port Ellen and Paul John. The range also includes a handful of blended malts, blends, single grains, bourbons and even ryes.

Port Ellen 33 years old, batch 6, 47.5%

Nose: Dried peat stored in a barn, sweet lemon and lime, toasted cereal notes and sticky toffee.

Palate: It has an elegant palate, sweet peat, chewy toffee and hints of toasted hazelnuts with a lick of black liquorice.

Finish: Super long length.

The Blended Whisky Company

www.theblendedwhiskycompany.com

The Blended Whisky Company, also established in 2012, produces The Lost Distilleries Blend, The Golden Age Blend and The Half-Century Blend. The Lost Distilleries Blend is made exclusively from whiskies produced at now closed distilleries. The ninth batch contains malts from Port Ellen, Brora, Rosebank Caperdonich, Mosstowie, Glenisla, Glen Mhor, Craigduff, Glenlochy and Imperial. The Golden Age Blend harks back to the early 1960s to mid 1970s and is made exclusively with whiskies that are at least 40 years old. Malts from Macallan, Glenrothes and Tamdhu are used as well as a little peated Bunnahabhain (with a ratio of four parts malt to just one part grain). The Half-Century Blend is made exclusively with whiskies over 50 years old and harks back to a time when distilleries were home to less efficient barley-strains, on-site floor maltings and inefficient brewer's yeast.

The Half-Century Blend, 45.5%

Nose: Brandy notes with freshly roasted chestnuts, baked apples, honey, oak and vanilla.

Palate: A creamy seductive dram with notes of warm apple pie drizzled with honey and toasted almonds. Add cigar leaves and a touch of bourbon sweetness.

Finish: Medium to long length with fresh orange.

Darkness!

www.darknesswhisky.com

The first whiskies from Darkness! were released in spring 2014 and the key words for these expressions are dark and heavily sherried. To create the character, single malts are filled into specially commissioned 50 litre first fill Sherry casks where they are finished for more than 3 months. Pedro Ximénez, Oloroso, Palo Cortado, Fino and Moscatel Sherry casks have all been used (specified on each bottling) as well as hybrid PX and Oloroso casks made up with staves from each. Recent releases include a 27 year old Bladnoch finished in an PX cask and a 22 year old Tobermory finished in a Moscatel cask.

Bladnoch 27 yeard old PX cask, 56.5%

Nose: Notes of gingerbread covered in toffee sauce, fresh apple, a flicker of orange and a mix of raisins and sultanas.

Palate: Pedro Ximénez sherry hits first swiftly followed by the raisins and sultanas mixed with spice. Autumnal fruits add a nice weight to the body.

Finish: Long expanding length.

A Dewar Rattray Ltd

www.adrattray.com

This company was founded by Andrew Dewar Rattray in 1868. In 2004 the company was revived by Tim Morrison, previously of Morrison Bowmore Distillers and fourth generation descendent of Andrew Dewar, with a view to bottling single cask malts from different regions in Scotland. One of its best-sellers is a single malt named Stronachie which is actually sourced from Benrinnes. Each Stronachie bottling is a batch of 6-10 casks and there is currently just the one expression, a 10 year old, but a special sherry finished version is also in the plans. A peated, blended malt, Cask Islay, became available in 2011 and released again in 2013 but this time as a single malt. In 2012 a new, 5 year old blend was launched under the name Bank Note. The AD Rattray´s Cask Collection is a range of single cask whiskies bottled at cask strength and without colouring or chill-filtration. This range was recently complemented by Vintage Cask Collection, including rare and older whiskies. AD Rattray is currently working on an extensive re-rack programme which includes finishing the same whisky in a variety of different cask types. In 2011, the company opened A Dewar Rattray´s Whisky Experience & Shop in Kirkoswald, South Ayrshire. Apart from having a large choice of whiskies for sale, there is a sample room, as well as a cask room. All the products in the shop, including per-sonalised own label single cask bottlings, are also available on-line from thewhiskyangel.com.

Bunnahabhain 30 years old, 48.3%
Nose: A tropical fruit basket of mandarin, nectarine, kiwi and walnut with notes of new leather and Aloe vera.
Palate: Lime, mango and coconut with toasted whole grain oats.
Finish: Fresh, fruity and opulent with bright green notes.

House Malt No. 8 - Macduff 2009
Nose: A likeable dram with Werthers Original toffee and vanilla pod.
Palate: Spiced oak, butterscotch, boiled cream sweets and Scotch tablet.
Finish: Light delicate spices linger.

The Whisky Agency
www.whiskyagency.de

The man behind this company is Carsten Ehrlich, to many whisky aficionados known as one of the founders of the annual Whisky Fair in Limburg, Germany. His experience from sourcing casks for limited Whisky Fair bottlings led him to start as an independent bottler in 2008 under the name The Whisky Agency. There are se-veral ranges including The Whisky Agency, The Perfect Dram and Specials with some unusual bottlings. One of the latest ranges is Good Vibes including both old expressions (Speyside region 40 and 43 years old) as well as younger bottlings (Caol Ila 8 years old).

Douglas Laing & Co
www.douglaslaing.com

Established in 1948 by Douglas Laing, this firm was run for many years by his two sons, Fred and Stewart. In 2013, the brothers decided to go their separate ways. Douglas Laing & Co is now run by Fred Laing and his daughter, Cara. Douglas Laing has the fol-lowing brands in their portfolio; Provenance (single casks typically aged between 8 and 20 years and bottled at 46%), Director´s Cut (old and rare single malts bottled at cask strength), Premier Barrel (single malts in ceramic decanters bottled at 46%), Clan Denny (two blended malts and a selection of old single grains), Double Barrel (two malts vatted together and bottled at 46%), Big Peat (a vatting of selected Islay malts) and Old Particular, a range of single malts and grains.

New releases in recent years include Scallywag, a blended malt influenced by sherried whiskies from Speyside and recently com-plemented by Scallywag Cask Strength Edition and Scallywag 13 years old. Timorous Beastie is a blended Highland malt with four expressions released so far - no age statement, 18, 21 and 40 years old while Rock Oyster (with a sherry edition released in 2017) is a blended malt combining whiskies from Islay, Arran, Orkney and

Jura and which can be found without age statement or as an 18 year old. All these whiskies are part of a range called Remarkable Regional Malts and in 2016, a fifth region was added when The Epicurean, a blended Lowland malt was released. In spring 2017, a new collection was introduced, themed around a deck of playing cards. The first release was Queen of the Hebrides (an 18 year old Laphroaig) followed by King of the Hills (Ben Nevis 20 years old).

In July 2017, it was announced that Douglas Laing would also become distillers. Their chosen site in Glasgow is on the banks of the river Clyde just opposite the new Clydeside Distillery which opened in 2017. Initial capacity will be 100,000 litres and the hope is that the distillery will be operational by the end of 2018. The total cost for the distillery is £10.7m but this also includes a bottling complex, a new corporate head office, a visitor centre, whisky laboratory and archive.

Timorous Beastie 18 years old, 46.8%
Nose: Roasted and dried corn leads onto leafy, honey notes with a touch of white peach.
Palate: A touch of jasmine rice with jeweled fruits. A flicker of lemongrass and meadow honey add another layer.
Finish: Long lingering length.

Scallywag 13 years old, 46%
Nose: Sweetened sultanas and candied ginger with a hint of blueberries kick start this energetic whisky.
Palate: Chewy toffee and raisins mingle with nutmeg and cigar notes. Ripe with good weight. Bit of a mini sherry bomb.
Finish: Medium to long length.

Malts of Scotland
www.malts-of-scotland.com

Thomas Ewers from Germany, bought casks from Scottish distil-leries and decided in the spring of 2009 to start releasing them as single casks bottled at cask strength and with no colouring or chill filtration. Apart from ranges of Scotch single malts, Ewers has also added three ranges called Malts of Ireland, Malts of India and Whiskeys of America. At the moment he has released more than 100 bottlings and apart from a large number of single casks, there are two special series, Amazing Casks and Angel´s Choice, both dedicated to very special and superior casks.

Hunter Laing & Co
www.hunterlaing.com

This company was formed after the demerger between Fred and Stewart Laing in 2013 (see Douglas Laing). It is run by Stewart Laing and his two sons, Scott and Andrew. The relatively new company Edition Spirits, founded by the sons has also been absor-bed into Hunter Laing with the range of single malts called First Editions.

From the demerger, the following ranges and brands ended up in the Hunter Laing portfolio; The Old Malt Cask (rare and old malts, bottled at 50%), The Old and Rare Selection (an exclusive range of old malts offered at cask strength) and The Sovereign (a range of old and rare grain whiskies). A new range with the name Hepburn´s Choice was launched in spring 2014. These single malts are younger than The Old Malt Cask expressions and bottled at 46%. A little later in the year, the blended malt Highland Journey was re-leased. In January 2016, the company announced their intentions of building a distillery on Islay and the construction work is now well

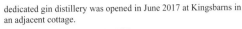

underway. Ardnahoe on the northeast coast near Bunnahabhain. will have a capacity of 500,000 litres and Jim McEwan, who retired from Bruichladdich in 2015, joined the team in 2017 as production director. McEwan was also responsible for selecting six single casks of rare Islay whiskies that were released in May under the label Feis Ile 2017 Kinship. The bottles are very limited and only available at Hunter Laing´s shop in Bridgend which will remain open until Ardnahoe opens in April 2018.

First Editions Braes of Glenlivet 1989, 27 years old, 54.9%
Nose: Yellow plums, a faint hint of chocolate, over ripe banana and dandelions flow slowly into the nose.
Palate: A warm seductive whisky with maple tones hitting the palate first, then the notes from the nose followed by orange.
Finish: Long ripe palate.

The Kinship Port Ellen 34 yers old, 61.6%
Nose: Quite fragrant with a touch of jasmine rice. White roses, limes and lilies mingle with bruised golden delicious and light chocolate tones.
Palate: White chocolate and melon pop first followed by jasmine, Turkish delight and a sweet smoke tone.
Finish: Long developing length.

Wemyss Malts
www.wemyssmalts.com

This family-owned company, a relative newcomer to the whisky world, was founded in 2005. The family owns another two companies in the field of wine and gin and in November 2014 they opened up their own whisky distillery at Kingsbarns in Fife. Based in Edinburgh, Wemyss Malts takes advantage of Charles MacLean´s experienced nose when choosing their casks. The family is mainly known for its range of blended malts of which there are three core expressions – The Hive, Spice King and Peat Chimney. These are available at 46% un chill-filtered and also in limited edition batch strength around 55%. In 2017, the family bottled a new part of their blended malt range called The Family Collection consisting of spirit sourced and fully matured by the family. There are two releases in 2017 – Vanilla Burst and Treacle Chest.

Another side of the business involves single malts. There are two ranges; one of which consists of single casks bottled at 46% or the occasional cask strength. The names of the whiskies reflect what they taste like although for some time now, the distillery name is also printed on the label. All whiskies are un chill-filtered and without colouring. In 2012, the company released its first premium blended whisky based on a selection of malt and grain whiskies aged a minimum of 15 years. The whisky is named Lord Elcho after the eldest son of the 5th Earl of Wemyss. The Lord Elcho range has since then been expanded with a no age statement version. Finally, the family has also had great success with their Darnley´s Gin and a

dedicated gin distillery was opened in June 2017 at Kingsbarns in an adjacent cottage.

Treacle Chest blended malt, 46%
Nose: Filled with plump dried fruits such as apricots, sultanas and apricots with a peppery, spicy edge.
Palate: Big robust flavours of nutmeg, cloves and cinnamon lead onto some sizeable sherry and plum jam tones.
Finish: Medium in length with the spice lingering on.

The Hive Batch Strength, 54.5%
Nose: Soot and orange peel hit first with sherry notes following along with a gentle hit of spice.
Palate: The orange peel packs a warming punch initially, followed by sherry, spice, honeycomb and a hint of milk chocolate.
Finish: Long citrus peel length.

Jewish Whisky Company
www.singlecasknation.com

A few years ago, Jason Johnstone-Yellin and Joshua Hatton, two well-known whisky bloggers, started, in alliance with Seth Klaskin, a new carer as independent bottlers. The idea with Single Cask Nation somewhat reminds you of Scotch Malt Whisky Society in the sense that you have to become a member of the nation in order to buy the bottlings. Some of the more recent bottlings include a 9 year old from The English Whisky Company, a 5 year old Laphroaig and a 12 year old Glen Moray. They have also included American and Indian whiskies in the range where some of the latest bottlings come from new American distilleries such as Westland, Koval, Catoctin Creek and FEW Spirits. Since 2013 the company also arranges popular whisky events under the name Whisky Jewbilee in New York, Chicago and Seattle. In 2017, the owners decided to launch a special range of whiskies that could also be found at retailers in California, Illinois, Massachusetts, New Jersey and New York. The plan is to bottle 12-18 single casks a year for the retail range.

Meadowside Blending
www.meadowsideblending.com

The company may be a newcomer to the family of independent bottlers but the founder certainly isn´t. Donald Hart, a Keeper of the Quaich and co-founder of the well-known bottler Hart Brothers, runs the Glasgow company together with his son, Andrew. There are three sides to the business – blends sold under the name The Royal Thistle, single malts labelled The Maltman and, most recently, single cask single grains under the label The Grainman.

Elixir Distillers
www.elixirdistillers.com

What at first sight seems like a newcomer in the business is in fact an expansion of what used to be Speciality Drinks which is owned by Sukhinder Singh. He is known by most for his very well-stocked shop in London, The Whisky Exchange. In the beginning of October every year, he is also hosting The Whisky Show in London, one of the best whisky festivals in the world. In 2005 he started as an independent bottler of malt whiskies operating under the brand name The Single Malts of Scotland. There are around 50 bottlings on offer at any time, either as single casks or as batches bottled at cask strength or at 46%. In 2009 a new range of Islay single malts under the name Port Askaig was introduced, starting with a cask strength, a 17 year old and a 25 year old. Over the years, a large number of new releases have been made while others have been discontinued. Some of the more recent are 100 proof, 8 year old and 15 year old Sherry.

Elements of Islay, a series of cask strength single malts in which all Islay distilleries are, or will be, represented was introduced a few years before Port Askaig. The list of the product range is cleverly constructed with periodical tables in mind in which each distillery has a two-letter acronym followed by a batch number, for example Ar_8 (Ardbeg) or Lp_7 (Laphroaig). Two of the new releases in 2016 were Ma_1 where Ma stands for Margadale indicating a heavily peated Bunnahabhain and Ln_1, Lochindaal, a medium peated Bruichladdich. In spring 2016, Elements of Islay Peat, the first blended malt version of the range, was launched, bottled at cask strength and it was followed up by a version bottled at 45%. Some of the most recent bottlings from Elixir Distillers appeared in June 2017 when two very rare expressions of Karuizawa, 31 and 33 years old, were released.

Elements of Islay Peat (blended malt), 45%
Nose: A seductive, malty dram with honeyed peat, ripe yellow plums and dry grass.
Palate: The sweet barley interacts with fruity smokiness with apricots, citrus, vanilla and toffee in the background.
Finish: Medium long where the sweetness turns into dry vanilla smoke and pear drops.

Port Askaig 15 years old sherry, 45.8%
Nose: As suspected, prunes and raisins are there but tropical fruits steal the show. Hints of eucalyptus and a very subdued smokiness.
Palate: More smoke and slightly peppery paired with raisins, ripe mango and pineapple.
Finish: Medium with slowly fading sherry notes.

are undoubtedly two single Islay malts called Finlaggan and The Ileach. The latter comes in two versions, bottled at 40% and 58%. The Finlaggan range was recently repackaged and now consists of Old Reserve (40%), Eilean Mor (46%), Port Finish (46%), Sherry Finish (46%) and Cask Strength (56%). Recent additions to the range include the single malt Islay Storm and, launched in autumn 2017, the blended malt Smokestack which contains only peated malts from Islay and the Highlands. Other expressions include two blended malts, Glenalmond and Black Cuillin and, not least, a wide range of single cask single malts under the name The Cooper's Choice. They are bottled at 46% or at cask strength and are all non coloured and non chill-filtered.

SmokeStack, 46%
Nose: A nose of peaty smoke. Over roasted chestnuts, sweet candied bacon, leather and gorse grass round it round.
Palate: Peat smoked bacon tones mingle with the peaty grass and gentle pops of sultanas.
Finish: Long, peaty finish.

Glenalmond, 40%
Nose: Warmed toffee, fruit spice, yellow plum, almond's and toast tickle the nose.
Palate: There are soft ginger tones in sticky toffee pudding with a sprinkle of lightly toasted nuts.
Finish: A mellow whisky with medium length.

North Star Spirits

www.northstarspirits.com

Founded in 2016, by Iain Croucher who was sales manager and brand ambassador for AD Rattray before deciding to go it alone. Based just North of Glasgow, Iain operates North Star from a shed at the bottom of his garden! Releases so far include a 30 year old Bunnahabhain, a 27 year old Tormore, a 20 year old Arran and his new range of blended malts and blended Scotch called 'Vega'. A new range called Phoenix is also on the horizon, with unique casks from interesting distilleries. North Star is not focused on just whisky from Scotland. Iain has bottled a Pedro Ximenez that spent some time in Islay casks and a 13 year old Tennessee Whiskey and there will be a small batch of Glasgow gin in the not too distant future.

The Ultimate Whisky Company

www.ultimatewhisky.com

Founded in 1994 by Han van Wees and his son Maurice, this Dutch independent bottler has until now bottled more than 500 single malts. All whiskies are un chill-filtered, without colouring and bottled at either 46% or cask strength. Recent bottlings include older whiskies such as a 27 year old Blair Athol and a 28 year old Balmenach but also younger malts (7-10 years) can be found. The van Wees family also operate one of the finest spirits shops in Europe - Van Wees Whisky World in Amersfoort - with i.a. more than 1,000 different whiskies including more than 500 single malts.

The Vintage Malt Whisky Company

www.vintagemaltwhisky.com

Founded in 1992 by Brian Crook, who previously had twenty years experience in the malt whisky industry, the company today is run by his two children, Andrew and Caroline. The company also owns and operates a sister company called The Highlands & Islands Scotch Whisky Co. The most famous brands in the range

Svenska Eldvatten

www.eldvatten.se

Founded in 2011 by Tommy Andersen and Peter Sjögren. They both have extensive experience from whisky and other spirits, which they have gained from arranging tastings for many years. Since the start, more than 50 single casks, bottled at cask strength, have been released. The owners have also released their own blended malt, bottled at 50%, under the name Glenn (a humorous tip of the hat to their home town Gothenburg where Glenn is one of the most common names). In their range of spirits they also have aged tequila and rum from the famous and sadly closed Trinidadian distillery Caroni. They have also launched their own rum, WeiRon Super Premium Aged Carribean Rum (both vatted and as a single cask), as well as gin and aquavit.

Wm Cadenhead & Co

www.wmcadenhead.com

This company was established in 1842 and is owned by J & A Mitchell (who also owns Springbank) since 1972. The single malts from Cadenheads are neither chill filtered nor coloured. In 2012, Mark Watt, who had been working for Duncan Taylor for several years, joined the company. His mission was to revamp the portfolio of whiskies and a number of new ranges were created. Today there is Authentic Collection (single cask cask strength whiskies, exclusively sold in their own shops), World Whiskies (single malts from non Scottish distillers as well as from Scottish grain distillers) and Small Batch, a range which can be divided into three separate ranges; Gold Label (single casks bottled at cask strength), Small Batch Cask Strength (2-4 casks of whisky from the same vintage, bottled at cask strength) and Small Batch 46% (same as the previous but diluted to 46%). A fourth range has recently been introduced, William Cadenhead Range, which consists of blended whisky as well as single malts from undisclosed distilleries.

In 2017 the company celebrated its 175th anniversary as Scotland's oldest independent bottler in quite a spectacular way with rare and old whiskies being released throughout the year. The first release in spring was made up of the following six whiskies; Banff 40yo, Convalmore 40yo, Caperdonich 39yo, Rosebank 25yo, Littlemill 26yo and a Heaven Hill 20yo distilled before the great fire. This was followed in August by a release of ten single cask bottlings – one for each of their ten shops.

Banff 40 years old, 51.2%

Nose: Pencil shavings, tangerines and tinned apricots, perfumed herbal notes and a touch of heather hop onto the nose.

Palate: A touch of ginger and gooseberries hit first followed by bruised pears, moist banana bread and flickers of crushed nuts.

Finish: Long intriguing length with hints of perfumed brambly apple.

Convalmore 40 years old, 56.8%

Nose: Pineapple and coconut along with hints of mango tea, white peach and herbal notes.

Palate: It is super juicy, with ripe pineapple, mango and coconut hitting first. Ripe peaches and juicy apricots follow on with white pepper and floral tones.

Finish: Long developing length.

Adelphi Distillery

www.adelphidistillery.com

Adelphi Distillery is named after a distillery which closed in 1902. The company is owned by Keith Falconer and Donald Houston, who recruited Alex Bruce from the wine trade to act as Managing Director. Their whiskies are always bottled at cask strength, uncoloured and non chill-filtered. Adelphi bottles around 50 casks a year. Two of their recurrent brands over the years have been Fascadale and Liddesdale which are in batches of approximately 1,500 bottles. They also have their own blended Scotch, Adelphi Private Stock, which is bottled at 40%. In October 2015, the first two bottlings of a new brand were launched. The Glover is a unique vatting of single malt from the closed Japanese distillery Hanyu and two Scottish single malts, Longmorn and Glen Garioch. A 14 and a 22 year old sold out almost instantaneously and they were followed in autumn 2016 by an 18 year old. The name of the whisky honours Thomas Blake Glover, an influential Scottish businessman working in Japan in the second half of the 19th century. Since 2014, Adelphi is also operating its own distillery in Glenbeg on the Ardnamurchan peninsula, a couple of miles from the company's office. Since the opening, the owners have released a year old malt spirit named Spirit 2016 AD which sold out instantly and so a second release at a higher age was due in September 2017. There are no plans to release the first Ardnamurchan single malt whisky until 2021.

Ardnamurchan Spirit 2017/AD, 53.6%

Nose: Fresh and lush, with aromas of citrus fruits, apples, raisins with a sprinkle of spice. Earthy tones and touches of peat add to the layers.

Palate: Citrus notes mingle with herbal touches and cloves. Raisins soaked in maple syrup, and peat give weight to the body.

Finish: Long length.

Deerstalker Whisky Co

www.deerstalkerwhisky.com

The Deerstalker brand, which dates from 1880 was originally owned by J.G. Thomson & Co of Leith and subsequently Tennent Caledonian Breweries. It was purchased by Glasgow based Aberko Ltd in 1994 and is managed by former Tennent's Export Director Paul Aston. The Deerstalker range covers single cask as well as blended malt whiskies. The 12 year old single malt (46%, un chill-filtered, natural colour) is the best known and has sourced its malt from Balmenach distillery for over 35 years. More recent additions are 'Limited Release' single cask bottlings of Auchentoshan (19 year old), Ben Nevis (18 year old), Speyside (18 years old) and Auchroisk (16 year old) at 48%. A Deerstalker Blended Malt (Highland Edition) was launched in 2014 and in autumn 2016 the Peated Edition of Deerstalker was released.

Deerstalker Blended Malt Peated Edition, 43%

Nose: Lemons and limes blend with peated saline aromas. The warm darkness of treacle and blood oranges are in the background.

Palate: Almost liquid peat, with dark molten chocolate cake and some fresh, wild blackberries giving a lovely soft fruity edge.

Finish: Long, with chocolate peaty tones.

Deerstalker Blended Malt Highland Edition, 43%

Nose: Sweet perfume hits with dried apricots, clover, dark roasted nuts, cloves and cinnamon.

Palate: The palate is darker than the nose with the spice mingling with spent coffee beans, a hint of ferns and dark leather.

Finish: Medium length, with crushed cloves and cinnamon.

Morrison & MacKay Whisky

www.mandmwhisky.co.uk

A relative newcomer as an independent bottler, there is nonetheless plenty of experience in the company. The Morrison part of the business name is represented by Brian Morrison (as well as his son Jamie) who's father was the legendary Stanley P Morrison, founder of Morrison Bowmore Distilleries and at one time owner of Bowmore, Auchentoshan and Glen Garioch. When Stanley P died, his two sons, Brian and Tim took over and ran the business until Suntory acquired the entire company. Tim went on to form AD Rattray independent bottler and has just recently opened a distillery in Glasgow. Brian on the other hand started the Scottish Liqueur Centre north of Perth and he is also nurturing plans to build a distillery in Aberargie, just south of Perth. Meanwhile his liqueur business has been expanded to also include malt whisky under the name Carn Mor. Currently there are three ranges; Carn Mor Strictly Limited, usually bottled at 46%, Celebration of the Cask which are single casks bottled at cask strength and Celebration of the Cask Black Gold with heavily sherried whiskies in focus. All whiskies are non chill-filtered.

Sansibar Whisky

www.sansibar-whisky.com

Started in 2012, this was the brainchild of the current majority owner and CEO Jens Drewitz and Carsten Ehrlich, the organizer of the famous Whisky Fair Limburg. Their idea was to create a range of high quality single malts from Scotland and to market them in connection with the well known Sansibar restaurant on the island of Sylt in northern Germany. Around 60 bottlings are produced per year and the range also includes rum.

Whisky
shops

AUSTRALIA
The Odd Whisky Coy
PO Box 2045
Glynde, SA, 5070
Phone: +61 (0)417 85 22 96
www.theoddwhiskycoy.com.au
Founded and owned by Graham Wright,
this on-line whisky specialist has an
impressive range. They are agents for
famous brands such as Springbank,
Benromach and Berry Brothers and
arrange recurrent seminars on the subject.

World of Whisky
Shop G12, Cosmopolitan Centre
2-22 Knox Street
Double Bay NSW 2028
Phone: +61 (0)2 9363 4212
www.worldofwhisky.com.au
A whisky specialist which offers a range
of 300 different expressions, most of them
single malts. The shop is also organising
and hosting regular tastings.

AUSTRIA
Potstill
Laudongasse 18
1080 Wien
Phone: +43 (0)664 118 85 41
www.potstill.org
Austria's premier whisky shop with over
1100 kinds of which c 900 are malts,
including some real rarities. Arranges
tastings and seminars and ships to several
European countries. On-line ordering.

Cadenhead Austria
Alter Markt 1
5020 Salzburg
Phone: +43 (0)662 84 53 05
www.cadenhead.at
Number 8 in the famous Cadenhead's
chain of whisky shops. At the moment
they offer 350 different whiskies, mostly
single malts and they also arrange monthly
tastings.

BELGIUM
Whiskycorner
Kraaistraat 16
3530 Houthalen
Phone: +32 (0)89 386233
www.whiskycorner.be
A very large selection of single malts,
no less than 2000 different! Also other
whiskies, calvados and grappas. The site is
in both French and English. Mail ordering,
but not on-line. Shipping worldwide.

Jurgen's Whiskyhuis
Gaverland 70
9620 Zottegem
Phone: +32 (0)9 336 51 06
www.whiskyhuis.be
An absolutely huge assortment of more
than 2,000 different single malts with 700
in stock and the rest delivered within the
week. Also 40 different grain whiskies and
120 bourbons. Worldwide shipping

Huis Crombé
Doenaertstraat 20
8510 Marke
Phone: +32 (0)56 21 19 87
www.crombewines.com
A wine retailer which also covers all kinds
of spirits. The whisky range is very nice
where a large assortment of Scotch is
supplemented with whiskies from Japan,
the USA and Ireland to mention a few.

Anverness Whisky & Spirits
Grote Steenweg 74
2600 Berchem – Antwerpen
Phone: +32 (0)3 218 55 90
www.anverness.be
Peter de Decker has established himself
as one of the best Belgian whisky retailers
where, apart from an impressive range of
whiskies, recurrent tastings and whisky
dinners play an important role.

We Are Whisky
Avenue Rodolphe Gossia 33
1350 Orp-Jauche (Jauche)
Phone: +32 (0)471 134556
www.wearewhisky.com
A fairly new shop and on-line retailer
with a range of more than 400 different
whiskies. They also arrange 3-4 tasting
every month.

Dram 242
Opwijksestraat 242
9280 Lebbeke
Phone: +32 (0)477 260993
www.dram242.be
Started in 2012 by Dirk Verleysen, this
shop has a wide range of whiskies. Apart
from the core official bottlings, Dirk has
focused on rare, old expressions as well as
whiskies from small, independent bottlers.

CANADA
Kensington Wine Market
1257 Kensington Road NW
Calgary
Alberta T2N 3P8
Phone: +1 403 283 8000
www.kensingtonwinemarket.com
A very large range of single malt bottlings

as well as other spirits and wines. Regular
tastings in the shop. Celebrating their 25th
anniversary this year, they are also the
home of the Scotch Malt Whisky Society
in Canada.

World of Whisky
Unit 240, 333 5 Avenue SW
Calgary
Alberta T2P 3B6
Phone: +1 587 956 8511
www.coopwinespiritsbeer.com/stores/
world-of-whisky/
Part of the Co-op Wine Spirits Beer (with
24 liquor stores in the Calgary area), Chris
Sikorsky recently opened this shop in
downtown Calgary specialising in whisky
from all corners of the world. Currently
there are close to 900 different whiskies in
the range including some extremely rare
ones from Scotland.

DENMARK
Juul's Vin & Spiritus
Værnedamsvej 15
1819 Frederiksberg
Phone: +45 33 31 13 29
www.juuls.dk
A very large range of wines, fortified
wines and spirits. Around 500 single malts.
Also a good selection of drinking glasses.

Cadenhead's WhiskyShop Denmark
Kongensgade 69 F
5000 Odense C
Phone: +45 66 13 95 05
www.cadenheads.dk
Whisky specialist with a very good range,
not least from Cadenhead's. Nice range
of champagne, cognac and rum. Arranges
whisky and beer tastings. On-line ordering
with worldwide shipping.

Whisky.dk
Sjølund Gade 12
6093 Sjølund
Phone: +45 5210 6093
www.whisky.dk
Henrik Olsen and Ulrik Bertelsen are
well-known in Denmark for their whisky
shows but they also run an on-line spirits
shop with an emphasis on whisky but also
including an impressive stock of rums.

ENGLAND
The Whisky Exchange
2 Bedford Street, Covent Garden
London WC2E 9HH
Phone: +44 (0)20 7100 0088
www.thewhiskyexchange.com

An excellent whisky shop owned by
Sukhinder Singh. Started off as a mail
order business, run from a showroom in
Hanwell, but later opened up at Vinopolis
in downtown London. Recently the
shop was re-located to a new and bigger
location in Covent Garden. The assortment
is huge with well over 1000 single malts
to choose from. Some rarities which can
hardly be found anywhere else are offered
thanks to Singh's great interest for antique
whisky. There are also other types of
whisky and cognac, calvados, rum etc. On-
line ordering and ships all over the world.

The Whisky Shop
(See also Scotland, The Whisky Shop)
11 Coppergate Walk
York YO1 9NT
Phone: +44 (0)1904 640300

510 Brompton Walk
Lakeside Shopping Centre
Thurrock Grays, Essex RM20 2ZL
Phone: +44 (0)1708 866255

7 Turl Street
Oxford OX1 3DQ
Phone: +44 (0)1865 202279

3 Swan Lane
Norwich NR2 1HZ
Phone: +44 (0)1603 618284

70 Piccadilly
London W1J 8HP
Phone: +44 (0)207 499 6649

Unit 7 Queens Head Passage
Paternoster
London EC4M 7DZ
Phone: +44 (0)207 329 5117

3 Exchange St
Manchester M2 7EE
Phone: +44 (0)161 832 6110

25 Chapel Street
Guildford GU1 3UL
Phone: +44 (0)1483 450900

Unit 9 Great Western Arcade
Birmingham B2 5HU
Phone: +44 (0)121 233 4416

64 East Street
Brighton BN1 1HQ
Phone: +44 (0)1273 327 962

3 Cheapside
Nottingham NG1 2HU
Phone: +44 (0)115 958 7080

9-10 High Street
Bath BA1 5AQ
Phone: +44 (0)1225 423 535

Unit 1/9 Red Mall,
Intu Metro Centre
Gateshead NE11 9YP
Phone: +44 (0)191 460 3777

Unit 201 Trentham Gardens
Stoke on Trent ST4 8AX
Phone: +44 (0)1782 644 483
www.whiskyshop.com
The first shop opened in 1992 in
Edinburgh and this is now the UK's largest
specialist retailer of whiskies with 20
outlets (plus one in Paris). A large product
range with over 700 kinds, including 400
malt whiskies and 140 miniature bottles, as

well as accessories and books. They also
run The W Club, the leading whisky club
in the UK where the excellent Whiskeria
magazine is one of the member's benefits.
On-line ordering and shipping all over the
world except to the USA.

Royal Mile Whiskies
3 Bloomsbury Street
London WC1B 3QE
Phone: +44 (0)20 7436 4763
www.royalmilewhiskies.com
The London branch of Royal Mile
Whiskies. See also Scotland, Royal Mile
Whiskies.

Berry Bros. & Rudd
63 Pall Mall
London SW1Y 5HZ
Phone: +44 (0)800 280 2440

The Warehouse Shop
Hamilton Close, Houndmills
Basingstoke RG21 6YB
Phone: +44 (0)800 280 2440
www.bbr.com/whisky
A legendary company that recently
opned a new shop in Pall Mall. One of
the world's most reputable wine shops
but with an exclusive selection of malt
whiskies. Also shops in Hong Kong,
Singapore and Japan.

The Wright Wine
and Whisky Company
The Old Smithy, Raikes Road, Skipton,
North Yorkshire BD23 1NP
Phone: +44 (0)1756 700886
www.wineandwhisky.co.uk
An eclectic selection of near to 1000
different whiskies. 'Tasting Cupboard' of
nearly 100 opened bottles for sampling
with regular hosted tasting evenings. Great
'Collector to Collector' selection of old
whiskies plus a fantastic choice of 1200+
wines, premium spirits and liqueurs.

Master of Malt
Unit 5, Chapman Way
Tunbridge Wells TN2 3EF
Phone: +44 (0)1892 888 376
www.masterofmalt.com
Online retailer and independent bottler
with a very impressive range of more
than 2,500 whiskies, including over 1,500
Scotch whiskies and over 1,500 single
malts. In addition to whisky there is an
enormous selection of rum, Cognac,
Armagnac, gin, tequila and more. The
website contains a wealth of information
on the distilleries and innovative perso-
nalised gift ideas. Drinks by the Dram
30ml samples of more than 3,000 different
whiskies are also available to try before
you buy a full bottle as well as a Build
Your Own Tasting Set option and Dram
Club monthly subscription services.

Whiskys.co.uk
The Square, Stamford Bridge
York YO4 11AG
Phone: +44 (0)1759 371356
www.whiskys.co.uk
Good assortment with more than 600
different whiskies. Also a nice range of
armagnac, rum, calvados etc. On-line
ordering, ships outside of the UK. The

owners also have another website, www.
whiskymerchants.co.uk with a huge
amount of information on just about every
whisky distillery in the world.

The Wee Dram
5 Portland Square, Bakewell
Derbyshire DE45 1HA
Phone: +44 (0)1629 812235
www.weedram.co.uk
Large range of Scotch single malts (c
450) with whiskies from other parts of the
world and a good range of whisky books.
Run 'The Wee Drammers Whisky Club'
with tastings and seminars. End of October
they arrange the yearly Wee Dram Fest
whisky festival.

Hard To Find Whisky
1 Spencer Street
Birmingham B18 6DD
Phone: +44 (0)8456 803 489
www.htfw.com
As the name says, this family owned shop
specialises in rare, collectable and new
releases of single malt whisky. The range
is astounding - almost 3,000 different bottlings including no less than 263 different
Macallan. World wide shipping.

Nickolls & Perks
37 High Street, Stourbridge
West Midlands DY8 1TA
Phone: +44 (0)1384 394518
www.nickollsandperks.co.uk
Mostly known as wine merchants but
also has a good range of whiskies with c
300 different kinds including 200 single
malts. On-line ordering with shipping
also outside of UK. Since 2011, they also
organize the acclaimed Midlands Whisky
Festival, see www.whiskyfest.co.uk

Gauntleys of Nottingham
4 High Street
Nottingham NG1 2ET
Phone: +44 (0)115 9110555
www.gauntley-wine.co.uk
A fine wine merchant established in 1880.
The range of wines are among the best
in the UK. All kinds of spirits, not least
whisky, are taking up more and more
space and several rare malts can be found.
Mail order service available.

Hedonism Wines
3-7 Davies St.
London W1K 3LD
Phone: +44 (020) 729 078 70
www.hedonism.co.uk
Located in the heart of London's Mayfair,
this is a new temple for wine lovers but
also with an impressive range of whiskies
and other spirits. They have over 1,200
different bottlings from Scotland and the
rest of the world! The very elegant shop is
in itself well worth a visit.

The Lincoln Whisky Shop
87 Bailgate
Lincoln LN1 3AR
Phone: +44 (0)1522 537834
www.lincolnwhiskyshop.co.uk
Mainly specialising in whisky with more
than 400 different whiskies but also 500
spirits and liqueurs and some 100 wines.
Mailorder only within UK.

Milroys of Soho

3 Greek Street
London W1D 4NX
Phone: +44 (0)207 734 2277
shop.milroys.co.uk
A classic whisky shop in Soho with a very
good range with over 700 malts and a
wide selection of whiskies from around the
world. On-line ordering.

Arkwrights

114 The Dormers
Highworth
Wiltshire SN6 7PE
Phone: +44 (0)1793 765071
www.whiskyandwines.com
A good range of whiskies (over 700 in
stock) as well as other spirits.
Regular tastings in the shop. On-line
ordering with shipping all over the world
except USA and Canada.

Edencroft Fine Wines

8-10 Hospital Street, Nantwich
Cheshire, CW5 5RJ
Phone: +44 (0)1270 629975
www.edencroft.co.uk
Family owned wine and spirits shop since
1994. Around 250 whiskies and also a
nice range of gin, cognac and other spirits
including cigars. Worldwide shipping.

Cadenhead´s Whisky Shop

26 Chiltern Street
London W1U 7QF
Phone: +44 (0)20 7935 6999
www.whiskytastingroom.com
One in a chain of shops owned by
independent bottlers Cadenhead. Sells
Cadenhead's product range and c. 200
other whiskies. Regular tastings.

Constantine Stores

30 Fore Street
Constantine, Falmouth
Cornwall TR11 5AB
Phone: +44 (0)1326 340226
www.drinkfinder.co.uk
A full-range wine and spirits dealer with a
good selection of whiskies from the whole
world (around 800 different, of which
600 are single malts).Worldwide shipping
except for USA and Canada.

House of Malt

12 Crosby Street
Carlisle CA1 1DQ
Phone: +44 (0)1228 739 713
www.houseofmalt.co.uk
Ben Turnbull offers a wide selection of
whiskies from Scotland and the world
as well as other spirits and craft ales.
There are three exclusive malts selected
by themselves and they also have online
ordering.

The Vintage House

42 Old Compton Street
London W1D 4LR
Phone: +44 (0)20 7437 5112
www.sohowhisky.com
A huge range of 1400 kinds of malt
whisky, many of them rare. Supplementing this is also a selection of fine wines.

Whisky On-line

Units 1-3 Concorde House, Charnley
Road, Blackpool, Lancashire FY1 4PE
Phone: +44 (0)1253 620376
www.whisky-online.com
A good selection of whisky and also
cognac, rum, port etc. On-line ordering
with shipping all over the world.

FRANCE

La Maison du Whisky

20 rue d´Anjou
75008 Paris
Phone: +33 (0)1 42 65 03 16

6 carrefour d l´Odéon
75006 Paris
Phone: +33 (0)1 46 34 70 20

(2 shops outside France)
47 rue Jean Chatel
97400 Saint-Denis, La Réunion
Phone: +33 (0)2 62 21 31 19

The Pier at Robertson Quay
80 Mohamed Sultan Road, #01-10
Singapore 239013
Phone: +65 6733 0059
www.whisky.fr
France's largest whisky specialist with
over 1200 whiskies in stock. Also a
number of own-bottled single malts. La
Maison du Whisky acts as a EU distributor
for many whisky producers around the
world. Four shops and on-line ordering.

The Whisky Shop

7 Place de la Madeleine
75008 Paris
Phone: +33 (0)1 45 22 29 77
The large chain of whisky shops in the UK
has now opened up a store in Paris as well.

GERMANY

Celtic Whisk(e)y & Versand

Otto Steudel
Bulmannstrasse 26
90459 Nürnberg
Phone: +49 (0)911 45097430
celtic.whiskymania.de
A very impressive single malt range with
well over 1000 different single malts and
a good selection from other parts of the
world. On-line ordering.

SCOMA

Am Bullhamm 17
26441 Jever
Phone: +49(0)4461 912237
www.scoma.de
Very large range of c 750 Scottish malts
and many from other countries. Holds
regular seminars and tastings. The
excellent, monthly whisky newsletter
SCOMA News is produced and can be
downloaded as a pdf-file from the website.
On-line ordering.

The Whisky Store

Am Grundwassersee 4
82402 Seeshaupt
Phone: +49 (0)8801 30 20 000
www.whisky.de
A very large range comprising c 700
kinds of whisky of which 550 are malts.
Also sells whisky liqueurs, books and

accessories. The website is a goldmine of
information. On-line ordering.

Cadenhead´s Whisky Market

Luxemburger Strasse 257
50939 Köln
Phone: +49 (0)221-2831834
www.cadenheads.de
Good range of malt whiskies (c 350
different kinds) with emphasis on
Cadenhead's own bottlings. Other
products include wine, cognac and rum
etc. Arranges recurring tastings and also
has an on-line shop.

Cadenhead´s Whisky Market

Mainzer Strasse 20
10247 Berlin-Friedrichshain
Phone: +49 (0)30-30831444
www.cadenhead-berlin.de
Excellent product range with more than
700 different kinds of whiskies with
emphasis on Cadenhead's own bottlings
as well as cognac and rum. Arranges
recurrent tastings.

Home of Malts

Hosegstieg 11
22880 Wedel
Phone: +49 (0)4103 965 9695
www.homeofmalts.com
Large assortment with over 800 different
single malts as well as whiskies from
many other countries. Also a nice selection
of cognac, rum etc. On-line ordering.

Reifferscheid

Mainzer Strasse 186
53179 Bonn / Mehlem
Phone: +49 (0)228 9 53 80 70
www.whisky-bonn.de
A well-stocked shop with a large range of
whiskies, wine, spirit, cigars and a delicatessen. Regular tastings.

Whisky-Doris

Germanenstrasse 38
14612 Falkensee
Phone: +49 (0)3322-219784
www.whisky-doris.de
Large range of over 300 whiskies and also
sells own special bottlings. Orders via
email. Shipping also outside Germany.

Finlays Whisky Shop

Hofheimer Str. 30
65719 Hofheim-Lorsbach
Phone: +49 (0)6192 30 90 335
www.finlayswhiskyshop.de
Whisky specialists with a large range of
over 1,400 whiskies. Finlays also work as
the importer to Germany of Douglas laing,
James MacArthur and Wilson & Morgan.
On-line ordering.

Weinquelle Lühmann

Lübeckerstrasse 145
22087 Hamburg
Phone: +49 (0)40-300 672 950
www.weinquelle.com
An impressive selection of both wines and
spirits with over 1000 different whiskies of
which 850 are malt whiskies. Also an impressive range of rums. On-line ordering.

The Whisky-Corner
Reichertsfeld 2
92278 Illschwang
Phone: +49 (0)9666-951213
www.whisky-corner.de
A small shop but large on mail order.
A very large assortment of over 1600
whiskies. Also sells blended and American
whiskies. The website is very informative
with features on, among others, whisky-
making, tasting and independent bottlers.
On-line ordering.

World Wide Spirits
Hauptstrasse 12
84576 Teising
Phone: +49 (0)8633 50 87 93
www.worldwidespirits.de
A nice range of c 500 whiskies with some
rarities from the twenties. Also large
selection of other spirits.

WhiskyKoch
Weinbergstrasse 2
64285 Darmstadt
Phone: +49 (0)6151 99 27 105
www.whiskykoch.de
A combination of a whisky shop and
restaurant. The shop has a nice selection
of single malts as well as other Scottish
products and the restaurant has specialised
in whisky dinners and tastings.

Kierzek
Weitlingstrasse 17
10317 Berlin
Phone: +49 (0)30 525 11 08
www.kierzek-berlin.de
Over 400 different whiskies in stock. In
the product range 50 kinds of rum and
450 wines from all over the world are
found among other products. Mail order
is available.

House of Whisky
Ackerbeeke 6
31683 Obernkirchen
Phone: +49 (0)5724-399420
www.houseofwhisky.de
Aside from over 1,200 different malts
also sells a large range of other spirits
(including over 100 kinds of rum).
On-line ordering.

World Wide Whisky (2 shops)
Eisenacher Strasse 64
10823 Berlin-Schöneberg
Phone: +49 (0)30-7845010
Hauptstrasse 58
10823 Berlin-Schöneberg
www.world-wide-whisky.de
Large range of 1,500 different whiskies.
Arranges tastings and seminars. Has a
large number of rarities. Orders via email.

HUNGARY

Whisky Net / Whisky Shop
Kovács Làszlò Street 21
2000 Szentendre

Veres Pálné utca 8.
1053 Budapest
Phone: +36 1 267-1588
www.whiskynet.hu
www.whiskyshop.hu
The largest selction of whisky in Hungary.
Agents for Arran, Benriach, Glenfarclas,

Gordon & MacPhail, Benromach, Douglas
Laing, Springbank, Angus Dundee, Ian
Macleod, Kilchoman among others. Also
mailorder.

IRELAND

Celtic Whiskey Shop
27-28 Dawson Street
Dublin 2
Phone: +353 (0)1 675 9744
www.celticwhiskeyshop.com
More than 350 kinds of Irish whiskeys but
also a good selection of Scotch, wines and
other spirits. World wide shipping.

ITALY

Whisky Shop
by Milano Whisky Festival
Via Cavaleri 6, Milano
Phone: +39 (0)2 48753039
www.whiskyshop.it
The team behind the excellent
Milano Whisky Festival also have an on-
line whiskyshop with almost 500 different
single malts including several special
festival bottlings.

Whisky Antique S.R.L.
Via Giardini Sud
41043 Formigine (MO)
Phone: +39 (0)59 574278
www.whiskyantique.com
Long-time whisky enthusiast and collector
Massimo Righi owns this shop specialising
in rare and collectable spirits – not only
whisky but also cognac, rum, armagnac
etc. They are also the Italian importer for
brands like Jack Wiebers, The Whisky
Agency and Perfect Dram.

Whisky & Co.
Via Margutta, 29
00187 Rome
Phone: +39 (0)6 3265 0514
www.whiskyandco.it
A new and very elegant whiskyshop has
recently been opened in the heart of Rome
by Massimo Righi, knwon from Whisky
Antique in Modena.

Cadenhead's Whisky Bar
Via Poliziano, 3
20154 Milano
Phone: +39 (0)2 336 055 92
www.cadenhead.it
This is the newest addition in the Caden-
head´s chain of shops. Concentrating
mostly on the Cadenhead´s range but they
also stock whiskies from other producers.

JAPAN

Liquor Mountain Co.,Ltd.
4F Kyoto Kowa Bldg.
82 Tachiurinishi-Machi,
Takakura-Nishiiru,
Shijyo-Dori, Shimogyo-Ku,
Kyoto, 600-8007
Phone: +81 (0)75 213 8880
www.likaman.co.jp
The company has more than 150 shops
specialising in spirits, beer and food.
Around 20 of them are designated whisky
shops under the name Whisky Kingdom

(although they have a full range of other
spirits) with a range of 500 different whiskies. The three foremost shops are;

Rakzan Sanjyo Onmae
1-8, HigashiGekko-cho, Nishinokyo,
Nakagyo-ku, Kyoto-shi
Kyoto
Phone: +81 (0)75-842-5123

Nagakute
2-105, Ichigahora, Nagakute-shi
Aichi
Phone: +81 (0)561-64-3081

Kabukicho 1chome
1-2-16, Kabuki-cho, Shinjuku-ku
Tokyo
Phone: +81 (0)3-5287-2080

THE NETHERLANDS

Whiskyslijterij De Koning
Hinthamereinde 41
5211 PM 's Hertogenbosch
Phone: +31 (0)73-6143547
www.whiskykoning.nl
An enormous assortment with more than
1400 kinds of whisky including
c 800 single malts. Arranges recurring
tastings. On-line ordering. Shipping all
over the world.

Van Wees - Whiskyworld.nl
Leusderweg 260
3817 KH Amersfoort
Phone: +31 (0)33-461 53 19
www.whiskyworld.nl
A very large range of 1000 whiskies
including over 500 single malts. Also have
their own range of bottlings (The Ultimate
Whisky Company). On-line ordering.

Wijnhandel van Zuylen
Loosduinse Hoofdplein 201
2553 CP Loosduinen (Den Haag)
Phone: +31 (0)70-397 1400
www.whiskyvanzuylen.nl
Excellent range of whiskies (circa 1100)
and wines. Email orders with shipping to
some ten European countries.

Wijnwinkel-Slijterij
Ton Overmars
Hoofddorpplein 11
1059 CV Amsterdam
Phone: +31 (0)20-615 71 42
www.tonovermars.nl
A very large assortment of wines, spirits
and beer which includes more than 400
single malts. Arranges recurring tastings.
Orders via email.

Wijn & Whisky Schuur
Blankendalwei 4
8629 EH Scharnegoutem
Phone: +31 (0)515-522706
www.wijnwhiskyschuur.nl
Large assortment with 1000 different
whiskies and a good range of other spirits
as well. Arranges recurring tastings. On-
line ordering.

Versailles Dranken
Lange Hezelstraat 83
6511 Cl Nijmegen
Phone: +31 (0)24-3232008
www.versaillesdranken.nl
A very impressive range with more than

1500 different whiskies, most of them from Scotland but also a surprisingly good selection (more than 60) of Bourbon. Arranges recurring tastings. On-line ordering.

Alba Malts
Kloosterstraat 15
6981 CC Doesburg
Phone: +31 (0)65-4295905
www.albamalts.com
A new whisky shop situated in an old chapel dating back to 1441. Marnix Okel has a passion for Scotland and will focus on Scotch single malt only, with a range of 400 whiskies to start with.

NEW ZEALAND
Whisky Galore
834 Colombo Street
Christchurch 8013
Phone: +64 (0) 800 944 759
www.whiskygalore.co.nz
The best whisky shop in New Zealand with 550 different whiskies, approximately 350 which are single malts. There is also online mail-order with shipping all over the world except USA and Canada.

POLAND
George Ballantine´s
Krucza str 47 A, Warsaw
Phone: +48 22 625 48 32

Pulawska str 22, Warsaw
Phone: +48 22 542 86 22

Marynarska str 15, Warsaw
Phone: +48 22 395 51 60

Zygmunta Vogla str 62, Warsaw
Phone: +48 22 395 51 64
www.sklep-ballantines.pl
The biggest assortment in Poland with more than 500 different single malts. Apart from whisky there is a full range of spirits and wines from all over the world. Recurrent tastings and mailorder.

RUSSIA
Whisky World Shop
9, Tverskoy Boulevard
123104 Moscow
Phone: +7 495 787 9150
www.whiskyworld.ru
Huge assortment with more than 1,000 different single malts. The range is supplemented with a nice range of cognac, armagnac, calvados, grappa and wines. Tastings are also arranged.

SCOTLAND
Gordon & MacPhail
58 - 60 South Street, Elgin
Moray IV30 1JY
Phone: +44 (0)1343 545110
www.gordonandmacphail.com
This legendary shop opened already in 1895 in Elgin. The owners are perhaps the most well-known among independent bottlers. The shop stocks more than 800 bottlings of whisky and more than 600 wines and there is also a delicatessen counter with high-quality products.

Tastings are arranged in the shop and there are shipping services within the UK and overseas. The shop attracts visitors from all over the world.

Royal Mile Whiskies (2 shops)
379 High Street, The Royal Mile
Edinburgh EH1 1PW
Phone: +44 (0)131 2253383

3 Bloomsbury Street
London WC1B 3QE
Phone: +44 (0)20 7436 4763
www.royalmilewhiskies.com
Royal Mile Whiskies is one of the most well-known whisky retailers in the UK. It was established in Edinburgh in 1991. There is also a shop in London since 2002 and a cigar shop close to the Edinburgh shop. The whisky range is outstanding with many difficult to find elsewhere. They have a comprehensive site regarding information on regions, distilleries, production, tasting etc. Royal Mile Whiskies also arranges 'Whisky Fringe' in Edinburgh, a two-day whisky festival which takes place annually in mid August. On-line ordering with worldwide shipping.

The Whisky Shop
(See also England, The Whisky Shop)
Unit L2-02 Buchanan Galleries
220 Buchanan Street
Glasgow G1 2GF
Phone: +44 (0)141 331 0022

17 Bridge Street
Inverness IV1 1HD
Phone: +44 (0)1463 710525

93 High Street
Fort William PH33 6DG
Phone: +44 (0)1397 706164

52 George Street
Oban PA34 5SD
Phone: +44 (0)1631 570896

Unit 23 Waverley Mall
Waverley Bridge
Edinburgh EH1 1BQ
Phone: +44 (0)131 558 7563

28 Victoria Street
Edinburgh EH1 2JW
Phone: +44 (0)131 225 4666
www.whiskyshop.com
The first shop opened in 1992 in Edinburgh and this is now the United Kingdom's largest specialist retailer of whiskies with 20 outlets (plus one in Paris). A large product range with over 700 kinds, including 400 malt whiskies and 140 miniature bottles, as well as accessories and books. The own range 'Glenkeir Treasures' is a special assortment of selected malt whiskies. The also run The W Club, the leading whisky club in the UK where the excellent Whiskeria magazine is one of the member´s benefits. On-line ordering.

Loch Fyne Whiskies
Main Street, Inveraray
Argyll PA32 8UD
Phone: +44 (0)800 107 1936
www.lochfynewhiskies.com
A legendary shop! The range of malt whiskies is large and they have their own

house blend, the prize-awarded Loch Fyne, as well as their 'The Loch Fyne Whisky Liqueur'. There is also a range of house malts called 'The Inverarity'. On-line ordering with worldwide shipping.

Single Malts Direct
36 Gordon Street
Huntly
Aberdeenshire AB54 8EQ
Phone: +44 (0) 845 606 6145
www.singlemaltsdirect.com
Owned by independent bottler Duncan Taylor. In the assortment is of course the whole Duncan Taylor range but also a selection of their own single malt bottlings called Whiskies of Scotland. A total of almost 700 different expressions. On-line shop with shipping worldwide.

The Whisky Shop Dufftown
1 Fife Street, Dufftown
Moray AB55 4AL
Phone: +44 (0)1340 821097
www.whiskyshopdufftown.co.uk
Whisky specialist in Dufftown in the heart of Speyside, wellknown to many of the Speyside festival visitors. More than 500 single malts as well as other whiskies. Arranges tastings as well as special events during the Festivals. On-line ordering.

Cadenhead's Whisky Shop
30-32 Union Street
Campbeltown PA28 6JA
Phone: +44 (0)1586 551710

9 Bolgam Street,
Campbeltown PA28 6HZ
Phone: +44 (0)1586 554761
www.wmcadenhead.com
Part of the chain of shops owned by independent bottlers Cadenhead. Sells Cadenhead's products and other whiskies with a good range of Springbank. On-line ordering.

Cadenhead´s Whisky Shop
172 Canongate, Royal Mile
Edinburgh EH8 8BN
Phone: +44 (0)131 556 5864
www.wmcadenhead.com
The oldest shop in the chain owned by Cadenhead. Sells Cadenhead's product range and a good selection of other whiskies and spirits. Recurrent tastings. On-line ordering.

The Good Spirits Co.
23 Bath Street,
Glasgow G2 1HW
Phone: +44 (0)141 258 8427
www.thegoodspiritsco.com
A newly opened specialist spirits store selling whisky, bourbon, rum, vodka, tequila, gin, cognac and armagnac, liqueurs and other spirits. They also stock quality champagne, fortified wines and cigars.

The Carnegie Whisky Cellars
The Carnegie Courthouse, Castle Street
IV25 3SD Dornoch
Phone: +44 (0)1862 811791
www.thecarnegiecourthouse.co.uk/whisky-cellars/
Opened by Michael Hanratty in 2016, this shop has already become a destination for whisky enthusiasts from the UK

and abroad. The interior of the shop is ravishing and the extensive range includes all the latest releases as well as rare and collectable bottles. UK and international shipping.

Abbey Whisky
Dunfermline KY11 3BZ
Phone: +44 (0)800 051 7737
www.abbeywhisky.com
Family run online whisky shop specialising in exclusive, rare and old whiskies from Scotland and the world. Apart from a wide range of official and independent bottlings, Abbey Whisky also selects their own casks and bottle them under the name 'The Rare Casks' and 'The Secret Casks'.

The Scotch Whisky Experience
354 Castlehill, Royal Mile
Edinburgh EH1 2NE
Phone: +44 (0)131 220 0441
www.scotchwhiskyexperience.co.uk
The Scotch Whisky Experience is a must for whisky devotees visiting Edinburgh. An interactive visitor centre dedicated to the history of Scotch whisky. This five-star visitor attraction has an excellent whisky shop with almost 300 different whiskies in stock. Recently, after extensive refurbishment, a brand new and interactive shop was opened.

Whiski Shop
4 North Bank Street
Edinburgh EH1 2LP
Phone: +44 (0)131 225 1532
www.whiskishop.com
www.whiskirooms.co.uk
A new concept located near Edinburgh Castle, combining a shop, a tasting room and a bistro. Also regular whisky tastings. Online mail order with worldwide delivery.

Robbie's Drams
3 Sandgate, Ayr
South Ayrshire KA7 1BG
Phone: +44 (0)1292 262 135
www.robbieswhiskymerchants.com
Over 600 whiskies available in store and over 900 available from their on-line shop. Specialists in single cask bottlings, closed distillery bottlings, rare malts, limited edition whisky and a nice range of their own bottlings. Worldwide shipping.

The Whisky Barrel
PO Box 23803, Edinburgh, EH6 7WW
Phone: +44 (0)845 2248 156
www.thewhiskybarrel.com
Online specialist whisky shop based in Edinburgh. They stock over 1,000 single malt and blended whiskies including Scotch, Japanese, Irish, Indian, Swedish and their own casks. Worldwide shipping.

The Scotch Malt Whisky Society
www.smws.com
A society with more than 20 000 members worldwide, specialised in own bottlings of single casks and release between 150 and 200 bottlings a year.

Drinkmonger
100 Atholl Road
Pitlochry PH16 5BL
Phone: +44 (0)1796 470133

11 Bruntsfield Place
Edinburgh EH10 4HN
Phone: +44 (0)131 229 2205
www.drinkmonger.com
Two new shops opened in 2011 by the well-known Royal Mile Whiskies. The idea is to have a 50:50 split between wine and specialist spiritswith the addition of a cigar assortment. The whisky range is a good cross-section with some rarities and a focus on local distilleries.

A.D. Rattray´s Whisky Experience & Whisky Shop
32 Main Road
Kirkoswald
Ayrshire KA19 8HY
Phone: +44 (0) 1655 760308
www.adrattray.com
A combination of whisky shop, sample room and educational center owned by the independent bottler A D Rattray. Tasting menus with different themes are available.

Robert Graham Ltd (3 shops)
194 Rose Street
Edinburgh EH2 4AZ
Phone: +44 (0)131 226 1874

Robert Graham´s Global Whisky Shop
111 West George Street
Glasgow G2 1QX
Phone: +44 (0)141 248 7283

Robert Graham's Treasurer 1874
254 Canongate
Royal Mile
Edinburgh EH8 8AA
Phone: +44 (0)131 556 2791
www.whisky-cigars.co.uk
Established in 1874 this company specialises in Scotch whisky and cigars. They have a nice assortment of malt whiskies and their range of cigars is impressive.

SOUTH AFRICA

Aficionados Premium Spirits Online
M5 Freeway Park
Cape Town
Phone: +27 21 511 7337
www.aficionados.co.za
An online liquor retailer specialising in single malt whisky. They claim to offer the widest of range of whiskies available in South Africa and hold regular tastings around the country. Shipping only within South Africa.

WhiskyBrother
Hyde Park Corner
(middle level inside shopping mall)
Johannesburg
Phone: +27 (0)11 325 6261
www.whiskybrother.com
A shop specialising in all things whisky - apart from 400 different bottlings they also sell glasses, books etc. Also sell whiskies bottled exclusively for the shop. Regular tastings and online shop.

SWITZERLAND

P. Ullrich AG
Schneidergasse 27
4051 Basel
Phone: +41 (0)61 338 90 91
Another two shops in Basel:
Laufenstrasse 16 & Unt. Rebgasse 18
and one in Talacker 30 in Zürich
www.ullrich.ch
A very large range of wines, spirits, beers, accessories and books. Over 800 kinds of whisky with almost 600 single malt. On-line ordering. Recently, they also founded a whisky club with regular tastings (www.whiskysinn.ch).

Eddie's Whiskies
Dorfgasse 27
8810 Horgen
Phone: +41 (0)43 244 63 00
www.eddies.ch
A whisky specialist with more than 700 different whiskies in stock with emphasis on single malts (more than 500 different). Also arranges tastings.

Angels Share Shop
Unterdorfstrasse 15
5036 Oberentfelden
Phone: +41 (0)62 724 83 74
www.angelsshare.ch
A combined restaurant and whisky shop. More than 400 different kinds of whisky as well as a good range of cigars. Scores extra points for short information and photos of all distilleries. On-line ordering.

UKRAINE

WINETIME
Mykoly Bazhana 1E
Kyiv 02068
Phone: +38 (0)44 338 08 88
www.winetime.ua
WINETIME is the largest specialized chain of wine and spirits shops in Ukraine. The company runs 18 stores in 14 regions of Ukraine. An impressive selection of spirits with over 1000 whiskies of which 600 are malt whiskies. On-line ordering. Also regular whisky tastings.

USA

Binny´s Beverage Depot
5100 W. Dempster (Head Office)
Skokie, IL 60077
Phone:
Internet orders, 888-942-9463 (toll free)
Whiskey Hotline, 888-817-5898 (toll free)
www.binnys.com
A chain of no less than 38 stores in the Chicago area, covering everything within wine and spirits. Some of the stores also have a gourmet grocery, cheese shop and, for cigar lovers, a walk-in humidor. Also lots of regular events in the stores. The range is impressive with more than 2100 whisk(e)y (700 single malts, 320 bourbons) and more. Among other products more than 400 kinds of tequila and mezcal, 450 vodkas and 350 rums should be mentioned. And, on top of that more than 10,000 different wines! Online mail order service.

Statistics

The following pages have been made possible,
first and foremost thanks to kind cooperation from The IWSR.
Data has also been provided by Drinks International, The Scotch Whisky
Industry Review and the Scotch Whisky Association.

Whisk(e)y forecast (volume)
by region and category 2016-2021

■ = positive volume growth   ▨ = negative volume growth

SW=Scotch Whisky, IW=Irish Whiskey, UW=US Whiskey, CW=Canadian Whisky, JW=Japanese whisky, TOT=Total.
The figures show CAGR% (Compound Annual Growth Rate) i. e. year-over-year growth rate.

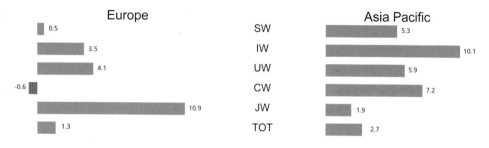

Europe
Category	CAGR%
SW	0.5
IW	3.5
UW	4.1
CW	-0.6
JW	10.9
TOT	1.3

Asia Pacific
Category	CAGR%
SW	5.3
IW	10.1
UW	5.9
CW	7.2
JW	1.9
TOT	2.7

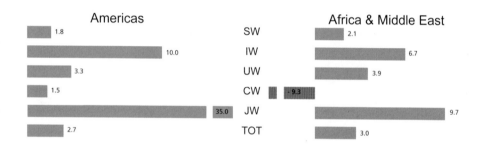

Americas
Category	CAGR%
SW	1.8
IW	10.0
UW	3.3
CW	1.5
JW	35.0
TOT	2.7

Africa & Middle East
Category	CAGR%
SW	2.1
IW	6.7
UW	3.9
CW	-9.3
JW	9.7
TOT	3.0

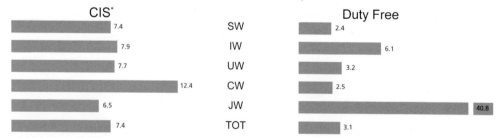

CIS*
Category	CAGR%
SW	7.4
IW	7.9
UW	7.7
CW	12.4
JW	6.5
TOT	7.4

Duty Free
Category	CAGR%
SW	2.4
IW	6.1
UW	3.2
CW	2.5
JW	40.8
TOT	3.1

* Russia and other former Soviet Socialist Republic states

The World
Category	CAGR%
SW	2.2
IW	7.4
UW	3.8
CW	1.5
JW	2.5
TOT	2.6

The Top 30 Whiskies of the World

Sales figures for 2016 (units in million 9-litre cases)

Officer's Choice (Allied Blenders & Distillers), Indian whisky — 32,9
McDowell's No. 1 (United Spirits), Indian whisky — 25,5
Imperial Blue (Pernod Ricard), Indian whisky — 18,0
Royal Stag (Pernod Ricard), Indian whisky — 18,0
Johnnie Walker (Diageo), Scotch whisky — 17,4
Jack Daniel's (Brown-Forman), Tennessee whiskey — 12,4
Original Choice (John Distilleries), Indian whisky — 10,8
Old Tavern (United Spirits), Indian whisky — 8,8
Hayward's Fine (United Spirits), Indian whisky — 8,2
Jim Beam (Beam Suntory), Bourbon — 8,0
Bagpiper (United Spirits), Indian whisky — 7,0
Crown Royal (Diageo), Canadian whisky — 6,8
Ballantine's (Pernod Ricard), Scotch whisky — 6,7
Jameson (Pernod Ricard), Irish whiskey — 6,2
Blenders Pride (Pernod Ricard), Indian whisky — 6,2
8PM (Radico Khaitan), Indian whisky — 5,7
Royal Challenge (United Spirits), Indian whisky — 4,7
William Grant's (William Grant & Sons), Scotch whisky — 4,5
Chivas Regal (Pernod Ricard), Scotch whisky — 4,3
J&B Rare (Diageo), Scotch whisky — 3,5
Kakubin (Suntory), Japanese whisky — 3,3
William Peel (Bélvedère), Scotch whisky — 3,0
Famous Grouse (Edrington), Scotch whisky — 3,0
William Lawson's (Bacardi), Scotch whisky — 3,0
Dewar's (Bacardi), Scotch whisky — 2,8
Director's Special Black (United Spirits), Indian whisky — 2,8
Black Nikka Clear (Asahi Breweries), Japanese whisky — 2,7
Label 5 (La Martiniquaise), Scotch whisky — 2,6
Evan Williams (Heaven Hill), Bourbon — 2,3
Bell's (Diageo), Scotch whisky — 2,1

Source: Drinks International, The Millionaires Club 2017

Global Exports of Scotch by Region

Volume (litres of pure alcohol)			chg	Value (£ Sterling)			chg
Region	2016	2015	%	Region	2016	2015	%
Africa	18,308,038	20,252,487	-10	Africa	166,699,435	193,676,818	-14
Asia	67,396,763	63,654,973	+6	Asia	785,752,330	772,386,515	+2
Australasia	8,945,599	9,235,830	-3	Australasia	108,781,275	97,559,266	+12
C&S America	37,538,506	35,544,962	+6	C&S America	339,208,739	332,667,493	+2
Eastern Europe	2,762,120	888,625	+210	Eastern Europe	17,406,537	9,776,958	+78
Europe (other)	5,822,396	6,653,246	-12	Europe (other)	91,136,702	102,696,130	-11
European Union	132,377,878	121,844,623	+9	European Union	1,241,689,593	1,198,393,010	+4
Middle East	14,037,184	14,174,307	-1	Middle East	217,917,206	207,231,516	+5
North America	52,769,877	52,115,294	+1	North America	1,040,648,531	941,136,341	+11
Total	339,958,361	324,364,347	+5	Total	4,009,240,348	3,855,525,047	+4

Source: Scotch Whisky Association

World Consumption of Blended Scotch

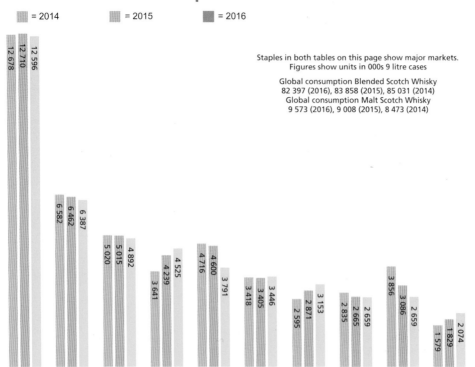

= 2014   = 2015   = 2016

Staples in both tables on this page show major markets.
Figures show units in 000s 9 litre cases

Global consumption Blended Scotch Whisky
82 397 (2016), 83 858 (2015), 85 031 (2014)
Global consumption Malt Scotch Whisky
9 573 (2016), 9 008 (2015), 8 473 (2014)

France: 12 678, 12 710, 12 596
USA: 6 582, 6 462, 6 387
UK: 5 020, 5 015, 4 892
Mexico: 3 641, 4 239, 4 525
Brazil: 4 716, 4 600, 3 791
Spain: 3 418, 3 405, 3 446
India: 2 595, 2 871, 3 153
South Africa: 2 835, 2 665, 2 659
Russia: 3 856, 3 086, 2 659
Poland: 1 579, 1 829, 2 074

Source: © The IWSR 2017

World Consumption of Malt Scotch

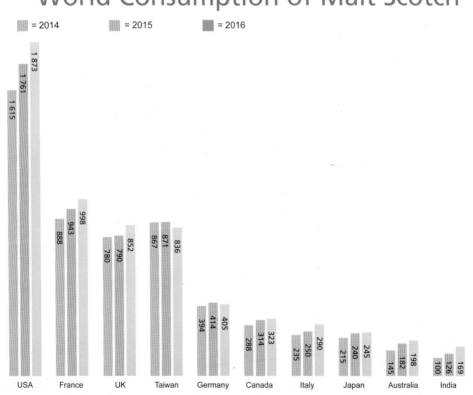

= 2014   = 2015   = 2016

USA: 1 615, 1 761, 1 873
France: 888, 943, 998
UK: 780, 790, 852
Taiwan: 867, 871, 836
Germany: 394, 414, 405
Canada: 288, 314, 323
Italy: 235, 250, 290
Japan: 215, 240, 245
Australia: 145, 182, 198
India: 100, 126, 169

Source: © The IWSR 2017

Top 10 Scotch Malt Whisky brands - world market share %

Brand	Year	Share
Glenfiddich	2016	12,5
	2015	12,1
	2014	12,1
The Glenlivet	2016	11,2
	2015	12,1
	2014	12,1
The Macallan	2016	8,7
	2015	8,8
	2014	9,5
Glenmorangie	2016	5,5
	2015	5,7
	2014	5,8
The Singleton (Dufftown, Glendullan, Glen Ord)	2016	5,2
	2015	5,4
	2014	4,8
Aberlour	2016	3,6
	2015	3,5
	2014	3,4
Laphroaig	2016	3,2
	2015	3,4
	2014	3,1
Balvenie	2016	3,1
	2015	3,0
	2014	2,8
Glen Grant	2016	3,1
	2015	3,2
	2014	3,3
Talisker	2016	2,3
	2015	2,4
	2014	2,2

Top 10 Scotch Blended Whisky brands - world market share %

Brand	Year	Share
Johnnie Walker	2016	21,5
	2015	21,5
	2014	21,5
Ballantine's	2016	7,8
	2015	7,1
	2014	6,8
Chivas Regal	2016	5,5
	2015	5,4
	2014	5,5
Grant's	2016	5,4
	2015	5,2
	2014	5,2
J&B	2016	4,2
	2015	4,2
	2014	4,2
Famous Grouse	2016	3,7
	2015	3,5
	2014	3,6
William Peel	2016	3,6
	2015	3,4
	2014	3,1
William Lawson's	2016	3,5
	2015	3,6
	2014	3,4
Dewar's	2016	3,2
	2015	3,1
	2014	3,2
Label 5	2016	2,7
	2015	2,7
	2014	2,7

Source: © The IWSR 2017

Distillery Capacity

Litres of pure alcohol - Scottish, active distilleries only

Glenfiddich	13 700 000	The Borders	2 000 000	Kingsbarns	600 000
Roseisle	12 500 000	Bowmore	2 000 000	Speyside	600 000
Ailsa Bay	12 000 000	Inchdairnie	2 000 000	Annandale	500 000
Glen Ord	11 000 000	Knockdhu	2 000 000	Ardnamurchan	500 000
Macallan	11 000 000	Balblair	1 800 000	The Clydeside	500 000
Glenlivet	10 500 000	Pulteney	1 800 000	Royal Lochnagar	500 000
Teaninich	10 200 000	Bruichladdich	1 500 000	Torabhaig	500 000
Dalmunach	10 000 000	Bladnoch	1 500 000	Lone Wolf	450 000
Balvenie	7 000 000	Glendronach	1 400 000	Glenturret	340 000
Caol Ila	6 500 000	Glen Spey	1 400 000	Glasgow	270 000
Glen Grant	6 200 000	Knockando	1 400 000	Harris	230 000
Dufftown	6 000 000	Ardbeg	1 400 000	Arbikie	200 000
Glenmorangie	6 000 000	Glen Garioch	1 370 000	Isle of Raasay	200 000
Mannochmore	6 000 000	Glencadam	1 300 000	Kilchoman	200 000
Auchroisk	5 900 000	Scapa	1 300 000	Lindores Abbey	150 000
Glen Keith	5 800 000	Arran	1 200 000	Wolfburn	135 000
Miltonduff	5 800 000	Glenglassaugh	1 100 000	Edradour	130 000
Glen Moray	5 700 000	Glengoyne	1 100 000	Ballindalloch	100 000
Glenrothes	5 600 000	Tobermory	1 000 000	Ncn´ean	100 000
Linkwood	5 600 000	Oban	870 000	Eden Mill	80 000
Ardmore	5 550 000	Glen Scotia	800 000	Daftmill	65 000
Dailuaine	5 200 000	Glengyle	750 000	Dornoch	30 000
Glendullan	5 000 000	Springbank	750 000	Strathearn	30 000
Loch Lomond	5 000 000	Benromach	700 000	Abhainn Dearg	20 000
Tomatin	5 000 000				
Clynelish	4 800 000				
Kininvie	4 800 000				
Tormore	4 800 000				
Longmorn	4 500 000				
Speyburn	4 500 000				
Dalmore	4 300 000				
Allt-a-Bhainne	4 200 000				
Braeval	4 200 000				
Glenburgie	4 200 000				
Glentauchers	4 200 000				
Craigellachie	4 100 000				
Royal Brackla	4 100 000				
Glenallachie	4 000 000				
Tamdhu	4 000 000				
Tamnavulin	4 000 000				
Aberlour	3 800 000				
Mortlach	3 800 000				
Glenlossie	3 700 000				
Benrinnes	3 500 000				
Glenfarclas	3 500 000				
Aberfeldy	3 400 000				
Cardhu	3 400 000				
Macduff	3 400 000				
Laphroaig	3 300 000				
Talisker	3 300 000				
Tomintoul	3 300 000				
Aultmore	3 200 000				
Fettercairn	3 200 000				
Inchgower	3 200 000				
Deanston	3 000 000				
Tullibardine	3 000 000				
Balmenach	2 800 000				
Benriach	2 800 000				
Blair Athol	2 800 000				
Bunnahabhain	2 700 000				
Glen Elgin	2 700 000				
Strathmill	2 600 000				
Lagavulin	2 530 000				
Glenkinchie	2 500 000				
Highland Park	2 500 000				
Jura	2 400 000				
Strathisla	2 200 000				
Cragganmore	2 200 000				
Dalwhinnie	2 200 000				
Auchentoshan	2 000 000				
Ben Nevis	2 000 000				

Summary of Malt Distillery Capacity by Owner

Owner (number of distilleries)	Litres of alcohol	% of Industry
Diageo (28)	121 300 000	31,7
Pernod Ricard (13)	65 500 000	17,1
William Grant (4)	37 500 000	9,8
Edrington Group (4)	19 440 000	5,1
Bacardi (John Dewar & Sons) (5)	18 200 000	4,8
Beam Suntory (5)	14 220 000	3,7
Emperador Inc (Whyte & Mackay) (4)	13 900 000	3,6
Pacific Spirits (Inver House) (5)	12 900 000	3,4
Moët Hennessy (Glenmorangie) (2)	7 400 000	1,9
Distell (Burn Stewart) (3)	6 700 000	1,8
Campari (Glen Grant) (1)	6 200 000	1,6
Loch Lomond Group (2)	5 800 000	1,5
La Martiniquaise (Glen Moray) (1)	5 700 000	1,5
Benriach Distillery Co (3)	5 300 000	1,4
Ian Macleod Distillers (2)	5 100 000	1,3
Tomatin Distillery Co (1)	5 000 000	1,3
Angus Dundee (2)	4 600 000	1,2
The Glenallachie Consortium (1)	4 000 000	1,0
J & G Grant (Glenfarclas) (1)	3 500 000	0,9
Picard (Tullibardine) (1)	3 000 000	0,8
John Fergus & Co. (Inchdairnie) (1)	2 000 000	0,5
Nikka (Ben Nevis Distillery) (1)	2 000 000	0,5
The Three Stills Co. (The Borders) (1)	2 000 000	0,5
Rémy Cointreau (Bruichladdich) (1)	1 500 000	< 0,5
J & A Mitchell (2)	1 500 000	< 0,5
David Prior (Bladnoch) (1)	1 500 000	< 0,5
Isle of Arran Distillers (1)	1 200 000	< 0,5
Gordon & MacPhail (Benromach) (1)	700 000	< 0,5
Wemyss Malts (Kingsbarns) (1)	600 000	< 0,5
Harvey´s of Edinburgh (Speyside) (1)	600 000	< 0,5
Adelphi Distillery (Ardnamurchan) (1)	500 000	< 0,5
Annandale Distillery Co. (1)	500 000	< 0,5
Morrison Glasgow Distillers (1)	500 000	< 0,5
Mossburn Distillers (Torabhaig) (1)	500 000	< 0,5
BrewDog plc (Lone Wolf) (1)	450 000	< 0,5
Glasgow Distillery Company (1)	270 000	< 0,5
Isle of Harris Distillers (1)	230 000	< 0,5
Kilchoman Distillery Co (1)	200 000	< 0,5
R&B Distillers (Isle of Raasay) (1)	200 000	< 0,5
Stirling family (Arbikie) (1)	200 000	< 0,5
Others (9)	740 000	< 0,5
Total	**382 740 000**	

Do you want to find out more in detail where the different distilleries are situated? We suggest that you pay a visit to **bit.ly/daNJMP** where Steffen Bräuner has plotted not only all the Scottish and Irish distilleries but there are also maps for the Americas and for distilleries from the rest of the world.

ORKNEY ISLANDS

NORTH HIGHLANDS

Wick

Isle of Lewis

Isle of Harris

SPEYSIDE

Inverness

SKYE

Kyle of Lockalsh

Loch Ness

Aberdeen

CENTRAL HIGHLANDS

Fort William

EAST HIGHLANDS

WEST HIGHLANDS

Pitlochry

Dundee

MULL

Oban

Loch Tay

Loch Lomond

Perth

St. Andrews

Stirling

JURA

Glasgow

Edinburgh

ISLAY

ARRAN

Campbeltown

Ayr

THE LOWLANDS

Dumfries

Stranraer

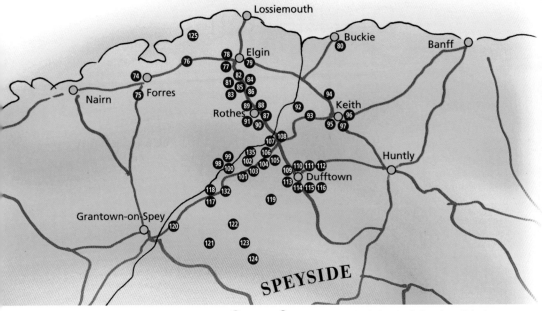

Distilleries in red letters are Speyside ● Active ● Closed, mothballed, dismantled or demolished

c = Closed, m = Mothballed, dm = Dismantled, d = Demolished

39 Aberfeldy	110 Dufftown	100 Knockando	2 Highland Park	51 Kinclaith (d)	100 Knockando
106 Aberlour	136 Eden Mill	21 Knockdhu	3 Scapa	52 Glen Flagler (d)	101 Glenfarclas
129 Abhainn Dearg	38 Edradour	56 Ladyburn (dm)	4 Pulteney	53 Rosebank (c)	102 Imperial (d)
127 Ailsa Bay	32 Fettercairn	63 Lagavulin	5 Brora (c)	54 St Magdalene (dm)	103 Dailuaine
119 Allt-a-Bhainne	141 Glasgow	64 Laphroaig	6 Clynelish	55 Glenkinchie	104 Benrinnes
128 Annandale	13 Glen Albyn (d)	137 Lindores Abbey	7 Balblair	56 Ladyburn (dm)	105 Glenallachie
134 Arbikie	105 Glenallachie	79 Linkwood	8 Glenmorangie	57 Bladnoch	106 Aberlour
62 Ardbeg	76 Glenburgie	48 Littlemill (d)	9 Ben Wyvis (c)	58 Arran	107 Macallan
25 Ardmore	34 Glencadam	46 Loch Lomond	10 Teaninich	59 Springbank	108 Craigellachie
131 Ardnamurchan	23 Glendronach	36 Lochside (d)	11 Dalmore	60 Glengyle	109 Convalmore (dm)
58 Arran	116 Glendullan	143 Lone Wolf	12 Glen Ord	61 Glen Scotia	110 Dufftown
49 Auchentoshan	85 Glen Elgin	84 Longmorn	13 Glen Albyn (d)	62 Ardbeg	111 Pittyvaich (d)
92 Auchroisk	35 Glenesk (dm)	107 Macallan	14 Glen Mhor (d)	63 Lagavulin	112 Glenfiddich
94 Aultmore	101 Glenfarclas	20 Macduff	15 Millburn (dm)	64 Laphroaig	113 Balvenie
7 Balblair	112 Glenfiddich	81 Mannochmore	16 Royal Brackla	65 Port Ellen (dm)	114 Kininvie
132 Ballindalloch	52 Glen Flagler (d)	15 Millburn (dm)	17 Tomatin	66 Bowmore	115 Mortlach
120 Balmenach	24 Glen Garioch	77 Miltonduff	18 Glenglassaugh	67 Bruichladdich	116 Glendullan
113 Balvenie	18 Glenglassaugh	115 Mortlach	19 Banff (d)	68 Kilchoman	117 Tormore
19 Banff (d)	50 Glengoyne	145 Ncn´ean	20 Macduff	69 Caol Ila	118 Cragganmore
30 Ben Nevis	87 Glen Grant	33 North Port (d)	21 Knockdhu	70 Bunnahabhain	119 Allt-a-Bhainne
82 Benriach	60 Glengyle	40 Oban	22 Glenugie (dm)	71 Jura	120 Balmenach
104 Benrinnes	96 Glen Keith	111 Pittyvaich (d)	23 Glendronach	72 Tobermory	121 Tomintoul
74 Benromach	55 Glenkinchie	65 Port Ellen (dm)	24 Glen Garioch	73 Talisker	122 Glenlivet
9 Ben Wyvis (c)	122 Glenlivet	4 Pulteney	25 Ardmore	74 Benromach	123 Tamnavulin
57 Bladnoch	31 Glenlochy (d)	53 Rosebank (c)	26 Speyside	75 Dallas Dhu (c)	124 Braeval
37 Blair Athol	83 Glenlossie	125 Roseisle	27 Royal Lochnagar	76 Glenburgie	125 Roseisle
138 Borders	14 Glen Mhor (d)	16 Royal Brackla	28 Glenury Royal (d)	77 Miltonduff	126 Ailsa Bay
66 Bowmore	8 Glenmorangie	27 Royal Lochnagar	29 Dalwhinnie	78 Glen Moray	127 Abhainn Dearg
124 Braeval	78 Glen Moray	54 St Magdalene (dm)	30 Ben Nevis	79 Linkwood	128 Annandale
5 Brora (c)	12 Glen Ord	3 Scapa	31 Glenlochy (d)	80 Inchgower	129 Wolfburn
67 Bruichladdich	89 Glenrothes	88 Speyburn	32 Fettercairn	81 Mannochmore	130 Strathearn
70 Bunnahabhain	61 Glen Scotia	26 Speyside	33 North Port (d)	82 Benriach	131 Ardnamurchan
69 Caol Ila	91 Glenspey	59 Springbank	34 Glencadam	83 Glenlossie	132 Ballindalloch
90 Caperdonich (c)	93 Glentauchers	130 Strathearn	35 Glenesk (dm)	84 Longmorn	133 Inchdairnie
99 Cardhu	41 Glenturret	97 Strathisla	36 Lochside (d)	85 Glen Elgin	134 Arbikie
142 Clydeside	22 Glenugie (dm)	95 Strathmill	37 Blair Athol	86 Coleburn (dm)	135 Dalmunach
6 Clynelish	28 Glenury Royal (d)	73 Talisker	38 Edradour	87 Glen Grant	136 Eden Mill
86 Coleburn (dm)	140 Harris	98 Tamdhu	39 Aberfeldy	88 Speyburn	137 Lindores Abbey
109 Convalmore (dm)	2 Highland Park	123 Tamnavulin	40 Oban	89 Glenrothes	138 Borders
118 Cragganmore	133 Inchdairnie	10 Teaninich	41 Glenturret	90 Caperdonich (c)	139 Torabhaig
108 Craigellachie	102 Imperial (d)	72 Tobermory	42 Daftmill	91 Glenspey	140 Harris
42 Daftmill	80 Inchgower	17 Tomatin	43 Kingsbarns	92 Auchroisk	141 Glasgow
103 Dailuaine	47 Inverleven (d)	121 Tomintoul	44 Tullibardine	93 Glentauchers	142 Clydeside
75 Dallas Dhu (c)	146 Isle of Raasay	139 Torabhaig	45 Deanston	94 Aultmore	143 Lone Wolf
11 Dalmore	71 Jura	117 Tormore	46 Loch Lomond	95 Strathmill	144 Dornoch
135 Dalmunach	68 Kilchoman	44 Tullibardine	47 Inverleven (d)	96 Glen Keith	145 Ncn´ean
29 Dalwhinnie	51 Kinclaith (d)	129 Wolfburn	48 Littlemill (d)	97 Strathisla	146 Isle of Raasay
45 Deanston	43 Kingsbarns		49 Auchentoshan	98 Tamdhu	
144 Dornoch	114 Kininvie		50 Glengoyne	99 Cardhu	

Distillery Index

2nd Street distilling Co 242
3 Howls Distillery 239
11 Wells Distillery 240

A

Aberfeldy 53
Aberlour 54
Abhainn Dearg distillery 174
Adnams Copper House Distillery 210
Aerø Whisky 209
Ailsa Bay 175
Akkeshi Distillery 196
Alazana Distillery, La 256
Alley 6 Craft Distillery 243
Allt-a-Bhainne 55
Alp Spirits 215
Alt Enderle Brennerei 218
Altstadthof, Hausbrauerei 220
Amrut Distilleries 252
Annandale distillery 173
Applewood Distillery 251
Arbikie 179
Archie Rose Distilling 250
Arcus distillery 227
Ardbeg 56-57
Ardmore 58
Ardnamurchan distillery 172
Arizona Distilling Company 244
Arran 59
Asaka 196
ASW Distillery 242
Auchentoshan 60
Auchroisk 61
Aultmore 62
Aurora Spirit 227
AV Brennerei 218

B

Bakery Hill Distillery 247
Balblair 63
Balcones Distillery 232
Ballindalloch distillery 172
Balmenach 64
Balvenie 65
Banff 184
Bellerhof Brennerei 221
Ben Nevis 66
BenRiach 67
Benrinnes 68
Benromach 69
Bent Brewstillery 241
Ben Wyvis 184
Bercloux 214
Bertrand, Distillerie 213
Bimber 211
Birkenhof-Brennerei 218
Black Gate Distillery 249
Bladnoch 70
Blair Athol 71
Blaue Maus, Destillerie 216
Blaum Bros. Distilling 240
Blue Ridge Distilling Co. 236
Boann Distillery 224

Borders, The 182
Boston Harnor Distillery 242
Bowmore 72-73
Bows 215
BOX Destilleri 228
Braeval 74
Braunstein 208
Brickway Brewery & Distillery 240
Broger Privatbrennerei 206
Brora 185
Brothers Spirits 244
Bruichladdich 76-77
Brûlerie du Revermont 213
Brunet, Distillerie 213
Bull Run Distillery 236
Bunnahabhain 78
Burger Hofbrennerei 220
Bushmills Distillery 226

C

Cannon Beach Distillery 242
Caol Ila 79
Caperdonich 186
Cardhu 80
Cardrona Distillery 251
Castle Glen Distillery 250
Castor, Distillerie du 215
Castan 215
Cedar Ridge Distillery 234
Central City Brewers & Distillers 246
Charbay Winery & Distillery 235
Chase Distillery 210
Chichibu 197
Civilized Spirits 239
Claeyssens, Distillerie 212
Clear Creek Distillery 233
Clydeside, The 181
Clynelish 82
Coleburn 186
Connacht Whiskey Company, The 224
Convalmore 186
Cooley 223
Coppercraft Distillery 240
Copper Fox Distillery 236
Copper Rivet 211
Coppersea Distilling 244
Copper Works Distilling Co. 237
Cornelius Pass Roadhouse 239
Corsair Artisan 234
Cotherman Distilling 242
Cotswolds Distillery, The 210
Cragganmore 83
Craigellachie 84
Cut Spike Distillery 236
Cutwater Spirits 235

D

Dachstein Destillerie 207
Daftmill 174
Dailuaine 85
Dallas Dhu 186
Dallas Distilleries 243
Dalmore 86

Dalmunach 177
Dalwhinnie 87
Damnation Alley Distillery 241
Dartmoor 211
Deanston 88
Deerhammer Distilling Co 238
Destilerias Liber 228
Dingle Distillery 224
Dirty Water Distillery 244
DoGood Distillery 236
Domaine de Bourjac 215
Domaine des Hautes-Glaces 214
Door County Distillery 237
Dornoch 182
DownSlope Distilling 236
Dreumont 214
Drexler, Destillerie 219
Druffel, Brennerei Josef 220
Dry Fly Distilling 234
Dubh Glas Distillery 246
Dufftown 89
DYC 227
Dürr Edelbranntweine 219

E

Ebner, Brennerei 207
Echlinville distillery 226
Eden Mill distillery 176
Edgefield Distillery 233
Edradour 90
Eifel Destillate 221
Eimwerk Distillery 222
Emilio Mignone Distillery 256
English Whisky Co, The see St George's Distillery
Ergaster 215
Etter Distillerie 230

F

Faber, Brennerei 218
Fanny's Bay Distillery 251
Fary Lochan Destilleri 208
Feller, Brennerei 219
Fettercairn 91
FEW Spirits 236
Finch Whiskydestillerie 221
Fitzke, Kleinbrennerei 218
Franz Kostenzer 207
Fuji-Gotemba 197

G

Gammelstilla Whisky 229
Gemmer, Landgasthof 219
Geuting, Gutsbrennerei Joh. B 220
Gilbert Holl, Distillerie 213
Glann ar Mor 212
Glasgow Distillery 177
Glen Albyn 187
Glenallachie 92
Glenburgie 93
Glencadam 94
Glendalough 224

Distillery Index

Glen Deveron see Macduff
Glendronach 95
Glendullan 96
Glen Elgin 97
Glenesk 187
Glenfarclas 98-99
Glenfiddich 100-101
Glen Flagler 187
Glen Garioch 102
Glenglassaugh 104
Glengoyne 105
Glen Grant 106-107
Glengyle 108
Glen Keith 110
Glenkinchie 111
Glenlivet 112-113
Glenlochy 187
Glenlossie 114
Glen Mhor 188
Glenmorangie 116-117
Glen Moray 118
Glenora Distillery 245
Glen Ord 119
Glenrothes 120
Glen Scotia 122
Glen Spey 123
Glentauchers 124
Glenturret 125
Glenugie 188
Glenury Royal 188
Glina Whiskydestillerie 220
Gold Cock distillery 208
Gotland Whisky 230
Gray Skies Distillery 243
Great Lakes Distillery 239
Great Northern Distillery 223
Great Southern Distilling Company 248
Great Wagon Distilling 239

H

Habbel, Destillerie Heinrich 219
Hagen, Brennerei 231
Haider, Whiskydistillery J 206
Hakushu 198
Hamilton Distillers 239
Hammerschmiede 217
Hard Times Distillery 243
Harris Distillery, Isle of 178
Hartmannsberg, Schaubrennerei Am 221
Hauer, Destillerie Ralf 221
d´Hautefeuille 215
Hellyers Road Distillery 248
Helsinki Distilling Company 211
Hepp, Distillerie 213
Hermann Pfanner, Destillerie 207
Het Anker Distillery 207
Hewn Spirits 241
Highland Park 126-127
High West Distillery 233
Hillrock Estate Distillery 238
Hollen, Whisky Brennerei 231
House Spirits Distillery 233
Höhler, Brennerei 217

I

Idlewild Spirits 244
III Spirits 245
Immortal Spirits 237
Imperial 188
Inchdairnie 173
Inchgower 128
Inverleven 189
Isle of Wight 211

J

James Sedgwick Distillery 255
Joadja Distillery 250
John Distilleries 252
John Emerald Distilling Company 240
Journeyman Distillery 236
Jura 129

K

Kalkwijck Distillers 226
Kammer-Kirsch, Destillerie 218
Kavalan Distillery 254
Keckeis Destillerie 207
Kempisch Vuur 208
Key West Distilling 241
Kilbeggan 224
Kilchoman 130
Kilkerran see Glengyle
Killara Distillery 251
Killyloch 189
Kinclaith 189
Kingsbarns Distillery 171
Kings County Distillery 239
Kininvie 131
Kinzigbrennerei 218
Knockando 132
Knockdhu 133
KyMar Farm Winery & Distillery 244

L

Ladyburn 189
Lagavulin 134-135
Lakes Distillery 210
Langatun Distillery 230
Laphroaig 136-137
Lark Distillery 247
Launceston Distillery 249
L B Distillers 246
Ledaig see Tobermory
Lehmann, Distillerie 213
Liebl, Bayerwald-Bärwurzerei und
Spezialitäten-Brennerei 217
Limfjorden, Braenderiet 209
Lindores Abbey 181
Linkwood 138
Liquid Riot 242
Littlemill 190
Loch Distillery 251
Locher, Brauerei 230
Loch Lomond 140
Lochside 190

Lohberg, Brauhaus am 220
London Distillery Company, The 210
Lone Wolf 178
Long Island Spirits 238
Longmorn 141
Long Road Distillers 244
Lyon Distilling Co. 244
Lübbehusen Malt Distillery 220
Lüthy, Bauernhofbrennerei 230

M

Macallan 142-143
McDowell´s 253
Macduff 144
McHenry & Sons Distillery, William 249
Mackey´s/Shene Distillery 250
Mackmyra 229
Madoc Distillery 256
Maine Craft Distilling 239
Mannochmore 145
Marder Edelbrände 219
Mavela, Domaine 212
Menhirs, Distillerie 213
Meyer, Distillerie 212
Michard, Brasserie 214
Miclo 215
Midleton Distillery 222
Milk & Honey Distillery 253
Millburn 190
Miltonduff 146
Mine d´Or, La 215
Miyagikyo 198
Montgomery Distillery 239
Moon Harbour 216
Mortlach 147
Mosgaard 209
Motor City Gas 244
Moutard-Diligent 216
Mt Uncle Distillery 251
Muraro Bebidas 256
Murree Brewery 253
Myken Distillery 227
Märkische Spez. Brennerei 219
Mönchguter Hofbrennerei 221
Mösslein, Destillerie 220

N

Nagahama 199
Nant Distillery 249
Nantou Distillery 255
Nashoba Valley Winery 234
Ncn´ean 182
New Holland Brewing 235
New Zealand Malt Whisky Co 251
Ninkasi, Distillerie 214
Nordmarkens Destilleri 230
Nordpfälzer
Edelobst & Whiskydestille 219
Norrtelje Brenneri 229
Norske Brenneri, Det 227
Northmaen, Distillerie de 213
North Port 190
Nukada 199

Distillery Index

Number Nine Spirituosen-Mnufaktur 220
Nyborg 209

O

Oak N´Harbor Distillery 241
Oban 148
Obsthof am Berg 217
Okanagan Spirits 246
Okayama 200
Old Hobart Distillery 248
Old Home Distillers 245
Old Line Spirits 242
Old Raven 206
Old Sandhill Whisky 221
Orange County Distillery 241
Ouche Nanon 216
Owl Distillery, The 207

P

Painted Stave Distilling 238
Paris, Distillerie de 214
Parkmore 192
Pemberton Distillery 246
Penderyn Distillery 231
Piautre, La 216
Pittyvaich 192
Port Ellen 191
Preussische Whiskydestillerie 217
Prichard´s Distillery 233
Pulteney 149
Puni Distillery 225

Q

Quincy Street Distillery 242
Quintessence, La 215

R

Raasay, Isle of 180
Rademon Estate 226
Rampur Distillery 253
Ranger Creek Brewing & Distilling 239
Redlands Estate Distillery 249
Reisetbauer 206
Rennaisance Artisan Distillers 240
Rieger & Hofmeister 218
River Sands Distillery 244
Roche Aux Fées 215
Rogner, Destillerie 206
Rogue Ales & Spirits 236
Rosebank 192
Roseisle distillery 175
Rouget de Lisle 213
RoughStock distillery 234
Royal Brackla 150
Royal Lochnagar 151
Rozelieures, Distillerie 213

S

Saburomaru 200
St George Distillery (USA) 234

St George´s Distillery (UK) 209
St Kilian Distillers 221
St Magdalene 192
San Diego Distillery 243
Santa Fe Spirits 237
Sauerländer Edelbrennerei 220Scapa 152
Schloss Neuenburg, Edelbrennerei 220
Seattle Distilling 241
Seger, Brennerei Walter 219
Senft, Edelbrände 219
Seven Stills Distillery 240
Shed Distillery, The 224
Shelter Point Distillery 245
Shene Distillery 250
Shinshu 201
Shizuoka 201
Sippel, Destillerie Thomas 221
Slane Castle Distillery 225
Slyrs Destillerie 216
Smögen Whisky 229
Sons of Liberty Spirits Company 236
Sound Spirits 242
Sperbers Destillerie 219
Speyburn 153
Speyside 154
Spirit Hound Distillers 244
Spirit of Hven 229
Spirit of Yorkshire 211
Spreewood 217
Springbank 156-157
Square One Brewery & Distillery 239
Stadelmann, Brennerei 230
Stark Spirits 242
Starward Distillery 248
Stauning Whisky 208
Steinhauser Destillerie 218
Steinwälder Hausbrennerei 221
Stickum Brennerei 217
StilltheOne Distillery Two 245
Still Waters Distillery 246
Stokerij Sculte 226
Stranahans Colorado Whiskey 232
Strathearn 176
Strathisla 158
Strathmill 159
Sugarhouse Distillery 241
Sullivans Cove Distillery 247

T

Talisker 160-161
Tamdhu 162
Tamnavulin 163
Teaninich 164
Tecker Whisky-Destillerie 219
Teeling Distillery 223
Teerenpeli 211
Telser, Brennerei 225
Telluride Distilling 245
Tevsjö Destilleri 230
Theurer, Brennerei Volker 220
Thomson Whisky Distillery 251
Thumb Butte Distillery 241
Thy Whisky 209

Timber Creek Distillery 244
Timboon Railway Shed Distillery 250
Tin Shed Distilling 250
Tobermory 165
Tomatin 166
Tomintoul 167
Torabhaig 180
Tormore 168
Town Branch Distillery 233
Triple Eight Distillery 234
Trolden Distillery 209
Tsunuki 202
Tualatin Valley Distilling 240
Tullamore Distillery 2213
Tullibardine 169
Tuthilltown Spirits 233
Two James Distillery 240

U

Union Distillery 256
Uppsala Destilleri 230
Us Heit Distillery 226

V

Valamo Distillery 211
Van Brunt Stillhouse 239
Venus Spirits 241
Vercors, La Distillerie du 216
Victoria Caledonian Distillery 245
Victoria Spirits 246
Vikre Distillery 240
Virginia Distillery 234

W

Waldviertler Granit Destillerie 207
Walsh Distillery 223
Warenghem, Distillerie 212
Waterford Distillery 224
Weingut Simons 218
Westland Distillery 232
West Cork Distillers 224
Weutz, Destillerie 206
Whisky Castle 230
White Oak 202
Wild Brennerei 220
Witherspoon Distillery 242
Wolfburn Distillery 171
Wood´s High Mountain Distillery 237
Woodstone Creek Distillery 235
Wright & Brown Distilling 241

Y

Yamazaki 203
Yoichi 203
Yukon Spirits 246

Z

Ziegler, Brennerei 218
Zuidam Distillers 225
Zürcher, Spezialitätenbrennerei 231